Mastering Spark for Data Science

Master the techniques and sophisticated analytics used to construct Spark-based solutions that scale to deliver production-grade data science products

Andrew Morgan
Antoine Amend
David George
Matthew Hallett

Pack‹t›

BIRMINGHAM - MUMBAI

Mastering Spark for Data Science

First published: March 2017

Production reference: 1240317

Published by Packt Publishing Ltd.
Livery Place
35 Livery Street
Birmingham
B3 2PB, UK.
ISBN 978-1-78588-214-2

www.packtpub.com

Credits

Authors

Andrew Morgan
Antoine Amend
David George
Matthew Hallett

Reviewer

Sumit Pal

Commissioning Editor

Akram Hussain

Acquisition Editor

Vinay Argekar

Content Development Editor

Amrita Noronha

Technical Editor

Sneha Hanchate

Copy Editor

Safis Editing

Project Coordinator

Shweta H Birwatkar

Proofreader

Safis Editing

Indexer

Pratik Shirodkar

Graphics

Tania Dutta

Production Coordinator

Arvindkumar Gupta

Foreword

The impact of Spark on the world of data science has been startling. It is less than 3 years since Spark 1.0 was released and yet Spark is already accepted as the omni-competent kernel of any big data architecture. We adopted Spark as our core technology at Barclays around this time and this was considered a bold (read 'rash') move. Now it is taken as a given that Spark is your starting point for any big data science project.

As data science has developed both as an activity and as an accepted term, there has been much talk about the unicorn data scientist. This is the unlikely character who can do both the maths and the coding. They are apparently hard to find, and harder to keep. My team likes to think more in terms of three data science competencies: pattern recognition, distributed computation, and automation. If data science is about exploiting insights from data in production, then you need to be able to develop applications with these three competencies in mind from the start. There is no point using a machine learning methodology that won't scale with your data, or building an analytical kernel that needs to be re-coded to be production quality. And so you need either a unicorn or a unicorn-team (my preference) to do the work.

Spark is your unicorn technology. No other language not only expresses analytical concepts elegantly but also moves effortlessly from the small scale to big data, and so naturally facilitates production-ready code as Spark (with the Scala API). We chose Spark because we could compose a model in a few lines, run the same code on the cluster as we had tried out on the laptop, and build robust unit-tested JVM applications that we could be confident would run in business-critical use cases. The combination of functional programming in Scala with the Spark abstractions is uniquely powerful, and choosing it has been a significant cause of the success of the team over the last 3 years.

So here's the conundrum. Why are there no books which present Spark in this way, recognizing that one of the best reasons to work in Spark is its application to production data science? If you scan the bookshelves (or look at tutorials online) all you will find is toy models and a review of the Spark APIs and libs. You will find little or nothing about how Spark fits into the wider architecture, or about how to manage data ETL in a sustainable way.

I think you will find that the practical approach taken by the authors in this book is different. Each chapter takes on a new challenge, and each reads as a voyage of discovery where the outcome was not necessarily known in advance of the exploration. And the value of doing data science properly is set out clearly from the start. This is one of the first books on Spark for grown-ups who want to do real data science that will make an impact on their organisation. I hope you enjoy it.

Harry Powell

Head of Advanced Analytics, Barclays

About the Authors

Andrew Morgan is a specialist in data strategy and its execution, and has deep experience in the supporting technologies, system architecture, and data science that bring it to life. With over 20 years of experience in the data industry, he has worked designing systems for some of its most prestigious players and their global clients – often on large, complex and international projects. In 2013, he founded ByteSumo Ltd, a data science and big data engineering consultancy, and he now works with clients in Europe and the USA. Andrew is an active data scientist, and the inventor of the TrendCalculus algorithm. It was developed as part of his ongoing research project investigating long-range predictions based on machine learning the patterns found in drifting cultural, geopolitical and economic trends. He also sits on the Hadoop Summit EU data science selection committee, and has spoken at many conferences on a variety of data topics. He also enjoys participating in the Data Science and Big Data communities where he lives in London.

This book is dedicated to my wife Steffy, to my children Alice and Adele, and to all my friends and colleagues who have been endlessly supportive. It is also dedicated to the memory of one my earliest mentors whom I studied under at the University of Toronto, a Professor Ferenc Csillag. Back in 1994, Ferko inspired me with visions of a future where we could use planet-wide data collection and sophisticated algorithms to monitor and optimize the world around us. It was an idea that changed my life, and his dream of a world saved by Big Data Science, is one I'm still chasing.

Antoine Amend is a data scientist passionate about big data engineering and scalable computing. The book's theme of torturing astronomical amounts of unstructured data to gain new insights mainly comes from his background in theoretical physics. Graduating in 2008 with a Msc. in Astrophysics, he worked for a large consultancy business in Switzerland before discovering the concept of big data at the early stages of Hadoop. He has embraced big data technologies ever since, and is now working as the Head of Data Science for cyber security at Barclays Bank. By combining a scientific approach with core IT skills, Antoine qualified two years running for the Big Data World Championships finals held in Austin TX. He Placed in the top 12 in both 2014 and 2015 edition (over 2000+ competitors) where he additionally won the Innovation Award using the methodologies and technologies explained in this book.

I would like to thank my wife for standing beside me, she has been my motivation for continuing to improve my knowledge and move my career forward. I thank my wonderful kids for always teaching me how to step back whenever it is necessary to clear my mind and get fresh new ideas.

I would like to extend my thanks to my co-workers, especially Dr. Samuel Assefa, Dr. Eirini Spyropoulou and Will Hardman for their patience listening to my crazy theories, and everyone else I had the pleasure to work with over the past few years. Finally, I want to address a special thanks to all my previous managers and mentors who helped me shape up my career in data and analytics; thanks to Manu, Toby, Gary and Harry.

David George is a distinguished distributed computing expert with 15+ years of data systems experience, mainly with globally recognized IT consultancies and brands. Working with core Hadoop technologies since the early days, he has delivered implementations at the largest scale. David always takes a pragmatic approach to software design and values elegance in simplicity.

Today he continues to work as a lead engineer, designing scalable applications for financial sector customers with some of the toughest requirements. His latest projects focus on the adoption of advanced AI techniques for increasing levels of automation across knowledge-based industries.

For Ellie, Shannon, Pauline and Pumpkin – here's to the sequel!

Matthew Hallett is a Software Engineer and Computer Scientist with over 15 years of industry experience. He is an expert Object Oriented programmer and systems engineer with extensive knowledge of low level programming paradigms and, for the last 8 years, has developed an expertise in Hadoop and distributed programming within mission critical environments, comprising multithousandnode data centres. With consultancy experience in distributed algorithms and the implementation of distributed computing architectures, in a variety of languages, Matthew is currently a Consultant Data Engineer in the Data Science & Engineering team at a top four audit firm.

Lynnie, thanks for your understanding and sacrifices that afforded me the time during late nights, weekends and holidays to write this book. Nugget, you make it all worthwhile.

We would also like to thank Gary Richardson, Dr David Pryce, Dr Helen Ramsden, Dr Sima Reichenbach and Dr Fabio Petroni for their invaluable advice and guidance that has led to the completion of this huge project – without their help and contributions this book may never have been completed!

About the Reviewer

Sumit Pal is an author who has published SQL on Big Data - Technology, Architecture and Innovations with Apress. Sumit has more than 22 years of experience in the software industry in various roles spanning companies from startups to enterprises.

He is an independent consultant working with big data, data visualization, and data science and a software architect building end-to-end, data-driven analytic systems.

Sumit has worked for Microsoft (SQL server development team), Oracle (OLAP development team), and Verizon (Big Data analytics team) in a career spanning 22 years. Currently, he works for multiple clients advising them on their data architectures and big data solutions and does hands-on coding with Spark, Scala, Java, and Python.

Sumit has spoken at big data conferences in Boston, Chicago, Las Vegas, and Vancouver. Sumit is also the author of the book on the same topic published by Apress in October 2016.

He has extensive experience in building scalable systems across the stack from middletier, data tier, to visualization for analytics applications, using BigData and NoSQL DB. Sumit has deep expertise in DataBase Internals, Data Warehouses, Dimensional Modeling, Data Science with Java, Python, and SQL.

Sumit started his career being a part of SQLServer development team at Microsoft in 1996-97 and then as a core server engineer for Oracle Corporation at their OLAP development team in Burlington, MA.

Sumit has also worked at Verizon as an associate director for big data architecture, where he strategized, managed, architected, and developed platforms and solutions for analytics and machine learning applications.

Sumit has also served as a chief architect at ModelN/LeapfrogRX (2006-2013), where he architected the middle tier core analytics platform with open source olap engine (Mondrian) on J2EE and solved some complex dimensional ETL, modeling, and performance optimization problems.

Sumit has done his MS and BS in computer science.

Sumit has hiked to Mt. Everest Base Camp in October 2016.

www.PacktPub.com

For support files and downloads related to your book, please visit www.PacktPub.com.

Did you know that Packt offers eBook versions of every book published, with PDF and ePub files available? You can upgrade to the eBook version at www.PacktPub.com and as a print book customer, you are entitled to a discount on the eBook copy. Get in touch with us at service@packtpub.com for more details.

At www.PacktPub.com, you can also read a collection of free technical articles, sign up for a range of free newsletters and receive exclusive discounts and offers on Packt books and eBooks.

Mapt

https://www.packtpub.com/mapt

Get the most in-demand software skills with Mapt. Mapt gives you full access to all Packt books and video courses, as well as industry-leading tools to help you plan your personal development and advance your career.

Why subscribe?

- Fully searchable across every book published by Packt
- Copy and paste, print, and bookmark content
- On demand and accessible via a web browser

Customer Feedback

Thanks for purchasing this Packt book. At Packt, quality is at the heart of our editorial process. To help us improve, please leave us an honest review on this book's Amazon page at `https://www.amazon.in/Mastering-Spark-Science-Andrew-Morgan-ebook/dp/B01BWNXA82?_encoding=UTF8&keywords=mastering%20spark%20for%20data%20science&qid=1490239942&ref_=sr_1_1&sr=8-1`.

If you'd like to join our team of regular reviewers, you can e-mail us at `customerreviews@packtpub.com`. We award our regular reviewers with free eBooks and videos in exchange for their valuable feedback. Help us be relentless in improving our products!

Table of Contents

Foreword   4

Preface   1

Chapter 1: The Big Data Science Ecosystem   9

  Introducing the Big Data ecosystem   10
    Data management   10
    Data management responsibilities   10
    The right tool for the job   12
  Overall architecture   13
    Data Ingestion   13
    Data Lake   15
      Reliable storage   15
      Scalable data processing capability   15
    Data science platform   16
    Data Access   16
  Data technologies   17
    The role of Apache Spark   18
  Companion tools   19
    Apache HDFS   19
      Advantages   20
      Disadvantages   20
      Installation   21
    Amazon S3   21
      Advantages   22
      Disadvantages   22
      Installation   22
    Apache Kafka   23
      Advantages   23
      Disadvantages   24
      Installation   24
    Apache Parquet   24
      Advantages   24
      Disadvantages   25
      Installation   25
    Apache Avro   25
      Advantages   25
      Disadvantages   26
      Installation   26

Apache NiFi   26
  Advantages   27
  Disadvantages   27
  Installation   27
Apache YARN   27
  Advantages   28
  Disadvantages   28
  Installation   28
Apache Lucene   28
  Advantages   29
  Disadvantages   29
  Installation   29
Kibana   29
  Advantages   30
  Disadvantages   30
  Installation   30
Elasticsearch   30
  Advantages   30
  Disadvantages   31
  Installation   31
Accumulo   31
  Advantages   32
  Disadvantages   32
  Installation   32
Summary   33

Chapter 2: Data Acquisition   35
Data pipelines   36
  Universal ingestion framework   36
  Introducing the GDELT news stream   38
    Discovering GDELT in real-time   38
    Our first GDELT feed   43
    Improving with publish and subscribe   45
Content registry   47
  Choices and more choices   47
  Going with the flow   48
  Metadata model   49
  Kibana dashboard   50
Quality assurance   51
    Example 1 – Basic quality checking, no contending users   52
    Example 2 – Advanced quality checking, no contending users   52
    Example 3 – Basic quality checking, 50% utility due to contending users   53
Summary   54

Chapter 3: Input Formats and Schema   55

A structured life is a good life	56
GDELT dimensional modeling	57
GDELT model	57
First look at the data	58
Core global knowledge graph model	58
Hidden complexity	60
Denormalized models	60
Challenges with flattened data	61
Issue 1 – Loss of contextual information	62
Issue 2: Re-establishing dimensions	62
Issue 3: Including reference data	64
Loading your data	65
Schema agility	67
Reality check	69
GKG ELT	70
Position matters	72
Avro	73
Spark-Avro method	74
Pedagogical method	76
When to perform Avro transformation	80
Parquet	81
Summary	82
Chapter 4: Exploratory Data Analysis	85
The problem, principles and planning	86
Understanding the EDA problem	86
Design principles	87
General plan of exploration	87
Preparation	88
Introducing mask based data profiling	88
Introducing character class masks	94
Building a mask based profiler	96
Setting up Apache Zeppelin	97
Constructing a reusable notebook	98
Exploring GDELT	110
GDELT GKG datasets	110
The files	110
Special collections	111
Reference data	112
Exploring the GKG v2.1	112
The Translingual files	113
A configurable GCAM time series EDA	114
Plot.ly charting on Apache Zeppelin	123

Exploring translation sourced GCAM sentiment with plot.ly 124
Concluding remarks 130
A configurable GCAM Spatio-Temporal EDA 131
Introducing GeoGCAM 132
Does our spatial pivot work? 137
Summary 138

Chapter 5: Spark for Geographic Analysis 139

GDELT and oil 140
GDELT events 141
GDELT GKG 142
Formulating a plan of action 142
GeoMesa 143
Installing 144
GDELT Ingest 145
GeoMesa Ingest 145
MapReduce to Spark 146
Geohash 149
GeoServer 152
Map layers 153
CQL 155
Gauging oil prices 156
Using the GeoMesa query API 157
Data preparation 159
Machine learning 165
Naive Bayes 166
Results 167
Analysis 168
Summary 169

Chapter 6: Scraping Link-Based External Data 171

Building a web scale news scanner 172
Accessing the web content 172
The Goose library 174
Integration with Spark 175
Scala compatibility 175
Serialization issues 176
Creating a scalable, production-ready library 177
Build once, read many 177
Exception handling 177
Performance tuning 179
Named entity recognition 180
Scala libraries 181

NLP walkthrough   181
   Extracting entities   182
   Abstracting methods   184
Building a scalable code   185
   Build once, read many   185
   Scalability is also a state of mind   186
   Performance tuning   187
GIS lookup   187
  GeoNames dataset   188
  Building an efficient join   189
    Offline strategy – Bloom filtering   191
    Online strategy – Hash partitioning   193
  Content deduplication   194
    Context learning   194
    Location scoring ·   194
Names de-duplication   195
  Functional programming with Scalaz   195
    Our de-duplication strategy   195
    Using the mappend operator   197
  Simple clean   198
  DoubleMetaphone   199
News index dashboard   201
Summary   202
Chapter 7: Building Communities   205
  Building a graph of persons   206
   Contact chaining   206
   Extracting data from Elasticsearch   208
  Using the Accumulo database   211
   Setup Accumulo   211
   Cell security   213
   Iterators   213
   Elasticsearch to Accumulo   214
    A graph data model in Accumulo   214
    Hadoop input and output formats   214
   Reading from Accumulo   217
   AccumuloGraphxInputFormat and EdgeWritable   218
   Building a graph   219
  Community detection algorithm   220
   Louvain algorithm   221
   Weighted Community Clustering (WCC)   222
    Description   223

Preprocessing stage	224
Initial communities	226
Message passing	226
Community back propagation	228
WCC iteration	233
Gathering community statistics	234
WCC Computation	235
WCC iteration	238
GDELT dataset	240
The Bowie effect	241
Smaller communities	243
Using Accumulo cell level security	244
Summary	246

Chapter 8: Building a Recommendation System — 247

Different approaches	248
Collaborative filtering	248
Content-based filtering	249
Custom approach	249
Uninformed data	250
Processing bytes	250
Creating a scalable code	253
From time to frequency domain	254
Fast Fourier transform	254
Sampling by time window	256
Extracting audio signatures	258
Building a song analyzer	261
Selling data science is all about selling cupcakes	261
Using Cassandra	262
Using the Play framework	263
Building a recommender	267
The PageRank algorithm	267
Building a Graph of Frequency Co-occurrence	267
Running PageRank	269
Building personalized playlists	270
Expanding our cupcake factory	271
Building a playlist service	271
Leveraging the Spark job server	273
User interface	277
Summary	278

Chapter 9: News Dictionary and Real-Time Tagging System — 281

The mechanical Turk	282
Human intelligence tasks	282

Bootstrapping a classification model 282
Learning from Stack Exchange 283
Building text features 284
Training a Naive Bayes model 287
Laziness, impatience, and hubris 289
Designing a Spark Streaming application 291
A tale of two architectures 292
The CAP theorem 292
The Greeks are here to help 294
Importance of the Lambda architecture 295
Importance of the Kappa architecture 297
Consuming data streams 298
Creating a GDELT data stream 299
Creating a Kafka topic 299
Publishing content to a Kafka topic 299
Consuming Kafka from Spark Streaming 300
Creating a Twitter data stream 301
Processing Twitter data 302
Extracting URLs and hashtags 303
Keeping popular hashtags 303
Expanding shortened URLs 305
Fetching HTML content 307
Using Elasticsearch as a caching layer 308
Classifying data 311
Training a Naive Bayes model 311
Thread safety 313
Predict the GDELT data 314
Our Twitter mechanical Turk 316
Summary 318
Chapter 10: Story De-duplication and Mutation 319
Detecting near duplicates 319
First steps with hashing 322
Standing on the shoulders of the Internet giants 323
Simhashing 323
The hamming weight 326
Detecting near duplicates in GDELT 327
Indexing the GDELT database 332
Persisting our RDDs 332
Building a REST API 333
Area of improvement 336
Building stories 337

Building term frequency vectors 337
The curse of dimensionality, the data science plague 339
Optimizing KMeans 340
Story mutation 344
The Equilibrium state 344
Tracking stories over time 345
Building a streaming application 346
Streaming KMeans 348
Visualization 351
Building story connections 355
Summary 359

Chapter 11: Anomaly Detection on Sentiment Analysis 361
Following the US elections on Twitter 361
Acquiring data in stream 362
Acquiring data in batch 364
The search API 364
Rate limit 365
Analysing sentiment 366
Massaging Twitter data 367
Using the Stanford NLP 369
Building the Pipeline 371
Using Timely as a time series database 373
Storing data 373
Using Grafana to visualize sentiment 376
Number of processed tweets 376
Give me my Twitter account back 377
Identifying the swing states 378
Twitter and the Godwin point 380
Learning context 380
Visualizing our model 382
Word2Graph and Godwin point 384
Building a Word2Graph 384
Random walks 387
A Small Step into sarcasm detection 389
Building features 389
#LoveTrumpsHates 390
Scoring Emojis 391
Training a KMeans model 392
Detecting anomalies 394
Summary 395

Chapter 12: TrendCalculus 397

Studying trends	398
The TrendCalculus algorithm	400
Trend windows	400
Simple trend	403
User Defined Aggregate Functions	404
Simple trend calculation	409
Reversal rule	411
Introducing the FHLS bar structure	413
Visualize the data	415
FHLS with reversals	417
Edge cases	419
Zero values	420
Completing the gaps	421
Stackable processing	425
Practical applications	426
Algorithm characteristics	426
Advantages	426
Disadvantages	427
Possible use cases	427
Chart annotation	427
Co-trending	427
Data reduction	427
Indexing	427
Fractal dimension	428
Streaming proxy for piecewise linear regression	428
Summary	428
Chapter 13: Secure Data	429
Data security	430
The problem	430
The basics	431
Authentication and authorization	432
Access control lists (ACL)	433
Role-based access control (RBAC)	434
Access	435
Encryption	435
Data at rest	436
Java KeyStore	442
S3 encryption	444
Data in transit	444
Obfuscation/Anonymizing	446
Masking	450

Tokenization	452
Using a Hybrid approach	454
Data disposal	455
Kerberos authentication	456
Use case 1: Apache Spark accessing data in secure HDFS	457
Use case 2: extending to automated authentication	460
Use case 3: connecting to secure databases from Spark	460
Security ecosystem	462
Apache sentry	462
RecordService	463
Apache ranger	464
Apache Knox	465
Your Secure Responsibility	465
Summary	466
Chapter 14: Scalable Algorithms	469
General principles	470
Spark architecture	472
History of Spark	473
Moving parts	474
Driver	475
SparkSession	475
Resilient distributed datasets (RDDs)	475
Executor	476
Shuffle operation	476
Cluster Manager	476
Task	476
DAG	477
DAG scheduler	477
Transformations	477
Stages	478
Actions	478
Task scheduler	479
Challenges	479
Algorithmic complexity	479
Numerical anomalies	480
Shuffle	482
Data schemes	483
Plotting your course	484
Be iterative	485
Data preparation	485
Scale up slowly	486
Estimate performance	487

Step through carefully 488
Tune your analytic 491
Design patterns and techniques 496
Spark APIs 496
Problem 496
Solution 497
Example 497
Summary pattern 498
Problem 498
Solution 498
Example 499
Expand and Conquer Pattern 499
Problem 499
Solution 499
Lightweight Shuffle 500
Problem 500
Solution 500
Wide Table pattern 502
Problem 502
Solution 502
Example 503
Broadcast variables pattern 503
Problem 503
Solution 503
Creating a broadcast variable 504
Accessing a broadcast variable 504
Removing a broadcast variable 504
Example 504
Combiner pattern 504
Problem 504
Solution 505
Example 507
Optimized cluster 510
Problem 510
Solution 510
Redistribution pattern 512
Problem 512
Solution 512
Example 513
Salting key pattern 513
Problem 513
Solution 514
Secondary sort pattern 515
Problem 515
Solution 515

Example   516
Filter overkill pattern   517
Problem   517
Solution   517
Probabilistic algorithms   517
Problem   517
Solution   518
Example   518
Selective caching   518
Problem   518
Solution   519
Garbage collection   520
Problem   520
Solution   520
Graph traversal   521
Problem   521
Solution   522
Example   522
Summary   522
Index   523

Preface

The purpose of data science is to transform the world using data, and this goal is mainly achieved through disrupting and changing real processes in real industries. To operate at that level we need to be able to build data science solutions of substance; ones that solve real problems, and which can run reliably enough for people to trust and act upon.

This book explains how to use Spark to deliver production grade data science solutions that are innovative, disruptive, and reliable enough to be trusted. Whilst writing this book it was the authors' intention to deliver a work that transcends the traditional cookbook style: providing not just examples of code, but developing the techniques and mind-set that are needed to explore content like a master; as they say, *Content is King*! Readers will notice that the book has a heavy emphasis on news analytics, and occasionally pulls in other datasets such as Tweets and financial data. This emphasis on news is not an accident; much effort has been spent on trying to focus on datasets that offer context at a global scale.

The implicit problem that this book is dedicated to is the lack of data offering proper context around how and why people make decisions. Often, directly accessible data sources are very focused on problem specifics and, as a consequence, can be very light on broader datasets offering the behavioral context needed to really understand what's driving the decisions that people make.

Considering a simple example where website users' key information such as age, gender, location, shopping behavior, purchases and so on are known, we might use this data to recommend products based on what others "like them" have been buying.

But to be exceptional, more context is required as to why people behave as they do. When news reports suggest a massive Atlantic hurricane is approaching the Florida coastline, and could reach the coast in say 36 hours, perhaps we should be recommending products people might need. Items such as USB enabled battery packs for keeping phones charged, candles, flashlights, water purifiers, and the like. By understanding the context in which decisions are being made, we can conduct better science.

Therefore, whilst this book certainly contains useful code and, in many cases, unique implementations, it further dives deep into the techniques and skills required to truly master data science; some of which are often overlooked or not considered at all. Drawing on many years of commercial experience, the authors have leveraged their extensive knowledge to bring the real, and exciting world of data science to life.

What this book covers

Chapter 1, *The Big Data Science Ecosystem*, this chapter is an introduction to an approach and accompanying ecosystem for achieving success with data at scale. It focuses on the data science tools and technologies that will be used in later chapters as well as introducing the environment and how to configure it appropriately. Additionally it explains some of the non-functional considerations relevant to the overall data architecture and long-term success.

Chapter 2, *Data Acquisition*, as a data scientist, one of the most important tasks is to accurately load data into a data science platform. Rather than having uncontrolled, ad hoc processes, this chapter explains how a general data ingestion pipeline in Spark can be constructed that serves as a reusable component across many feeds of input data.

Chapter 3, *Input Formats and Schema*, this chapter demonstrates how to load data from its raw format onto different schemas, therefore enabling a variety of different kinds of downstream analytics to be run over the same data. With this in mind, we will look at the traditionally well-understood area of data schemas. We will cover key areas of traditional database modeling and explain how some of these cornerstone principles are still applicable to Spark today. In addition, whilst honing our Spark skills we will analyze the GDELT data model and show how to store this large dataset in an efficient and scalable manner.

Chapter 4, *Exploratory Data Analysis*, a common misconception is that an EDA is only for discovering the statistical properties of a dataset and providing insights about how it can be exploited. In practice, this isn't the full story. A full EDA will extend that idea, and include a detailed assessment of the "feasibility of using this Data Feed in production." It requires us to also understand how we would specify a production grade data loading routine for this dataset, one that might potentially run in a "lights out mode" for many years. This chapter offers a rapid method for doing Data Quality assessment using a "data profiling" technique to accelerate the process.

Chapter 5, *Spark for Geographic Analysis*, geographic processing is a powerful new use case for Spark, and this chapter demonstrates how to get started. The aim of this chapter is to explain how Data Scientists can process geographic data, using Spark, to produce powerful map based views of very large datasets. We demonstrate how to process spatio-temporal datasets easily via Spark integrations with Geomesa, which helps turn Spark into a sophisticated geographic processing engine. The chapter later leverages this spatio-temporal data to apply machine learning with a view to predicting oil prices.

Chapter 6, *Scraping Link-Based External Data*, this chapter aims to explain a common pattern for enhancing local data with external content found at URLs or over APIs, such as GDELT and Twitter. We offer a tutorial using the GDELT news index service as a source of news URLS, demonstrating how to build a web scale News Scanner that scrapes global breaking news of interest from the internet. We further explain how to use the specialist web-scraping component in a way that overcomes the challenges of scale, followed by the summary of this chapter.

Chapter 7, *Building Communities*, this chapter aims to address a common use case in data science and big data. With more and more people interacting together, communicating, exchanging information, or simply sharing a common interest in different topics, the entire world can be represented as a Graph. A data scientist must be able to detect communities, find influencers / top contributors, and detect possible anomalies.

Chapter 8, *Building a Recommendation System*, if one were to choose an algorithm to showcase data science to the public, a recommendation system would certainly be in the frame. Today, recommendation systems are everywhere; the reason for their popularity is down to their versatility, usefulness and broad applicability. In this chapter, we will demonstrate how to recommend music content using raw audio signals.

Chapter 9, *News Dictionary and Real-Time Tagging System*, while a hierarchical data warehouse stores data in files of folders, a typical Hadoop based system relies on a flat architecture to store your data. Without a proper data governance or a clear understanding of what your data is all about, there is an undeniable chance of turning data lakes into swamps, where an interesting dataset such as GDELT would be nothing more than a folder containing a vast amount of unstructured text files. In this chapter, we will be describing an innovative way of labeling incoming GDELT data in a non-supervised way and in near real time.

Chapter 10, *Story De-duplication and Mutation*, in this chapter, we de-duplicate and index the GDELT database into stories, before tracking stories over time and understanding the links between them, how they may mutate and if they could lead to any subsequent events in the near future. Core to this chapter is the concept of Simhash to detect near duplicates and building vectors to reduce dimensionality using Random Indexing.

Chapter 11, *Anomaly Detection and Sentiment Analysis*, perhaps the most notable occurrence of the year 2016 was the tense US presidential election and its eventual outcome: the election of President Donald Trump, a campaign that will long be remembered; not least for its unprecedented use of social media and the stirring up of passion among its users, most of whom made their feelings known through the use of hashtags. In this chapter, instead of trying to predict the outcome itself, we will aim to detect abnormal tweets during the US election using a real-time Twitter feed.

Chapter 12, *TrendCalculus*, long before the concept of "what's trending" became a popular topic of study by data scientists, there was an older one that is still not well served by data science; it is that of Trends. Presently, the analysis of trends, if it can be called that, is primarily carried out by people "eyeballing" time series charts and offering interpretations. But what is it that people's eyes are doing? This chapter describes an implementation in Apache Spark of a new algorithm for studying trends numerically: TrendCalculus.

Chapter 13, *Secure Data*, throughout this book we visit many areas of data science, often straying into those that are not traditionally associated with a data scientist's core working knowledge. In this chapter we will visit another of those often overlooked fields, Secure Data; more specifically, how to protect your data and analytic results at all stages of the data life cycle. Core to this chapter is the construction of a commercial grade encryption codec for Spark.

Chapter 14, *Scalable Algorithms*, in this chapter we learn about why sometimes even basic algorithms, despite working at small scale, will often fail in "big data". We'll see how to avoid issues when writing Spark jobs that run over massive Datasets and will learn about the structure of algorithms and how to write custom data science analytics that scale over petabytes of data. The chapter features areas such as: parallelization strategies, caching, shuffle strategies, garbage collection optimization and probabilistic models; explaining how these can help you to get the most out of the Spark paradigm.

What you need for this book

Spark 2.0 is used throughout the book along with Scala 2.11, Maven and Hadoop. This is the basic environment required, there are many other technologies used which are introduced in the relevant chapters.

Who this book is for

We presume that the data scientists reading this book are knowledgeable about data science, common machine learning methods, and popular data science tools, and have in the course of their work run proof of concept studies, and built prototypes. We offer a book that introduces advanced techniques and methods for building data science solutions to this audience, showing them how to construct commercial grade data products.

Conventions

In this book, you will find a number of text styles that distinguish between different kinds of information. Here are some examples of these styles and an explanation of their meaning.

Code words in text, database table names, folder names, filenames, file extensions, pathnames, dummy URLs, user input, and Twitter handles are shown as follows: "The next lines of code read the link and assign it to the to the `BeautifulSoup` function."

A block of code is set as follows:

```
import org.apache.spark.sql.functions._

val rdd = rawDS map GdeltParser.toCaseClass
val ds = rdd.toDS()
// DataFrame-style API
ds.agg(avg("goldstein")).as("goldstein").show()
```

When we wish to draw your attention to a particular part of a code block, the relevant lines or items are set in bold:

```
spark.sql("SELECT V2GCAM FROM GKG LIMIT 5").show
spark.sql("SELECT AVG(GOLDSTEIN) AS GOLDSTEIN FROM GKG WHERE GOLDSTEIN IS
NOT NULL").show()
```

Any command-line input or output is written as follows:

```
$ cat 20150218230000.gkg.csv | gawk -F"\t" '{print $4}'
```

New terms and **important words** are shown in bold. Words that you see on the screen, for example, in menus or dialog boxes, appear in the text like this: "In order to download new modules, we will go to **Files** | **Settings** | **Project Name** | **Project Interpreter**."

> Warnings or important notes appear in a box like this.

> Tips and tricks appear like this.

Reader feedback

Feedback from our readers is always welcome. Let us know what you think about this book-what you liked or disliked. Reader feedback is important for us as it helps us develop titles that you will really get the most out of. To send us general feedback, simply e-mail feedback@packtpub.com, and mention the book's title in the subject of your message. If there is a topic that you have expertise in and you are interested in either writing or contributing to a book, see our author guide at www.packtpub.com/authors.

Customer support

Now that you are the proud owner of a Packt book, we have a number of things to help you to get the most from your purchase.

Downloading the example code

You can download the example code files for this book from your account at http://www.packtpub.com. If you purchased this book elsewhere, you can visit http://www.packtpub.com/support and register to have the files e-mailed directly to you.

You can download the code files by following these steps:

1. Log in or register to our website using your e-mail address and password.
2. Hover the mouse pointer on the **SUPPORT** tab at the top.
3. Click on **Code Downloads & Errata**.
4. Enter the name of the book in the **Search** box.
5. Select the book for which you're looking to download the code files.
6. Choose from the drop-down menu where you purchased this book from.
7. Click on **Code Download**.

Once the file is downloaded, please make sure that you unzip or extract the folder using the latest version of:

- WinRAR / 7-Zip for Windows
- Zipeg / iZip / UnRarX for Mac
- 7-Zip / PeaZip for Linux

The code bundle for the book is also hosted on GitHub at `https://github.com/PacktPubl ishing/Mastering-Spark-for-Data-Science`. We also have other code bundles from our rich catalog of books and videos available at `https://github.com/PacktPublishing/`. Check them out!

Downloading the color images of this book

We also provide you with a PDF file that has color images of the screenshots/diagrams used in this book. The color images will help you better understand the changes in the output. You can download this file from `https://www.packtpub.com/sites/default/files/down loads/MasteringSparkforDataScience_ColorImages.pdf`.

Errata

Although we have taken every care to ensure the accuracy of our content, mistakes do happen. If you find a mistake in one of our books-maybe a mistake in the text or the code-we would be grateful if you could report this to us. By doing so, you can save other readers from frustration and help us improve subsequent versions of this book. If you find any errata, please report them by visiting http://www.packtpub.com/submit-errata, selecting your book, clicking on the **Errata Submission Form** link, and entering the details of your errata. Once your errata are verified, your submission will be accepted and the errata will be uploaded to our website or added to any list of existing errata under the Errata section of that title.

To view the previously submitted errata, go to https://www.packtpub.com/books/content/support and enter the name of the book in the search field. The required information will appear under the **Errata** section.

Piracy

Piracy of copyrighted material on the Internet is an ongoing problem across all media. At Packt, we take the protection of our copyright and licenses very seriously. If you come across any illegal copies of our works in any form on the Internet, please provide us with the location address or website name immediately so that we can pursue a remedy.

Please contact us at copyright@packtpub.com with a link to the suspected pirated material.

We appreciate your help in protecting our authors and our ability to bring you valuable content.

Questions

If you have a problem with any aspect of this book, you can contact us at questions@packtpub.com, and we will do our best to address the problem.

1
The Big Data Science Ecosystem

As a data scientist, you'll no doubt be very familiar with handling files and processing perhaps even large amounts of data. However, as I'm sure you will agree, doing anything more than a simple analysis over a single type of data requires a method of organizing and cataloguing data so that it can be managed effectively. Indeed, this is the cornerstone of a great data scientist. As the data volume and complexity increases, a consistent and robust approach can be the difference between generalized success and over-fitted failure!

This chapter is an introduction to an approach and ecosystem for achieving success with data at scale. It focuses on the data science tools and technologies. It introduces the environment, and how to configure it appropriately, but also explains some of the nonfunctional considerations relevant to the overall data architecture. While there is little actual data science at this stage, it provides the essential platform to pave the way for success in the rest of the book.

In this chapter, we will cover the following topics:

- Data management responsibilities
- Data architecture
- Companion tools

Introducing the Big Data ecosystem

Data management is of particular importance, especially when the data is in flux; either constantly changing or being routinely produced and updated. What is needed in these cases is a way of storing, structuring, and auditing data that allows for the continuous processing and refinement of models and results.

Here, we describe how to best hold and organize your data to integrate with Apache Spark and related tools within the context of a data architecture that is broad enough to fit the everyday requirement.

Data management

Even if, in the medium term, you only intend to play around with a bit of data at home; then without proper data management, more often than not, efforts will escalate to the point where it is easy to lose track of where you are and mistakes will happen. Taking the time to think about the organization of your data, and in particular, its ingestion, is crucial. There's nothing worse than waiting for a long running analytic to complete, collating the results and producing a report, only to discover you used the wrong version of data, or data is incomplete, has missing fields, or even worse you deleted your results!

The bad news is that, despite its importance, data management is an area that is consistently overlooked in both commercial and non-commercial ventures, with precious few off-the-shelf solutions available. The good news is that it is much easier to do great data science using the fundamental building blocks that this chapter describes.

Data management responsibilities

When we think about data, it is easy to overlook the true extent of the scope of the areas we need to consider. Indeed, most data "newbies" think about the scope in this way:

1. Obtain data
2. Place the data somewhere (anywhere)
3. Use the data
4. Throw the data away

In reality, there are a large number of other considerations, it is our combined responsibility to determine which ones apply to a given work piece. The following data management building blocks assist in answering or tracking some important questions about the data:

- File integrity
    - Is the data file complete?
    - How do you know?
    - Was it part of a set?
    - Is the data file correct?
    - Was it tampered with in transit?
- Data integrity
    - Is the data as expected?
    - Are all of the fields present?
    - Is there sufficient metadata?
    - Is the data quality sufficient?
    - Has there been any data drift?
- Scheduling
    - Is the data routinely transmitted?
    - How often does the data arrive?
    - Was the data received on time?
    - Can you prove when the data was received?
    - Does it require acknowledgement?
- Schema management
    - Is the data structured or unstructured?
    - How should the data be interpreted?
    - Can the schema be inferred?
    - Has the data changed over time?
    - Can the schema be evolved from the previous version?
- Version Management
    - What is the version of the data?
    - Is the version correct?
    - How do you handle different versions of the data?
    - How do you know which version you're using?

- Security
    - Is the data sensitive?
    - Does it contain personally identifiable information (PII)?
    - Does it contain personal health information (PHI)?
    - Does it contain payment card information (PCI)?
    - How should I protect the data?
    - Who is entitled to read/write the data?
    - Does it require anonymization/sanitization/obfuscation/encryption?
- Disposal
    - How do we dispose of the data?
    - When do we dispose of the data?

If, after all that, you are still not convinced, before you go ahead and write that bash script using the `gawk` and `crontab` commands, keep reading and you will soon see that there is a far quicker, flexible, and safer method that allow you to start small and incrementally create commercial grade ingestion pipelines!

The right tool for the job

Apache Spark is the emerging de facto standard for scalable data processing. At the time of writing this book, it is the most active **Apache Software Foundation** (**ASF**) project and has a rich variety of companion tools available. There are new projects appearing every day, many of which overlap in functionality. So it takes time to learn what they do and decide whether they are appropriate to use. Unfortunately, there's no quick way around this. Usually, specific trade-offs must be made on a case-by-case basis; there is rarely a one-size-fits-all solution. Therefore, the reader is encouraged to explore the available tools and choose wisely!

Various technologies are introduced throughout this book, and the hope is that they will provide the reader with a taster of some of the more useful and practical ones to a level where they may start utilizing them in their own projects. And further, we hope to show that if the code is written carefully, technologies may be interchanged through clever use of **Application Program Interface** (**APIs**) (or high order functions in Spark Scala) even when a decision is proved to be incorrect.

Overall architecture

Let's start with a high-level introduction to data architectures: what they do, why they're useful, when they should be used, and how Apache Spark fits in.

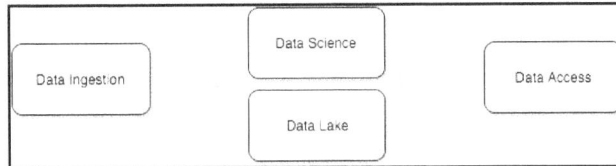

At their most general, modern data architectures have four basic characteristics:

- Data Ingestion
- Data Lake
- Data Science
- Data Access

Let's introduce each of these now, so that we can go into more detail in the later chapters.

Data Ingestion

Traditionally, data is ingested under strict rules and formatted according to a predetermined schema. This process is known as **Extract, Transform, Load** (**ETL**), and is still a very common practice supported by a large array of commercial tools as well as some open source products.

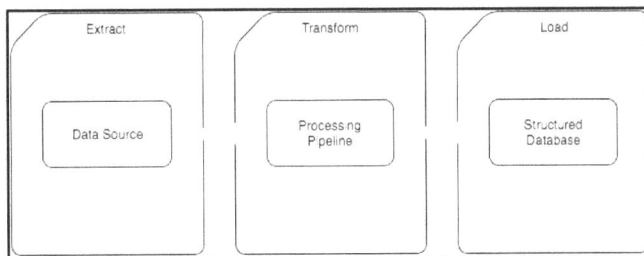

The ETL approach favors performing up-front checks, which ensure data quality and schema conformance, in order to simplify follow-on online analytical processing. It is particularly suited to handling data with a specific set of characteristics, namely, those that relate to a classical entity-relationship model. However, it is not suitable for all scenarios.

During the big data revolution, there was a metaphorical explosion of demand for structured, semi-structured, and unstructured data, leading to the creation of systems that were required to handle data with a different set of characteristics. These came to be defined by the phrase, *4 Vs: Volume, Variety, Velocity, and Veracity* `http://www.ibmbigdatahub.com` `/infographic/four-vs-big-data`. While traditional ETL methods floundered under this new burden-because they simply required too much time to process the vast quantities of data, or were too rigid in the face of change, a different approach emerged. Enter the **schema-on-read** paradigm. Here, data is ingested in its original form (or at least very close to) and the details of normalization, validation, and so on are done at the time of analytical processing.

This is typically referred to as **Extract Load Transform** (**ELT**), a reference to the traditional approach:

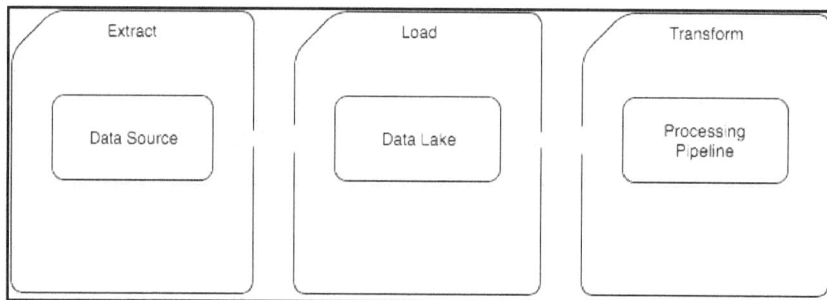

This approach values the delivery of data in a timely fashion, delaying the detailed processing until it is absolutely required. In this way, a data scientist can gain access to the data immediately, searching for insight using a range of techniques not available with a traditional approach.

Although we only provide a high-level overview here, this approach is so important that throughout the book we will explore further by implementing various schema-on-read algorithms. We will assume the ELT method for data ingestion, that is to say we encourage the loading of data at the user's convenience. This may be every n minute, overnight or during times of low usage. The data can then be checked for integrity, quality, and so forth by running batch processing jobs offline, again at the user's discretion.

Data Lake

A data lake is a convenient, ubiquitous store of data. It is useful because it provides a number of key benefits, primarily:

- Reliable storage
- Scalable data processing capability

Let's take a brief look at each of these.

Reliable storage

There is a good choice of underlying storage implementations for a data lake, these include **Hadoop Distributed File System (HDFS)**, **MapR-FS**, and **Amazon AWS S3**.

Throughout the book, HDFS will be the assumed storage implementation. Also, in this book the authors use a distributed Spark setup, deployed on **Yet Another Resource Negotiator (YARN)** running inside a Hortonworks HDP environment. Therefore, HDFS is the technology used, unless otherwise stated. If you are not familiar with any of these technologies, they are discussed further on in this chapter.

In any case, it's worth knowing that Spark references HDFS locations natively, accesses local file locations via the prefix `file://` and references S3 locations via the prefix `s3a://`.

Scalable data processing capability

Clearly, Apache Spark will be our data processing platform of choice. In addition, as you may recall, Spark allows the user to execute code in their preferred environment, be that local, standalone, YARN or Mesos, by configuring the appropriate cluster manager; in `masterURL`. Incidentally, this can be done in any one of the three locations:

- Using the `--master` option when issuing the `spark-submit` command
- Adding the `spark.master` property in the `conf/spark-defaults.conf` file
- Invoking the `setMaster` method on the `SparkConf` object

If you're not familiar with HDFS, or if you do not have access to a cluster, then you can run a local Spark instance using the local filesystem, which is useful for testing. However, beware that there are often bad behaviors that only appear when executing on a cluster. So, if you're serious about Spark, it's worth investing in a distributed cluster manager why not try Spark standalone cluster mode, or Amazon AWS EMR? For example, Amazon offers a number of affordable paths to cloud computing, you can explore the idea of spot instances at `https://aws.amazon.com/ec2/spot/`.

Data science platform

A data science platform provides services and APIs that enable effective data science to take place, including explorative data analysis, machine learning model creation and refinement, image and audio processing, natural language processing, and text sentiment analysis.

This is the area where Spark really excels and forms the primary focus of the remainder of this book, exploiting a robust set of native machine learning libraries, unsurpassed parallel graph processing capabilities and a strong community. Spark provides truly scalable opportunities for data science.

The remaining chapters will provide insight into each of these areas, including `Chapter 6`, *Scraping Link-Based External Data*, `Chapter 7`, *Building Communities*, and `Chapter 8`, *Building a Recommendation System*.

Data Access

Data in a data lake is most frequently accessed by data engineers and scientists using the Hadoop ecosystem tools, such as Apache Spark, Pig, Hive, Impala, or Drill. However, there are times when other users, or even other systems, need access to the data and the normal tools are either too technical or do not meet the demanding expectations of the user in terms of real-world latency.

In these circumstances, the data often needs to be copied into data marts or index stores so that it may be exposed to more traditional methods, such as a report or dashboard. This process, which typically involves creating indexes and restructuring data for low-latency access, is known as data egress.

Fortunately, Apache Spark has a wide variety of adapters and connectors into traditional databases, BI tools, and visualization and reporting software. Many of these will be introduced throughout the book.

Data technologies

When Hadoop first started, the word Hadoop referred to the combination of HDFS and the MapReduce processing paradigm, as that was the outline of the original paper `http://research.google.com/archive/mapreduce.html`. Since that time, a plethora of technologies have emerged to complement Hadoop, and with the development of Apache YARN we now see other processing paradigms emerge such as Spark.

Hadoop is now often used as a colloquialism for the entire big data software stack and so it would be prudent at this point to define the scope of that stack for this book. The typical data architecture with a selection of technologies we will visit throughout the book is detailed as follows:

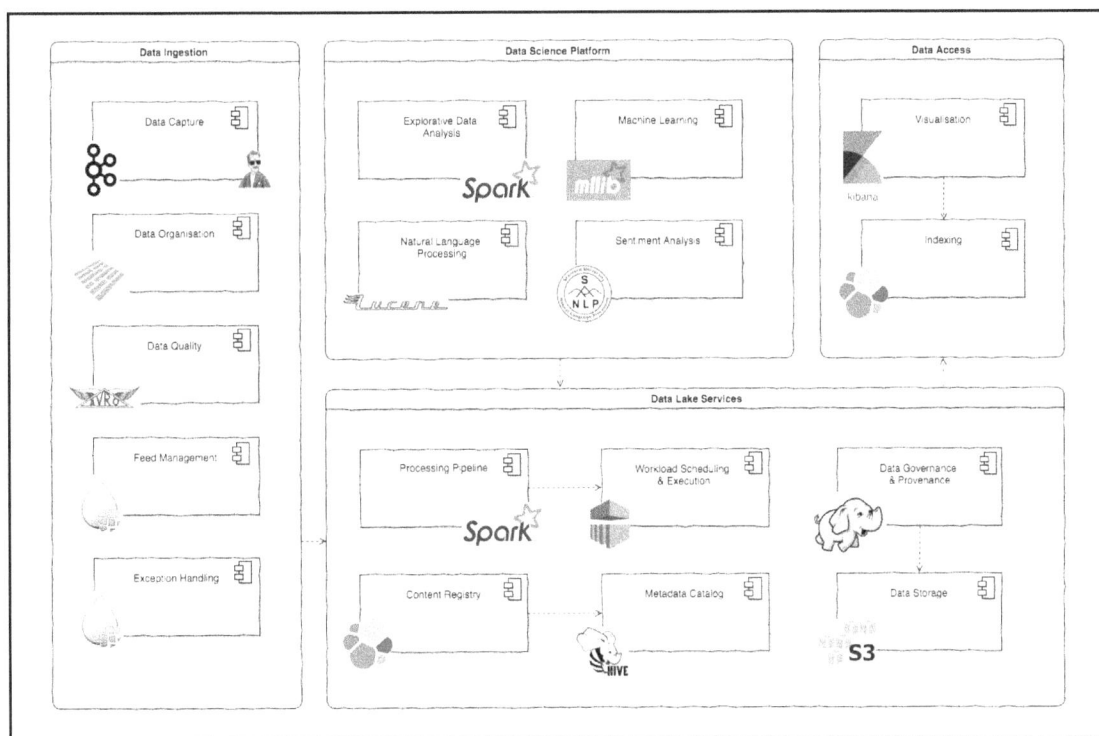

The relationship between these technologies is a dense topic as there are complex interdependencies, for example, Spark depends on GeoMesa, which depends on Accumulo, which depends on Zookeeper and HDFS! Therefore, in order to manage these relationships, there are platforms available, such as Cloudera or Hortonworks HDP `http://hortonworks.com/products/sandbox/`. These provide consolidated user interfaces and centralized configuration. The choice of platform is that of the reader, however, it is not recommended to install a few of the technologies initially and then move to a managed platform as the version problems encountered will be very complex. Therefore, it is usually easier to start with a clean machine and make a decision upfront as to which direction to take.

All of the software we use in this book is platform-agnostic and therefore fits into the general architecture described earlier. It can be installed independently and it is relatively straightforward to use with single or multiple server environment without the use of a managed product.

The role of Apache Spark

In many ways, Apache Spark is the glue that holds these components together. It increasingly represents the hub of the software stack. It integrates with a wide variety of components but none of them are hard-wired. Indeed, even the underlying storage mechanism can be swapped out. Combining this feature with the ability to leverage different processing frameworks means the original Hadoop technologies effectively become components, rather than an imposing framework. The logical diagram of our architecture appears as follows:

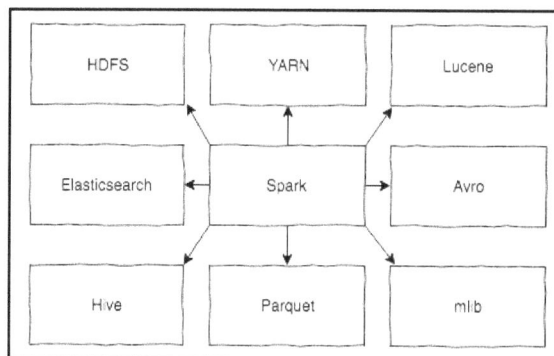

As Spark has gained momentum and wide-scale industry acceptance, many of the original Hadoop implementations for various components have been refactored for Spark. Thus, to add further complexity to the picture, there are often several possible ways to programmatically leverage any particular component; not least the imperative and declarative versions depending upon whether an API has been ported from the original Hadoop Java implementation. We have attempted to remain as true as possible to the Spark ethos throughout the remaining chapters.

Companion tools

Now that we have established a technology stack to use, let's describe each of the components and explain why they are useful in a Spark environment. This part of the book is designed as a reference rather than a straight read. If you're familiar with most of the technologies, then you can refresh your knowledge and continue to the next section, Chapter 2, *Data Acquisition*.

Apache HDFS

The **Hadoop Distributed File System** (**HDFS**) is a distributed filesystem with built-in redundancy. It is optimized to work on three or more nodes by default (although one will work fine and the limit can be increased), which provides the ability to store data in replicated blocks. So not only is a file split into a number of blocks but three copies of those blocks exist at any one time. This cleverly provides data redundancy (if one is lost two others still exist) but also provides *data locality*. When a distributed job is run against HDFS, not only will the system attempt to gather all of the blocks required for the data input to that job, it will also attempt to only use the blocks which are physically close to the server running that job; so it has the ability to reduce network bandwidth using only the blocks on its local storage, or those on nodes close to itself. This is achieved in practice by allocating HDFS physical disks to nodes, and nodes to racks; blocks are written in a node-local, rack-local, and cluster-local method. All instructions to HDFS are passed through a central server called **NameNode**, so this provides a possible central point of failure; there are various methods for providing NameNode redundancy.

Furthermore, in a multi-tenanted HDFS scenario, where many processes are accessing the same file at the same time, load balancing can also be achieved through the use of multiple blocks; for example, if a file takes up one block, this block is replicated three times and, therefore, potentially can be read from three different physical locations concurrently. Although this may not seem like a big win, on clusters of hundreds or thousands of nodes the network IO is often the single most limiting factor to a running job–the authors have certainly experienced times on multi-thousand node clusters where jobs have had to wait hours to complete purely because the network bandwidth has been maxed out due to the large number of other threads calling for data.

If you are running a laptop, require data to be stored locally, or wish to use the hardware you already have, then HDFS is a good option.

Advantages

The following are the advantages of using HDFS:

- **Redundancy**: Configurable replication of blocks provides tolerance for node and disk failure
- **Load balancing**: Block replication means the same data can be accessed from different physical locations
- **Data locality**: Analytics try to access the closest relevant physical block, reducing network IO.
- **Data balance**: An algorithm is available to re-balance the data blocks as they become too clustered or fragmented.
- **Flexible storage**: If more space is needed, further disks and nodes can be added; although this is not a hot process, the cluster will require outage to add these resources
- **Additional costs**: No third-party costs are involved
- **Data encryption**: Implicit encryption (when turned on)

Disadvantages

The following are the disadvantages:

- The NameNode provides for a central point of failure; to mitigate this, there are secondary and high availability options available
- A cluster requires basic administration and potentially some hardware effort

Installation

To use HDFS, we should decide whether to run Hadoop in a local, pseudo-distributed or fully-distributed manner; for a single server, pseudo-distributed is useful as analytics should translate directly from this machine to any Hadoop cluster. In any case, we should install Hadoop with at least the following components:

- NameNode
- Secondary NameNode (or High Availability NameNode)
- DataNode

Hadoop can be installed via `http://hadoop.apache.org/releases.html`.

Spark needs to know the location of the Hadoop configuration, specifically the following files: `hdfs-site.xml`, `core-site.xml`. This is then set in the configuration parameter `HADOOP_CONF_DIR` in your Spark configuration.

HDFS will then be available natively, so the file `hdfs://user/local/dir/text.txt` can be addressed in Spark simply using `/user/local/dir/text.txt`.

Amazon S3

S3 abstracts away all of the issues related to parallelism, storage restrictions, and security allowing very large parallel read/write operations along with a great **Service Level Agreement** (**SLA**) for a very small cost. This is perfect if you need to get up and running quickly, can't store data locally, or don't know what your future storage requirements might be. It should be recognized that `s3n` and `S3a` utilize an object storage model, not file storage, and therefore there are some compromises:

- Eventual consistency is where changes made by one application (creation, updates, and deletions) will not be visible until some undefined time, although most AWS regions now support read-after-write consistency.
- `s3n` and `s3a` utilize nonatomic rename and delete operations; therefore, renaming or deleting large directories takes time proportional to the number of entries. However, target files can remain visible to other processes during this time, and indeed, until the eventual consistency has been resolved.

S3 can be accessed through command-line tools (s3cmd) via a webpage and via APIs for most popular languages; it has native integration with Hadoop and Spark through a basic configuration.

Advantages

The following are the advantages:

- Infinite storage capacity
- No hardware considerations
- Encryption available (user stored keys)
- 99.9% availability
- Redundancy

Disadvantages

The following are the disadvantages:

- Cost to store and transfer data
- No data locality
- Eventual consistency
- Relatively high latency

Installation

You can create an AWS account: https://aws.amazon.com/free/. Through this account, you will have access to S3 and will simply need to create some credentials.

The current S3 standard is s3a; to use it through Spark requires some changes to the Spark configuration:

```
spark.hadoop.fs.s3a.impl=org.apache.hadoop.fs.s3a.S3AFileSystem
spark.hadoop.fs.s3a.access.key=MyAccessKeyID
spark.hadoop.fs.s3a.secret.key=MySecretKey
```

If using HDP, you may also need:

```
spark.driver.extraClassPath=${HADOOP_HOME}/extlib/hadoop-aws-
currentversion.jar:${HADOOP_HOME}/ext/aws-java-sdk-1.7.4.jar
```

All S3 files will then be accessible within Spark using the prefix `s3a://` to the S3 object reference:

```
val rdd = spark.sparkContext.textFile("s3a://user/dir/text.txt")
```

We can also use the AWS credentials inline assuming that we have set `spark.hadoop.fs.s3a.impl`:

```
spark.sparkContext.textFile("s3a://AccessID:SecretKey@user/dir/file")
```

However, this method will not accept the forward-slash character / in either of the keys. This is usually solved by obtaining another key from AWS (keep generating a new one until there are no forward-slashes present).

We can also browse the objects through the web interface located under the S3 tab in your AWS account.

Apache Kafka

Apache Kafka is a distributed, message broker written in Scala and available under the Apache Software Foundation license. The project aims to provide a unified, high-throughput, low-latency platform for handling real-time data feeds. The result is essentially a massively scalable publish-subscribe message queue, making it highly valuable for enterprise infrastructures to process streaming data.

Advantages

The following are the advantages:

- Publish-subscribe messaging
- Fault-tolerant
- Guaranteed delivery
- Replay messages on failure
- Highly-scalable, shared-nothing architecture
- Supports back pressure
- Low latency
- Good Spark-streaming integration
- Simple for clients to implement

Disadvantages

The following are the disadvantages:

- At least once semantics – cannot provide exactly-once messaging due to lack of a transaction manager (as yet)
- Requires Zookeeper for operation

Installation

As Kafka is a pub-sub tool, its purpose is to manage messages (publishers) and direct them to the relevant endpoints (subscribers). This is done using a broker, which is installed when implementing Kafka. Kafka is available through the Hortonworks HDP platform, or can be installed independently from this link `http://kafka.apache.org/downloads.html`.

Kafka uses Zookeeper to manage leadership election (as Kafka can be distributed thus allowing for redundancy), the quick start guide found in the preceding link can be used to set up a single node Zookeeper instance, and also provide a client and consumer to publish and subscribe to topics, which provide the mechanism for message handling.

Apache Parquet

Since the inception of Hadoop, the idea of columnar-based formats (as opposed to row based) has been gaining increasing support. Parquet has been developed to take advantage of compressed, efficient columnar data representation and is designed with complex nested data structures in mind; taking the lead from algorithms discussed in the Apache Dremel paper `http://research.google.com/pubs/pub36632.html`. Parquet allows compression schemes to be specified on a per-column level, and is future-proofed for adding more encodings as they are implemented. It has also been designed to provide compatibility throughout the Hadoop ecosystem and, like Avro, stores the data schema with the data itself.

Advantages

The following are the advantages:

- Columnar storage
- Highly storage efficient
- Per column compression

- Supports predicate pushdown
- Supports column pruning
- Compatible with other formats, for example, Avro
- Read efficient, designed for partial data retrieval

Disadvantages

The following are the disadvantages:

- Not good for random access
- Potentially computationally intensive for writes

Installation

Parquet is natively available in Spark and can be accessed directly as follows:

```
val ds = Seq(1, 2, 3, 4, 5).toDS
ds.write.parquet("/data/numbers.parquet")
val fromParquet = spark.read.parquet("/data/numbers.parquet")
```

Apache Avro

Apache Avro is a data serialization framework originally developed for Hadoop. It uses JSON for defining data types and protocols (although there is an alternative IDL), and serializes data in a compact binary format. Avro provides both a serialization format for persistent data, and a wire format for communication between Hadoop nodes, and from client programs to the Hadoop services. Another useful feature is its ability to store the data schema along with the data itself, so any Avro file can always be read without the need for referencing external sources. Further, Avro supports schema evolution and therefore backwards compatibility between Avro files written with older schema versions being read with a newer schema version.

Advantages

The following are the advantages:

- Schema evolution
- Disk space savings

- Supports schemas in JSON and IDL
- Supports many languages
- Supports compression

Disadvantages

The following are the disadvantages:

- Requires schema to read and write data
- Serialization computationally heavy

Installation

As we are using Scala, Spark, and Maven environments in this book, Avro can be imported as follows:

```
<dependency>
    <groupId>org.apache.avro</groupId>
    <artifactId>avro</artifactId>
    <version>1.7.7</version>
</dependency>
```

It is then a matter of creating a schema and producing the Scala code to write data to Avro using the schema. This is explained in detail in `Chapter 3`, *Input Formats and Schema*.

Apache NiFi

Apache NiFi originated from the United States **National Security Agency** (**NSA**) where it was released to open source in 2014 as part of their Technology Transfer Program. NiFi enables the production of scalable directed graphs of data routing and transformation, within a simple user interface. It also supports data provenance, a wide range of prebuilt processors and the ability to build new processors quickly and efficiently. It has prioritization, tunable delivery tolerances, and back-pressure features included, which allow the user to tune processors and pipelines for specific requirements, even allowing flow modification at runtime. All of this adds up to an incredibly flexible tool for building everything from one-off file download data flows through to enterprise grade ETL pipelines. It is generally quicker to build a pipeline and download files with NiFi than even writing a quick bash script, adding in the feature-rich processors used for this and it makes for a compelling proposition.

Advantages

The following are the advantages:

- Wide range of processors
- Hub and spoke architecture
- **Graphical User Interface** (**GUI**)
- Scalable
- Simplifies parallel processing
- Simplifies thread handling
- Allows runtime modifications
- Redundancy through clusters

Disadvantages

The following are the disadvantages:

- No cross-cutting error handler
- Expression language is only partially implemented
- Flowfile version management lacking

Installation

Apache NiFi can be installed with Hortonworks and is known as Hortonworks Dataflow. It is also available as a standalone install from Apache, `https://nifi.apache.org/`. There is an introduction to NiFi in `Chapter 2`, *Data Acquisition*.

Apache YARN

YARN is the principle component of Hadoop 2.0, which essentially allows Hadoop to plug in processing paradigms rather than being limited to just the original MapReduce. YARN consists of three main components: the resource manager, node manager, and application manager. It is out of the scope of this book to dive into YARN; the main thing to understand is that if we are running a Hadoop cluster, then our Spark jobs can be executed using YARN in client mode, as follows:

```
spark-submit --class package.Class /
             --master yarn /
             --deploy-mode client [options] <app jar> [app options]
```

Advantages

The following are the advantages:

- Supports Spark
- Supports prioritized scheduling
- Supports data locality
- Job history archive
- Works out of the box with HDP

Disadvantages

The following are the disadvantages:

- No CPU resource control
- No support for data lineage

Installation

YARN is installed as part of Hadoop; this could either be Hortonworks HDP, Apache Hadoop, or one of the other vendors. In any case, we should install Hadoop with at least the following components:

- ResourceManager
- NodeManager (1 or more)

To ensure that Spark can use YARN, it simply needs to know the location of `yarn-site.xml`, which is set using the `YARN_CONF_DIR` parameter in your Spark configuration.

Apache Lucene

Lucene is an indexing and search library tool originally built with Java, but now ported to several other languages, including Python. Lucene has spawned a number of subprojects in its time, including Mahout, Nutch, and Tika. These have now become top-level Apache projects in their own right while Solr has more recently joined as a subproject. Lucene has a comprehensive capability, but is particularly known for its use in Q&A search engines and information-retrieval systems.

Advantages

The following are the advantages:

- Highly efficient full-text searches
- Scalable
- Multilanguage support
- Excellent out-of-the-box functionality

Disadvantages

The disadvantage is databases are generally better for relational operations.

Installation

Lucene can be downloaded from `https://lucene.apache.org/` if you wish to learn more and interact with the library directly.

When utilizing Lucene, we only really need to include `lucene-core-<version>.jar` in our project. For example, when using Maven:

```
<dependency>
    <groupId>org.apache.lucene</groupId>
    <artifactId>lucene-core</artifactId>
    <version>6.1.0</version>
</dependency>
```

Kibana

Kibana is an analytics and visualization platform that also provides charting and streaming data summarization. It uses Elasticsearch for its data source (which in turn uses Lucene) and can therefore leverage very powerful search and indexing capabilities at scale. Kibana can be used to visualize data in many different ways, including bar charts, histograms, and maps. We have mentioned Kibana briefly towards the end of this chapter and it will be used extensively throughout this book.

Advantages

The following are the advantages:

- Visualize data at scale
- Intuitive interface to quickly develop dashboards

Disadvantages

The following are the disadvantages:

- Only integrates with Elasticsearch
- Kibana releases are tied to specific Elasticsearch versions

Installation

Kibana can easily be installed as a standalone piece since it has its own web server. It can be downloaded from `https://www.elastic.co/downloads/kibana`. As Kibana requires Elasticsearch, this will also need to be installed; see preceding link for more information. The Kibana configuration is handled in `config/kibana.yml`, if you have installed a standalone version of Elasticsearch, then no changes are required, it will work out of the box!

Elasticsearch

Elasticsearch is a web-based search engine based on Lucene (see previously). It provides a distributed, multitenant-capable full-text search engine with schema-free JSON documents. It is built in Java but can be utilized from any language due to its HTTP web interface. This makes it particularly useful for transactions and/or data-intensive instructions that are to be displayed via web pages.

Advantages

The advantages are as follows:

- Distributed
- Schema free
- HTTP interface

Disadvantages

The disadvantages are as follows

- Unable to perform distributed transactions
- Lack of frontend tooling

Installation

Elasticsearch can be installed from `https://www.elastic.co/downloads/elasticsearch`. To provide access to the Rest API, we can import the Maven dependency:

```
<dependency>
    <groupId>org.elasticsearch</groupId>
    <artifactId>elasticsearch-spark_2.10</artifactId>
    <version>2.2.0-m1</version>
</dependency>
```

There is also a great tool to help with administering Elasticsearch content. Search for the Chrome extension, Sense, at `https://chrome.google.com/webstore/category/extensions`. With a further explanation found at:
`https://www.elastic.co/blog/found-sense-a-cool-json-aware-interface-to-elasticsearch`. Alternatively, it is available for Kibana at
`https://www.elastic.co/guide/en/sense/current/installing.html`.

Accumulo

Accumulo is a no-sql database based on Google's Bigtable design and was originally developed by the American National Security Agency, subsequently being released to the Apache community in 2011. Accumulo offers us the usual big data advantages such as bulk loading and parallel reading but also has some additional capabilities; iterators, for efficient server and client side pre-computation, data aggregation and, most importantly, cell level security. The security aspect of Accumulo makes it very useful for Enterprise usage as it enables flexible security in a multitenant environment. Accumulo is powered by Apache Zookeeper, in the same way as Kafka, and also leverages Apache Thrift, `https://thrift.apache.org/`, which enables a cross language **Remote Procedural Call (RPC)** capability.

Advantages

The advantages are as follows:

- Pure implementation of Google Bigtable
- Cell level security
- Scalable
- Redundancy
- Provides iterators for server-side computation

Disadvantages

The disadvantages are as follows:

- Zookeeper not universally popular with DevOps
- Not always the most efficient choice for bulk relational operations

Installation

Accumulo can be installed as part of the Hortonworks HDP release, or may be installed as a standalone instance from `https://accumulo.apache.org/`. The instance should then be configured using the installation documentation, at the time of writing `https://accumulo.apache.org/1.7/accumulo_user_manual#_installation`.

In `Chapter 7`, *Building Communities*, we demonstrate the use of Accumulo with Spark, along with some of the more advanced features such as `Iterators` and `InputFormats`. We also show how to work with data between Elasticsearch and Accumulo.

Summary

In this chapter, we introduced the idea of data architecture and explained how to group responsibilities into capabilities that help manage data throughout its lifecycle. We explained that all data handling requires a level of due diligence, whether this is enforced by corporate rules or otherwise, and without this, analytics and their results can quickly become invalid.

Having scoped our data architecture, we have walked through the individual components and their respective advantages/disadvantages, explaining that our choices are based upon collective experience. Indeed, there are always options when it comes to choosing components and their individual features should always be carefully considered before any commitment.

In the next chapter, we will dive deeper into how to source and capture data. We will advise on how to bring data onto the platform and discuss aspects related to processing and handling data through a pipeline.

2
Data Acquisition

As a data scientist, one of the most important tasks is to load data into your data science platform. Rather than having uncontrolled, ad hoc processes, this chapter explains how a general data ingestion pipeline in Spark can be constructed that serves as a reusable component across many feeds of input data. We walk through a configuration and demonstrate how it delivers vital feed management information under a variety of running conditions.

Readers will learn how to construct a *content register* and use it to track all input loaded to the system and to deliver metrics on ingestion pipelines, so that these flows can be reliably run as an automated, lights-out process.

In this chapter, we will cover the following topics:

- Introduce the **Global Database of Events, Language, and Tone** (**GDELT**) dataset
- Data pipelines
- Universal ingestion framework
- Real-time monitoring for new data
- Receiving streaming data via Kafka
- Registering new content and vaulting for tracking purposes
- Visualization of content metrics in Kibana to monitor ingestion processes and data health

Data pipelines

Even with the most basic of analytics, we always require some data. In fact, finding the *right data* is probably among the hardest problems to solve in data science (but that's a whole topic for another book!). We have already seen in the last chapter that the way in which we obtain our data can be as simple or complicated as is needed. In practice, we can break this decision down into two distinct areas: *ad hoc* and *scheduled*.

- **Ad hoc data acquisition**: is the most common method during prototyping and small scale analytics as it usually doesn't require any additional software to implement. The user acquires some data and simply downloads it from source as and when required. This method is often a matter of clicking on a web link and storing the data somewhere convenient, although the data may still need to be versioned and secure.

- **Scheduled data acquisition**: is used in more controlled environments for large scale and production analytics; there is also an excellent case for ingesting a dataset into a data lake for possible future use. With the **Internet of Things** (**IoT**) on the increase, huge volumes of data are being produced in many cases, if the data is not ingested immediately it is lost forever. Much of this data may not have an apparent use today, but could have in the future; so the mindset is to gather all of the data in case it is needed and delete it later when we are sure it is not.

It's clear we need a flexible approach to data acquisition that supports a variety of procurement options.

Universal ingestion framework

There are many ways to approach data acquisition, ranging from home-grown bash scripts through to high-end commercial tools. The aim of this section is to introduce a highly-flexible framework that we can use for small-scale data ingest, and then grow as our requirements change all the way through to a full, corporately-managed workflow if needed. That framework will be built using **Apache NiFi**. NiFi enables us to build large-scale, integrated data pipelines that move data around the planet. In addition, it's also incredibly flexible and easy to build simple pipelines usually quicker even than using bash or any other traditional scripting method.

> If an ad hoc approach is taken to source the same dataset on a number of occasions, then some serious thought should be given as to whether it falls into the scheduled category, or at least whether a more robust storage and versioning setup should be introduced.

We have chosen to use Apache NiFi as it offers a solution that provides the ability to create many pipelines of varying complexity that can be scaled to truly big data and IoT levels, and it also provides a great drag and drop interface (using what's known as *flow-based programming* `https://en.wikipedia.org/wiki/Flow-based_programming`). With patterns, templates, and modules for workflow production, it automatically takes care of many of the complex features that traditionally plague developers such as multithreading, connection management, and scalable processing. For our purposes, it will enable us to quickly build simple pipelines for prototyping, and scale these to full production where required.

It's pretty well documented and easy to get running by following the information on `https://nifi.apache.org/download.html`. It runs in a browser and looks like this:

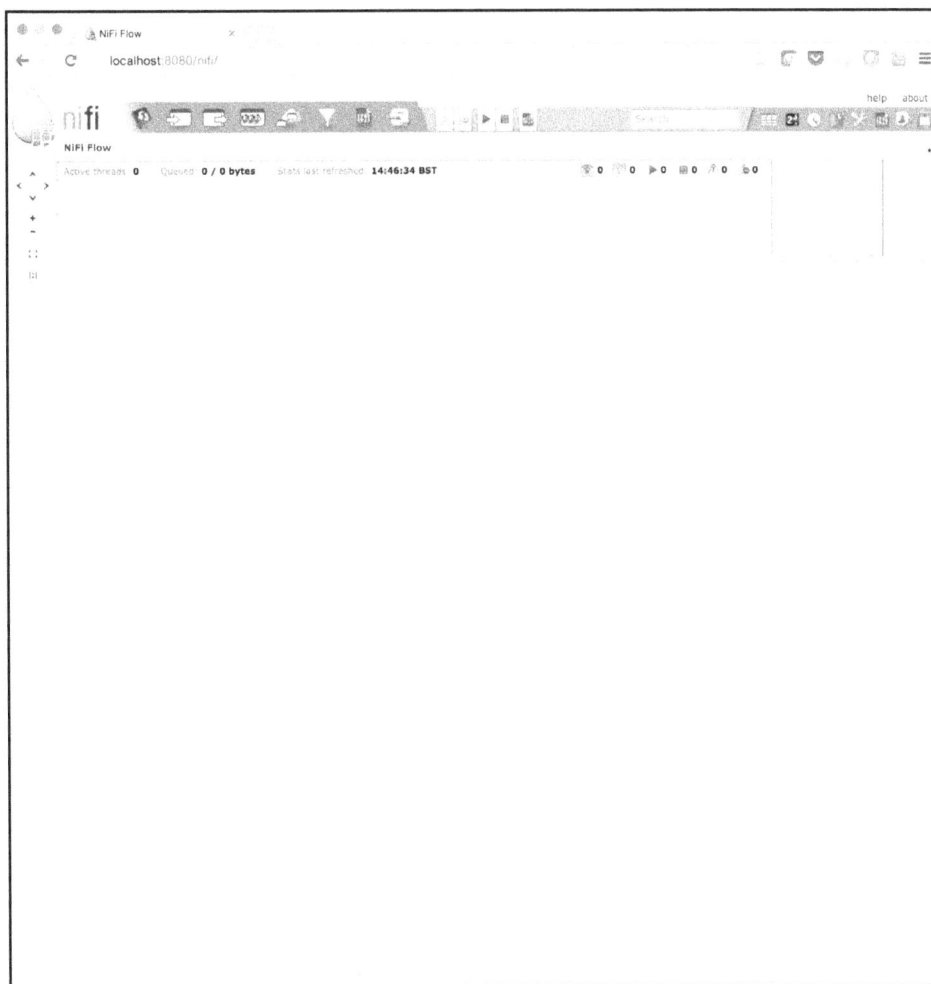

We leave the installation of NiFi as an exercise for the reader, which we would encourage you to do as we will be using it in the following section.

Introducing the GDELT news stream

Hopefully, we have NiFi up and running now and can start to ingest some data. So, let's start with some global news media data from GDELT. Here's our brief, taken from the GDELT website,

`http://blog.gdeltproject.org/gdelt-2-0-our-global-world-in-realtime/`:

> *"Within 15 minutes of GDELT monitoring a news report breaking anywhere the world, it has translated it, processed it to identify all events, counts, quotes, people, organizations, locations, themes, emotions, relevant imagery, video, and embedded social media posts, placed it into global context, and made all of this available via a live open metadata firehose enabling open research on the planet itself.*

> *[As] the single largest deployment in the world of sentiment analysis, we hope that by bringing together so many emotional and thematic dimensions crossing so many languages and disciplines, and applying all of it in realtime to breaking news from across the planet, that this will spur an entirely new era in how we think about emotion and the ways in which it can help us better understand how we contextualize, interpret, respond to, and understand global events."*

Quite a challenging remit I think you'd agree! Therefore, rather than delay, pausing to specify the details here, let's get going straight away. We'll introduce the aspects of GDELT as we use them throughout the coming chapters.

In order to start consuming this open data, we'll need to hook into that metadata firehose and ingest the news streams onto our platform. How do we do this? Let's start by finding out what data is available.

Discovering GDELT in real-time

GDELT publishes a list of the latest files on their website. This list is updated every 15 minutes. In NiFi, we can set up a dataflow that will poll the GDELT website, source a file from this list, and save it to HDFS so we can use it later.

Inside the NiFi dataflow designer, create a HTTP connector by dragging a processor onto the canvas and selecting `GetHTTP` function.

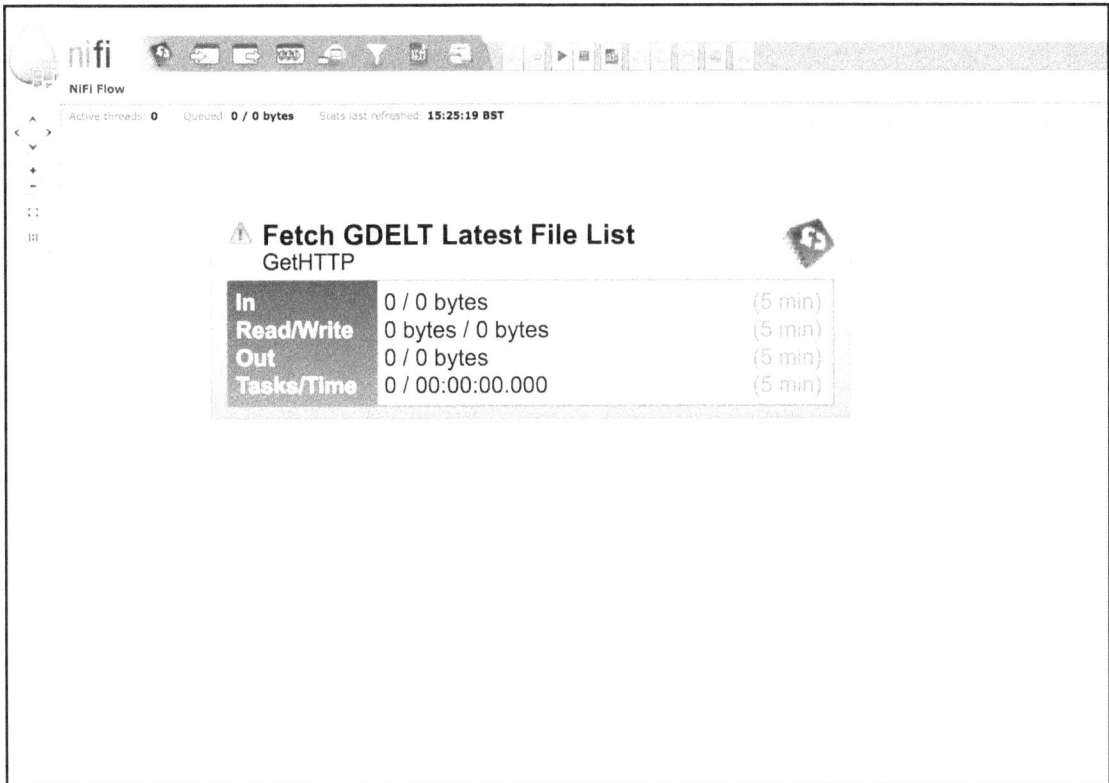

To configure this processor, you'll need to enter the URL of the file list as:

```
http://data.gdeltproject.org/gdeltv2/lastupdate.txt
```

Also, provide a temporary filename for the file list you will download. In the example below, we've used NiFi's expression language to generate a universally unique key so that files are not overwritten (UUID()).

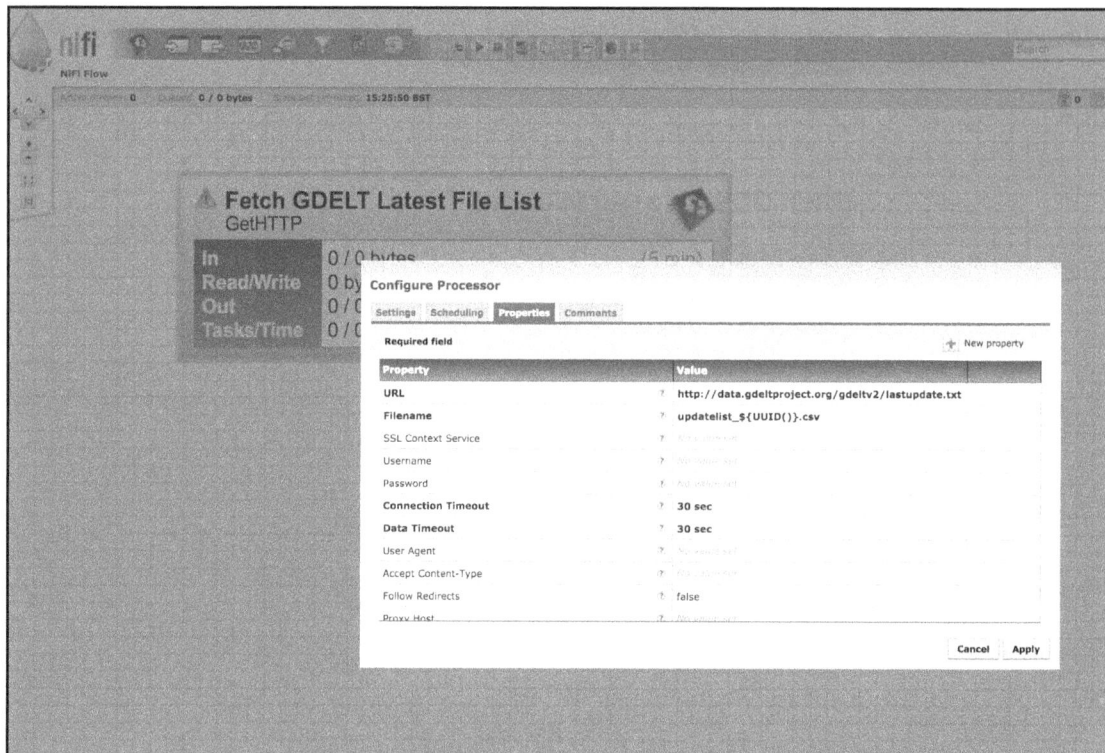

It's worth noting that with this type of processor (GetHTTP method), NiFi supports a number of scheduling and timing options for the polling and retrieval. For now, we're just going to use the default options and let NiFi manage the polling intervals for us.

An example of the latest file list from GDELT is shown as follows:

Next, we will parse the URL of the GKG news stream so that we can fetch it in a moment. Create a regular expression parser by dragging a processor onto the canvas and selecting ExtractText. Now, position the new processor underneath the existing one and drag a line from the top processor to the bottom one. Finish by selecting the success relationship in the connection dialog that pops up.

This is shown in the following example:

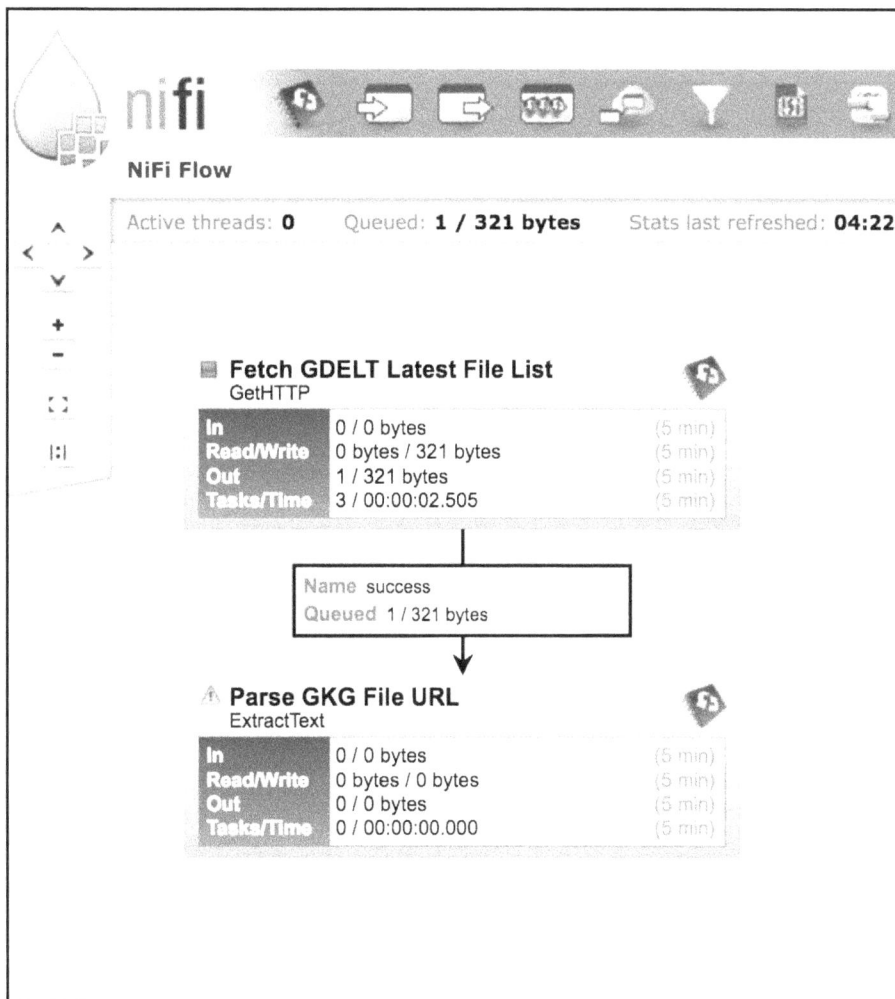

Next, let's configure the `ExtractText` processor to use a regular expression that matches only the relevant text of the file list, for example:

```
([^ ]*gkg.csv.*)
```

From this regular expression, NiFi will create a new property (in this case, called `url`) associated with the flow design, which will take on a new value as each particular instance goes through the flow. It can even be configured to support multiple threads.

Again, this is example is shown as follows:

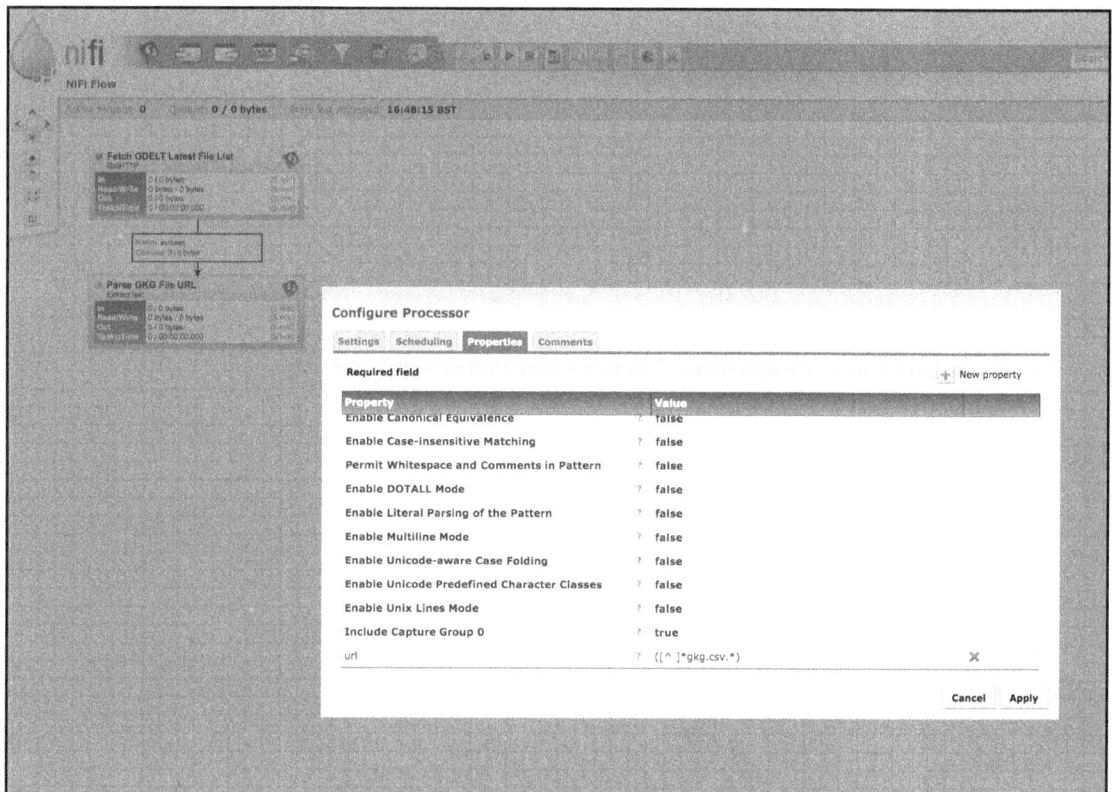

It's worth noting here, that while this is a fairly specific example, the technique is deliberately general purpose and can be used in many situations.

Our first GDELT feed

Now that we have the URL of the GKG feed, we fetch it by configuring an `InvokeHTTP` processor to use the `url` property we previously created as it's remote endpoint, and dragging the line as before.

All that remains is to decompress the zipped content with an `UnpackContent` processor (using the basic `.zip` format) and save to HDFS using a `PutHDFS` processor, like so:

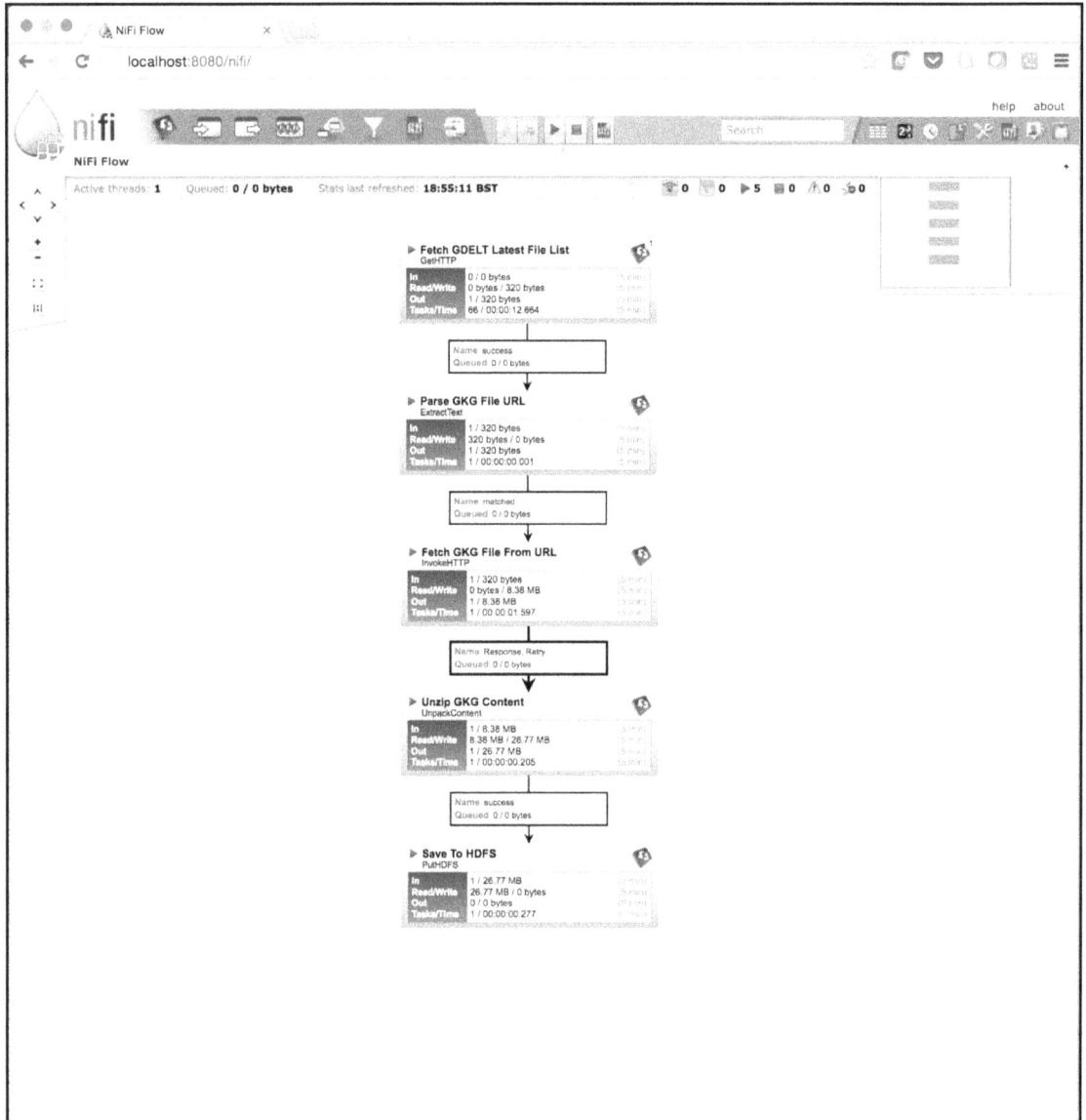

Improving with publish and subscribe

So far, this flow looks very *point-to-point*, meaning that if we were to introduce a new consumer of data, for example, a Spark-streaming job, the flow must be changed. For example, the flow design might have to change to look like this:

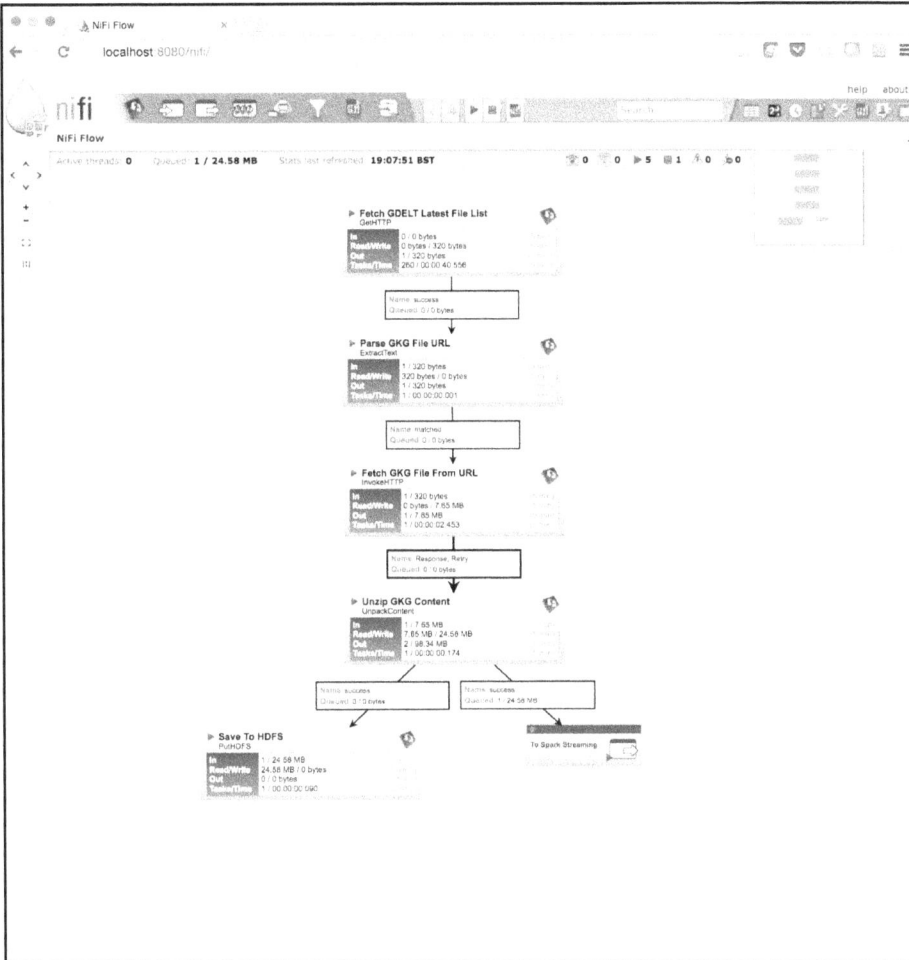

If we add yet another, the flow must change again. In fact, each time we add a new consumer, the flow gets a little more complicated, particularly when all the error handling is added. This is clearly not always desirable, as introducing or removing consumers (or producers) of data, might be something we want to do often, even frequently. Plus, it's also a good idea to try to keep your flows as simple and reusable as possible.

Therefore, for a more flexible pattern, instead of writing directly to HDFS, we can publish to *Apache Kafka*. This gives us the ability to add and remove consumers at any time without changing the data ingestion pipeline. We can also still write to HDFS from Kafka if needed, possibly even by designing a separate NiFi flow, or connect directly to Kafka using the Spark-streaming.

To do this, we create a Kafka writer by dragging a processor onto the canvas and selecting `PutKafka`.

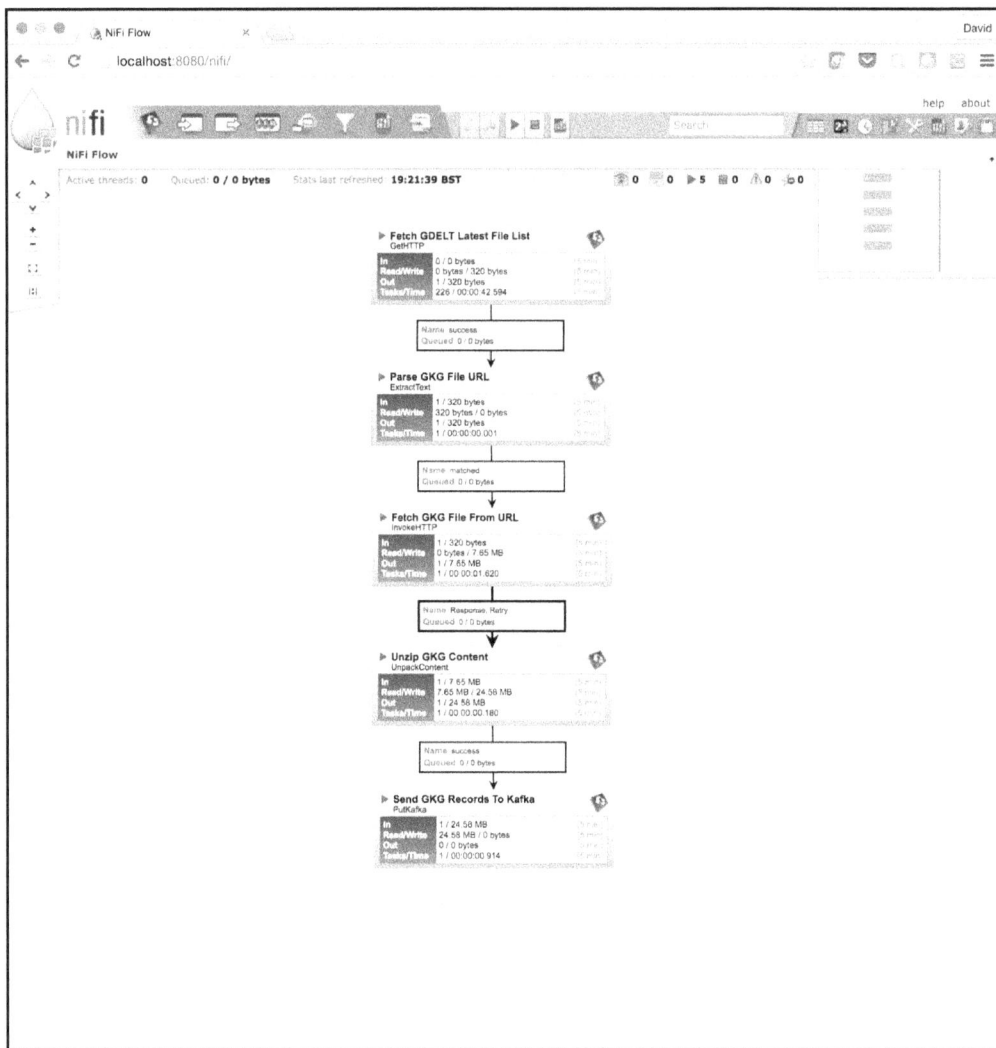

We now have a simple flow that continuously polls for an available file list, routinely retrieving the latest copy of a new stream over the web as it becomes available, decompressing the content, and streaming it record-by-record into Kafka, a durable, fault-tolerant, distributed message queue, for processing by the Spark-streaming or storage in HDFS. And what's more, without writing a single line of bash!

Content registry

We have seen in this chapter that data ingestion is an area that is often overlooked, and that its importance cannot be underestimated. At this point, we have a pipeline that enables us to ingest data from a source, schedule that ingest, and direct the data to our repository of choice. But the story does not end there. Now we have the data, we need to fulfil our data management responsibilities. Enter the *content registry*.

We're going to build an index of metadata related to that data we have ingested. The data itself will still be directed to storage (HDFS, in our example) but, in addition, we will store metadata about the data, so that we can track what we've received and understand basic information about it, such as, when we received it, where it came from, how big it is, what type it is, and so on.

Choices and more choices

The choice of which technology we use to store this metadata is, as we have seen, one based upon knowledge and experience. For metadata indexing, we will require at least the following attributes:

- Easily searchable
- Scalable
- Parallel write ability
- Redundancy

There are many ways to meet these requirements, for example we could write the metadata to Parquet, store in HDFS, and search using Spark SQL. However, here we will use *Elasticsearch* as it meets the requirements a little better, most notably because it facilitates low latency queries of our metadata over a REST API, very useful for creating dashboards. In fact, Elasticsearch has the advantage of integrating directly with **Kibana**, meaning it can quickly produce rich visualizations of our content registry. For this reason, we will proceed with Elasticsearch in mind.

Going with the flow

Using our current NiFi pipeline flow, let's fork the output from "Fetch GKG files from URL" to add an additional set of steps to allow us to capture and store this metadata in Elasticsearch. These are:

1. Replace the flow content with our metadata model.
2. Capture the metadata.
3. Store directly in Elasticsearch.

Here's what this looks like in NiFi:

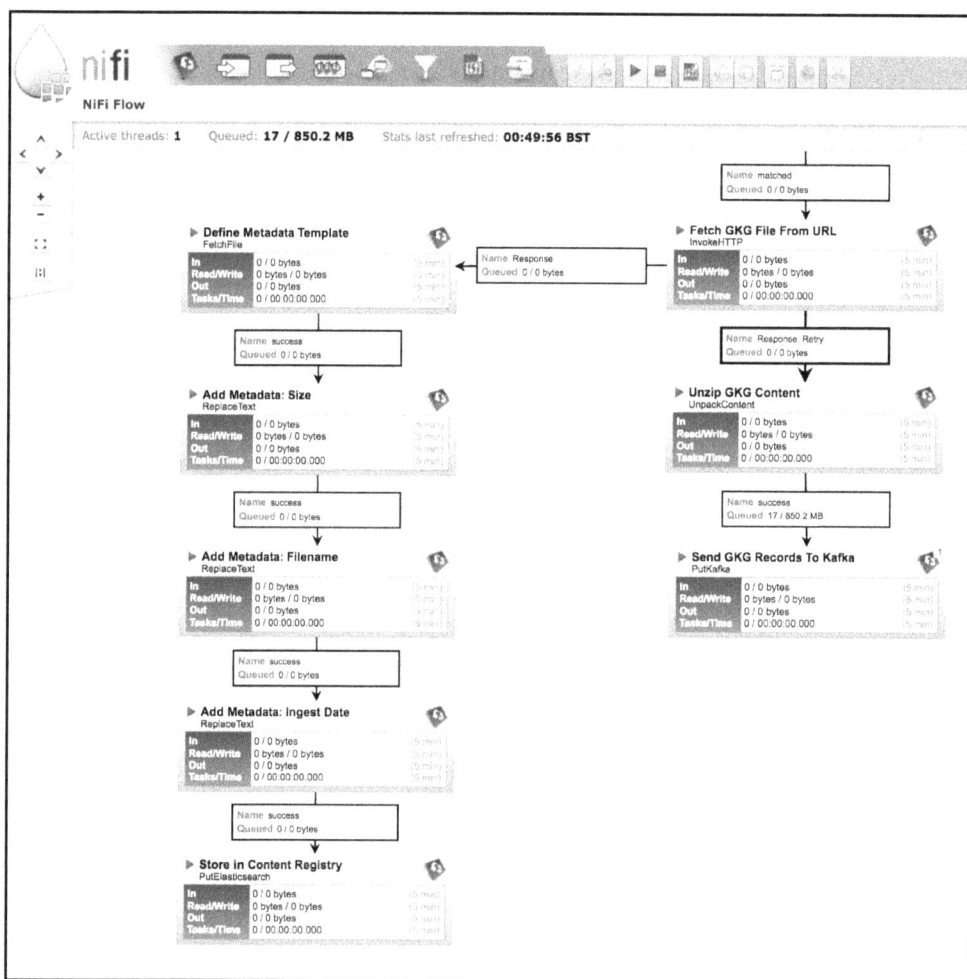

Metadata model

So, the first step here is to define our metadata model. And there are many areas we could consider, but let's select a set that helps tackle a few key points from earlier discussions. This will provide a good basis upon which further data can be added in the future, if required. So, let's keep it simple and use the following three attributes:

- File size
- Date ingested
- File name

These will provide basic registration of received files.

Next, inside the NiFi flow, we'll need to replace the actual data content with this new metadata model. An easy way to do this, is to create a JSON template file from our model. We'll save it to local disk and use it inside a `FetchFile` processor to replace the flow's content with this skeleton object. This template will look something like:

```
{
  "FileSize": SIZE,
  "FileName": "FILENAME",
  "IngestedDate": "DATE"
}
```

Note the use of placeholder names (`SIZE`, `FILENAME`, `DATE`) in place of the attribute values. These will be substituted, one-by-one, by a sequence of `ReplaceText` processors, that swap the placeholder names for an appropriate flow attribute using regular expressions provided by the NiFi Expression Language, for example `DATE` becomes `${now()}`.

The last step is to output the new metadata payload to Elasticsearch. Once again, NiFi comes ready with a processor for this; the `PutElasticsearch` processor.

An example metadata entry in Elasticsearch:

```
{
        "_index": "gkg",
        "_type": "files",
        "_id": "AVZHCvGIV6x-JwdgvCzW",
        "_score": 1,
        "source": {
           "FileSize": 11279827,
           "FileName": "20150218233000.gkg.csv.zip",
           "IngestedDate": "2016-08-01T17:43:00+01:00"
        }
```

Now that we have added the ability to collect and interrogate metadata, we now have access to more statistics that can be used for analysis. This includes:

- Time-based analysis, for example, file sizes over time
- Loss of data, for example, are there data holes in the timeline?

If there is a particular analytic that is required, the NIFI metadata component can be adjusted to provide the relevant data points. Indeed, an analytic could be built to look at historical data and update the index accordingly if the metadata does not exist in current data.

Kibana dashboard

We have mentioned Kibana a number of times in this chapter. Now that we have an index of metadata in Elasticsearch, we can use the tool to visualize some analytics. The purpose of this brief section is to demonstrate that we can immediately start to model and visualize our data. To see Kibana used in a more complex scenario, have a look at Chapter 9, *News Dictionary and Real-Time Tagging System*. In this simple example, we have completed the following steps:

1. Added the Elasticsearch index for our GDELT metadata to the **Settings** tab.
2. Selected file size under the **Discover** tab.
3. Selected **Visualize** for file size.
4. Changed the Aggregation field to Range.
5. Entered values for the ranges.

The resulting graph displays the file size distribution:

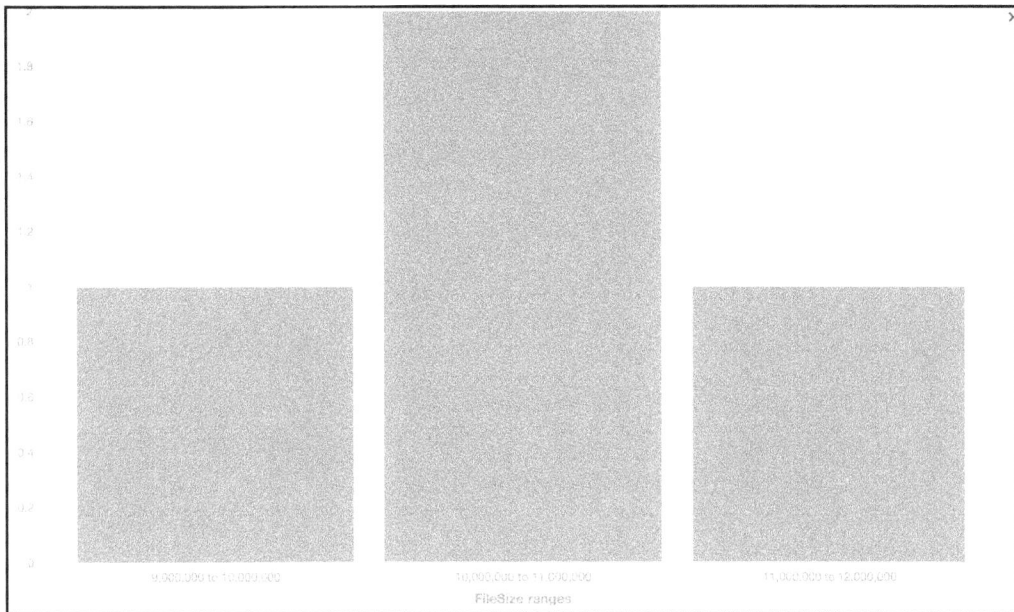

From here, we are free to create new visualizations or even a fully-featured dashboard that can be used to monitor the status of our file ingest. By increasing the variety of metadata written to Elasticsearch from NiFi, we can make more fields available in Kibana and even start our data science journey right here with some ingest-based actionable insights.

Now that we have a fully-functioning data pipeline delivering us real-time feeds of data, how do we ensure data quality of the payload we are receiving? Let's take a look at the options.

Quality assurance

With an initial data ingestion capability implemented, and data streaming onto your platform, you will need to decide how much quality assurance is required at the "front door". It's perfectly viable to start with no initial quality controls and build them up over time (retrospectively scanning historical data as time and resources allow). However, it may be prudent to install a basic level of verification to begin with. For example, basic checks such as file integrity, parity checking, completeness, checksums, type checking, field counting, overdue files, security field pre-population, denormalization, and so on.

You should take care that your up-front checks do not take too long. Depending on the intensity of your examinations and the size of your data, it's not uncommon to encounter a situation where there is not enough time to perform all processing before the next dataset arrives. You will always need to monitor your cluster resources and calculate the most efficient use of time.

Here are some examples of the types of rough capacity planning calculations you can perform:

Example 1 – Basic quality checking, no contending users

- Data is ingested every 15 minutes and takes 1 minute to pull from the source
- Quality checking (integrity, field count, field pre-population) takes 4 minutes
- There are no other users on the compute cluster

There are 10 minutes of resources available for other tasks.

As there are no other users on the cluster, this is satisfactory – no action needs to be taken.

Example 2 – Advanced quality checking, no contending users

- Data is ingested every 15 minutes and takes 1 minute to pull from the source
- Quality checking (integrity, field count, field pre-population, denormalization, sub dataset building) takes 13 minutes
- There are no other users on the compute cluster

There is only 1 minute of resource available for *other tasks.*

You probably need to consider, either:

- Configuring a resource scheduling policy
- Reducing the amount of data ingested
- Reducing the amount of processing we undertake
- Adding additional compute resources to the cluster

Example 3 – Basic quality checking, 50% utility due to contending users

- Data is ingested every 15 minutes and takes 1 minute to pull from the source
- Quality checking (integrity, field count, field pre-population) takes 4 minutes (100% utility)
- There are other users on the compute cluster

*There are 6 minutes of resources available for other tasks (15 – 1 – (4 * (100 / 50))). Since there are other users, there is a danger that, at least some of the time, we will not be able to complete our processing and a backlog of jobs will occur.*

When you run into timing issues, you have a number of options available to you in order to circumvent any backlog:

- Negotiating sole use of the resources at certain times
- Configuring a resource scheduling policy, including:
    - YARN fair scheduler: allows you to define queues with differing priorities and target your Spark jobs by setting the `spark.yarn.queue` property on start-up so your job always takes precedence
    - Dynamic resource allocation: allows concurrently running jobs to automatically scale to match their utilization
    - Spark scheduler pool: allows you to define queues when sharing a `SparkContext` using a multithreading model, and target your Spark job by setting the `spark.scheduler.pool` property per execution thread so your thread takes precedence
    - Running processing jobs overnight when the cluster is quiet

In any case, you will eventually get a good idea of how the various parts to your jobs perform and will then be in a position to calculate what changes could be made to improve efficiency. There's always the option of throwing more resources at the problem, especially when using a cloud provider, but we would certainly encourage the intelligent use of existing resources – this is far more scalable, cheaper, and builds data expertise.

Summary

In this chapter, we walked through the full setup of an Apache NiFi GDELT ingest pipeline, complete with metadata forks and a brief introduction to visualizing the resulting data. This section is particularly important as GDELT is used extensively throughout the book and the NiFi method is a highly effective way to source data in a scalable and modular way.

In the next chapter, we will get to grips with what to do with the data once it's landed, by looking at schemas and formats.

3
Input Formats and Schema

The aim of this chapter is to demonstrate how to load data from its raw format onto different schemas, therefore enabling a variety of different kinds of downstream analytics to be run over the same data. When writing analytics, or even better, building libraries of reusable software, you generally have to work with interfaces of fixed input types. Therefore, having flexibility in how you transition data between schemas, depending on the purpose, can deliver considerable downstream value, both in terms of widening the type of analysis possible and the re-use of existing code.

Our primary objective is to learn about the data format features that accompany Spark, although we will also delve into the finer points of data management by introducing proven methods that will enhance your data handling and increase your productivity. After all, it is most likely that you will be required to formalize your work at some point, and an introduction to how to avoid the potential long-term pitfalls is invaluable when writing analytics, and long after.

With this is mind, we will use this chapter to look at the traditionally well understood area of *data schemas*. We will cover key areas of traditional database modeling and explain how some of these cornerstone principles are still applicable to Spark.

In addition, while honing our Spark skills, we will analyze the GDELT data model and show how to store this large dataset in an efficient and scalable manner.

We will cover the following topics:

- Dimensional modeling: benefits and weaknesses in relation to Spark
- Focus on the GDELT model
- Lifting the lid on schema-on-read
- Avro object model
- Parquet storage model

Let's start with some best practice.

A structured life is a good life

When learning about the benefits of Spark and big data, you may have heard discussions about *structured* data versus *semi-structured* data versus *unstructured* data. While Spark promotes the use of structured, semi-structured, and unstructured data, it also provides the basis for its consistent treatment. The only constraint being that it should be *record-based*. Providing they are record-based, datasets can be transformed, enriched and manipulated in the same way, regardless of their organization.

However, it is worth noting that having unstructured data does not necessitate taking an unstructured *approach*. Having identified techniques for exploring datasets in the previous chapter, it would be tempting to dive straight into stashing data somewhere accessible and immediately commencing simple profiling analytics. In real life situations, this activity often takes precedence over due diligence. Once again, we would encourage you to consider several key areas of interest, for example, file integrity, data quality, schedule management, version management, security, and so on, before embarking on this exploration. These should not be ignored and many are large topics in their own right.

Therefore, while we have already covered many of these concerns in Chapter 2, *Data Acquisition*, and will study more later, for example in Chapter 13, *Secure Data*, in this chapter we are going to focus on data input and output formats specifically, exploring some of the methods that we can employ to ensure better data handling and management.

GDELT dimensional modeling

As we have chosen to use GDELT for analysis purposes in this book, we will introduce our first example using this dataset. First, let's select some data.

There are two streams of data available: **Global Knowledge Graph** (**GKG**) and **Events**.

For this chapter, we are going to use GKG data to create a time-series dataset queryable from Spark SQL. This will give us a great starting point to create some simple introductory analytics.

In the next chapters, `Chapter 4`, *Exploratory Data Analysis* and `Chapter 5`, *Spark for Geographic Analysis*, we'll go into more detail but stay with GKG. Then, in `Chapter 7`, *Building Communities*, we will explore events by producing our own network graph of persons and using it in some cool analytics.

GDELT model

GDELT has been around for more than 20 years and, during that time, has undergone some significant revisions. For our introductory examples, to keep things simple, let's limit our range of data from 1st April 2013, when GDELT had a major file structure overhaul, introducing the GKG files. It's worth noting that the principles discussed in this chapter are applicable to all versions of GDELT data, however, the specific schemas and **Uniform Resource Identifiers** (**URIs**) prior to this date may be different to the ones described. The version we will use is GDELT v2.1, which is the latest version at the time of writing. But again, it's worth noting that this varies only slightly from GDELT 2.0.

There are two data tracks within GKG data:

1. The entire knowledge graph, along with all of its fields.
2. The subset of the graph, which contains a set of predefined categories.

We'll look at the first track.

First look at the data

We discussed how to download GDELT data in Chapter 2, *Data Acquisition*, so if you already have a NiFi pipeline configured to download the GKG data, just ensure that it's available in HDFS. However, if you have not completed that chapter, then we would encourage you to do this first, as it explains why you should take a structured approach to obtaining data.

While we have gone to great lengths to discourage the use of ad hoc data downloading, the scope of this chapter is of course known and therefore, if you are interested in following the examples seen here, you can skip the use of NiFi and obtain the data directly (in order to get started as quickly as possible).

If you do wish to download a sample, here's a reminder of where to find the GDELT 2.1 GKG master file list:

> http://data.gdeltproject.org/gdeltv2/masterfilelist.txt

Make a note of a couple of the latest entries that match .gkg.csv.zip, copy them using your favorite HTTP tool, and upload them into HDFS. For example:

```
wget http://data.gdeltproject.org/gdeltv2/20150218230000.gkg.csv.zip -o
log.txt
unzip 20150218230000.gkg.csv.zip
hdfs dfs -put 20150218230000.gkg.csv /data/gdelt/gkg/2015/02/21/
```

Now that you have unzipped your CSV file and loaded it into HDFS, let's get on and look at the data.

> It is not actually necessary to unzip data before loading to HDFS. Spark's TextInputFormat class supports compressed types and will decompress transparently. However, as we unzipped the content in our NiFi pipeline in the previous chapter, decompression is performed here for consistency.

Core global knowledge graph model

There are some important principles to understand which will certainly save time in the long run, whether in terms of computing or human effort. Like many CSVs, this file is hiding some complexity that, if not understood well at this stage, could become a real problem during our large scale analytics later. The GDELT documentation describes the data. It can be found here: http://data.gdeltproject.org/documentation/GDELT-Global_Knowledge_Graph_Codebook-V2.1.pdf.

It indicates that each CSV line is newline delimite, and structured as in *Figure 1*:

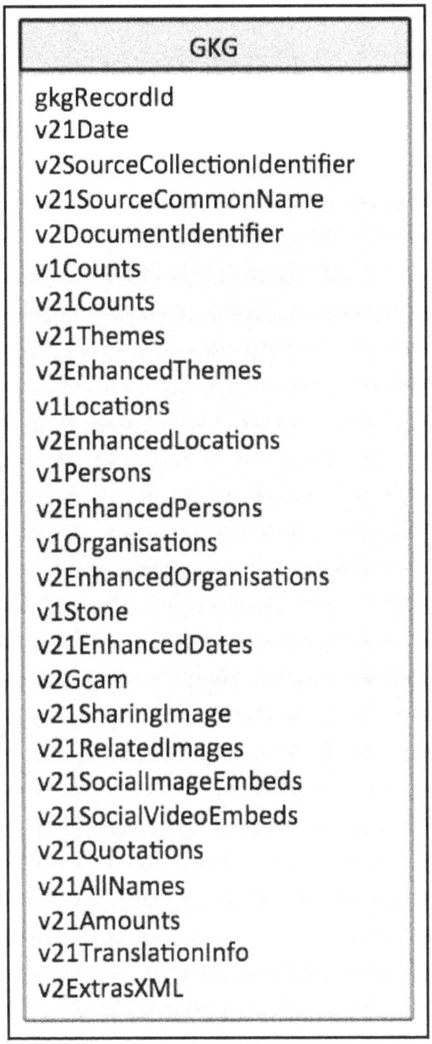

GKG
gkgRecordId
v21Date
v2SourceCollectionIdentifier
v21SourceCommonName
v2DocumentIdentifier
v1Counts
v21Counts
v21Themes
v2EnhancedThemes
v1Locations
v2EnhancedLocations
v1Persons
v2EnhancedPersons
v1Organisations
v2EnhancedOrganisations
v1Stone
v21EnhancedDates
v2Gcam
v21SharingImage
v21RelatedImages
v21SocialImageEmbeds
v21SocialVideoEmbeds
v21Quotations
v21AllNames
v21Amounts
v21TranslationInfo
v2ExtrasXML

Figure 1 GDELT GKG v2.1

On the face of it, this appears to be a nice, simple model whereby we can simply query a field and use the enclosed data-exactly like the CSV files we import and export to Microsoft Excel every day. However, if we examine the fields in more detail, it becomes clear that some of the fields are actually references to external sources and others are flattened data, actually represented by other tables.

Hidden complexity

The flattened data structures in a core GKG model represent hidden complexity. For example, looking at field V2GCAM in the documentation, it outlines the idea that this is a series of comma-delimited blocks containing colon-delimited key-value pairs, the pairs representing GCAM variables, and their respective counts. Like so:

```
wc:125,c2.21:4,c10.1:40,v10.1:3.21111111
```

If we reference the GCAM specification, `http://data.gdeltproject.org/documentation/GCAM-MASTER-CODEBOOK.TXT` we can translate this to:

Type	Count
WordCount	125
General Inquirer Bodypt	4
SentiWordNet	40
SentiWordNet average	3.21111111

There are also other fields that work in the same way, such as `V2Locations`, `V2Persons`, `V2Organizations`, and so on. So, what's really going on here? What are all these nested structures and why would you choose to represent data in this way? Actually, it turns out that this is a convenient way to collapse a **dimensional model** so that it can be represented in single line records without any loss of data or cross-referencing. In fact, it's a frequently used technique, known as *denormalization*.

Denormalized models

Traditionally, a dimensional model is a database table structure that comprises many fact and dimension tables. They are often referred to as having star or snowflake schemas due to their appearance in entity-relation diagrams. In such a model, a *fact* is a value that can be counted or summed and typically provides a measurement at a given point in time. As they are often based on transactions, or repeating events, the number of facts are prone to growing very large. A *dimension* on the other hand is a logical grouping of information whose purpose is to qualify or contextualize facts. They usually provide an entry point for interpreting facts by means of grouping or aggregation. Also, dimensions can be hierarchical and one dimension can reference another. We can see a diagram of the expanded GKG dimensional structure in *Figure 2*.

In our GCAM example, the facts are the entries found in the above table, and the dimension is the GCAM reference itself. While this may seem like a simple, logical abstraction, it does mean that we have an important area of concern that we should consider carefully: dimensional modeling is great for traditional databases where data can be split into tables–in this case, GKG and GCAM tables–as these types of databases, by their very nature, are optimized for that structure. For example, the operations for looking up values or aggregating facts are available natively. When using Spark, however, some of the operations that we take for granted can be very expensive. For example, if we wanted to average all of the GCAM fields for millions of entries, then we would have a very large computation to perform. We will discuss this in more detail in the following diagram:

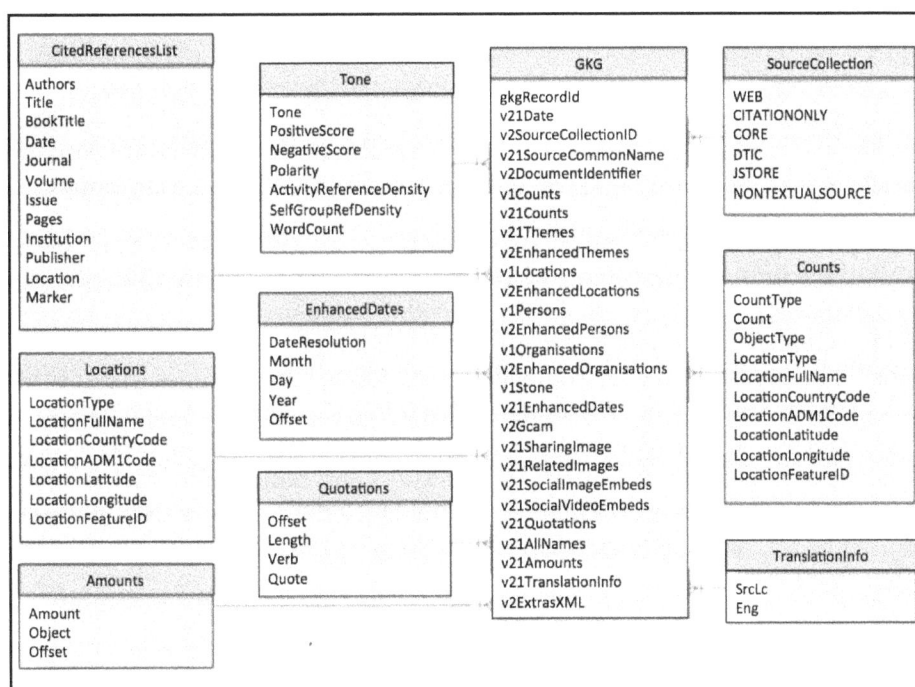

Figure 2 GDELT GKG 2.1 expanded

Challenges with flattened data

Having explored the GKG data schema, we now know that the taxonomy is a typical star schema with a single fact table referencing multiple dimension tables. With this hierarchical structure, we will certainly struggle should we need to slice-and-dice data in the same way a traditional database would allow.

But what makes it so difficult to process on Spark? Let's look at three different issues inherent with this type of organization.

Issue 1 – Loss of contextual information

First, there is the matter of the various arrays used within each record of the dataset. For example, `V1Locations`, `V1Organizations`, and `V1Persons` fields all contain a list of 0 or more objects. As we do not have the original body of the text used to derive this information (although we can sometimes obtain it if the source is WEB, JSTOR, and so on, since those will contain links to the source document), we lose the context of the relationships between the entities.

For example, if we have [Barack Obama, David Cameron, Francois Hollande, USA, France, GB, Texaco, Esso, Shell] in our data, then we could make the assumption that the source article is related to a meeting between heads of state over an oil crisis. However, this is only an assumption and may not be the case, if we were truly objective, we could equally assume that the article was related to companies who had employees with famous names.

To help us to infer these relationships between entities, we can develop a time series model that takes all of the individual contents of a GDELT field, over a certain time period, and performs an expansion join. Thus, on a simple level, those pairs that are seen more often are more likely to actually relate to each other and we can start to make some more concrete assumptions. For example, if we see [Barack Obama, USA] 100,000 times in our timeseries and [Barack Obama, France] only 5000 times, then it is very likely that there is a strong relationship between the first pair, and a secondary relationship between the second. In other words, we can identify the tenuous relationships and remove them when needed. This method can be used at scale to identify relationships between apparently unrelated entities. In `Chapter 7`, *Building Communities*, we use this principle to identify relationships between some very unlikely people!

Issue 2: Re-establishing dimensions

With any denormalized data it should be possible to reconstruct, or inflate, the original dimensional model. With this in mind, let's look at a useful Spark function that will help us to expand our arrays and produce a flattened result; it's called `DataFrame.explode`, and here's an illustrative example:

```
case class Grouped(locations:Array[String], people:Array[String])

val group = Grouped(Array("USA","France","GB"),
        Array("Barack Obama","David Cameron", "Francois Hollande"))

val ds = Seq(group).toDS
```

```
ds.show

+-----------------+--------------------+
|        locations|              people|
+-----------------+--------------------+
|[USA, France, GB]|[Barack Obama, Da...|
+-----------------+--------------------+

val flatLocs = ds.withColumn("locations",explode($"locations"))
flatLocs.show

+---------+--------------------+
|Locations|              People|
+---------+--------------------+
|      USA|[Barack Obama, Da...|
|   France|[Barack Obama, Da...|
|       GB|[Barack Obama, Da...|
+---------+--------------------+


val flatFolk = flatLocs.withColumn("people",explode($"people"))
flatFolk.show

+---------+------------------+
|Locations|            People|
+---------+------------------+
|      USA|      Barack Obama|
|      USA|     David Cameron|
|      USA|Francois Hollande|
|   France|      Barack Obama|
|   France|     David Cameron|
|   France|Francois Hollande|
|       GB|      Barack Obama|
|       GB|     David Cameron|
|       GB|Francois Hollande|
+---------+------------------+
```

Using this method, we can easily expand arrays and then perform the grouping of our choice. Once expanded, the data is readily aggregated using the `DataFrame` methods and can even be done using SparkSQL. An example of this can be found in the Zeppelin notebooks in our repository.

It is important to understand that, while this function is simple to implement, it is not necessarily performant and may hide the underlying processing complexity required. In fact, there is an example of the explode function using GKG data within the Zeppelin notebook that accompanies this chapter, whereby, if the explode functions are not reasonably scoped, then the function returns a heap space issue as it runs out of memory.

This function does not solve the inherent problem of consuming large amounts of system resources, and so you should still take care when using it. And while this general problem cannot be solved, it can be managed by performing only the groupings and joins necessary, or by calculating them ahead of time and ensuring they complete within the resources available. You may even wish to write an algorithm that splits a dataset and performs the grouping sequentially, persisting each time. We explore methods to help us with this problem, and other common processing issues, in `Chapter 14`, *Scalable Algorithms*.

Issue 3: Including reference data

For this issue, let's look at the GDELT event data, which we have expanded in *Figure 3*:

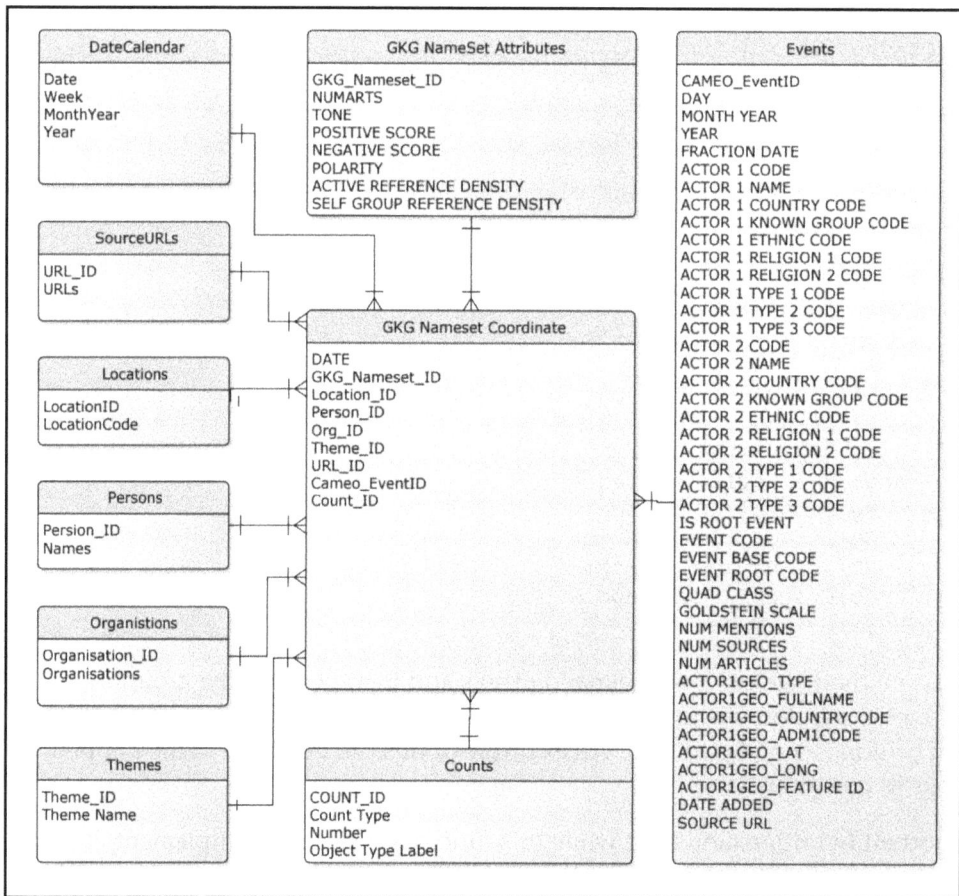

Figure 3 GDELT Events Taxonomy

This type of diagrammatic representation draws attention to the relationships in the data and gives an indication of how we might want to inflate it. Here, we see many fields that are just codes and would require translation back into their original descriptions in order to present anything meaningful. For example, in order to interpret the `Actor1CountryCode` (GDELT events), we will need to join the event data with one or more separate reference datasets that provide the translation text. In this case, the documentation tells us to reference the CAMEO dataset located here: `http://data.gdeltproject.org/documentation/CAMEO.Manual.1.1b3.pdf`.

This type of join has always presented a serious problem at data scale and there are various ways to handle it depending upon the given scenario – it is important at this stage to understand exactly how your data will be used, which joins may be required immediately, and which may be deferred until sometime in the future.

In the case where we choose to completely denormalize, or flatten, the data before processing, then it makes sense to do the join upfront. In this case, follow-on analytics will certainly be more efficient, as the relevant joins have already been completed:

So, in our example:

```
wc:125,c2.21:4,c10.1:40,v10.1:3.21111111
```

For each code in the record, there is a join to the respective reference table, and the entire record becomes:

```
WordCount:125, General_Inquirer_Bodypt:4, SentiWordNet:40, SentiWordNet
average: v10.1:3.21111111
```

This is a simple change, but is one that uses a lot of disk space if performed across large numbers of rows. The trade-off is that the joins have to be performed at some point, perhaps at ingest or as a regular batch job after ingest; it is perfectly reasonable to ingest the data as is, and perform flattening of the dataset at a time that is convenient to the user. In any case, the flattened data can be consumed by any analytic and data analysts need not concern themselves with this potentially hidden issue.

On the other hand, often, deferring the join until later in the processing can mean that there are fewer records to join with – as there may have been aggregation steps in the pipeline. In this case, joining to tables at the last possible opportunity pays off because, often, the reference or dimension tables are small enough to be broadcast joins, or map-side joins. As this is such an important topic, we will continue to look at different ways of approaching join scenarios throughout the book.

Loading your data

As we have outlined in previous chapters, traditional system engineering commonly adopts a pattern to move the data from its source to its destination, that is, ETL, whereas Spark tends to rely on schema-on-read. As it's important to understand how these concepts relate to schemas and input formats, let's describe this aspect in more detail:

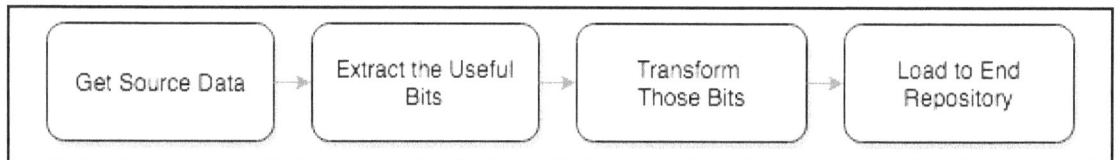

Get Source Data	→	Extract the Useful Bits	→	Transform Those Bits	→	Load to End Repository

On the face of it, the ETL approach seems to be sensible, and indeed has been implemented by just about every organization that stores and handles data. There are some very popular, feature-rich products out there that perform the ETL task very well - not to mention Apache's open source offering, Apache Camel `http://camel.apache.org/etl-example.html`.

However, this apparently straightforward approach belies the true effort required to implement even a simple data pipeline. This is because we must ensure that all data complies with a fixed schema before we can use it. For example, if we wanted to ingest some data from a starting directory, the minimal work is as follows:

1. Ensure we are always looking at the pickup directory.
2. When data arrives, collect it.
3. Ensure the data is not missing anything and validate according to a predefined ruleset.
4. Extract the parts of the data that we are interested in, according to a predefined ruleset.
5. Transform these selected parts according to a predefined schema.
6. Load the data to a repository (for example, a database) using the correct versioned schema.
7. Deal with any failed records.

We can immediately see a number of formatting issues here that must be addressed:

1. We have a predefined ruleset and, therefore, this must be version controlled. Any mistakes will mean bad data in the end database and a re-ingest of that data through the ETL process to correct it (very time and resource expensive). Any change to the format of the inbound dataset, and this ruleset must be changed.

2. Any change to the target schema will require very careful management. At the very least, a version control change in the ETL, and possibly even a reprocessing of some or all of the previous data (which could be a very time consuming and expensive backhaul).

3. Any change to the end repository will result in at least a version control schema change, and perhaps even a new ETL module (again, very time and resource intensive).

4. Inevitably, there will be some bad data that makes it through to the database. Therefore, an administrator will need set rules to monitor the referential integrity of tables to ensure damage is kept to a minimum and arrange for the re-ingestion of any corrupted data.

If we now consider these issues and massively increase the volume, velocity, variety, and veracity of the data, it is easy to see that our straightforward ETL system has quickly grown into a near unmanageable system. Any formatting, schema, and business rule changes will have a negative impact. In some cases, there may not be enough processor and memory resources to even keep pace, due to all the processing steps required. Data cannot be ingested until all of the ETL steps have been agreed and are in place. In large corporations it can take months to agree schema transforms before any implementation even commences, thus resulting in a large backlog, or even loss of data. All this results in a brittle system that is difficult to change.

Schema agility

To overcome this, schema-on-read encourages us to shift to a very simple principle: *apply schema to the data at runtime, as opposed to applying it on load (that is, at ingest)*. In other words, a schema is applied to the data when it is read in for processing. This simplifies the ETL process somewhat:

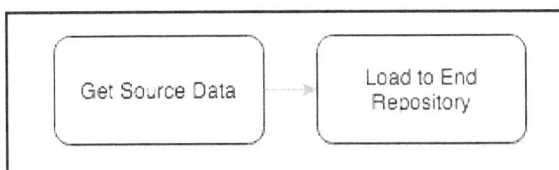

Of course, it does not mean you eliminate the transform step entirely. You're simply *deferring* the act of validation, applying business rules, error handling, ensuring referential integrity, enriching, aggregating, and otherwise inflating the model until the point you are ready to use it. The idea is that, by this point, you should know more about the data and certainly about the way you wish to use it. Therefore, you can use this increased knowledge of the data to effect efficiencies in the loading method. Again, this is a trade-off. What you save in upfront processing costs, you may lose in duplicate processing and potential inconsistency. However, techniques such as persistence, indexing, memorization, and caching can all help here. As mentioned in the previous chapter, this process is commonly known as ELT due to the reversal in the order of processing steps.

One benefit of this approach is that it allows greater freedom to make appropriate decisions about the way you represent and model data for any given use case. For example, there are a variety of ways that data can be structured, formatted, stored, compressed, or serialized, and it makes sense to choose the most appropriate method given the set of specific requirements related to the particular problem you are trying to solve.

One of the most important opportunities that this approach provides is that you can choose how to physically lay out the data, that is, decide on the directory structure where data is kept. It is generally not advised to store all your data in a single directory because, as the number of files grows, it takes punitively longer amounts of time for the underlying filesystem to address them. But, ideally, we want to be able to specify the smallest possible data split to fulfill the functionality and efficiently store and retrieve at the volumes required. Therefore, data should be logically grouped depending upon the analysis that is required and the amount of data that you expect to receive. In other words, data may be divided across directories based upon type, subtype, date, time, or some other relevant property, but it should be ensured that no single directory bears undue burden. Another important point to realize here is that, once the data is landed, it can always be reformatted or reorganized at a later date, whereas, in an ETL paradigm, this is usually far more difficult.

In addition to this, ELT can also have a surprising benefit on **change management** and **version control**. For example, if external factors cause the data schema to change, you can simply load different data to a new directory in your data store and use a flexible schema tolerant serialization library, such as Avro or Parquet, which both support **schema evolution** (we will look at these later in this chapter); or, if the results of a particular job are unsatisfactory, we need only change the internals of that one job before rerunning it. This means that schema changes become something that can be managed on a per analytic basis, rather than on a per feed basis, and the impact of change is better isolated and managed.

By the way, it's worth considering a hybrid approach, particularly useful in streaming use cases, whereby some processing can be done during collection and ingest, and others during runtime. The decision around whether to use ETL or ELT is not necessarily a binary one. Spark provides features that give you control over your data pipelines. In turn, this affords you the flexibility to transform or persist data when it makes sense to do so, rather than adopting a one-size-fits-all approach.

The best way to determine which approach to take is to learn from the actual day-to-day use of a particular dataset and adjust its processing accordingly, identifying bottlenecks and fragility as more experience is gained. There may also be corporate rules levied, such as virus scanning or data security, which will determine a particular route. We'll look more into this at the end of the chapter.

Reality check

As with most things in computing, there's no silver bullet. ELT and schema-on-read will not fix all your data formatting problems, but they are useful tools in the toolbox and, generally speaking, the pros usually outweigh the cons. It is worth noting, however, that there are situations where you can actually introduce difficulties if you're not careful.

In particular, it can be more involved to perform ad hoc analysis on complex data models (as opposed to in databases). For example, in the simple case of extracting a list of all of the names of the cities mentioned in news articles, in a SQL database you could essentially run `select CITY from GKG`, whereas, in Spark, you first need to understand the data model, parse and validate the data, and then create the relevant table and handle any errors on-the-fly, sometimes each time you run the query.

Again, this is a trade-off. With schema-on-read you lose the built-in data representation and inherent knowledge of a fixed schema, but you gain the flexibility to apply different models or views as required. As usual, Spark provides features designed to assist in exploiting this approach, such as, transformations, `DataFrames`, `SparkSQL`, and REPL, and when used properly, they allow you to maximize the benefits of schema-on-read. We'll learn more about this as we go furthur.

GKG ELT

As our NiFi pipeline writes data as is to HDFS, we can take full advantage of schema-on-read and immediately start to use it without having to wait for it to be processed. If you would like to be a bit more advanced, then you could load the data in a splittable and/or zipped format such as `bzip2` (native to Spark). Let's take a look at a simple example.

> HDFS uses a block system to store data. In order to store and leverage data in the most efficient way, HDFS files should be splittable where possible. If the CSV GDELT files are loaded using `TextOutputFormat` class, for example, then files larger than the block size will be split across filesize/blocksize blocks. Partial blocks do not occupy a full block size on disk.

By using `DataFrames`, we can write SQL statements to explore the data or with datasets we can chain fluent methods, but in either case there is some initial preparation required.

The good news is that usually this can be done entirely by Spark, as it supports the transparent loading of data into Datasets via case classes, using **Encoders** and so most of the time you won't need to worry too much about the inner workings. Indeed, when you have a relatively simple data model, it's usually enough to define a case class, map your data onto it, and convert to a dataset using `toDS` method. However, in most real-world scenarios, where data models are more complex, you will be required to write your own custom parser. Custom parsers are nothing new in data engineering, but in a schema-on-read setting, they are often required to be used by data scientists, as the interpretation of data is done at runtime and not load time. Here's an example of the use of the custom GKG parser to be found in our repository:

```
import org.apache.spark.sql.functions._

val rdd = rawDS map GdeltParser.toCaseClass
val ds = rdd.toDS()
// DataFrame-style API
ds.agg(avg("goldstein")).as("goldstein").show()
// Dataset-style API
ds.groupBy(_.eventCode).count().show()
```

You can seen preceding that, once the data is parsed, it can be used in the full variety of Spark APIs.

If you're more comfortable using SQL, you can define your own schema, register a table, and use SparkSQL. In either approach, you can choose how to load the data based on how it will be used, allowing for more flexibility over which aspects you spend time parsing. For example, the most basic schema for loading GKG is to treat every field as a String, like so:

```
import org.apache.spark.sql.types._

val schema = StructType(Array(
    StructField("GkgRecordId"          , StringType, true),
    StructField("V21Date"              , StringType, true),
    StructField("V2SrcCollectionId"    , StringType, true),
    StructField("V2SrcCmnName"         , StringType, true),
    StructField("V2DocId"              , StringType, true),
    StructField("V1Counts"             , StringType, true),
    StructField("V21Counts"            , StringType, true),
    StructField("V1Themes"             , StringType, true),
    StructField("V2Themes"             , StringType, true),
    StructField("V1Locations"          , StringType, true),
    StructField("V2Locations"          , StringType, true),
    StructField("V1Persons"            , StringType, true),
    StructField("V2Persons"            , StringType, true),
    StructField("V1Orgs"               , StringType, true),
    StructField("V2Orgs"               , StringType, true),
    StructField("V15Tone"              , StringType, true),
    StructField("V21Dates"             , StringType, true),
    StructField("V2GCAM"               , StringType, true),
    StructField("V21ShareImg"          , StringType, true),
    StructField("V21RelImg"            , StringType, true),
    StructField("V21SocImage"          , StringType, true),
    StructField("V21SocVideo"          , StringType, true),
    StructField("V21Quotations"        , StringType, true),
    StructField("V21AllNames"          , StringType, true),
    StructField("V21Amounts"           , StringType, true),
    StructField("V21TransInfo"         , StringType, true),
    StructField("V2ExtrasXML"          , StringType, true)
))

val filename="path_to_your_gkg_files"

val df = spark
    .read
    .option("header", "false")
    .schema(schema)
    .option("delimiter", "t")
    .csv(filename)

df.createOrReplaceTempView("GKG")
```

And now you can execute SQL queries, like so:

```
spark.sql("SELECT V2GCAM FROM GKG LIMIT 5").show
spark.sql("SELECT AVG(GOLDSTEIN) AS GOLDSTEIN FROM GKG WHERE GOLDSTEIN IS
NOT NULL").show()
```

With this approach, you can start profiling the data straight away and it's useful for many data engineering tasks. When you're ready, you can choose other elements of the GKG record to expand. We'll see more about this in the next chapter.

Once you have a DataFrame, you can convert it into a Dataset by defining a case class and casting, like so:

```
val ds = df.as[GdeltEntity]
```

Position matters

It's worth noting here that, when loading data from CSV, Spark's schema matching is entirely *positional*. This means that, when Spark tokenizes a record based on the given separator, it assigns each token to a field in the schema using its position, even if a header is present. Therefore, if a column is omitted in the schema definition, or your dataset changes over time due to data drift or data versioning, you may get a misalignment that Spark will not necessarily warn you about!

Therefore, we recommend doing basic data profiling and data quality checks on a routine basis to mitigate these situations. You can use the built-in functions in `DataFrameStatFunctions` to assist with this. Some examples are shown as follows:

```
df.describe("V1Themes").show

df.stat.freqItems(Array("V2Persons")).show

df.stat.crosstab("V2Persons","V2Locations").show
```

Next, let's explain a great way to put some structure around our code, and also reduce the amount of code written, by using Avro or Parquet.

Avro

We have seen how easy it can be to ingest some data and use Spark to analyze it without the need for any traditional ETL tools. While it is very useful to work in an environment where schemas are all but ignored, this is not realistic in the commercial world. There is, however, a good middle ground, which gives us some great advantages over both ETL and unbounded data processing-Avro.

Apache Avro is serialization technology, similar in purpose to Google's protocol buffers. Like many other serialization technologies, Avro uses a schema to describe data, but the key to its usefulness is that it provides the following features:

- **It stores the schema alongside the data**. This allows for efficient storage because the schema is only stored once, at the top of the file. It also means that data can be read even if the original class files are no longer available.
- **It supports schema-on-read and schema evolution**. This means it can implement different schemas for the reading and writing of data, providing the advantages of schema versioning without the disadvantages of large administrative overhead every time we wish to make data amendments.
- **It is language agnostic**. Therefore, it can be used with any tool or technology that allows custom serialization framework. It is particularly useful for writing directly to Hive, for example.

As Avro stores the schema with the enclosed data, it is *self-describing*. So instead of struggling to read the data because you have no classes, or trying to guess which version of a schema applies, or in the worst case having to throw away the data altogether, we can simply interrogate the Avro file for the schema that the data was written with.

Avro also allows amendments to a schema in the form of additive changes, or appends, that can be accommodated thus making a specific implementation backwards compatible with older data.

As Avro represents data in a binary form, it can be transferred and manipulated more efficiently. Also, it takes up less space on disk due to its inherent compression.

For the reasons stated above, Avro is an incredibly popular serialization format, used by a wide variety of technologies and end-systems, and you will no doubt have cause to use it at some point. Therefore, in the next sections we will demonstrate two different ways to read and write Avro-formatted data. The first is an elegant and simple method that uses a third party, purpose-built library, called `spark-avro`, and the second is an under-the-covers method, useful for understanding how the mechanics of Avro work.

Spark-Avro method

To address the complexities of implementing Avro, the `spark-avro` library has been developed. This can be imported in the usual ways, using maven:

```
<dependency>
    <groupId>com.databricks</groupId>
    <artifactId>spark-avro_2.11</artifactId>
    <version>3.1.0</version>
</dependency>
```

For this implementation, we will create the Avro schema using a `StructType` object, transform the input data using an `RDD`, and create a `DataFrame` from the two. Finally, the result can be written to file, in Avro format, using the `spark-avro` library.

The `StructType` object is a variation on the `GkgCoreSchema` used above and in `Chapter 4`, *Exploratory Data Analysis*, and is constructed as follows:

```
val GkgSchema = StructType(Array(
  StructField("GkgRecordId", GkgRecordIdStruct, true),
  StructField("V21Date", LongType, true),
  StructField("V2SrcCollectionId", StringType, true),
  StructField("V2SrcCmnName", StringType, true),
  StructField("V2DocId", StringType, true),
  StructField("V1Counts", ArrayType(V1CountStruct), true),
  StructField("V21Counts", ArrayType(V21CountStruct), true),
  StructField("V1Themes", ArrayType(StringType), true),
  StructField("V2EnhancedThemes",ArrayType(EnhancedThemes),true),
  StructField("V1Locations", ArrayType(V1LocationStruct), true),
  StructField("V2Locations", ArrayType(EnhancedLocations), true),
  StructField("V1Persons", ArrayType(StringType), true),
  StructField("V2Persons", ArrayType(EnhancedPersonStruct), true),
  StructField("V1Orgs", ArrayType(StringType), true),
  StructField("V2Orgs", ArrayType(EnhancedOrgStruct), true),
  StructField("V1Stone", V1StoneStruct, true),
  StructField("V21Dates", ArrayType(V21EnhancedDateStruct), true),
  StructField("V2GCAM", ArrayType(V2GcamStruct), true),
  StructField("V21ShareImg", StringType, true),
  StructField("V21RelImg", ArrayType(StringType), true),
  StructField("V21SocImage", ArrayType(StringType), true),
  StructField("V21SocVideo", ArrayType(StringType), true),
  StructField("V21Quotations", ArrayType(QuotationStruct), true),
  StructField("V21AllNames", ArrayType(V21NameStruct), true),
  StructField("V21Amounts", ArrayType(V21AmountStruct), true),
  StructField("V21TransInfo", V21TranslationInfoStruct, true),
```

```
    StructField("V2ExtrasXML", StringType, true)
  ))
```

We have used a number of custom `StructTypes`, which could be specified inline for `GkgSchema`, but which we have broken out for ease of reading.

For example, `GkgRecordIdStruct` is:

```
val GkgRecordIdStruct = StructType(Array(
  StructField("Date", LongType),
  StructField("TransLingual", BooleanType),
  StructField("NumberInBatch";, IntegerType)
))
```

Before we use this schema, we must first produce an RDD by parsing the input GDELT data into a Row:

```
val gdeltRDD = sparkContext.textFile("20160101020000.gkg.csv")

val gdeltRowOfRowsRDD = gdeltRDD.map(_.split("\t"))
  .map(attributes =>
    Row(
      createGkgRecordID(attributes(0)),
      attributes(1).toLong,
      createSourceCollectionIdentifier(attributes(2),
      attributes(3),
      attributes(4),
      createV1Counts(attributes(5),
      createV21Counts(attributes(6),
      .
      .
      .
    )
  ))
```

Here you see a number of custom parsing functions, for instance, `createGkgRecordID`, that take raw data and contain the logic for reading and interpreting each field. As GKG fields are complex and often contain *nested data structures*, we need a way to embed them into the Row. To help us out, Spark allows us to treat them as `Rows` inside `Rows`. Therefore, we simply write parsing functions that return `Row` objects, like so:

```
def createGkgRecordID(str: String): Row = {
  if (str != "") {
    val split = str.split("-")
    if (split(1).length > 1) {
      Row(split(0).toLong, true, split(1).substring(1).toInt)
    }
```

```
    else {
      Row(split(0).toLong, false, split(1).toInt)
    }
  }
  else {
    Row(0L, false, 0)
  }
}
```

Putting the code together, we see the entire solution in just a few lines:

```
import org.apache.spark.sql.types._
import com.databricks.spark.avro._
import org.apache.spark.sql.Row

val df = spark.createDataFrame(gdeltRowOfRowsRDD, GkgSchema)

df.write.avro("/path/to/avro/output")
```

Reading the Avro files into a `DataFrame` is similarly simple:

```
val avroDF = spark
  .read
  .format("com.databricks.spark.avro")
  .load("/path/to/avro/output")
```

This gives a neat solution for dealing with Avro files, but what's going on under the covers?

Pedagogical method

In order to explain how Avro works, let's take a look at a roll your own solution. In this case, the first thing we need to do is to create an Avro schema for the version or versions of data that we intend to ingest.

There are Avro implementations for several languages, including Java. These implementations allow you to generate bindings for Avro so that you can serialize and deserialize your data objects efficiently. We are going to use a maven plugin to help us automatically compile these bindings using an Avro IDL representation of the GKG schema. The bindings will be in the form of a Java class that we can use later on to help us build Avro objects. Use the following imports in your project:

```
<dependency>
    <groupId>org.apache.avro</groupId>
    <artifactId>avro</artifactId>
    <version>1.7.7</version>
</dependency>
```

```
<plugin>
    <groupId>org.apache.avro</groupId>
    <artifactId>avro-maven-plugin</artifactId>
    <version>1.7.7</version>
    <executions>
        <execution>
            <phase>generate-sources</phase>
            <goals>
                <goal>schema</goal>
            </goals>
            <configuration>
                <sourceDirectory>
                ${project.basedir}/src/main/avro/
                </sourceDirectory>
                <outputDirectory>
                    ${project.basedir}/src/main/java/
                </outputDirectory>
            </configuration>
        </execution>
    </executions>
</plugin>
```

We can now take a look at our Avro IDL schema created from a subset of the available Avro types:

```
+---------------+-------------+
|      primitive|      complex|
+---------------+-------------+
|null           |       record|
|Boolean        |         enum|
|int            |        array|
|long           |          map|
|float          |        union|
|double         |        fixed|
|bytes          |             |
|string         |             |
+---------------+-------------+
```

The full Avro IDL schema for GDELT 2.1 can be found in our code repo, but here's a snippet:

```
@namespace("org.io.gzet.gdelt.gkg")
protocol Gkg21
{

    @namespace("org.io.gzet.gdelt.gkg.v1")
    record Location
    {
```

```
        int locationType = 0;
        union { null , string } fullName = null;
        union { null , string } countryCode = null;
        union { null , string } aDM1Code = null;
        float locationLatitude = 0.0;
        float locationLongitude = 0.0;
        union { null , string } featureId = null;
    }

    @namespace("org.io.gzet.gdelt.gkg.v1")
    record Count
    {
        union { null , string } countType = null;
        int count = 0;
        union { null , string } objectType = null;
        union { null , org.io.gzet.gdelt.gkg.v1.Location } v1Location =
null;
    }

@namespace("org.io.gzet.gdelt.gkg.v21")
 record Specification
 {
    GkgRecordId gkgRecordId;
    union { null , long } v21Date = null;
    union { null , org.io.gzet.gdelt.gkg.v2.SourceCollectionIdentifier }
v2SourceCollectionIdentifier = null;
    union { null , string } v21SourceCommonName = null;
    union { null , string } v2DocumentIdentifier = null;
    union { null , array<org.io.gzet.gdelt.gkg.v1.Count> } v1Counts = null;
    union { null , array<org.io.gzet.gdelt.gkg.v21.Count> } v21Counts =
null;
    union { null , array<string> } v1Themes = null;
 }
```

Avro provides an extensible type system that supports **custom types**. It's also modular and offers namespaces, so that we can add new types and reuse custom types as the schema evolves. In the preceding example, we can see primitive types extensively used, but also custom objects such as `org.io.gzet.gdelt.gkg.v1.Location`.

To create Avro files, we can use the following code (full example in our code repository):

```
    val inputFile = new File("gkg.csv");
    val outputFile = new File("gkg.avro");

    val userDatumWriter = new
        SpecificDatumWriter[Specification](classOf[Specification])

    val dataFileWriter = new
```

```
      DataFileWriter[Specification](userDatumWriter)

  dataFileWriter.create(Specification.getClassSchema, outputFile)


  for (line <- Source.fromFile(inputFile).getLines())
      dataFileWriter.append(generateAvro(line))

  dataFileWriter.close()


  def generateAvro(line: String): Specification = {

    val values = line.split("\t",-1)
    if(values.length == 27){
      val specification = Specification.newBuilder()
        .setGkgRecordId(createGkgRecordId(values{0}))
        .setV21Date(values{1}.toLong)
        .setV2SourceCollectionIdentifier(
          createSourceCollectionIdentifier(values{2}))
        .setV21SourceCommonName(values{3})
        .setV2DocumentIdentifier(values{4})
        .setV1Counts(createV1CountArray(values{5}))
        .setV21Counts(createV21CountArray(values{6}))
        .setV1Themes(createV1Themes(values{7}))
        .setV2EnhancedThemes(createV2EnhancedThemes(values{8}))
        .setV1Locations(createV1LocationsArray(values{9}))
    .
    .
    .

    }
  }
```

The `Specification` object is created for us once we compile our IDL (using the maven plugin). It contains all of the methods required to access the Avro model, for example `setV2EnhancedLocations`. We are then left with creating the functions to parse our GKG data; two examples are shown, as follows:

```
  def createSourceCollectionIdentifier(str: String) :
  SourceCollectionIdentifier = {
    str.toInt match {
    case 1 => SourceCollectionIdentifier.WEB
    case 2 => SourceCollectionIdentifier.CITATIONONLY
    case 3 => SourceCollectionIdentifier.CORE
    case 4 => SourceCollectionIdentifier.DTIC
    case 5 => SourceCollectionIdentifier.JSTOR
    case 6 => SourceCollectionIdentifier.NONTEXTUALSOURCE
```

```
      case _ => SourceCollectionIdentifier.WEB
  }
    }
  def createV1LocationsArray(str: String): Array[Location] = {
    val counts = str.split(";")
    counts map(createV1Location(_))
  }
```

This approach creates the required Avro files, but it is shown here to demonstrate how Avro works. As it stands, this code does not operate in parallel and, therefore, should not be used on big data. If we wanted to parallelize it, we could create a custom `InputFormat`, wrap the raw data into an RDD, and perform the processing on that basis. Fortunately, we don't have to, as `spark-avro` has already done it for us.

When to perform Avro transformation

In order to make best use of Avro, next, we need to decide when it is best to transform the data. Converting to Avro is a relatively expensive operation, so it should be done at the point when it makes most sense. Once again, it's a tradeoff. This time, it's between a flexible data model supporting unstructured processing, exploratory data analysis, ad hoc querying, and a structured type system. There are two main options to consider:

1. **Convert as late as possible**: it is possible to perform Avro conversion in each and every run of a job. There are some obvious drawbacks here, so it's best to consider persisting Avro files at some point, to avoid the recalculation. You could do this lazily upon the first time, but chances are this would get confusing quite quickly. The easier option is to periodically run a batch job over the data at rest. This job's only task would be to create Avro data and write it back to disk. This approach gives us full control over when the conversion jobs are executed. In busy environments, jobs can be scheduled for quiet periods and priority can be allocated on an ad hoc basis. The downside is that we need to know how long the processing is going to take in order to ensure there is enough time for completion. If processing is not completed before the next batched data arrives, then a backlog builds and it can be difficult to catch up.

2. **Convert as early as possible**: the alternative approach is to create an ingest pipeline, whereby the incoming data is converted to Avro on the fly (particularly useful in streaming scenarios). By doing this, we are in danger of approaching an ETL-style scenario, so it is really a judgment call as to which approach best suits the specific environment in use at the time.

Now, let's look at a related technology that is used extensively throughout Spark, that is Apache Parquet.

Parquet

Apache Parquet is a columnar storage format specifically designed for the Hadoop ecosystem. Traditional row-based storage formats are optimized to work with one record at a time, meaning they can be slow for certain types of workload. Instead, Parquet serializes and stores data by column, thus allowing for optimization of storage, compression, predicate processing, and bulk sequential access across large datasets – exactly the type of workload suited to Spark!

As Parquet implements per column data compaction, it's particularly suited to CSV data, especially with fields of low cardinality, and file sizes can see huge reductions when compared to Avro.

```
+--------------------------+-------------+
|                 File Type|         Size|
+--------------------------+-------------+
|20160101020000.gkg.csv    |     20326266|
|20160101020000.gkg.avro   |     13557119|
|20160101020000.gkg.parquet|      6567110|
|20160101020000.gkg.csv.bz2|      4028862|
+--------------------------+-------------+
```

Parquet also integrates with Avro natively. Parquet takes an Avro in-memory representation of data and maps to its internal data types. It then serializes the data to disk using the Parquet columnar file format.

We have seen how to apply Avro to the model, now we can take the next step and use this Avro model to persist data to disk via the Parquet format. Again, we will show the current method and then some lower-level code for demonstrative purposes. First, the recommended method:

```
val gdeltAvroDF = spark
    .read
    .format("com.databricks.spark.avro")
    .load("/path/to/avro/output")

gdeltAvroDF.write.parquet("/path/to/parquet/output")
```

Now for the detail behind how Avro and Parquet relate to each other:

```
val inputFile = new File("("/path/to/avro/output ")
 val outputFile = new Path("/path/to/parquet/output")

val schema = Specification.getClassSchema
val reader =  new GenericDatumReader[IndexedRecord](schema)
val avroFileReader = DataFileReader.openReader(inputFile, reader)

val parquetWriter =
    new AvroParquetWriter[IndexedRecord](outputFile, schema)

while(avroFileReader.hasNext)  {
    parquetWriter.write(dataFileReader.next())
}


dataFileReader.close()
parquetWriter.close()
```

As before, the lower-level code is quite verbose, although it does give some insight into the various steps required. You can find the full code in our repository.

We now have a great model to store and retrieve our GKG data that uses Avro and Parquet and can easily be implemented using `DataFrames`.

Summary

In this chapter, we have seen why datasets should always be thoroughly understood before too much exploration work is undertaken. We have discussed the details of structured data and dimensional modeling, particularly with respect to how this applies to the GDELT dataset, and have expanded the GKG model to show its underlying complexity.

We have explained the difference between the traditional ETL and newer schema-on-read ELT techniques, and have touched upon some of the issues that data engineers face regarding data storage, compression, and data formats – specifically the advantages and implementations of Avro and Parquet. We have also demonstrated that there are several ways to explore data using the various Spark API, including examples of how to use SQL on the Spark shell.

We can conclude this chapter by mentioning that the code in our repository pulls everything together and is a full model for reading in raw GKG files (use the Apache NiFi GDELT data ingest pipeline from `Chapter 1`, *Data Acquisition* if you require some data).

In the next chapter, we will dive deeper into the GKG model by exploring the techniques used to explore and analyze data at scale. We will see how to develop and enrich our GKG data model using SQL, and investigate how Apache Zeppelin notebooks can provide a richer data science experience.

4
Exploratory Data Analysis

Exploratory Data Analysis (**EDA**) performed in commercial settings is generally commissioned as part of a larger piece of work that is organized and executed along the lines of a feasibility assessment. The aim of this feasibility assessment, and thus the focus of what we can term an *extended EDA*, is to answer a broad set of questions about whether the data examined is fit for purpose and thus worthy of further investment.

Under this general remit, the data investigations are expected to cover several aspects of feasibility that include the practical aspects of using the data in production, such as its timeliness, quality, complexity, and coverage, as well as being appropriate for the intended hypothesis to be tested. While some of these aspects are potentially less fun from a data science perspective, these data quality led investigations are no less important than purely statistical insights. This is especially true when the datasets in question are very large and complex and when the investment needed to prepare the data for the data science might be significant. To illustrate this point, and to bring the topic to life, we present methods for doing an EDA of the vast and complex **Global Knowledge Graph** (**GKG**) data feeds, made available by the **Global Database of Events, Language and Tone** (**GDELT**) project.

In this chapter, we will create and interpret an EDA while covering the following topics:

- Understanding the problems and design goals for planning and structuring an Extended Exploratory Data Analysis
- What data profiling is, with examples, and how a general framework for data quality can be formed around the technique for continuous data quality monitoring
- How to construct a general *mask-based* data profiler around the method
- How to store the exploratory metrics to a standard schema, to facilitate the study of data drift in the metrics over time, with examples

- How to use Apache Zeppelin notebooks for quick EDA work, and for plotting charts and graphs
- How to extract and study the GCAM sentiments in GDELT, both as time series and as spatio-temporal datasets
- How to extend Apache Zeppelin to generate custom charts using the `plot.ly` library

The problem, principles and planning

In this section, we will explore why an EDA might be required and discuss the important considerations for creating one.

Understanding the EDA problem

A difficult question that precedes an EDA project is: *Can you give me an estimate and breakdown of your proposed EDA costs, please?*

How we answer this question ultimately shapes our EDA strategy and tactics. In days gone by, the answer to this question typically started like this: *Basically you pay by the column....* This rule of thumb is based on the premise that there is *an iterable unit of data exploration work*, and these units of work drive the estimate of effort and thus the rough price of performing the EDA.

What's interesting about this idea is that the units of work are quoted in terms of the *data structures to investigate* rather than *functions that need writing*. The reason for this is simple. Data processing pipelines of functions are assumed to exist already, rather than being new work, and so the quotation offered is actually the implied cost of configuring the new inputs' data structures to our standard data processing pipelines for exploring data.

This thinking brings us to the main EDA problem, that *exploring* seems hard to pin down in terms of planning tasks and estimating timings. The recommended approach is to consider explorations as configuration driven tasks. This helps us to structure and estimate the work more effectively, as well as helping to shape the thinking around the effort so that configuration is the central challenge, rather than the writing of a lot of ad hoc throw-away code.

The process of configuring data exploration also drives us to consider the processing templates we might need. We would need to configure these based on the form of the data we explore. For instance, we would need a standard exploration pipeline for structured data, for text data, for graph shaped data, for image data, for sound data, for time series data, and for spatial data. Once we have these templates, we need to simply map our input data to them and configure our ingestion filters to deliver a focused lens over the data.

Design principles

Modernizing these ideas for Apache Spark based EDA processing means that we need to design our configurable EDA functions and code with some general principles in mind:

- **Easily reusable functions/features**: We need to define our functions to work on general data structures in general ways so they produce good exploratory features and deliver them in ways that minimize the effort needed to configure them for new datasets
- **Minimize intermediate data structures**: We need to avoid proliferating intermediate schemas, helping to minimize intermediate configurations, and where possible create reusable data structures
- **Data driven configuration**: Where possible, we need to have configurations that can be generated from metadata to reduce the manual boilerplate work
- **Templated visualizations**: General reusable visualizations driven from common input schemas and metadata

Lastly, although it is not a strict principle per se, we need to construct exploratory tools that are flexible enough to discover data structures rather than depend on rigid pre-defined configurations. This helps when things go wrong, by helping us to reverse engineer the file content, the encodings, or the potential errors in the file definitions when we come across them.

General plan of exploration

The early stages of all EDA work are invariably based on the simple goal of establishing whether the data is of good quality. If we focus here, to create a general *getting started* plan that is widely applicable, then we can lay down a general set of tasks.

These tasks create the general shape of a proposed EDA project plan, which is as follows:

- Prepare source tools, source our input datasets, review the documentation, and so on. Review security of data where necessary.
- Obtain, decrypt, and stage the data in HDFS; collect **non-functional requirements** (**NFRs**) for planning.
- Run code point level frequency reports on the file content.
- Run a population check on the amount of missing data in the files' fields.
- Run a low grain format profiler to check on the high cardinality fields in the files.
- Run a high grain format profiler check on format-controlled fields in the files.
- Run referential integrity checks, where appropriate.
- Run in-dictionary checks, to verify external dimensions.
- Run basic numeric and statistical explorations of numeric data.
- Run more visualization-based explorations of key data of interest.

> In character encoding terminology, a code point or code position is any of the numerical values that make up the code space. Many code points represent single characters, but they can also have other meanings, such as for formatting.

Preparation

Now that we have a general plan of action, before exploring our data, we must first invest in building the reusable tools for conducting the early mundane parts of the exploration pipeline that help us validate data; then as a second step investigate GDELT's content.

Introducing mask based data profiling

A simple but effective method for quickly exploring new types of data is to make use of mask based data profiling. A *mask* in this context is a transformation function for a string that generalizes a data item into a feature, that, as a collection of masks, will have a lower cardinality than the original values in the field of study.

When a column of data is summarized into mask frequency counts, a process commonly called *data profiling*, it can offer rapid insights into the common structures and content of the strings, and hence reveal how the raw data was encoded. Consider the following mask for exploring data:

- Translate uppercase letters to *A*
- Translate lowercase letters to *a*
- Translate numbers, 0 through 9, to *9*

It seems like a very simple transformation at first glance. As an example, let's apply this mask to a high cardinality field of data, such as the GDELT GKG file's *V2.1 Source Common Name* field. The documentation suggests it records the common name of the source of the news article being studied, which typically is the name of the website the news article was scraped from. Our expectation is that it contains domain names, such as `nytimes.com`.

Before implementing the production solution in Spark, let's prototype a profiler on the Unix command line to provide an example that we can run anywhere:

```
$ cat 20150218230000.gkg.csv | gawk -F"\t" '{print $4}' | \
  sed "s/[0-9]/9/g; s/[a-z]/a/g; s/[A-Z]/A/g" | sort |    \
  uniq -c | sort -r -n | head -20

232 aaaa.aaa
195 aaaaaaaaaa.aaa
186 aaaaaa.aaa
182 aaaaaaaa.aaa
168 aaaaaaa.aaa
167 aaaaaaaaaaaa.aaa
167 aaaaa.aaa
153 aaaaaaaaaaaaa.aaa
147 aaaaaaaaaa.aaa
120 aaaaaaaaaaaaaa.aaa
```

The output is a sorted count of records found in the Source Common Name column alongside the mask generated by the regular expression (regex). It should be very clear looking at the results of this *profiled data* that the field contains domain names – or does it? As we have only looked at the most common masks (the top 20 in this case) perhaps the long tail of masks at the other end of the sorted list holds potential data quality issues at a lower frequency.

Rather than looking at just the top 20 masks, or even the bottom 20, we can introduce a subtle change to improve the generalization ability of our mask function. By making the regex collapse multiple adjacent occurrences of lower case letters into a single a character, the mask's cardinality can be reduced without really diminishing our ability to interpret the results. We can prototype this improvement with just a small change to our regex and hopefully view all the masks in one page of output:

```
$ # note: on a mac use gsed, on linux use sed.
$ hdfs dfs -cat 20150218230000.gkg.csv |                    \
  gawk -F"\t" '{print $4}' | sed "s/[0-9]/9/g; s/[A-Z]/A/g; \
  s/[a-z]/a/g; s/a*a/a/g"| sort | uniq -c | sort -r -n

2356 a.a
 508 a.a.a
  83 a-a.a
  58 a99.a
  36 a999.a
  24 a-9.a
  21 99a.a
  21 9-a.a
  15 a9.a
  15 999a.a
  12 a9a.a
  11 a99a.a
   8 a-a.a.a
   7 9a.a
   3 a-a-a.a
   2 AAA Aa      <---note here the pattern that stands out
   2 9a99a.a
   2 9a.a.a
   1 a9.a.a
   1 a.99a.a
   1 9a9a.a
   1 9999a.a
```

Very quickly, we have prototyped a mask that reduces the three thousand or so raw values down to a very short list of 22 values that are easily inspected by eye. As the long tail is now a much shorter tail, we can easily spot any possible outliers in this data field that could represent quality issues or special cases. This type of inspection, although manual, can be very powerful.

Notice, for instance, there is a particular mask in the output, AAA Aa, which doesn't have a *dot* within it, as we would expect in a domain name. We interpret this finding to mean we've spotted two rows of raw data that are not valid domain names, but perhaps general descriptors. Perhaps this is an error, or an example of what is known as, *illogical field use*, meaning there could be other values slipping into this column that perhaps should logically go elsewhere.

This is worth investigating, and it is easy to inspect those exact two records. We do so by generating the masks alongside the original data, then filtering on the offending mask to locate the original strings for manual inspection.

Rather than code a very long one liner on the command line, we can inspect these records using a legacy data profiler called bytefreq (short for *byte frequencies*) written in awk. It has switches to generate formatted reports, database ready metrics, and also a switch to output masks and data side by side. We have open-sourced bytefreq specifically for readers of this book, and suggest you play with it to really understand how useful this technique can be: https://bitbucket.org/bytesumo/bytefreq.

```
$ # here is a Low Granularity report from bytefreq
$ hdfs dfs -cat 20150218230000.gkg.csv |            \
gawk -F"\t" '{print $4}' | awk -F"," -f         \
~/bytefreq/bytefreq_v1.04.awk -v header="0" -v report="0"  \
  -v grain="L"

-   ##column_100000001  2356  a.a      sfgate.com
-   ##column_100000001  508   a.a.a     theaustralian.com.au
-   ##column_100000001  109   a9.a     france24.com
-   ##column_100000001  83    a-a.a    news-gazette.com
-   ##column_100000001  44    9a.a     927thevan.com
-   ##column_100000001  24    a-9.a    abc-7.com
-   ##column_100000001  23    a9a.a    abc10up.com
-   ##column_100000001  21    9-a.a    4-traders.com
-   ##column_100000001  8     a-a.a.a  gazette-news.co.uk
-   ##column_100000001  3     9a9a.a    8points9seconds.com
-   ##column_100000001  3     a-a-a.a  the-american-interest.com
-   ##column_100000001  2     9a.a.a    9news.com.au
-   ##column_100000001  2     A Aa      BBC Monitoring
-   ##column_100000001  1     a.9a.a    vancouver.24hrs.ca
-   ##column_100000001  1     a9.a.a    guide2.co.nz

$ hdfs dfs -cat 20150218230000.gkg.csv | gawk                \
-F"\t" '{print $4}'|gawk -F"," -f ~/bytefreq/bytefreq_v1.04.awk\
-v header="0" -v report="2" -v grain="L" | grep ",A Aa"

BBC Monitoring,A Aa
BBC Monitoring,A Aa
```

When we inspect the odd mask, `A Aa`, we can see the offending text found is `BBC Monitoring`, and in re-reading the GDELT documentation we will see that this is not an error, but a known special case. It means when using this field, we must remember to handle this special case. One way to handle it could be by including a correction rule to swap this string value for a value that works better, for example, the valid domain name `www.monitor.bbc.co.uk`, which is the data source to which the text string refers.

The idea we are introducing here is that a mask can be used as a *key* to retrieve offending records in particular fields. This logic leads us to the next major benefit of mask based profiling: the output masks are a form of *Data Quality Error Code*. These error codes can fall into two categories: a whitelist of *good* masks, and a blacklist of *bad* masks that are used to find poor quality data. Thought of this way, masks then form the basis for searching and retrieving data cleansing methods, or perhaps for throwing an alarm or rejecting a record.

The lesson is that we can create *Treatment functions* to remediate raw strings that are found using a particular mask calculated over data in a particular field. This thinking leads to the following conclusion: we can create a general framework around mask based profiling for doing data quality control and remediation *as we read data within our data reading pipeline*. This has some really advantageous solution properties:

- Generating data quality masks is an *on read* process; we can accept new raw data and write it to disk then, on read, we can generate masks only when needed at query time – so data cleansing can be a dynamic process.
- Treatment functions can then be dynamically applied to targeting remediation efforts that help to cleanse our data at the time of read.
- Because previously unseen strings are generalized into masks, new strings can be flagged as having quality issues even if that exact string has never been seen before. This generality helps us to reduce complexity, simplify our processes, and create reusable smart solutions – even across subject areas.
- Data items that create masks that do not fall either into mask white-lists, fix-lists, or blacklists can potentially be quarantined for attention; human analysts can inspect the records and hopefully whitelist them, or perhaps create new Treatments Functions that help to get the data out of quarantine and back into production.
- Data quarantines can be implemented simply as an on-read filter, and when new remediation functions are created to cleanse or fix data, the dynamic treatments applied at read time will automatically *release* the corrected data to users without long delays.

- Eventually a data quality Treatment library will be created that stabilizes over time. New work is mainly done by mapping and applying the existing treatments to new data. A phone number reformatting Treatment function, for example, can be widely reused over many datasets and projects.

With the method and architectural benefits now explained, the requirements for building a generalized mask based profiler should be clearer. Note that the mask generation process is a classic Hadoop MapReduce process: map input's data out to masks, and reduce those masks back down to summarized frequency counts. Note also how, even in this short example, we have already used two types of masks and each is made up of a pipeline of underlying transformations. It suggests we need a tool that supports a library of predefined masks as well as allowing for user defined masks that can be created quickly and on demand. It also suggests there should be ways to *stack* the masks to build them up into complex pipelines.

What may not be so obvious yet is that all data profiling done in this way can write profiler metrics to *a common output format.* This helps to improve reusability of our code through simplifying the logging, storing, retrieval, and consumption of the profiling data.

As an example we should be able to report all mask based profiler metrics using the following schema:

```
Metric Descriptor
Source Studied
IngestTime
MaskType
FieldName
Occurrence Count
KeyCount
MaskCount
Description
```

Once our metrics are captured in this single schema format, we can then build secondary reports using a user interface, such as Zeppelin notebook.

Before we walk through implementing these functions, an introduction to the character class masks is needed as these differ slightly from the normal profiling masks.

Introducing character class masks

There is another simple type of data profiling that we can also apply that helps with file inspection. It involves profiling the actual bytes that make up a whole file. It is an old method, one that originally comes from cryptography where frequency analysis of letters in texts was used to gain an edge on deciphering substitution codes.

While not a common technique in data science circles today, byte level analysis is surprisingly useful when it's needed. In the past, data encodings were a massive problem. Files were encoded in a range of code pages, across ASCII and EBCDIC standards. Byte frequency reporting was often critical to discover the actual encoding, delimiters, and line endings used in the files. Back, then the number of people who could create files, but not technically describe them, waqs surprising. Today, as the world moves increasingly to Unicode-based character encodings, these old methods need updating. In Unicode, the concept of a byte is modernized to multi-byte *code points*, which can be revealed in Scala using the following function:

```scala
val tst = "Andrew 漢字"

def toCodePointVector(input: String) = input.map{
    case (i) if i > 65535 =>
        val hchar = (i - 0x10000) / 0x400 + 0xD800
        val lchar = (i - 0x10000) % 0x400 + 0xDC00
        f"\\u$hchar%04x\\u$lchar%04x"
    case (i) if i > 0 => f"\\u$i%04x"
    // kudos to Ben Reich: http://k.bytefreq.com/1MjyvNz
    }

val out = toCodePointVector(tst)

val rows = sc.parallelize(out)
rows.countByValue().foreach(println)

// results in the following: [codepoint], [Frequency_count]
(\u0065,1)
(\u03d6,1)
(\u006e,1)
(\u0072,1)
(\u0077,1)
(\u0041,1)
(\u0020,2)
(\u6f22,1)
(\u0064,1)
(\u5b57,1)
```

Using this function, we can begin to profile any international character level data we receive in our GDELT dataset and start to understand the complexities we might face in exploiting the data. But, unlike the other masks, to create interpretable results from code points, we require a dictionary that we can use to look up meaningful contextual information, such as unicode category and the unicode character names.

To generate a contextual lookup, we can use this quick command line hack to generate a reduced dictionary from the main one found at unicode.org, which should help us to better report on our findings:

```
$ wget ftp://ftp.unicode.org/Public/UNIDATA/UnicodeData.txt
$ cat UnicodeData.txt | gawk -F";" '{OFS=";"} {print $1,$3,$2}' \
  | sed 's/-/ /g'| gawk '{print $1,$2}'| gawk -F";" '{OFS="\t"} \
  length($1) < 5 {print $1,$2,$3}' > codepoints.txt

# use "hdfs dfs -put" to load codepoints.txt to hdfs, so
# you can use it later

head -1300 codepoints.txt | tail -4
0513      Ll    CYRILLIC SMALL
0514      Lu    CYRILLIC CAPITAL
0515      Ll    CYRILLIC SMALL
0516      Lu    CYRILLIC CAPITAL
```

We will use this dictionary, joined to our discovered code points, to report on the character class frequencies of each byte in the file. While it seems like a simple form of analysis, the results can often be surprising and offer a forensic level of understanding of the data we are handling, its source, and the types of algorithms and methods we can apply successfully to it. We will also look up the general Unicode Category to simplify our reports using the following lookup table:

```
Cc   Other, Control
Cf   Other, Format
Cn   Other, Not Assigned
Co   Other, Private Use
Cs   Other, Surrogate
LC   Letter, Cased
Ll   Letter, Lowercase
Lm   Letter, Modifier
Lo   Letter, Other
Lt   Letter, Titlecase
Lu   Letter, Uppercase
Mc   Mark, Spacing Combining
Me   Mark, Enclosing
Mn   Mark, Nonspacing
```

```
Nd  Number, Decimal Digit
Nl  Number, Letter
No  Number, Other
Pc  Punctuation, Connector
Pd  Punctuation, Dash
Pe  Punctuation, Close
Pf  Punctuation, Final quote
Pi  Punctuation, Initial quote
Po  Punctuation, Other
Ps  Punctuation, Open
Sc  Symbol, Currency
Sk  Symbol, Modifier
Sm  Symbol, Math
So  Symbol, Other
Zl  Separator, Line
Zp  Separator, Paragraph
Zs  Separator, Space
```

Building a mask based profiler

Let's walk through creating a notebook-based toolkit for profiling data in Spark. The mask functions we will implement are set out over several grains of detail, moving from file level to row level, and then to field level:

1. Character level masks applied across whole files are:
   - Unicode Frequency, UTF-16 multi-byte representation (aka Code Points), at file level
   - UTF Character Class Frequency, at file level
   - Delimiter Frequency, at row level

2. String level masks applied to fields within files are:
   - ASCII low grain profile, per field
   - ASCII high grain profile, per field
   - Population checks, per field

Setting up Apache Zeppelin

As we are going to be exploring our data visually, a product that could be very useful for mixing and matching technologies with relative ease is Apache Zeppelin. Apache Zeppelin is an Apache Incubator product that enables us to create a notebook, or worksheet, containing a mix of a number of different languages including Python, Scala, SQL, and Bash, which makes it ideal for working with Spark for running exploratory data analysis.

Code is written in a notebook style using *paragraphs* (or cells) where each cell can be independently executed making it easy to work on a small piece of code without having to repeatedly compile and run entire programs. It also serves as a record of the code used to produce any given output, and helps us to integrate visualizations.

Zeppelin can be installed and run very quickly, a minimal installation process is explained as follows:

- Download and extract Zeppelin from here:
  `https://zeppelin.incubator.apache.org/download.html`
- Find the conf directory and make a copy of `zeppelin-env.sh.template` named `zeppelin-env.sh`.
- Alter the `zeppelin-env.sh` file, uncomment and set the `JAVA_HOME` and `SPARK_HOME` entries to the relevant locations on your machine.
- Should you want Zeppelin to use HDFS in Spark, set the `HADOOP_CONF_DIR` entry to the location of your Hadoop files; `hdfs-site.xml`, `core-site.xml`, and so on.
- Start the Zeppelin service: `bin/zeppelin-daemon.sh start`. This will automatically pick up the changes made in `conf/zeppelin-env.sh`.

On our test cluster, we are using Hortonworks HDP 2.6, and Zeppelin comes as part of the installation.

One thing to note when using Zeppelin is that the first paragraph should always be a declaration of external packages. Any Spark dependencies can be added in this way using the `ZeppelinContext`, to be run right after each restart of the interpreter in Zeppelin; for example:

```
%dep
z.reset
// z.load("groupId>:artifactId:version")
```

After this we can write code in any of the available languages. We are going to use a mix of Scala, SQL, and Bash across the notebook by declaring each cell using a type of interpreter, that is, `%spark`, `%sql`, and `%shell`. Zeppelin defaults to Scala Spark if no interpreter is given (`%spark`).

You can find the Zeppelin notebooks to accompany this chapter, as well as others in our code repository.

Constructing a reusable notebook

In our code repository we have created a simple, extensible, open source data profiler library that can also be found here:
`https://bytesumo@bitbucket.org/gzet_io/profilers.git`

The library takes care of the framework needed to apply masks to data frames, including the special case where raw lines of a file are cast to a data frame of just one column. We won't go through all the details of that framework line by line, but the class of most interest is found in the file `MaskBasedProfiler.scala`, which also contains the definitions of each of the available mask functions.

A great way to use this library is by constructing a user-friendly notebook application that allows for visual exploration of data. We have prepared just such a notebook for our profiling using Apache Zeppelin. Next, we will walk through how to build our own notebook using the preceding section as a starting point. The data in our examples is the GDELT `event` files, which have a simple tab delimited format.

The first step to building up a notebook (or even just to play with our readymade one), is to copy the `profilers-1.0.0.jar` file from our library into a local directory that the Zeppelin user on our cluster can access, which on a Hortonworks installation is the Zeppelin user's home directory on the Namenode:

```
git clone https://bytesumo@bitbucket.org/gzet_io/profilers.git
sudo cp profilers-1.0.0.jar /home/zeppelin/.
sudo ls /home/zeppelin/
```

Then we can visit `http://{main.install.hostname}:9995` to access the Apache Zeppelin homepage. From that page, we can upload our notebook and follow along, or we can create a new one and build our own by clicking **Create new note**.

In Zeppelin, the first paragraph of a notebook is where we execute our Spark code dependencies. We'll import the profiler jars that we'll need later:

```
%dep
// you need to put the profiler jar into a directory
// that Zeppelin has access to.
// For example, /home/zeppelin, a non-hdfs directory on
// the namenode.
z.load("/home/zeppelin/profilers-1.0.0.jar")
// you may need to restart your interpreter, then run
// this paragraph
```

In paragraph two, we include a small shell script to inspect the file(s) we want to profile to verify that we're picking up the right ones. Note the use of `column` and `colrm`, both very handy Unix commands for inspecting columnar table data on the command line:

```
%sh
# list the first two files in the directory, make sure the header file
exists
# note - a great trick is to write just the headers to a delimited file
# that sorts to the top of your file glob, a trick that works well with
# Spark's csv reader where headers are not on each file you
# hold in hdfs.
# this is a quick inspection check, see we use column and
# colrm to format it:

hdfs dfs -cat "/user/feeds/gdelt/events/*.export.CSV" \
|head -4|column -t -s $'\t'|colrm 68

GlobalEventID  Day       MonthYear  Year  FractionDate  Actor1Code
610182939      20151221  201512     2015  2015.9616
610182940      20151221  201512     2015  2015.9616
610182941      20151221  201512     2015  2015.9616     CAN
```

In paragraph 3, 4, 5, and 6, we use Zeppelin's facility for user input boxes to allow the user to configure the EDA notebook like it's a proper web-based application. This allows users to configure four variables that can be reused in the notebook to drive further investigations: **YourMask**, **YourDelimiter**, **YourFilePath**, and **YourHeaders**. These look great when we hide the editors and adjust the alignment and size of the windows:

Configure the Profiler's Mask	Configure Delimiter	Configure the CSV file to profile	Headers?
YourMask	YourDelimiter	YourFilePath	YourHeaders
STRING HIGH	\t	user/feeds/gdelt/eve	✓ Has Header / No Header
YourMask: String = ASCIICLASS_HIGHGRAIN	YourDelimiter: String = \t	YourFilePath: String = /user/feeds/gdelt/events/*.export.CSV	YourHeader: String = true

If we open the prepared notebook and click on **show editor** on any of these input paragraphs, we'll see how we set those up to provide drop-down boxes in Zeppelin, for example:

```
val YourHeader = z.select("YourHeaders", Seq(  ("true", "HasHeader"),
("false", "No Header"))).toString
```

Next, we have a paragraph that is used to import the functions we need:

```
import io.gzet.profilers._
import sys.process._
import org.apache.spark.sql.SQLContext
import org.apache.spark.sql.functions.udf
import org.apache.spark.sql.types.{StructType, StructField, StringType,
IntegerType}
import org.apache.spark.sql.SaveMode
import sqlContext.implicits._
```

Then we move on to a new paragraph that configures and ingests the data we read in:

```
val InputFilePath = YourFilePath
// set our input to user's file glob
val RawData = sqlContext.read
// read in tabular data
        .option("header", YourHeader)
// configurable headers
        .option("delimiter", YourDelimiter )
// configurable delimiters
        .option("nullValue", "NULL")
// set a default char if nulls seen
        .option("treatEmptyValuesAsNulls", "true")
// set to null
        .option("inferschema", "false")
// do not infer schema, we'll discover it
        .csv(InputFilePath)
// file glob path. Can use wildcards
RawData.registerTempTable("RawData")
// register data for Spark SQL access to it
RawData.cache()
// cache the file for use
val RawLines = sc.textFile(InputFilePath)
// read the file lines as a string
RawLines.toDF.registerTempTable("RawLines")
// useful to check for schema corruption
RawData.printSchema()
// print out the schema we found

// define our profiler apps
```

```
val ASCIICLASS_HIGHGRAIN     =
MaskBasedProfiler(PredefinedMasks.ASCIICLASS_HIGHGRAIN)
val CLASS_FREQS              =
MaskBasedProfiler(PredefinedMasks.CLASS_FREQS)
val UNICODE                  = MaskBasedProfiler(PredefinedMasks.UNICODE)
val HEX                      = MaskBasedProfiler(PredefinedMasks.HEX)
val ASCIICLASS_LOWGRAIN      =
MaskBasedProfiler(PredefinedMasks.ASCIICLASS_LOWGRAIN)
val POPCHECKS                = MaskBasedProfiler(PredefinedMasks.POPCHECKS)

// configure our profiler apps
val Metrics_ASCIICLASS_HIGHGRAIN    =
ASCIICLASS_HIGHGRAIN.profile(YourFilePath, RawData)
val Metrics_CLASS_FREQS             = CLASS_FREQS.profile(YourFilePath,
RawLines.toDF)
val Metrics_UNICODE                 = UNICODE.profile(YourFilePath,
RawLines.toDF)
val Metrics_HEX                     = HEX.profile(YourFilePath,
RawLines.toDF)
val Metrics_ASCIICLASS_LOWGRAIN     =
ASCIICLASS_LOWGRAIN.profile(YourFilePath, RawData)
val Metrics_POPCHECKS               = POPCHECKS.profile(YourFilePath,
RawData)
// note some of the above read tabular data, some read rawlines of string
data

// now register the profiler output as sql accessible data frames

Metrics_ASCIICLASS_HIGHGRAIN.toDF.registerTempTable("Metrics_ASCIICLASS_HIG
HGRAIN")
Metrics_CLASS_FREQS.toDF.registerTempTable("Metrics_CLASS_FREQS")
Metrics_UNICODE.toDF.registerTempTable("Metrics_UNICODE")
Metrics_HEX.toDF.registerTempTable("Metrics_HEX")
Metrics_ASCIICLASS_LOWGRAIN.toDF.registerTempTable("Metrics_ASCIICLASS_LOWG
RAIN")
Metrics_POPCHECKS.toDF.registerTempTable("Metrics_POPCHECKS")
```

Now that we've done the configuration steps, we can start to examine our tabular data and discover if our reported column names match our input data. In a new paragraph window, we use the SQL context to simplify calling SparkSQL and running a query:

```
%sql
select * from RawData
limit 10
```

The great thing about Zeppelin is that the output is formatted into a proper HTML table, which we can easily use to inspect wide files having many columns (for example, GDELT Event files):

We can see from this displayed data that our columns match the input data; therefore we can proceed with our analysis.

> If you wish to read the GDELT event files, you can find the header file in our code repository.

If there are errors in the data alignment between columns and content at this point, it is also possible to select the first 10 rows of the RawLines Dataframe, configured earlier, which will display just the first 10 rows of the raw string based data inputs. If the data happens to be tab delimited, we'll see immediately a further benefit that the Zeppelin formatted output will align the columns for us on the raw strings automatically, much like the way that we did earlier using the bash command *column*.

Now we will move on to study the file's bytes, to discover details about the encodings within it. To do so we load our lookup tables, and then join them to the output of our profiler functions, which we registered earlier as a table. Notice how the output of the profiler can be treated directly as an SQL callable table:

```
// load the UTF lookup tables

val codePointsSchema = StructType(Array(
    StructField("CodePoint"  , StringType, true),      //$1
    StructField("Category"   , StringType, true),      //$2
    StructField("CodeDesc"   , StringType, true)       //$3
    ))
```

```
val UnicodeCatSchema = StructType(Array(
    StructField("Category"        , StringType, true), //$1
    StructField("Description"     , StringType, true)  //$2
    ))

val codePoints = sqlContext.read
    .option("header", "false")     // configurable headers
    .schema(codePointsSchema)
    .option("delimiter", "\t" )   // configurable delimiters
    .csv("/user/feeds/ref/codepoints2.txt")  // configurable path

codePoints.registerTempTable("codepoints")
codePoints.cache()
val utfcats = sqlContext.read
     .option("header", "false")     // configurable headers
     .schema(UnicodeCatSchema)
     .option("delimiter", "\t" )   // configurable delimiters
     .csv("/user/feeds/ref/UnicodeCategory.txt")

utfcats.registerTempTable("utfcats")
utfcats.cache()

// Next we build the different presentation layer views for the codepoints
val hexReport = sqlContext.sql("""
select
  r.Category
, r.CodeDesc
, sum(maskCount) as maskCount
from
    ( select
             h.*
            ,c.*
       from Metrics_HEX h
       left outer join codepoints c
           on ( upper(h.MaskType) = c.CodePoint)
    ) r
group by r.Category, r.CodeDesc
order by r.Category, r.CodeDesc, 2 DESC
""")
hexReport.registerTempTable("hexReport")
hexReport.cache()
hexReport.show(10)
+--------+----------------+---------+
|Category|        CodeDesc|maskCount|
+--------+----------------+---------+
|      Cc|  CTRL: CHARACTER|   141120|
|      Ll|      LATIN SMALL|   266070|
|      Lu|    LATIN CAPITAL|   115728|
```

```
  |       Nd|       DIGIT EIGHT|    18934|
  |       Nd|        DIGIT FIVE|    24389|
  |       Nd|        DIGIT FOUR|    24106|
  |       Nd|        DIGIT NINE|    17204|
  |       Nd|         DIGIT ONE|    61165|
  |       Nd|       DIGIT SEVEN|    16497|
  |       Nd|         DIGIT SIX|    31706|
  +--------+-----------------+---------+
```

In a new paragraph, we can use the SQLContext to visualize the output. To help view the values that are skewed, we can use the SQL statement to calculate the log of the counts. This produces a graphic, which we could include in a final report, where we can toggle between raw frequencies and log frequencies.

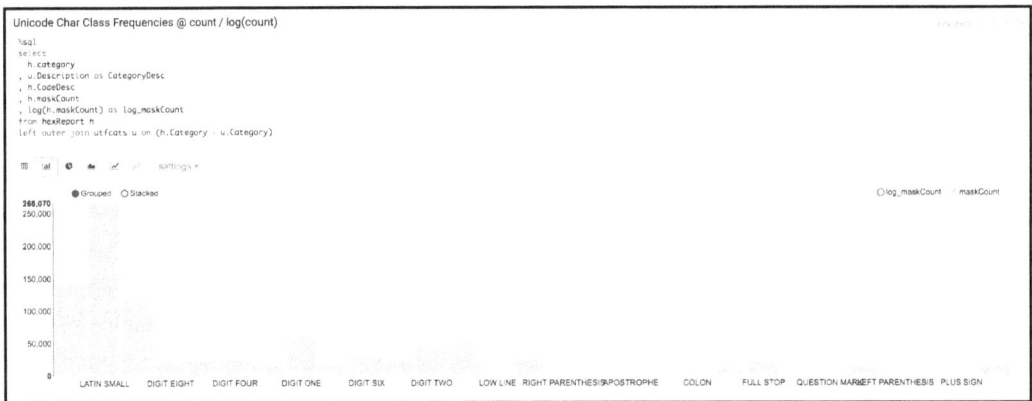

Because we have loaded the category of character classes, we can also adjust the visualization to further simplify the chart:

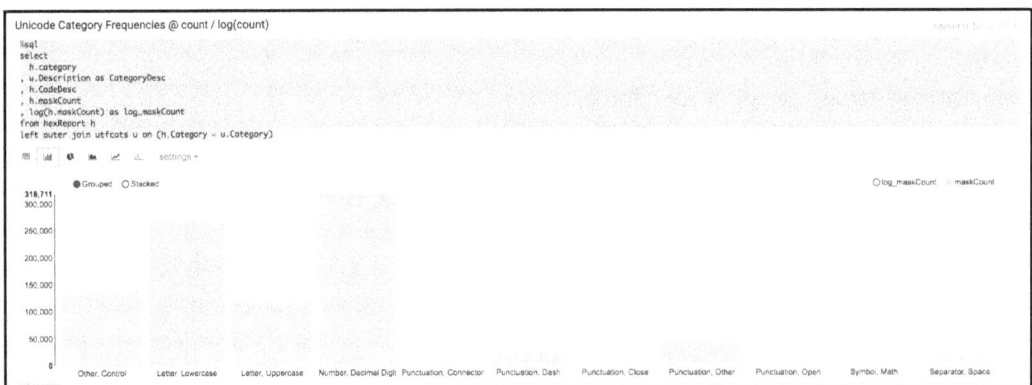

A basic check we must always run when doing an EDA is population checks, which we calculate using POPCHECKS. POPCHECKS is a special mask we defined in our Scala code that returns a `1` if a field is populated, or a `0` if it is not. When we inspect the result, we notice we'll need to do some final report writing to present the numbers in a more directly interpretable way:

```
Metrics_POPCHECKS.toDF.show(1000, false)
```

```
Metrics_POPCHECKS.toDF.show(1000, false)

+---------------------------------+-------------+----------+----------------+----------------+--------+--------+---------+-----------+
|metricDescriptor                 |sourceStudied|ingestTime|maskType|fieldName      |occurrenceCount|keyCount|maskCount|description|
+---------------------------------+-------------+----------+----------------+----------------+--------+--------+---------+-----------+
|/user/feeds/gdelt/events/*.export.CSV|2016-12-23|0|Actor1Type2Code |100525|61|59  |<function1>|
|/user/feeds/gdelt/events/*.export.CSV|2016-12-23|0|Actor1Geo_Lat   |100525|61|2122|<function1>|
|/user/feeds/gdelt/events/*.export.CSV|2016-12-23|0|Actor2Type2Code |100525|61|58  |<function1>|
|/user/feeds/gdelt/events/*.export.CSV|2016-12-23|0|NumSources      |100525|61|2351|<function1>|
|/user/feeds/gdelt/events/*.export.CSV|2016-12-23|0|ActionGeo_Long  |100525|61|2315|<function1>|
|/user/feeds/gdelt/events/*.export.CSV|2016-12-23|0|Actor1Geo_FullName|100525|61|2122|<function1>|
|/user/feeds/gdelt/events/*.export.CSV|2016-12-23|0|AvgTone         |100525|61|2351|<function1>|
|/user/feeds/gdelt/events/*.export.CSV|2016-12-23|0|Actor1Geo_Type  |100525|61|2351|<function1>|
|/user/feeds/gdelt/events/*.export.CSV|2016-12-23|0|ActionGeo_ADM2Code|100525|61|1343|<function1>|
|/user/feeds/gdelt/events/*.export.CSV|2016-12-23|0|DateAdded       |100525|61|2351|<function1>|
```

We can do that in two steps. Firstly, we can use an SQL case expression to convert the data into values of *populated* or *missing,* which should help. Then we can pivot this aggregate dataset by performing a `groupby` on the filename, `metricDescriptor`, and `fieldname` while performing a sum over the populated and the missing values. When we do this we can also include default values of zero where the profiler did not find any cases of data either being populated or missing. It's important to do this when we calculate percentages, to ensure that we never have null numerators or denominators. While this code is not as short as it could be, it illustrates a number of techniques for manipulating data in `SparkSQL`.

Notice also that in `SparkSQL` we can use the SQL `coalesce` statement, which is not to be confused with Spark native `coalesce` functionality, for manipulating RDDs. In the SQL sense this function converts nulls into default values, and it is often used gratuitously to trap special cases in production grade code where data is not particularly trusted. Notable also is that sub-selects are well supported in `SparkSQL`. You can even make heavy use of these and Spark will not complain. This is particularly useful as they are the most natural way to program for many traditional database engineers as well as people with experience of databases of all kinds:

```
val pop_qry = sqlContext.sql("""
select * from (
    select
            fieldName as rawFieldName
    ,       coalesce( cast(regexp_replace(fieldName, "C", "") as INT),
    fieldName) as fieldName
```

```
        ,    case when maskType = 0 then "Populated"
                  when maskType = 1 then "Missing"
             end as PopulationCheck
        ,     coalesce(maskCount, 0) as maskCount
        ,    metricDescriptor as fileName
        from Metrics_POPCHECKS
   ) x
   order by fieldName
   """)
   val pivot_popquery =
   pop_qry.groupBy("fileName","fieldName").pivot("PopulationCheck").sum("maskC
   ount")
    pivot_popquery.registerTempTable("pivot_popquery")
    val per_pivot_popquery = sqlContext.sql("""
    Select
    x.*
    , round(Missing/(Missing + Populated)*100,2) as PercentMissing
    from
        (select
            fieldname
            , coalesce(Missing, 0) as Missing
            , coalesce(Populated,0) as Populated
            , fileName
        from pivot_popquery) x
    order by x.fieldname ASC
    """)
    per_pivot_popquery.registerTempTable("per_pivot_popquery")
    per_pivot_popquery.select("fieldname","Missing","Populated","PercentMissing
    ","fileName").show(1000,false)
```

The output of the preceding code is a clean reporting table about field level population counts in our data:

```
+--------------------+-------+---------+--------------+------------------------------------+
|fieldname           |Missing|Populated|PercentMissing|fileName                            |
+--------------------+-------+---------+--------------+------------------------------------+
|ActionGeo_ADM1Code  |36     |2315     |1.53          |/user/feeds/gdelt/events/*.export.CSV|
|ActionGeo_ADM2Code  |1008   |1343     |42.88         |/user/feeds/gdelt/events/*.export.CSV|
|ActionGeo_CountryCode|36    |2315     |1.53          |/user/feeds/gdelt/events/*.export.CSV|
|ActionGeo_FeatureID |36     |2315     |1.53          |/user/feeds/gdelt/events/*.export.CSV|
|ActionGeo_FullName  |36     |2315     |1.53          |/user/feeds/gdelt/events/*.export.CSV|
|ActionGeo_Lat       |36     |2315     |1.53          |/user/feeds/gdelt/events/*.export.CSV|
|ActionGeo_Long      |36     |2315     |1.53          |/user/feeds/gdelt/events/*.export.CSV|
|ActionGeo_Type      |0      |2351     |0.0           |/user/feeds/gdelt/events/*.export.CSV|
|Actor1Code          |198    |2153     |8.42          |/user/feeds/gdelt/events/*.export.CSV|
|Actor1CountryCode   |937    |1414     |39.86         |/user/feeds/gdelt/events/*.export.CSV|
|Actor1EthnicCode    |2332   |19       |99.19         |/user/feeds/gdelt/events/*.export.CSV|
|Actor1Geo_ADM1Code  |229    |2122     |9.74          |/user/feeds/gdelt/events/*.export.CSV|
|Actor1Geo_ADM2Code  |979    |1372     |41.64         |/user/feeds/gdelt/events/*.export.CSV|
|Actor1Geo_CountryCode|229   |2122     |9.74          |/user/feeds/gdelt/events/*.export.CSV|
|Actor1Geo_FeatureID |229    |2122     |9.74          |/user/feeds/gdelt/events/*.export.CSV|
|Actor1Geo_FullName  |229    |2122     |9.74          |/user/feeds/gdelt/events/*.export.CSV|
|Actor1Geo_Lat       |229    |2122     |9.74          |/user/feeds/gdelt/events/*.export.CSV|
|Actor1Geo_Long      |229    |2122     |9.74          |/user/feeds/gdelt/events/*.export.CSV|
|Actor1Geo_Type      |0      |2351     |0.0           |/user/feeds/gdelt/events/*.export.CSV|
```

When graphically displayed in our Zeppelin notebook using the `stacked` bar chart functionality, the data produces excellent visualizations that instantly tell us about the levels of data population in our files:

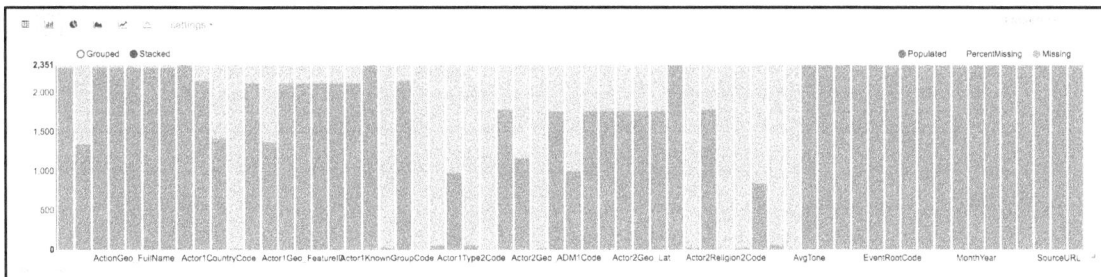

As Zeppelin's bar charts support tooltips, we can use the pointer to observe the full names of the columns, even if they display poorly in the default view.

Lastly, we can also include further paragraphs in our notebook to reveal the results of the `ASCII_HighGrain` and `ASCII_LowGrain` masks, explained earlier. This can be done by simply viewing the profiler outputs as a table, or using more advanced functionality in Zeppelin. As a table, we can try the following:

```
val proReport = sqlContext.sql("""
 select * from (
 select
     metricDescriptor as sourceStudied
 ,   "ASCII_LOWGRAIN" as metricDescriptor
 , coalesce(cast( regexp_replace(fieldName, "C", "") as INT),fieldname) as
fieldName
 , ingestTime
 , maskType as maskInstance
 , maskCount
 , description
 from Metrics_ASCIICLASS_LOWGRAIN
 ) x
 order by fieldNAme, maskCount DESC
 """)
 proReport.show(1000, false)
```

```
proReport: org.apache.spark.sql.DataFrame = [sourceStudied: string, metricDescriptor: string, fieldName: string, ingestTime: date, maskInstance: string, maskCount: bigint, description: st
+----------------------------------------------------+---------------------------+----------------------+-------------------------+-------------+
|sourceStudied                                       |metricDescriptor|fieldName|ingestTime|maskInstance                       |maskCount|
+----------------------------------------------------+---------------------------+----------------------+-------------------------+-------------+
|/user/feeds/gdelt/events/*.export.CSV|ASCII_LOWGRAIN |ActionGeo_ADM1Code    |2016-12-23|A9                            |1207      |
|/user/feeds/gdelt/events/*.export.CSV|ASCII_LOWGRAIN |ActionGeo_ADM1Code    |2016-12-23|A                             |1108      |
|/user/feeds/gdelt/events/*.export.CSV|ASCII_LOWGRAIN |ActionGeo_ADM1Code    |2016-12-23|                              |36        |
|/user/feeds/gdelt/events/*.export.CSV|ASCII_LOWGRAIN |ActionGeo_ADM2Code    |2016-12-23|9                             |1204      |
|/user/feeds/gdelt/events/*.export.CSV|ASCII_LOWGRAIN |ActionGeo_ADM2Code    |2016-12-23|                              |1008      |
|/user/feeds/gdelt/events/*.export.CSV|ASCII_LOWGRAIN |ActionGeo_ADM2Code    |2016-12-23|A9                            |139       |
|/user/feeds/gdelt/events/*.export.CSV|ASCII_LOWGRAIN |ActionGeo_CountryCode|2016-12-23|A                             |2315      |
|/user/feeds/gdelt/events/*.export.CSV|ASCII_LOWGRAIN |ActionGeo_CountryCode|2016-12-23|                              |36        |
|/user/feeds/gdelt/events/*.export.CSV|ASCII_LOWGRAIN |ActionGeo_FeatureID   |2016-12-23|-9                            |1108      |
|/user/feeds/gdelt/events/*.export.CSV|ASCII_LOWGRAIN |ActionGeo_FeatureID   |2016-12-23|A                             |810       |
|/user/feeds/gdelt/events/*.export.CSV|ASCII_LOWGRAIN |ActionGeo_FeatureID   |2016-12-23|9                             |397       |
|/user/feeds/gdelt/events/*.export.CSV|ASCII_LOWGRAIN |ActionGeo_FeatureID   |2016-12-23|                              |36        |
```

To build an interactive viewer, which is useful when we look at ASCII_HighGrain masks that may have very high cardinalities, we can set up an SQL statement that accepts the value of a Zeppelin user input box, where users can type in the column number or the field name to retrieve just the relevant section of the metrics we collected.

We do that in a new SQL paragraph like this, with the SQL predicate being `x.fieldName like '%${ColumnName}%'`:

```
%sql
 select x.* from (
 select
     metricDescriptor as sourceStudied
 ,   "ASCII_HIGHGRAIN" as metricDescriptor
 , coalesce(cast( regexp_replace(fieldName, "C", "")
   as INT),fieldname) as fieldName
```

```
    , ingestTime
    , maskType as maskInstance
    , maskCount
    , log(maskCount) as log_maskCount
    from Metrics_ASCIICLASS_HIGHGRAIN
    ) x
    where  x.fieldName like '%${ColumnName}%'
    order by fieldName, maskCount DESC
```

This creates an interactive user window that refreshes on user input, creating a dynamic profiling report having several output configurations. Here we show the output not as a table, but as a chart of the log of the frequency counts for a field that should have low cardinality, the longitude of *Action* identified in the event file:

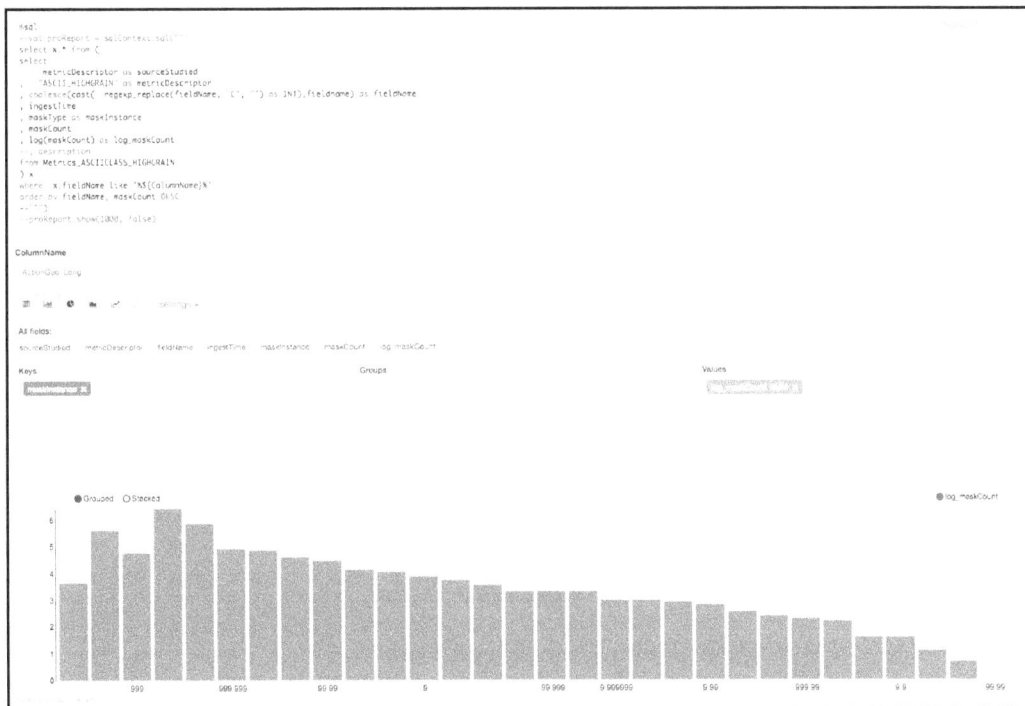

The result shows us that even a simple field like Longitude has a large spread of formats in the data.

The techniques reviewed so far should help create a very reusable notebook for performing exploratory data profiling on all our input data, both quickly and efficiently, producing graphical outputs that we can use to produce great reports and documentation about input file quality.

Exploring GDELT

A large part of the EDA journey is obtaining and documenting the sources of data, and GDELT content is no exception. After researching the GKG datasets, we discovered that it was challenging just to document the actual sources of data we should be using. In the following sections, we provide a comprehensive listing of the resources we located for use, which will need to be run in the examples.

> A cautionary note on download times: using a typical 5 Mb home broadband, 2000 GKG files takes approximately 3.5 hours to download. Given that the GKG English language files alone have over 40,000 files, this could take a while to download.

GDELT GKG datasets

We should be using the latest GDELT data feed, version 2.1 as of December 2016. The main documentation for this data is here:

```
http://data.gdeltproject.org/documentation/GDELT-Global_Knowledge_Graph_Codeboo
k-V2.1.pdf
```

In the following section, we have included the data and secondary references to look up tables, and further documentation.

The files

GKG-English Language Global Knowledge Graph (v2.1)

```
http://data.gdeltproject.org/gdeltv2/masterfilelist.txt
```

```
http://data.gdeltproject.org/gdeltv2/lastupdate.txt
```

GKG-Translated – Non-English Global Knowledge Graph

```
http://data.gdeltproject.org/gdeltv2/lastupdate-translation.txt
```

```
http://data.gdeltproject.org/gdeltv2/masterfilelist-translation.txt
```

GKG-TV (Internet Archive – American Television Global Knowledge Graph)

```
http://data.gdeltproject.org/gdeltv2_iatelevision/lastupdate.txt
```

```
http://data.gdeltproject.org/gdeltv2_iatelevision/masterfilelist.txt
```

GKG-Visual – CloudVision

`http://data.gdeltproject.org/gdeltv2_cloudvision/lastupdate.txt`

Special collections

GKG-AME – Africa And Middle East Global Knowledge Graph

`http://data.gdeltproject.org/gkgv2_specialcollections/AME-GKG.CIA.gkgv2.csv.zip`

`http://data.gdeltproject.org/gkgv2_specialcollections/AME-GKG.CORE.gkgv2.csv.zip`

`http://data.gdeltproject.org/gkgv2_specialcollections/AME-GKG.DTIC.gkgv2.csv.zip`

`http://data.gdeltproject.org/gkgv2_specialcollections/AME-GKG.IADISSERT.gkgv2.csv.zip`

`http://data.gdeltproject.org/gkgv2_specialcollections/AME-GKG.IANONDISSERT.gkgv2.csv.zip`

`http://data.gdeltproject.org/gkgv2_specialcollections/AME-GKG.JSTOR.gkgv2.csv.zip`

GKG-HR (Human Rights Collection)

`http://data.gdeltproject.org/gkgv2_specialcollections/HR-GKG.AMNESTY.gkgv2.csv.zip`

`http://data.gdeltproject.org/gkgv2_specialcollections/HR-GKG.CRISISGROUP.gkgv2.csv.zip`

`http://data.gdeltproject.org/gkgv2_specialcollections/HR-GKG.FIDH.gkgv2.csv.zip`

`http://data.gdeltproject.org/gkgv2_specialcollections/HR-GKG.HRW.gkgv2.csv.zip`

`http://data.gdeltproject.org/gkgv2_specialcollections/HR-GKG.ICC.gkgv2.csv.zip`

`http://data.gdeltproject.org/gkgv2_specialcollections/HR-GKG.OHCHR.gkgv2.csv.zip`

`http://data.gdeltproject.org/gkgv2_specialcollections/HR-GKG.USSTATE.gkgv2.csv.zip`

Reference data

http://data.gdeltproject.org/documentation/GCAM-MASTER-CODEBOOK.TXT

http://data.gdeltproject.org/supportingdatasets/GNS-GAUL-ADM2-CROSSWALK.TXT.zip

http://data.gdeltproject.org/supportingdatasets/DOMAINSBYCOUNTRY-ENGLISH.TXT

http://data.gdeltproject.org/supportingdatasets/DOMAINSBYCOUNTRY-ALLLANGUAGES.TXT

http://www.unicode.org/Public/UNIDATA/UnicodeData.txt

http://www.geonames.org/about.html

Exploring the GKG v2.1

When we review existing articles that explore the GDELT data feeds, we find many studies that focus on the people, themes, and tone of the articles, and some that focus on the earlier event files. But there is not much published that explores the **Global Content Analysis Measures** (**GCAM**) content that is now included in the GKG files. When we try to use the data quality workbook we've built to examine the GDELT data feed, we discover that the Global Knowledge Graph is hard to work with, as the files are encoded using multiple nested delimiters. Working with this nested format data quickly is the key challenge in working with the GKG, and indeed the GCAM, and is the focus of the rest of this chapter.

There are some obvious questions we need to answer as part of exploring the GCAM data in the GKG files:

- What are the differences between the English language GKG files and the translated *Translingual* international files? Are there differences in how the data is populated between these feeds, given that some of the entity recognition algorithms might not work well on translated files?
- If the translated data is well populated for the GCAM sentiment metrics dataset, included in the GKG files, can it (or indeed the English versions) be trusted? How can we access and normalize this data, and does it hold valuable signals rather than noise?

If we can answer just these two questions alone, we will have established much about the usefulness of GDELT as a source of signals from which to perform data science. However, *how* we answer those questions is important, and we need to try and template our code as we obtain those answers, to create reusable configuration driven EDA components. If we can create re-purposable explorations in line with our principles, we will drive out far more value than hardcoding our analysis.

The Translingual files

Let's reuse our earlier work to reveal some of the quality issues, then extend our explorations to these more detailed and complex questions. By running some of the population count (POPCHECK) metrics to a temporary file, for both the normal GKG data and the translated files, we can import and union the results together. This is a benefit of having a standardized metrics format that we reuse; we can easily perform comparisons across datasets!

Rather than go through the code in detail, we'll deliver some headline answers. When we examine the population counts between the English and the translated GKG files we do expose some differences in the content available:

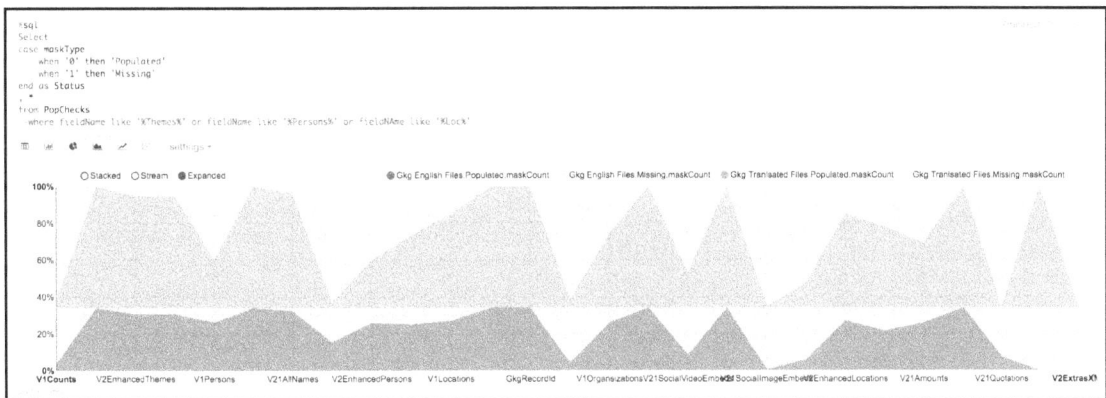

We see here that the translated GKG translingual files have no Quotations data at all and that they are very under populated when identifying Persons versus the population counts we are seeing in the general English language news feed. So there are definitely some differences to be mindful of.

As a consequence, we should examine carefully any content in the translingual data feeds that we wish to rely on in production. Later we'll see how the translated information in the GCAM sentiment content measures up against the native English language sentiments.

A configurable GCAM time series EDA

The GCAM's content is primarily made up of *Word Counts*, created by filtering news articles using dictionary filters and doing word counts on the synonyms that characterize the theme of interest. The resulting count can be normalized through dividing the count by the total words in the document. It also includes *Scored Values* delivering sentiment scores that appear to be based on directly studying the original language text.

We can quickly summarize the range of sentiment variables to study and explore in the GCAM in a couple of lines of code, the output of which is annotated with the name of the language:

```
wget http://data.gdeltproject.org/documentation/GCAM-MASTER-CODEBOOK.TXT
cat GCAM-MASTER-CODEBOOK.TXT | \
gawk 'BEGIN{OFS="\t"} $4 != "Type" {print $4,$5}' | column -t -s $'\t' \
| sort | uniq -c | gawk ' BEGIN{print "Lang Type Count" }{print $3, $2,\
$1}' | column -t -s $' '
```

```
Lang  Type         Count  Annotation
ara   SCOREDVALUE  1      Arabic
cat   SCOREDVALUE  16     Catalan
deu   SCOREDVALUE  1      German
eng   SCOREDVALUE  30     English
fra   SCOREDVALUE  1      French
glg   SCOREDVALUE  16     Galician
hin   SCOREDVALUE  1      Hindi
ind   SCOREDVALUE  1      Indonesian
kor   SCOREDVALUE  1      Korean
por   SCOREDVALUE  1      Portuguese
rus   SCOREDVALUE  1      Russian
spa   SCOREDVALUE  29     Spanish
urd   SCOREDVALUE  1      Urdu
zho   SCOREDVALUE  1      Chinese
ara   WORDCOUNT    1      Arabic
cat   WORDCOUNT    16     Catalan
deu   WORDCOUNT    44     German
eng   WORDCOUNT    2441   English
fra   WORDCOUNT    78     French
glg   WORDCOUNT    16     Galician
hin   WORDCOUNT    1      Hindi
hun   WORDCOUNT    36     Hungarian
```

```
ind    WORDCOUNT    1          Indonesian
kor    WORDCOUNT    1          Korean
por    WORDCOUNT    46         Portuguese
rus    WORDCOUNT    65         Russian
spa    WORDCOUNT    62         Spanish
swe    WORDCOUNT    64         Swedish
urd    WORDCOUNT    1          Urdu
zho    WORDCOUNT    1          Chinese
```

The GCAM word count based time series seems to be most fully developed, especially in the English language where there are 2441 sentiment measures! Working with such a large number of measures seems hard, even to do simple analysis. We'll need some tools to simplify things, and we'll need to focus our scope.

To help, we've created a simple SparkSQL-based explorer to extract and visualize time series data from the GCAM block of data, which specifically targets the word count based sentiments. It's created by cloning and adjusting our original data quality explorer in Zeppelin.

It works by adjusting it to read in the GKG file glob using a defined schema, and previewing just the raw data we want to focus on:

```
val GkgCoreSchema = StructType(Array(
    StructField("GkgRecordId"          , StringType, true), //$1
    StructField("V21Date"              , StringType, true), //$2
    StructField("V2SrcCollectionId"    , StringType, true), //$3
    StructField("V2SrcCmnName"         , StringType, true), //$4
    StructField("V2DocId"              , StringType, true), //$5
    StructField("V1Counts"             , StringType, true), //$6
    StructField("V21Counts"            , StringType, true), //$7
    StructField("V1Themes"             , StringType, true), //$8
    StructField("V2Themes"             , StringType, true), //$9
    StructField("V1Locations"          , StringType, true), //$10
    StructField("V2Locations"          , StringType, true), //$11
    StructField("V1Persons"            , StringType, true), //$12
    StructField("V2Persons"            , StringType, true), //$13
    StructField("V1Orgs"               , StringType, true), //$14
    StructField("V2Orgs"               , StringType, true), //$15
    StructField("V15Tone"              , StringType, true), //$16
    StructField("V21Dates"             , StringType, true), //$17
    StructField("V2GCAM"               , StringType, true), //$18
    StructField("V21ShareImg"          , StringType, true), //$19
    StructField("V21RelImg"            , StringType, true), //$20
    StructField("V21SocImage"          , StringType, true), //$21
    StructField("V21SocVideo"          , StringType, true), //$22
    StructField("V21Quotations"        , StringType, true), //$23
    StructField("V21AllNames"          , StringType, true), //$24
```

```
        StructField("V21Amounts"          , StringType, true), //$25
        StructField("V21TransInfo"         , StringType, true), //$26
        StructField("V2ExtrasXML"          , StringType, true)  //$27
        ))

val InputFilePath = YourFilePath

val GkgRawData = sqlContext.read
                          .option("header", "false")
                          .schema(GkgCoreSchema)
                          .option("delimiter", "\t")
                          .csv(InputFilePath)

GkgRawData.registerTempTable("GkgRawData")

// now we register slices of the file we want to explore quickly

val PreRawData = GkgRawData.select("GkgRecordID","V21Date","V2GCAM",
"V2DocId")
// we select the GCAM, plus the story URLs in V2DocID, which later we can
//filter on.

PreRawData.registerTempTable("PreRawData")
```

The results of the early column selections isolate our content on the areas to explore; time (V21Date), sentiment(V2GCAM), and Source URL (V2DocID):

```
+----+-------------+-------------------+-------------------+
| ID|      V21Date|            V2GCAM|           V2DocId|
+----+-------------+-------------------+-------------------+
|...0|20161101000000|wc:77,c12.1:2,c12...|http://www.tampab...|
|...1|20161101000000|wc:57,c12.1:6,c12...|http://regator.co...|
|...2|20161101000000|wc:740,c1.3:2,c12...|http://www.9news....|
|...3|20161101000000|wc:1011,c1.3:1,c1...|http://www.gaming...|
|...4|20161101000000|wc:260,c1.2:1,c1....|http://cnafinance...|
+----+-------------+-------------------+-------------------+
```

In a new Zeppelin paragraph, we create an SQLContext and carefully unravel the nested structure of the GCAM records. Notice the first of the inner comma delimited rows in the V2GCAM field hold the wc dimension and a measure representing the word count of the story for this GkgRecordID, then the other sentiment measures are listed. We need to unfurl this data into actual rows, as well as divide all word count based sentiments by the total word count for the article in wc to normalize the scores.

In the following snippets, we have designed a `SparkSQL` statement to do this in a typical *onion* fashion, using subselects. This is a coding style you may wish to learn to read if you don't know it already. It works like this – create the innermost selection/query and then run it to test it, then wrap it in brackets and continue by selecting the data into the next query process, and so on. Then the catalyst optimizer does its magic and optimizes the whole pipeline. It results in an ETL process that is both declarative and readable, and which also offers an ability to troubleshoot and isolate issues in any part of the pipeline, if that's needed. If we want to understand how to handle the nested array process, we can easily rebuild the following SQL, running the innermost fragment first, then reviewing its outputs, then expanding on it to include the next query that wraps it, and so on. Step by step we can then review the staged outputs to review how the whole statement works together to deliver the final result.

The key trick in the following query is how to apply the word count denominator to each of the other sentiment word counts, to normalize the values. This method of normalization is actually suggested in the GKG documentation, although no implementation hints are provided.

Also of note, is how the V21Date field is converted from an integer to a date, which is needed to plot the time series effectively. The conversion requires that we pre-import the following library in addition to the others imported in the notebook:

```
import org.apache.spark.sql.functions.{Unix_timestamp, to_date}
```

Using the `Unix_timestamp` functions, we convert the V21Date into a `Unix_timestamp`, which is an integer, and then convert that integer again into a date field, all using native Spark libraries to configure the formatting and temporal resolution.

The following SQL query achieves our desired investigation:

```
%sql
  -- for urls containing "trump" build 15min "election fraud" sentiment time
series chart.
 select
   V21Date
 , regexp_replace(z.Series, "\\.", "_") as Series
 , sum(coalesce(z.Measure, 0) / coalesce (z.WordCount, 1)) as
Sum_Normalised_Measure
 from
 (
     select
       GkgRecordID
     , V21Date
     , norm_array[0] as wc_norm_series
     , norm_array[1] as WordCount
```

```
        , ts_array[0] as Series
        , ts_array[1] as Measure
        from
        (
            select
              GkgRecordID
            ,   V21Date
            , split(wc_row, ":")     as norm_array
            , split(gcam_array, ":") as ts_array
            from
                (
                select
                  GkgRecordID
                ,   V21Date
                , gcam_row[0] as wc_row
                , explode(gcam_row) as gcam_array
                from
                    (
                     select
                            GkgRecordID
                        ,   from_Unixtime(
                                Unix_timestamp(
                                    V21Date, "yyyyMMddHHmmss")
                                , 'YYYY-MM-dd-HH-mm'
                                ) as V21Date
                        ,   split(V2GCAM, ",")  as gcam_row
                        from PreRawData
                        where length(V2GCAM) >1
                        and V2DocId like '%trump%'
                    ) w
                ) x
            ) y
        ) z
        where z.Series <> "wc" and z.Series = 'c18.134'
                        -- c18.134 is "ELECTION_FRAUD"
        group by z.V21Date, z.Series
        order by z.V21Date ASC
```

The results of the query are illustrated here using Zeppelin's time series viewer. It shows that the time series data is building up properly and that it looks very credible, having a short-lived peak on November 8 2016: the day of the US presidential election:

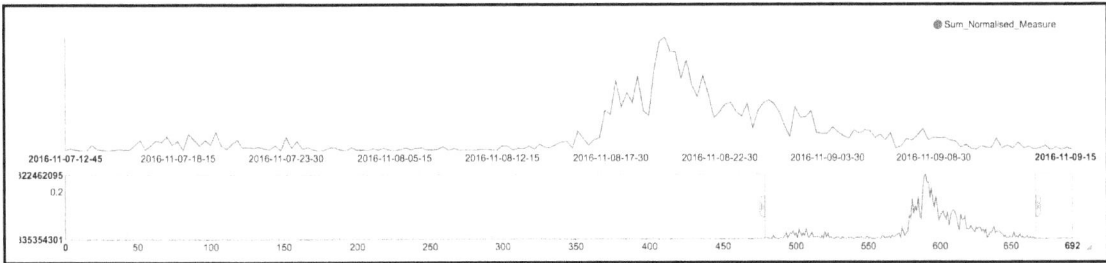

Now we have a working SQL statement to examine the GCAM sentiment scores, perhaps we should double-check some other measures, for example on a different but related topic, such as the Brexit vote in the UK.

We've selected three GCAM sentiment measures that look interesting, in addition to the *Election Fraud* measure, which hopefully will provide an interesting comparison to the results we've seen for the US election. The measures we'll look at are:

- 'c18.101' — Immigration
- 'c18.100' — Democracy
- 'c18.140' — Election

To include them, we need to extend our query to pick up multiple normalized Series, and we may also need to be mindful that the results may not all fit into Zeppelin's viewer, which defaults to only taking in the first 1000 results, so we may need to further summarize to hours or days. While not a large change, it will be interesting to see how extensible our existing work is:

```
val ExtractGcam = sqlContext.sql("""
select
    a.V21Date
, a.Series
, Sum(a.Sum_Normalised_Measure) as Sum_Normalised_Measure
from (
    select
    z.partitionkey
    , z.V21Date
    , regexp_replace(z.Series, "\\.", "_") as Series
    , sum(coalesce(z.Measure, 0) / coalesce (z.WordCount, 1))
     as Sum_Normalised_Measure
    from
    (
        select
        y.V21Date
        , cast(cast(round(rand(10) *1000,0) as INT) as string)
```

```
             as partitionkey
           , y.norm_array[0] as wc_norm_series
           , y.norm_array[1] as WordCount
           , y.ts_array[0] as Series
           , y.ts_array[1] as Measure
           from
           (
               select
                 x.V21Date
               , split(x.wc_row, ":")      as norm_array
               , split(x.gcam_array, ":") as ts_array
               from
                   (
                   select
                     w.V21Date
                   , w.gcam_row[0] as wc_row
                   , explode(w.gcam_row) as gcam_array
                   from
                       (
                       select
                           from_Unixtime(Unix_timestamp(V21Date,
        "yyyyMMddHHmmss"), 'YYYY-MM-dd-HH-mm')
            as V21Date
                           ,   split(V2GCAM, ",")  as gcam_row
                           from PreRawData
                           where length(V2GCAM) > 20
                           and V2DocId like '%brexit%'
                       ) w
                       where gcam_row[0] like '%wc%'
                         OR gcam_row[0] like '%c18.1%'
                   ) x

           ) y
       ) z
       where z.Series <> "wc"
           and
           (   z.Series = 'c18.134' -- Election Fraud
            or z.Series = 'c18.101' -- Immigration
            or z.Series = 'c18.100' -- Democracy
            or z.Series = 'c18.140' -- Election
           )
       group by z.partitionkey, z.V21Date, z.Series
) a
group by a.V21Date, a.Series
""")
```

In this second example, we further refine our base query, removing the unnecessary GKGRecordIDs that we didn't use. This query also demonstrates how to filter results against many `Series` names using a simple set of predicates. Notice we have also added in a pre-grouping step using the following:

```
group by z.partitionkey, z.V21Date, z.Series

-- Where the partition key is:
-- cast(cast(round(rand(10) *1000,0) as INT) as string) as partitionkey
```

This random number is used to create a partition prefix key that we use in our inner group by statement, before going on to group again without this prefix. The query is written in this way as it helps to subdivide and pre-summarize *hotspotting* data and smooth out any pipeline bottlenecks.

When we look at the results of this query in Zeppelin's time series viewer we have the chance to further summarize up to hourly counts, and to translate the cryptic GCAM series codes into proper names using a case statement. We can do this in a new query, helping to isolate *specific* reporting configurations away from the general dataset construction query:

```
Select
a.Time
, a.Series
, Sum(Sum_Normalised_Measure) as Sum_Normalised_Measure
from
(
        select
        from_Unixtime(Unix_timestamp(V21Date,
                    "yyyy-MM-dd-HH-mm"),'YYYY-MM-dd-HH')
         as Time
       , CASE
           when Series = 'c18_134' then 'Election Fraud'
           when Series = 'c18_101' then 'Immigration'
           when Series = 'c18_100' then 'Democracy'
           when Series = 'c18_140' then 'Election'
       END as Series
       , Sum_Normalised_Measure
       from ExtractGcam
       -- where Series = 'c18_101' or Series = 'c18_140'
) a
group by a.Time, a.Series
order by a.Time
```

This final query reduces the data to hourly values, which is less than the default 1000 row maximum that Zeppelin handles by default, additionally it generates a comparative time series chart:

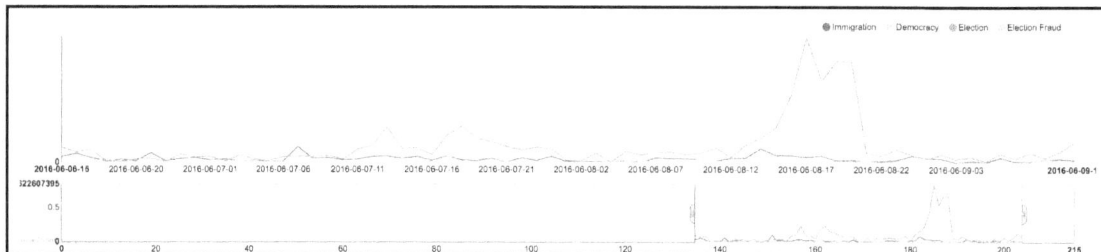

The resulting chart illustrates that there is almost no discussion at all about *Election Fraud* preceding the Brexit vote, but there are however spikes on *Election*, and that Immigration is a hotter theme than Democracy. Again, the GCAM English language sentiment data seems to hold real signal.

Now that we have shed some light on the English language records, we can extend our work to explore them against the translated data in GCAM.

As a final way to complete the analysis in this notebook, we can comment out the filters on the specific `Series` and write a timeseries database of all the GCAM series data for Brexit to a parquet file in our HDFS filesystem. This allows us to permanently store our GCAM data to disk and even to append new data to it over time. The following is the code needed to either overwrite, or to append to a parquet file:

```
// save the data as a parquet file
val TimeSeriesParqueFile =
"/user/feeds/gdelt/datastore/BrexitTimeSeries2016.parquet"

// *** uncomment to append to an existing parquet file ***
// ExtractGcam.save(TimeSeriesParqueFile
              //, "parquet"
              //, SaveMode.Append)
// ************************************************************
// *** uncomment to initially load a new parquet file ***
   ExtractGcam.save(TimeSeriesParqueFile
         , "parquet"
   , SaveMode.Overwrite)
// ************************************************************
```

With the parquet files written to disk, we have now built a lightweight GCAM time series data store that allows us to quickly retrieve a GCAM sentiment, for exploration across language groups.

Plot.ly charting on Apache Zeppelin

For our next exploration we will also extend our use of Apache Zeppelin notebooks to include producing `%pyspark` charts using an external charting library called plotly, open sourced by `https://plot.ly/`, which can be used to create print quality visualizations. To use plotly in our notebook, we can upgrade our Apache Zeppelin installation, using the code found at `https://github.com/beljun/zeppelin-plotly`, which provides the integration needed. On its GitHub page, there are detailed installation instructions, and within their code base, they provide a very helpful example notebook. Here are some tips for installing plotly for use on an HDP cluster with Zeppelin:

- Log into the Namenode as the Zeppelin user and change the directory to the Zeppelin home directory at `/home/zeppelin` where we will download the external code:

  ```
  git clone https://github.com/beljun/zeppelin-plotly
  ```

- Change the directory to where the Zeppelin `*.war` file is kept. This location is revealed in the Zeppelin **Configuration** tab. For example:

  ```
  cd /usr/hdp/current/zeppelin-server/lib
  ```

Now, as per the instructions, we need to edit the index.html document found in the Zeppelin `war` file:

```
ls *war    # zeppelin-web-0.6.0.2.4.0.0-169.war
cp zeppelin-web-0.6.0.2.4.0.0-169.war \
    bkp_zeppelin-web-0.6.0.2.4.0.0-169.war
jar xvf zeppelin-web-0.6.0.2.4.0.0-169.war \
    index.html
vi index.html
```

- Once the `index.html` page is extracted we can use an editor such as vim to insert the `plotly-latest.min.js` script tag (as per the instructions), just before the body tag, and save and execute the document.

- Put the edited `index.html` document back into the war file using:

```
jar uvf zeppelin-web-0.6.0.2.4.0.0-169.war index.html
```

- Finally, log into Ambari, and use it to restart the Zeppelin service.
- Follow the rest of the instructions to generate a test chart in Zeppelin.
- We may need to install or update old libraries if there are issues. Log into the Namenode and use pip to install the packages:

```
sudo pip install plotly
sudo pip install plotly --upgrade
sudo pip install colors
sudo pip install cufflinks
sudo pip install pandas
sudo pip install Ipython
sudo pip install -U pyOpenSSL
# note also install pyOpenSSL to get things running.
```

With the installation complete, we should now be able to create Zeppelin notebooks that generate inline plot.ly charts from the `%pyspark` paragraphs, and these will be created offline using the local libraries rather than the online service.

Exploring translation sourced GCAM sentiment with plot.ly

For this comparison, let's focus on an interesting measure found in the GCAM documentation: *c6.6; Financial Uncertainty*. This measure counts word-matches made between a news story and a financially oriented *uncertainty dictionary*. If we trace its provenance online, we can discover the academic paper and actual dictionary driving the metric. However, will that dictionary based measure work with translated news text? To investigate this, we can review how this financial *Uncertainty* metric differs across six major European language groups: English, French, German, Spanish, Italian, and Polish with respect to the subject of Brexit.

We create a new notebook, include a *pyspark* paragraph to load plot.ly libraries and set them to run in offline mode:

```
%pyspark
# Instructions here: https://github.com/beljun/zeppelin-plotly
import sys
sys.path.insert(0, "/home/zeppelin/zeppelin-plotly")

import offline
```

```
sys.modules["plotly"].offline = offline
sys.modules["plotly.offline"] = offline

import cufflinks as cf
cf.go_offline()

import plotly.plotly as py
import plotly.graph_objs as go

import pandas as pd
import numpy as np
```

Then we create a paragraph to read in our cached data from parquet:

```
%pyspark

GcamParquet =
sqlContext.read.parquet("/user/feeds/gdelt/datastore/BrexitTimeSeries2016.p
arquet")

# register the content as a python data frame
sqlContext.registerDataFrameAsTable(GcamParquet, "BrexitTimeSeries")
```

We then can create an SQL query that reads and prepares it for plot, and registers it for use:

```
%pyspark
FixedExtractGcam = sqlContext.sql("""
select
  V21Date
, Series
, CASE
    when LangLen = 0 then "eng"
    when LangLen > 0 then SourceLanguage
  END as SourceLanguage
, FIPS104Country
, Sum_Normalised_Measure
from
(   select *,length(SourceLanguage) as LangLen
    from BrexitTimeSeries
    where V21Date like "2016%"
) a
""")

sqlContext.registerDataFrameAsTable(FixedExtractGcam, "Brexit")
# pyspark accessible registration of the data
```

Now that we've defined an adaptor, we can create the query that summarizes the data in our parquet file to something that will fit more easily into memory:

```
%pyspark

timeplot = sqlContext.sql("""
Select
from_Unixtime(Unix_timestamp(Time, "yyyy-MM-dd"), 'YYYY-MM-dd
HH:mm:ss.ssss') as Time
, a.Series
, SourceLanguage as Lang
--, Country
, sum(Sum_Normalised_Measure) as Sum_Normalised_Measure
from
(       select
          from_Unixtime(Unix_timestamp(V21Date,
                        "yyyy-MM-dd-HH"), 'YYYY-MM-dd') as Time
        , SourceLanguage
        , CASE
          When Series = 'c6_6' then "Uncertainty"
          END as Series
        , Sum_Normalised_Measure
        from Brexit
        where Series in ('c6_6')
        and SourceLanguage in ( 'deu', 'fra', 'ita', 'eng', 'spa', 'pol')
        and V21Date like '2016%'
) a
group by a.Time, a.Series, a.SourceLanguage order by a.Time, a.Series,
a.SourceLanguage
""")

sqlContext.registerDataFrameAsTable(timeplot, "timeplot")
# pyspark accessible registration of the data
```

This main payload query generates a set of data that we can load to a `pandas` array in `pyspark`, and which has timestamps with a plot.ly ready format:

```
+------------------------+----------+----+--------------------+
|Time                    |Series    |Lang|Sum_Normalised_Measure|
+------------------------+----------+----+--------------------+
|2016-01-04 00:00:00.0000|Uncertainty|deu |0.0375              |
|2016-01-04 00:00:00.0000|Uncertainty|eng |0.5603189694252122  |
|2016-01-04 00:00:00.0000|Uncertainty|fra |0.08089269454114742 |
+------------------------+----------+----+--------------------+
```

To feed this data to plot.ly we must convert the Spark Dataframe that we generated into a `pandas` one:

```
%pyspark
explorer = pd.DataFrame(timeplot.collect(), columns=['Time', 'Series',
'SourceLanguage','Sum_Normalised_Measure'])
```

When we perform this step, we must remember to `collect()` the dataframe, as well as reset the column names for `pandas` to pick up. With a `pandas` array now in our Python environment, we can pivot the data easily into a form that will facilitate time series plotting:

```
pexp = pd.pivot_table(explorer, values='Sum_Normalised_Measure',
index=['Time'], columns=['SourceLanguage','Series'], aggfunc=np.sum,
fill_value=0)
```

Lastly, we include a call to generate the chart:

```
pexp.iplot(title="BREXIT: Daily GCAM Uncertainty Sentiment Measures by
Language", kind ="bar", barmode="stack")
```

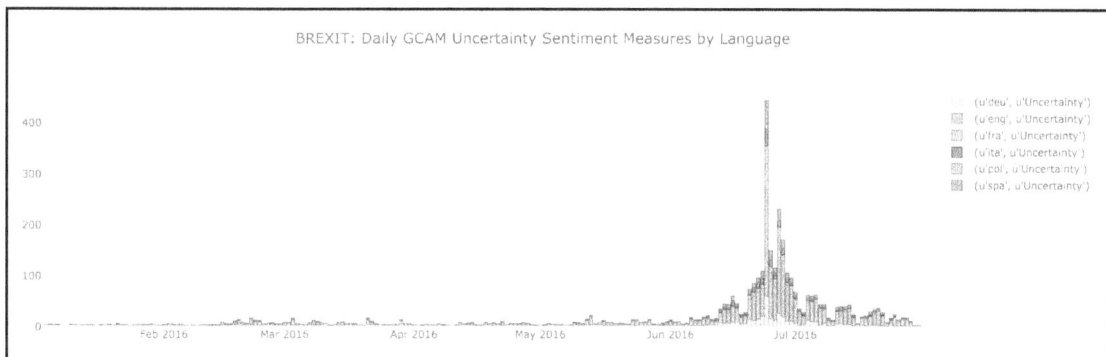

Now that we have produced a working plot.ly chart of our data, we should create a custom visualization, which was not possible with the standard Zeppelin notebook, to illustrate the value that the plotly library brings to our exploration. A simple example is to generate some *small multiples* like this:

```
pexp.iplot(title="BREXIT: Daily GCAM Uncertainty by Language, 2016-01
through 2016-07",subplots=True, shared_xaxes=True, fill=True,  kind ="bar")
```

Which generates the following chart:

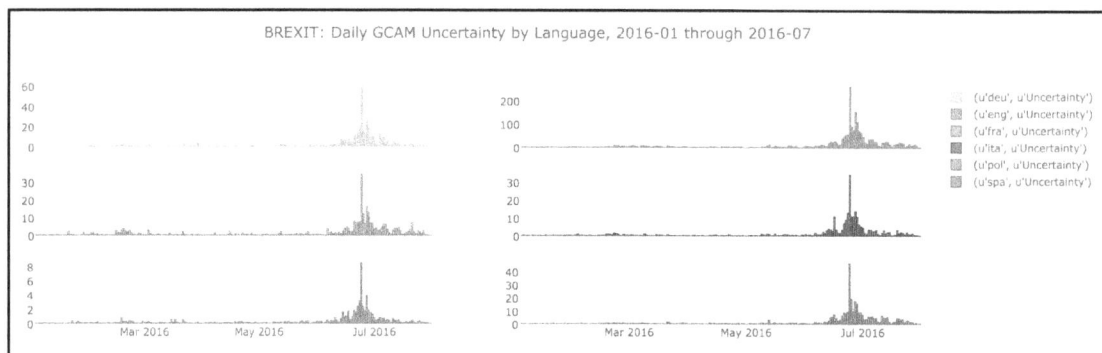

This small multiple chart helps us to see that, in the Italian press, there seems to have been a local spike in financial Uncertainty on June 15 2016; just a week or so before the election. This is something we might wish to investigate as it is also present, to a lesser degree, in Spanish language news too.

Plotly also offers many other interesting visualizations. If you have been carefully reading the code snippets, you may have noticed that the parquet file includes the FIPS10-4 country code from the GKG files. We should be able to leverage these location codes to plot a choropleth map of the Uncertainty metric, using Plotly, and at the same time leverage our previous data processing.

To create this geographical map, we reuse our parquet file reader query that we registered earlier. Unfortunately, the GKG files use FIPS 10-4 two-character country encoding, and Plotly uses ISO-3166 three-character country codes to automatically geotag the user records it processes for plotting. We can address this by using a case statement in our SQL to remap our codes, before summarizing them over the whole period of enquiry:

```pyspark
%pyspark
mapplot = sqlContext.sql("""
Select
  CountryCode
, sum(Sum_Normalised_Measure) as Sum_Normalised_Measure
from (  select
        from_Unixtime(Unix_timestamp(V21Date, "yyyy-MM-dd-HH"),
                                    'YYYY-MM') as Time
      , CASE
          when FIPS104Country = "AF" then "AFB"
          when FIPS104Country = "AL" then "ALB"
            -- I have excluded the full list of
            -- countries in this code snippet
          when FIPS104Country = "WI" then "ESH"
```

```
                when FIPS104Country = "YM" then "YEM"
                when FIPS104Country = "ZA" then "ZMB"
                when FIPS104Country = "ZI" then "ZWE"
              END as CountryCode
            , Sum_Normalised_Measure
            from Brexit
            where Series in ('c6_6')
            and V21Date like '2016%'
    ) a
    group by a.CountryCode order by a.CountryCode
    """)

    sqlContext.registerDataFrameAsTable(mapplot, "mapplot") # python

    mapplot2 = pd.DataFrame(mapplot.collect(), columns=['Country',
    'Sum_Normalised_Measure'])
```

With our data now prepared in a `pandas` dataframe, we can invoke the visualization using the following line of Python:

```
    mapplot2.iplot( kind = 'choropleth', locations = 'Country', z =
    'Sum_Normalised_Measure', text = 'Country', locationmode = 'ISO-3',
    showframe = True, showcoastlines = False, projection = dict(type =
    'equirectangular'), colorscale = [[0,"rgb(5, 10, 172)"],[0.9,"rgb(40, 60,
    190)"],[0.9,"rgb(70, 100, 245)"],[1,"rgb(90, 120, 245)"],[1,"rgb(106, 137,
    247)"],[1,"rgb(220, 220, 220)"]])
```

The final result is an interactive, zoomable map of the world. We will leave its political interpretation to the reader, but conclude technically that perhaps this map shows an effect to do with news volume that we could later normalize on; for instance by dividing our values by total stories per country.

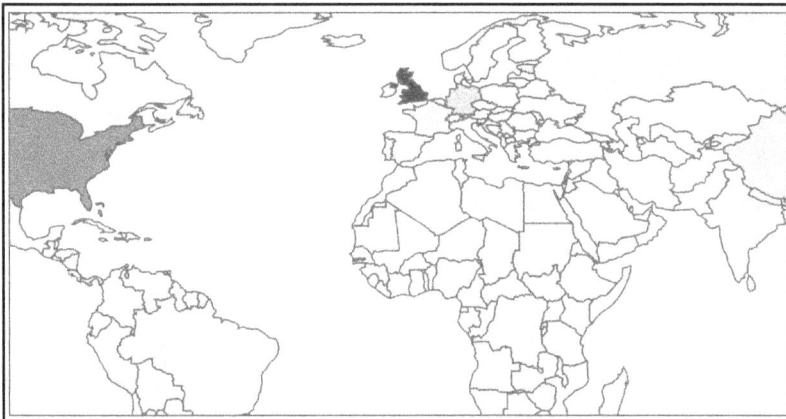

Concluding remarks

It is worth pointing out that there are a number of parameters that drove our EDA across all of our investigations, and we could consider how these might be parameterized to build proper exploration products for monitoring GDELT. Parameters for consideration are as follows:

- We can select a non-GCAM field to filter on. In the preceding examples, it is configured to the V2DocID, which is the URL of the story. Finding words in the URL such as BREXIT or TRUMP will help to scope our investigations to stories that are relevant to particular subject areas. We could also reuse this technique to filter on BBC or NYTIMES, for example. Alternatively, if we swapped this column for another, such as Theme or Person, then these columns would offer new ways to focus our study on particular subjects or people of interest.
- We have converted and generalized the granularity of the timestamp, V21Date, to deliver hourly time series increments, but we could reconfigure this to create our time series on a monthly, weekly, or daily basis – or indeed on any other increment.
- We first selected and scoped our investigation to one timeseries of interest, *c18_134*, which is *Election Fraud*, but we can easily reconfigure this to look at *Immigration* or *Hate Speech* or any of the other 2400+ sentiment scores that are word count based.
- We have introduced a file glob at the start of our notebook, which scopes the amount of time that we include in the summary output. To keep costs low, we've kept it small to start with, but we could refocus this time range on key events, or even open it up to all of the available files, given enough processing budget (time and money).

We have now illustrated that our code can be easily adjusted to build a notebook-based GCAM time-series explorer, from which we would be able to construct huge numbers of focused investigations on demand; each exploring the content of the GCAM data in a configurable way.

If you have been carefully following the SQL code throughout the notebook, and were wondering why it had not been written using the Python API, or perhaps using idiomatic Scala, we will complete this section with one final observation: it is precisely because it is constructed from SQL that it can be moved between the Python, R, or Scala contexts with almost no cost in code refactoring. Should a new charting facility in R become available, it can be ported easily over to R, and then effort can be focused solely on the visualization. Indeed, with the arrival of Spark 2.0+, it is perhaps the SQL code that requires the least review when porting. The importance of code portability cannot be stressed enough. The most valuable benefit of using SQL in the EDA context, however, is that it makes generating parameter driven notebooks in Zeppelin so easy, as we have seen in the earlier profiler section. Drop-down boxes, and other UI widgets, can all be created in conjunction with string processing to customize the code before execution, irrespective of backend language. This is an extremely fast way to build interactivity and configuration into our analysis, without dipping into complex meta programming methods. It also helps us to avoid solving those meta programming complexities across the different language back ends available in Apache Zeppelin/Spark.

With respect to building broad data explorations, if we wished to use our cached results in parquet more broadly, there is also an opportunity to remove the need for "eyeballs looking at charts" altogether. See `Chapter 12`, *TrendCalculus* to get an idea for how we could programmatically study trends across all of the data in GKG programmatically.

A final trick of note when using Zeppelin, to produce graphics for EDA reports, is one that is purely practical. If we wish to extract our graphics to files, to include them in our final report for example, rather than taking screenshots of our notebook, we can directly extract the scalable vector graphics files (SVG) from Zeppelin and download them to files using the *bookmarklet* found here `http://nytimes.github.io/svg-crowbar/`.

A configurable GCAM Spatio-Temporal EDA

Another question about the GCAM remains unanswered; how do we start to understand how it subdivides spatially? Could a geospatial pivot of the GCAM expose how the global news media presents its aggregate geopolitical views, as detailed geographies that get beneath country level analysis?

If we can construct such a dataset as part of our EDA, it would have many and varied applications. At a city level for example, it would be a general geopolitical signals library that could enrich a wide range of other data science projects. Consider holiday travel booking patterns, shown against the backdrop of geopolitical themes emerging in the news. Would we discover that global news signals at city level predicts rising or falling tourism rates in places of media interest? The possibilities for this type of data are nearly endless when we consider the resulting information as a source of geopolitical situational awareness.

With such an opportunity in front of us, we need to consider carefully our investment in this more complex EDA. It will need, as before, a common data structure from which to start our explorations.

As a target, we will aim to construct the following dataframe from which to explore the geopolitical trends, which we will call "*GeoGcam*":

```
val GeoGcamSchema = StructType(Array(
        StructField("Date"          , StringType, true),  //$1
        StructField("CountryCode"   , StringType, true),  //$2
        StructField("Lat"           , DoubleType, true),  //$3
        StructField("Long"          , DoubleType, true),  //$4
        StructField("Geohash"       , StringType, true),  //$5
        StructField("NewsLang"      , StringType, true),  //$6
        StructField("Series"        , StringType, true),   //$7
        StructField("Value"         , DoubleType, true),  //$8
        StructField("ArticleCount"  , DoubleType, true),  //$9
        StructField("AvgTone"       , DoubleType, true)  //$10
    ))
```

Introducing GeoGCAM

GeoGcam is a global spatio-temporal signals dataset that is derived from the raw GDELT Global Knowledge Graph (2.1). It enables the exploration of evolving geopolitical trends in global news media sentiment quickly and easily. The data itself is created using a transformation pipeline that casts the raw GKG files into a standard, reusable, global time/space/sentiment signals format that allows for direct downstream spatio-temporal analysis, cartographic visualization, and further wide scale geopolitical trend analysis.

It can be used as a source of external covariates for predictive models, especially ones that require improved geopolitical situational awareness.

It is constructed by recasting the GKG's GCAM sentiment data into a spatially oriented schema. This is performed by *placing* each news story's sentiments against each of the fine-grained city/town level locations identified in its GKG record.

The data is then aggregated by city, across all of the indexed stories in a 15 minute GKG time window. The result is a file that delivers an aggregate news media *sentiment consensus* across all stories in that space and time window, for that place. Although there will be noise, our hypothesis is that big broad geopolitical themes will emerge.

A sample of the dataset (which matches the target schema) is:

```
+--------------+-------+------+--------+------------+
|Date          |Country|Lat   |Long    |Geohash     |
|              |Code   |      |        |            |
+--------------+-------+------+--------+------------+
|20151109103000|CI     |-33.45|-70.6667|66j9xyw5ds13|
|20151109103000|CI     |-33.45|-70.6667|66j9xyw5ds13|
|20151109103000|CI     |-33.45|-70.6667|66j9xyw5ds13|
|20151109103000|CI     |-33.45|-70.6667|66j9xyw5ds13|
|20151109103000|CI     |-33.45|-70.6667|66j9xyw5ds13|
|20151109103000|CI     |-33.45|-70.6667|66j9xyw5ds13|
|20151109103000|CI     |-33.45|-70.6667|66j9xyw5ds13|
|20151109103000|CI     |-33.45|-70.6667|66j9xyw5ds13|
|20151109103000|CI     |-33.45|-70.6667|66j9xyw5ds13|
|20151109103000|CI     |-33.45|-70.6667|66j9xyw5ds13|
+--------------+-------+------+--------+------------+

+----+------+-----+-------+----------------+
|News|Series|SUM  |Article|AvgTone         |
|Lang|      |Value|Count  |                |
+----+------+-----+-------+----------------+
|E   |c12_1 |16.0 |1.0    |0.24390243902439|
|E   |c12_10|26.0 |1.0    |0.24390243902439|
|E   |c12_12|12.0 |1.0    |0.24390243902439|
|E   |c12_13|3.0  |1.0    |0.24390243902439|
|E   |c12_14|11.0 |1.0    |0.24390243902439|
|E   |c12_3 |4.0  |1.0    |0.24390243902439|
|E   |c12_4 |3.0  |1.0    |0.24390243902439|
|E   |c12_5 |10.0 |1.0    |0.24390243902439|
|E   |c12_7 |15.0 |1.0    |0.24390243902439|
|E   |c12_8 |6.0  |1.0    |0.24390243902439|
+----+------+-----+-------+----------------+
```

Technical notes on the dataset:

- Only news articles tagged with specific city locations are included, meaning only those tagged by GKG as having a location type code of 3=USCITY or 4=WORLDCITY.
- We have calculated and included the full GeoHash for each city (see Chapter 5, *Spark for Geographic Analysis* for more information), simplifying how the data can be indexed and summarized for larger geographic regions.
- The granularity of the file is based on the aggregation key used to produce the dataset, which is: V21Date, LocCountryCode, Lat, Long, GeoHash, Language, Series.
- We have carried forward the primary location country code field, identified in the GKG feed, into the city level aggregation function; this allows us to quickly examine the data by countries without having to perform complex lookups.
- The provided data is un-normalized. We should later normalize it via the total article word count for the location, which is available in the series called wc. But this should only be done for word count based sentiment measures. We also carry a count of the articles so we can test different types of normalization.
- The feed is built from the English language GKG records, but we plan to include the international *Translingual* feeds in the same data format. In readiness, we've included a field denoting the original news story language.
- We have an ingestion routine for this dataset to GeoMesa, a scalable data store that allows us to geographically explore the resulting data; this is available in our code repository. For an in-depth exploration of GeoMesa, see Chapter 5, *Spark for Geographic Analysis.*

The following is a pipeline to build up the GeoGCAM files:

```
// be sure to include a dependency to the geohash library
// here in the 1st para of zeppelin:
// z.load("com.github.davidmoten:geo:0.7.1")
// to use the geohash functionality in your code

val GcamRaw = GkgFileRaw.select("GkgRecordID","V21Date","V15Tone","V2GCAM",
"V1Locations")
    GcamRaw.cache()
    GcamRaw.registerTempTable("GcamRaw")

def vgeoWrap (lat: Double, long: Double, len: Int): String = {
    var ret = GeoHash.encodeHash(lat, long, len)
    // select the length of the geohash, less than 12..
    // it pulls in the library dependency from
    //    com.github.davidmoten:geo:0.7.1
```

```
      return(ret)
} // we wrap up the geohash function locally

// we register the vGeoHash function for use in SQL
sqlContext.udf.register("vGeoHash", vgeoWrap(_:Double,_:Double,_:Int))

val ExtractGcam = sqlContext.sql("""
    select
        GkgRecordID
    ,   V21Date
    ,   split(V2GCAM, ",")                    as Array
    ,   explode(split(V1Locations, ";"))     as LocArray
    ,   regexp_replace(V15Tone, ",.*$", "") as V15Tone
        -- note we truncate off the other scores
    from GcamRaw
    where length(V2GCAM) >1 and length(V1Locations) >1
""")


val explodeGcamDF = ExtractGcam.explode("Array", "GcamRow"){c: Seq[String]
=> c }



val GcamRows =
explodeGcamDF.select("GkgRecordID","V21Date","V15Tone","GcamRow",
"LocArray")
// note ALL the locations get repeated against
// every GCAM sentiment row

    GcamRows.registerTempTable("GcamRows")

val TimeSeries = sqlContext.sql("""
select   -- create geohash keys
  d.V21Date
, d.LocCountryCode
, d.Lat
, d.Long
 , vGeoHash(d.Lat, d.Long, 12)        as GeoHash
, 'E' as NewsLang
, regexp_replace(Series, "\\.", "_") as Series
, coalesce(sum(d.Value),0) as SumValue
         -- SQL's "coalesce" means "replaces nulls with"
, count(distinct  GkgRecordID )       as ArticleCount
, Avg(V15Tone)                        as AvgTone
from
(   select  -- build Cartesian join of the series
              -- and granular locations
      GkgRecordID
    , V21Date
```

```
    , ts_array[0]  as Series
    , ts_array[1]  as Value
    , loc_array[0] as LocType
    , loc_array[2] as LocCountryCode
    , loc_array[4] as Lat
    , loc_array[5] as Long
    , V15Tone
    from
        (select -- isolate the data to focus on
          GkgRecordID
        , V21Date
        , split(GcamRow,   ":") as ts_array
        , split(LocArray,  "#") as loc_array
        , V15Tone
        from GcamRows
        where length(GcamRow)>1
        ) x
    where
    (loc_array[0] = 3 or  loc_array[0] = 4) -- city level filter
) d
group by
    d.V21Date
, d.LocCountryCode
, d.Lat
, d.Long
, vGeoHash(d.Lat, d.Long, 12)
, d.Series
order by
    d.V21Date
, vGeoHash(d.Lat, d.Long, 12)
, d.Series
""")
```

This query essentially does the following: It builds a Cartesian join between all the GCAM sentiments and the granular locations identified in the records (cities / places), and then proceeds to *place* the Tone and sentiment values on those locations for all news stories in a 15 minute window. The output is a spatio-temporal dataset that allows us to geographically map the GCAM sentiments. For instance, it is possible to quickly export and plot this data in QGIS, which is an open source mapping tool.

Does our spatial pivot work?

When the preceding GeoGCAM dataset is filtered to look at the GCAM *immigration* sentiment as a theme over the first two weeks of GKG data in February 2015, we can generate the following map:

This illustrates the tone of global English language news media, using light (positive average tone) and dark (negative average tone), which is found in the GKG files over that period, and explores how that tone maps over each geographic tile on the map (the pixel size calculated mirrors fairly accurately the size of the truncated GeoHash that is grouped on) with respect to the sentiment for immigration as a theme.

We can see very clearly on this map that immigration is not only a hot topic associated with places in the UK, but also has strong spatial concentrations in other places too. For instance, we can see the strong negative tone associated with parts of the Middle East that clearly stands out in a concentrated dark block. We also see details that we perhaps would have missed before. For example, there is a concentrated negative tone on immigration around Dublin, which is not immediately explainable, and something seems to be happening in the north east of Nigeria

The map shows that there may also be an English language bias to watch out for, as there is little discussion in non-English speaking places, which seems odd, until we realize we've not yet included the Translingual GKG feed. This suggests that we should extend our processing to include the translingual data source, in order to obtain a more rounded and full set of signals including non-English news media.

The full list of the GCAM time series available is listed in the GCAM master codebook found here: `http://data.gdeltproject.org/documentation/GCAM-MASTER-CODEBOOK.TXT`.

For the moment, the English language news data examined in the GeoGCAM format provides a fascinating view of the world, and we discover that GDELT does offer real signals we can leverage. Using the GeoGCAM formatted data developed in this chapter, you should now be able to construct your own specific geopolitical explorations easily and quickly, even integrating this content with your own datasets.

Summary

In this chapter, we've reviewed many ideas for exploring data quality and data content. We have also introduced the reader to tools and techniques for working with GDELT, which are aimed at encouraging the reader to expand their own investigations. We have demonstrated rapid development in Zeppelin, and written much of our code in SparkSQL to demonstrate the excellent portability of this method. As the GKG files are so complex in terms of content, much of the rest of this book is dedicated to in-depth analyses that move beyond exploration, and we step away from SparkSQL as we dig deeper into the Spark codebase.

In the next chapter,that is, `Chapter 5`, *Spark for Geographic Analysis*, we will explore GeoMesa; an ideal tool for managing and exploring the GeoGCAM dataset created in this chapter, as well as GeoServer and the GeoTools toolsets to further expand our knowledge of spatio-temporal exploration and visualization.

5
Spark for Geographic Analysis

Geographic processing is a powerful use case for Spark and therefore the aim of this chapter is to explain how data scientists can process geographic data using Spark to produce powerful, map-based views of very large datasets. We will demonstrate how to process spatio-temporal datasets easily via Spark integrations with GeoMesa, which helps turn Spark into a sophisticated geographic processing engine. As the **Internet of Things** (**IoT**) and other location-aware datasets become ever more common, and *moving objects* data volumes climb, Spark will become a critical tool that closes the geoprocessing gap that exists between spatial functionality and processing scalability. This chapter reveals how to conduct advanced geopolitical analysis of global news with a view to leveraging the data to analyze and perform data science on oil prices.

In this chapter, we will cover the following topics:

- Using Spark to ingest and preprocess geolocated data
- Storing geodata which is appropriately indexed, using Geohash indexing inside GeoMesa
- Running complex spatio-temporal queries, filtering data across time and space
- Using Spark and GeoMesa together to perform advanced geographic processing in order to study change over time
- Using Spark to calculate density maps and to visualize changes in these maps over time
- Querying and integrating spatial data across map layers to build new insights

GDELT and oil

The premise of this chapter is that we can manipulate GDELT data to determine, to a greater or lesser extent, the price of oil based on historic events. The accuracy of our predictor will depend on many variables including the detail of our events, the number used and our hypotheses surrounding the nature of the relationship between oil and these events.

The oil industry is very complex and is driven by many factors. It has been found however, that most major oil price fluctuations are largely explained by shifts in the demand of crude oil. The price also increases during times of greater demand for stock, and historically has been high in times of geopolitical tension in the Middle East. In particular, political events have a strong influence on the oil price and it is this aspect that we will concentrate on.

Crude oil is produced by many countries around the world; there are however, three main benchmarks that are used by producers for pricing:

- Brent: Produced by various entities in the North Sea
- WTI: **West Texas Intermediate** (**WTI**) covering entities in the mid-west and Gulf Coast regions of North America
- OPEC: Produced by members of OPEC:

  Algeria, Angola, Ecuador, Gabon, Indonesia, Iran, Iraq, Kuwait, Libya, Nigeria, Qatar, Saudi Arabia, UAE, and Venezuela

It becomes clear that the first thing we need to do is to obtain the historical pricing data for the three baselines. By searching the Internet, downloadable data can be found in many places, for example:

- Brent: `https://fred.stlouisfed.org/`
- WTI: `https://fred.stlouisfed.org/`
- OPEC: `http://opec.org`

Now we know that oil prices are primarily determined by supply and demand, our first hypothesis will be that the supply and demand is affected, to a greater extent, by world events and thus we can predict what that supply and demand is likely to be.

We want to try and determine whether the oil price will rise or fall during the next day, week, or month and, as we have used GDELT throughout the book, we will take that knowledge and expand it to run some very large processing jobs. Before we start, it's worth discussing the path we are going to take, and the reasons for the decisions made. The first area of concern is how GDELT relates to oil; this will define the scope of the initial work, and provide a base upon which we can build later. It is important here that we decide how to leverage GDELT and what the consequences of that decision will be; for example, we could decide to use all of the data for all of the time, but the processing time required for that is very large indeed since just one day of GDELT events data can average 15 MB, and 1.5 GB for GKG. Therefore, we should analyze the contents of the two sets and try to establish what our initial data input will be.

GDELT events

Looking through the GDELT schema, there are a number of points that could be useful; the events schema primarily revolves around identifying the two primary actors in a story and relating an event to them. There is also the ability to look at events at different levels, so we will have good flexibility to work at higher or lower levels of complexity, depending upon how our results work out. For example:

The `EventCode` field is a CAMEO action code: 0251 (Appeal for easing of administrative sanctions) and can also be used at the levels 02 (Appeal) and 025 (Appeal to yield).

Our second hypothesis is therefore, that the level of detail of the event will provide better or worse accuracy from our algorithm.

Other interesting labels are `GoldsteinScale`, `NumMentions` and `Lat/Lon`. The `GoldsteinScale` label is a number from -10 to +10 and it attempts to capture the theoretical potential impact that type of event can have on the stability of a country; a great match based on what we have already established about the stability of oil prices. The `NumMentions` label gives us an indication of how often the event has appeared across all source documents; this could help us to assign an importance to events if we find that we need to reduce the number of assessed events in our processing. For example, we could process the data and find the top 10, 100, or 1000 events in the last hour, day, or week based upon how often they have been mentioned. Finally, the `lat/lon` label information attempts to assign a geographical point of reference for the event, making this very useful for when we want to produce maps in GeoMesa.

GDELT GKG

The GKG schema is related to summarizing the content of the events and providing enhanced information specific to that content. Areas of interest for our purposes include `Counts`, `Themes`, `GCAM`, and `Locations`; the `Counts` field maps any numeric mention, thus potentially allowing us to calculate a severity, for example KILLS=47. The `Themes` field lists all of the themes based on the GDELT category list; this could help us to machine learn particular areas, over time, which affect oil prices. The `GCAM` field is the result of content analysis of the event; a quick perusal of the GCAM list shows us that there are some possibly useful dimensions to look out for:

```
c9.366   9    366    WORDCOUNT    eng    Roget's Thesaurus 1911 Edition    CLASS
III - RELATED TO MATTER/3.2 INORGANIC MATTER/3.2.3 IMPERFECT FLUIDS/366 OIL

c18.172  18   172    WORDCOUNT    eng    GDELT    GKG    Themes    ENV_OIL
c18.314  18   314    WORDCOUNT    eng    GDELT    GKG    Themes
ECON_OILPRICE
```

And finally, we have the `Locations` field, which provides similar information to the Events, and thus also can be used for visualization of maps.

Formulating a plan of action

Having inspected the GDELT schemas, we now need to make some decisions around what data we are going to use, and make sure we justify that usage based on our hypotheses. This is a critical stage as there are many areas to consider, and at the very least we need to:

- Ensure that our hypotheses are clear so that we have a known starting point
- Ensure that we are clear about how we are going to implement the hypotheses, and determine an action plan
- Ensure that we use enough appropriate data to meet our action plan; scope the data usage to ensure we can produce a conclusion within a given time frame, for example, using all GDELT data would be great, but is probably not reasonable unless a large processing cluster is available. On the other hand using one day is clearly not enough to gauge any patterns over time
- Formulate a plan B in case our initial results are not conclusive

Our second hypothesis is about the detail of the events; for the purposes of clarity, in this chapter, we are going to choose just one of the data sources initially, with a view to adding further complexity if our model does not perform well. Therefore, we can choose the GDELT events as the fields mentioned above provide for an excellent base upon which to prove our algorithms; in particular, the `gcam` field will be very useful to determine the nature of an event and the `NumMentions` field will be quick to implement when considering the importance of an event. While the GKG data also looks useful, we want to try and use general events at this stage; so, the GCAM oil data, for example, is considered too specific as there is a good chance that articles related to these fields will often be about the reaction to oil price change, and therefore too late to consider for our model.

Our initial processing flow (action plan) will involve the following steps:

- Obtain oil price data for the last 5 years
- Obtain GDELT events for the last 5 years
- Install GeoMesa and related tools
- Load the GDELT data to GeoMesa
- Build a visualization to show some of the events on a world map
- Use an appropriate machine learning algorithm to learn event types against oil price rise/fall
- Use the model to predict the rise or fall in price of oil

GeoMesa

GeoMesa is an open source product designed to leverage the distributed nature of storage systems, such as Accumulo and Cassandra, to hold a distributed spatio-temporal database. With this design, GeoMesa is capable of running the large-scale geospatial analytics that are required for very large data sets, including GDELT.

We are going to use GeoMesa to store GDELT data and run our analytics across a large proportion of that data; this should give us access to enough data to train our model so that we can predict the future rise and fall of oil prices. Also, GeoMesa will enable us to plot large amounts of points on a map, so that we can visualize GDELT and any other useful data.

Installing

There is a very good tutorial on the GeoMesa website (`www.geomesa.org`) that guides the user through the installation process. Therefore, it is not our intention here to produce another how-to guide; there are, however, a few points worth noting that may save you time in getting everything up and running:

- GeoMesa has a lot of components, and many of these have a lot of versions. It is very important to ensure that all of the versions of the software stack match exactly with the versions specified in the GeoMesa maven POMs. Of particular interest are Hadoop, Zookeeper, and Accumulo; the version locations can be found in the root `pom.xml` file in the GeoMesa tutorial and other related downloads.

- At the time of writing, there are some additional issues when integrating GeoMesa with some of the Hadoop vendor stacks. If you are able, use GeoMesa with your own stack of Hadoop/Accumulo and so on, to ensure version compatibility.

- The GeoMesa version dependency labeling has changed from version 1.3.0. It is very important that you ensure all of the versions line up with your chosen version of GeoMesa; if there are any conflicting classes then there will definitely be problems at some point down the line.

- If you have not used Accumulo before, we have discussed it in detail in other chapters within this book. An initial familiarization will help greatly when using GeoMesa (see `Chapter 7`, *Building Communities*).

- When using Accumulo 1.6 or greater with GeoMesa, there is the option to use Accumulo namespaces. If you are unfamiliar with this, then opt to not use namespaces and simply copy the GeoMesa runtime JAR into `/lib/text` in your Accumulo root folder.

- GeoMesa uses a few shell scripts; due to the nature of operating systems there may be the odd problem with running these scripts, depending upon your platform. The issues are minor and can be fixed with some quick Internet searches; for example when running `jai-image.sh` there was a minor issue with user confirmation on an Mac OSX.

- The GeoMesa maven repository can be found at `https://repo.locationtech.org/content/repositories/releases/org/locationtech/geomesa/`

Once you are able to successfully run GeoMesa from the command line, we can move on to the next section.

GDELT Ingest

The next stage is to obtain the GDELT data and load it into GeoMesa. There are a number of options here, depending upon how you plan to proceed; if you are just working through this chapter, then you can use a script to download the data in one go:

```
$ mkdir gdelt && cd gdelt
$ wget http://data.gdeltproject.org/events/md5sums
$ for file in `cat md5sums | cut -d' ' -f3 | grep '^201[56]'` ; do wget
http://data.gdeltproject.org/events/$file ; done
$ md5sum -c md5sums 2>&1 | grep '^201[56]'
```

This will download and verify all of the GDELT events data for 2015 and 2016. The amount of data required is something we need to estimate at this stage, as we do not know how our algorithm is going to work out, so we have chosen two years worth to start with.

An alternative to the script is to read `Chapter 2`, *Data Acquisition*, which explains in detail how to configure Apache NiFi to download the GDELT data in real time, and further it loads it to HDFS ready for use. Otherwise, a script to allow the preceding data to be transferred to HDFS is shown as follows:

```
$ ls -1 *.zip | xargs -n 1 unzip
$ rm *.zip
$ hdfs dfs -copyFromLocal *.CSV hdfs:///data/gdelt/
```

> HDFS uses data blocks; we want to ensure that files are stored as efficiently as possible. Writing a method to aggregate files to the HDFS block size (64 MB by default) will ensure the NameNode memory is not filled with many entries for lots of small files, and will make processing more efficient also. Large files that use more than one block (file size > 64 MB) are known as split files.

We have a substantial amount of data in HDFS (approximately 48 GB for 2015/16). Now, we will load this to Accumulo via GeoMesa.

GeoMesa Ingest

The GeoMesa tutorials discuss the idea of loading the data from HDFS to Accumulo using a `MapReduce` job. Let's take a look at this and create a Spark equivalent.

MapReduce to Spark

Since **MapReduce** (**MR**) is generally considered dead, or at least dying, it is very useful to know how to create Spark jobs from those existing in MR. The following method can be applied to any MR job. We will consider the GeoMesa Accumulo loading job described in the GeoMesa tutorial (`geomesa-examples-gdelt`) for this case.

An MR job is typically made up of three parts: the mapper, the reducer, and the driver. The GeoMesa example is a map-only job and therefore requires no reducer. The job takes a GDELT input line, creates a (Key,Value) pair from an empty `Text` object and the created GeoMesa `SimpleFeature`, and uses the `GeoMesaOutputFormat` to load the data to Accumulo. The full code of the MR job can be found in our repository; next this we will work through the key parts and suggest the changes required for Spark.

The job is initiated from the `main` method; the first few lines are related to parsing the required options from the command line, such as the Accumulo username and password. We then reach:

```
SimpleFeatureType featureType =
    buildGDELTFeatureType(featureName);
DataStore ds = DataStoreFinder.getDataStore(dsConf);
ds.createSchema(featureType);
runMapReduceJob(featureName, dsConf,
    new Path(cmd.getOptionValue(INGEST_FILE)));
```

The GeoMesa `SimpleFeatureType` is the primary mechanism used to store data in a GeoMesa data store and it needs to be initialized once, along with the data store initialization. Once this is done we execute the MR job itself. In Spark, we can pass the arguments via the command line as before, and then do the one-off setup:

```
spark-submit --class io.gzet.geomesa.ingest /
             --master yarn /
             geomesa-ingest.jar <accumulo-instance-id>
...
```

The contents of the jar contain a standard Spark job:

```
val conf = new SparkConf()
val sc = new SparkContext(conf.setAppName("Geomesa Ingest"))
```

Parse the command line arguments as before, as well as performing the initialization:

```
val featureType = buildGDELTFeatureType(featureName)
val ds = DataStoreFinder
   .getDataStore(dsConf)
   .createSchema(featureType)
```

Now we can load the data from HDFS, using wildcards if required. This creates one partition for each block of the file (64 MB default), resulting in an RDD[String]:

```
val distDataRDD = sc.textFile(/data/gdelt/*.CSV)
```

Or we can fix the number of partitions, depending upon our available resources:

```
val distDataRDD = sc.textFile(/data/gdelt/*.CSV, 20)
```

Then we can perform the map, where we can embed the function to replace the process in the original MR map method. We create a tuple (Text,SimpleFeatureType) to replicate a (Key, Value) pair so that we can use the OutputFormat in the next step. When Scala Tuples are created in this way, the resulting RDD gains extra methods, such as ReduceByKey, which is functionally equivalent to the MR Reducer (see below for further information on what we should really be using, mapPartitions):

```
val processedRDD = distDataRDD.map(s =>{
    // Processing as before to build the SimpleFeatureType
    (new Text, simpleFeatureType)
})
```

Then, we can finally output to Accumulo using the GeomesaOutputFormat from the original job:

```
processedRDD.saveAsNewAPIHadoopFile("output/path", classOf[Text],
classOf[SimpleFeatureType], classOf[GeomesaOutputFormat])
```

At this stage, we have not mentioned the setup method in the MR job; this method is called before any input is processed to allocate an expensive resource like a database connection, or in our case, a reusable object, and a cleanup method is then used to release that resource if it were to persist when out of scope. In our case, the setup method is used to create a SimpleFeatureBuilder which can be reused during each call of the mapper to build SimpleFeatures for output; there is no cleanup method as the memory is automatically released when the object is out of scope (the code has completed).

The Spark map function only operates on one input at a time, and provides no means to execute code before or after transforming a batch of values. It looks reasonable to simply put the setup and cleanup code before and after a call to map:

```
// do setup work
val processedRDD = distDataRDD.map(s =>{
    // Processing as before to build the SimpleFeatureType
    (new Text, simpleFeatureType)
})
// do cleanup work
```

But, this fails for several reasons:

- It puts any objects used in map into the map function's closure, which requires that it be serializable (for example, by implementing java.io.Serializable). Not all objects will be serializable, thus exceptions may be thrown.
- The map function is a transformation, rather than an operation, and is lazily evaluated. Thus, instructions after the map function are not guaranteed to be executed immediately.
- Even if the preceding issues were covered for a particular implementation, we would only be executing code on the driver, not necessarily freeing resources allocated by serialized copies.

The closest counterpart to a mapper in Spark is the mapPartitions method. This method does not map just one value to another value, but maps an Iterator of values to an Iterator of other values, akin to a bulk-map method. This means that the mapPartitions can allocate resources locally at its start:

```
val processedRDD = distDataRDD.mapPartitions { valueIterator =>
  // setup code for SimpleFeatureBuilder
  val transformed = valueIterator.map( . . . )
  transformed
}
```

However, releasing resources (cleanup) is not straightforward as we still experience the lazy evaluation problem; if resources are freed after the map, then the iterator may not have evaluated before the disappearance of those resources. One solution to this is as follows:

```
val processedRDD = distDataRDD.mapPartitions { valueIterator =>
  if (valueIterator.isEmpty) {
    // return an Iterator
  } else {
    //  setup code for SimpleFeatureBuilder
    valueIterator.map { s =>
// Processing as before to build the SimpleFeatureType
      val simpleFeature =
      if (!valueIterator.hasNext) {
        // cleanup here
      }
      simpleFeature
    }
  }
}
```

Now that we have the Spark code for ingest, there is an additional change that we could make, which is to add a `Geohash` field (see the following for more information on how to produce this field). To insert this field into the code, we will need an additional entry at the end of the GDELT attributes list:

```
Geohash:String
```

And a line to set the value of the `simpleFeature` type:

```
simpleFeature.setAttribute(Geomesa, calculatedGeoHash)
```

Finally, we can run our Spark job to load the GeoMesa Accumulo instance with the GDELT data from HDFS. The two years of GDELT is around 100 million entries! You can check how much data is in Accumulo by using the Accumulo shell, run from the `accumulo/bin` directory:

```
./accumulo shell -u username -p password -e "scan -t gdelt_records -np" |
wc
```

Geohash

Geohash is a geocoding system invented by Gustavo Niemeyer. It is a hierarchical, spatial data structure that subdivides space into buckets of grid shape, which is one of the many applications of what is known as a Z-order curve and generally space-filling curves.

Geohashes offer properties like arbitrary precision and the possibility of gradually removing characters from the end of the code to reduce its size (and gradually lose precision).

As a consequence of the gradual precision degradation, nearby geographical locations will often (but not always) present similar prefixes. The longer a shared prefix is, the closer the two locations are; this is very useful in GeoMesa should we want to use points from a particular area, as we can use the `Geohash` field added in the preceding ingest code .

The main usages of Geohashes are:

- As a unique identifier
- To represent point data, for example, in databases

When used in a database, the structure of geo-hashed data has two advantages. First, data indexed by Geohash will have all points for a given rectangular area in contiguous slices (the number of slices depends on the precision required and the presence of Geohash *fault lines*). This is especially useful in database systems where queries on a single index are much easier or faster than multiple-index queries: Accumulo, for example. Second, this index structure can be used for a quick-and-dirty proximity search: the closest points are often among the closest Geohashes. These advantages make Geohashes ideal for use in GeoMesa. The following is an extract of code from David Allsopp's excellent Geohash scala implementation https://github.com/davidallsopp/geohash-scala. This code can be used to produce Geohashes based on a lat/lon input:

```
/** Geohash encoding/decoding as per http://en.wikipedia.org/wiki/Geohash
*/
object Geohash {

  val LAT_RANGE = (-90.0, 90.0)
  val LON_RANGE = (-180.0, 180.0)

  // Aliases, utility functions
  type Bounds = (Double, Double)
  private def mid(b: Bounds) = (b._1 + b._2) / 2.0
  implicit class BoundedNum(x: Double) { def in(b: Bounds): Boolean = x >=
b._1 && x <= b._2 }

  /**
   * Encode lat/long as a base32 geohash.
   *
   * Precision (optional) is the number of base32 chars desired; default is
12, which gives precision well under a meter.
   */
  def encode(lat: Double, lon: Double, precision: Int=12): String = { //
scalastyle:ignore
    require(lat in LAT_RANGE, "Latitude out of range")
    require(lon in LON_RANGE, "Longitude out of range")
    require(precision > 0, "Precision must be a positive integer")
    val rem = precision % 2 // if precision is odd, we need an extra bit so
the total bits divide by 5
    val numbits = (precision * 5) / 2
    val latBits = findBits(lat, LAT_RANGE, numbits)
    val lonBits = findBits(lon, LON_RANGE, numbits + rem)
    val bits = intercalatelonBits, latBits)
    bits.grouped(5).map(toBase32).mkString // scalastyle:ignore
  }

  private def findBits(part: Double, bounds: Bounds, p: Int): List[Boolean]
= {
```

```
    if (p == 0) Nil
    else {
      val avg = mid(bounds)
      if (part >= avg) true :: findBits(part, (avg, bounds._2), p - 1)
// >= to match geohash.org encoding
      else false :: findBits(part, (bounds._1, avg), p - 1)
    }
  }

  /**
   * Decode a base32 geohash into a tuple of (lat, lon)
   */
  def decode(hash: String): (Double, Double) = {
    require(isValid(hash), "Not a valid Base32 number")
    val (odd, even) =toBits(hash).foldRight((List[A](), List[A]())) { case
(b, (a1, a2)) => (b :: a2, a1) }
    val lon = mid(decodeBits(LON_RANGE, odd))
    val lat = mid(decodeBits(LAT_RANGE, even))
    (lat, lon)
  }

  private def decodeBits(bounds: Bounds, bits: Seq[Boolean]) =
    bits.foldLeft(bounds)((acc, bit) => if (bit) (mid(acc), acc._2) else
(acc._1, mid(acc)))
}

def intercalate[A](a: List[A], b: List[A]): List[A] = a match {
 case h :: t => h :: intercalate(b, t)
 case _ => b
}
```

One limitation of the Geohash algorithm is in attempting to utilize it to find points in proximity to each other based on a common prefix. Edge case locations that are close to each other, but on opposite sides of the 180 degrees meridian, will result in Geohash codes with no common prefix (different longitudes for near physical locations). Points that are close by at the North and South poles will have very different Geohashes (different longitudes for near physical locations).

Also, two close locations on either side of the equator (or Greenwich meridian) will not have a long common prefix since they belong to different halves of the world; one location's binary latitude (or longitude) will be 011111… and the other 100000… so they will not have a common prefix and most bits will be flipped.

In order to do a proximity search, we could compute the southwest corner (low Geohash with low latitude and longitude) and northeast corner (high Geohash with high latitude and longitude) of a bounding box and search for Geohashes between those two. This will retrieve all points in the Z-order curve between the two corners; this also breaks down at the 180 meridians and the poles.

Finally, since a Geohash (in this implementation) is based on coordinates of longitude and latitude, the distance between two Geohashes reflects the distance in latitude/longitude coordinates between two points, which does not translate to actual distance. In this case, we can use the **Haversine** formula:

$$2r \arcsin\left(\sqrt{\sin^2\left(\frac{\varphi_2 - \varphi_1}{2}\right) + \cos(\varphi_1)\cos(\varphi_2)\sin^2\left(\frac{\lambda_2 - \lambda_1}{2}\right)}\right)$$

This gives us the actual distance between the two points taking into account the curvature of the earth, where:

- **r** is the radius of the sphere,
- **φ1**, **φ2**: latitude of point 1 and latitude of point 2, in radians
- **λ1**, **λ2**: longitude of point 1 and longitude of point 2, in radians

GeoServer

Now that we have successfully loaded GDELT data to Accumulo via GeoMesa, we can work towards visualizing that data on a map; this feature is very useful for plotting results of analytics on world maps, for example. GeoMesa integrates well with GeoServer for this purpose. GeoServer is an **Open Geospatial Consortium** (**OGC**) compliant with the implementation of a number of standards including **Web Feature Service** (**WFS**) and **Web Map Service** (**WMS**). "It publishes data from any major spatial data source".

We are going to use GeoServer to view the results from our analytics in a clean, presentable way. Again, we are not going to delve into getting GeoServer up and running, as there is a very good tutorial in the GeoMesa documentation that enables the integration of the two. A couple of common points to watch out for are as follows:

- The system uses **Java Advanced Imaging** (**JAI**) libraries; if you have issues with these, specifically on a Mac, then these can often be fixed by removing the libraries from the default Java installation:

```
rm /System/Library/Java/Extensions/jai_*.
```

This will then allow the GeoServer versions to be used, located in
`$GEOSERVER_HOME/webapps/geoserver/WEB-INF/lib/`

- Again, we cannot stress the importance of versions. You must be very clear about which versions of the main modules you are using, for example, Hadoop, Accumulo, Zookeeper, and most importantly, GeoMesa. If you mix versions you will see problems and the stack traces often mask the true issue. If you do have exceptions, check and double-check your versions.

Map layers

Once GeoServer is running, we can create a layer for visualization. GeoServer enables us to publish a single or a group of layers to produce a graphic. When we create a layer, we can specify the bounding box, view the feature (which is the `SimpleFeature` we created in the Spark code previously), and even run a **Common Query Language** (**CQL**) query to filter the data (more about this as follows). After a layer has been created, selecting layer preview and the JPG option will produce a URL with a graphic similar to the following; temporal bounding here is for January 2016 so that the map is not overcrowded:

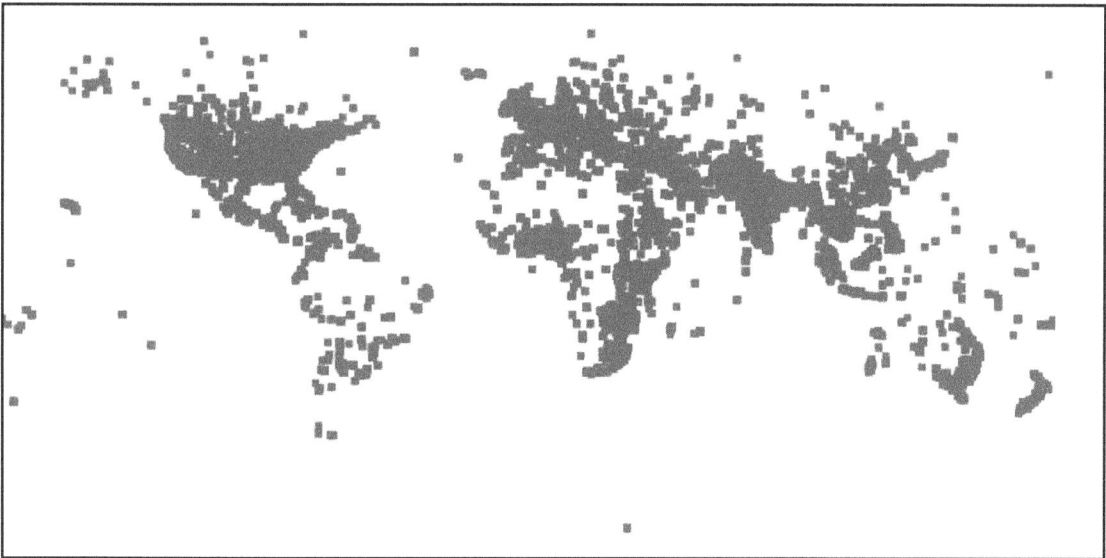

The URL can be used to produce other graphics, simply by manipulating the arguments. A brief breakdown of the URL is given as follows:

The `geoserver` URL with the standard:

```
http://localhost:8080/geoserver/geomesa/wms?
```

The `request` type:

```
service=WMS&version=1.1.0&request=GetMap&
```

The `layers` and `styles`:

```
layers=geomesa:event&styles=&
```

Set the layer `transparency`, if required:

```
transparency=true&
```

The `cql` statement, in this case any row that has an entry with `GoldsteinScale>8`:

```
cql_filter=GoldsteinScale>8&
```

The bounding box `bbox`:

```
bbox=-180.0,-90.0,180.0,90.0&
```

The `height` and `width` of the graphic:

```
width=768&height=384&
```

Source and `image` type:

```
srs=EPSG:4326&format=image%2Fjpeg&
```

Filter the content by temporal query bounds:

```
time=2016-01-01T00:00:00.000Z/2016-01-30T23:00:00.000Z
```

The final step for this section is to attach a world map to this layer so that the image becomes more readable. If you search the Internet for world map shape files, there are a number of options; we have used one from `http://thematicmapping.org`. Adding one of these into GeoServer as a shape-file store, and then creating and publishing a layer before creating a layer group of our GDELT data and the shape-file, will produce an image similar to this:

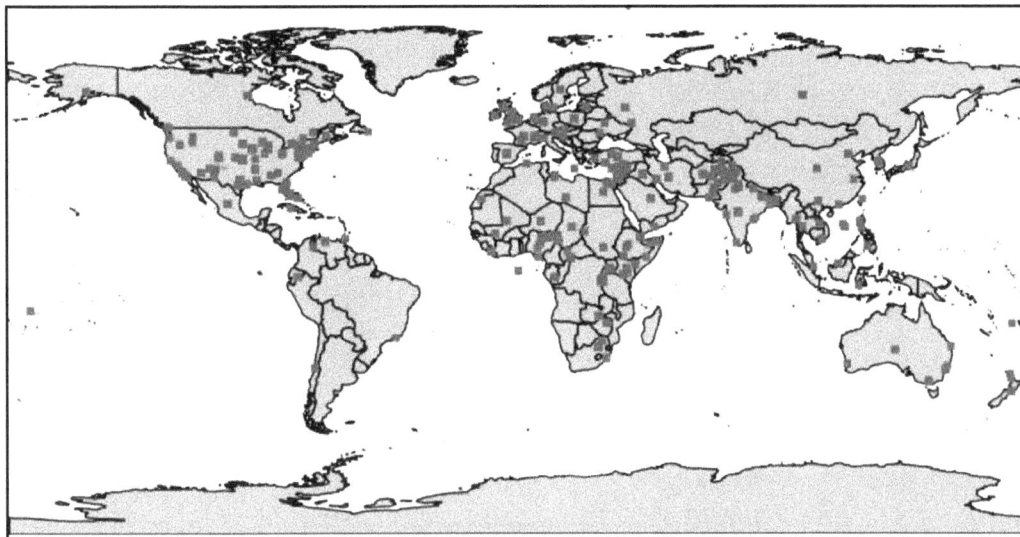

To make things a bit more interesting, we have filtered the events based on the
`GoldsteinScale` field in the `FeatureType`. By adding `cql_filter=GoldsteinScale >
8` to the URL, we can plot all of the points where the `GoldsteinScale` score was greater
than eight; so essentially, the above image shows us where the highest levels of positive
sentiment were located in the world, in January 2016!

CQL

Common Query Language (**CQL**) is a plain text query language created by the OGC for the
`Catalogue Web Services specification`. It is a human-readable query language (unlike,
for example, `OGC filters`) and uses a similar syntax to SQL. Although similar to SQL, CQL
has much less functionality; for example, it is quite strict in requiring an attribute to be on
the left side of any comparison operator.

The following lists the CQL supported operators:

- Comparison operators: =, <>, >, >=, <, <=
- ID, list and other operators: BETWEEN, BEFORE, AFTER, LIKE, IS, EXISTS,
  NOT, IN
- Arithmetic expression operators: +, -, *, /
- Geometric operators: EQUALS, DISJOINT, INTERSECTS, TOUCHES, CROSSES,
  WITHIN, CONTAINS, OVERLAPS, RELATE, DWITHIN, BEYOND

Due to the limitations of CQL, GeoServer provides an extended version of CQL called ECQL. ECQL provides much of the missing functionality of CQL, providing a more flexible language that has more in common with SQL. GeoServer supports the use of both CQL and ECQL in WMS and WFS requests.

The quickest way to test CQL queries is to amend the URL of a layer such as the one we created above, when using JPGs for example, or to use the CQL box at the bottom of the layer option within GeoMesa.

If we have several layers defined in one WMS request, such as:

```
http://localhost:8080/geoserver/wms?service=WMS&version=1.1.0&request=GetMa
p&layers=layer1,layer2,layer3   ...
```

Then we may want to filter just one of those layers with the CQL query. In this case, CQL filters must be ordered in the same way that the layers are; we use the `INCLUDE` keyword for the layers that we don't want to filter and delimit them using a ";". For example, to filter only `layer2` in our example, the WMS request would appear thus:

```
http://localhost:8080/geoserver/wms?service=WMS&version=1.1.0&request=GetMa
p&layers=layer1,layer2,layer3&cql_filter=INCLUDE;(LAYER2_COL='value');INCLU
DE...
```

> Be aware when using columns of type `Date`; we need to determine their format before attempting any CQL with them. Usually they will be in ISO8601 format; 2012-01-01T00:00:00Z. However, different formats may be present depending upon how the data was loaded. In our example, we have ensured the SQLDATE is in the correct format.

Gauging oil prices

Now that we have a substantial amount of data in our data store (we can always add more data using the preceding Spark job) we will proceed to query that data, using the GeoMesa API, to get the rows ready for application to our learning algorithm. We could of course use raw GDELT files, but the following method is a useful tool to have available.

Using the GeoMesa query API

The GeoMesa query API enables us to query for results based upon spatio-temporal attributes, whilst also leveraging the parallelization of the data store, in this case Accumulo with its iterators. We can use the API to build `SimpleFeatureCollections`, which we can then parse to realize GeoMesa `SimpleFeatures` and ultimately the raw data that matches our query.

At this stage we should build code that is generic, such that we can change it easily should we decide later that we have not used enough data, or perhaps if we need to change the output fields. Initially, we will extract a few fields; `SQLDATE`, `Actor1Name`, `Actor2Name`, and `EventCode`. We should also decide on the bounding box for our queries; as we are looking at three different oil indexes there is a decision to be made about how we suppose the geographical influence of events relates to the oil price itself. This is one of the most difficult variables to evaluate, as there are so many factors involved in the price determination; arguably the bounding box is the whole world. However, as we are using three indexes, we are going to make the assumption that each index has its own geographic limitations, based on research regarding the areas of oil supply and the areas of demand. We can always vary these bounds later should we have more relevant information, or if the results are not favorable and we need to re-evaluate. The proposed initial bounding boxes are:

- Brent: North Sea and the UK (Supply) and Central Europe (Demand): 34.515610, -21.445313 – 69.744748, 36.914063

- WTI: America (Supply) and Western Europe (Demand): -58.130121, -162.070313, 71.381635, -30.585938

- OPEC: The Middle East (Supply) and Europe (Demand): -38.350273, -20.390625, 38.195022, 149.414063

The code to extract our results from GeoMesa is as follows (Brent Oil):

```scala
object CountByWeek {

  // specify the params for the datastore
  val params = Map(
    "instanceId" -> "accumulo",
    "zookeepers" -> "127.0.0.1:2181",
    "user"       -> "root",
    "password"   -> "accumulo",
    "tableName"  -> "gdelt")

  // matches the params in the datastore loading code
  val typeName     = "event"
  val geom         = "geom"
  val date         = "SQLDATE"
  val actor1       = "Actor1Name"
  val actor2       = "Actor2Name"
  val eventCode    = "EventCode"
  val numArticles  = "NumArticles"

  // specify the geographical bounding
  val bbox   = "34.515610, -21.445313, 69.744748, 36.914063"

  // specify the temporal bounding
  val during = "2016-01-01T00:00:00.000Z/2016-12-30T00:00:00.000Z"

  // create the filter
  val filter = s"bbox($geom, $bbox) AND $date during $during"

  def main(args: Array[String]) {
    // Get a handle to the data store
    val ds = DataStoreFinder
      .getDataStore(params)
      .asInstanceOf[AccumuloDataStore]

    // Construct a CQL query to filter by bounding box
    val q = new Query(typeName, ECQL.toFilter(filter))

    // Configure Spark
    val sc = new SparkContext(GeoMesaSpark.init(
      new SparkConf(true), ds))

    // Create an RDD from the query
    val simpleFeaureRDD = GeoMesaSpark.rdd(new Configuration,
      sc, params, q)

    // Convert RDD[SimpleFeature] to RDD[Row] for DataFrame creation below
```

```
val gdeltAttrRDD = simpleFeaureRDD.mapPartitions { iter =>
  val df = new SimpleDateFormat("yyyy-MM-dd")
  val ff = CommonFactoryFinder.getFilterFactory2
  val dt = ff.property(date)
  val a1n = ff.property(actor1)
  val a2n = ff.property(actor2)
  val ec = ff.property(eventCode)
  val na = ff.property(numArticles)
  iter.map { f =>
    Row(
      df.format(dt.evaluate(f).asInstanceOf[java.util.Date]),
      a1n.evaluate(f),
      a2n.evaluate(f),
      ec.evaluate(f),
      na.evaluate(f)
    )
  }
}
```

The `RDD[Row]` collection can be written to disk for future use as follows:

```
gdeltAttrRDD.saveAsTextFile("/data/gdelt/brent-2016-rdd-row)
```

We should read in as much data as possible at this point in order to provide our algorithm with a large amount of training data. We will split our input data between training and test data at a later stage. Therefore, there is no need to hold any data back.

Data preparation

At this stage, we have obtained our data from GeoMesa based on the bounding box, and the date range, for a particular oil index. The output has been organized such that we have a collection of rows, each one containing the supposed important details for one event. We are not sure whether the fields we have chosen for each event are entirely relevant in providing enough information to build a reliable model so, depending upon our results, this is something that we may have to experiment with at a later date. We next need to transform the data into something that can be used by our learning process. In this case, we will aggregate the data into one-week blocks and transform the data into a typical *bag of words*, starting by loading the data from the previous step:

```
val gdeltAttrRDD = sc.textFile("/data/gdelt/brent-2016-rdd-row)
```

Within this RDD, we have the `EventCodes` (CAMEO codes): these will need to be transformed into their respective descriptions, so that the bag of words can be built. By downloading the CAMEO codes from `http://gdeltproject.org/data/lookups/CAMEO.e ventcodes.txt`, we can create a `Map` object for use in the next step:

```
var cameoMap = scala.collection.mutable.Map[String, String]()

val linesRDD = sc.textFile("file://CAMEO.eventcodes.txt")
linesRDD.collect.foreach(line => {
  val splitsArr = line.split("\t")
  cameoMap += (splitsArr(0) -> splitsArr(1).
    replaceAll("[^A-Za-z0-9 ]", ""))
})
```

Note that we normalize the output by removing any non-standard characters; the aim of this is to try and avoid erroneous characters affecting our training model.

We can now create our `bagOfWordsRDD` by appending the actor codes either side of the `EventCode` mapped description, and create a DataFrame from the date and formed sentence:

```
val bagOfWordsRDD = gdeltAttrRDD.map(f => Row(
    f.get(0),
    f.get(1).toString.replaceAll("\\s","").
      toLowerCase + " " + cameoMap(f.get(3).toString.
      toLowerCase + " " + f.get(2).toString.replaceAll("\\s","").
      toLowerCase)
 )

 val gdeltSentenceStruct = StructType(Array(
    StructField("Date", StringType, true),
    StructField("sentence", StringType, true)
 ))

 val gdeltSentenceDF
 spark.createDataFrame(bagOfWordsRDD,gdeltSentenceStruct)
 gdeltSentenceDF.show(false)

 +----------+---------------------------------------------------+
 |Date      |sentence                                           |
 +----------+---------------------------------------------------+
 |2016-01-02|president demand not specified below unitedstates  |
 |2016-01-02|vladimirputin engage in negotiation beijing        |
 |2016-01-02|northcarolina make pessimistic comment neighborhood|
 +----------+---------------------------------------------------+
```

We have previously mentioned that we could work with our data at a daily, weekly, or even yearly level; by choosing weekly, we will next need to group our DataFrame by week. In Spark 2.0, we can achieve this easily using window functions:

```
val windowAgg = gdeltSentenceDF.
    groupBy(window(gdeltSentenceDF.col("Date"),
      "7 days", "7 days", "1 day"))
val sentencesDF = windowAgg.agg(
    collect_list("sentence") as "sentenceArray")
```

As we will produce the oil price data for the end of each week, we should ensure that our sentence data is grouped for the days Friday to Thursday, so that we can later join this with the price data for that Friday. This is achieved by altering the fourth argument of the `window` function; in this case, one day provided the correct grouping. If we run the command `sentencesDF.printSchema`, we will see that the `sentenceArray` column is an array of strings, while we need just a `String` for the input to our learning algorithms. The next code extract demonstrates this change, as well as producing the column `commonFriday`, which gives us a reference for the date we are working around for each row, as well as a unique key that we can join with later:

```
val convertWrappedArrayToStringUDF = udf {(array: WrappedArray[String]) =>
  array.mkString(" ")
  }

val dateConvertUDF = udf {(date: String) =>
  new SimpleDateFormat("yyyy-MM-dd").
    format(new SimpleDateFormat("yyyy-MM-dd hh:mm:ss").
      parse(date))
  }

val aggSentenceDF = sentencesDF.withColumn("text",
 convertWrappedArrayToStringUDF(
    sentencesDF("sentenceArray"))).
      withColumn("commonFriday", dateConvertUDF(sentencesDF("window.end")))

aggSentenceDF.show

+--------------------+-----------------+--------------+------------+
|              window|    sentenceArray|          text|commonFriday|
+--------------------+-----------------+--------------+------------+
|[2016-09-09 00:00...|[unitedstates app|unitedstates a|  2016-09-16|
|[2016-06-24 00:00...|[student make emp|student make e|  2016-07-01|
|[2016-03-04 00:00...|[american provide|american provi|  2016-03-11|
+--------------------+-----------------+--------------+------------+
```

The next step is to collect our data and label it for use in the next stage. In order to label it, we must normalize the oil price data we downloaded. Earlier in this chapter we mentioned the frequency of data points; at the moment the data contains a date and the price at the end of that day. We need to transform our data into tuples of (Date, change) where the Date is the Friday of that week and the change is a rise or fall based on the average of the daily prices from the previous Monday onwards; if the price stays the same, we'll take this to be a fall so that we can implement binary value learning algorithms later.

We can again use the window feature in Spark DataFrames to easily group the data by week; we will also reformat the date as follows, so that the window group function performs correctly:

```
// define a function to reformat the date field
def convert(date:String) : String = {
  val dt = new SimpleDateFormat("dd/MM/yyyy").parse(date)
  new SimpleDateFormat("yyyy-MM-dd").format(dt)
}

val oilPriceDF = spark
  .read
  .option("header","true")
  .option("inferSchema", "true")
  .csv("oil-prices.csv")

// create a User Defined Function for the date changes
val convertDateUDF = udf {(Date: String) => convert(Date)}

val oilPriceDatedDF = oilPriceDF.withColumn("DATE",
convertDateUDF(oilPriceDF("DATE")))

// offset to start at beginning of week, 4 days in this case
val windowDF =
oilPriceDatedDF.groupBy(window(oilPriceDatedDF.col("DATE"),"7 days", "7
days", "4 days"))

// find the last value in each window, this is the trading close price for
that week
val windowLastDF = windowDF.agg(last("PRICE") as "last(PRICE)"
).sort("window")

windowLastDF.show(20, false)
```

This will produce something similar to this:

```
+-------------------------------------------+----------+
|window                                     |last(PRICE)|
+-------------------------------------------+----------+
|[2011-11-21 00:00:00.0,2011-11-28 00:00:00.0]|106.08    |
|[2011-11-28 00:00:00.0,2011-12-05 00:00:00.0]|109.59    |
|[2011-12-05 00:00:00.0,2011-12-12 00:00:00.0]|107.91    |
|[2011-12-12 00:00:00.0,2011-12-19 00:00:00.0]|104.0     |
+-------------------------------------------+----------+
```

Now we can calculate the rise or fall from the previous week; first by adding the previous week's last(PRICE) to each row (using the Spark lag function), and then by calculating the result:

```scala
val sortedWindow = Window.orderBy("window.start")

// add the previous last value to each row
val lagLastCol = lag(col("last(PRICE)"), 1).over(sortedWindow)
val lagLastColDF = windowLastDF.withColumn("lastPrev(PRICE)", lagLastCol)

// create a UDF to calculate the price rise or fall
val simplePriceChangeFunc = udf{(last : Double, prevLast : Double) =>
  var change = ((last - prevLast) compare 0).signum
  if(change == -1)
    change = 0
  change.toDouble
}

// create a UDF to calculate the date of the Friday for that week
val findDateTwoDaysAgoUDF = udf{(date: String) =>
  val dateFormat = new SimpleDateFormat( "yyyy-MM-dd" )
  val cal = Calendar.getInstance
  cal.setTime( dateFormat.parse(date))
  cal.add( Calendar.DATE, -3 )
  dateFormat.format(cal.getTime)
}

val oilPriceChangeDF = lagLastColDF.withColumn("label",
simplePriceChangeFunc(
  lagLastColDF("last(PRICE)"),
  lagLastColDF("lastPrev(PRICE)")
)).withColumn("commonFriday",
findDateTwoDaysAgoUDF(lagLastColDF("window.end")))


oilPriceChangeDF.show(20, false)
```

```
+-------------------+----------+--------------+-----+-----------+
|             window|last(PRICE)|lastPrev(PRICE)|label|commonFriday|
+-------------------+----------+--------------+-----+-----------+
|[2015-12-28 00:00...|      36.4|          null| null|  2016-01-01|
|[2016-01-04 00:00...|     31.67|          36.4|  0.0|  2016-01-08|
|[2016-01-11 00:00...|      28.8|         31.67|  0.0|  2016-01-15|
+-------------------+----------+--------------+-----+-----------+
```

You will notice the use of the `signum` function; this is very useful for comparison as it produces the following outcomes:

- If the first value is less than the second, output -1

- If the first value is greater than the second, output +1

- If the two values are equal, output 0

Now that we have the two DataFrames, `aggSentenceDF` and `oilPriceChangeDF`, we can join the two using the `commonFriday` column to produce a labeled dataset:

```
val changeJoinDF = aggSentenceDF
  .drop("window")
  .drop("sentenceArray")
  .join(oilPriceChangeDF, Seq("commonFriday"))
  .withColumn("id", monotonicallyIncreasingId)
```

We also drop the window and `sentenceArray` columns, as well as add an ID column, so that we can uniquely reference each row:

```
changeJoinDF.show
+------------+--------+--------+-----------+--------+-----+------+
|commonFriday|    text|  window|last(PRICE)|lastPrev|label|    id|
+------------+--------+--------+-----------+--------+-----+------+
|  2016-09-16|unitedsta|[2016-09-|      45.26|   48.37|  0.0|   121|
|  2016-07-01|student m|[2016-06-|      47.65|   46.69|  1.0|   783|
|  2016-03-11|american |[2016-03-|      39.41|   37.61|  1.0|   356|
+------------+--------+--------+-----------+--------+-----+------+
```

Machine learning

We now have input data and the weekly price change; next, we will turn our GeoMesa data into numerical vectors that a machine-learning model can work with. The Spark machine learning library, MLlib, has a utility called `HashingTF` to do just that. `HashingTF` transforms a bag of words into a vector of term frequencies by applying a hash function to each term. Because the vector has a finite number of elements, it's possible that two terms will map to the same, hashed term; the hashed, vectorized features may not exactly represent the actual content of the input text. So, we'll set up a relatively large feature vector, accommodating 10,000 different hashed values, to reduce the chance of these collisions. The logic behind this is that there are only so many possible events (regardless of their size) and therefore a repeat of a previously seen event should produce a similar outcome. Of course, the combination of events may change this, which is accounted for by initially taking one-week blocks. To format the input data correctly for `HashingTF`, we will also execute a `Tokenizer` over the input text:

```
val tokenizer = new Tokenizer().
   setInputCol("text").
   setOutputCol("words")
val hashingTF = new HashingTF().
   setNumFeatures(10000).
   setInputCol(tokenizer.getOutputCol).
   setOutputCol("rawFeatures")
```

The final preparation step is to implement an **Inverse Document Frequency (IDF)**, this is a numerical measure of how much information each term provides:

```
val idf = new IDF().
   setInputCol(hashingTF.getOutputCol).
   setOutputCol("features")
```

For the purposes of this exercise, we will implement a Naive Bayes implementation to perform the machine learning part of our functionality. This algorithm is a good initial fit to learn outcomes from a series of inputs; in our case, we hope to learn an increase or decrease in oil price given a set of events from the previous week.

Naive Bayes

Naive Bayes is a simple technique for constructing classifiers: models that assign class labels to problem instances, represented as vectors of feature values, where the class labels are drawn from some finite set. Naive Bayes is available in Spark MLlib, thus:

```
val nb = new NaiveBayes()
```

We can tie all of the above steps together using an MLlib Pipeline; a Pipeline can be thought of as a workflow that simplifies the combination of multiple algorithms. From the Spark documentation some definitions are as follows:

- DataFrame: This ML API uses DataFrames from Spark SQL as an ML dataset, which can hold a variety of data types. For example, a DataFrame could have different columns storing text, feature vectors, true labels, and predictions.

- Transformer: A Transformer is an algorithm that can transform one DataFrame into another DataFrame. For example, an ML model is a Transformer that transforms a DataFrame with features into a DataFrame with predictions.

- Estimator: An Estimator is an algorithm that can "fit" a DataFrame to produce a Transformer. For example, a learning algorithm is an Estimator that trains on a DataFrame and produces a model.

- Pipeline: A Pipeline chains multiple Transformers and Estimators together to specify an ML workflow.

The `pipeline` is declared thus:

```
val pipeline = new Pipeline().
  setStages(Array(tokenizer, hashingTF, idf, nb))
```

We noted previously, that all of the available data should be read from GeoMesa, as we would split the data at a later stage in order to provide training and test data sets. This is performed here:

```
val splitDS = changeJoinDF.randomSplit(Array(0.75,0.25))
val (trainingDF,testDF) = (splitDS(0),splitDS(1))
```

And finally, we can execute the full model:

```
val model = pipeline.fit(trainingDF)
```

The model can be saved and loaded easily:

```
model.save("/data/models/gdelt-naivebayes-2016")
val naivebayesModel = PipelineModel.load("/data/models/Gdelt-
naivebayes-2016")
```

Results

To test our model, we should execute the `model` transformer, mentioned as follows:

```
model
  .transform(testDF)
  .select("id", "prediction", "label").
  .collect()
  .foreach {
    case Row(id: Long, pred: Double, label: Double) =>
      println(s"$id --> prediction=$pred --> should be: $label")
  }
```

This provides a prediction for each of the input rows:

```
8847632629761 --> prediction=1.0 --> should be: 1.0
1065151889408 --> prediction=0.0 --> should be: 0.0
1451698946048 --> prediction=1.0 --> should be: 1.0
```

The results, having been taken from the resultant DataFrame
(`model.transform(testDF).select("rawPrediction", "probability",
"prediction").show`), are as follows:

```
+--------------------+--------------------+----------+
|       rawPrediction|         probability|prediction|
+--------------------+--------------------+----------+
|[-6487.5367247911...|[2.26431216092671...|       1.0|
|[-8366.2851849035...|[2.42791395068146...|       1.0|
|[-4309.9770937765...|[3.18816589322004...|       1.0|
+--------------------+--------------------+----------+
```

Analysis

In a problem space such as oil price prediction, it is always going to be very difficult/near impossible to create a truly successful algorithm, so this chapter was always geared towards more of a demonstration piece. However, we have results and their legitimacy is not irrelevant; we trained the above algorithms with several years of data from the oil indexes and GDELT, and then gleaned the results from the outcome of the model execution before comparing it to the correct label.

In tests, the previous model showed a 51% accuracy. This is marginally better than what we would expect from simply selecting results at random, but provides a firm base upon which to make improvements. With the ability to save data sets and models, it would be straightforward to make changes to the model during efforts to improve accuracy.

There are many areas of improvement that can be made and we have already mentioned some of them during this chapter. In order to improve our model, we should address the specific areas in a systematic manner. As we can only make an educated guess as to which changes will affect an improvement, it is important to try and address the areas of greatest concern first. Following, is a brief summary of how we might approach these changes. We should always visit our hypotheses and determine whether they are still valid, or where changes should be made.

Hypothesis 1: *"The supply and demand [of oil] is affected, to a greater extent, by world events and thus we can predict what that supply and demand is likely to be."* Our initial attempt at a model has shown 51% accuracy; although this is not enough to determine that this hypothesis is valid, it is worth continuing with other areas of the model and to attempt to improve accuracy before discounting the hypothesis altogether.

Hypothesis 2: *"The level of detail of the event will provide better or worse accuracy from our algorithm."* We have huge scope for change here; there are several areas where we could amend the code and re-run the model quickly, for example:

- Number of events: does an increase affect accuracy?
- Daily/Weekly/Monthly data roundups: weekly round-ups may not ever give good results
- Limited data sets: we currently only use a few fields from GDELT, would more fields help with the accuracy?
- Preclusion of any other types of data: would the introduction of GKG data help with accuracy?

In conclusion, we perhaps have more questions than we started with; however, we have now done the ground work to produce an initial model upon which we can build, hopefully improving accuracy and leading to a further understanding of the data and its potential effect on oil prices.

Summary

In this chapter, we have introduced the concepts of storing data in a spatio-temporal way so that we can use GeoMesa and GeoServer to create and run queries. We have shown these queries executed in both the tools themselves and in a programmatic way, leveraging GeoServer to display results. Further, we have demonstrated how to merge different artifacts to create insights purely from the raw GDELT events, before any follow-on processing. Following on from GeoMesa, we have touched upon the highly complex world of oil pricing and worked on a simple algorithm to estimate weekly oil changes. Whilst it is not reasonable to create an accurate model with the time and resources available, we have explored a number of areas of concern and attempted to address these, at least at a high level, in order to give an insight into possible approaches that can be made in this problem space.

Throughout the chapter, we have introduced a number of key Spark libraries and functions, the key area being MLlib which we will see in further detail during the course of the rest of this book.

In the next chapter, Chapter 6, *Scraping Link-Based External Data*, we further implement the GDELT dataset to build a web scale news scanner for tracking trends.

6
Scraping Link-Based External Data

This chapter aims to explain a common pattern for enhancing local data with external content found at URLs or over APIs. Examples of this are when URLs are received from GDELT or Twitter. We offer readers a tutorial using the GDELT news index service as a source of news URLs, demonstrating how to build a web scale news scanner that scrapes global breaking news of interest from the Internet. We explain how to build this specialist web scraping component in a way that overcomes the challenges of scale. In many use cases, accessing the raw HTML content is not sufficient enough to provide deeper insights into emerging global events. An expert data scientist must be able to extract entities out of that raw text content to help build the context needed track broader trends.

In this chapter, we will cover the following topics:

- Create a scalable web content fetcher using the *Goose* library
- Leverage the Spark framework for Natural Language Processing (NLP)
- De-duplicate names using the double metaphone algorithm
- Make use of GeoNames dataset for geographic coordinates lookup

Building a web scale news scanner

What makes data science different from statistics is the emphasis on scalable processing to overcome complex issues surrounding the quality and variety of the collected data. While statisticians work on samples of clean datasets, perhaps coming from a relational database, data scientists in contrast, work at scale with unstructured data coming from a variety of sources. While the former focuses on building models having high degrees of precision and accuracy, the latter often focuses on constructing rich integrated datasets that offer the discovery of less strictly defined insights. The data science journey usually involves torturing the initial sources of data, joining datasets that were theoretically not meant to be joined, enriching content with publicly available information, experimenting, exploring, discovering, trying, failing, and trying again. No matter the technical or mathematical skills, the main difference between an average and an expert data scientist is the level of curiosity and creativity employed in extracting the value latent in the data. For instance, you could build a simple model and provide business teams with the minimum they asked for, or you could notice and leverage all these URLs mentioned in your data, then scrape that content, and use these extended results to discover new insights that exceed the original questions business teams asked.

Accessing the web content

Unless you have been working really hard in early 2016, you will have heard about the death of the singer *David Bowie*, aged 69, on January 10, 2016. This news has been widely covered by all media publishers, relayed on social networks, and followed by lots of tributes paid from the greatest artists around the world. This sadly is a perfect use case for the content of this book, and a good illustration for this chapter. We will use the following article from the BBC as a reference in this section:

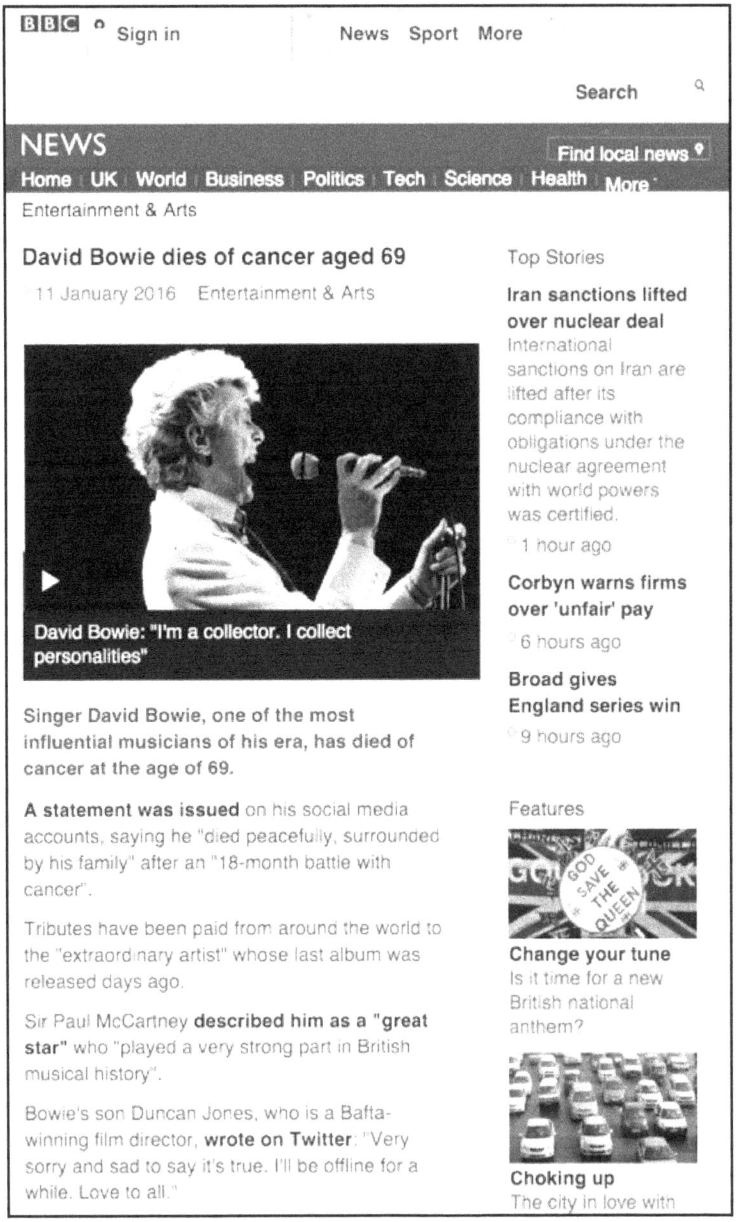

BBC Sign in News Sport More

Search

NEWS

Find local news

Home | UK | World | Business | Politics | Tech | Science | Health | More

Entertainment & Arts

David Bowie dies of cancer aged 69

11 January 2016 Entertainment & Arts

David Bowie: "I'm a collector. I collect personalities"

Singer David Bowie, one of the most influential musicians of his era, has died of cancer at the age of 69.

A statement was issued on his social media accounts, saying he "died peacefully, surrounded by his family" after an "18-month battle with cancer".

Tributes have been paid from around the world to the "extraordinary artist" whose last album was released days ago.

Sir Paul McCartney **described him as a "great star"** who "played a very strong part in British musical history".

Bowie's son Duncan Jones, who is a Bafta-winning film director, **wrote on Twitter**: "Very sorry and sad to say it's true. I'll be offline for a while. Love to all."

Top Stories

Iran sanctions lifted over nuclear deal

International sanctions on Iran are lifted after its compliance with obligations under the nuclear agreement with world powers was certified.

1 hour ago

Corbyn warns firms over 'unfair' pay

6 hours ago

Broad gives England series win

9 hours ago

Features

Change your tune

Is it time for a new British national anthem?

Choking up

The city in love with

Figure 1: BBC article about David Bowie. Source: http://www.bbc.co.uk/news/entertainment-arts-35278872

Looking at the HTML source code behind this article, the first thing to notice is that most of the content does not contain any valuable information. This includes the header, footer, navigation panels, sidebar, and all the hidden JavaScript code. While we are only interested in the title, some references (such as the publishing date), and at most, really only a dozens lines for the article itself, analyzing the page will require parsing more than 1500 lines of HTML code. Although we can find plenty of libraries designed for parsing HTML file content, creating a parser generic enough that can work with unknown HTML structures from random articles might become a real challenge on its own.

The Goose library

We delegate this logic to the excellent Scala library **Goose** (`https://github.com/GravityLabs/goose`). This library opens a URL connection, downloads the HTML content, cleanses it from all its junk, scores the different paragraphs using some clustering of English stop words, and finally returns the pure text content stripped of any of the underlying HTML code. With a proper installation of *imagemagick*, this library can even detect the most representative picture of a given website (out of the scope here). The `goose` dependency is available on Maven central:

```
<dependency>
  <groupId>com.gravity</groupId>
  <artifactId>goose</artifactId>
  <version>2.1.23</version>
</dependency>
```

Interacting with the Goose API is as pleasant as the library itself. We create a new Goose configuration, disable the image fetching, modify some optional settings such as the user agent and time out options, and create a new `Goose` object:

```
def getGooseScraper(): Goose = {
  val conf: Configuration = new Configuration
  conf.setEnableImageFetching(false)
  conf.setBrowserUserAgent(userAgent)
  conf.setConnectionTimeout(connectionTimeout)
  conf.setSocketTimeout(socketTimeout)
  new Goose(conf)
}

val url = "http://www.bbc.co.uk/news/entertainment-arts-35278872"
val goose: Goose = getGooseScraper()
val article: Article = goose.extractContent(url)
```

Calling the `extractContent` method returns an Article class with the following values:

```
val cleanedBody: String = article.cleanedArticleText
val title: String = article.title
val description: String = article.metaDescription
val keywords: String = article.metaKeywords
val domain: String = article.domain
val date: Date = article.publishDate
val tags: Set[String] = article.tags

/*
Body: Singer David Bowie, one of the most influential musicians...
Title: David Bowie dies of cancer aged 69
Description: Tributes are paid to David Bowie...
Domain: www.bbc.co.uk
*/
```

Using such a library, opening a connection and parsing the HTML content did not take us more than a dozen lines of code, and the technique can be applied to a random list of articles' URLs regardless of their source or HTML structure. The final output is a cleanly parsed dataset that is consistent, and highly useable in downstream analysis.

Integration with Spark

The next logical step is to integrate such a library and make its API available within a scalable Spark application. Once integrated, we will explain how to efficiently retrieve the remote content from a large collection of URLs and how to make use of non-serializable classes inside of a Spark transformation, and in a way that is performant.

Scala compatibility

The Goose library on Maven has been compiled for Scala 2.9, and therefore is not compatible with Spark distribution (requires Scala 2.11 for version 2.0+ of Spark). To use it, we had to recompile the Goose distribution for Scala 2.11 and, for your convenience, we made it available on our main GitHub repository. This can be quickly installed using the commands below:

```
$ git clone git@bitbucket.org:gzet_io/goose.git
$ cd goose && mvn clean install
```

Note, you will have to modify your project `pom.xml` file using this new dependency.

```
<dependency>
  <groupId>com.gravity</groupId>
  <artifactId>goose_2.11</artifactId>
  <version>2.1.30</version>
</dependency>
```

Serialization issues

Any Spark developer working with third-party dependencies should have experienced a `NotSerializableException` at least once. Although it might be challenging to find the exact root cause on a large project with lots of transformations, the reason is quite simple. Spark tries to serialize all its transformations before sending them to the appropriate executors. Since the `Goose` class is not serializable, and since we built an instance outside of a closure, this code is a perfect example of a `NotSerializableException` being thrown.

```
val goose = getGooseScraper()
def fetchArticles(urlRdd: RDD[String]): RDD[Article] = {
  urlRdd.map(goose.extractContent)
}
```

We simply overcome this constraint by creating an instance of a `Goose` class inside of a `map` transformation. By doing so, we avoid passing any reference to a non-serializable object we may have created. Spark will be able to send the code *as-is* to each of its executors without having to serialize any referenced object.

```
def fechArticles(urlRdd: RDD[String]): RDD[Article] = {
  urlRdd map { url =>
    val goose = getGooseScraper()
    goose.extractContent(url)
  }
}
```

Creating a scalable, production-ready library

Improving performance of a simple application that runs on a single server is sometimes not easy; but doing so on a distributed application running on several nodes that processes a large amount of data in parallel is often vastly more difficult, as there are so many additional factors to consider that affect performance. We show next, the principles we used to tune the content fetching library, so it can be confidently run on clusters at any scale without issues.

Build once, read many

It is worth mentioning that in the previous example, a new Goose instance was created for each URL, making our code particularly inefficient when running at scale. As a naive example to illustrate this point, it may take around 30 ms to create a new instance of a `Goose` class. Doing so on each of our millions of records would require 1 hour on a 10 node clusters, not to mention the garbage collection performance that would be significantly impacted. This process can be significantly improved using a `mapPartitions` transformation. This closure will be sent to the Spark executors (just like a `map` transformation would be) but this pattern allows us to create a single Goose instance per executor and call its `extractContent` method for each of the executor's records.

```
def fetchArticles(urlRdd: RDD[String]): RDD[Article] = {
  urlRdd mapPartitions { urls =>
    val goose = getGooseScraper()
    urls map goose.extractContent
  }
}
```

Exception handling

Exception handling is a cornerstone of proper software engineering. This is especially true in distributed computing, where we are potentially interacting with a large number of external resources and services that are out of our direct control. If we were not handling exceptions properly, for instance, any error occurring while fetching external website content would make Spark reschedule the entire task on other nodes several times before throwing a final exception and aborting the job. In a production-grade, lights-out web scraping operation, this type of issue could compromise the whole service. We certainly do not want to abort our whole web scraping content handling process because of a simple 404 error.

To harden our code against these potential issues, any exceptions should be properly caught, and we should ensure that all returned objects should consistently be made optional, being undefined for all the failed URLs. In this respect, the only bad thing that could be said about the Goose library is the inconsistency of its returned values: null can be returned for titles and dates, while an empty string is returned for missing descriptions and bodies. Returning null is a really bad practice in Java/Scala as it usually leads to `NullPointerException` – despite the fact most developers usually write a This should not happen comment next to it. In Scala, it is advised to return an option instead of null. In our example code, any field we harvest from the remote content should be returned optionally, as it may not exist on the original source page. Additionally, we should address other areas of consistency too when we harvest data, for example we can convert dates into strings as it might lead to serialization issues when calling an action (such as **collect**). For all these reasons, we should redesign our `mapPartitions` transformation as follows.

- We test for the existence of each object and return optional results
- We wrap the article content into a serializable case class `Content`
- We catch any exception and return a default object with undefined values

The revised code is shown as follows:

```
case class Content(
    url: String,
    title: Option[String],
    description: Option[String],
    body: Option[String],
    publishDate: Option[String]
)

def fetchArticles(urlRdd: RDD[String]): RDD[Content] = {

  urlRdd mapPartitions { urls =>

    val sdf = new SimpleDateFormat("yyyy-MM-dd'T'HH:mm:ssZ")
    val goose = getGooseScraper()

    urls map { url =>

      try {

        val article = goose.extractContent(url)
        var body = None: Option[String]
        var title = None: Option[String]
        var description = None: Option[String]
        var publishDate = None: Option[String]
```

```
        if (StringUtils.isNotEmpty(article.cleanedArticleText))
          body = Some(article.cleanedArticleText)

        if (StringUtils.isNotEmpty(article.title))
          title = Some(article.title)

        if (StringUtils.isNotEmpty(article.metaDescription))
          description = Some(article.metaDescription)

        if (article.publishDate != null)
          publishDate = Some(sdf.format(article.publishDate))

        Content(url, title, description, body, publishDate)

      } catch {
        case e: Throwable => Content(url, None, None, None, None)
      }
    }
  }

}
```

Performance tuning

Although most of the time, the performance of a Spark application can greatly be improved from changes to the code itself (we have seen the concept of using `mapPartitions` instead of a `map` function for that exact same purpose), you may also have to find the right balance between the total number of executors, the number of cores per executor, and the memory allocated to each of your containers.

When doing this second kind of application tuning, the first question to ask yourself is whether your application is I/O bound (lots of read/write access), network bound (lots of transfer between nodes), memory, or CPU bound (your tasks usually take too much time to complete).

It is easy to spot the main bottleneck in our web scraper application. It takes around 30 ms to create a `Goose` instance, and fetching the HTML of a given URL takes around 3 seconds to complete. We basically spend 99% of our time waiting for a chunk of content to be retrieved, mainly because of the Internet connectivity and website availability. The only way to overcome this issue is to drastically increase the number of executors used in our Spark job. Note that since executors usually sit on different nodes (assuming a correct Hadoop setup), a higher degree of parallelism will not hit the network limit in terms of bandwidth (as it would certainly do on a single node with multiple threads).

Furthermore, it is key to note that no reduce operation (no shuffle) is involved at any stage of this process as this application is a *map-only* job, making it linearly scalable by nature. Logically speaking, two times more executors would make our scraper two times more performant. To reflect these settings on our application, we need to make sure our data set is partitioned evenly with at least as many partitions as the number of executors we have defined. If our dataset were to fit on a single partition only, only one of our many executors would be used, making our new Spark setup both inadequate and highly inefficient. Repartitioning our collection is a one-off operation (albeit an expensive one) assuming we properly cache and materialize our RDD. We use parallelism of 200 here:

```
val urlRdd = getDistinctUrls(gdeltRdd).repartition(200)
urlRdd.cache()
urlRdd.count()

val contentRdd: RDD[Content] = fetchArticles(urlRdd)
contentRdd.persist(StorageLevel.DISK_ONLY)
contentRdd.count()
```

The last thing to remember is to thoroughly cache the returned RDD, as this eliminates the risk that all its lazily defined transformations (including the HTML content fetching) might be re-evaluated on any further action we might call. To stay on the safe side, and because we absolutely do not want to fetch HTML content over the internet twice, we force this caching to take place explicitly by persisting the returned dataset to DISK_ONLY.

Named entity recognition

Building a web scraper that enriches an input dataset containing URLs with external web-based HTML content is of great business value within a big data ingestion service. But while an average data scientist should be able to study the returned content by using some basic clustering and classification techniques, an expert data scientist will bring this data enrichment process to the next level, by further enriching and adding value to it in post processes. Commonly, these value-added, post processes include disambiguating the external text content, extracting entities (like People, Places, and Dates), and converting raw text into its simplest grammatical form. We will explain in this section how to leverage the Spark framework in order to create a reliable **Natural Language Processing** (**NLP**) pipeline that includes these valuable post-processed outputs, and which handles English language-based content at any scale.

Scala libraries

ScalaNLP (`http://www.scalanlp.org/`) is the parent project of breeze (among others), and is a numerical computational framework heavily used in Spark MLlib. This library would have been the perfect candidate for NLP on Spark if it was not causing such a number of dependency issues between the different versions of breeze and epic. To overcome these core dependency mismatches, we would have to recompile either the entire Spark distribution or the full ScalaNLP stack, neither of them being a walk in the park. Instead, our preferred candidate is thus a suite of Natural Language processors from the Computational Language Understanding Lab (`https://github.com/clulab/processors`). Written in Scala 2.11, it provides three different APIs: A Stanford **CoreNLP** processor, a fast processor, and one for processing biomedical text. Within this library, we can use `FastNLPProcessor` that is both accurate enough for basic **Named Entity Recognition** (**NER**) functionalities and licensed under Apache v2.

```
<dependency>
    <groupId>org.clulab</groupId>
    <artifactId>processors-corenlp_2.11</artifactId>
    <version>6.0.1</version>
</dependency>

<dependency>
    <groupId>org.clulab</groupId>
    <artifactId>processors-main_2.11</artifactId>
    <version>6.0.1</version>
</dependency>

<dependency>
    <groupId>org.clulab</groupId>
    <artifactId>processors-models_2.11</artifactId>
    <version>6.0.1</version>
</dependency>
```

NLP walkthrough

A NLP processor annotates a document and returns a list of lemma (words in their simplest grammatical form), a list of named entities types such as [ORGANIZATION], [LOCATION], [PERSON] and a list of normalized entities (such as actual date values).

Extracting entities

In the following example, we initialize a `FastNLPProcessor` object, annotate and tokenize the document into a list of `Sentence`, zip both the lemma and NER types, and finally return an array of recognized entities for each given sentence.

```scala
case class Entity(eType: String, eVal: String)

def processSentence(sentence: Sentence): List[Entity] = {
  val entities = sentence.lemmas.get
    .zip(sentence.entities.get)
    .map {
      case (eVal, eType) =>
        Entity(eType, eVal)
    }
}

def extractEntities(processor: Processor, corpus: String) = {
  val doc = processor.annotate(corpus)
  doc.sentences map processSentence
}

val t = "David Bowie was born in London"
val processor: Processor = new FastNLPProcessor()
val sentences = extractEntities(processor, t)

sentences foreach { sentence =>
  sentence foreach println
}

/*
Entity(David,PERSON)
Entity(Bowie,PERSON)
Entity(was,O)
Entity(born,O)
Entity(in,O)
Entity(London,LOCATION)
*/
```

Looking at the above output, you may notice that all the retrieved entities are not linked together, both `David` and `Bowie` being two distinct entities of a type `[PERSON]`. We recursively aggregate consecutive similar entities using the following methods.

```
def aggregate(entities: Array[Entity]) = {
  aggregateEntities(entities.head, entities.tail, List())
}

def aggregateEntity(e1: Entity, e2: Entity) = {
  Entity(e1.eType, e1.eVal + " " + e2.eVal)
}

def aggEntities(current: Entity, entities: Array[Entity], processed :
List[Entity]): List[Entity] = {
  if(entities.isEmpty) {
    // End of recusion, no additional entity to process
    // Append our last un-processed entity to our list
    current :: processed
  } else {
    val entity = entities.head
    if(entity.eType == current.eType) {
      // Aggregate consecutive values only of a same entity type
      val aggEntity = aggregateEntity(current, entity)
      // Process next record
      aggEntities(aggEntity, entities.tail, processed)
    } else {
      // Add current entity as a candidate for a next aggregation
      // Append our previous un-processed entity to our list
      aggEntities(entity, entities.tail, current :: processed)
    }
  }
}

def processSentence(sentence: Sentence): List[Entity] = {
  val entities = sentence.lemmas.get
    .zip(sentence.entities.get)
    .map {
      case (eVal, eType) =>
        Entity(eType, eVal)
    }
  aggregate(entities)
}
```

Printing out the same content now gives us a much more consistent output.

```
/*
(PERSON,David Bowie)
(O,was born in)
(LOCATION,London)
*/
```

> In a functional programming context, try to limit the use of any mutable object (such as using `var`). As a rule of thumb, any mutable object can always be avoided using preceding recursive functions.

Abstracting methods

We appreciate that working on an array of sentences (sentences being themselves an array of entities) might sound quite blurry. By experience, this will be much more confusing when running at scale, when several `flatMap` functions will be required for a simple transformation on a RDD. We wrap the results into a class `Entities` and expose the following methods:

```
case class Entities(sentences: Array[List[(String, String)]])
  {

  def getSentences = sentences

  def getEntities(entity: String) = {
    sentences flatMap { sentence =>
      sentence
    } filter { case (entityType, entityValue) =>
      entityType == entity
    } map { case (entityType, entityValue) =>
      entityValue
    } toSeq
  }
```

Building a scalable code

We have now defined our NLP framework and abstracted most of the complex logic into a set of methods and convenient classes. The next step is to integrate this code within a Spark context and to start processing text content at scale. In order to write scalable code, one needs to take extra care addressing the following points:

- Any use of a non-serializable class within a Spark job must be carefully declared inside of a closure in order to avoid a `NotSerializableException` being raised. Please refer to the Goose library serialization issues we have been discussing in the previous section.
- Whenever we create a new instance of `FastNLPProcessor` (whenever we first hit its `annotate` method because of lazy defined), all the required models will be retrieved from classpath, deserialized, and loaded into memory. This process takes around 10 seconds to complete.
- In addition to the instantiation process being quite slow, it is worth mentioning that the models can be very large (around a gigabyte), and that keeping all these models in memory will be incrementally consuming our available Heap space.

Build once, read many

For all these reasons, embedding our code *as-is* within a `map` function would be terribly inefficient (and would probably blow all our available heap space). As per the below example, we leverage the `mapPartitions` pattern in order to optimize both the overhead time of loading and deserializing the models, as well as reducing the amount of memory used by our executors. Using `mapPartitions` forces the processing of the first record of each partition to evaluate the models inducing the model loading and deserializing process, and all subsequent calls on that executor will reuse those models within that partition, helping to limit the expensive model transfer and initialization costs to once per executor.

```
def extract(corpusRdd: RDD[String]): RDD[Entities] = {
  corpusRdd mapPartitions {
    case it=>
      val processor = new FastNLPProcessor()
      it map {
        corpus =>
          val entities = extractEntities(processor, corpus)
          new Entities(entities)
      }
  }
}
```

The ultimate goal of this NLP scalability problem is to load the least possible number of models while processing as many records as possible. With one executor, we would load the models only once but would totally lose the point of parallel computing. With lots of executors, we will spend much more time deserializing models than actually processing our text content. This is discussed in the performance tuning section.

Scalability is also a state of mind

Because we designed our code locally before integrating it into Spark, we kept in mind writing things in the most convenient way. It is important because scalability is not only how fast you code works in a big data environment, but also how people feel about it, and how efficiently developers interact with your API. As a developer, if you need to chain nested `flatMap` functions in order to perform what should be a simple transformation, your code simply does not scale! Thanks to our data structure being totally abstracted inside of an `Entities` class, deriving the different RDDs from our NLP extraction can be done from a simple map function.

```
val entityRdd: RDD[Entities] = extract(corpusRdd)
entityRdd.persist(StorageLevel.DISK_ONLY)
entityRdd.count()

val perRdd = entityRdd.map(_.getEntities("PERSON"))
val locRdd = entityRdd.map(_.getEntities("LOCATION"))
val orgRdd = entityRdd.map(_.getEntities("ORGANIZATION"))
```

> **TIP**
>
> It is key to note the use of `persist` here. As previously done on the HTML fetcher process, we thoroughly cache the returned RDD to avoid situations where all its underlying transformations will be re-evaluated on any further action we might be calling. NLP processing being quite an expensive process, you have to make sure it won't be executed twice, hence the `DISK_ONLY` cache here.

Performance tuning

In order to bring this application to scale, you need to ask yourself the same key questions: Is this job I/O, memory, CPU, or network bound? NLP extraction is an expensive task, and loading a model is memory intensive. We may have to reduce the number of executors while allocating much more memory to each of them. To reflect these settings, we need to make sure our dataset will be evenly partitioned using at least as many partitions as the number of executors. We also need to enforce this repartitioning by caching our RDD and calling a simple `count` action that will evaluate all our previous transformations (including the partitioning itself).

```scala
val corpusRdd: RDD[String] = inputRdd.repartition(120)
corpusRdd.cache()
corpusRdd.count()

val entityRdd: RDD[Entities] = extract(corpusRdd)
```

GIS lookup

In the previous section, we were covering an interesting use case, how to extract location entities from unstructured data. In this section, we will make our enrichment process even smarter by trying to retrieve the actual geographical coordinate information (such as latitude and longitude) based on the locations of entities we were able to identify. Given an input string `London`, can we detect the city of London – UK together with its relative latitude and longitude? We will be discussing how to build an efficient geo lookup system that does not rely on any external API and which can process location data of any scale by leveraging the Spark framework and the *Reduce-Side-Join* pattern. When building this lookup service, we will have to bear in mind many places around the world might be sharing the same name (there are around 50 different places called Manchester in the US alone), and that an input record may not use the official name of the place it would be referring to (the official name of commonly used Geneva/Switzerland is Geneva).

GeoNames dataset

GeoNames (`http://www.geonames.org/`) is a geographical database that covers all countries, contains over 10 million place names with geographic coordinates, and is available for download free of charge. In this example, we will be using the `AllCountries.zip` dataset (1.5 GB) together with `admin1CodesASCII.txt` reference data in order to turn our location strings into valuable location objects with geo coordinates. We will be keeping only the records related to continents, countries, states, districts, and cities together with major oceans, seas, rivers, lakes, and mountains, thus reducing by half, the entire dataset. Although the admin codes dataset easily fits in memory, the Geo names must be processed within an RDD and need to be converted into the following case classes:

```
case class GeoName(
  geoId: Long,
  name: String,
  altNames: Array[String],
  country: Option[String],
  adminCode: Option[String],
  featureClass: Char,
  featureCode: String,
  population: Long,
  timezone: Array[String],
  geoPoint: GeoPoint
)

case class GeoPoint(
  lat: Double,
  lon: Double
)
```

We will not be describing the process of parsing a flat file into a `geoNameRDD` here. The parser itself is quite straightforward, processing a tab delimited records file and converting each value as per the above case class definition. We expose the following static method instead:

```
val geoNameRdd: RDD[GeoName] = GeoNameLookup.load(
  sc,
  adminCodesPath,
  allCountriesPath
)
```

Building an efficient join

The main lookup strategy will rely on a `join` operation to be executed against both our Geo names and our input data. In order to maximize the chance of getting a location match, we will be expanding our initial data using a `flatMap` function over all the possible alternative names, hence drastically increasing the initial size of 5 million to approximately 20 million records. We also make sure to clean names from any accents, dashes, or fuzzy characters they might contain:

```
val geoAltNameRdd = geoNameRdd.flatMap {
  geoName =>
    altNames map { altName =>
      (clean(altName), geoName)
    }
} filter { case (altName, geoName) =>
  StringUtils.isNotEmpty(altName.length)
} distinct()

val inputNameRdd = inputRdd.map { name =>
  (clean(name), name)
} filter { case (cleanName, place) =>
  StringUtils.isNotEmpty(cleanName.length)
  }
```

And voila, the remaining process is a simple `join` operation between both a cleaned input and a cleaned `geoNameRDD`. Finally, we can group all the matching places into a simple set of `GeoName` objects:

```
def geoLookup(
  inputNameRdd: RDD[(String, String)],
  geoNameRdd: RDD[(String, GeoName)]
): RDD[(String, Array[GeoName])] = {

  inputNameRdd
    .join(geoNameRdd)
    .map { case (key, (name, geo)) =>
      (name, geo)
    }
    .groupByKey()
    .mapValues(_.toSet)

}
```

An interesting pattern can be discussed here. How does Spark perform a `join` operation on large datasets? Called the *Reduce-Side-Join* pattern in legacy MapReduce, it requires the framework to hash all the keys from both RDDs and send all elements with a same key (same hash) on a dedicated node in order to locally `join` their values. The principle of *Reduce-Side-Join* is illustrated in *Figure 2* as follows. Because a *Reduce-Side-Join* is an expensive task (network bound), we must take special care addressing the following two points:

- *GeoNames* dataset is much larger than our input RDD. We will be wasting lots of effort shuffling data that wouldn't match anyway, making our `join` not only inefficient, but mainly useless.
- *GeoNames* dataset does not change over time. It wouldn't make sense to re-shuffle this immutable dataset on a pseudo real-time system (such as Spark Streaming) where location events are received in batch.

We can build two different strategies, an offline and an online strategy. The former will make use of a *Bloom filter* to drastically reduce the amount of data to be shuffled while the latter will partition our RDD by key in order to reduce the network cost associated to a `join` operation.

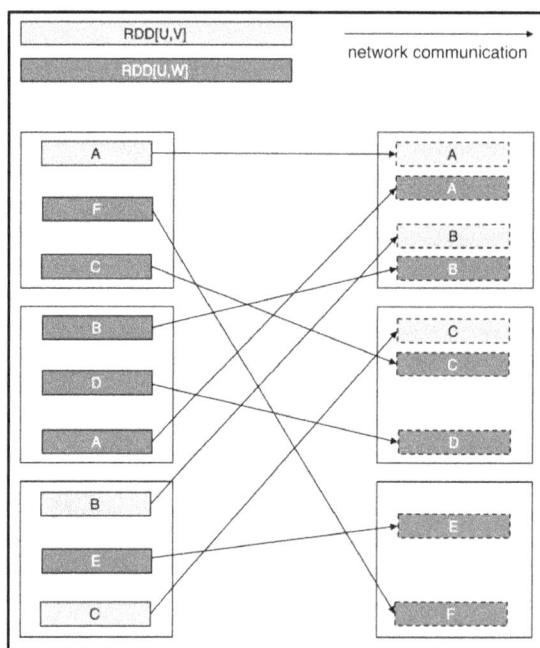

Figure 2: The Reduce-Side-Join

Offline strategy – Bloom filtering

Bloom filter is a space efficient probabilistic data structure that is used to test whether an element is a member of a set with a limited probability of false positives. Heavily used in legacy MapReduce, some implementations have been compiled for Scala. We will use the Bloom filter of breeze library, available on maven central (breeze itself can be used without much of dependency mismatches compared to the ScalaNLP models we were discussing earlier).

```
<dependency>
  <groupId>org.scalanlp</groupId>
  <artifactId>breeze_2.11</artifactId>
  <version>0.12</version>
</dependency>
```

Because our input dataset is much smaller than our `geoNameRDD`, we will train a Bloom filter against the former by leveraging the `mapPartitions` function. Each executor will build its own Bloom filter that we can aggregate, thanks to its associative property, into a single object using a bitwise operator within a `reduce` function:

```
val bfSize = inputRdd.count()
val bf: BloomFilter[String] = inputRdd.mapPartitions { it =>
  val bf = BloomFilter.optimallySized[String](bfSize, 0.001)
  it.foreach { cleanName =>
    bf += cleanName
  }
  Iterator(bf)
} reduce(_ | _)
```

We test our filter against the full `geoNameRDD` in order to remove the places we know will not match, and finally execute our same `join` operation, but this time with much less data:

```
val geoNameFilterRdd = geoAltNameRdd filter {
  case(name, geo) =>
    bf.contains(name)
}

val resultRdd = geoLookup(inputNameRdd, geoNameFilterRdd)
```

By reducing the size of our `geoNameRDD`, we have been able to release a lot of pressure from the shuffling process, making our `join` operation much more efficient. The resulting *Reduce-Side-Join* is reported on following *Figure 3*:

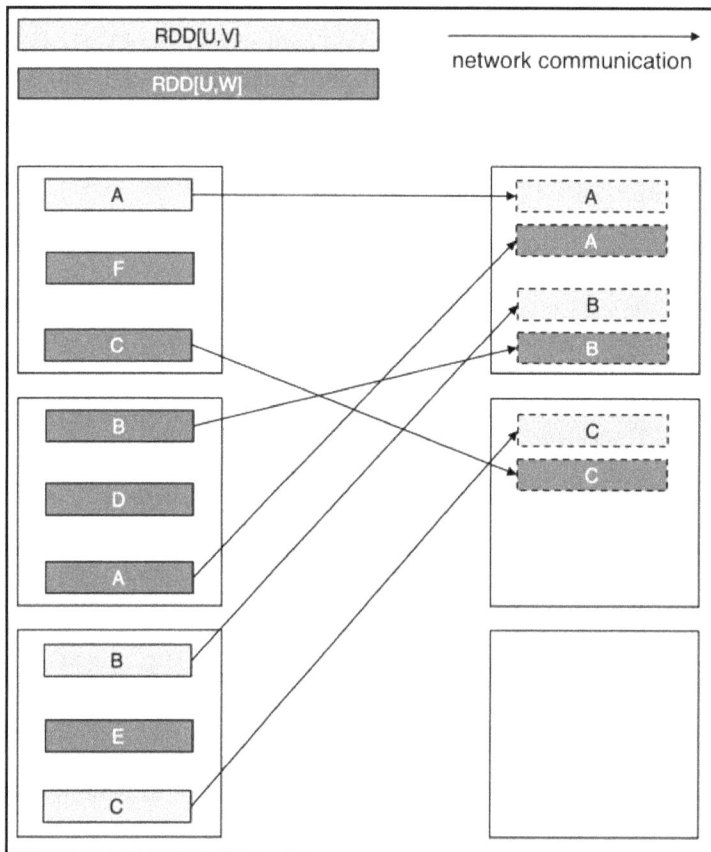

Figure 3: Reduce-Side-Join with Bloom filter

Online strategy – Hash partitioning

In an offline process, we were reducing the amount of data to be shuffled by pre-processing our `geoNameRDD`. In a streaming process, because any new batch of data is different, it wouldn't be worth filtering our reference data over and over. In such a scenario, we can greatly improve the `join` performance by pre-partitioning our `geoNameRDD` data by key, using a `HashPartitioner` with the number of partitions being at least the number of executors. Because the Spark framework knows about the repartitioning used, only the input RDD would be sent to the shuffle, making our lookup service significantly faster. This is illustrated in *Figure 4*. Note the `cache` and `count` methods used to enforce the partitioning. Finally, we can safely execute our same `join` operation, this time with much less pressure on the network:

```
val geoAltNamePartitionRdd = geoAltNameRdd.partitionBy(
  new HashPartitioner(100)
).cache()

geoAltNamePartitionRdd.count()
val resultRdd = geoLookup(inputNameRdd, geoAltNamePartitionRdd)
```

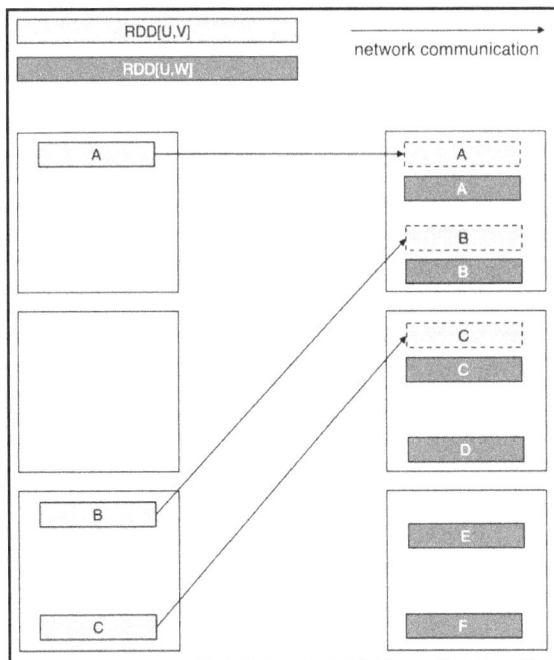

Figure 4: Reduce-Side-Join with Hash partitioning

Content deduplication

With cities like Manchester being found 100 times in our dataset, we need to work on a deduplication strategy for similar names, taking into account some cities might not be as important as others in terms of probability of being found within a random text content.

Context learning

The most accurate method for de-duplicating locations content would probably be to study location records in their contexts, similar to Apple – the company – being to Google and Yahoo! what Apple – the fruit – is to banana and orange. By machine learning locations in their context, we would probably discover that words *beavers* and *bears* are contextually close to the city of London in Ontario, Canada. As far as we know, the risk of bumping into a wild bear in London, UK is pretty small. Assuming one can access the text content, training a model shouldn't be difficult, but accessing the geo coordinates would require building an indexed dictionary of every single place with both its geographical values and its most describing topics. Because we do not have access to such a dataset (we could be scraping *Wikipedia* though), and that we do not want to assume one gets access to text content, we will simply be ranking places as an order of importance.

Location scoring

Given the different codes we pulled from the GeoNames website, we assume a continent will be more important than a country, a country will be more important than a state or a capital, and so on. This naive approach will make sense for 80% of the time, but might return irrelevant results in some edge cases. Given the Manchester example, we will find Manchester as being the parish of Manchester, a major state in Jamaica, instead of Manchester city, a *simple* city in the UK. We can fix this issue by being less restrictive in term of scoring and by sorting places of a same score by descending order of population. Returning the most important and relevant place makes sense, and such an approach is done by most online APIs anyway, but is that fair for the less important cities? We improve our scoring engine by adding a unique reference ID to a context where several locations may be mentioned together. If a document is only focused on cities in Canada, and if nothing is mentioning the United Kingdom, then *London* would most likely be the place in Canada. If no country or state is mentioned, or if both Canada and United Kingdom are found, we take the most important city of London in our dataset being London in the UK. The de-duplication occurs by sorting all our matching records by similar continent/country/states mentioned in the context, then by importance, and finally by population. The first result will be returned as our best candidate.

Names de-duplication

As we were pulling entities from an NLP extraction process without any validation, the name we were able to retrieve may be written in many different ways. They can be written in different order, might contain middle names or initials, a salutation or a nobility title, nicknames, or even some typos and spelling mistakes. Although we do not aim to fully de-duplicate the content (such as learning that both *Ziggy Stardust* and *David Bowie* stand for the same person), we will be introducing two simple techniques used to de-duplicate a large amount of data at a minimal cost by combining the concept MapReduce paradigm and functional programming.

Functional programming with Scalaz

This section is all about enriching data as part of an ingestion pipeline. We are therefore less interested in building the most accurate system using advanced machine learning techniques, but rather the most scalable and efficient one. We want to keep a dictionary of alternative names for each record, to merge and update them really fast, with the least possible code, and at very large scale. We want these structures to behave like monoids, algebraic associative structures properly supported on **Scalaz** (https://github.com/scalaz/scalaz), a library used for doing pure functional programming:

```
<dependency>
  <groupId>org.scalaz</groupId>
  <artifactId>scalaz-core_2.11</artifactId>
  <version>7.2.0</version>
</dependency>
```

Our de-duplication strategy

We use a simple example below to justify the need of using Scalaz programming for building a scalable, deduplication pipeline made of multiple transformations. Using a RDD of person, `personRDD`, as a test dataset shown as follows:

```
personRDD.take(8).foreach(println)

/*
David Bowie
david bowie
david#Bowie
David Bowie
david bowie
```

```
David Bowie
David Bowie
Ziggy Stardust
*/
```

Here, we first count the number of occurrences for each entry. This is in fact a simple Wordcount algorithm, the *101* of MapReduce programming:

```
val wcRDD = personRDD
  .map(_ -> 1)
  .reduceByKey(_+_)

wcRDD.collect.foreach(println)

/*
(David Bowie, 4)
(david bowie, 2)
(david#Bowie, 1)
(Ziggy Stardust, 1)
*/
```

Here, we apply a first transformation, such as `lowercase`, and produce an updated report:

```
val lcRDD = wcRDD.map { case (p, tf) =>
  (p.lowerCase(), tf)
}
.reduceByKey(_+_)

lcRDD.collect.foreach(println)

/*
(david bowie, 6)
(david#bowie, 1)
(ziggy stardust, 1)
*/
```

Here, we then apply a second transformation that removes any special character:

```
val reRDD = lcRDD.map { case (p, tf) =>
  (p.replaceAll("[^a-z]", ""), tf)
}
.reduceByKey(_+_)

reRDD.collect.foreach(println)

/*
(david bowie, 7)
(ziggy stardust, 1)
```

```
*/
```

We now have reduced our list of six entries to only two, but since we've lost the original records across our transformations, we cannot build a dictionary in the form of [original value] -> [new value].

Using the mappend operator

Instead, using the Scalaz API, we initialize a names' frequency dictionary (as a Map, initialized to 1) upfront for each original record and merge these dictionaries using the mappend function (accessed through the |+| operator). The merge occurs after each transformation, within a reduceByKey function, taking the result of the transformation as a key and the term frequency map as a value:

```
import scalaz.Scalaz._

def initialize(rdd: RDD[String]) = {
  rdd.map(s => (s, Map(s -> 1)))
    .reduceByKey(_ |+| _)
}

def lcDedup(rdd: RDD[(String, Map[String, Int])]) = {
  rdd.map { case (name, tf) =>
    (name.toLowerCase(), tf)
  }
  .reduceByKey(_ |+| _)
}

def reDedup(rdd: RDD[(String, Map[String, Int])]) = {
  rdd.map { case (name, tf) =>
    (name.replaceAll("\\W", ""), tf)
  }
  .reduceByKey(_ |+| _)
}

val wcTfRdd = initialize(personRDD)
val lcTfRdd = lcDedup(wcTfRdd)
val reTfRdd = reDedup(lcTfRdd)

reTfRdd.values.collect.foreach(println)

/*
Map(David Bowie -> 4, david bowie -> 2, david#Bowie -> 1)
Map(ziggy stardust -> 1)
*/
```

For each de-duplication entry, we find the most frequent item and build our dictionary RDD as follows:

```
val dicRDD = fuTfRdd.values.flatMap {
  alternatives =>
    val top = alternatives.toList.sortBy(_._2).last._1
    tf.filter(_._1 != top).map { case (alternative, tf) =>
      (alternative, top)
    }
}

dicRDD.collect.foreach(println)

/*
david bowie, David Bowie
david#Bowie, David Bowie
*/
```

In order to fully de-duplicate our person RDD, one needs to replace all `david bowie` and `david#bowie` occurrences with `David Bowie`. Now that we have explained the de-duplication strategy itself, let us dive deeply into the set of transformations.

Simple clean

The first deduplication transformation is obviously to clean names from all their fuzzy characters or extra spaces. We replace accents with their matching ASCII characters, handle camel case properly, and remove any stop words such as [mr, miss, sir]. Applying this function to the prime minister of Tonga, [Mr. Siale◉ataongo Tu◉ivakanō], we return [siale ataongo tu ivakano], a much cleaner version of it, at least in the context of string deduplication. Executing the deduplication itself will be as simple as a few lines of code using both the MapReduce paradigm and the monoids concept introduced earlier:

```
def clean(name: String, stopWords: Set[String]) = {

  StringUtils.stripAccents(name)
    .split("\\W+").map(_.trim).filter { case part =>
      !stopWords.contains(part.toLowerCase())
    }
    .mkString(" ")
    .split("(?<=[a-z])(?=[A-Z])")
    .filter(_.length >= 2)
    .mkString(" ")
    .toLowerCase()

}
```

```
def simpleDedup(rdd: RDD[(String, Map[String, Int])], stopWords:
Set[String]) = {

  rdd.map { case (name, tf) =>
    (clean(name, stopWords), tf)
  }
  .reduceByKey(_ |+| _)

}
```

DoubleMetaphone

DoubleMetaphone is a useful algorithm that can index names by their English pronunciation. Although it does not produce an exact phonetic representation of a name, it creates a simple hash function that can be used to group names with similar phonemes.

> For more information about DoubleMetaphone algorithm, please refer to:
> *Philips, L. (1990). Hanging on the Metaphone (Vol. 7). Computer Language.)*

We turn to this algorithm for performance reasons, as finding potential typos and spelling mistakes in large dictionaries is usually an expensive operation; it often requires a candidate name to be compared with each of the others we are tracking. This type of comparison is challenging in a big data environment as it usually requires a Cartesian `join` which can generate excessively large intermediate datasets. The metaphone algorithm offers a greater, and much faster alternative.

Using the `DoubleMetaphone` class from the Apache commons package, we simply leverage the MapReduce paradigm by grouping names sharing a same pronunciation. [david bowie], [david bowi] and [davide bowie], for example, are all sharing the same code [TFT#P] and will all be grouped together. In the example below, we compute the double metaphone hash for each record and call a `reduceByKey` that merges and updates all our names' frequency maps:

```
def metaphone(name: String) = {
  val dm = new DoubleMetaphone()
  name.split("\\s")
    .map(dm.doubleMetaphone)
    .mkString("#")
}

def metaphoneDedup(rdd: RDD[(String, Map[String, Int])]) = {
  rdd.map { case (name, tf) =>
```

```
    (metaphone(name), tf)
  }
  .reduceByKey(_ |+| _)
}
```

We can also greatly improve this simple technique by keeping a list of common English nicknames (bill, bob, will, beth, al, and so on) and their associated primary names, so that we can match across non-phonetic synonyms. We can do this by pre-processing our name RDD by replacing the hash codes for known nicknames with the hash codes of the associated primary names, and then we can run the same deduplication algorithm to resolve duplicates across both phonetic and synonym based matches. This will detect both spelling mistakes and alternative nicknames as follows:

```
persons.foreach(p => println(p + "\t" + metaphoneAndNickNames(p))

/*
David Bowie    TFT#P
David Bowi     TFT#P
Dave Bowie     TFT#P
*/
```

Once again, we want to highlight the fact this algorithm (and the simple cleansing routine shown above) will not be as accurate as a proper, fuzzy string matching approach that would, for example, compute a *Levenshtein* distance between each possible pair of names. By sacrificing accuracy, we do however create a method that is highly scalable, and that finds most common spelling mistakes at a minimal cost, especially spelling mistakes made on silent consonants. Once all the alternative names have been grouped on the resulting hash codes, we can output the best alternative to the presented name as the most frequent name we return from our term frequency objects. This best alternate is applied through a join with the initial name RDD in order to replace any record with its preferred alternative (if any):

```
def getBestNameRdd(rdd: RDD[(String, Map[String, Int])]) = {
  rdd.flatMap { case (key, tf) =>
    val bestName = tf.toSeq.sortBy(_._2).last._1
    tf.keySet.map { altName =>
      (altName, bestName)
    }
  }
}

val bestNameRdd = getBestNameRdd(nameTfRdd)

val dedupRdd = nameRdd
  .map(_ -> 1)
  .leftOuterJoin(bestNameRdd)
```

```
.map { case (name, (dummy, optBest)) =>
  optBest.getOrElse(name)
}
```

News index dashboard

Since we were able to enrich the content found at input URLs with valuable information, the natural next step is to start visualizing our data. Although the different techniques of Exploratory Data Analysis have been thoroughly discussed within *Chapter 4, Exploratory Data Analysis*, we believe it is worth wrapping up what we have covered so far using a simple dashboard in Kibana. From around 50,000 articles, we were able to fetch and analyze on January 10-11, we filter any record mentioning *David Bowie* as a NLP entity and containing the word *death*. Because all our text content is properly indexed in Elasticsearch, we can pull 209 matching articles with their content in just a few seconds.

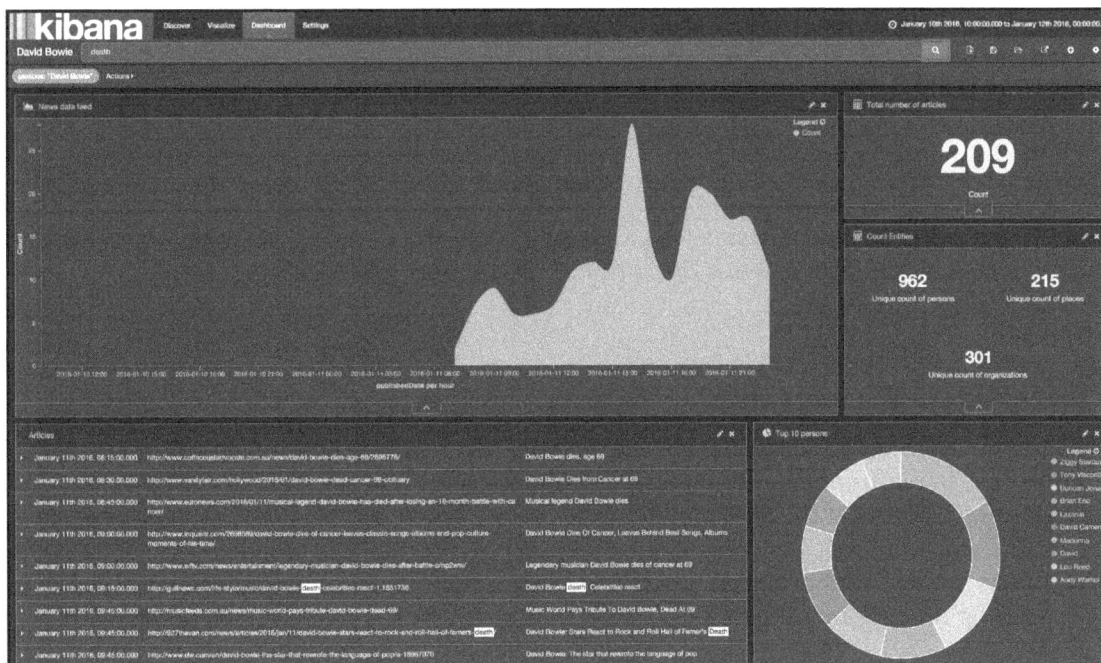

Figure 5: News Index Dashboard

We can quickly get the top ten persons mentioned alongside **David Bowie**, including his stage name *Ziggy Stardust*, his son *Duncan Jones*, his former producer *Tony Visconti*, or the British prime minister *David Cameron*. Thanks to the *GeoLookup* service we built, we display all the different places mentioned, discovering a clique around the Vatican City state where the cardinal **Gianfranco Ravasi**, head of the pontifical council of culture, tweeted about *David Bowie's* famous lyrics of *Space Oddity*.

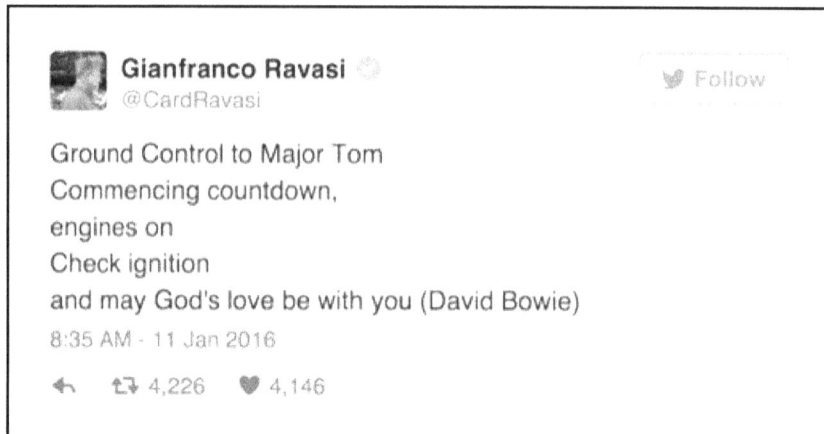

Gianfranco Ravasi
@CardRavasi

Ground Control to Major Tom
Commencing countdown,
engines on
Check ignition
and may God's love be with you (David Bowie)
8:35 AM - 11 Jan 2016

4,226   4,146

Follow

Figure 6: Vatican paid tribute from Twitter

Finally, in the race to be the first news publishing company covering breaking news, finding the first one who published about *David Bowie's* death is as easy as a simple click!

Summary

Data science is not just about machine learning. In fact, machine learning is only a small portion of it. In our understanding of what modern data science is, the science often happens exactly here, at the data enrichment process. The real magic occurs when one can transform a meaningless dataset into a valuable set of information and get new insights out of it. In this section, we have been describing how to build a fully functional data insight system using nothing more than a simple collection of URLs (and a bit of elbow grease).

In this chapter, we demonstrated how to create an efficient web scraper with Spark using the Goose library and how to extract and de-duplicate features out of raw text using NLP techniques and the GeoNames database. We also covered some interesting design patterns such as *mapPartitions* and *Bloom filters* that will be discussed further in Chapter 14, *Scalable Algorithms*.

In the next chapter, we will be focusing on the people we were able to extract from all these news articles. We will be describing how to create connections among them using simple contact chaining techniques, how to efficiently store and query a large graph from a Spark context, and how to use *GraphX* and *Pregel* to detect communities.

7
Building Communities

With more and more people interacting together and communicating, exchanging information, or simply sharing a common interest in different topics, most data science use cases can be addressed using graph representations. Although very large graphs were, for a long time, only used by the Internet giants, government, and national security agencies, it is becoming more common place to work with large graphs containing millions of vertices. Hence, the main challenge of a data scientist will not necessarily be to detect communities and find influencers on graphs, but rather to do so in a fully distributed and efficient way in order to overcome the constraint of scale. This chapter progresses through building a graph example, at scale, using the persons we identified using NLP extraction described in `Chapter 6`, *Scraping Link-Based External Data*.

In this chapter, we will cover the following topics:

- Use Spark to extract content from Elasticsearch, build a Graph of person entities and learn the benefits of using Accumulo as a secure graph database
- Write a community detection algorithm from A to Z using *GraphX* and triangle optimization
- Leverage Accumulo specific features, including cell-level security to observe the changes in communities, and iterators to provide server and client-side computation

This chapter being quite technical, we expect the reader to be already familiar with graph theory, message passing, and *Pregel* API. We also invite the reader to go through every white paper mentioned in the chapter.

Building a graph of persons

We previously used NLP entity recognition to identify persons from an HTML raw text format. In this chapter, we move to a lower level by trying to infer relations between these entities and detect the possible communities surrounding them.

Contact chaining

Within the context of news articles, we first need to ask ourselves a fundamental question. What defines a relation between two entities? The most elegant answer would probably be to study words using the Stanford NLP libraries described in Chapter 6, *Scraping Link-Based External Data*. Given the following input sentence, which is taken from http://www.ibtime s.co.uk/david-bowie-yoko-ono-says-starmans-death-has-left-big-empty-space-1545160:

> *"Yoko Ono said she and late husband John Lennon shared a close relationship with David Bowie"*

We could easily extract the syntactic tree, a structure that linguists use to model how sentences are grammatically built and where each element is reported with its type such as a noun (NN), a verb (VR), or a determiner (DT) and its relative position in the sentence:

```
val processor = new CoreNLPProcessor()
val document = processor.annotate(text)

document.sentences foreach { sentence =>
  println(sentence.syntacticTree.get)
}

/*
(NNP Yoko)
(NNP Ono)
(VBD said)
        (PRP she)
      (CC and)
        (JJ late)
        (NN husband)
          (NNP John)
          (NNP Lennon)
      (VBD shared)
        (DT a)
        (JJ close)
        (NN relationship)
        (IN with)
```

```
(NNP David)
(NNP Bowie)
*/
```

A thorough study of each element, its type, its predecessors, and successors would help build a directed graph with edges being the true definitions of the relations that exist between all these three entities. An example of a graph built out of that sentence is reported as follows:

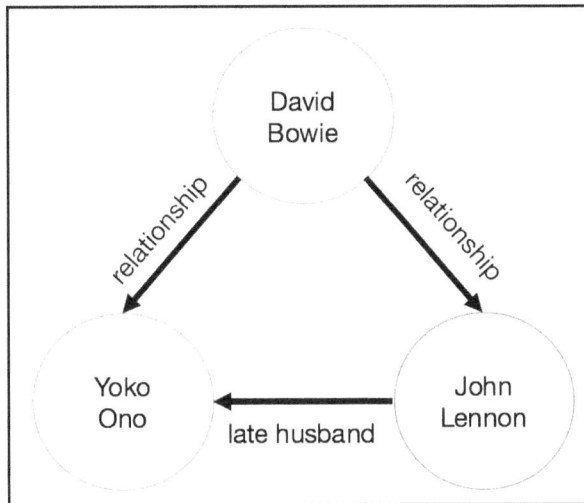

Figure 1: Syntactic graph for David Bowie, Yoko Ono, and John Lennon

Although it makes perfect sense (grammatically speaking), building a graph out of syntactic trees would require excessive amount of coding, would probably deserve a whole chapter on its own, and does not bring much added value since most of the relations we would build (in the context of news articles) would not be based on true facts taken from history books, but rather need to be put in their context. To illustrate this point we have two sentences which are taken from `http://www.digitalspy.com/music/news/a779577/paul-mccartney-pays-tribute-to-great-star-david-bowie-his-star-will-shine-in-the-sky-forever/`:

"Sir Paul McCartney described [David Bowie] as a great star"

"[Sir Paul McCartney] treasure[s] the moments they had together"

It would create the same grammatical link between vertices [Paul McCartney] and [David Bowie], while only the latter assumes a physical connection between them (they actually spent time together).

Instead, we use a much faster approach by grouping names based on their positions within a text. Our Naive assumption is that most of the authors usually start mentioning the names of important people first, then write about secondary characters, and lastly about less important persons. Our contact chaining is therefore a simple nested loop across all the names in a given article, names being sorted from the most to the least important ones using their actual position. Because of its relative time complexity $O(n^2)$ this approach will only be valid for hundreds of records per article and will certainly be a limiting factor with text mentioning hundreds of thousands of different entities.

```
def buildTuples(p: Array[String]): Array[(String, String)] = {
    for(i <- 0 to p.length - 2; j <- i + 1 to p.length - 1) yield {
      (p(i), p(j))
    }
}
```

In our code repository, you will see an alternative: `Combinations`, which is a more generic solution that allows the specification of a variable `r`; this allows us to specify the number of entities that need to appear in each output combination, that is, 2 for this chapter but more in other contexts. Using `Combinations.buildTuples` is functionally equal to the `buildTuples` code given earlier.

Extracting data from Elasticsearch

Elasticsearch is a perfect tool for storing and indexing text content together with its metadata attributes, and was therefore a logical choice for our online data store using the text content we extracted in the previous chapter. As this section is more batch-process oriented, we get the data from Elasticsearch into our Spark cluster using the excellent Spark Elasticsearch API as shown in the following code:

```
<dependency>
  <groupId>org.elasticsearch</groupId>
  <artifactId>elasticsearch-spark_2.11</artifactId>
  <version>2.4.0<version>
</dependency>
```

Given an index type and name, a convenient way for interacting with the Elasticsearch API is using Spark DataFrame. Efficient enough in most use cases (a simple example is shown next), this might become a challenge when working on more complex and nested schemas:

```
val spark = SparkSession
  .builder()
  .config("es.nodes", "localhost")
  .config("es.port", "9200")
  .appName("communities-es-download")
  .getOrCreate()

spark
  .read
  .format("org.elasticsearch.spark.sql")
  .load("gzet/news")
  .select("title", "url")
  .show(5)


+--------------------+--------------------+
|               title|                 url|
+--------------------+--------------------+
|Sonia Meets Mehbo...|http://www.newind...|
|"A Job Well Done ...|http://daphneanso...|
|New reading progr...|http://www.mailtr...|
|Barrie fire servi...|http://www.simcoe...|
|Paris police stat...|http://www.dailym...|
+--------------------+--------------------+
```

In fact, the Elasticsearch API is not flexible enough to read nested structures and complex arrays. Using latest versions of Spark, one will quickly run into errors such as *"Field 'persons' is backed by an array but the associated Spark Schema does not reflect this"*. With some experimentation, we can see that accessing nested and complex structures from Elasticsearch is usually much easier using a set of standard JSON parsers (such as `json4s` in the following code):

```
<dependency>
  <groupId>org.json4s</groupId>
  <artifactId>json4s-native_2.11</artifactId>
  <version>3.2.11</version>
</dependency>
```

We query Elasticsearch using the implicit `esJsonRdd` function from a spark context:

```
import org.elasticsearch.spark._
import org.json4s.native.JsonMethods._
import org.json4s.DefaultFormats

def readFromES(query: String = "?q=*"): RDD[Array[String]] = {

  sc.esJsonRDD("gzet/news", query)
    .values
    . map {
      jsonStr =>
        implicit val format = DefaultFormats
        val json = parse(jsonStr)
        (json \ "persons").extract[Array[String]]
    }

}

readFromEs("?persons='david bowie'")
   .map(_.mkString(","))
   .take(3)
   .foreach(println)

/*
david bowie,yoko ono,john lennon,paul mc cartney
duncan jones,david bowie,tony visconti
david bowie,boris johnson,david cameron
*/
```

Using the `query` parameter, we can access all the data from Elasticsearch, a sample of it, or even all of the records matching a specific query. We can finally build our list of tuples using the simple contact chaining method explained earlier.

```
val personRdd = readFromES()
val tupleRdd = personRdd flatMap buildTuples
```

Using the Accumulo database

We have seen a method to read our `personRdd` object from Elasticsearch and this forms a simple and neat solution for our storage requirements. However, when writing commercial applications, we must always be mindful of security and, at the time of writing, Elasticsearch security is still in development; so it would be useful at this stage to introduce a storage mechanism with native security. This is an important consideration we are using GDELT data that is, of course, open source by definition. In a commercial environment, it is very common for datasets to be confidential or commercially sensitive in some way, and clients will often request details of how their data will be secured long before they discuss the data science aspect itself. It is the authors experience that many a commercial opportunity is lost due to the inability of solution providers to demonstrate a robust and secure data architecture.

Accumulo (`http://accumulo.apache.org`) is a NoSQL database based on Google's Bigtable design (`http://research.google.com/archive/bigtable.html`) and was originally developed by the United States National Security Agency, which was subsequently released to the Apache community in 2011. Accumulo offers us the usual big data advantages such as bulk loading and parallel reading but also has some additional capabilities such as Iterators, for efficient server and client-side precomputation, data aggregation and, most importantly, cell-level security.

For our work in community detection, we will use Accumulo to take advantage specifically of its iterator and cell-level security features. First of all, we should set up an Accumulo instance and then load some data from Elasticsearch to Accumulo you can find the full code in our GitHub repository.

Setup Accumulo

The steps required to install Accumulo are out of the scope of this book; there are several tutorials available on the Web. A vanilla installation with a root user is all that is required to continue with this chapter, although we need to pay particular attention to the initial security setup in the Accumulo configuration. Once you run the Accumulo shell successfully, you are ready to proceed.

Use the following code as a guideline to creating users. The aim is to create several users with different security labels so that when we load the data, the users will have varying access to it.

```
# set up some users
createuser matt
createuser ant
createuser dave
createuser andy

# create the persons table
createtable persons

# switch to the persons table
table persons

# ensure all of the users can access the table
grant -s System.READ_TABLE -u matt
grant -s System.READ_TABLE -u ant
grant -s System.READ_TABLE -u dave
grant -s System.READ_TABLE -u andy

# allocate security labels to the users
addauths -s unclassified,secret,topsecret -u matt
addauths -s unclassified,secret -u ant
addauths -s unclassified,topsecret -u dave
addauths -s unclassified -u andy

# display user auths
getauths -u matt

# create a server side iterator to sum values
setiter -t persons -p 10 -scan -minc -majc -n sumCombiner -class
org.apache.accumulo.core.iterators.user.SummingCombiner

# list iterators in use
listiter -all

# once the table contains some records ...
user matt

# we'll see all of the records that match security labels for the user
scan
```

Cell security

Accumulo protects its cells using tokens. Tokens are made up of labels; in our case, these are [unclassified], [secret], and [topsecret], but you can use any comma-delimited values. Accumulo rows are written with a visibility field (refer to the following code) that is simply a string representation of the labels required to access a row value. The visibility field can contain Boolean logic to combine different labels and also allows for basic precedence, for instance:

```
secret&topsecret (secret AND topsecret)
secret|topsecret (secret OR topsecret)
unclassified&(secret|topsecret) (unclassified AND secret, or unclassified
AND topsecret)
```

A user has to match at least the visibility field in order to be granted access, and must supply labels that are a subset of his token stored in Accumulo (or the query will be rejected). Any values that are not matched will simply not be returned in the user query, this is an important point because if there is some indication to the user that data is missing, it is often possible for the user to draw logical, correct (or often worse, incorrect) conclusions about the nature of the data, for example, in a contact chain of people, if some vertices are available to a user and some not, but the unavailable vertices are marked as such, then the user might be able to determine information about those missing entities based on the surrounding graph. For example, a government agency investigating organized crime may allow senior employees to view an entire graph, but junior employees to only view parts of it. Let's say some well-known persons are shown in the graph, and there is a blank entry for a vertex, then it might be straightforward to workout who the missing entity is; if this placeholder is absent altogether, then there is no obvious indication that the chain stretches any further, thus allowing the agency to control dissemination of information. The graph is still of use to analysts, however, who are oblivious to the link and can continue working on specific areas of the graph.

Iterators

Iterators are a very important feature in Accumulo and provide a real-time processing framework, which leverages the power and parallelization of Accumulo, to produce modified versions of data at very low latency. We won't go into great detail here as the Accumulo documentation has plenty of examples, but we will use an iterator to keep a sum of the values for the same Accumulo row, that is, the number of times we have seen the same person pair; and this will be stored in that row value. This iterator will then appear to take effect whenever the table is scanned; we will also demonstrate how to invoke the same Iterator from the client side (for use when it has not been applied to the server).

Elasticsearch to Accumulo

Let's take advantage of Spark's ability to use Hadoop input and output formats, which leverage the native Elasticsearch and Accumulo libraries. It is worth noting that there are different routes that we could take here, the first is to use the Elasticsearch code given earlier to produce an array of string tuples and feed that into `AccumuloLoader` (found in the code repository); the second is to explore an alternative using additional Hadoop `InputFormat`; we can produce code that reads from Elasticsearch using `EsInputFormat` and writes to Accumulo using `AccumuloOutputFormat` class.

A graph data model in Accumulo

Before delving into the code, it is worth describing the schema we will be using to store a graph of persons in Accumulo. Each source node (`person A`) will be stored as a row key, the association name (such as "is also known as") as a column family, the destination node (`person B`) as a column qualifier, and a default value of `1` as a column value (that will be aggregated thanks to our iterator). This is reported here in Figure 2:

row key	column families					
	relationA			relationB		
	qualifier	value	visibility	qualifier	value	visibility
personA	personB	1	INTERNAL	personD	1	SECRET
	personC	1	CONFIDENTIAL			
personB	personC	1	INTERNAL	personD	1	CONFIDENTIAL

Figure 2: Graph data model on Accumulo

The main advantage of such a model is that given an input vertex (a person's name), one can quickly access all its known relationships through a simple GET query. The reader will surely appreciate the cell level security where we hide a particular edge triplet `[personA]` `<= [relationB] => [personD]` from most Accumulo users with no [`SECRET`] authorization granted.

The downside of such a model is that, compared to a graph database (such as Neo4J or OrientDB), traversing queries such as a depth first search would be terribly inefficient (we would need multiple recursive queries). We delegate any graph processing logic to GraphX later in this chapter.

Hadoop input and output formats

We use the following maven dependency in order to build both our input/output formats and our Spark client. The version obviously depends on the distribution of Hadoop and Accumulo installed.

```
<dependency>
  <groupId>org.apache.accumulo</groupId>
  <artifactId>accumulo-core</artifactId>
  <version>1.7.0<version>
</dependency>
```

We configure for reading from Elasticsearch through the `ESInputFormat` class. We extract a key-value pair RDD of `Text` and `MapWritable`, where the key contains the document ID and the value of all the JSON documents wrapped inside of a serializable HashMap:

```
val spark = SparkSession
  .builder()
  .appName("communities-loader")
  .getOrCreate()

val sc = spark.sparkContext
val hdpConf = sc.hadoopConfiguration

// set the ES entry points
hdpConf.set("es.nodes", "localhost:9200")
hdpConf.set("es.resource", "gzet/articles")

// Read map writable objects
import org.apache.hadoop.io.Text
import org.apache.hadoop.io.MapWritable
import org.elasticsearch.hadoop.mr.EsInputFormat

val esRDD: RDD[MapWritable] = sc.newAPIHadoopRDD(
  hdpConf,
  classOf[EsInputFormat[Text, MapWritable]],
  classOf[Text],
  classOf[MapWritable]
).values
```

An Accumulo `mutation` is similar to a `put` object in HBase, and contains the table's coordinates such as row key, column family, column qualifier, column value, and visibility. This object is built as follows:

```
def buildMutations(value: MapWritable) = {

  // Extract list of persons
```

```
val people = value
  .get("person")
  .asInstanceOf[ArrayWritable]
  .get()
  .map(_.asInstanceOf[Text])
  .map(_.toString)

// Use a default Visibility
val visibility = new ColumnVisibility("unclassified")

// Build mutation on tuples
buildTuples(people.toArray)
  .map {
    case (src, dst) =>
      val mutation = new Mutation(src)
      mutation.put("associated", dst, visibility, "1")
      (new Text(accumuloTable), mutation)
  }
```

We use the aforementioned `buildTuples` method to calculate our person pairs and write them to Accumulo using the Hadoop `AccumuloOutputFormat`. Note that we can optionally apply a security label to each of our output rows using `ColumnVisibility`; refer to *Cell security*, which we saw earlier.

We configure for writing to Accumulo. Our output RDD will be a key-value pair RDD of `Text` and `Mutation`, where the key contains the Accumulo table and the value the mutation to insert:

```
// Build Mutations
val accumuloRDD = esRDD flatMap buildMutations

// Save Mutations to Accumulo
accumuloRDD.saveAsNewAPIHadoopFile(
  "",
  classOf[Text],
  classOf[Mutation],
  classOf[AccumuloOutputFormat]
)
```

Reading from Accumulo

Now that we have our data in Accumulo, we can use the shell to inspect it (assuming we select a user that has enough privileges to see the data). Using the `scan` command in Accumulo shell, we can simulate a specific user and query, therefore validating the results of `io.gzet.community.accumulo.AccumuloReader`. When using the Scala version, we must ensure that the correct Authorization is used-it is passed into the read function via a `String`, an example might be `"secret,topsecret"`:

```
def read(
  sc: SparkContext,
  accumuloTable: String,
  authorization: Option[String] = None
)
```

This method of applying Hadoop input/output format utilizes `static` methods within the Java Accumulo library (`AbstractInputFormat` is subclassed by `InputFormatBase`, which is subclassed by `AccumuloInputFormat`). Spark users must pay particular attention to these utility methods that alter the Hadoop configuration via an instance of a `Job` object. This can be set as follows:

```
val hdpConf = sc.hadoopConfiguration
val job = Job.getInstance(hdpConf)

val clientConfig = new ClientConfiguration()
  .withInstance(accumuloInstance)
  .withZkHosts(zookeeperHosts)

AbstractInputFormat.setConnectorInfo(
  job,
  accumuloUser,
  new PasswordToken(accumuloPassword)
)

AbstractInputFormat.setZooKeeperInstance(
  job,
  clientConfig
)

if(authorization.isDefined) {
  AbstractInputFormat.setScanAuthorizations(
    job,
    new Authorizations(authorization.get)
  )
}
```

```
InputFormatBase.addIterator(job, is)
InputFormatBase.setInputTableName(job, accumuloTable)
```

You will also notice the configuration of an Accumulo iterator:

```
val is = new IteratorSetting(
  1,
  "summingCombiner",
  "org.apache.accumulo.core.iterators.user.SummingCombiner"
)

is.addOption("all", "")
is.addOption("columns", "associated")
is.addOption("lossy", "TRUE")
is.addOption("type", "STRING")
```

We can use client or server-side iterators and we have previously seen an example of server-side when configuring Accumulo via the shell. The key difference is that client-side Iterators are executed within the client JVM, as opposed to server-side, which leverage the power of the Accumulo tablet servers. A full explanation can be found in the Accumulo documentation. However, there are many reasons for selecting a client or server-side Iterator including choices over whether tablet server performance should be compromised, JVM memory usage, and so on. These decisions should be made when creating your Accumulo architecture. At the end of our `AccumuloReader` code, we can see the calling function that produces an RDD of `EdgeWritable`:

```
val edgeWritableRdd: RDD[EdgeWritable] = sc.newAPIHadoopRDD(
  job.getConfiguration,
  classOf[AccumuloGraphxInputFormat],
  classOf[NullWritable],
  classOf[EdgeWritable]
) values
```

AccumuloGraphxInputFormat and EdgeWritable

We have implemented our own Accumulo `InputFormat` to enable us to read Accumulo rows and automatically output our own Hadoop `Writable`; `EdgeWritable`. This provides for a convenience wrapper to hold our source vertex, our destination vertex, and the count as edge weight, which can then be used when building the graph. This is extremely useful as Accumulo uses the iterator discussed earlier to calculate the total count for each unique row, thereby removing the need to do this manually. As Accumulo is written in Java, our `InputFormat` uses Java to extend `InputFormatBase`, thus inheriting all of the Accumulo `InputFormat` default behavior, but outputting our choice of schema.

We are only interested in outputting `EdgeWritables`; therefore, we set all of the keys to be null (`NullWritable`) and the values to `EdgeWritable`, an additional advantage being that values in Hadoop only need to inherit from the `Writable` Interface (although we have inherited `WritableComparable` for completeness, and `EdgeWritable` can therefore be used as a key, if required).

Building a graph

Because GraphX uses long objects as an underlying type for storing vertices and edges, we first need to translate all of the persons we fetched from Accumulo into a unique set of IDs. We assume our list of unique persons does not fit in memory, or wouldn't be efficient to do so anyway, so we simply build a distributed dictionary using the `zipWithIndex` function as shown in the following code:

```
val dictionary = edgeWritableRdd
  .flatMap {
    edge =>
      List(edge.getSourceVertex, edge.getDestVertex)
  }
  .distinct()
  .zipWithIndex()
  .mapValues {
    index =>
      index + 1L
  }
}

dictionary.cache()
dictionary.count()

dictionary
  .take(3)
  .foreach(println)

/*
(david bowie, 1L)
(yoko ono, 2L)
(john lennon, 3L)
*/
```

We create an edge RDD using two successive join operations onto our person tuples and finally build our weighted and directed graph of persons with vertices containing the person name, and edge attributes the frequency count of each tuple.

```
val vertices = dictionary.map(_.swap)

val edges = edgeWritableRdd
  .map {
    edge =>
      (edge.getSourceVertex, edge)
  }
  .join(dictionary)
  .map {
    case (from, (edge, fromId)) =>
      (edge.getDestVertex, (fromId, edge))
  }
  .join(dictionary)
  .map {
    case (to, ((fromId, edge), toId)) =>
      Edge(fromId, toId, edge.getCount.toLong)
  }

val personGraph = Graph.apply(vertices, edges)

personGraph.cache()
personGraph.vertices.count()

personGraph
  .triplets
  .take(2)
  .foreach(println)

/*
((david bowie,1),(yoko ono,2),1)
((david bowie,1),(john lennon,3),1)
((yoko ono,2),(john lennon,3),1)
*/
```

Community detection algorithm

Community detection has become a popular field of research over the past few decades. Sadly, it did not move as fast as the digital world that a true data scientist lives in, with more and more data collected every second. As a result, most of the proposed solutions are simply not suitable for a big data environment.

Although a lot of algorithms suggest a new scalable way for detecting communities, none of them is actually meaning scalable in a sense of distributed algorithms and parallel computing.

Louvain algorithm

Louvain algorithm is probably the most popular and widely used algorithm for detecting communities on undirected weighted graphs.

> For more information about Louvain algorithm, refer to the publication: *Fast unfolding of communities in large networks. Vincent D. Blondel, Jean-Loup Guillaume, Renaud Lambiotte, Etienne Lefebvre. 2008*

The idea is to start with each vertex being the center of its own community. At each step, we look for community neighbors and check whether or not merging both communities together would result in any gain in the modularity values. Going through each vertex, we compress the graph so that all nodes being part of the same community become a unique community vertex, with all community internal edges becoming a self-edge with aggregated weights. We repeat this process until the modularity can no longer be optimized. The process is reported as follows in *Figure 3*:

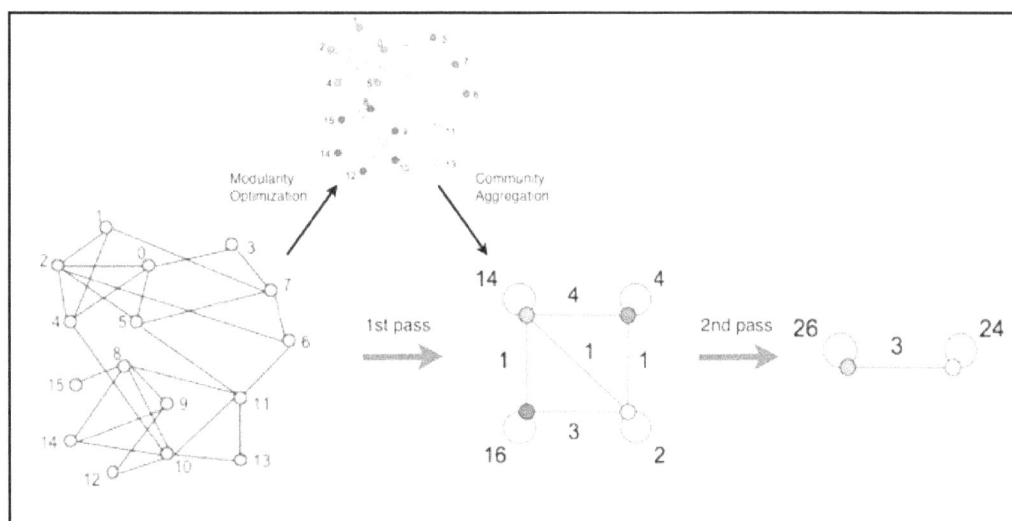

Figure 3: Fast unfolding of communities in large networks-Vincent D. Blondel, Jean-Loup Guillaume, Renaud Lambiotte, Etienne Lefebvre, 2008

Because modularity will be updated any time a vertex changes, and because the change of each vertex will be driven by the global modularity update, vertices need to be processed in a serial order; making the modularity optimization a cut-off point to the nature of parallel computing. Recent studies have reported that the quality of results may decrease as the size of graph increases excessively so that modularity is unable to detect small and well-defined communities.

To the very best of our knowledge, the only distributed version of Louvain that is publicly available has been created by Sotera, a national security technology supplier (`https://gith ub.com/Sotera/distributed-graph-analytics/tree/master/dga-graphx`). With different implementations on either MapReduce, Giraph, or GraphX, their idea is to make vertices choices simultaneously and update the graph state after each change. Because of the parallel nature, some of the vertex choices will be incorrect as they may not maximize a global modularity, but eventually become more and more consistent after repeated iterations.

This (potentially) slightly less accurate, but definitely highly scalable, algorithm was worth investigating, but because there is no right or wrong solution to the community detection problem and because each data science use case is different, we decided to build our own distributed version of a different algorithm rather than describing an existing one. For convenience, we repackaged this distributed version of Louvain and made it available in our GitHub repository.

Weighted Community Clustering (WCC)

By searching for some documentation material on graph algorithms, we came across a fantastic and recent white paper mentioning both scalability and parallel computing. We invite our readers to read this paper first before moving forward in the implementation.

> For more information about WCC algorithm, refer to the publication: *A. Prat-Perez, D. Dominguez-Sal, and J.-L. Larriba-Pey, "High quality, scalable and parallel community detection for large real graphs," in Proceedings of the 23rd International Conference on World Wide Web, ser. WWW '14. New York, NY, USA: ACM, 2014, pp. 225-236*

Although no implementation could be found, and the authors are discrete about the technologies they were using, we were particularly interested by the heuristic used as a measure of the graph partitioning since detection can be done in parallel without having to re-compute a global metric such as the graph modularity.

Description

Also interesting is the assumption they use, inspired from real-life social networks, as a quality measure for detecting communities. Because communities are groups of vertices that are tightly connected together and loosely connected with the rest of the graph, there should be a high concentration of triangles closed within each community. In other words, vertices that form part of a community should be closing many more triangles in their own community than they would be closing outside:

$$WCC(x, C) = \begin{cases} \frac{t(x,C)}{t(x,V)} \cdot \frac{vt(x,V)}{|C\setminus\{x\}|+vt(x,V\setminus C)} & \text{if } t(x, V) \neq 0; \\ 0 & \text{if } t(x, V) = 0. \end{cases}$$

As per the preceding equation, the clustering coefficient (WCC) for a given vertex **x** in a community **C** will be maximized when **x** will be closing more triangles inside of its community than outside (communities will be well defined) and/or when the number of its neighbors where it does not close any triangle with will be minimal (all nodes are interconnected). As reported in the following equation, the **WCC** of a community **S** will be the average **WCC** of each of its vertices:

$$WCC(S) = \frac{1}{|C|} \sum_{x \in S} WCC(x, C).$$

Similarly, the **WCC** of a graph partition **P** will be the weighted average of each community's WCC:

$$WCC(\mathcal{P}) = \frac{1}{|V|} \sum_{i=1}^{n} (|C_i| \cdot WCC(C_i)).$$

The algorithm consists of three different phases explained next. A preprocessing step that creates an initial set of communities, a community-back propagation to ensure initial communities are consistent, and finally an iterative algorithm that optimizes the global clustering coefficient value.

Preprocessing stage

The first step is to define a graph structure with vertices containing all the variables we need to compute the WCC metrics locally, including the current community a vertex belongs to, the number of triangles each vertex is closing inside and outside of its communities, the number of nodes it shares triangles with and the current WCC metric. All these variables will be wrapped into a `VState` class:

```
class VState extends Serializable {
  var vId = -1L
  var cId = -1L
  var changed = false
  var txV = 0
  var txC = 0
  var vtxV = 0
  var vtxV_C = 0
  var wcc = 0.0d
}
```

In order to compute the initial WCC, we first need to count the number of triangles any vertex is closing within its neighborhood. Counting the number of triangles usually consists of aggregating the neighbors IDs for each vertex, sending this list to each of its neighbors, and searching for common IDs in both vertex neighbors and vertex neighbors' neighbors. Given two connected vertices A and B, the intersection between A's and B's respective list of neighbors is the number of triangles vertex A closes with B, and the aggregation in A returns the total number of triangles vertex A is closing across the graph.

In large networks with highly connected vertices, sending a list of adjacent vertices to each neighbor can be time consuming and network intensive. In GraphX, the `triangleCount` function has been optimized so that for each edge, only the least important vertex (in term of degrees) will be sending its list to its adjacent nodes, hence minimizing the associated cost. This optimization requires the graph to be canonical (a source ID is lower than a destination ID) and partitioned. Using our graph of persons, this can be done as follows:

```
val cEdges: RDD[Edge[ED]] = graph.edges
  .map { e =>
    if(e.srcId > e.dstId) {
      Edge(e.dstId, e.srcId, e.attr)
    } else e
  }

val canonicalGraph = Graph
  .apply(graph.vertices, cEdges)
  .partitionBy(PartitionStrategy.EdgePartition2D)

canonicalGraph.cache()
```

```
canonicalGraph.vertices.count()
```

A prerequisite of the WCC optimization is to remove edges that are not part of any triangle since they will not be contributing to communities. We therefore need to count the number of triangles, the degree of each vertex, the neighbor's IDs, and we finally remove edges where the intersection of neighbor's IDs is empty. Filtering out these edges can be done using the subGraph method that takes both a filter function for edges' triplets and a filter function for vertices as input arguments:

```
val triGraph = graph.triangleCount()
val neighborRdd = graph.collectNeighborIds(EdgeDirection.Either)

val subGraph = triGraph.outerJoinVertices(neighborRdd)({ (vId, triangle,
neighbors) =>
  (triangle, neighbors.getOrElse(Array()))
}).subgraph((t: EdgeTriplet[(Int, Array[Long]), ED]) => {
  t.srcAttr._2.intersect(t.dstAttr._2).nonEmpty
}, (vId: VertexId, vStats: (Int, Array[Long])) => {
  vStats._1 > 0
})
```

Because we removed all edges that were not closing any triangle, the number of degrees for each vertex becomes the number of distinct vertices a given vertex is closing triangles with. Finally, we create our initial VState graph as follows, where each vertex becomes a center node of its own community:

```
val initGraph: Graph[VState, ED] =
subGraph.outerJoinVertices(subGraph.degrees)((vId, vStat, degrees) => {
  val state = new VState()
  state.vId = vId
  state.cId = vId
  state.changed = true
  state.txV = vStat._1
  state.vtxV = degrees.getOrElse(0)
  state.wcc = degrees.getOrElse(0).toDouble / vStat._1
  state
})

initGraph.cache()
initGraph.vertices.count()

canonicalGraph.unpersist(blocking = false)
```

Initial communities

The second step of this phase is to initialize communities using these initial WCC values. We define our initial set of communities as being consistent if and only if the following three requirements are all met:

- Any community must contain a single center node and border nodes, and all border vertices must be connected to the community center
- Any community center must have the highest clustering coefficient in its community
- A border vertex that is connected to two different centers (therefore two different communities according to rule 1) must be part of the community whose center has the highest clustering coefficient

Message passing

In order to define our initial communities, each vertex needs to send information to its neighbors, including its ID, its clustering coefficient, its degrees, and the current community it belongs to. For convenience, we will send the main vertex attribute VState class as a message as it already contains all this information. Vertices will receive these messages from their neighborhood, will select the best one with the highest WCC score (within our getBestCid method), highest degree, highest ID, and will update their community accordingly.

This communication across vertices is a perfect use case for the aggregateMessages function, the equivalent of the map-reduce paradigm in GraphX. This function requires two functions to be implemented, one that sends a message from one vertex to its adjacent node, and one that aggregates multiple messages at the vertex level. This process is called *message passing* and is described as follows:

```
def getBestCid(v: VState, msgs: Array[VState]): VertexId = {

  val candidates = msgs filter {

    msg =>
      msg.wcc > v.wcc ||
      (msg.wcc == v.wcc && msg.vtxV > v.vtxV) ||
      (msg.wcc == v.wcc && msg.vtxV > v.vtxV && msg.cId > v.cId)
  }

  if(candidates.isEmpty) {

    v.cId
```

```
    } else {

      candidates
       .sortBy {
         msg =>
           (msg.wcc, msg.vtxV, msg.cId)
         }
         .last
         .cId
    }

}

def sendMsg = (ctx: EdgeContext[VState, ED, Array[VState]]) => {

  ctx.sendToDst(
    Array(ctx.srcAttr)
  )

  ctx.sendToSrc(
    Array(ctx.dstAttr)
  )
}

def mergeMsg = (m1: Array[VState], m2: Array[VState]) => {
  m1 ++ m2
}

def msgs = subGraph.aggregateMessages(sendMsg, mergeMsg)

val initCIdGraph = subGraph.outerJoinVertices(msgs)((vId, vData, msgs) => {
  val newCId = getBestCid(vData, msgs.getOrElse(Array()))
  vData.cId = newCId
  vData
})

initCIdGraph.cache()
initCIdGraph.vertices.count()
initGraph.unpersist(blocking = false)
```

An example of this community initialization process is reported in *Figure 4*. The left graph, with its nodes proportionally resized to reflect their true WCC coefficients, has been initialized with four different communities, **1**, **11**, **16**, and **21**.

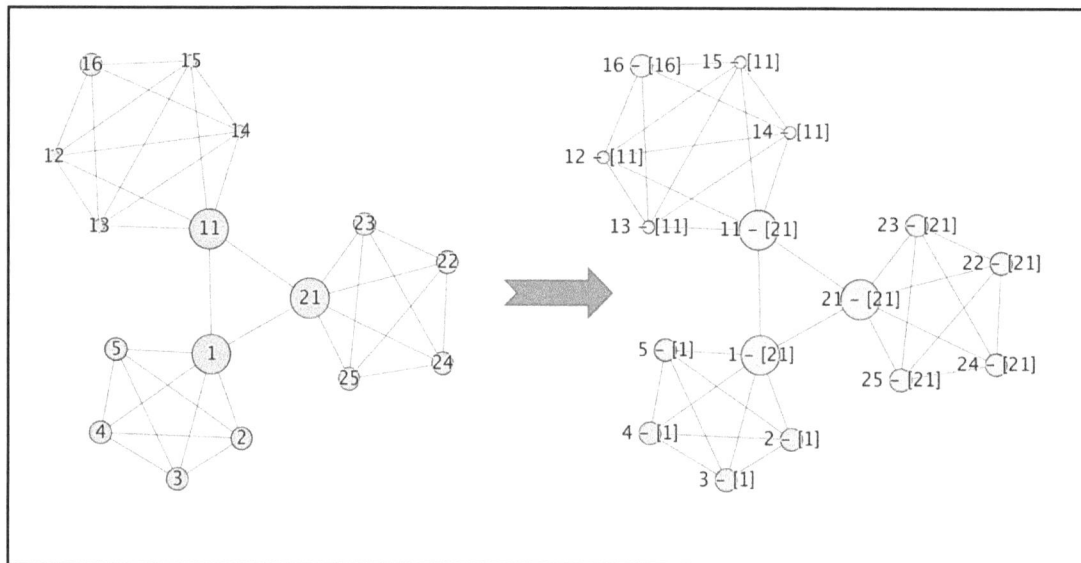

Figure 4: WCC community initialization

Although one will surely appreciate that a single `aggregateMessages` function was returning relatively consistent communities, this initial partitioning violates the third of the rules we defined earlier. Some vertices (such as **2**, **3**, **4**, and **5**) belongs to a community whose center is not a center node (vertex **1** belongs to community **21**). This same issue is noticed for community **11**.

Community back propagation

In order to address this inconsistency and respect our third requirement, any vertex *x* must broadcast its updated community to all of its neighbors having a lower coefficient, as, according to our second rule, only these lower ranked vertices could potentially become a border node of *x*. Any further update will result in a new message to be passed to lower rank vertices, and so on, until no vertices will change community, at which point the third of our rules will be satisfied.

Since no global knowledge of the graph is required between iterations (such as counting the global WCC value), community updates can be extensively parallelized using the Pregel API of GraphX. Initially developed at Google, Pregel allows vertices to receive messages from previous iterations, send new messages to their neighborhood and modify their own state until no further messages could be sent.

> For more information about *Pregel* algorithm, refer to the publication: *G. Malewicz, M. H. Austern, A. J. Bik, J. C. Dehnert, I. Horn, N. Leiser, and G. Czajkowski, "Pregel: A system for large-scale graph processing," in Proceedings of the 2010 ACM SIGMOD International Conference on Management of Data, ser. SIGMOD '10. New York, NY, USA: ACM, 2010, pp. 135-146. [Online]. Available: http://doi.acm.org/10.1145/1807167.1807184*

Similar to the `aggregateMessages` function mentioned earlier, we will send the vertex attribute `VState` as a message across vertices, with, as an initial message for Pregel super step, a new object initialized with default values (WCC of 0).

```
val initialMsg = new VState()
```

When more than one message is received at the vertex level, we only keep the one with the highest clustering coefficient, and given the same coefficient, the one with the highest degree (and then the highest ID). We create an implicit ordering on `VState` for that purpose:

```
implicit val VSOrdering: Ordering[VState] = Ordering.by({ state =>
  (state.wcc, state.vtxV, state.vId)
})

def compareState(c1: VState, c2: VState) = {
  List(c1, c2).sorted(VStateOrdering.reverse)
}

val mergeMsg = (c1: VState, c2: VState) => {
  compareState(c1, c2).head
}
```

Following the same principle as per recursive algorithms, we need to properly define a breaking clause at which point Pregel should stop sending and processing messages. This will be done within the send function that takes an edge triplet as an input and returns an iterator of messages. A vertex will send its `VState` attribute if and only if its community has changed over the previous iteration. In that case, the vertex will inform its lower ranked neighbors about its community update but will also send a signal to itself to acknowledge this successful broadcast. The latter is our breaking clause as it ensures no further message will be sent from that given node (unless its community gets updated in the further steps):

```
def sendMsg = (t: EdgeTriplet[VState, ED]) => {

  val messages = mutable.Map[Long, VState]()
  val sorted = compareState(t.srcAttr, t.dstAttr)
  val (fromNode, toNode) = (sorted.head, sorted.last)
  if (fromNode.changed) {
    messages.put(fromNode.vId, fromNode)
    messages.put(toNode.vId, fromNode)
  }

  messages.toIterator

}
```

The last function to implement is the core function of the Pregel algorithm. Here we define the logic to be applied at the vertex level given the unique message we selected from the `mergeMsg` function. We identify four different possibilities of messages, each of them defined with the logic to be applied on the vertex status.

1. If the message is the initial message sent from Pregel (vertex ID is not set, WCC is null), we do not update the vertex community ID.
2. If the message comes from the vertex itself, this is an acknowledgement from the `sendMsg` function, we set the vertex status to silent.
3. If the message (with higher WCC) comes from a center node of a community, we update the vertex attribute to be a border node of this new community.
4. If the message (with higher WCC) comes from a border node of a community, this vertex becomes a center of its own community and will broadcast this update further to its lower-ranked network.

```
def vprog = (vId: VertexId, state: VState, message: VState) => {

  if (message.vId >= 0L) {

    // message comes from myself
    // I stop spamming people
```

```
  if (message.vId == vId) {
    state.changed = false
  }

  // Sender is a center of its own community
  // I become a border node of its community
  if (message.cId == message.vId) {
    state.changed = false
    state.cId = message.cId
  }

  // Sender is a border node of a foreign community
  // I become a center of my own community
  // I broadcast this change downstream
  if (message.cId != message.vId) {
    state.changed = true
    state.cId = vId
  }

}
state

}
```

Finally, we chain all these three functions together using the `apply` function of the `Pregel` object. We set the maximum number of iterations to infinity as we rely on the breaking clause we defined using an acknowledgment type message:

```
val pregelGraph: Graph[VState, ED] = Pregel.apply(
  initCIdGraph,
  initialMsg,
  Int.MaxValue
)(
  vprog,
  sendMsg,
  mergeMsg
)

pregelGraph.cache()
pregelGraph.vertices.count()
```

Although the concept of Pregel is fascinating, its implementation is certainly not. As a reward to this tremendous effort, we display the resulting graph in *Figure 5* next. Vertices **1** and **11** are still part of community **21** which remains valid, but communities **1** and **11** have now been replaced with communities **15** and **5** respectively, vertices having the highest clustering coefficient, degree, or ID in their community, hence validating the third requirement:

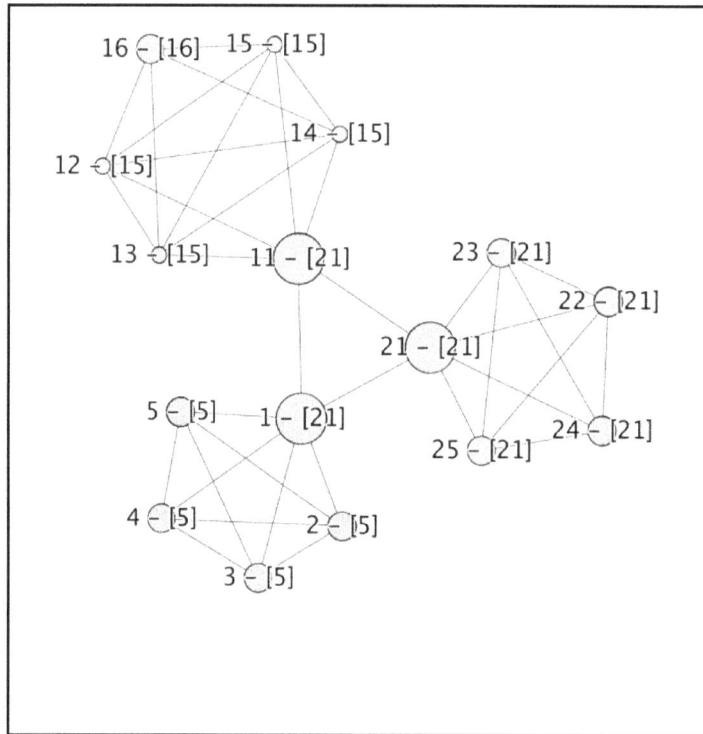

Figure 5: Community back propagation update

We used the Pregel API to create our initial set of communities with respect to the rules introduced earlier, but we are not set yet. The preceding figure definitely suggests some improvements that will be addressed in the following subsection. However, before moving forward, one can notice that no particular partitioning was used here. If we were to send multiple messages across communities' nodes, and if those vertices were located on different partitions (hence different executors), we would certainly not optimize the network traffic related to message passing. Different sorts of partitioning exist in GraphX, but none of them allow us to use a vertex attribute such as the community ID as a measure of the partitioning.

In the following simple function, we extract all graph triplets, build a hashcode out of a community tuple and repartition this edge RDD using the standard key value `HashPartitioner` class. We finally build a new graph out of this repartitioned set so that we guarantee all vertices connected from a community C1 to a community C2 will all belong to the same partition:

```
def repartition[ED: ClassTag](graph: Graph[VState, ED]) = {


  val partitionedEdges = graph
    .triplets
    .map {
      e =>
        val cId1 = e.srcAttr.cId
        val cId2 = e.dstAttr.cId
        val hash = math.abs((cId1, cId2).hashCode())
        val partition = hash % partitions
        (partition, e)
    }
    .partitionBy(new HashPartitioner(partitions))
    .map {
      pair =>
        Edge(pair._2.srcId, pair._2.dstId, pair._2.attr)
    }

  Graph(graph.vertices, partitionedEdges)

}
```

WCC iteration

The purpose of this stage is to iteratively let all vertices choose between the following three options until the WCC value cannot be longer optimized, at which point our community detection algorithm would converge to its optimal graph structure:

- **STAY**: To stay in its community
- **TRANSFER**: To move from its community and become part of its neighbor's community
- **REMOVE**: To leave its community and become part of its own community

For each vertex, the best movement is the one that maximizes the total WCC value. Similar to the Louvain approach, each movement depends on a global score to be computed, but the reason we turned to this algorithm is that this score can be approximated using a heuristic defined in *High quality, scalable and parallel community detection for large real graphs* from Arnau Prat-Pérez et. al. Because this heuristic does not require the computation of all internal triangles, vertices can all move simultaneously and this process can therefore be designed in a fully decentralized and highly scalable way.

Gathering community statistics

In order to compute this heuristic, we first need to aggregate basic statistics at the community level such as the number of elements and the number of inbound and outbound links, both of them expressed as a simple word count function here. We combine them in memory as the number of communities will be considerably smaller than the number of vertices:

```
case class CommunityStats(
    r: Int,
    d: Double,
    b: Int
)

def getCommunityStats[ED: ClassTag](graph: Graph[VState, ED]) = {

  val cVert = graph
    .vertices
    .map(_._2.cId -> 1)
    .reduceByKey(_+_)
    .collectAsMap()

  val cEdges = graph
    .triplets
    .flatMap { t =>
      if(t.srcAttr.cId == t.dstAttr.cId){
        Iterator((("I", t.srcAttr.cId), 1))
      } else {
        Iterator(
          (("O", t.srcAttr.cId), 1),
          (("O", t.dstAttr.cId), 1)
        )
      }
    }
    .reduceByKey(_+_)
    .collectAsMap()

  cVert.map {
```

```
    case (cId, cCount) =>
      val intEdges = cEdges.getOrElse(("I", cId), 0)
      val extEdges = cEdges.getOrElse(("O", cId), 0)
      val density = 2 * intEdges / math.pow(cCount, 2)
      (cId, CommunityStats(cCount, density, extEdges))
  }

}
```

Finally, we collect both the number of vertices and the community statistics (including the community edge density) and broadcast the results to all of our Spark executors:

```
var communityStats = getCommunityStats(pregelGraph)
val bCommunityStats = sc.broadcast(communityStats)
```

> **TIP**
>
> It is important to understand the use of the `broadcast` method here. If the community statistics are used within a Spark transformation, this object will be sent to the executors for each record the latter has to process. We compute them once, broadcast the result to the executors' caches so that any closure can locally make use them, hence saving lots of unnecessary network transfer.

WCC Computation

According to the set of equations defined earlier, each vertex must have access to the community statistics it belongs to and the number of triangles it closes with any vertex inside of its community. For that purpose, we collect neighbors via a simple message passing, but only on the vertices within the same community, thus limiting the network traffic:

```
def collectCommunityEdges[ED: ClassTag](graph: Graph[VState, ED]) = {

  graph.outerJoinVertices(graph.aggregateMessages((e: EdgeContext[VState,
ED, Array[VertexId]]) => {
    if(e.dstAttr.cId == e.srcAttr.cId){
      e.sendToDst(Array(e.srcId))
      e.sendToSrc(Array(e.dstId))
    }
  }, (e1: Array[VertexId], e2: Array[VertexId]) => {
    e1 ++ e2
  }))(((vid, vState, vNeighbours) => {
    (vState, vNeighbours.getOrElse(Array()))
  })

}
```

Similarly, we count the number of shared triangles using the following function. Note that we use the same optimization as per the default `triangleCount` method using the smallest set only to send messages to the largest one.

```
def collectCommunityTriangles[ED: ClassTag](graph: Graph[(VState,
Array[Long]), ED]) = {

  graph.aggregateMessages((ctx: EdgeContext[(VState, Array[Long]), ED,
Int]) => {
    if(ctx.srcAttr._1.cId == ctx.dstAttr._1.cId){
      val (smallSet, largeSet) = if (ctx.srcAttr._2.length <
ctx.dstAttr._2.length) {
        (ctx.srcAttr._2.toSet, ctx.dstAttr._2.toSet)
      } else {
        (ctx.dstAttr._2.toSet, ctx.srcAttr._2.toSet)
      }
      val it = smallSet.iterator
      var counter: Int = 0
      while (it.hasNext) {
        val vid = it.next()
        if (
          vid != ctx.srcId &&
          vid != ctx.dstId &&
          largeSet.contains(vid)
        ) {
          counter += 1
        }
      }

      ctx.sendToSrc(counter)
      ctx.sendToDst(counter)

    }
  }, (e1: Int, e2: Int) => (e1 + e2))

}
```

We compute and update the new WCC score of each vertex as a function of the community neighborhood size and the number of community triangles. This equation is the one described earlier while introducing the WCC algorithm. We compute a score as a ratio of triangles closed inside versus outside of a community C given a vertex x:

```
def updateGraph[ED: ClassTag](graph: Graph[VState, ED], stats:
Broadcast[Map[VertexId, CommunityStats]]) = {

  val cNeighbours = collectCommunityEdges(graph)
  val cTriangles = collectCommunityTriangles(cNeighbours)
```

```
cNeighbours.outerJoinVertices(cTriangles)(
  (vId, vData, tri) => {
    val s = vData._1
    val r = stats.value.get(s.cId).get.r

    // Core equation: compute WCC(v,C)
    val a = s.txC * s.vtxV
    val b = (s.txV * (r - 1 + s.vtxV_C).toDouble)
    val wcc = a / b

    val vtxC = vData._2.length
    s.vtxV_C = s.vtxV - vtxC

    // Triangles are counted twice (incoming / outgoing)
    s.txC = tri.getOrElse(0) / 2
    s.wcc = wcc
    s
  })

}

val wccGraph = updateGraph(pregelGraph, bCommunityStats)
```

The global WCC value is a simple aggregation of each vertex WCC normalized with the number of elements in each community. This value must be broadcast to Spark executors too as it will be used inside of a Spark transformation:

```
def computeWCC[ED: ClassTag](graph: Graph[VState, ED], cStats:
Broadcast[Map[VertexId, CommunityStats]]): Double = {

  val total = graph.vertices
    .map {
      case (vId, vState) =>
        (vState.cId, vState.wcc)
    }
    .reduceByKey(_+_)
    .map {
      case (cId, wcc) =>
        cStats.value.get(cId).get.r * wcc
    }
    .sum

  total / graph.vertices.count

}

val wcc = computeWCC(wccGraph, bCommunityStats)
val bWcc = sc.broadCast(wcc)
```

WCC iteration

Given the cost of inserting a vertex x into a community $\mathbf{C}$, the costs of removing/transferring x from/to a community $\mathbf{C}$ can be expressed as a function of the former, and can be derived from three parameters Θ_1, Θ_2, and Θ_3. This heuristic states that for each vertex x, a single computation is needed for each of its surrounding communities $\mathbf{C}$, and can be done in parallel assuming we gathered all the community statistics in the first place:

$$WCC(P') - WCC(P) = WCC'_I(v, C)$$
$$= \frac{1}{V} \cdot (d_{in} \cdot \Theta_1 + (r - d_{in}) \cdot \Theta_2 + \Theta_3)$$

The computation of Θ_1, Θ_2, and Θ_3 will not be reported here (it is available on our GitHub), but depends on the community density, the external edges, and the number of elements, all of them available within our broadcasted set of `CommunityStats` objects defined earlier. Finally, it is worth mentioning that this computation has a linear time complexity.

At each iteration, we will collect the different communities surrounding any vertex, and will aggregate the number of edges using the `mappend` aggregation from Scalaz that we introduced in `Chapter 6`, *Scraping Link-Based External Data*. This helps us to limit the amount of code written and avoids using mutable objects.

```
val cDegrees = itGraph.aggregateMessages((ctx: EdgeContext[VState, ED,
Map[VertexId, Int]]) => {

  ctx.sendToDst(
    Map(ctx.srcAttr.cId -> 1)
  )

  ctx.sendToSrc(
    Map(ctx.dstAttr.cId -> 1)
  )

}, (e1: Map[VertexId, Int], e2: Map[VertexId, Int]) => {
  e1 |+| e2
})
```

Using the community statistics, the WCC value from the previous iteration, the number of vertices and the above edges count, we can now estimate the cost of inserting each vertex x into a surrounding community $\mathbf{C}$. We find the local best movement for each vertex and for each of its surrounding communities, and finally apply the best one that maximizes the WCC value.

Finally, we call back the set of methods and functions defined earlier in order to update the new WCC value for each vertex, for each community, and then for the graph partition itself to see whether or not all these changes resulted in any WCC improvement. If the WCC value cannot be optimized any longer, the algorithm has converged to its optimal structure and we finally return a vertex RDD containing both the vertex ID and the final community ID this vertex belongs to.

Our test community graph has been optimized (not without its fair share of effort) and reported as shown in *Figure 6*:

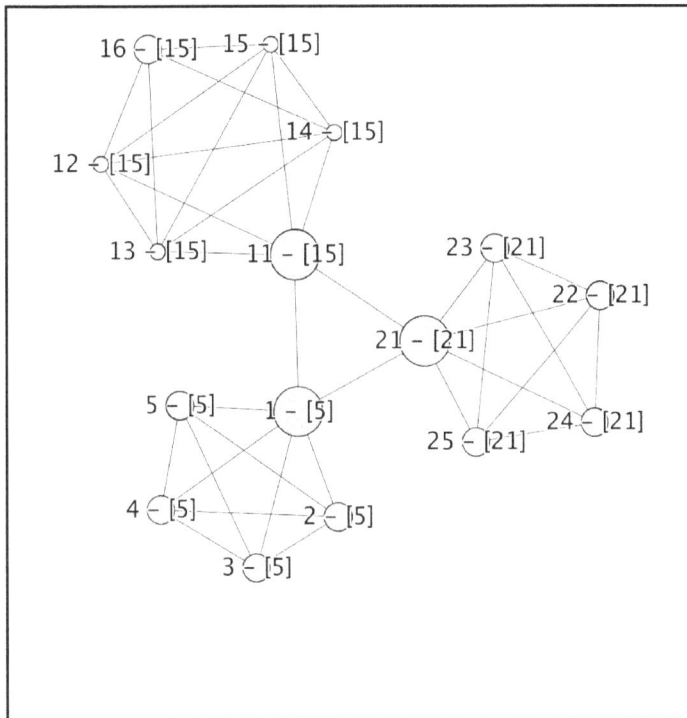

Figure 6: WCC optimized communities

We observe all the changes we were expecting from the previous figures. Vertices **1** and **11** are now part of their expected communities, respectively **5** and **11**. We also note that vertex 16 has now been included within its community 11.

GDELT dataset

In order to validate our implementation, we use the GDELT dataset we analyzed in the previous chapter. We extracted all of the communities and spent some time looking at the person names to see whether or not our community clustering was consistent. The full picture of the communities is reported in *Figure 7* and has been realized using the Gephi software, where only the top few thousand connections have been imported:

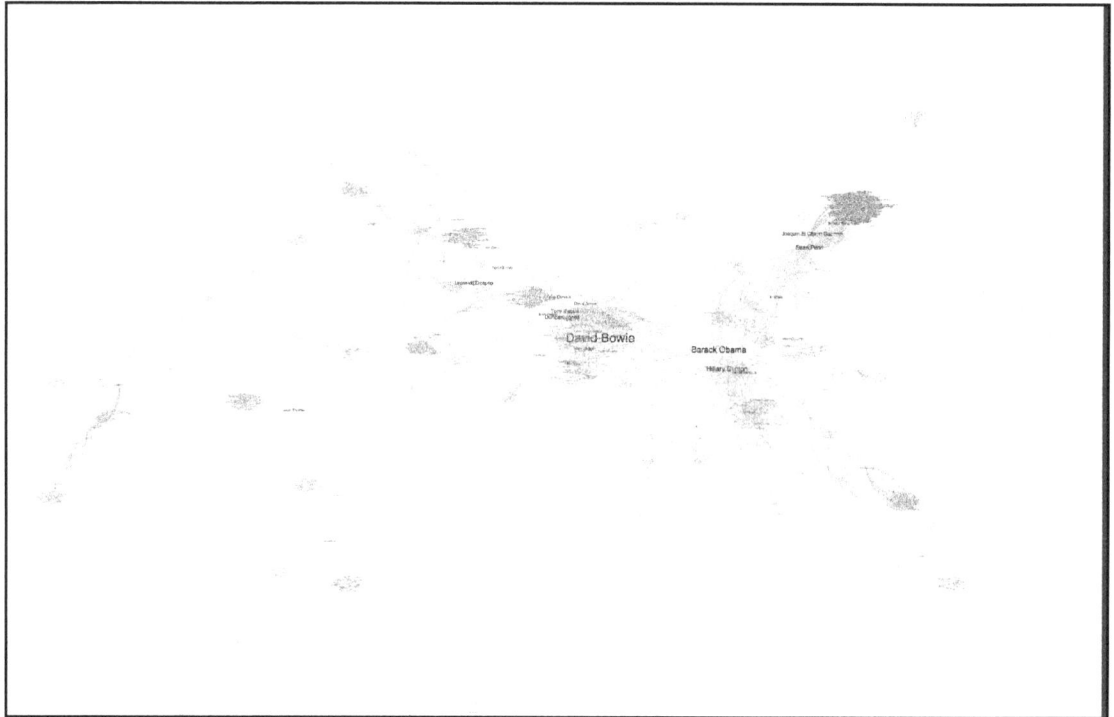

Figure 7: Community detection on January 12

We first observe that most of the communities we detected are totally aligned with the ones we could eyeball on a force-directed layout, giving a good confidence level about the algorithm accuracy.

The Bowie effect

Any well-defined community has been properly identified, and the less obvious ones are the ones surrounding highly connected vertices such as David Bowie. The name David Bowie being heavily mentioned in GDELT articles alongside so many different persons that, on that day of January 12, 2016, it became too large to be part of its logical community (music industry) and formed a broader community impacting all its surrounding vertices. There is definitely an interesting pattern here as this community structure gives us clear insights about a potential breaking news article for a particular person on a particular day.

Looking at the David Bowie's closest communities in *Figure 8*, we observe the nodes to be highly interconnected because of what we will be calling the *Bowie effect*. In fact, there have been so many tributes paid from so many various communities that the number of triangles formed across different communities has been abnormally high. As a result, it brought different logical communities closer to each other, communities that were theoretically not meant to be, such as the *70s* rock star idols close enough to religious people.

The small world phenomenon, as defined in the 60s by Stanley Milgram, states that everyone is connected through a short number of acquaintances. Kevin Bacon, an American actor, even suggested he would be connected to every other actor by a maximum depth of 6 connections, also known as its *Bacon Number* (`https://oracleofbacon.org/`).

On that day, the *Kevin Bacon Number* of Pope Francis and Mick Jagger was only 1 thanks to the Cardinal Gianfranco Ravasi who tweeted about David Bowie.

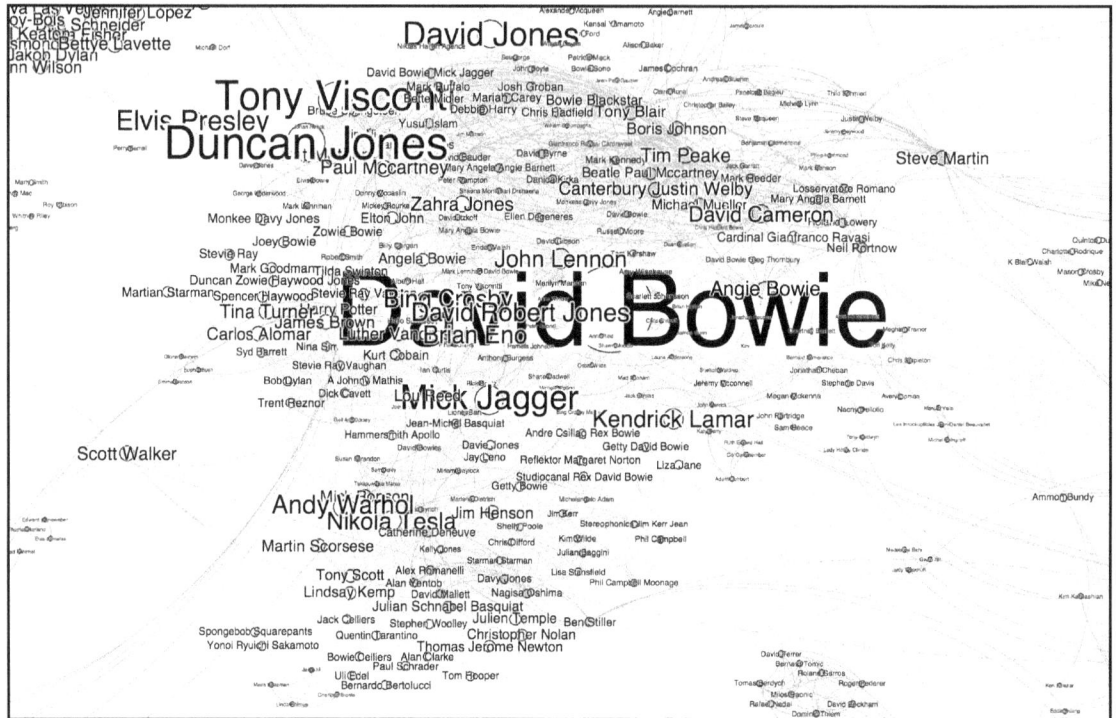

Figure 8: Communities surrounding David Bowie, January 12

Although the Bowie's effect, by its nature of a breaking news article, is a true pattern on that particular graph structure, its effect could have been minimized using weighted edges based on names frequency count. Indeed, some random noise from the GDELT dataset could be enough to close critical triangles from two different communities and therefore bring them close to each other, no matter the weight of this critical edge. This limitation is common for all un-weighted algorithms and would require a preprocessing phase to reduce this unwanted noise.

Smaller communities

We can, however, observe some more defined communities here, such as the UK politicians Tony Blair, David Cameron, and Boris Johnson or the movie directors Christopher Nolan, Martin Scorsese, or Quentin Tarantino. Looking at a broader level, we can detect well-defined communities, such as tennis players, footballers, artists, or politicians of a specific country. As an undeniable proof of accuracy, we even detected Matt Leblanc, Courtney Cox, Matthew Perry, and Jennifer Anniston as being part of a same Friends community and Luke Skywalker, Anakin Skywalker, Chewbacca, and Emperor Palpatine as part of the Star Wars community and its recently lost actress, Carrie Fisher. An example of professional boxer's communities is reported in *Figure 9*:

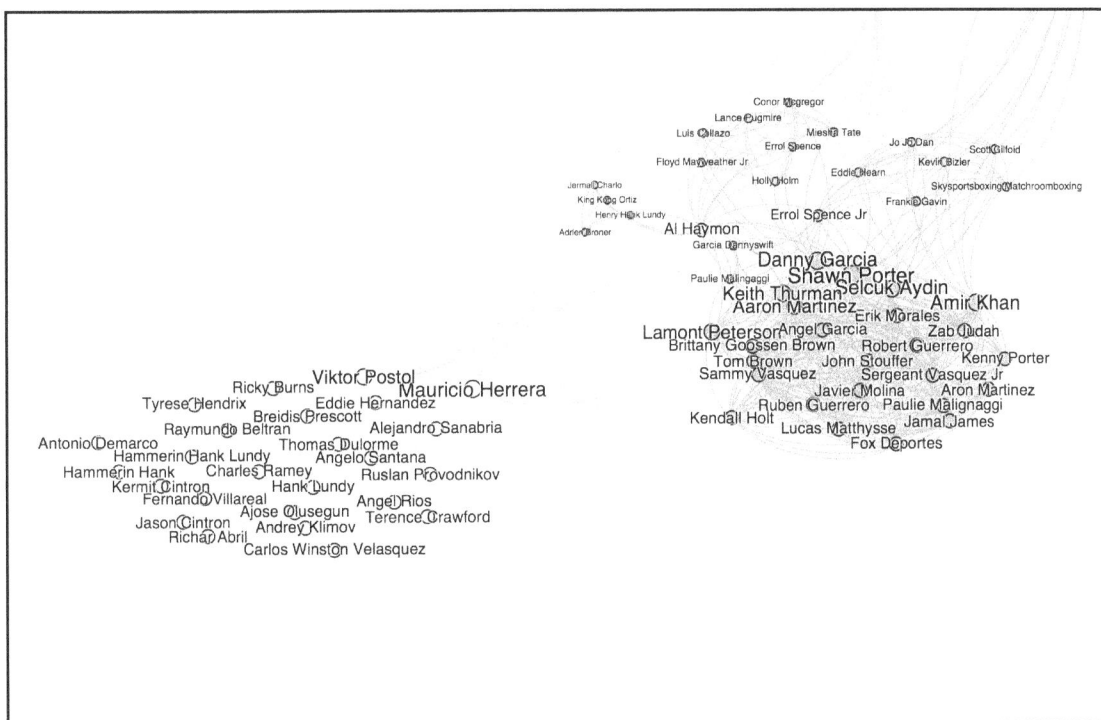

Figure 9: Professional boxer communities

Using Accumulo cell level security

We have previously discussed the nature of cell-level security in Accumulo. In the context of the graphs that we have produced here, the usefulness of security can be well simulated. If we configure Accumulo such that rows containing David Bowie are securely labeled differently to all other rows, then we can turn on and off the Bowie's effect. Any Accumulo user with full access will see the complete graph provided earlier. If we then restrict that user to everything other than David Bowie (a simple change to the Authorization in `AccumuloReader`), then we see the following figure. This new graph is very interesting as it serves a number of purposes:

- It removes the noise created by the social media effect of David Bowie's death, thereby revealing the true communities involved
- It removes many of the false links between entities, thereby increasing their Bacon number and showing their true relationship
- It demonstrates that it is possible to remove a key figure in a graph and still retain a large amount of useful information, thereby demonstrating the point made earlier regarding the removal of key entities for security reasons (as discussed in *Cell security*)

It also has to be said, of course, that by removing an entity, we may also be removing key relationships between entities; that is, the contact chaining effect and this is a negative aspect when specifically trying to relate individual entities-overall, the communities, however, remain intact.

Kendrick Lamar

Cardinal Gianfranco Ravasi

Mark Bleeder

Beatle Paul Mccartney

Neil Portnow

Losservatore Romano

Mick Jagger

Mary Angela Barnettier

Canterbury Justin Welby

Boris Johnson

Bing Crosby

Tim Peake Blair

David Cameron

James Brown

Stevie Ray

Luther Vandross

John Lennon

Brian Eno

Paul Mccartney

Yusuf Islam

Mariah Carey

Pat Metheny   Bruce Springsteen

Josh Groban

Harry Potter

Jim Nicole

Debbie Harry Bette Midler

Andy Warhol

Pharrell Williams

Chris Hadfield

Nikola Tesla

Tony Visconti
Duncan Jones

Ricky Gervais

Martin Scorsese

Elvis Presley

Bob Moore

Marie Osmond

Millie Kirsta Fisher

Cyndi L Mikkey Dee

Donny Edwards   Bennetts Holland Dubois

Shia Labeouf

Jamie Foxx   Pepe Dee Dave Grohl

Michael Keaton

Jack Daniels   Zicock Gallagher

Jennifer Lopez

Tom Hanks Baron Anne Wilson

Tony Steve Alejandro Gonz

Viva Las Vegas

Helen Mirren Dylan avette

Jakob Dylan

Taylor Kinney

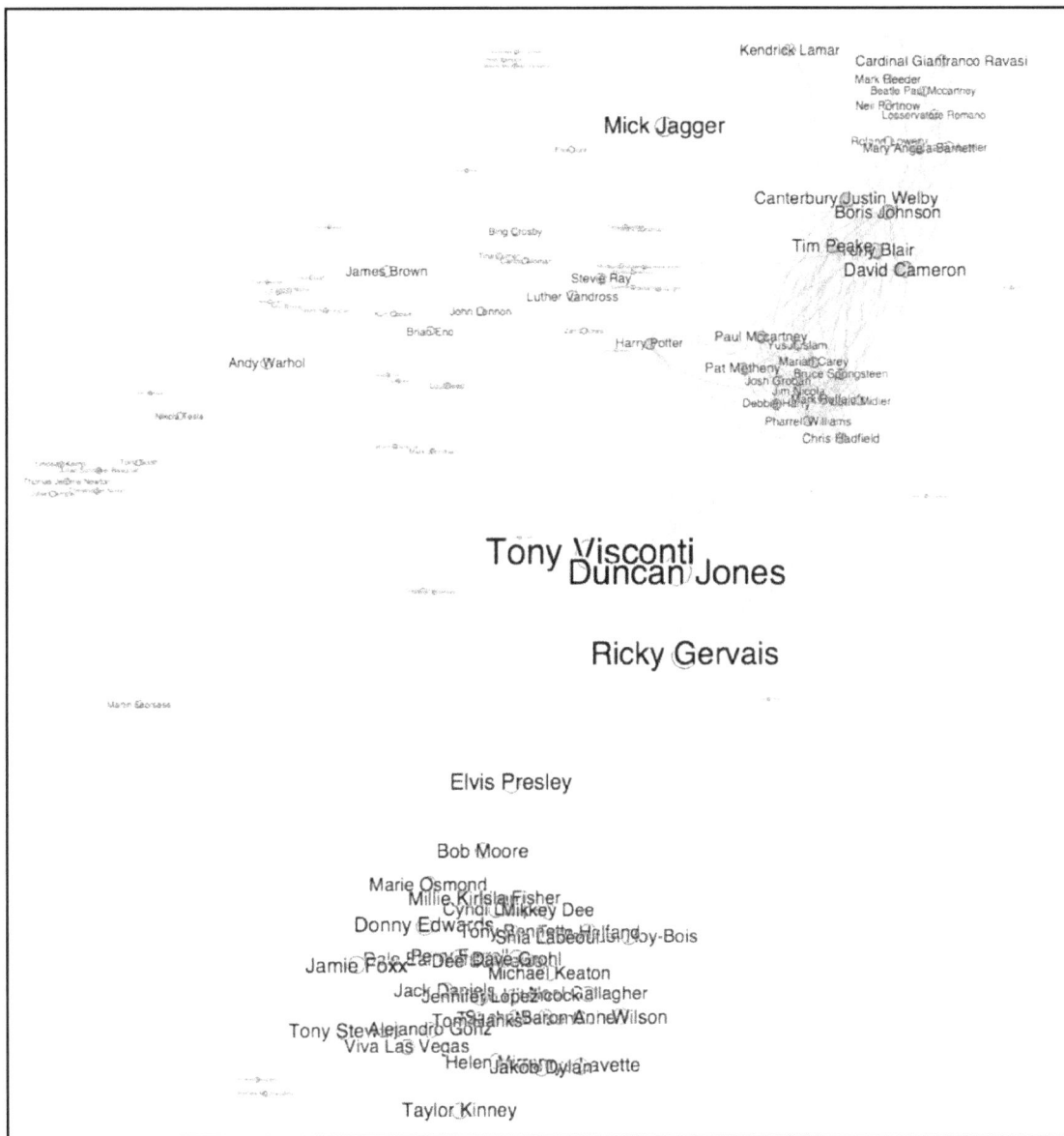

Figure 10: David Bowie's communities with restricted access

Summary

We have discussed and built a real-world implementation of graph communities leveraging the power of a secure and robust architecture. We have outlined the idea that there is no right or wrong solution in the community detection problem space, as it strongly depends on the use case. In a social network context, for example, where vertices are tightly connected together (an edge represents a true connection between two users), the edge weight does not really matter while the triangle approach probably does. In the telecommunication industry, one could be interested in the communities based on the frequency call of a given user A to a user B, hence turning to a weighted algorithm such as Louvain.

We appreciate that building this community algorithm was far from an easy task, and perhaps stretches the goals of this book, but it involves all of the techniques of graph processing in Spark that makes GraphX a fascinating and extensible tool. We introduced the concepts of message passing, Pregel, graph partitioning, and variable broadcast, backed by a real-world implementation in Elasticsearch and Accumulo.

In the next chapter, we will apply the concepts of graph theory we learned here to the music industry, learning how to build a music recommendation engine using audio signal, Fourier transforms, and *PageRank* algorithm.

8
Building a Recommendation System

If one were to choose an algorithm to showcase data science to the public, a recommendation system would certainly be in the frame. Today, recommendation systems are everywhere. The reason for their popularity is down to their versatility, usefulness, and broad applicability. Whether they are used to recommend products based on user's shopping behavior or to suggest new movies based on viewing preferences, recommenders are now a fact of life. It is even possible that this book was magically suggested based on what marketing companies know about you, such as your social network preferences, your job status, or your browsing history.

In this chapter, we will demonstrate how to recommend music content using raw audio signal. For that purpose, we will cover the following topics:

- Using Spark to process audio files stored on HDFS
- Learning about *Fourier transform* for audio signal transformation
- Using Cassandra as a caching layer between online and offline layers
- Using *PageRank* as an unsupervised recommendation algorithm
- Integrating Spark Job Server with the Play framework to build an end-to-end prototype

Different approaches

The end goal of a recommendation system is to suggest new items based on a user's historical usage and preferences. The basic idea is to use a ranking for any product that a customer has been interested in in the past. This ranking can be explicit (asking a user to rank a movie from 1 to 5) or implicit (how many times a user visited this page). Whether it is a product to buy, a song to listen to, or an article to read, data scientists usually address this issue from two different angles: *collaborative filtering* and *content-based filtering*.

Collaborative filtering

Using this approach, we leverage big data by collecting more information about the behavior of people. Although an individual is by definition unique, their shopping behavior is usually not, and some similarities can always be found with others. The recommended items will be targeted for a particular individual, but they will be derived by combining the user's behavior with that of similar users. This is the famous quote from most retail websites:

> *"People who bought this also bought that..."*

Of course, this requires prior knowledge about the customer, their past purchases and you must also have enough information about other customers to compare against. Therefore, a major limiting factor is that items must have been viewed at least once in order to be shortlisted as a potential recommended item. In fact, we cannot recommend an item until it has been seen/bought at least once.

> The iris dataset of collaborative filtering is usually done using samples of the LastFM
> dataset: `http://labrosa.ee.columbia.edu/millionsong/lastfm`.

Content-based filtering

An alternative approach, rather than using similarities with other users, involves looking at the product itself and the type of products a customer has been interested in in the past. If you are interested in both *classical music* and *speed metal*, it is safe to assume that you would probably buy (at least consider) any new albums mixing up both classical rhythms with heavy metal riffs. Such a recommendation would be difficult to find in a collaborative filtering approach as no one in your neighborhood shares your musical taste.

The main advantage of this approach is that, assuming we have enough knowledge about the content to recommend (such as the categories, labels, and so on), we can recommend a new item even when no one has seen it before. The downside is that the model can be more difficult to build and selecting the right features with no loss of information can be challenging.

Custom approach

As the focus of this book is *Mastering Spark for Data Science* we wish to provide the reader with a new and innovative way of addressing the recommendation issue, rather than just explaining the standard collaborative filtering algorithm that anyone could build using the out-of-the-box Spark APIs and following a basic tutorial `http://spark.apache.org/docs/latest/mllib-collaborative-filtering.html`. Let's start with a hypothesis:

If we were to recommend songs to end-users, couldn't we build a system that would recommend songs, not based on what people like or dislike, nor on the song attributes (genre, artist), but rather on how the song really sounds and how you feel about it?

In order to demonstrate how to build such a system, (and since you likely do not have access to a public dataset containing both music content and ranking a legitimate one at least), we will explain how to construct it locally using your own personal music library. Feel free to play along!

Uninformed data

The following technique could be seen as something of a game changer in how most modern data scientists work. While it is common to work with structured and unstructured text, it is less common to work on raw binary data the reason being the gap between computer science and data science. Textual processing is limited to a standard set of operations that most will be familiar with, that is, acquiring, parsing and storing, and so on. Instead of restricting ourselves to these operations, we will work directly with audio transforming and enrich the uninformed signal data into informed transcription. In doing this, we enable a new type of data pipeline that is analogous to teaching a computer to *hear* the voice from audio files.

A second (breakthrough) idea that we encourage here is a shift in thinking around how data scientists engage with Hadoop and big data nowadays. While many still consider these technologies as just *yet another database*, we want to showcase the vast array of possibilities that become available with these tools. After all, no one laughs at the data scientist who can train a machine to talk to customers or make sense of call center recordings.

Processing bytes

The first thing to consider is the audio file format. The `.wav` files can be processed pretty much as they are using the `AudioSystem` library (from `javax.sound`), while an `.mp3` would require pre-processing using external codec libraries. If we read a file from an `InputStream`, we can create an output byte array containing audio signals as follows:

```
def readFile(song: String) = {
  val is = new FileInputStream(song)
   processSong(is)
}
def processSong(stream: InputStream): Array[Byte] = {

  val bufferedIn = new BufferedInputStream(stream)
  val out = new ByteArrayOutputStream
  val audioInputStream = AudioSystem.getAudioInputStream(bufferedIn)

  val format = audioInputStream.getFormat
  val sizeTmp = Math.rint((format.getFrameRate *
              format.getFrameSize) /
              format.getFrameRate)
            .toInt

  val size = (sizeTmp + format.getFrameSize) -
            (sizeTmp % format.getFrameSize)
```

```
val buffer = new Array[Byte](size)

var available = true
var totalRead = 0
while (available) {
  val c = audioInputStream.read(buffer, 0, size)
  totalRead += c
  if (c > -1) {
    out.write(buffer, 0, c)
  } else {
    available = false
  }
}

audioInputStream.close()
out.close()
out.toByteArray
}
```

Songs are usually encoded using a sample rate of 44KHz, which, according to the **Nyquist** theorem, is twice as large as the highest frequency that the human ear can perceive (covering ranges from 20Hz to 20KHz).

> For more information about the Nyquist theorem, please visit: `http://red` `wood.berkeley.edu/bruno/npb261/aliasing.pdf`.

In order to represent the sound that a human being can hear, we would need around 44,000 samples per seconds, hence 176,400 bytes per second for stereo (two channels). The latter is the following byte frequency:

```
val format = audioInputStream.getFormat

val sampleRate = format.getSampleRate

val sizeTmp = Math.rint((format.getFrameRate *
             format.getFrameSize) /
             format.getFrameRate)
           .toInt

  val size = (sizeTmp + format.getFrameSize) -
         (sizeTmp % format.getFrameSize)

  val byteFreq = format.getFrameSize * format.getFrameRate.toInt
```

Finally, we access the audio signal by processing the output byte array and plotting the first few bytes of our sample data (in this case, *Figure 1*, shows the Mario Bros theme song). Note the timestamp that can be retrieved using both the byte index and the byte frequency values, like so:

```
val data: Array[Byte] = processSong(inputStream)

val timeDomain: Array[(Double, Int)] = data
  .zipWithIndex
  .map { case (b, idx) =>
      (minTime + idx * 1000L / byteFreq.toDouble, b.toInt)
  }
```

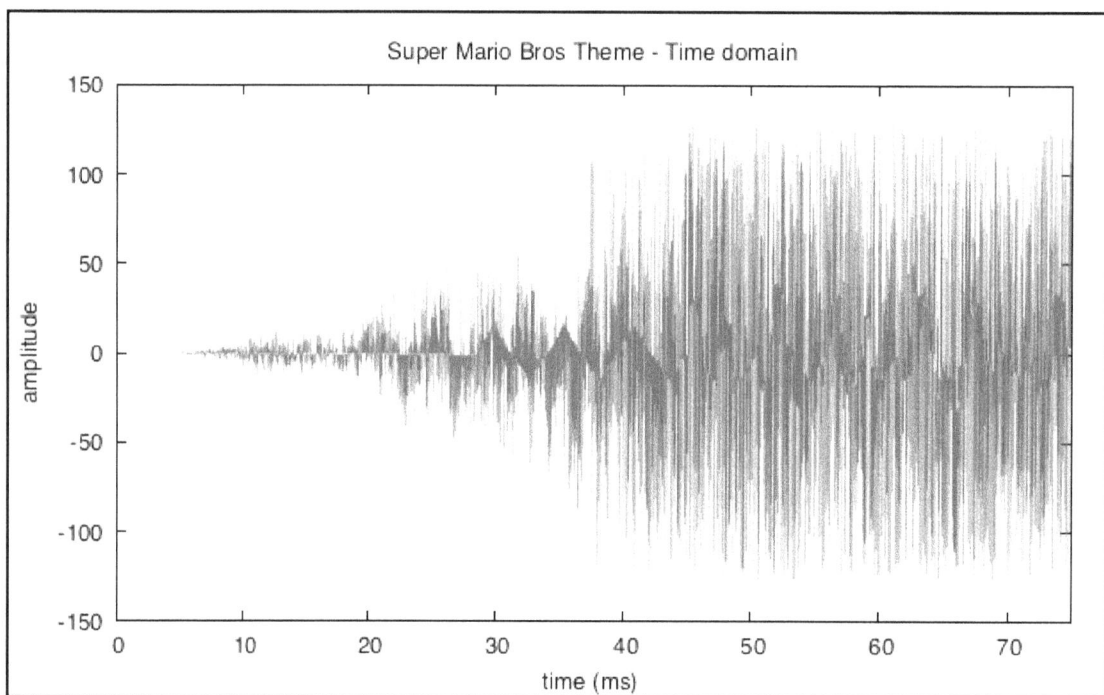

Figure 1: Mario Bros theme – time domain

For convenience, we wrap all these audio characteristics into a case class `Audio` (shown in the following snippet) to which we will add additional utility methods as we go along in the chapter:

```
case class Audio(data: Array[Byte],
                 byteFreq: Int,
                 sampleRate: Float,
```

```
                    minTime: Long,
                    id: Int= 0) {

    def duration: Double =
      (data.length + 1) * 1000L / byteFreq.toDouble

    def timeDomain: Array[(Double, Int)] = data
      .zipWithIndex
      .map { case (b, idx) =>
          (minTime + idx * 1000L / byteFreq.toDouble, b.toInt)
      }

    def findPeak: Float = {
      val freqDomain = frequencyDomain()
      freqDomain
        .sortBy(_._2)
        .reverse
        .map(_._1)
        .head
    }

    // Next to come

}
```

Creating a scalable code

Now that we have created functions to extract audio signals from `.wav` files (via a `FileInputStream`), naturally the next step is to use it to process the remaining records stored on HDFS. As already highlighted in previous chapters, this isn't a difficult task once the logic works on a single record. In fact, Spark comes with a utility to process binary data out of the box, so we simply plug in the following function:

```
def read(library: String, sc: SparkContext) = {
  sc.binaryFiles(library)
    .filter { case (filename, stream) =>
      filename.endsWith(".wav")
    }
    .map { case (filename, stream) =>
      val audio =  processSong(stream.open())
      (filename, audio)
    }
}

val audioRDD: RDD[(String, Audio)] = read(library, sc)
```

We make sure we only send `.wav` files to our processor and get a new RDD made of a filename (the song name) and its corresponding `Audio` case class (including the extracted audio signal).

> The `binaryFiles` method of Spark reads a file whole (without splitting it) and outputs an RDD containing both the file path and its corresponding input stream. Therefore, it is advised to work on relatively small files (perhaps just a few megabytes) as it clearly affects memory consumption and hence performance.

From time to frequency domain

Accessing the audio time domain is a great achievement, but sadly it's not much value on its own. However, we can use it to better understand what the signal truly represents, that is, to extract the hidden frequencies it comprises. Naturally, we can convert the time domain signal to a frequency domain using *Fourier transform*.

> You can learn more about *Fourier transform* at `http://www.phys.hawaii.e du/~jgl/p274/fourier_intro_Shatkay.pdf`.

As a summary, without going into too much detail or having to tackle the complex equations, the basic assumption that Joseph Fourier makes in his legendary and eponymous formula is that all signals are made of an infinite accumulation of sine waves from different frequencies and phases.

Fast Fourier transform

Discrete Fourier transform (**DFT**) is the summation of different sine waves and can be represented using the following equation:

$$F(n) = \sum_{k=0}^{N-1} x(k)e^{\frac{-j2\pi kn}{N}}$$

Although this algorithm is trivial to implement using a brute force approach, it is highly inefficient $O(n^2)$ since for each data point n, we have to compute the sum of n exponents. Therefore, a three-minute song would generate $(3 \times 60 \times 176,400)^2 \approx 10^{15}$ number of operations. Instead, Cooley and Tukey contributed a **Fast Fourier transform** (**FFT**) using a divide and conquer approach to the DFT that reduces the overall time complexity to $O(n.log(n))$.

The official paper describing the Cooley and Tukey algorithm can be found online: http://www.ams.org/journals/mcom/1965-19-090/S0025-5718-19 65-0178586-1/S0025-5718-1965-0178586-1.pdf

Fortunately for us, there are existing FFT implementations available, and so we will compute the FFT using a Java-based library provided by `org.apache.commons.math3`. When using this library, we need only to ensure that our input data is padded with zeros so that the total length is a power of two and can be divided into odd and even sequences:

```
def fft(): Array[Complex] = {

  val array = Audio.paddingToPowerOf2(data)
  val transformer = new FastFourierTransformer(
                        DftNormalization.STANDARD)

  transformer.transform(array.map(_.toDouble),
      TransformType.FORWARD)

}
```

This returns an array of `Complex` numbers that are made of real and imaginary parts and can be easily converted to a frequency and amplitude (or magnitude) as follows. According to the Nyquist theorem, we only need half the frequencies:

```
def frequencyDomain(): Array[(Float, Double)] = {

  val t = fft()
  t.take(t.length / 2) // Nyquist
  .zipWithIndex
  .map { case (c, idx) =>
    val freq = (idx + 1) * sampleRate / t.length
    val amplitude =  sqrt(pow(c.getReal, 2) +
                        pow(c.getImaginary, 2))
    val db = 20 * log10(amplitude)
    (freq, db)
  }

}
```

Finally, we include these functions in the `Audio` case class and plot the frequency domain for the first few seconds of the Mario Bros theme song:

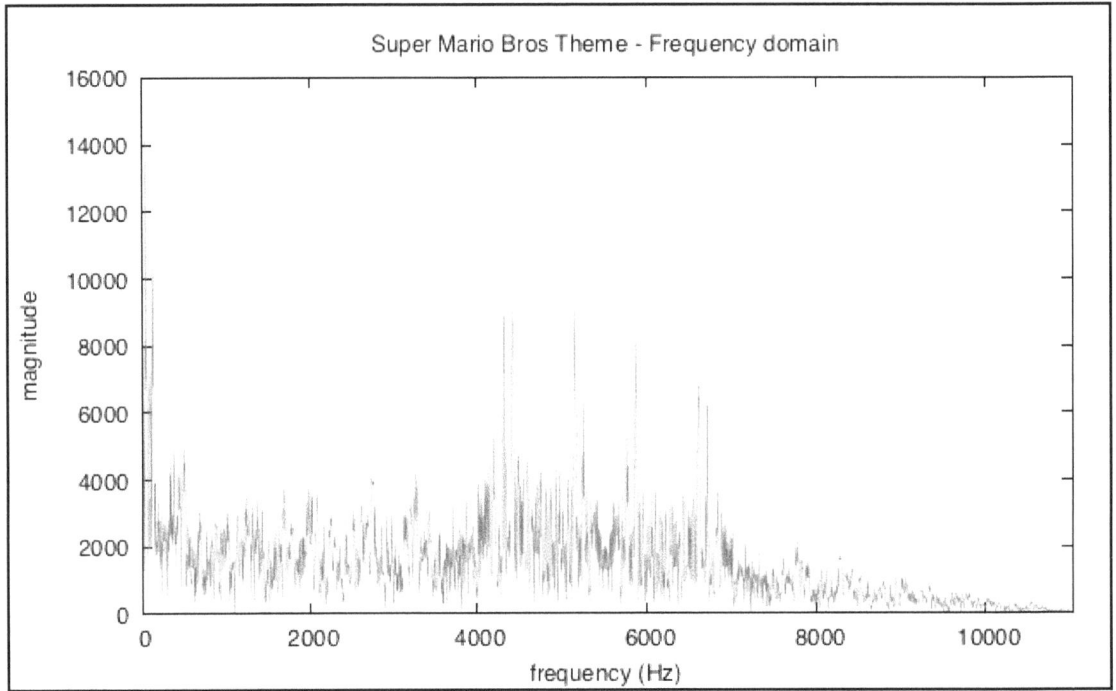

Figure 2: Mario Bros theme – frequency domain

In Figure 2, significant peaks can be seen in the medium-high frequency range (between 4KHz and 7KHz) and we will use these as a fingerprint for the song.

Sampling by time window

Although more efficient, the FFT is still an expensive operation due to its high memory consumption (remember, a typical three-minute song would have around *3 x 60 x 176,400* points to process). This becomes especially problematic when applied to a large number of data points and so must be taken into consideration for large scale processing.

Instead of looking at the full spectrum, we sample our songs using a time window. In fact, a full FFT wouldn't be of any use anyway since we want to know the time each major frequency was heard. Therefore, we iteratively split each `Audio` class into smaller case classes of 20 millisecond samples. This timeframe should be small enough for the purpose of analysis meaning small enough so that the FFT can be computed and dense enough to ensure that sufficient frequencies are extracted to provide an adequate audio fingerprint. The produced chunks of 20 milliseconds will drastically increase the overall size of our RDD:

```
def sampleByTime(duration: Double = 20.0d,
                 padding: Boolean = true): List[Audio] = {

  val  size = (duration * byteFreq / 1000.0f).toInt
  sample(size, padding)

}

def sample(size: Int= math.pow(2, 20).toInt,
         padding: Boolean = true): List[Audio] = {

  Audio
    .sample(data, size, padding)
    .zipWithIndex
    .map { case (sampleAudio, idx) =>
      val firstByte = idx * size
      val firstTime = firstByte * 1000L / byteFreq.toLong
      Audio(
          sampleAudio,
          byteFreq,
          sampleRate,
          firstTime,
          idx
      )
    }

}

val sampleRDD = audioRDDflatMap { case (song, audio) =>
  audio.sampleByTime()
    .map { sample =>
      (song, sample)
    }
}
```

> **TIP**
>
> While this is not our primary focus, one could rebuild the full FFT spectrum of the entire signal by recombining samples with inner and outer FFT and applying a twiddle factor `https://en.wikipedia.org/wiki/Twiddle_factor`. This could be useful when processing large records with a limited amount of available memory.

Extracting audio signatures

Now we have multiple samples at regular time intervals, we can extract frequency signatures using FFT. In order to generate a sample signature, instead of using the exact peak (which could be approximate), we try to find the closest note in different frequency bands. This offers an approximation, but in doing so it overcomes any noise issues present in the original signal, as noise interferes with our signatures.

We look at the following frequency bands 20-60 Hz, 60-250Hz, 250-2000Hz, 2-4Kz, and 4-6Kz and find the closest note according to the following frequency reference table. These bands are not random. They correspond to the different ranges of musical instruments (for example, double bass spans between 50 to 200Hz, piccolo from 500 to 5KHz).

	C	C#	D	Eb	E	F	F#	G	G#	A	Bb	B
0	16.35	17.32	18.35	19.45	20.60	21.83	23.12	24.50	25.96	27.50	29.14	30.87
1	32.70	34.65	36.71	38.89	41.20	43.65	46.25	49.00	51.91	55.00	58.27	61.74
2	65.41	69.30	73.42	77.78	82.41	87.31	92.50	98.00	103.8	110.0	116.5	123.5
3	130.8	138.6	146.8	155.6	164.8	174.6	185.0	196.0	207.7	220.0	233.1	246.9
4	261.6	277.2	293.7	311.1	329.6	349.2	370.0	392.0	415.3	440.0	466.2	493.9
5	523.3	554.4	587.3	622.3	659.3	698.5	740.0	784.0	830.6	880.0	932.3	987.8
6	1047	1109	1175	1245	1319	1397	1480	1568	1661	1760	1865	1976
7	2093	2217	2349	2489	2637	2794	2960	3136	3322	3520	3729	3951
8	4186	4435	4699	4978	5274	5588	5920	6272	6645	7040	7459	7902

Figure 3: Frequency note reference table

Figure 4, shows the first sample of our Mario Bros theme song in a lower frequency band. We can see that the highest magnitude of 43Hz corresponds to the prime octave of note **F**:

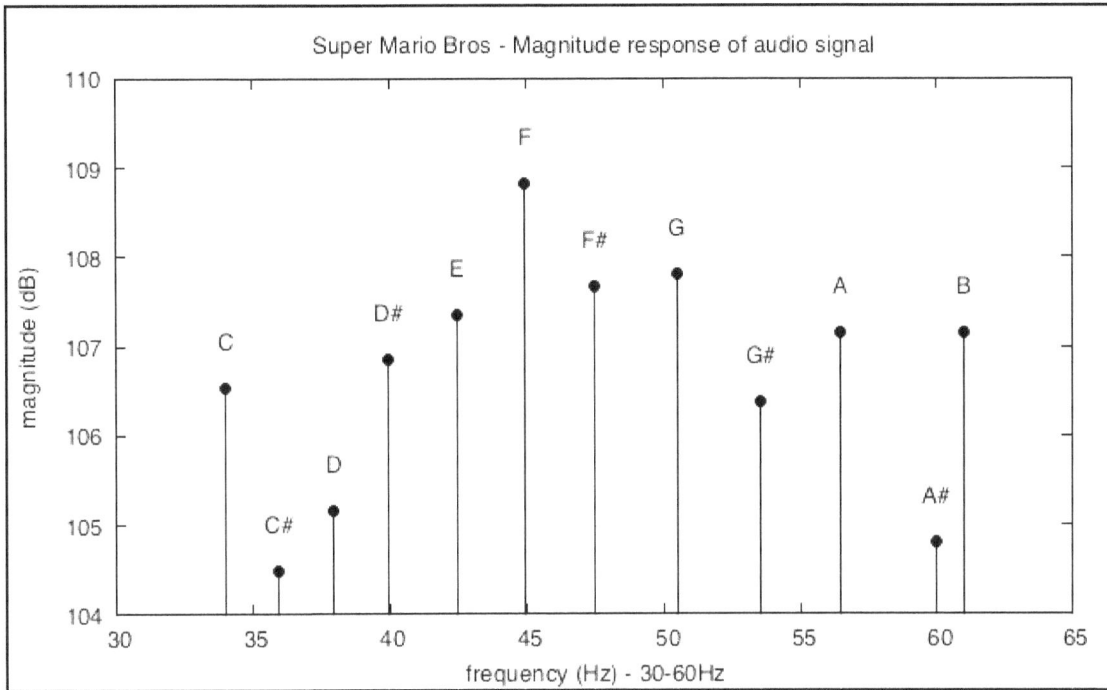

Figure 4: Mario Bros theme-lower frequencies

For each sample, we build a hash composed of five letters (such as [**E–D#–A–B–B–F**]) corresponding to the strongest note (the highest peak) in each of the preceding frequency bands. We consider this hash a fingerprint for that particular 20 milliseconds time window. We then build a new RDD made of hash values as follows (we include a hashing function within our `Audio` case class):

```
def hash: String = {
  val freqDomain = frequencyDomain()
  freqDomain.groupBy { case (fq, db) =>
    Audio.getFrequencyBand(fq)
  }.map { case (bucket, frequencies) =>
    val (dominant, _) = frequencies.map { case (fq, db) =>
      (Audio.findClosestNote(fq), db)
    }.sortBy { case (note, db) =>
      db
    }.last
    (bucket, dominant)
```

```
  }.toList
  .sortBy(_._1)
  .map(_._2)
  .mkString("-")
}


/*
001 Amadeus Mozart - Requiem (K. 626)          E-D#-A-B-B-F
001 Amadeus Mozart - Requiem (K. 626)          G#-D-F#-B-B-F
001 Amadeus Mozart - Requiem (K. 626)          F#-F#-C-B-C-F
001 Amadeus Mozart - Requiem (K. 626)          E-F-F#-B-B-F
001 Amadeus Mozart - Requiem (K. 626)          E-F#-C#-B-B-F
001 Amadeus Mozart - Requiem (K. 626)          B-E-F-A#-C#-F
*/
```

Now we group all song IDs sharing the same hash in order to build an RDD of unique hashes:

```
case class HashSongsPair(
                          id: String,
                          songs: List[Long]
                        )

val hashRDD = sampleRDD.map { case (id, sample) =>
  (sample.hash, id)
}
.groupByKey()
.map { case (id, songs) =>
  HashSongsPair(id, songs.toList)
}
```

Our assumption is that when a hash is defined in a song at a particular time window, similar songs could potentially share similar hashes, but two songs having all the same hashes (and in order) would be truly identical; one could share part of my DNA, but one having the exact same DNA would be a perfect clone of myself.

If a music aficionado is feeling blessed listening to the *concerto in D* by Tchaikovsky, can we recommend *Pachelbel's Canon in D* just because both of them share a musical cadence (that is, common frequencies around *D*)?

Is it valid (and feasible) to recommend playlists that are only based on certain frequency bands? Surely the frequencies themselves would not be enough to fully describe a song. What about tempo, timbre, or rhythm? Is this model complete enough to accurately represent all the nuances of musical diversity and range? Probably not, but for the purpose of data science, it's worth investigating anyway!

Building a song analyzer

However, before deep diving into the recommender itself, the reader may have noticed an important property that we were able to extract out of the signal data. Since we generated audio signatures at regular time intervals, we can compare signatures and find potential duplicates. For example, given a random song, we should be able to guess the title, based on previously indexed signatures. In fact, this is the exact approach taken by many companies when providing music recognition services. To take it one step further, we could potentially provide insight into a band's musical influences, or further, perhaps even identify song plagiarism, once and for all settling the *Stairway to Heaven* dispute between Led Zeppelin and the American rock band Spirit `http://consequenceofsound.net/2014/05/did-led-zeppelin-steal-stairway-to-heaven-legendary-rock-band-facing-lawsuit-from-former-tourmates/`.

With this in mind, we will take a detour from our recommendation use case by continuing our investigation into song identification a little further. Next, we build an analyzer system capable of anonymously receiving a song, analyzing its stream, and returning the title of the song (in our case, the original filename).

Selling data science is all about selling cupcakes

Sadly, an all too often neglected aspect of the data science journey is data visualization. In other words, how to present your results back to end users. While many data scientists are content to present their findings in an Excel spreadsheet, today's end users are keen for richer, more immersive experiences. Often they want to play around, *interacting* with data. Indeed, providing an end user with a full, end-to-end user experience even a simple one can be a great way to spark interest in your science; making a simple proof of concept into a prototype people can easily understand. And due to the prevalence of Web 2.0 technologies, user expectations are high, but thankfully, there are a variety of free, open source products that can help, for example, Mike Bostock's D3.js, is a popular framework that provides a toolkit for creating just such user interfaces.

Selling data science without rich data visualization is like trying to sell a cake without icing, few people will trust in the finished product. Therefore, we will build a user interface for our analyzer system. But first, let's get the audio data out of Spark (our hashes are currently stored in memory inside an RDD) and into a web-scale datastore.

Using Cassandra

We need a fast, efficient, and distributed key-value store to keep all our hash values. Although many databases are fit for this purpose, we'll choose Cassandra in order to demonstrate its integration with Spark. First, import the Cassandra input and output formats using the Maven dependency:

```
<dependency>
  <groupId>com.datastax.spark</groupId>
  <artifactId>spark-cassandra-connector_2.11</artifactId>
  <version>2.0.0</version>
</dependency>
```

As you would expect, persisting (and retrieving) RDDs from Spark to Cassandra is relatively trivial:

```
import com.datastax.spark.connector._

val keyspace = "gzet"
val table = "hashes"

// Persist RDD
hashRDD.saveAsCassandraTable(keyspace, table)

// Retrieve RDD
val retrievedRDD = sc.cassandraTable[HashSongsPair](
  keyspace,
  table
)
```

This will create a new table `hashes` on keyspace `gzet`, inferring the schema from the `HashSongsPair` object. The following is the equivalent SQL statement executed (provided here for information only):

```
CREATE TABLE gzet.hashes (
  id text PRIMARY KEY,
  songs list<bigint>
)
```

Using the Play framework

As our Web UI will front the complex processing required to transform a song into frequency hashes, we want it to be an interactive web application rather than a simple set of static HTML pages. Furthermore, this must be done in the exact same way and with the same functions as we did using Spark (that is, the same song should generate the same hashes). The Play framework (`https://www.playframework.com/`) will allow us to do this, and Twitter's bootstrap (`http://getbootstrap.com/`) will be used to put the icing on the cake, for a more professional look and feel.

Although this book is not about building user interfaces, we will introduce some concepts related to the Play framework, as if used well it can provide a source of great value for data scientists. As always, the full code is available in our GitHub repository.

First, we create a **data access layer**, responsible for handling connections and queries to Cassandra. For any given hash, we return the list of matching song IDs. Similarly, for any given ID, we return the song name:

```
val cluster = Cluster
  .builder()
  .addContactPoint(cassandraHost)
  .withPort(cassandraPort)
  .build()
val session = cluster.connect()

  def findSongsByHash(hash: String): List[Long] = {
    val stmt = s"SELECT songs FROM hashes WHERE id = '$hash';"
    val results = session.execute(stmt)
    results flatMap { row =>
      row.getList("songs", classOf[Long])
    }
    .toList
  }
```

Next, we create a simple **view**, made of three objects, a `text` field, a file `Upload`, and a `submit` button. These few lines are enough to provide our user interface:

```
<div>
    <input type="text" class="form-control">
    <span class="input-group-btn">
      <button class="btn-primary">Upload</button>
      <button class="btn-success">Analyze</button>
    </span>
</div>
```

Then we create a **controller** that will handle both GET and POST HTTP requests through the index and submit methods, respectively. The latter will process the uploaded file by converting a FileInputStream into an Audio case class, splitting it into 20 millisecond chunks, extracting the FFT signatures (hashes) and querying Cassandra for matching IDs:

```
def index = Action { implicit request =>
  Ok(views.html.analyze("Select a wav file to analyze"))
}

def submit = Action(parse.multipartFormData) { request =>
  request.body.file("song").map { upload =>
    val file = new File(s"/tmp/${UUID.randomUUID()}")
    upload.ref.moveTo(file)
    val song = process(file)
    if(song.isEmpty) {
      Redirect(routes.Analyze.index())
        .flashing("warning" -> s"No match")
    } else {
      Redirect(routes.Analyze.index())
        .flashing("success" -> song.get)
    }
  }.getOrElse {
    Redirect(routes.Analyze.index())
      .flashing("error" -> "Missing file")
  }
}

def process(file: File): Option[String] = {
  val is = new FileInputStream(file)
  val audio = Audio.processSong(is)
  val potentialMatches = audio.sampleByTime().map {a =>
    queryCassandra(a.hash)
  }
  bestMatch(potentialMatches)
}
```

Finally, we return the matching result (if any) through a flashing message and we chain both the view and controller together by defining our new routes for our `Analyze` service:

```
GET      /analyze        controllers.Analyze.index
POST     /analyze        controllers.Analyze.submit
```

The resulting UI is reported in *Figure 5*, and works perfectly with our own music library:

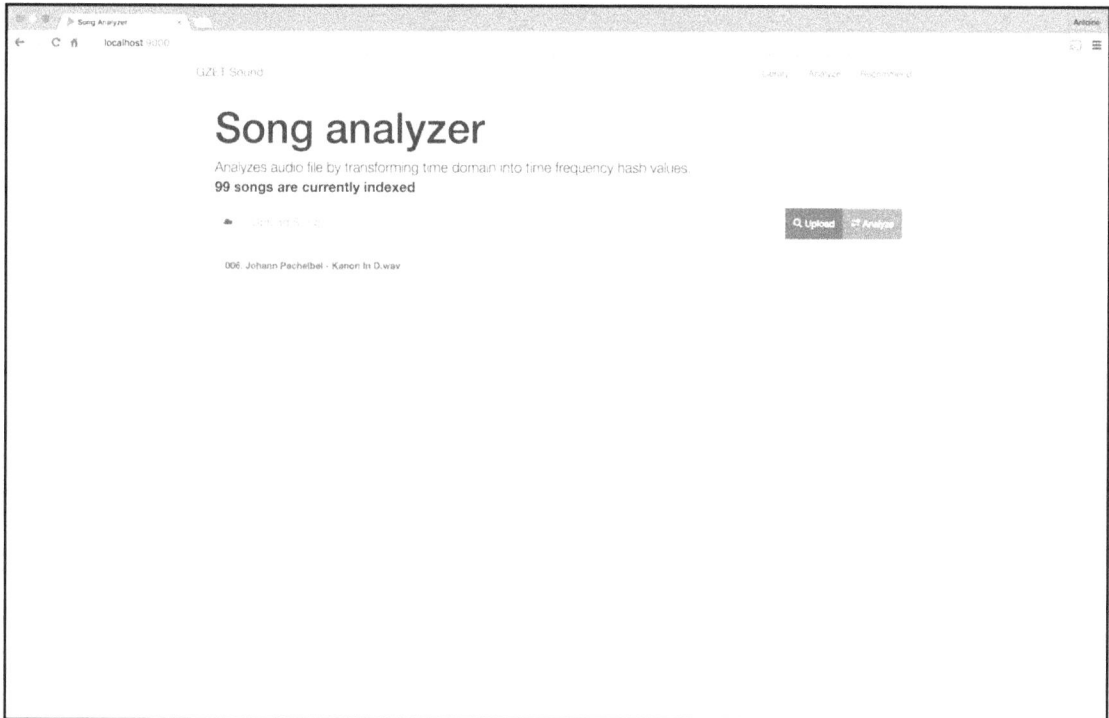

Figure 5: Sound analyser UI

The following *Figure 6* shows the end-to-end process:

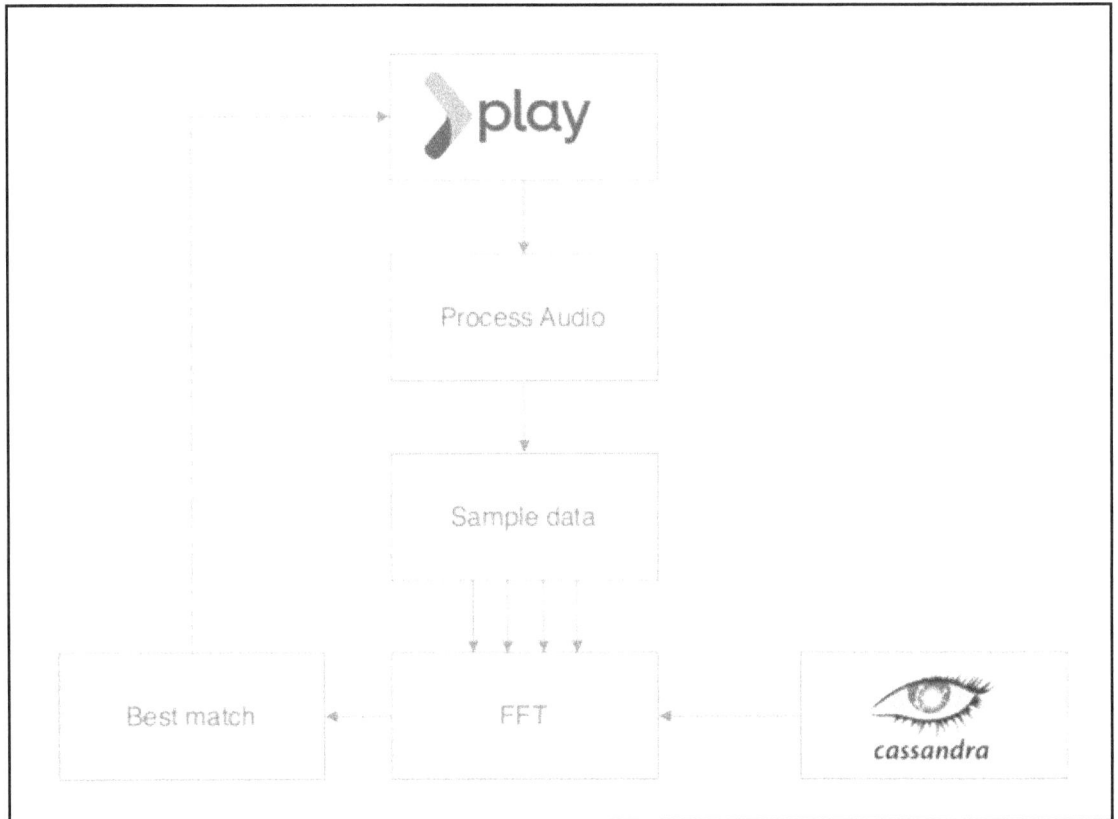

Figure 6: Sound analyser process

As mentioned, the Play framework shares some pieces of code with our offline Spark job. This is made possible because we are programming in a functional style and have applied a good separation of concerns. While the Play framework does not work natively with Spark (in terms of RDDs and Spark context objects), because they are not dependent on Spark, we can use any of the functions we created earlier (such as the ones in the Audio class). This is one of the many advantages of functional programming; functions, by definition, are stateless and represent a key component in the adoption of a hexagonal **architecture**: `http ://wiki.c2.com/?HexagonalArchitecture`. Isolated functions can always be called by different actors, whether it is inside of an RDD or within a Play controller.

Building a recommender

Now that we've explored our song analyzer, let's get back on track with the recommendation engine. As discussed earlier, we would like to recommend songs based on frequency hashes extracted from audio signals. Taking as an example the dispute between Led Zeppelin and Spirit, we would expect both songs to be relatively close to each other, as the allegation is that they share a melody. Using this thought as our main assumption, we could potentially recommend *Taurus* to someone interested in *Stairway to Heaven*.

The PageRank algorithm

Instead of recommending a specific song, we will recommend playlists. A playlist would consist of a list of all our songs ranked by relevance, most to least relevant. Let's begin with the assumption that people listen to music in a similar way to the way they browse articles on the web, that is, following a logical path from link to link, but occasionally switching direction, or teleporting, and browsing to a totally different website. Continuing with the analogy, while listening to music one can either carry on listening to music of a similar style (and hence follow their most expected journey), or skip to a random song in a totally different genre. It turns out that this is exactly how Google ranks websites by popularity using a **PageRank** algorithm.

> For more details on the PageRank algorithm visit: `http://ilpubs.stanfo rd.edu:8090/422/1/1999-66.pdf`.

The popularity of a website is measured by the number of links it points to (and is referred from). In our music use case, the popularity is built as the number hashes a given song shares with all its neighbors. Instead of popularity, we introduce the concept of song commonality.

Building a Graph of Frequency Co-occurrence

We start by reading our hash values back from Cassandra and re-establishing the list of song IDs for each distinct hash. Once we have this, we can count the number of hashes for each song using a simple `reduceByKey` function, and because the audio library is relatively small, we collect and broadcast it to our Spark executors:

```
val hashSongsRDD = sc.cassandraTable[HashSongsPair]("gzet", "hashes")

val songHashRDD = hashSongsRDD flatMap { hash =>
```

```
      hash.songs map { song =>
        ((hash, song), 1)
      }
    }

  val songTfRDD = songHashRDD map { case ((hash,songId),count) =>
      (songId, count)
    } reduceByKey(_+_)

  val songTf = sc.broadcast(songTfRDD.collectAsMap())
```

Next, we build a co-occurrence matrix by getting the cross product of every song sharing a same hash value, and count how many times the same tuple is observed. Finally, we wrap the song IDs and the normalized (using the term frequency we just broadcast) frequency count inside of an Edge class from GraphX:

```
  implicit class Crossable[X](xs: Traversable[X]) {
      def cross[Y](ys: Traversable[Y]) = for { x <- xs; y <- ys } yield (x,
  y)

  val crossSongRDD = songHashRDD.keys
      .groupByKey()
      .values
      .flatMap { songIds =>
          songIds cross songIds filter { case (from, to) =>
            from != to
      }.map(_ -> 1)
    }.reduceByKey(_+_)
      .map { case ((from, to), count) =>
        val weight = count.toDouble /
                    songTfB.value.getOrElse(from, 1)
        Edge(from, to, weight)
    }.filter { edge =>
      edge.attr > minSimilarityB.value
    }

  val graph = Graph.fromEdges(crossSongRDD, 0L)
```

We are only keeping edges with a weight (meaning a hash co-occurrence) greater than a predefined threshold in order to build our hash frequency graph.

Running PageRank

Contrary to what one would normally expect when running a PageRank, our graph is undirected. It turns out that for our recommender, the lack of direction does not matter, since we are simply trying to find similarities between Led Zeppelin and Spirit. A possible way of introducing direction could be to look at the song publishing date. In order to find musical influences, we could certainly introduce a chronology from the oldest to newest songs giving directionality to our edges.

In the following `pageRank`, we define a probability of 15% to skip, or **teleport** as it is known, to any random song, but this can be obviously tuned for different needs:

```
val prGraph = graph.pageRank(0.001, 0.15)
```

Finally, we extract the page ranked vertices and save them as a playlist in Cassandra via an RDD of the `Song` case class:

```
case class Song(id: Long, name: String, commonality: Double)
val vertices = prGraph
  .vertices
  .mapPartitions { vertices =>
    val songIds = songIdsB
  .value
  .vertices
  .map { case (songId, pr) =>
      val songName = songIds.get(vId).get
        Song(songId, songName, pr)
      }
  }

vertices.saveAsCassandraTable("gzet", "playlist")
```

The reader may be pondering the exact purpose of PageRank here, and how it could be used as a recommender? In fact, our use of PageRank means that the highest ranking songs would be the ones that share many frequencies with other songs. This could be due to a common arrangement, key theme, or melody; or maybe because a particular artist was a major influence on a musical trend. However, these songs should be, at least in theory, more popular (by virtue of the fact they occur more often), meaning that they are more likely to have mass appeal.

On the other end of the spectrum, low ranking songs are ones where we did not find any similarity with anything we know. Either these songs are so avant-garde that no one has explored these musical ideas before, or alternatively are so bad that no one ever wanted to copy them! Maybe they were even composed by that up-and-coming artist you were listening to in your rebellious teenage years. Either way, the chance of a random user liking these songs is treated as negligible. Surprisingly, whether it is a pure coincidence or whether this assumption really makes sense, the lowest ranked song from this particular audio library is Daft Punk's–*Motherboard* it is a title that is quite original (a brilliant one though) and a definite unique sound.

Building personalized playlists

We just have seen that a simple PageRank could help us create a general-purpose playlist. And although this isn't targeted towards any individual, it could serve as a playlist for a random user. It is the best recommendation we can make without any information about a user's preferences. The more we will learn about a user, the better we can personalize the playlist towards what they truly prefer. To do this, we would probably follow a content-based recommendation approach.

Without up-front information about a user's preferences, we can seek to collect our own information whenever a user plays a song, and hence personalize their playlist at runtime. To do this, we will assume that our user was enjoying the previous song that they listened to. We will also need to disable teleporting and generate a new playlist that is seeded from that particular song ID.

PageRank and personalized PageRank are identical in the way that they compute scores (using the weight of incoming/outgoing edges), but the personalized version only allows users to teleport to the provided ID. A simple modification of the code allows us to personalize PageRank using a certain community ID (see Chapter 7, *Building Communities*, for a definition of communities) or using a certain music attribute such as the artist or the genre. Given our previous graph, a personalized page rank is implemented as follows:

```
val graph = Graph.fromEdges(edgeRDD, 0L)
val prGraph = graph.personalizedPageRank(id, 0.001, 0.1)
```

Here, the chance of teleporting to a random song is zero. There is still a 10% chance of skipping, but within only a very small tolerance of the provided song ID. In other words, regardless of the song we are currently listening to, we essentially defined a 10% chance of playing the song that we provide as a seed.

Expanding our cupcake factory

Similar to our song analyzer prototype, we want to present our suggested playlist back to our imaginary customer in a nice and tidy user interface.

Building a playlist service

Still using the Play framework, our technology stack stays the same, this time we simply create a new endpoint (a new route):

```
GET        /playlist       controllers.Playlist.index
```

Just as before, we create an additional controller that handles simple GET requests (triggered when a user loads the playlist webpage). We load the generic playlist stored in Cassandra, wrap all these songs inside of a `Playlist` case class, and send it back to the `playlist.scala.html` view. The controller model looks as follows:

```
def getSongs: List[Song] = {
    val s = "SELECT id, name, commonality FROM gzet.playlist;"
    val results = session.execute(s)
    results map { row =>
      val id = row.getLong("id")
      val name = row.getString("name")
      val popularity = row.getDouble("commonality")
      Song(id, name, popularity)
    } toList
  }

  def index = Action { implicit request =>
    val playlist = models.Playlist(getSongs)
    Ok(views.html.playlist(playlist))
  }
```

The view remains reasonably simple, as we iterate through all the songs to display, ordered by commonality (from the most to least common ones):

```
@(playlist: Playlist)

@displaySongs(playlist: Playlist) = {
    @for(node <- playlist.songs.sortBy(_.commonality).reverse) {
      <a href="/playlist/@node.id" class="list-group-item">
        <iclass="glyphiconglyphicon-play"></i>
        <span class="badge">
          @node.commonality
        </span>
        @node.name
```

```
        </a>
    }
}

@main("playlist") {
  <div class="row">
    <div class="list-group">
      @displaySongs(playlist)
    </div>
  </div>
}
```

> Note the `href` attribute in each list item – any time a user clicks on a song from that list, we will be generating a new `REST` call to the /playlist/id endpoint (this is described in the following section).

Finally, we are pleased to unveil the recommended (generic) playlist in *Figure 7*. For some reason unknown to us, apparently a novice to classical music should start listening to *Gustav Mahler, Symphony No. 5*.

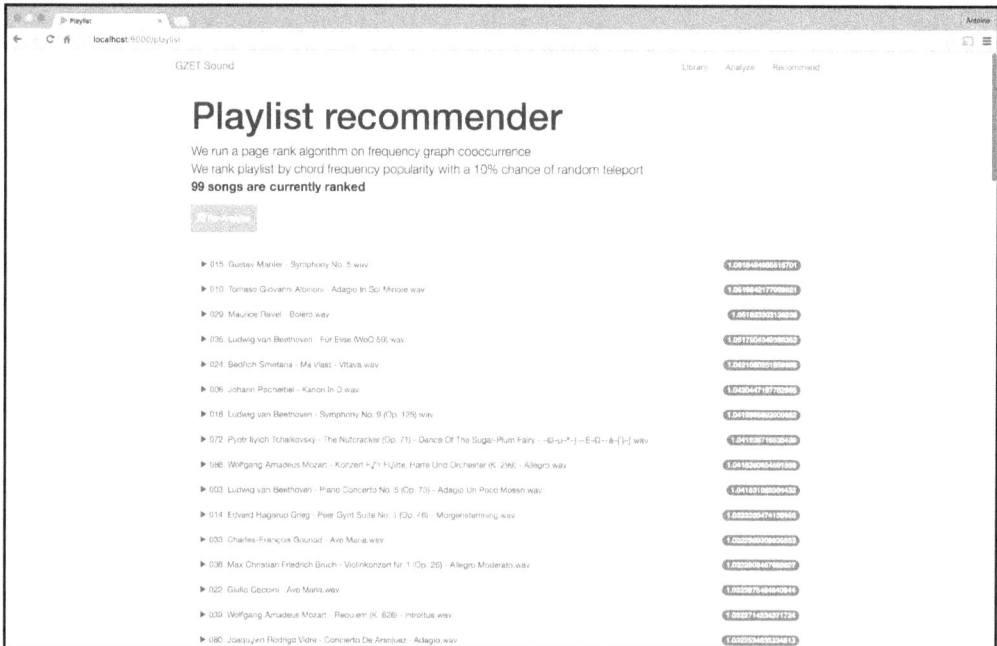

Figure 7: Playlist recommender

Leveraging the Spark job server

Here comes yet another interesting challenge. Although our list of songs for a generic playlist and PageRank score is stored on Cassandra, this is not feasible for personalized playlists, as it would require pre-computation of all the PageRank scores for all the possible song IDs. And as we want to build the personalized playlists in pseudo real time, and we might also be loading new songs fairly regularly, we need to find a better approach than starting up a `SparkContext` upon every request.

The first constraint is that the PageRank function by nature is a distributed process and cannot be used outside of the context of Spark (that is, inside our Play framework's JVM). We appreciate that creating a new Spark job on each http request would certainly be a bit of an overkill, so we would like to start one single Spark job and process new graphs only when needed, ideally through a simple REST API call.

The second challenge is that we do not wish to load the same graph dataset from Cassandra repeatedly. This should be loaded once and cached in Spark memory and shared across different jobs. In Spark terminology, this would require an RDD to be accessible from a shared context.

Luckily, both points are addressed with Spark **job server** (`https://github.com/spark-jobserver/spark-jobserver`). Although this project is fairly immature (or at least not quite production-ready yet), it is a perfectly viable solution for showcasing data science.

For the purpose of this book, we compile and deploy a Spark job server using a local configuration only. We strongly encourage the reader to have a deeper look at the job server website (see previous link) for more information about packaging and deployment. Once our server starts, we need to create a new context (meaning starting up a new Spark job) with additional configuration settings for handling connection to Cassandra. We give this context a name so that we can use it later on:

```
curl -XPOST 'localhost:8090/contexts/gzet?\
  num-cpu-cores=4&\
  memory-per-node=4g&\
  spark.executor.instances=2&\
  spark.driver.memory=2g&\
  passthrough.spark.cassandra.connection.host=127.0.0.1&\
  passthrough.spark.cassandra.connection.port=9042'
```

The next step is to modify our code to be Spark job server compliant. We need the following dependency:

```
<dependency>
    <groupId>spark.jobserver</groupId>
    <artifactId>job-server-api_2.11</artifactId>
    <version>spark-2.0-preview</version>
</dependency>
```

We modify our SparkJob using the signature of the `SparkJob` interface that comes with job server. This is a requirement of all Spark job server jobs:

```
object PlaylistBuilder extends SparkJob {

  override def runJob(
    sc: SparkContext,
    jobConfig: Config
  ): Any = ???

  override def validate(
    sc: SparkContext,
    config: Config
  ): SparkJobValidation = ???

}
```

In the `validate` method, we ensure that all the job requirements will be satisfied (such as the input configuration needed for that job), and in `runJob` we execute our normal Spark logic just as we did before. The last change is that, while we will still be storing our generic playlist into Cassandra, we will cache the nodes and edges RDDs in Spark shared memory where it will be made available to further jobs. This can be done by extending the `NamedRddSupport` trait.

We simply have to save both edges and node RDDs (note that saving a `Graph` object is not supported yet) to keep accessing the graph in subsequent jobs:

```
this.namedRdds.update("rdd:edges", edgeRDD)
this.namedRdds.update("rdd:nodes", nodeRDD)
```

From the personalized `Playlist` job, we retrieve and process our RDDs as follows:

```
val edgeRDD = this.namedRdds.get[Edge]("rdd:edges").get
val nodeRDD = this.namedRdds.get[Node]("rdd:nodes").get

val graph = Graph.fromEdges(edgeRDD, 0L)
```

We then execute our personalized PageRank, but instead of saving the results back to Cassandra, we will simply collect the first 50 songs. When deployed, this action will implicitly output this list back to the client thanks to the magic of the job server:

```
val prGraph = graph.personalizedPageRank(id, 0.001, 0.1)

prGraph
  .vertices
  .map { case(vId, pr) =>
    List(vId, songIds.value.get(vId).get, pr).mkString(",")
  }
  .take(50)
```

We compile our code and publish our shaded jar file into job server by giving it an application name as follows:

```
curl --data-binary @recommender-core-1.0.jar \
  'localhost:8090/jars/gzet'
```

Now that we are almost ready to deploy our recommendation system, let's recap over what we are going to demo. We will be executing the two different user flows shortly:

- When a user logs in to the recommendation page, we retrieve the latest generic playlist available in Cassandra. Alternatively, we start a new asynchronous job to create a new one if needed. This will load the required RDDs within the Spark context.
- When a user plays a new song from our recommended items, we spin up a synchronous call to the Spark job server and build the next playlist based around this song ID.

The flow for the generic PageRank playlist is shown in *Figure 8*:

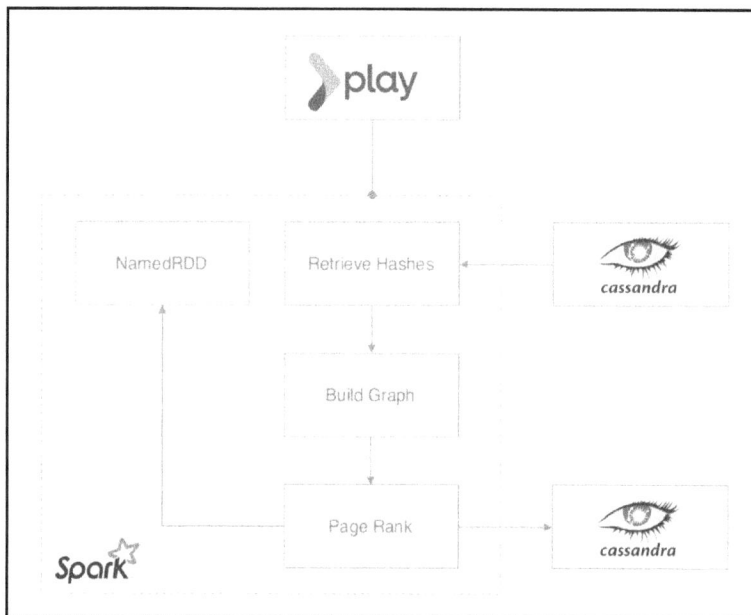

Figure 8: Playlist recommender process

The flow for the personalized PageRank playlist is shown in Figure 9:

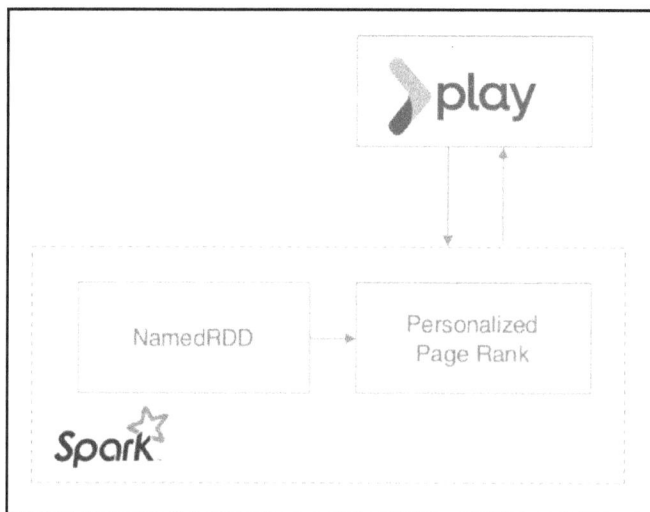

Figure 9: Personalized playlist recommender process

User interface

The final remaining piece of the puzzle is to make a call to the Spark job server from the service layer in Play Framework. Although this is done programmatically using the `java.net` package, as it's a REST API the equivalent `curl` requests are shown in the following snippet:

```
# Asynchronous Playlist Builder
curl -XPOST 'localhost:8090/jobs?\
 context=gzet&\
 appName=gzet&\
 classPath=io.gzet.recommender.PlaylistBuilder'

# Synchronous Personalized Playlist for song 12
curl -XPOST -d "song.id=12" 'localhost:8090/jobs?\
 context=gzet&\
 appName=gzet&\
 sync=true&\
 timeout=60000&\
 classPath=io.gzet.recommender.PersonalizedPlaylistBuilder'
```

Initially, when we built our HTML code, we introduced a link, or `href`, to `/playlist/${id}`. This REST call will be converted for you into a GET request to the `Playlist` controller and bound to your `personalize` function, like so:

```
GET /playlist/:id controllers.Playlist.personalize(id: Long)
```

The first call to the Spark job server will spin up a new Spark job synchronously, read the results back from the job output, and redirect to the same page view with an updated playlist, this time based around this song ID:

```
def personalize(id: Long) = Action { implicit request =>
  val name = cassandra.getSongName(id)
  try {
    val nodes = sparkServer.generatePlaylist(id)
    val playlist = models.Playlist(nodes, name)
    Ok(views.html.playlist(playlist))
  } catch {
    case e: Exception =>
      Redirect(routes.Playlist.index())
        .flashing("error" -> e.getMessage)
  }
}
```

And voila, the resulting UI is shown in *Figure 10*. Anytime a user plays a song, the playlist will be updated and displayed, acting as a full-blown ranking recommendation engine.

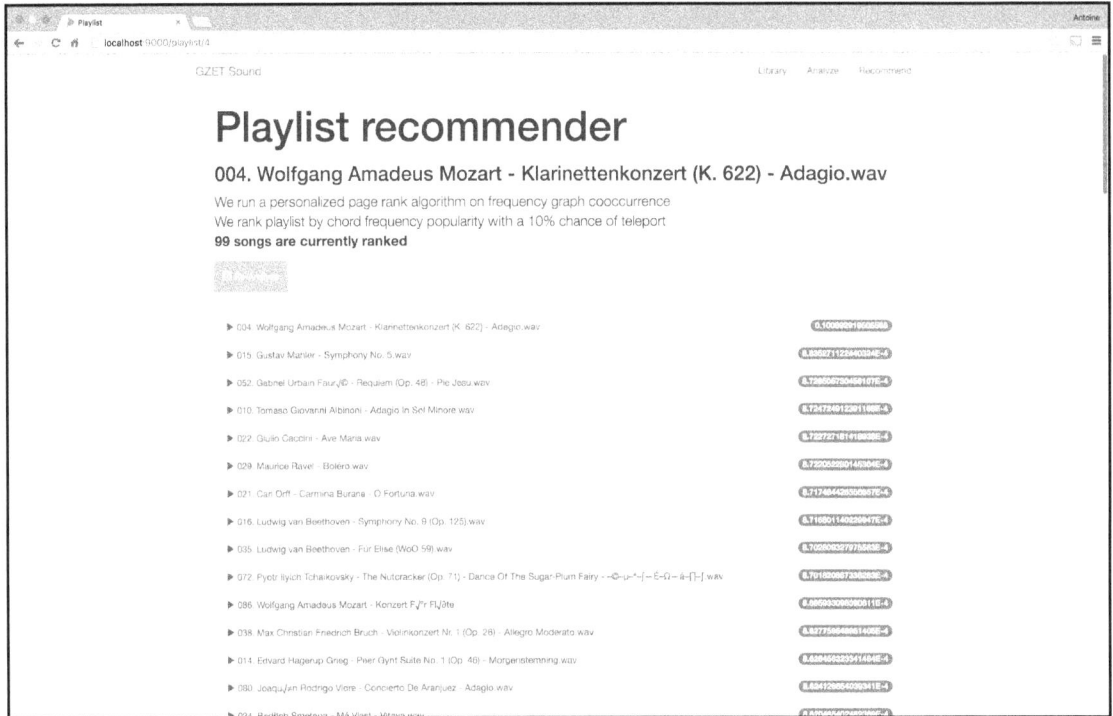

Figure 10: Personalized playlist recommender process

Summary

While our recommendation system may not have taken the typical textbook approach, nor may it be the most accurate recommender possible, it does represent a fully demonstrable and incredibly interesting approach to one of the most commonplace techniques in data science today. Further, with persistent data storage, a REST API interface, distributed shared memory caching, and a modern web 2.0-based user interface, it provides a reasonably complete and rounded candidate solution.

Of course, building a production-grade product out of this prototype would still require much effort and expertise. There are still improvements to be sought in the area of signal processing. For example, one could improve the sound pressure and reduce the signal noise by using a loudness filter, `http://languagelog.ldc.upenn.edu/myl/StevensJASA1955.pdf`, by extracting pitches and melodies, or most importantly, by converting stereo to a mono signal.

> All these processes are actually part of an active area of research – readers can look at some of the following publications: `http://www.justinsalamon.com/publications.html` and `http://www.mattmcvicar.com/publications/`.

In addition, we questioned how one can improve data science demonstrations by using simple (interactive) user interfaces. As mentioned, this is an often overlooked aspect and a key feature of presentation. Even in the early stages of a project, it's worth investing some time in data visualization, as it can be especially useful when convincing business people of the viability of your product.

One final thought, as an aspirational chapter we explored innovative ways to address data science use cases in a Spark environment. By balancing skills between mathematics and computer science, data scientists should feel free to explore, to be creative, to push back the frontier of what is feasible, to undertake what people say is not, but most importantly, to have fun with data. For this is the main reason why being a data scientist is considered the *sexiest job of the 21st century*.

This chapter was a musical interlude. In the next chapter, we will be looking at classifying GDELT articles by bootstrapping a classification model using Twitter data, another ambitious task to say the least.

9
News Dictionary and Real-Time Tagging System

While a hierarchical data warehouse stores data in files of folders, a typical Hadoop based system relies on a flat architecture to store your data. Without proper data governance or a clear understanding of what your data is all about, there is an undeniable chance of turning data lakes into swamps, where an interesting dataset such as GDELT would be nothing more than a folder containing a vast amount of unstructured text files. For that reason, data classification is probably one of the most widely used machine learning techniques in large scale organizations as it allows users to properly categorize and label their data, publish these categories as part of their metadata solutions, and therefore access specific information in the most efficient way. Without a proper tagging mechanism executed upfront, ideally at ingest, finding all news articles about a specific topic would require parsing the entire dataset looking for specific keywords. In this chapter, we will be describing an innovative way of labeling incoming GDELT data in a non-supervised way and in near real time using both Spark Streaming and the 1% Twitter firehose.

We will cover the following topics:

- Bootstrapping a Naive Bayes classifier using Stack Exchange data
- Lambda versus Kappa architecture for real-time streaming applications
- Kafka and Twitter4J within a Spark Streaming application
- Thread safety when deploying models
- Using Elasticsearch as a caching layer

The mechanical Turk

Data classification is a supervised learning technique. This means that you can only predict the labels and categories you have learned from a training dataset. Because the latter has to be properly labeled, this becomes the main challenge which we will be addressing in this chapter.

Human intelligence tasks

None of our data, within the context of news articles, has been properly labeled upfront; there is strictly nothing we can learn out of it. Common sense for data scientists is to start labeling some input records manually, records that will serve as a training dataset. However, because the number of classes may be relatively large, at least in our case (hundreds of labels), the amount of data to label could be significant (thousands of articles) and would require tremendous effort. A first solution is to outsource this laborious task to a "Mechanical Turk", the term being used as reference to one of the most famous hoaxes in history where an *automated* chess player fooled most of the world leaders (`https://en.wiki pedia.org/wiki/The_Turk`). This commonly describes a process that can be done by a machine, but in reality it is done by a hidden person, hence a Human Intelligence Task.

For the readers information, a Mechanical Turk initiative has been started at Amazon (`http s://www.mturk.com/mturk/welcome`), where individuals can register to perform human intelligence tasks such as labeling input data or detecting sentiment of a text content. Crowdsourcing this task could be one viable solution assuming you can share this internal (and potentially confidential) dataset to a third party. An alternative solution described here is to bootstrap a classification model using a pre-existing labeled dataset.

Bootstrapping a classification model

A text classification algorithm usually learns from term frequencies vectors; a possible approach is to train a model using external resources with a similar context. For instance, one could classify unlabeled IT related content using categories learned from a full dump of the Stack Overflow website. Because Stack Exchange is not only reserved for IT professionals, one could find various datasets in many different contexts that would serve many purposes (`https://archive.org/download/stackexchange`).

Learning from Stack Exchange

We will demonstrate here how to bootstrap a simple Naive Bayes classification model using the home brewing related dataset from the Stack Exchange website:

```
$ wget https://archive.org/download/stackexchange/beer.stackexchange.com.7z
$ 7z e beer.stackexchange.com.7z
```

We create a few methods that pull both the body and labels from all XML documents, extract the clean text content out of the HTML encoded body (using the Goose scraper introduced in Chapter 6, *Scraping Link-Based External Data*) and finally convert our RDD of XML documents into a Spark DataFrame. The different methods are not reported here, but they can be found in our code repository. One needs to note that Goose scraper can be used offline by providing the HTML content (as a string) alongside a dummy URL.

We provide the reader with a convenient `parse` method that can be used for pre-processing any `Post.xml` data from the Stack Exchange website. This function is part of our `StackBootstraping` code available in our code repository:

```
import io.gzet.tagging.stackoverflow.StackBootstraping

val spark = SparkSession.builder()
  .appName("StackExchange")
  .getOrCreate()

val sc = spark.sparkContext
val rdd = sc.textFile("/path/to/posts.xml")
val brewing = StackBootstraping.parse(rdd)

brewing.show(5)

+--------------------+--------------------+
|                body|                tags|
+--------------------+--------------------+
|I was offered a b...|             [hops]|
|As far as we know...|          [history]|
|How is low/no alc...|         [brewing]|
|In general, what'...|[serving, tempera...|
|Currently I am st...| [pilsener, storage]|
+--------------------+--------------------+
```

Building text features

With our beer content properly labeled, the remaining process is to bootstrap the algorithm itself. For that purpose, we use a simple Naive Bayes classification algorithm that determines the conditional probability of a label given an item's features. We first collect all distinct labels, assign a unique identifier (as `Double`), and broadcast our label dictionary to the Spark executors:

```
val labelMap = brewing
  .select("tags")
  .withColumn("tag", explode(brewing("tags")))
  .select("tag")
  .distinct()
  .rdd
  .map(_.getString(0)).zipWithIndex()
  .mapValues(_.toDouble + 1.0d)
labelMap.take(5).foreach(println)

/*
(imperal-stout,1.0)
(malt,2.0)
(lent,3.0)
(production,4.0)
(local,5.0)
*/
```

> **TIP**
>
> As introduced earlier, make sure that large collections that are used inside a Spark transformation have been broadcast to all Spark executors. This reduces the cost associated to network transfer.

A `LabeledPoint` is composed of both a label (as `Double`) and features (as `Vector`). A common practice to build features out of text content is to build term frequency vectors, where each word across all documents corresponds to a specific dimension. With around hundreds of thousands of dimensions (the estimated number of words in English is 1,025,109), this highly dimensional space will be particularly inefficient for most machine learning algorithms. In fact, when Naive Bayes multiplies probabilities (lower than 1), there is a certain risk of reaching 0 due to machine precision issue (numerical underflow as described in Chapter 14, *Scalable Algorithm*). Data scientists overcome that constraint using the principle of dimensionality reduction, projecting a sparse vector into a denser space while preserving distance measures (the principle of dimensionality reduction will be covered in Chapter 10, *Story De-duplication and Mutation*). Although we can find many algorithms and techniques for that purpose, we will use the hashing utility provided by Spark.

With a vector size of n (default of 2^{20}), its `transform` method groups all words in n different buckets in respect to their hash values, and sums up the bucket frequencies to build denser vectors.

Prior to a dimensionality reduction, which can be an expensive operation, vector size can be greatly reduced by stemming and cleaning the text content. We use the Apache Lucene analyzer here:

```
<dependency>
    <groupId>org.apache.lucene</groupId>
    <artifactId>lucene-analyzers-common</artifactId>
    <version>4.10.1</version>
</dependency>
```

We remove all punctuation and numbers and feed the plain text object to a Lucene analyzer, collecting each clean word as a `CharTermAttribute`:

```
def stem(rdd: RDD[(String, Array[String])]) = {

  val replacePunc = """\\W""".r
  val replaceDigitOnly = """\\s\\d+\\s""".r

  rdd mapPartitions { it =>

    val analyzer = new EnglishAnalyzer
    it map { case (body, tags) =>
      val content1 = replacePunc.replaceAllIn(body, " ")
      val content = replaceDigitOnly.replaceAllIn(content1, " ")
      val tReader = new StringReader(content)
      val tStream = analyzer.tokenStream("contents", tReader)
      val term = tStream.addAttribute(classOf[CharTermAttribute])
       tStream.reset()
      val terms = collection.mutable.MutableList[String]()
      while (tStream.incrementToken) {
        val clean = term.toString
        if (!clean.matches(".*\\d.*") && clean.length > 3) {
          terms += clean
        }
      }
      tStream.close()
      (terms.toArray, tags)
    }

  }
}
```

With this approach, we transform the text [Mastering Spark for Data Science – V1] into [master spark data science], hence reducing the number of words (therefore dimensions) from our input vectors. Finally, we normalize our term frequency vector using the MLlib `normalizer` class:

```
val hashingTf = new HashingTF()
val normalizer = new Normalizer()

val labeledCorpus = stem(df map { row =>
  val body = row.getString(0)
  val tags = row.getAs[mutable.WrappedArray[String]](1)
  (body, tags)
})

val labeledPoints = labeledCorpus flatMap { case (corpus, tags) =>
  val vector = hashingTf.transform(corpus)
  val normVector = normalizer.transform(vector)
  tags map { tag =>
    val label = bLabelMap.value.getOrElse(tag, 0.0d)
    LabeledPoint(label, normVector)
  }
}
```

Hash functions can lead to dramatic overestimates due to collisions (two different words of complete different meanings could share a same hash value). We will be discussing the Random Indexing technique in `Chapter 10`, *Story De-duplication and Mutation*, in order to limit the number of collisions while preserving the distance measure.

Training a Naive Bayes model

We train a Naive Bayes algorithm as follows and test our classifier using a test dataset that we did not include in the training data points. We finally display the first five predictions in the following example. The labels on the left-hand side are the original labels from our test content; on the right-hand side are the results of the Naive Bayes classification. An `ipa` has been predicted as `hangover`, validating with certainty the accuracy of our classification algorithm:

```
labeledPoints.cache()
val model: NaiveBayesModel = NaiveBayes.train(labeledPoints)
labeledPoints.unpersist(blocking = false)

model
  .predict(testPoints)
  .map { prediction =>
    bLabelMap.value.map(_.swap).get(prediction).get
  }
  .zip(testLabels)
  .toDF("predicted","original")
  .show(5)

+---------+----------+
| original|  predicted|
+---------+----------+
|  brewing|    brewing|
|      ipa|   hangover|
| hangover|   hangover|
| drinking|   drinking|
| pilsener|   pilsener|
+---------+----------+
```

For convenience, we abstract all these methods and expose the following ones within a `Classifier` object that will be used later:

```
def train(rdd: RDD[(String, Array[String])]): ClassifierModel
def predict(rdd: RDD[String]): RDD[String]
```

We have demonstrated how to export labeled data from external sources, how to build a term frequency vector, and how to train a simple Naive Bayes classification model. The high level workflow used here is represented in the following figure and is common for most classification use cases:

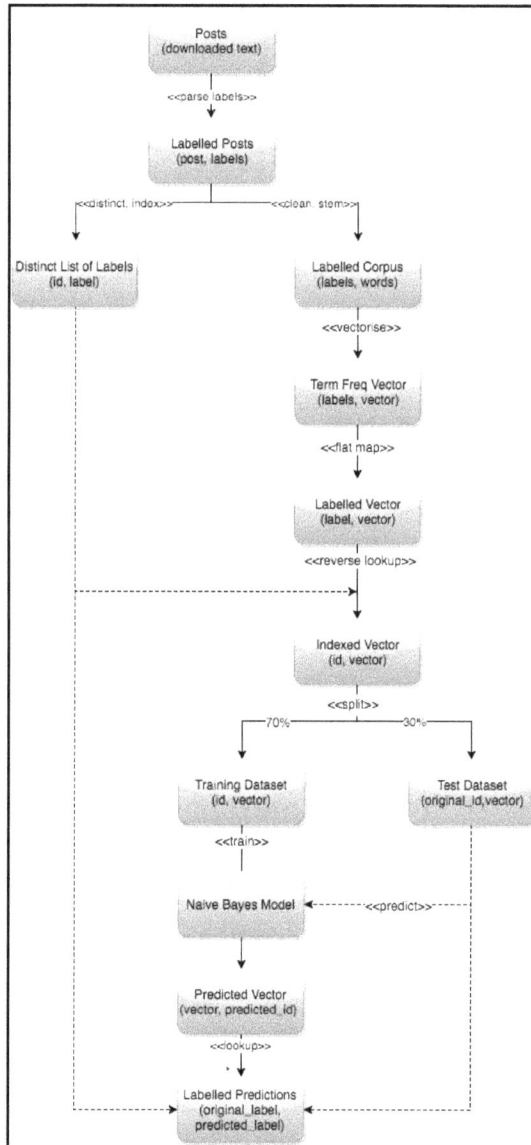

Figure 1: Classification workflow

The next step is to start classifying the original unlabeled data (assuming our content is still brewery related). This closes the introduction of Naive Bayes classification and how a bootstrapped model could steal ground truth from external resources. Both these techniques will be used in our classification system in the following section.

Laziness, impatience, and hubris

Here comes the second of our main challenges that we will be facing within our context of news articles. Assuming someone spent days manually labeling data, this would solve our classification problem for known categories at a particular point in time, and would probably only be valid when back-testing our data. Who knows what the news headline would be on tomorrow's newspaper; no one can define all the fine-grained labels and topics that will be covered in the near future (although broader categories can still be defined). This would require lots of effort to constantly re-evaluate, retrain and redeploy our model whenever a new trending topic arises. As a concrete example, no one was talking about the topic of Brexit a year ago; this topic is now heavily mentioned in news articles.

From our experience, data scientists should bear in mind a famous quote from Larry Wall, inventor of the Perl programming language:

> *"We will encourage you to develop the three great virtues of a programmer, laziness, impatience and hubris".*

- *Laziness* makes you go to great efforts to reduce overall energy expenditure
- *Impatience* makes you write programs that don't just react to your needs but anticipates them
- *Hubris* makes you write programs that people won't want to say bad things about

We want to avoid efforts related to both the preparation and the maintenance of a classification model (laziness) and to programmatically anticipate the arising of new topics (impatience), though this could sound like an ambitious task (but what is hubris if not an excessive pride in achieving the impossible?). Social networks are a fantastic place to steal ground truth from. In fact, when people tweet news articles, they unconsciously help us label our data. We do not need to pay for Mechanical Turks when we potentially have millions of users doing the job for us. In other terms, we crowdsource the labeling of GDELT data to Twitter users.

Any article mentioned on Twitter will help us build a term frequency vector while the associated hashtags will be used as proper labels. In the following example, adorable news about President Obama meeting Prince George wearing a bathrobe has been classified as [#Obama] and [#Prince] `http://www.wfmynews2.com/entertainment/adorable-prince-g eorge-misses-bedtime-meets-president-obama/149828772`:

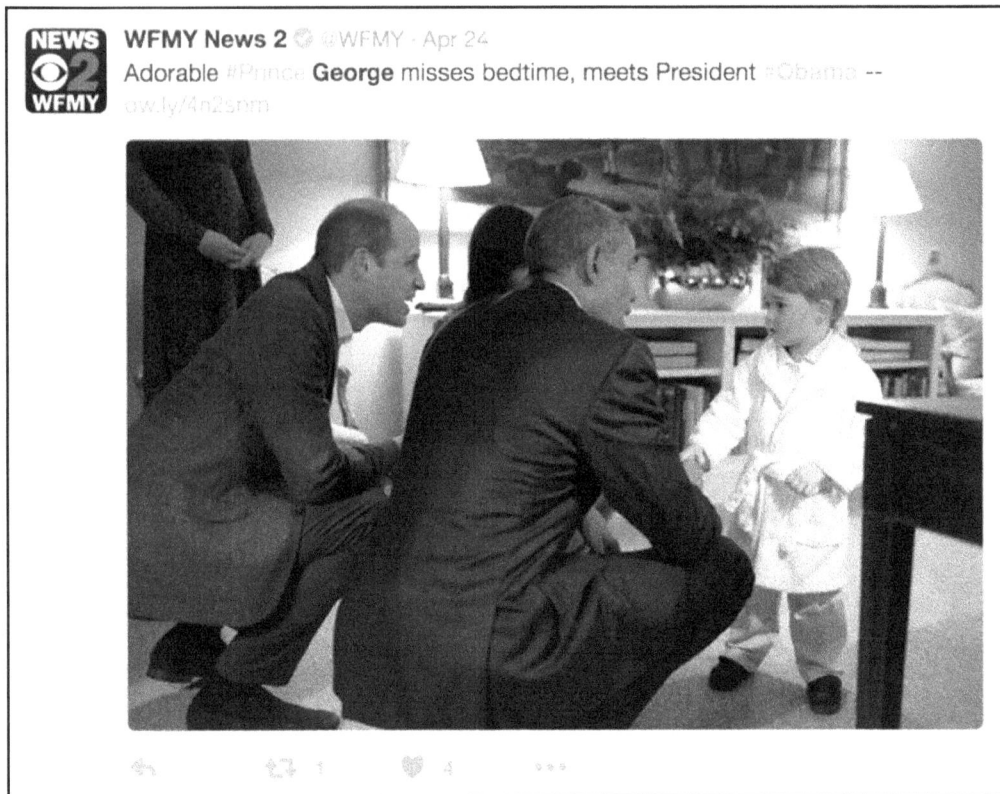

Figure 2: President Obama meets Prince George, #Obama, #Prince

In the following example, we pay tribute to all of music's great losses of 2016 by machine learning topics [#DavidBowie], [#Prince], [#GeorgeMichael], and [#LeonardCohen] within the same news article from The Guardian `https://www.theguardian.com/music /2016/dec/29/death-stars-musics-greatest-losses-of-2016`:

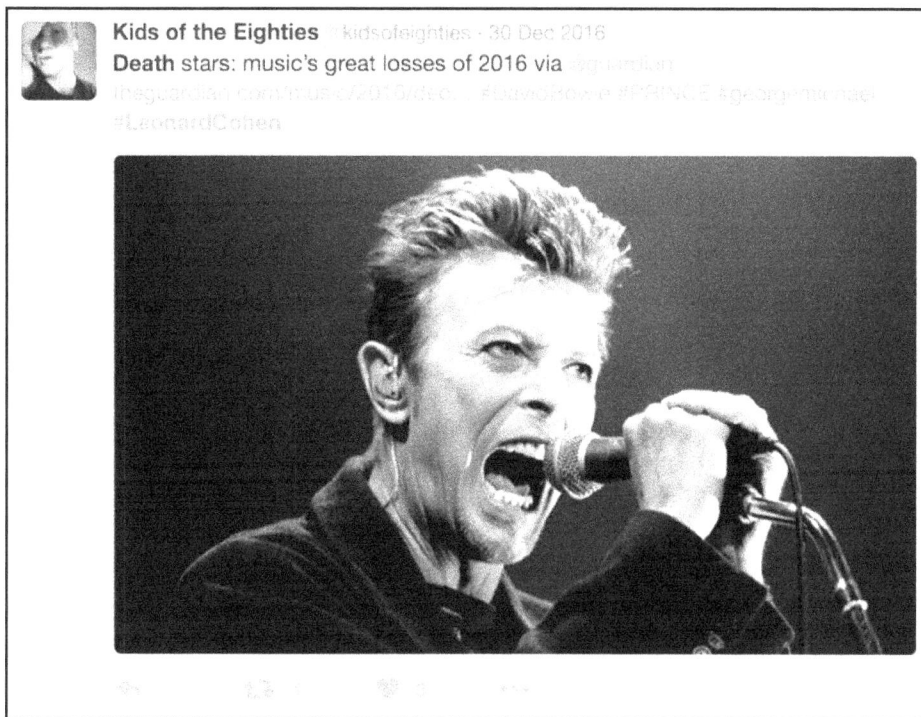

Figure 3: Music's great losses in 2016 – source

Using this approach, our algorithm will be constantly and automatically re-evaluated, learning from arising topics on its own, hence working in a non-supervised way (although being a supervised learning algorithm in the proper sense).

Designing a Spark Streaming application

Building a real-time application differs from batch processing in terms of architecture and components involved. While the latter can easily be built bottom-up, where programmers add functionalities and components when needed, the former usually needs to be built top-down with a solid architecture in place. In fact, due to the constraints of volume and velocity (or veracity in a streaming context), an inadequate architecture will prevent programmers from adding new functionalities. One always needs a clear understanding of how streams of data are interconnected, how and where they are processed, cached, and retrieved.

A tale of two architectures

In terms of stream processing using Apache Spark, there are two emerging architectures that should be considered: Lambda architecture and Kappa architecture. Before we delve into the details of the two architectures, let's discuss the problems they are trying to solve, what they have in common, and in what context you would use each.

The CAP theorem

For years, engineers working on highly-distributed systems have been concerned with handling network outages. The following is a scenario of particular interest, consider:

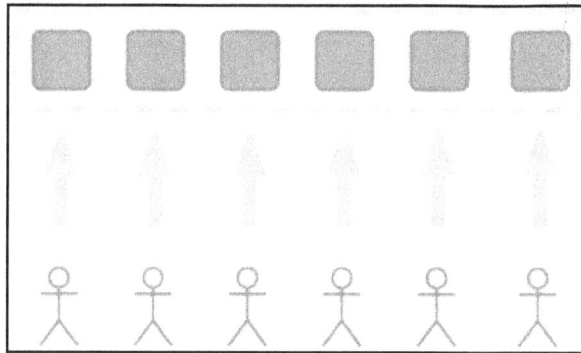

Figure 4: Distributed system outage

Normal operation of a typical distributed system is where users perform actions and the system uses techniques, such as replication, caching, and indexing, to ensure correctness and timely response. But what happens when something goes wrong:

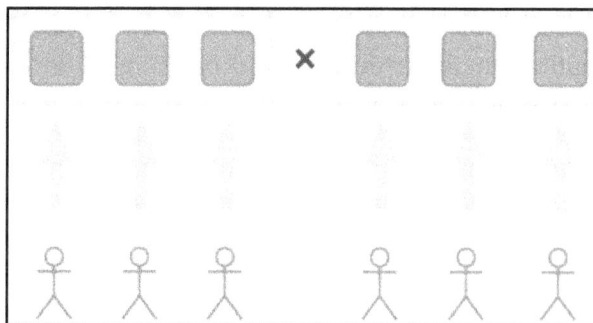

Figure 5: Distributed system split brain syndrome

Here, a network outage has effectively prevented users from performing their actions safely. Yes, a simple network failure causes a complication that not only affects the function and performance as you might expect but also the correctness of the system.

In fact, the system now suffers from what is known as *split brain syndrome*. In this situation, the two parts of the system are no longer able to talk to each other, so any modifications performed by users on one side are not visible on the opposite side. It's almost like there are two separate systems, each maintaining their own internal state, which would become quite different over time. Crucially, a user may report different answers when running the same queries on either side.

This is but one example in the general case of failure within a distributed system, and although much time has been devoted to solving these problems, there are still only three practical approaches:

1. Prevent users from making any updates until the underlying problem is resolved and in the meantime preserve the current state of the system (last known state before failure) as correct (that is, sacrifice *partition tolerance*).
2. Allow users to continue doing updates as before, but accept that answers may be different and will have to converge at some point when the underlying problem is corrected (that is, sacrifice *consistency*).
3. Shift all users onto one part of the system and allow them to continue doing updates as before. The other part of the system is treated as failed and a partial reduction of processing power is accepted until the problem is resolved – the system may become less responsive as a result (that is, sacrifice *Availability*).

The preceding conjuncture is more formally stated as CAP theorem (`http://nathanmarz.com/blog/how-to-beat-the-cap-theorem.html`). It reasons that in an environment where failures are a fact of life and you cannot sacrifice functionality (1) you must choose between having consistent answers (2) or full capability (3). You cannot have both as it's a trade-off.

> In fact, it's more correct here to describe "failures" as the more general term, "partition tolerance", as this type of failure could refer to any division of the system – a network outage, server reboot, a full disk, and so on – it is not necessarily specifically network problems.

Needless to say this is a simplification, but nonetheless, most data processing systems will fit into one of these broad categories in the event of a failure. Furthermore, it turns out that most traditional database systems favor consistency, achieving this using well-understood computer science methods such as transactions, write-ahead logs, and pessimistic locking.

However, in today's online world, where users expect 24/7 access to services, many of which are revenue-generating; Internet of Things or real-time decision making, a scalable fault-tolerant approach is required. Consequently, there has been a surge in efforts to produce alternatives that ensure availability in the event of failure (indeed the Internet itself was born from this very need).

It turns out that striking the right balance between implementing highly-available systems that also provide an acceptable level of consistency is a challenge. In order to manage the necessary trade-offs, approaches tend to provide weaker definitions of consistency, that is, *eventual consistency* where stale data is usually tolerated for a short while, and over time the correct data is agreed upon. Yet even with this compromise, they still require the use of far more complicated techniques hence they are more difficult to build and maintain.

> With more onerous implementations, vector-clocks and read-repair are involved in order to handle concurrency and prevent data corruption

The Greeks are here to help

Both Lambda and Kappa architectures provide simpler solutions to the previously described problems. They advocate the use of modern big data technologies, such as Apache Spark and Apache Kafka as the basis for consistent available processing systems, where logic can be developed without the need to reason about failure. They are applicable in situations with the following characteristics:

- An unbounded, inbound stream of information, potentially from multiple sources
- Analytical processing over a very large, cumulative dataset
- User queries with time-based guarantees on data consistency
- Zero-tolerance for degradation of performance or downtime

Where you have these conditions, you can consider either architecture as a general candidate. Each adheres to the following core principles that help simplify issues around data consistency, concurrent access, and prevention of data corruption:

- **Data immutability**: Data is only ever created or read. It is never updated or deleted. Treating data this way greatly simplifies the model required to keep your data consistent.

- **Human fault tolerance**: When fixing or upgrading software during the normal course of the software development lifecycle, it is often necessary to deploy new versions of analytics and replay historical data through the system in order to produce revised answers. Indeed, when managing systems dealing directly with data of this capability is often critical. The batch layer provides a durable store of historical data and hence allows for any mistakes to be recovered.

It's these principles that form the basis of their eventually-consistent solutions without the need to worry about complexities such as read-repairs or vector-clocks; they're definitely more developer-friendly architectures!

So, let's discuss some of the reasons to choose one over the other. Let's first consider the Lambda architecture.

Importance of the Lambda architecture

The Lambda architecture, as first proposed by Nathan Marz, typically ls something like this:

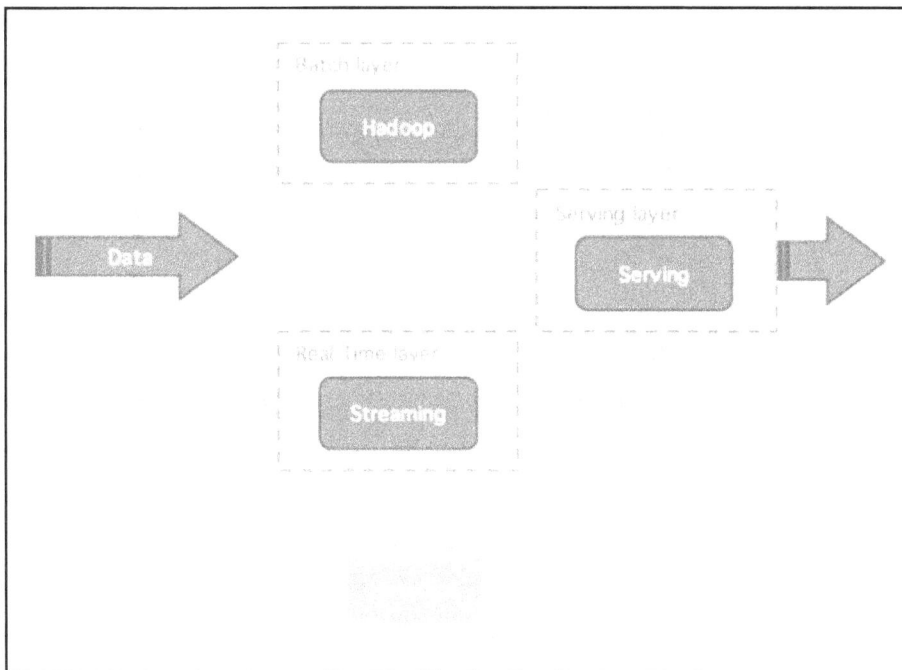

Figure 6: Lambda architecture

In essence, data is dual-routed into two layers:

- A **Batch layer** capable of computing a snapshot at a given point in time
- A **Real-Time layer** capable of processing incremental changes since the last snapshot

The **Serving layer** is then used to merge these two views of the data together producing a single up-to-date version of the truth.

In addition to the previously described general characteristics, Lambda architecture is most suitable when you have either of the following specific conditions:

- Complex or time-consuming bulk or batch algorithms that have no equivalent or alternative incremental iterative algorithm (and approximations are not acceptable) so you need a batch layer.
- Guarantees on data consistency cannot be met by the batch layer alone, regardless of parallelism of the system, so you need a real-time layer. For example, you have:
  - Low latency write-reads
  - Arbitrarily wide ranges of data, that is, years
  - Heavy data skew

Where you have either one of these conditions, you should consider using the Lambda architecture. However, before going ahead, be aware that it brings with it the following qualities that may present challenges:

- Two data pipelines: There are separate workflows for batch and stream processing and, although where possible you can attempt to reuse core logic and libraries, the flows themselves must be managed individually at runtime.
- Complex code maintenance: For all but simple aggregations, the algorithms in the batch and real time layers will need to be different. This is particularly true for machine learning algorithms, where there is an entire field devoted to this study called online machine learning (`https://en.wikipedia.org/wiki/Online_machine_learning`), which can involve implementing incremental iterative algorithms, or approximation algorithms, outside of existing frameworks.
- Increased complexity in the serving layer: Aggregations, unions, and joins are necessary in the serving layer in order to merge deltas with aggregations. Engineers should be careful that this does not split out into consuming systems.

Despite these challenges, the Lambda architecture is a robust and useful approach that has been implemented successfully in many institutions and organizations, including Yahoo!, Netflix, and Twitter.

Importance of the Kappa architecture

The Kappa architecture takes simplification one step further by putting the concept of a *distributed log* at its center. This allows the removal of the batch layer altogether and consequently creates a vastly simpler design. There are many different implementations of Kappa, but generally it looks like this:

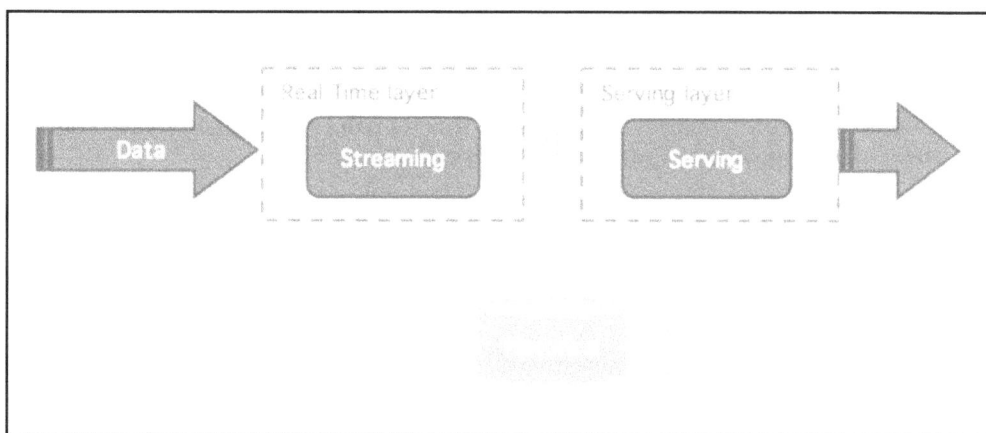

Figure 7: Kappa architecture

In this architecture, the distributed log essentially provides the characteristics of data immutability and re-playability. By introducing the concept of *mutable state store* in the processing layer, it unifies the computation model by treating all processing as stream processing, even batch, which is considered just a special case of stream. Kappa architecture is most suitable when you have either of the following specific conditions:

- Guarantees on data consistency can be met using the existing batch algorithm by increasing parallelism of the system to reduce latency
- Guarantees on data consistency can be met by implementing incremental iterative algorithms

If either one of these options is viable, then Kappa architecture should provide a modern, scalable approach to meet your batch and streaming requirements. However, it's worth considering the constraints and challenges of the technologies chosen for any implementation you may decide on. The potential limitations include:

- Exactly-once semantics: Many popular distributed messaging systems, such as Apache Kafka, don't currently support exactly-once message delivery semantics. This means that, for now, consuming systems have to deal with receiving data duplicates themselves. This is typically done by using checkpoints, unique keys, idempotent writes, or other such de-duplication techniques, but it does increase complexity and hence makes the solution more difficult to build and maintain.

- Out of order event handling: Many streaming implementations, such as Apache Spark, do not currently support updates ordered by the event time, instead they use the processing time, that is, the time the event was first observed by the system. Consequently, updates could be received out of order and the system needs to be able to handle this. Again, this increases code complexity and makes the solution more difficult to build and maintain.

- No strong consistency, that is, linearizability: As all updates are applied asynchronously, there are no guarantees that write will take effect immediately (although they will be eventually consistent). This means that in some circumstances you would not immediately be able to "read your writes".

In the next chapter, we will discuss incremental iterative algorithms, how data skew or server failures affect consistency, and how the back-pressure features in Spark Streaming can help reduce failures. With regards to what has been explained in this section, we will build our classification system following a Kappa architecture.

Consuming data streams

Similar to a batch processing job, we create a new Spark application using a `SparkConf` object and a context. In a streaming application, the context is created using a batch size parameter that will be used for any incoming stream (both GDELT and Twitter layers, part of the same context, will both be tied to the same batch size). GDELT data being published every 15 minutes, our batch size will be naturally 15 minutes as we want to predict categories in a pseudo real-time basis:

```
val sparkConf = new SparkConf().setAppName("GZET")
val ssc = new StreamingContext(sparkConf, Minutes(15))
val sc = ssc.sparkContext
```

Creating a GDELT data stream

There are many ways of publishing external data into a Spark streaming application. One could open a simple socket and start publishing data over the netcat utility, or could be streaming data through a Flume agent monitoring an external directory. Production systems usually use Kafka as a default broker for both its high throughput and its overall reliability (data is replicated over multiple partitions). Surely, we could be using the same Apache NiFi stack as described in `Chapter 10`, *Story De-duplication and Mutation*, but we want to describe here a much easier route simply by "piping" articles URLs (extracted from GDELT records) into our Spark application through a Kafka topic.

Creating a Kafka topic

Creating a new Kafka topic is quite easy (in a test environment). Extra care must be taken on production environments by choosing the right number of partitions and replication factors. Also note that a proper zookeeper quorum must be installed and configured. We start the Kafka server and create a topic named `gzet`, using one partition only and a replication factor of 1:

```
$ kafka-server-start /usr/local/etc/kafka/server.properties >
/var/log/kafka/kafka-server.log 2>&1 &

$ kafka-topics --create --zookeeper localhost:2181 --replication-factor 1 -
-partitions 1 --topic gzet
```

Publishing content to a Kafka topic

We can feed the Kafka queue by piping content to the `kafka-console-producer` utility. We use `awk`, `sort`, and `uniq` commands as we are only interested in the distinct URLs from GDELT records (URL is the last field of our tab separated values, hence the `$NF`):

```
$ cat ${FILE} | awk '{print $NF}' | sort | uniq | kafka-console-producer --
broker-list localhost:9092 --topic gzet
```

For convenience, we create a simple bash script that listens for new files on the GDELT website, downloads and extracts content to a temporary directory, and executes the preceding command. The script can be found in our code repository (`gdelt-stream.sh`).

Consuming Kafka from Spark Streaming

Kafka is an official source of Spark Streaming, available using the following dependency:

```
<dependency>
   <groupId>org.apache.spark</groupId>
   <artifactId>spark-streaming-kafka-0-8_2.11</artifactId>
   <version>2.0.0</version>
</dependency>
```

We define the number of Spark partitions that will be used for processing data from the gzet topic (10 here) together with the zookeeper quorum. We return the message itself (the URLs piped to our Kafka producer) in order to build our stream of article URLs:

```
def createGdeltStream(ssc: StreamingContext) = {
   KafkaUtils.createStream(
      ssc,
      "localhost:2181",
      "gzet",
      Map("gzet" -> 10)
   ).values
 }

val gdeltUrlStream: DStream[String] = createGdeltStream(ssc)
```

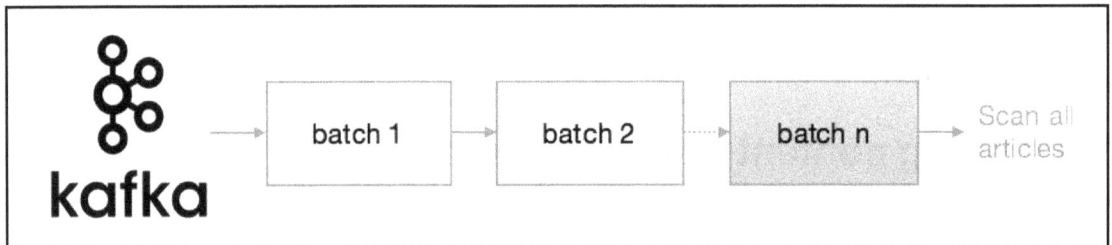

Figure 8: GDELT online layer

In the preceding figure we show how GDELT data will be processed in batches by listening to a Kafka topic. Each batch will be analyzed and the articles downloaded using the HTML parser described in `Chapter 6`, *Scraping Link-Based External Data*.

Creating a Twitter data stream

The obvious constraint of using Twitter is the constraint of scale. With over 500 million tweets a day, our application needs to be written in the most distributed and scalable way in order to handle the large amount of input data. Furthermore, if only 2% of these tweets contained a reference to an external URL, we would still have a million URLs to fetch and analyze per day (in addition to the thousands coming from GDELT). Because we do not have a dedicated architecture to handle this veracity of data for the purpose of this book, we will be using the 1% firehose provided for free by Twitter. One simply needs to register a new application on the Twitter website (`https://apps.twitter.com`) and retrieve both its associated application settings and authorization tokens. Note, however, that the Twitter connector is no longer part of core Spark Streaming since version `2.0.0`. As part of the Apache Bahir project (`http://bahir.apache.org/`), it can be used with the following maven `dependency`:

```
<dependency>
    <groupId>org.apache.bahir</groupId>
    <artifactId>spark-streaming-twitter_2.11</artifactId>
    <version>2.0.0</version>
</dependency>
```

Because Spark Streaming uses `twitter4j` in the background, the configuration is done using the `ConfigurationBuilder` object from the `twitter4j` libraries:

```
import twitter4j.auth.OAuthAuthorization
import twitter4j.conf.ConfigurationBuilder

def getTwitterConfiguration = {

  val builder = new ConfigurationBuilder()

  builder.setOAuthConsumerKey("XXXXXXXXXXXXXXX")
  builder.setOAuthConsumerSecret("XXXXXXXXXXXX")
  builder.setOAuthAccessToken("XXXXXXXXXXXXXXX")
  builder.setOAuthAccessTokenSecret("XXXXXXXXX")

  val configuration = builder.build()
  Some(new OAuthAuthorization(configuration))

}
```

We create our data stream by supplying an array of keywords (can be specific hashtags). In our case, we want to listen to all 1%, no matter the keywords or hashtags used (discovering new hashtags is actually part of our application), hence providing an empty array:

```
def createTwitterStream(ssc: StreamingContext) = {
   TwitterUtils.createStream(
     ssc,
     getTwitterConfiguration,
     Array[String]()
   )
}

val twitterStream: DStream[Status] = createTwitterStream(ssc)
```

The returned object is a stream of `status`, `twitter4j` class embedding all tweets properties such as the ones reported in the following snippet. In the scope of this application, we will only be interested in the `getText` method that returns the tweet body:

```
val body: String = status.getText()
val user: User = status.getUser()
val contributors: Array[Long] = status.getContributors()
val createdAt: Long = status.getCreatedAt()
../..
```

Processing Twitter data

The second main constraint of using Twitter is the constraint of noise. When most classification models are trained against dozens of different classes, we will be working against hundreds of thousands of distinct hashtags per day. We will be focusing on popular topics only, meaning the trending topics occurring within a defined batch window. However, because a 15 minute batch size on Twitter will not be sufficient enough to detect trends, we will apply a 24-hour moving window where all hashtags will be observed and counted, and where only the most popular ones will be kept.

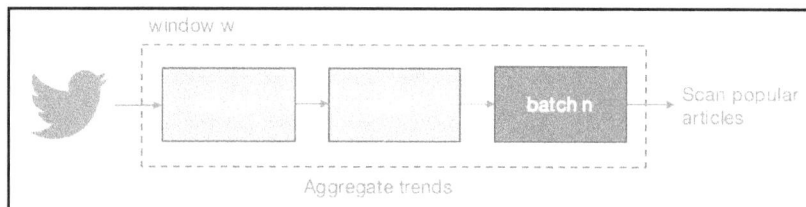

Figure 9: Twitter online layer, batch and window size

Using this approach, we reduce the noise of unpopular hashtags, making our classifier much more accurate and scalable, and significantly reducing the number of articles to fetch as we only focus on trending URLs mentioned alongside popular topics. This allows us to save lots of time and resources spent analyzing irrelevant data (with regards to a classification model).

Extracting URLs and hashtags

We extract both the clean hashtags (that are more than x characters long and that do not contain numbers; yet another measure of reducing noise) and references to valid URLs. Note the Scala `Try` method that catches any exception when testing a `URL` object. Only the tweets matching both of these two conditions will be kept:

```
def extractTags(tweet: String) = {
  StringUtils.stripAccents(tweet.toLowerCase())
    .split("\\s")
    .filter { word =>
      word.startsWith("#") &&
        word.length > minHashTagLength &&
        word.matches("#[a-z]+")
    }
}

def extractUrls(tweet: String) = {
  tweet.split("\\s")
    .filter(_.startsWith("http"))
    .map(_.trim)
    .filter(url => Try(new URL(url)).isSuccess)
}

def getLabeledUrls(twitterStream: DStream[Status]) = {
  twitterStream flatMap { tweet =>
    val tags = extractTags(tweet.getText)
    val urls = extractUrls(tweet.getText)
    urls map { url =>
      (url, tags)
    }
  }
}

val labeledUrls = getLabeledUrls(twitterStream)
```

Keeping popular hashtags

The basic idea of this step is to execute a simple word count over a 24h time window. We extract all hashtags, assign a value of 1, and count the number of occurrences using a reduce function. In a streaming context, the `reduceByKey` function can be applied over a window (that must be larger than the batch size) using `reduceByKeyAndWindow` method. Although this term frequency dictionary will always be available at each batch, the current top ten hashtags are printed out every 15 minutes, data will be counted over a larger period (24h):

```
def getTrends(twitterStream: DStream[Status]) = {

  val stream = twitterStream
    .flatMap { tweet =>
      extractTags(tweet.getText)
    }
    .map(_ -> 1)
    .reduceByKeyAndWindow(_ + _, Minutes(windowSize))

  stream.foreachRDD { rdd =>
    val top10 = rdd.sortBy(_._2, ascending = false).take(10)
    top10.foreach { case (hashTag, count) =>
      println(s"[$hashTag] - $count")
    }
  }

  stream
}

val twitterTrend = getTrends(twitterStream)
```

In a batch processing context, one could easily join an RDD of hashtags with the Twitter RDD in order to keep only the "hottest" tweets (tweets mentioning an article alongside a popular hashtag). In a streaming context, data streams cannot be joined as each stream contains several RDDs. Instead, we transform a `DStream` with another one using the `transformWith` function that takes an anonymous function as an argument and applies it on each of their RDDs. We transform our Twitter stream with our hashtag stream by applying a function that filters out the unpopular tweets. Note that we use Spark context to broadcast our current top *n* hashtags (limited to the top 100 here):

```
val joinFunc = (labeledUrls: RDD[(String, Array[String])], twitterTrend:
RDD[(String, Int)]) => {

  val sc = twitterTrend.sparkContext
  val leaderBoard = twitterTrend
    .sortBy(_._2, ascending = false)
    .take(100)
```

```
    .map(_._1)

  val bLeaderBoard = sc.broadcast(leaderBoard)

  labeledUrls
    .flatMap { case (url, tags) =>
      tags map (tag => (url, tag))
    }
    .filter { case (url, tag) =>
      bLeaderBoard.value.contains(tag)
    }
    .groupByKey()
    .mapValues(_.toArray.distinct)

}

val labeledTrendUrls = labeledUrls
  .transformWith(twitterTrend, joinFunc)
```

Because the returned stream will only contain the "hottest" URLs, the amount of data should be drastically reduced. Although we cannot guarantee at this stage whether or not the URL points to a proper text content (could be a YouTube video or a simple image), at least we know we won't waste effort fetching content about useless topics.

Expanding shortened URLs

URLs available on Twitter are shortened. The only way to detect the true source programmatically is to "open the box" for all of them, wasting, sadly, lots of time and effort on potentially irrelevant content. It is also worth mentioning that many web scrapers would not handle shortened URLs efficiently (including Goose scraper). We expand URLs by opening an HTTP connection, disabling redirects, and looking at the Location header. We also provide the method with a list of "untrusted" sources, sources that are, for the context of a classification model, not providing any useful content (such as videos from https://www.youtube.com):

```
def expandUrl(url: String) : String = {

  var connection: HttpURLConnection = null
  try {

    connection = new URL(url)
                   .openConnection
                   .asInstanceOf[HttpURLConnection]
```

```
        connection.setInstanceFollowRedirects(false)
        connection.setUseCaches(false)
        connection.setRequestMethod("GET")
        connection.connect()

        val redirectedUrl = connection.getHeaderField("Location")

        if(StringUtils.isNotEmpty(redirectedUrl)){
          redirectedUrl
        } else {
          url
        }

      } catch {
        case e: Throwable => url
      } finally {
        if(connection != null)
          connection.disconnect()
      }
    }

    def expandUrls(tStream: DStream[(String, Array[String])]) = {
      tStream
        .map { case (url, tags) =>
          (HtmlHandler.expandUrl(url), tags)
        }
        .filter { case (url, tags) =>
          !untrustedSources.value.contains(url)
        }
    }
  }

val expandedUrls = expandUrls(labeledTrendUrls)
```

Similar to what has been done in the previous chapter, we thoroughly catch any possible exceptions arising from an HTTP connection. Any uncaught exception (could be a simple 404 error) would make this task re-evaluate on different Spark executors before raising a fatal exception, exiting our Spark application.

Fetching HTML content

We've already introduced web scrapers in a previous chapter, using Goose library recompiled for Scala 2.11. We will create a method that takes a `DStream` as input instead of an RDD, and only keep the valid text content with at least 500 words. We will finally return a stream of text alongside the associated hashtags (the popular ones):

```
def fetchHtmlContent(tStream: DStream[(String, Array[String])]) = {

  tStream
    .reduceByKey(_++_.distinct)
    .mapPartitions { it =>

      val htmlFetcher = new HtmlHandler()
      val goose = htmlFetcher.getGooseScraper
      val sdf = new SimpleDateFormat("yyyyMMdd")

      it.map { case (url, tags) =>
        val content = htmlFetcher.fetchUrl(goose, url, sdf)
        (content, tags)
      }
      .filter { case (contentOpt, tags) =>
        contentOpt.isDefined &&
          contentOpt.get.body.isDefined &&
          contentOpt.get.body.get.split("\\s+").length >= 500
      }
      .map { case (contentOpt, tags) =>
        (contentOpt.get.body.get, tags)
      }

  }

  val twitterContent = fetchHtmlContent(expandedUrls)
```

We apply the same approach for GDELT data where all the content (text, title, description, and so on) will also be returned. Note the `reduceByKey` method, which acts as a distinct function for our data stream:

```
def fetchHtmlContent(urlStream: DStream[String]) = {

  urlStream
    .map(_ -> 1)
    .reduceByKey()
    .keys
    .mapPartitions { urls =>

      val sdf = new SimpleDateFormat("yyyyMMdd")
```

```
    val htmlHandler = new HtmlHandler()
    val goose = htmlHandler.getGooseScraper
    urls.map { url =>
        htmlHandler.fetchUrl(goose, url, sdf)
    }

}
.filter { content =>
  content.isDefined &&
    content.get.body.isDefined &&
    content.get.body.get.split("\\s+").length > 500
}
.map(_.get)
}

val gdeltContent = fetchHtmlContent(gdeltUrlStream)
```

Using Elasticsearch as a caching layer

Our ultimate goal is to train a new classifier at each batch (every 15 minutes). However, the classifier will be trained using more than just the few records we downloaded within that current batch. We somehow have to cache the text content over a larger period of time (set to 24h) and retrieve it whenever we need to train a new classifier. With Larry Wall's quote in mind, we will try to be as lazy as possible maintaining the data consistency over this online layer. The basic idea is to use a **Time to live** (**TTL**) parameter that will seamlessly drop any outdated record. The Cassandra database provides this feature out of the box (so does HBase or Accumulo), but Elasticsearch is already part of our core architecture and can easily be used for that purpose. We will create the following mapping for the gzet/twitter index with the _ttl parameter enabled:

```
$ curl -XPUT 'http://localhost:9200/gzet'
$ curl -XPUT 'http://localhost:9200/gzet/_mapping/twitter' -d '
{
    "_ttl" : {
            "enabled" : true
    },
    "properties": {
      "body": {
        "type": "string"
      },
      "time": {
        "type": "date",
        "format": "yyyy-MM-dd HH:mm:ss"
      },
      "tags": {
```

```
      "type": "string",
      "index": "not_analyzed"
    },
    "batch": {
      "type": "integer"
    }
  }
}'
```

Our records will exist on Elasticsearch for a period of 24h (the TTL value is defined on insert) after which any record will simply be discarded. As we delegate the maintenance tasks to Elasticsearch, we can safely pull all possible records from our online cache without worrying too much about any outdated value. All the retrieved data will be used as a training set for our classifier. The high level process is reported in the following figure:

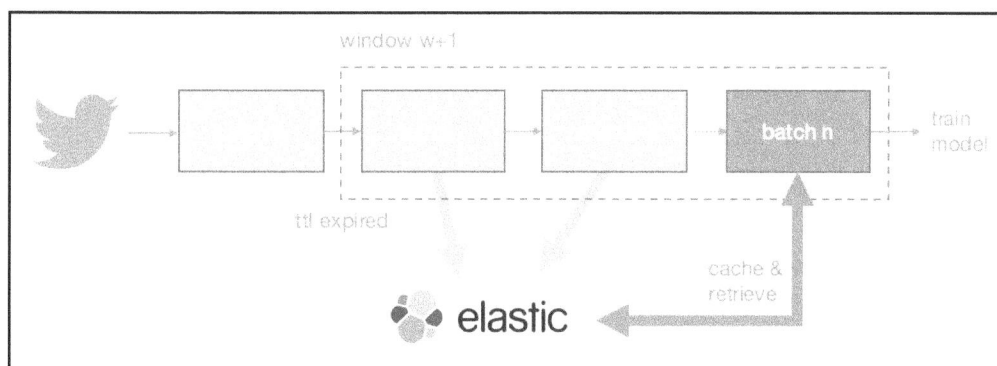

Figure 10: Using Elasticsearch as a caching layer

For each RDD in our data stream, we retrieve all existing records from the previous 24h, cache our current set of Twitter content, and train a new classifier. Converting a data stream into RDDs is a simple operation using the `foreachRDD` function.

We persist current records into Elasticsearch using the `saveToEsWithMeta` function from the Elasticsearch API. This function accepts the `TTL` parameter as part of the metadata map (set to 24h, in seconds, and formatted as String):

```
import org.elasticsearch.spark._
import org.elasticsearch.spark.rdd.Metadata._

def saveCurrentBatch(twitterContent: RDD[(String, Array[String])]) = {
  twitterContent mapPartitions { it =>
    val sdf = new SimpleDateFormat("yyyy-MM-dd HH:mm:ss")
    it map { case (content, tags) =>
      val data = Map(
```

```
        "time" -> sdf.format(new Date()),
        "body" -> content,
        "tags" -> tags
      )
      val metadata = Map(
        TTL -> "172800s"
      )
      (metadata, data)
    }
  } saveToEsWithMeta "gzet/twitter"
}
```

It is worth executing a simple check on Elasticsearch in order to make sure that the TTL parameter has been properly set, and is effectively decreasing every second. Once it has reached 0, the indexed document should be dropped. The following simple command prints out the _ttl value for document ID [AVRr9LaCoYjYhZG9lvBl] every second. This uses a simple jq utility (https://stedolan.github.io/jq/download/) to parse JSON objects from the command line:

```
$ while true ; do TTL=`curl -XGET
'http://localhost:9200/gzet/twitter/AVRr9LaCoYjYhZG9lvBl' 2>/dev/null | jq
"._ttl"`; echo "TTL is $TTL"; sleep 1; done

../..
TTL is 48366081
TTL is 48365060
TTL is 48364038
TTL is 48363016
../..
```

All the online records (records with unexpired TTL) can be retrieved into an RDD using the following function. Similar to what we've done in Chapter 7, *Building communities*, extracting lists from Elasticsearch is far easier using JSON parsing than Spark DataFrame:

```
import org.elasticsearch.spark._
import org.json4s.DefaultFormats
import org.json4s.jackson.JsonMethods._

def getOnlineRecords(sc: SparkContext) = {
  sc.esJsonRDD("gzet/twitter").values map { jsonStr =>
    implicit val format = DefaultFormats
    val json = parse(jsonStr)
    val tags = (json \ "tags").extract[Array[String]]
    val body = (json \ "body").extract[String]
    (body, tags)
  }
}
```

We download all Twitter contents from our caching layer while saving our current batch. The remaining process is to train our classification algorithm. This method is discussed in the following section:

```
twitterContent foreachRDD { batch =>

  val sc = batch.sparkContext
  batch.cache()

  if(batch.count() > 0) {
    val window = getOnlineRecords(sc)
    saveCurrentBatch(batch)
    val trainingSet = batch.union(window)
    //Train method described hereafter
    trainAndSave(trainingSet, modelOutputDir)
  }

  batch.unpersist(blocking = false)
}
```

Classifying data

The remaining part of our application is to start classifying data. As introduced earlier, the reason for using Twitter was to steal ground truth from external resources. We will train a Naive Bayes classification model using Twitter data while predicting categories of the GDELT URLs. The convenient side of using a Kappa architecture approach is that we do not have to worry much about exporting some common pieces of code across different applications or different environments. Even better, we do not have to export/import our model between a batch and a speed layer (both GDELT and Twitter, sharing the same Spark context, are part of the same physical layer). We could save our model to HDFS for auditing purposes, but we simply need to pass a reference to a Scala object between both classes.

Training a Naive Bayes model

We've already introduced both the concept of bootstrapping a Naive Bayes model using Stack Exchange datasets and the use of a `Classifier` object that builds `LabeledPoints` out of text content. We will create a `ClassifierModel` case class that wraps both a Naive Bayes model and its associated labels dictionary and exposes both a `predict` and a `save` method:

```
case class ClassifierModel(
  model: NaiveBayesModel,
```

```
    labels: Map[String, Double]
) {

  def predictProbabilities(vectors: RDD[Vector]) = {
    val sc = vectors.sparkContext
    val bLabels = sc.broadcast(labels.map(_.swap))
    model.predictProbabilities(vectors).map { vector =>
      bLabels.value
        .toSeq
        .sortBy(_._1)
        .map(_._2)
        .zip(vector.toArray)
        .toMap
    }
  }

  def save(sc: SparkContext, outputDir: String) = {
    model.save(sc, s"$outputDir/model")
    sc.parallelize(labels.toSeq)
      .saveAsObjectFile(s"$outputDir/labels")
  }

}
```

Because more than one hashtag could be necessary to fully describe an article content, we will predict instead a probability distribution using the `predictProbabilities` function. We convert our label identifier (as `Double`) to the original category (as `String`) using the label dictionary we saved alongside the model. Finally we can save, for auditing purposes only, both our model and the label dictionary into HDFS.

> All MLlib models support both a save and a load function. Data will be persisted as `ObjectFile` in HDFS, and can be easily retrieved and deserialized. Using ML library, objects are saved into parquet format. One would need, however, to save additional pieces of information; such as in our example, the label dictionary used for training that model.

Thread safety

Our `Classifier` is a singleton object, and, as per the singleton pattern, should be thread safe. That means that parallel threads should not modify a same state using, for instance, a setter method. In our current architecture, only Twitter will be training and updating a new model every 15 minutes, models that will be only used by the GDELT service (no concurrent update). However, there are two important things to take into consideration:

1. Firstly, our model has been trained using distinct labels (hashtags found in a 24h time window, extracted every 15 minutes). A new model will be trained against an updated dictionary. Both the model and the labels are tightly coupled, and therefore must be synchronized. In the unlikely event of GDELT pulling labels while Twitter is updating a model, our predictions will be inconsistent. We ensure thread safety by wrapping both labels and models within our same `ClassifierModel` case class.

2. The second (although less critical) concern is that our process is parallel. That means that similar tasks will be executed simultaneously from different executors, on different chunks of data. At a point in time, we would need to ensure that all models are the same version on each executor, although predicting a particular chunk of data with a slightly less up-to-date model will still technically be valid (as long as the model and labels are synchronized). We illustrate this statement with the two following examples. The first one cannot guarantee consistency of models across executors:

```
val model = NaiveBayes.train(points)
vectors.map { vector =>
  model.predict(vector)
  }
```

The second example (used by default by Spark) broadcasts a model to all executors at once, hence guaranteeing the overall consistency of the predicting phase:

```
val model = NaiveBayes.train(points)
val bcModel = sc.broadcast(model)
vectors mapPartitions { it =>
  val model = bcModel.value
  it.map { vector =>
    model.predict(vector)
  }
}
```

In our `Classifier` singleton object, we define our model as a global variable (as optional as it may not exist yet) that will be updated after each call to the `train` method:

```
var model = None: Option[ClassifierModel]

def train(rdd: RDD[(String, Array[String])]): ClassifierModel = {
  val labeledPoints = buildLabeledPoints(rdd)
  val labels = getLabels(rdd)
  labeledPoints.cache()
  val nbModel = NaiveBayes.train(labeledPoints)
  labeledPoints.unpersist(blocking = false)
  val cModel = ClassifierModel(nbModel, labels)
  model = Some(cModel)
  cModel
}
```

Coming back to our Twitter stream, for each RDD, we build our training set (abstracted within our `Classifier`), train a new model, and then save it to HDFS:

```
def trainAndSave(trainingSet: RDD[(String, Array[String])],
 modelOutputDir: String) = {
  Classifier
      .train(trainingSet)
      .save(batch.sparkContext, modelOutputDir)
}
```

Predict the GDELT data

Using the `Classifier` singleton object, we can access the latest model published from the Twitter processor. For each RDD, for each article, we simply predict the hashtags probability distribution that describes each article's text content:

```
gdeltContent.foreachRDD { batch =>

  val textRdd = batch.map(_.body.get)
  val predictions = Classifier.predictProbabilities(textRdd)

  batch.zip(predictions).map { case (content, dist) =>
    val hashTags = dist.filter { case (hashTag, proba) =>
      proba > 0.25d
    }
    .toSeq
    .map(_._1)
    (content, hashTags)
  }
  .map { case (content, hashTags) =>
```

```
    val sdf = new SimpleDateFormat("yyyy-MM-dd HH:mm:ss")
    Map(
      "time"  -> sdf.format(new Date()),
      "body"  -> content.body.get,
      "url"   -> content.url,
      "tags"  -> hashTags,
      "title" -> content.title
    )
  }
  .saveToEs("gzet/gdelt")

}
```

We only keep probabilities higher than 25% and publish each article together with its predicted hashtags into our Elasticsearch cluster. Publishing the results officially marks the end of our classification application. We report the full architecture here:

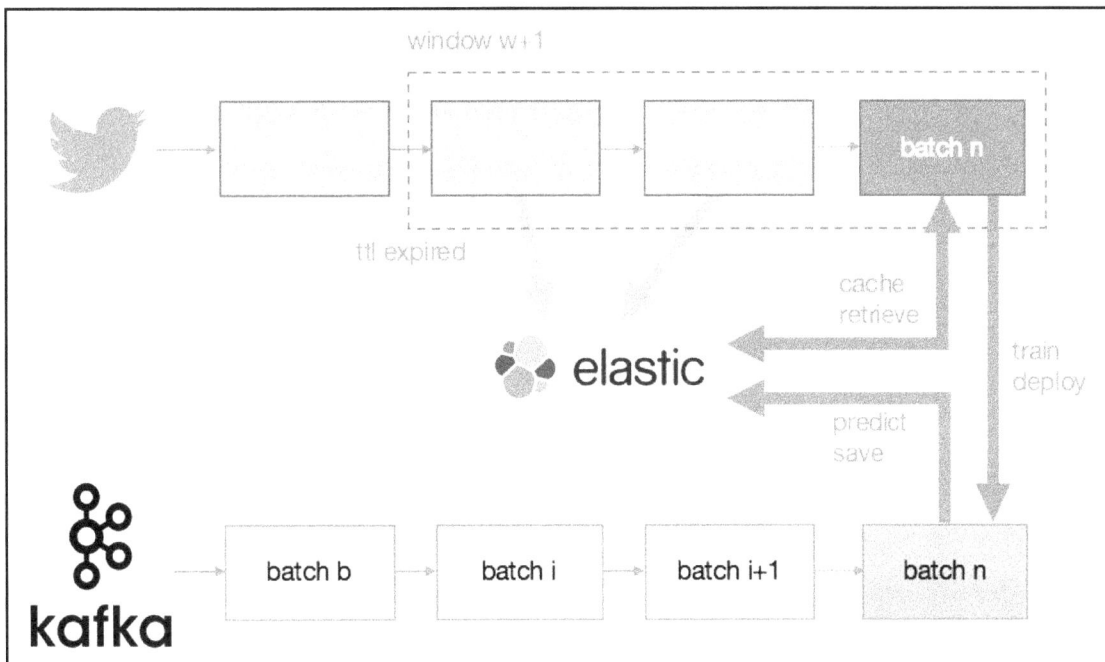

Figure 11: An innovative way of tagging news articles

Our Twitter mechanical Turk

The accuracy of a classification algorithm should be measured against a test dataset, meaning a labeled dataset that was not included in the training phase. We do not have access to such a dataset (this is the reason we bootstrapped our model initially), hence we cannot compare the original versus predicted categories. Instead of the true accuracy, we can estimate an overall confidence level by visualizing our results. With all our data on Elasticsearch, we build a Kibana dashboard with an additional plugin for tag cloud visualizations (`https://github.com/stormpython/tagcloud`).

The following figure shows the number of GDELT articles that were analyzed and predicted on May 1, 2016. Around 18,000 articles have been downloaded in less than 24h (by batch interval of 15 minutes). At each batch, we observe no more than 100 distinct predicted hashtags; this is fortunate as we only kept the top 100 popular hashtags occurring within a 24h time window. Besides, it gives us hints about both GDELT and Twitter following a relatively normal distribution (batches are not skewed around a particular category).

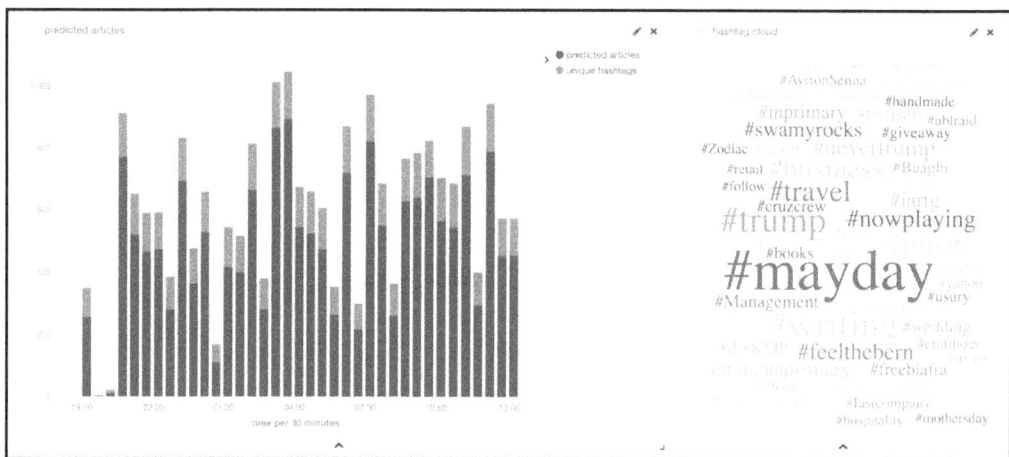

Figure 12: Predicted articles on May 1

In addition to these 18,000 articles, we also extracted around 700 Twitter text content labeled against our 100 popular hashtags, making each topic covered by seven articles on average. Although this training set is already a good start for the content of this book, we could probably expand it by being less restrictive in terms content or by grouping similar hashtags into broader categories. We could also increase the TTL value on Elasticsearch. Increasing the number of observations while limiting Twitter noise should definitely improve the overall model accuracy.

We observe the most popular hashtags in that particular window to be [#mayday] and [#trump]. We also observe at least as many [#nevertrump] as [#maga], hence satisfying both of the two US political parties. This will be confirmed using the US election data in `Chapter 11`, *Anomaly Detection on Sentiment Analysis*.

Finally, we select a particular hashtag and retrieve all its associated keywords. This is important as it basically validates the consistency of our classification algorithm. Our hope is that for each hashtag coming from Twitter, the significant terms from GDELT will be consistent enough and should all be related to the same hashtag meaning. We focus on the [#trump] tag and access the Trump cloud in the following figure:

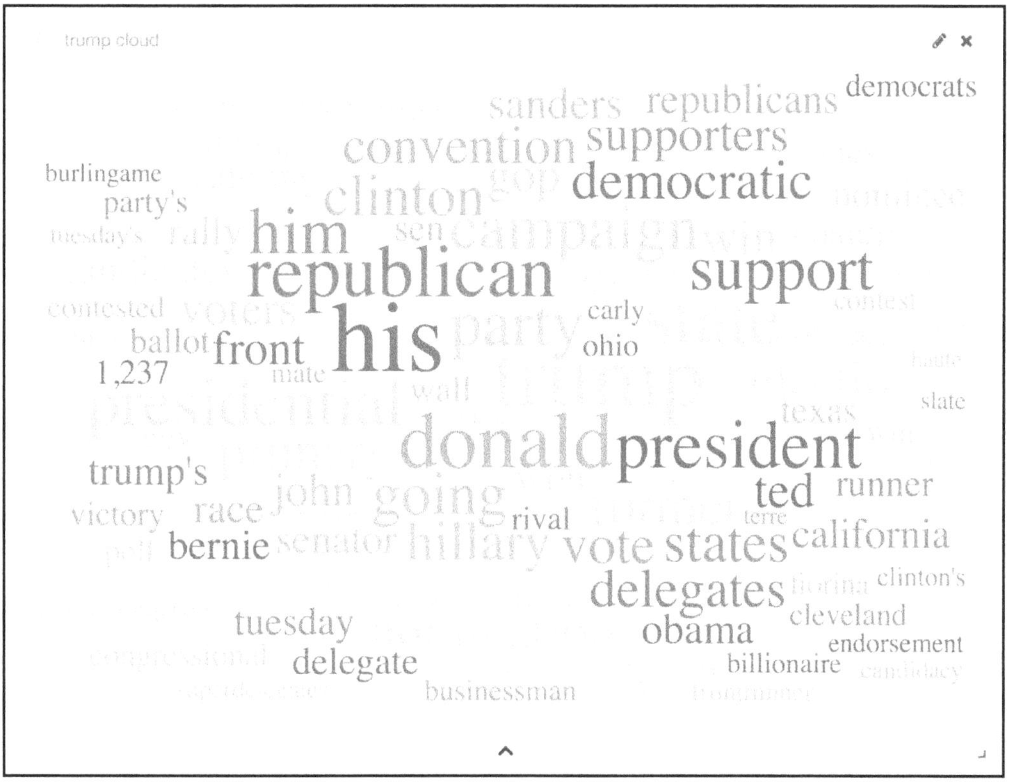

Figure 13: The #Trump cloud

We observe most of the significant terms (every article predicted as [#trump]) to be all about the presidential campaign, the United States, primary, and so on. It also contains names of candidates running for the presidential (Hillary Clinton and Ted Cruz). Although we still find some articles and keywords that are not Donald Trump related, this validates a certain consistency to our algorithm. For many records (more than 30% of them), the results were even above all our initial expectations.

Summary

Although we were impressed with many of the overall model consistencies, we appreciate that we certainly did not build the most accurate classification system ever. Crowd sourcing this task to millions of users was an ambitious task and by far not the easiest way of getting clearly defined categories. However, this simple proof of concept shows us a few important things:

1. It technically validates our Spark Streaming architecture.
2. It validates our assumption of bootstrapping GDELT using an external dataset.
3. It made us lazy, impatient, and proud.
4. It learns without any supervision and eventually gets better at every batch.

No data scientist can build a fully functional and highly accurate classification system in just a few weeks, especially not on dynamic data; a proper classifier needs to be evaluated, trained, re-evaluated, tuned, and retrained for at least the first few months, and then re-evaluated every half a year at the very least. Our goal here was to describe the components involved in a real-time machine learning application and to help data scientists sharpen their creative minds (out-of-the-box thinking is the #1 virtue of a modern data scientist).

In the next chapter, we will be focusing on article mutation and story de-duplication; how likely is a topic to evolve over time, how likely is a clique of people (or community) likely to mutate over time? By de-duplicating articles into stories, stories into epics, can we predict the possible outcomes based on previous observations?

10
Story De-duplication and Mutation

How large is the World Wide Web? Although it is impossible to know the exact size – not to mention the Deep and Dark Web – it was estimated to hold more than a trillion pages in 2008, that, in the data era, was somehow the middle age. Almost a decade later, it is safe to assume that the Internet's collective brain has more neurons than our actual gray matter that's stuffed between our *ears*. But out of these trillion plus URLs, how many web pages are truly identical, similar, or covering the same topic?

In this chapter, we will de-duplicate and index the GDELT database into stories. Then, we will track stories over time and understand the links between them, how they may mutate and if they could lead to any subsequent event in the near future.

We will cover the following topics:

- Understand the concept of *Simhash* to detect near duplicates
- Build an online de-duplication API
- Build vectors using TF-IDF and reduce dimensionality using *Random Indexing*
- Build stories connection in pseudo real-time using Streaming KMeans

Detecting near duplicates

While this chapter is about grouping articles into stories, this first section is all about detecting near duplicates. Before delving into the de-duplication algorithm itself, it is worth introducing the notion of story and de-duplication in the context of news articles. Given two distinct articles – by distinct we mean two different URLs – we may observe the following scenarios:

- The URL of article 1 actually redirects to article 2 or is an extension of the URL provided in article 2 (some additional URL parameters, for instance, or a shortened URL). Both articles with the same content are considered as *true duplicates* although their URLs are different.
- Both article 1 and article 2 are covering the exact same event, but could have been written by two different publishers. They share lots of content in common, but are not truly similar. Based on certain rules explained hereafter, they might be considered as *near-duplicates*.
- Both article 1 and article 2 are covering the same type of event. We observe major differences in style or different *flavors* of the same topic. They could be grouped into a common *story*.
- Both article 1 and article 2 are covering two different events. Both contents are *different* and should not be grouped within the same story, nor should they be considered as near duplicates.

Facebook users must have noticed the *related articles* feature. When you like a news article-click on an article's link or play an article's video, Facebook thinks this link is interesting and updates its timeline (or whatever it is called) to display more content that looks similar. In *Figure 1*, I was really amused to see the Samsung Galaxy Note 7 smartphone emitting smoke or catching fire, therefore banned from most of US flights. Facebook automatically suggested me similar articles around this Samsung fiasco. What probably happened is that by opening this link I may have queried the Facebook internal APIs and asked for similar content. Here comes the notion of finding near duplicates in real-time, and here is what we will try to build in the first section.

Antoine Amend
Just now · London · ⚐ ▼

http://www.forbes.com/.../samsung-south-korean-government-i.../...

Galaxy Note 7 Fiasco: Samsung, South Korean Government
Launches Investigation

Industry analysts say investigating why the Note 7 devices caught fire is crucial for
the world's largest smartphone maker.

FORBES.COM | BY JOHN KANG

👍 Like　　　💬 Comment　　　➤ Share

Write a comment...

RELATED ARTICLES

Why Samsung Abandoned Its Galaxy Note 7
Flagship Phone

The unprecedented move by the South Korean
electronics giant is an embarrassing reversal for a...

THE NEW YORK TIMES · 11,181 SHARES　　Share　Save

Singapore Airlines bans Samsung Galaxy Note 7
on its flights

SINGAPORE Singapore Airlines said on Saturday it
has banned Samsungs Galaxy Note 7 mobile phon...

GMA NEWS · 4,366 SHARES　　　Share　Save

Figure 1: Facebook suggesting related articles

First steps with hashing

Finding true duplicates is easy. Two articles will be considered as identical if their content is the same. But instead of comparing strings (that may be large and therefore not efficient), we can compare their hash values just like one would compare hand signatures; two articles having the same signature should be considered as identical. A simple `groupBy` function would detect the true duplicatess out of a string array as shown as follows:

```
Array("Hello Spark", "Hello Hadoop", "Hello Spark")
  .groupBy(a => Integer.toBinaryString(a.hashCode))
  .foreach(println)

11001100010111100111000111001111 List(Hello Spark, Hello Spark)
10101011110110000110101101110011 List(Hello Hadoop)
```

But even the most complex hash function leads to some collisions. Java's built-in `hashCode` function is encoding a string into a 32-bit integer, which means that, in theory, we *only* have 2^{32} possibilities of getting different words sharing the same hash value. In practice, collisions should always be handled carefully, as, according to the *birthday paradox*, they will appear much more often than once every 2^{32} values. To prove our point, the following example considers the four different strings to be identical:

```
Array("AaAa", "BBBB", "AaBB", "BBAa")
  .groupBy(a => Integer.toBinaryString(a.hashCode))
  .foreach(Sprintln)

11111000000001000000 List(AaAa, BBBB, AaBB, BBAa)
```

Also, some articles may sometimes only differ by a very small portion of text, for example, a piece of advertisement, an additional footer, or an extra bit in the HTML code that make a hash signature different from almost identical content. In fact, even a minor typo on one single word would result in a total different hash value, making two near-duplicate articles to be considered as totally different.

```
Array("Hello, Spark", "Hello Spark")
  .groupBy(a => Integer.toBinaryString(a.hashCode))
  .foreach(println)

11100001101000010101000011010111  List(Hello, Spark)
11001100010111100111000111001111  List(Hello Spark)
```

Although the strings `Hello Spark` and `Hello, Spark` are really close (they only differ by 1 character), their hash values differ by 16-bits (out of 32). Luckily, the elders of the Internet may have found a solution to detect near duplicates using hash values.

Standing on the shoulders of the Internet giants

Needless to say, Google is fairly good at indexing webpages. With more than a trillion distinct URLs, detecting duplicates is the key when it comes to indexing web content. Surely the Internet giants must have developed techniques over the years to solve this problem of scale, hence limiting the amount of computing resources needed to index the whole Internet. One of these techniques described here is called *Simhash* and is so simple and neat, albeit so efficient, that it is worth knowing if you truly want to *Master Spark for data science*.

> More information about *Simhash* could be found at
> `http://www.wwwconference.org/www2007/papers/paper215.pdf`.

Simhashing

The main idea behind **Simhash** is not to compute one single hash value at once, but rather to look at the article's content and compute multiple individual hashes. For each word, each pair of word, or even each two-character shingle, we can easily compute hash values using the simple Java built-in `hashCode` function described earlier. In the following *Figure 2*, we report all the 32-bit hash values (the first 20 zero values omitted) of the two characters set included in the string **hello simhash**:

	hashcodes											
he	1	1	0	0	1	1	1	1	1	1	0	1
el	1	1	0	0	1	0	1	0	0	1	1	1
ll	1	1	0	1	1	0	0	0	0	0	0	0
lo	1	1	0	1	1	0	0	0	0	0	1	1
si	1	1	1	0	0	1	0	1	0	1	1	0
im	1	1	0	1	0	0	1	0	0	1	0	0
mh	1	1	0	1	1	0	0	1	1	0	1	1
ha	1	1	0	0	1	1	1	1	1	0	0	1
as	1	1	0	0	0	0	1	1	0	0	1	0
sh	1	1	1	0	0	1	0	1	0	1	0	1

Figure 2: Building hello simhash shingles

A simple Scala implementation is reported next:

```scala
def shingles(content: String) = {
  content.replaceAll("\\s+", "")
    .sliding(2)
    .map(s => s.mkString(""))
    .map(s => (s, s.hashCode))
}

implicit class BitOperations(i1: Int) {
  def toHashString: String = {
    String.format(
      "%32s",
      Integer.toBinaryString(i1)
    ).replace(" ", "0")
  }
}

shingles("spark").foreach { case (shingle, hash) =>
  println("[" + shingle + "]\t" + hash.toHashString)
}

[sp]    00000000000000000000111001011101
[pa]    00000000000000000000110111110001
[ar]    00000000000000000000110000110001
[rk]    00000000000000000000111000111001
```

With all these hash values computed, we initialize a `Simhash` object as a zero integer. For each bit in that 32-bit integer, we count the number of hash values in our list with that particular bit set to 1 and subtract the number of values within that same list with that particular bit that is <u>not</u> set. This gives us the array reported in *Figure 3*. Finally, any value greater than 0 will be set to 1, any value lower or equal to 0 will be left as 0. The only tricky part here is to work on bit shifting operations, but the algorithm itself is fairly trivial. Note that we use recursion here to avoid the use of mutable variables (using `var`) or lists.

	10	10	-6	-2	2	-2	0	2	-4	0	0	2
hello simhash	1	1	0	0	1	0	0	1	0	0	0	1

Figure 3: Building hello simhash

```scala
implicit class BitOperations(i1: Int) {

  // ../..

  def isBitSet(bit: Int): Boolean = {
```

```
    ((i1 >> bit) & 1) == 1
  }
}

implicit class Simhash(content: String) {

  def simhash = {
    val aggHash = shingles(content).flatMap{ hash =>
      Range(0, 32).map { bit =>
        (bit, if (hash.isBitSet(bit)) 1 else -1)
      }
    }
    .groupBy(_._1)
    .mapValues(_.map(_._2).sum > 0)
    .toArray

    buildSimhash(0, aggHash)
  }

 private def buildSimhash(
     simhash: Int,
     aggBit: Array[(Int, Boolean)]
    ): Int = {

    if(aggBit.isEmpty) return simhash
    val (bit, isSet) = aggBit.head
    val newSimhash = if(isSet) {
      simhash | (1 << bit)
    } else {
      simhash
    }
    buildSimhash(newSimhash, aggBit.tail)

  }
}

val s = "mastering spark for data science"
println(toHashString(s.simhash))

00000000000000000000000110000110001
```

The hamming weight

It is easy to understand that the more words two articles have in common, the more both of them will share a same bit *b* set to 1 in their Simhash. But the beauty of Simhash comes with this aggregation step. Many other words in our corpus (hence other hashes) may not have this particular bit *b* set, hence making this value to also decrease when some different hashes are observed. Sharing a common set of words is not enough, similar articles must also share the same word frequency. The following example shows three Simhash values computed for the strings **hello simhash**, **hello minhash**, and **hello world**.

hello simhash	1	1	0	0	1	0	0	1	0	0	0	1
hello minhash	1	1	0	0	1	0	1	1	0	0	0	1
hello world	1	1	0	0	1	0	1	0	0	0	0	0

Figure 4: Comparing hello simhash

When both **hello simhash** and **hello world** differ by 3-bits, **hello simhash** and **hello minhash** only differ by **1**. In fact, we can express the distance between them as the hamming weight of their EXCLUSIVE OR (**XOR**) product. **Hamming weight** is the number of bits we need to change in order to turn a given number into the zero element. The hamming weight of the **XOR** operation of two numbers is therefore the number of bits that differ between these two elements, **1** in that case.

hello simhash	1	1	0	0	1	0	0	1	0	0	0	1
hello minhash	1	1	0	0	1	0	1	1	0	0	0	1
XOR	0	0	0	0	0	0	1	0	0	0	0	0

Figure 5: Hamming weight of hello simhash

We simply use Java's `bitCount` function that returns the number of one-bits in the two's complement binary representation of the specified integer value.

```
implicit class BitOperations(i1: Int) {

  // ../..

  def distance(i2: Int) = {
    Integer.bitCount(i1 ^ i2)
  }
}

val s1 = "hello simhash"
val s2 = "hello minhash"
val dist = s1.simhash.distance(s2.simhash)
```

We have been able to successfully build Simhash and perform some simple pairwise comparison. The next step is to scale this up and start detecting actual duplicates out of the GDELT database.

Detecting near duplicates in GDELT

We covered the data acquisition process in depth in Chapter 2, *Data Acquisition*. For this use case, we will use a NiFi flow in *Figure 6* that listens to the GDELT master URL, fetches and unzips the latest GKG archive, and stores this file on HDFS in a compressed format.

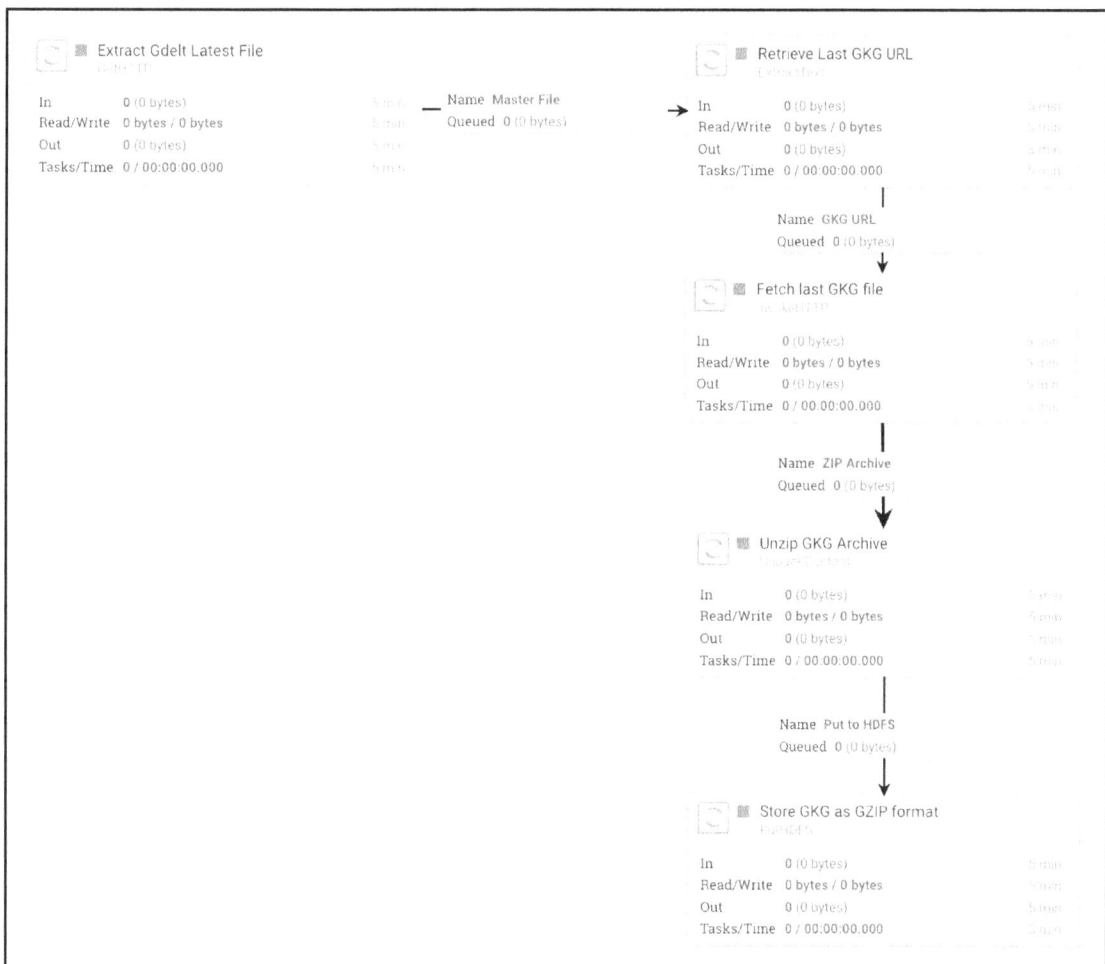

Figure 6: Downloading GKG data

We first parse our GKG records using the set of parsers we created earlier (available in our GitHub repo), extract all the distinct URLs and fetch the HTML content using the Goose extractor introduced in `Chapter 6`, *Scraping Link-Based External Data*.

```
val gdeltInputDir = args.head
val gkgRDD = sc.textFile(gdeltInputDir)
  .map(GKGParser.toJsonGKGV2)
  .map(GKGParser.toCaseClass2)

val urlRDD = gkgRDD.map(g => g.documentId.getOrElse("NA"))
  .filter(url => Try(new URL(url)).isSuccess)
  .distinct()
  .repartition(partitions)

val contentRDD = urlRDD mapPartitions { it =>
  val html = new HtmlFetcher()
  it map html.fetch
}
```

Because the `hashcode` function is case sensitive (*Spark* and *spark* result in total different hash values), it is strongly recommended to clean our text prior to a `simhash` function. Similar to what was described in `Chapter 9`, *News Dictionary and Real-Time Tagging System*, we first use the following Lucene analyzer to stem words:

```
<dependency>
  <groupId>org.apache.lucene</groupId>
  <artifactId>lucene-analyzers-common</artifactId>
  <version>4.10.1</version>
</dependency>
```

As you may have noticed earlier, we wrote our Simhash algorithm inside of an implicit class; we can apply our `simhash` function directly on a string using the following import statement. A bit of extra effort taken at an early stage of development always pays off.

```
import io.gzet.story.simhash.SimhashUtils._
val simhashRDD = corpusRDD.mapValues(_.simhash)
```

We now have an RDD of content (`Content` being a case class wrapping the article URL, title and body) together with its Simhash value and a unique identifier we may be using later. Let's first try to validate our algorithm and find our first duplicates. From now on, we only consider as duplicates the articles that have no more than 2-bits difference in their 32-bit Simhash values.

```
hamming match {
  case 0 => // identical articles - true-duplicate
  case 1 => // near-duplicate (mainly typo errors)
```

```
  case 2 => // near-duplicate (minor difference in style)
  case _ => // different articles
}
```

But here comes a scalability challenge: we certainly do not want to execute a Cartesian product to compare pairwise articles from our Simhash RDD. Instead, we want to leverage the MapReduce paradigm (using a `groupByKey` function) and only group articles that are duplicates. Our approach is following an *expand-and-conquer* pattern where we first expand our initial dataset, leverage the Spark shuffle and then solve our problem locally at the executor level. As we only need to deal with 1-bit difference (we will then apply the same logic for 2-bits), our strategy is to expand our RDD so that for each Simhash `s`, we output all the 31 other 1-bit combinations of **s** using the same 1-bit mask.

```
def oneBitMasks: Set[Int] = {
  (0 to 31).map(offset => 1 << offset).toSet
}

00000000000000000000000000000001
00000000000000000000000000000010
00000000000000000000000000000100
00000000000000000000000000001000
...
```

Taking a Simhash value `s`, we output the possible 1-bit combinations of **s** using a XOR between each preceding mask and the Simhash value `s`.

```
val s = 23423
oneBitMasks foreach { mask =>
  println((mask ^ s).toHashString)
}

00000000000000000101101101111111
00000000000000000101101101111110
00000000000000000101101101111101
00000000000000000101101101111011
...
```

Dealing with 2-bits is not that different, although a bit more aggressive in terms of scalability (we now have 496 possible combinations to output, meaning any combination of 2-bits out of 32).

```
def twoBitsMasks: Set[Int] = {
  val masks = oneBitMasks
  masks flatMap { e1 =>
    masks.filter( e2 => e1 != e2) map { e2 =>
      e1 | e2
    }
```

```
    }
}
```

```
00000000000000000000000000000011
00000000000000000000000000000101
00000000000000000000000000000110
00000000000000000000000000001001
. . .
```

Finally, we build our set of masks to apply (note that we also want to output the original Simhash by applying a 0-bit difference mask) in order to detect duplicates as follows:

```
val searchmasks = twoBitsMasks ++ oneBitMasks ++ Set(0)
```

This also helps us expand our initial RDD accordingly. This surely is an expensive operation as it increases the size of our RDD by a constant factor (496 + 32 + 1 possible combinations), but stays linear in terms of time complexity while Cartesian join is a quadratic operation - $O(n^2)$.

```
val duplicateTupleRDD = simhashRDD.flatMap {
  case ((id, _), simhash) =>
    searchmasks.map { mask =>
      (simhash ^ mask, id)
    }
}
.groupByKey()
```

We find that article A is a duplicate of article B, which is a duplicate of article C. This is a simple graph problem that can easily be solved through *GraphX* using a connected components algorithm.

```
val edgeRDD = duplicateTupleRDD
  .values
  .flatMap { it =>
    val list = it.toList
    for (x <- list; y <- list) yield (x, y)
  }
  .filter { case (x, y) =>
    x != y
  }
  .distinct()
  .map {case (x, y) =>
    Edge(x, y, 0)
  }

val duplicateRDD = Graph.fromEdges(edgeRDD, 0L)
  .connectedComponents()
```

```
.vertices
.join(simhashRDD.keys)
.values
```

Out of the 15,000 articles used for that test, we extracted around 3,000 different stories. We report an example in *Figure 7*, which includes two near-duplicate articles we were able to detect, both of them being highly similar but not truly identical.

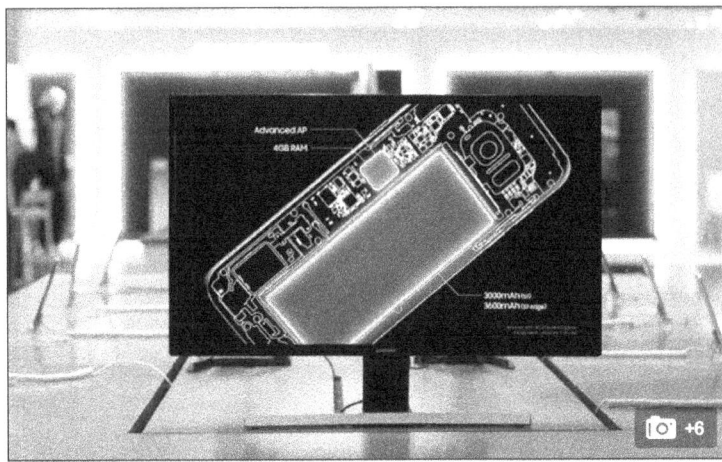

Figure 7: Galaxy Note 7 fiasco from the GDELT database

Indexing the GDELT database

The next step is to start building our online API so that any user can detect near-duplicate events in real time just like Facebook does on a user's timeline. We use the *Play Framework* here, but we will keep the description short as this has already been covered in Chapter 8, *Building a Recommendation System*.

Persisting our RDDs

Firstly, we need to extract data out of our RDD and persist it somewhere that is reliable, scalable, and highly efficient for search by key. As the main purpose of that database is to retrieve an article given a specific key (key being the Simhash), **Cassandra** (maven dependency as follows) sounds like a good fit for that job.

```
<dependency>
  <groupId>com.datastax.spark</groupId>
  <artifactId>spark-cassandra-connector_2.11</artifactId>
</dependency>
```

Our data model is fairly simple and consists of one simple table:

```
CREATE TABLE gzet.articles (
  simhash int PRIMARY KEY,
  url text,
  title text,
  body text
);
```

The easiest way to store our RDD into Cassandra is to wrap our result in a case class object that matches our earlier table definition and calls the `saveToCassandra` function:

```
import com.datastax.spark.connector._

corpusRDD.map { case (content, simhash) =>
  Article(
    simhash,
    content.body,
    content.title,
    content.url
  )
}
.saveToCassandra(cassandraKeyspace, cassandraTable)
```

Building a REST API

The next step is to work on the API itself. We create a new maven module (packaged as `play2`) and import the following dependencies:

```
<packaging>play2</packaging>

<dependencies>
  <dependency>
    <groupId>com.typesafe.play</groupId>
    <artifactId>play_2.11</artifactId>
  </dependency>
  <dependency>
    <groupId>com.datastax.cassandra</groupId>
    <artifactId>cassandra-driver-core</artifactId>
  </dependency>
</dependencies>
```

We first create a new **data access layer**, that, given an input Simhash, builds the list of all the possible 1-bit and 2-bit masks discussed earlier and pulls all the matching records from Cassandra:

```
class CassandraDao() {

  private val session = Cluster.builder()
                        .addContactPoint(cassandraHost)
                        .withPort(cassandraPort)
                        .build()
                        .connect()

  def findDuplicates(hash: Int): List[Article] = {
    searchmasks.map { mask =>
      val searchHash = mask ^ hash
      val stmt = s"SELECT simhash, url, title, body FROM gzet.articles
WHERE simhash = $searchHash;"
      val results = session.execute(stmt).all()
      results.map { row =>
        Article(
          row.getInt("simhash"),
          row.getString("body"),
          row.getString("title"),
          row.getString("url")
        )
      }
      .head
    }
    .toList
  }
}
```

In our **controller**, given an input URL, we extract the HTML content, tokenize the text, build a Simhash value, and call our service layer to finally return our matching records in a JSON format.

```
object Simhash extends Controller {

  val dao = new CassandraDao()
  val goose = new HtmlFetcher()

  def detect = Action { implicit request =>
    val url = request.getQueryString("url").getOrElse("NA")
    val article = goose.fetch(url)
    val hash = Tokenizer.lucene(article.body).simhash
    val related = dao.findDuplicates(hash)
    Ok(
        Json.toJson(
```

```
        Duplicate(
          hash,
          article.body,
          article.title,
          url,
          related
        )
      )
    )
  }
}
```

The following `play2` route will redirect any GET request to the `detect` method we saw earlier:

```
GET /simhash io.gzet.story.web.controllers.Simhash.detect
```

Finally, our API can be started and exposed to the end users as follows:

```
curl -XGET 'localhost:9000/simhash?url=
http://www.detroitnews.com/story/tech/2016/10/12/samsung-damage/91948802/'

{
  "simhash": 1822083259,
  "body": "Seoul, South Korea - The fiasco of Samsung's [...]
  "title": "Fiasco leaves Samsung's smartphone brand [...]",
  "url": "http://www.detroitnews.com/story/tech/2016/[...]",
  "related": [
    {
      "hash": 1821919419,
      "body": "SEOUL, South Korea - The fiasco of [...]
      "title": "Note 7 fiasco leaves Samsung's [...]",
      "url": "http://www.chron.com/business/technology/[...]"
    },
    {
      "hash": -325433157,
      "body": "The fiasco of Samsung's fire-prone [...]
      "title": "Samsung's Smartphone Brand [...]",
      "url": "http://www.toptechnews.com/[...]"
    }
  ]
}
```

Congratulations! You have now built an online API that can be used to detect near-duplicates such as the ones around Galaxy Note 7 fiasco; but how accurate our API is compared to the one from Facebook? This surely is accurate enough to start de-noising GDELT data by grouping highly similar events into stories.

Area of improvement

Although we are already satisfied with the overall quality of the results returned by our API, here we discuss a major improvement in the context of news articles. In fact, articles are not only made of different bag of words, but follow a clear structure where the order truly matters. In fact, the title is always a punch line, and the main content is well covered within the first few lines only. The rest of the article does matter, but may not be as important as the introduction. Given that assumption, we can slightly modify our Simhash algorithm to take the order into account by attributing a different weight to each word.

```
implicit class Simhash(content: String) {

  // ../..

  def weightedSimhash = {

    val features = shingles(content)
    val totalWords = features.length
    val aggHashWeight = features.zipWithIndex
      .map {case (hash, id) =>
        (hash, 1.0 - id / totalWords.toDouble)
      }
      .flatMap { case (hash, weight) =>
        Range(0, 32).map { bit =>
          (bit, if(hash.isBitSet(bit)) weight else -weight)
        }
      }
      .groupBy(_._1)
      .mapValues(_.map(_._2).sum > 0)
      .toArray

    buildSimhash(0, aggHashWeight)
  }

}
```

Instead of adding 1 or -1 any time the same bit value is set or not, we add the corresponding weight of that word according to its position in the article. Similar articles will have to share same words, same word frequency, but also a similar structure. In other words, we are much less permissive in any difference occurring in the first few lines of text than we are at the really bottom line of each article.

Building stories

Simhash should be used to detect near-duplicate articles only. Extending our search to a 3-bit or 4-bit difference becomes terribly inefficient (3-bit difference requires 5,488 distinct queries to Cassandra while 41,448 queries will be needed to detect up to 4-bit differences) and seems to bring much more noise than related articles. Should the user want to build larger stories, a typical clustering technique must be applied then.

Building term frequency vectors

We will start grouping events into stories using a KMeans algorithm, taking the articles' word frequencies as input vectors. TF-IDF is simple, efficient, and a proven technique to build vectors out of text content. The basic idea is to compute a word frequency that we normalize using the inverse document frequency across the dataset, hence decreasing the weight on common words (such as stop words) while increasing the weight of words specific to the definition of a document. Its implementation is part of the basics of MapReduce processing, the *Wordcount* algorithm. We first compute our RDD of term frequency for each word in each document.

```
val tfRDD = documentRDD.flatMap { case (docId, body) =>
  body.split("\\s").map { word =>
    ((docId, word), 1)
  }
}
.reduceByKey(_+_)
.map { case ((docId, word), tf) =>
  (docId, (word, tf))
}
```

The IDF is the logarithmic value of the total number of documents divided by the number of documents containing the letter w:

$$idf_i = log\left(\frac{n+1}{df_i+1}\right)$$

```
val n = sc.broadcast(documentRDD.count())
val dfMap = sc.broadcast(
  tfRDD.map { case (docId, (word, _)) =>
    (docId, word)
  }
  .distinct()
```

```
    .values
    .map { word =>
      (word, 1)
    }
    .reduceByKey(_+_)
    .collectAsMap()
)

val tfIdfRDD = tfRDD.mapValues { case (word, tf) =>
  val df = dfMap.value.get(word).get
  val idf = math.log((n.value + 1) / (df + 1))
  (word, tf * idf)
}
```

As our output vectors are made of words, we need to assign a sequence ID to each word in our corpus. We may have two solutions here. Either we build our dictionary and assign an ID for each word, or group different words in same buckets using a hash function. The former is ideal but results in vectors about a million features long (as many features as we do have unique words) while the latter is much smaller (as many features as the user specifies) but may lead to undesired effects due to hash collisions (the least features the more collisions).

```
val numFeatures = 256

val vectorRDD = tfIdfRDD.mapValues { case (word, tfIdf) =>
  val rawMod = word.hashCode % numFeatures
  rawMod + (if (rawMod < 0) numFeatures else 0)
  (word.hashCode / numFeatures, tfIdf)
}
.groupByKey()
.values
.map { it =>
  Vectors.sparse(numFeatures, it.toSeq)
}
```

Although we describe the TF-IDF technique in detail, this hashing TF can be done within only a couple of lines thanks to the MLlib utilities, which we'll see next. We built our RDD of 256 large vectors that can (technically) be fed in a KMeans clustering, but, due to the hashing properties we just explained earlier, we would be subject to dramatic hash collisions.

```
val tfModel = new HashingTF(1 << 20)
val tfRDD = documentRDD.values.map { body =>
  tfModel.transform(body.split("\\s"))
}

val idfModel = new IDF().fit(tfRDD)
```

```
val tfIdfRDD = idfModel.transform(tfRDD)
val normalizer = new Normalizer()
val sparseVectorRDD = tfIdfRDD map normalizer.transform
```

The curse of dimensionality, the data science plague

Increasing our feature size from 256 to say 2^{20} will strongly limit the number of collisions, but will come at a price, our data points are now embedded on a highly dimensional space.

Here we describe a clever approach to overcome the *curse of dimensionality* (http://www.stat.ucla.edu/~sabatti/statarray/textr/node5.html) without having to deep dive into fuzzy mathematical theories around matrix calculation (such as singular value decomposition) and without the need of compute-intensive operation. This approach is called *Random Indexing* and is similar to the *Simhash* concept described earlier.

> More information about Random Indexing can be found at
> http://eprints.sics.se/221/1/RI_intro.pdf.

The idea is to generate a sparse, randomly generated and unique representation of each distinct feature (a word here), composed of +1s, -1s, and mainly 0s. Then, each time we come across a word in a context (a document), we add this word's signature to a context vector. A document vector is then the sum of each of its words' vectors as per the following *Figure 8* (or the sum of each of its TF-IDF vectors, in our case):

	Random Contexts								
mastering	1	0	0	0	0	1	1	0	-1
spark	0	1	0	0	1	1	1	-1	0
for	1	0	0	0	1	1	-1	0	1
data	0	0	0	0	0	0	0	1	0
science	-1	1	1	0	1	1	0	0	-1

	Aggregated Context								
mastering spark for data science	1	2	1	0	3	4	1	0	-1

Figure 8: Building a Random Indexing vector

We invite our purist math geek readers to dive into the *Johnson-Lindenstrauss* (`http://ttic.uchicago.edu/~gregory/courses/LargeScaleLearning/lectures/jl.pdf`) lemma that basically states that *"if we project points in a vector space into a randomly selected subspace of sufficiently high dimensionality, the distances between the points are approximately preserved"*. Although the *Random Indexing* technique itself can be implemented (with its fair amount of effort), the *Johnson-Lindenstrauss* lemma is quite useful but by far more difficult to grasp. Luckily, an implementation is part of the excellent spark-package *generalized-kmeans-clustering* (`https://github.com/derrickburns/generalized-kmeans-clustering`) from *Derrick Burns*.

```
val embedding = Embedding(Embedding.MEDIUM_DIMENSIONAL_RI)
val denseVectorRDD = sparseVectorRDD map embedding.embed
denseVectorRDD.cache()
```

We were finally able to project our 2^{20} large vectors in *only* 256 dimensions. This technique offers huge benefits to say the least.

- We have a fixed number of features. Our vectors will never grow in size should we encounter a new word in the future that was not part of our initial dictionary. This will be particularly useful in a streaming context.
- Our input feature set is extremely large (2^{20}). Although the collisions will still occur, the risk is mitigated.
- The distances are preserved thanks to the *Johnson-Lindenstrauss* lemma.
- Our output vectors are relatively small (256). We overcame the curse of dimensionality.

As we cached our vector RDD into memory, we can now look at the KMeans clustering itself.

Optimizing KMeans

We assume our readers are familiar with KMeans clustering already as this algorithm is probably the most famous and widely used algorithm for unsupervised clustering. Any attempt at doing yet another explanation here will not be as good as the many resources you will be able to find out there after more than half a century of active research.

We previously created our vectors based on the articles' contents (TF-IDF). The next step is to start grouping articles into stories based on their similarity. In Spark implementation of KMeans, only the *Euclidean distance* measure is supported. One would argue the *Cosine distance* would be more suitable for text analysis, but we assume that the former is accurate enough as we do not want to repackage the MLlib distribution for that exercise.For more explanation regarding the use of cosine distance for text analysis, please refer to http://www .cse.msu.edu/~pramanik/research/papers/2003Papers/sac04.pdf. We report in the following code both the Euclidean and Cosine functions that can be applied on any array of double (the logical data structure behind dense vectors):

```
def euclidean(xs: Array[Double], ys: Array[Double]) = {
  require(xs.length == ys.length)
  math.sqrt((xs zip ys)
    .map { case (x, y) =>
      math.pow(y - x, 2)
    }
    .sum
  )
}

def cosine(xs: Array[Double], ys: Array[Double]) = {

  require(xs.length == ys.length)
  val magX = math.sqrt(xs.map(i => i * i).sum)
  val magY = math.sqrt(ys.map(i => i * i).sum)
  val dotP = (xs zip ys).map { case (x, y) =>
    x * y
  }.sum

  dotP / (magX * magY)
}
```

Training a new KMeans clustering is fairly simple using the MLlib package. We specify a threshold of 0.01 after which we consider our cluster centers to converge and set the maximum iterations to 1,000.

```
val model: KMeansModel = new KMeans()
  .setEpsilon(0.01)
  .setK(numberOfClusters)
  .setMaxIterations(1000)
  .run(denseVectorRDD)
```

But what is the right number of clusters in our particular use case? With between 500 to 1,000 different articles per 15mn batch, how many stories can we build? The right question is, *How many true events do we think happened over a 15mn batch window?* In fact, optimizing KMeans for news articles is not different from any other use case; this is done by optimizing its associated cost, cost being the **sum of the squared distances (SSE)** from the points to their respective centroids.

```
val wsse = model.computeCost(denseVectorRDD)
```

With *k* equal to the number of articles, the associated cost will be 0 (each article is the center of its own cluster). Similarly, with *k* equal to 1, the cost will be maximum. The best value of *k* is therefore the minimum possible value after which adding a new cluster would not bring any gain in the associated cost, usually represented as an elbow in the SSE curve shown in the next figure.

Using all the 15,000 articles we collected so far, the optimal number of clusters is not obvious here but would probably be around 300.

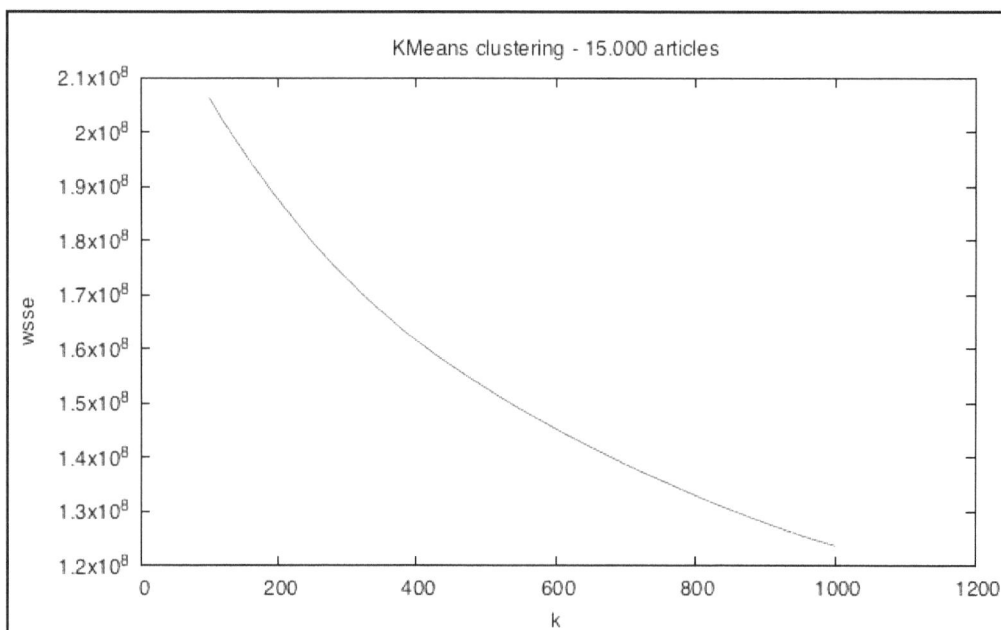

Figure 9: Elbow method using the cost function

A rule of thumb is to use k as a function of n (number of articles). With over 15,000 articles, following this rule would return $k \approx 100$.

$$k \approx \sqrt{\frac{n}{2}}$$

We use a value of 100 and start predicting our clusters for each of our data points.

```
val clusterTitleRDD = articleRDD
  .zip(denseVectorRDD)
  .map { case ((id, article), vector) =>
    (model.predict(vector), article.title)
  }
```

Although this could be greatly improved, we confirm many articles that look similar are grouped within same stories. We report some Samsung-related articles belonging to the same cluster here:

- *What Samsung can learn from Tylenol, Mattel, and JetBlue...*
- *Huawei Mate 9 Appears To Be A Samsung Galaxy Note 7 Clone...*
- *In light of the Note 7 debacle, Samsung may be poised to...*
- *Samsung's spiralling stock draws investors betting...*
- *Note 7 fiasco leaves Samsung's smartphone brand...*
- *Samsung's smartphone brand takes beating from Note 7 fiasco...*
- *Note 7 fiasco leaves Samsung's smartphone brand in question...*
- *Note 7 fiasco leaves Samsung's smartphone brand in question...*
- *Samsung's smartphone brand takes beating from Note 7 fiasco...*
- *Fiasco leaves Samsung's smartphone brand in question...*

Surely these similar articles were not eligible for a Simhash lookup as they differ by more than 1-bits or 2-bits. A clustering technique can be used to group similar (but not duplicate) articles into broader stories. It is worth mentioning that optimizing KMeans is a tedious task that requires many iterations and thorough analysis. This, however, is not part of the scope here as we will be focusing on much larger clusters and much smaller datasets in real time.

Story mutation

We now have enough material to enter the heart of the subject. We were able to detect near-duplicate events and group similar articles within a story. In this section, we will be working in real time (on a Spark Streaming context), listening for news articles, grouping them into stories, but also looking at how these stories may change over time. We appreciate that the number of stories is undefined as we do not know in advance what events may arise in the coming days. As optimizing KMeans for each batch interval (15 mn in GDELT) would not be ideal, neither would it be efficient, we decided to take this constraint not as a limiting factor but really as an advantage in the detection of breaking news articles.

The Equilibrium state

If we were to divide the world's news articles into say 10 or 15 clusters, and fix that number to never change over time, then training a KMeans clustering should probably group similar (but not necessarily duplicate) articles into generic stories. For convenience, we give the following definitions:

- An **article** is the news article covering a particular event at a time T
- A **story** is a group of similar articles covering an event at a time T
- A **topic** is a group of similar stories covering different events over a period P
- An **epic** is a group of similar stories covering the same event over a period P

We assume that after some time without any major news events, any story will be grouped into distinct *topics* (each covering one or several themes). As an example, any article about politics – regardless the nature of the political event – may be grouped into the politics bucket. This is what we call the *Equilibrium state*, where the world is equally divided into 15 distinct and clear categories (war, politics, finance, technology, education, and so on).

But what happens if a major event just breaks through? An event may become so important that, over time, (and because of the fixed number of clusters) it could shadow the least important *topic* and become part of its own *topic*. Similar to the BBC broadcast that is limited to a 30 mn window, some minor events like the *Oyster festival in Whitstable* may be skipped in favor of a major international event (to the very dismay of oysters' fans). This topic is not generic anymore but is now associated to a particular event. We called this topic an *epic*. As an example, the generic *topic* [terrorism, war, and violence] became an epic [**Paris Attacks**] in November last year when a major terrorist attack broke through; what was deemed to be a broad discussion about violence and terrorism in general became a branch dedicated to the articles covering the events held in Paris.

Now imagine an *epic* keeps growing in size; while the first articles about **Paris Attacks** were covering facts, few hours later, the entire world was paying tribute and condemning terrorism. At the same time, investigations were led by both French and Belgium police to track and dismantle the terrorism network. Both of these stories were massively covered, hence became two different versions of the same *epic*. This concept of branching is reported in the following *Figure 10*:

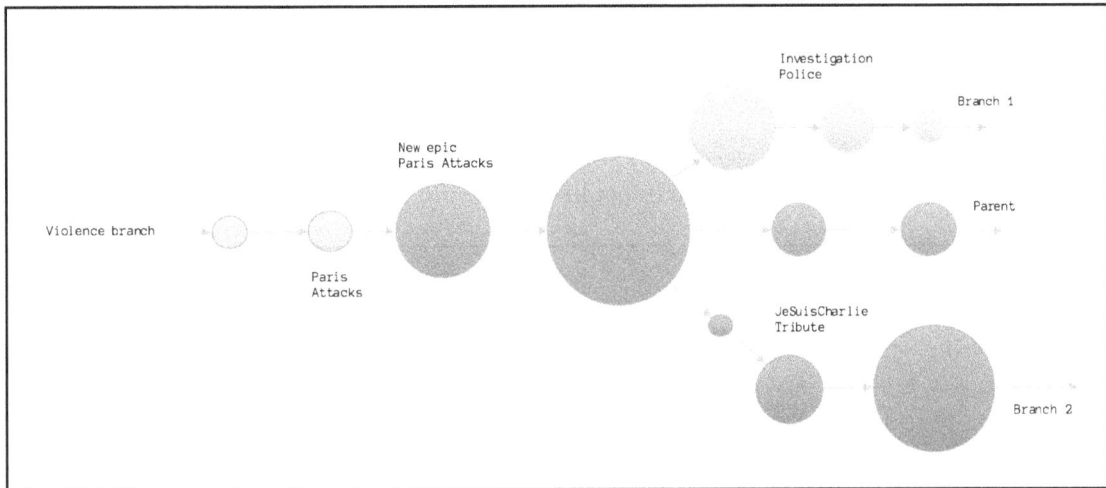

Figure 10: Concept of a story mutation branching

Surely some epics will last longer than others, but when they vanish – if they do – their branches may be recycled to cover new breaking articles (remember the fixed number of clusters) or be re-used to group generic stories back to their generic topics. At some point in time, we eventually reach a new Equilibrium state where the world nicely fits again within 15 different topics. We assume, though, that a new Equilibrium may not be a perfect clone of the previous one as this disturbance may have carved and re-shaped the world somehow. As a concrete example, we still mention 9/11-related articles nowadays; world trade center attacks that happened in NYC in 2001 are still contributing to the definition of [violence, war, and terrorism] *topic*.

Tracking stories over time

Although the preceding description is more conceptual than anything, and would probably deserve a subject for a PhD in data science applied to geo-politics, we would like to dig that idea further and see how Streaming KMeans could be a fantastic tool for that use case.

Building a streaming application

The first thing is to acquire our data in real time, hence modifying our existing NiFi flow to fork our downloaded archive to a Spark Streaming context. One could simply **netcat** the content of a file to an open socket, but we want this process to be resilient and fault tolerant. NiFi comes, by default, with the concept of output ports that provide a mechanism to transfer data to remote instances using *Site-To-Site*. In that case, the port works like a queue, and no data should be lost in transit, hopefully. We enable this functionality in the `nifi.properties` file by allocating a port number.

```
nifi.remote.input.socket.port=8055
```

We create a port called [Send_To_Spark] on our canvas, and every record (hence the `SplitText` processor) will be sent to it just like we would be doing on a Kafka topic.

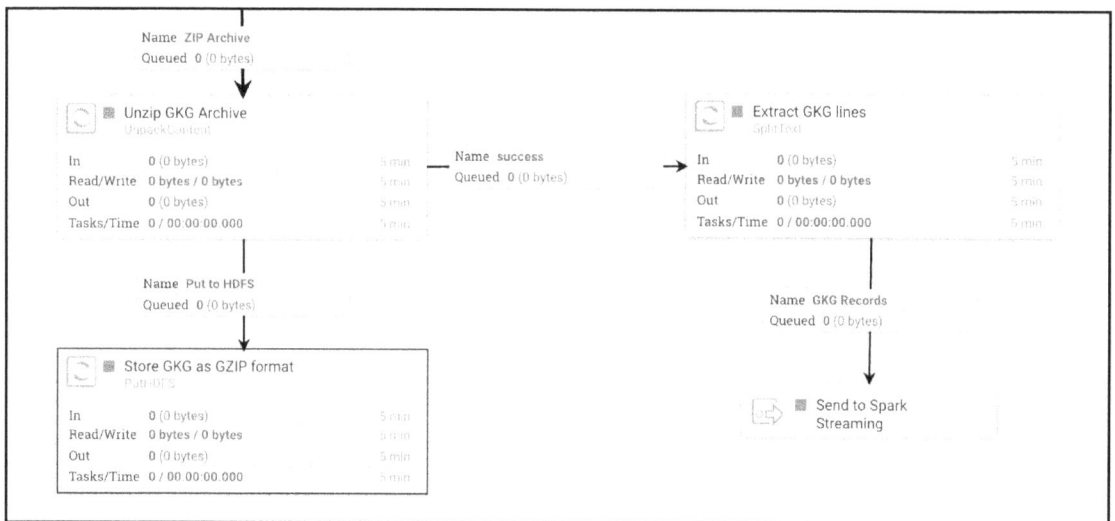

Figure 11: Sending GKG records to Spark Streaming

> 💡 **TIP**
>
> Although we are designing a streaming application, it is recommended to always keep an immutable copy of your data in a resilient data store (HDFS here). In our NiFi flow earlier, we did not modify our existing process, but forked it to also send records to our Spark Streaming. This will be particularly useful when/if we need to replay part of our dataset.

On the Spark side, we need to build a Nifi receiver. This can be achieved using the following maven dependency:

```
<dependency>
  <groupId>org.apache.nifi</groupId>
  <artifactId>nifi-spark-receiver</artifactId>
  <version>0.6.1</version>
</dependency>
```

We define the NiFi endpoint together with the port name [Send_To_Spark] we assigned earlier. Our stream of data will be received as packet stream that can easily be converted into a String using the getContent method.

```
def readFromNifi(ssc: StreamingContext): DStream[String] = {

  val nifiConf = new SiteToSiteClient.Builder()
    .url("http://localhost:8090/nifi")
    .portName("Send_To_Spark")
    .buildConfig()

  val receiver = new NiFiReceiver(nifiConf, StorageLevel.MEMORY_ONLY)
  ssc.receiverStream(receiver) map {packet =>
    new String(packet.getContent, StandardCharsets.UTF_8)
  }
}
```

We start our streaming context and listen to new GDELT data coming every 15 mn.

```
val ssc = new StreamingContext(sc, Minutes(15))
val gdeltStream: DStream[String] = readFromNifi(ssc)
val gkgStream = parseGkg(gdeltStream)
```

The next step is to download the HTML content for each article. The tricky part here is to download articles for distinct URLs only. As there is no built-in distinct operation on DStream, we need to access the underlying RDDs using a transform operation on top of which we pass an extractUrlsFromRDD function:

```
val extractUrlsFromRDD = (rdd: RDD[GkgEntity2]) => {
  rdd.map { gdelt =>
    gdelt.documentId.getOrElse("NA")
  }
  .distinct()
}
val urlStream = gkgStream.transform(extractUrlsFromRDD)
val contentStream = fetchHtml(urlStream)
```

Similarly, building vectors requires access to the underlying RDDs as we need to count the document frequency (used for TF-IDF) across the entire batch. This is also done within the `transform` function.

```
val buildVectors = (rdd: RDD[Content]) => {

  val corpusRDD = rdd.map(c => (c, Tokenizer.stem(c.body)))

  val tfModel = new HashingTF(1 << 20)
  val tfRDD = corpusRDD mapValues tfModel.transform

  val idfModel = new IDF() fit tfRDD.values
  val idfRDD = tfRDD mapValues idfModel.transform

  val normalizer = new Normalizer()
  val sparseRDD = idfRDD mapValues normalizer.transform

  val embedding = Embedding(Embedding.MEDIUM_DIMENSIONAL_RI)
  val denseRDD = sparseRDD mapValues embedding.embed

  denseRDD
}

val vectorStream = contentStream transform buildVectors
```

Streaming KMeans

Our use case perfectly fits in a **Streaming KMeans** algorithm. The concept of Streaming KMeans does not differ from the classic KMeans except that it applies on dynamic data and therefore needs to be constantly re-trained and updated.

At each batch, we find the closest center for each new data point, average the new cluster centers and update our model. As we track the true clusters and adapt to the changes in pseudo real-time, it will be particularly easy to track the same topics across different batches.

The second important feature of a Streaming KMeans is the forgetfulness. This ensures new data points received at time t will be contributing more to the definition of our clusters than any other point in the past history, hence allowing our cluster centers to smoothly drift over time (stories will mutate). This is controlled by the decay factor and its half-life parameter (expressed in the number of batches or number of points) that specifies the time after which a given point will only contribute half of its original weight.

- With an infinite decay factor, all the history will be taken into account, our cluster centers will be drifting slowly and will not be reactive if a major news event just breaks through
- With a small decay factor, our clusters will be too reactive towards any point and may drastically change any time a new event is observed

The third and most important feature of a Streaming KMeans is the ability to detect and recycle dying clusters. When we observe a drastic change in our input data, one cluster may become far from any known data point. Streaming KMeans will eliminate this dying cluster and split the largest one in two. This is totally in-line with our concept of story branching, where multiple stories may share a common ancestor.

We use a half-life parameter of two batches here. As we get new data every 15 mn, any new data point will stay *active* for 1 hour only. The process for training Streaming KMeans is reported in *Figure 12*:

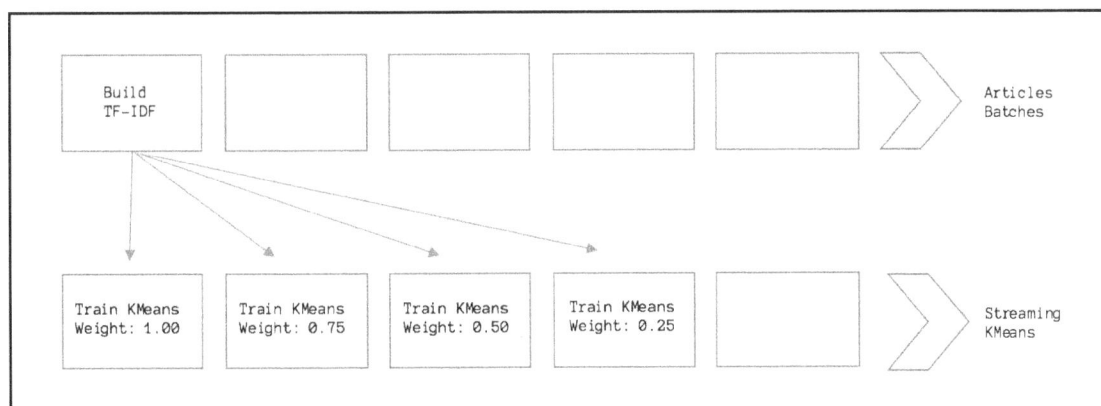

Figure 12: Training a Streaming KMeans

We create a new Streaming KMeans as follows. Because we did not observe any data point yet, we initialize it with 15 random centers of 256 large vectors (size of our TF-IDF vectors) and train it in real time using the `trainOn` method:

```
val model = new StreamingKMeans()
  .setK(15)
  .setRandomCenters(256, 0.0)
  .setHalfLife(2, "batches")

model.trainOn(vectorStream.map(_._2))
```

Finally, we predict our clusters for any new data point:

```
val storyStream = model predictOnValues vectorStream
```

We then save our results to our Elasticsearch cluster using the following attributes (accessed through a series of join operations). We do not report here how to persist RDD to Elasticsearch as we believe this has been covered in depth in the previous chapters already. Note that we also save the vector itself as we may re-use it later in the process.

```
Map(
  "uuid" -> gkg.gkgId,
  "topic" -> clusterId,
  "batch" -> batchId,
  "simhash" -> content.body.simhash,
  "date" -> gkg.date,
  "url" -> content.url,
  "title" -> content.title,
  "body" -> content.body,
  "tone" -> gkg.tones.get.averageTone,
  "country" -> gkg.v2Locations,
  "theme" -> gkg.v2Themes,
  "person" -> gkg.v2Persons,
  "organization" -> gkg.v2Organizations,
  "vector" -> v.toArray.mkString(",")
)
```

Visualization

As we stored our articles with their respective stories and *topics* on Elasticsearch, we can browse any events using a keyword search (as the articles are fully analyzed and indexed) or for a particular person, theme, organization, and so on. We build visualizations on top of our stories and try to detect their potential drifts on a Kibana dashboard. The different cluster IDs (our different *topics*) over time are reported in the following *Figure 13* for the 13th of November (35,000 articles indexed):

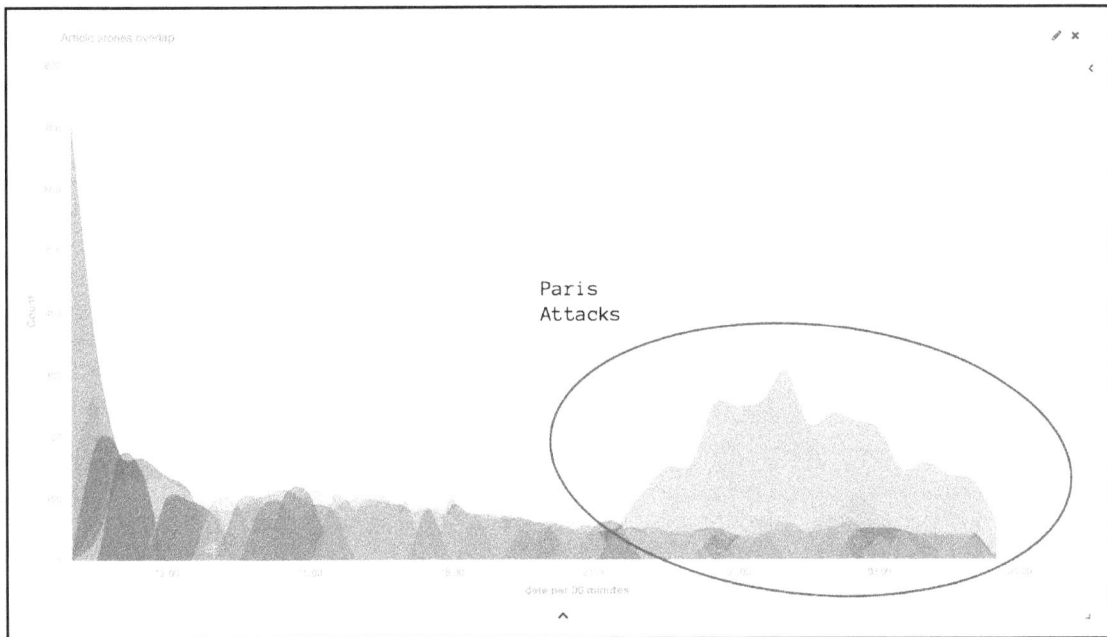

Figure 13: Kibana visualization of the Paris attacks

The results are quite promising. We were able to detect the **Paris Attacks** at around 9:30 p.m. on November 13th, only a few minutes after the first attacks started. We also confirm a relative good consistency of our clustering algorithm as a particular cluster was made of events related to the **Paris Attacks** only (5,000 articles) from 9:30 p.m. to 3:00 a.m.

But we may wonder what this particular cluster was about before the first attack took place. Since we indexed all the articles together with their cluster ID and their GKG attributes, we can easily track a story backwards in time and detect its mutation. It turns out this particular *topic* was mainly covering events related to [MAN_MADE_DISASTER] theme (among others) until 9 p.m. to 10 p.m. when it turned into the **Paris Attacks** *epic* with themes around [TERROR], [STATE_OF_EMERGENCY], [TAX_ETHNICITY_FRENCH], [KILL], and [EVACUATION].

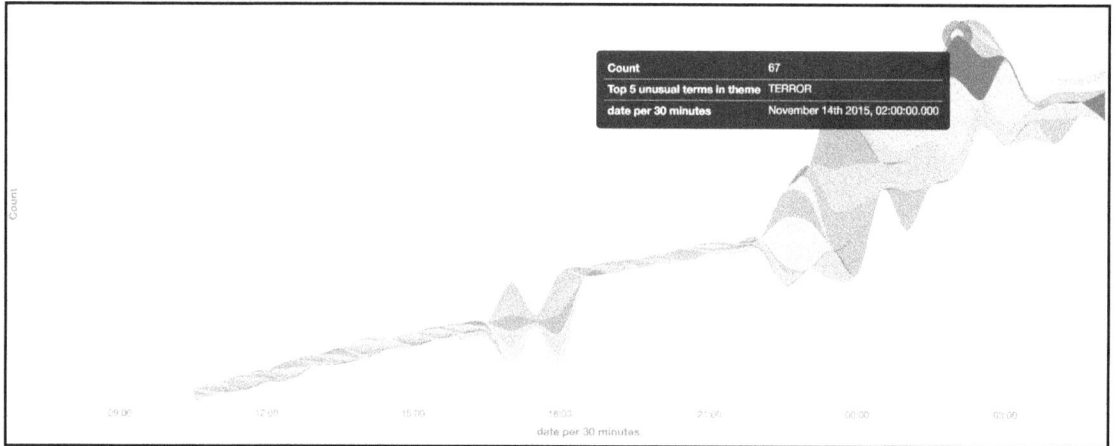

Figure 14: Kibana streamgraph of the Paris attacks cluster

Needless to say the 15 mn average tone we get from GDELT dropped drastically after 9 p.m. for that particular *topic*:

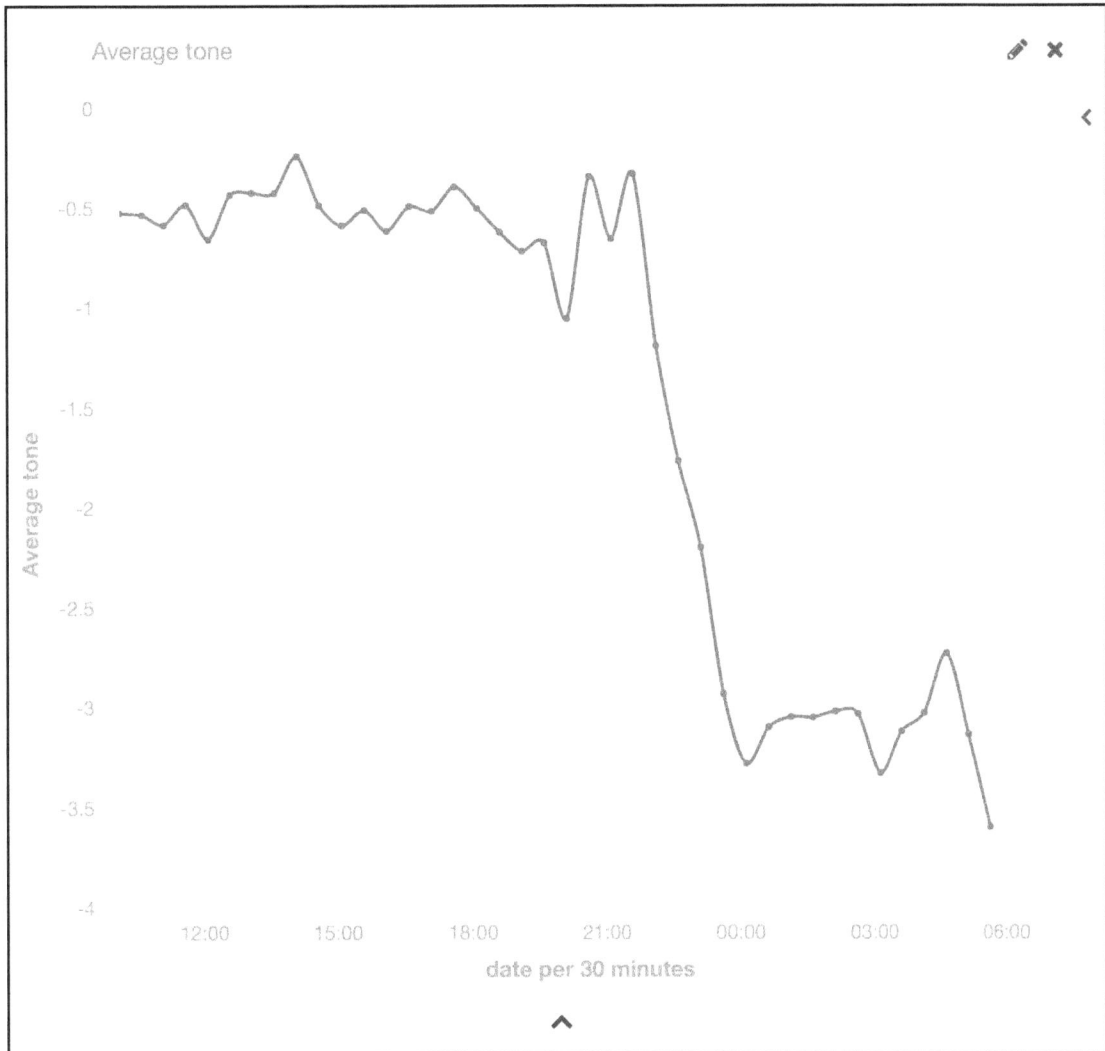

Figure 15: Kibana average tone-Paris attacks cluster

Using these three simple visualizations, we prove that we can track a story over time and study its potential mutation in genre, keywords, persons, or organizations (basically any entity we can extract from GDELT). But we could also look at the geolocation from the GKG records; with enough articles, we could possibly track the terrorist hunt held between Paris and Brussels on a map, in pseudo real time!

Although we found one main cluster that was specific to the Paris Attacks, and that this particular cluster was the first one to cover this series of events, this may not be the only one. According to the Streaming KMeans definition earlier, this *topic* became so big that it surely had triggered one or several subsequent *epics*. We report in the following *Figure 16* the same results as per *Figure 13*, but this time filtered out for any article matching the keyword *Paris*:

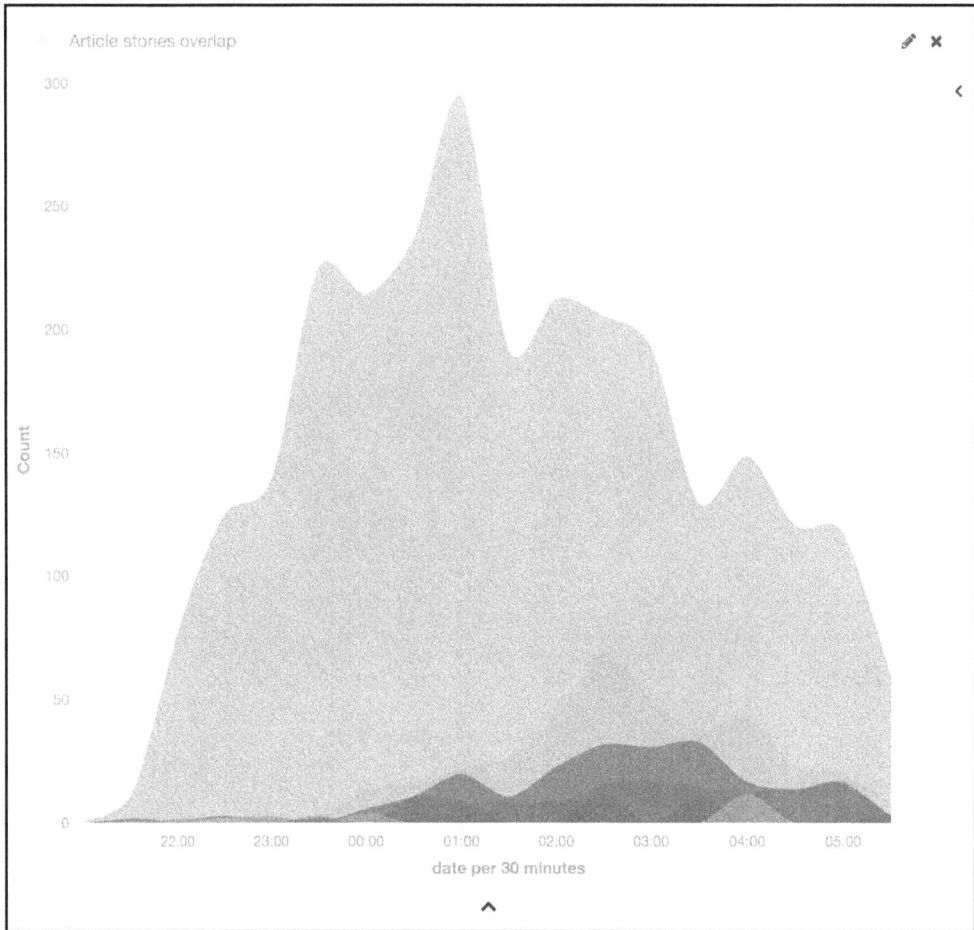

Figure 16: Kibana Paris Attacks multiple epics

It seems that around midnight, this *epic* gave rise to multiple versions of the same event (at least three major ones). After an hour following the attacks (1 hour is our decay factor), Streaming KMeans started to recycle dying clusters, hence creating new branches out of the most important event (our *Paris attack* cluster).

While the main *epic* was still covering the event itself (the facts), the second most important one was more about social network related articles. A simple word frequency analysis tells us this *epic* was about the #portesOuvertes (open doors) and #prayForParis hashtags where Parisians responded to terror with solidarity. We also detected another cluster focusing more on all the politicians paying tributes to France and condemning terrorism. All these new stories share the *Paris attack epic* as a common ancestor, but cover a different flavor of it.

Building story connections

How can we link these branches together? How can we track an *epic* over time and see when, if, how, or why it may split? Surely visualization helps, but we are looking at a graph problem to solve here.

Because our KMeans model keeps getting updated at each batch, our approach is to retrieve the articles that we predicted using an outdated version of our model, pull them from Elasticsearch, and predict them against our updated KMeans. Our assumption is as follows:

If we observe many articles at a time t that belonged to a story s, and now belong to a story s' at a time $t+\delta t$, then s most likely migrated to s' in δt time.

As a concrete example, the first #prayForParis article was surely belonging to the *Paris Attacks epic*. Few batches later, that same article belonged to the *Paris Attacks/Social Network* cluster. Therefore, the *Paris Attack epic* may have spawn the *Paris Attacks/Social Network epic*. This process is reported in the following *Figure 17*:

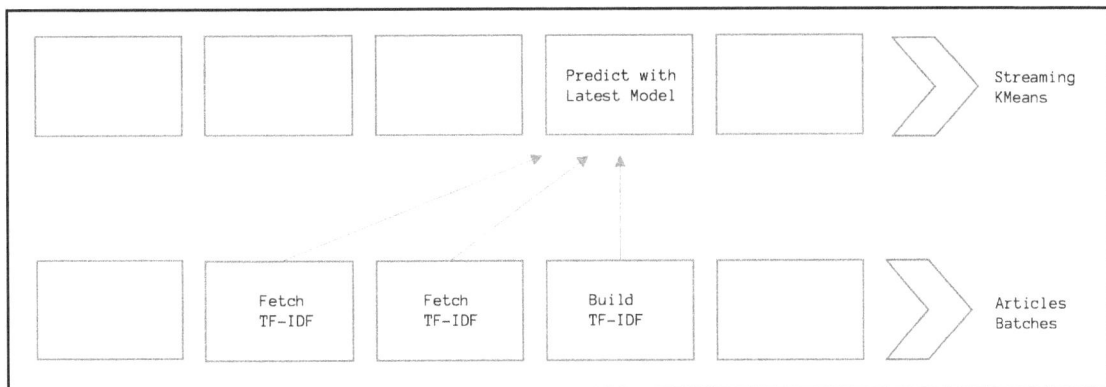

Figure 17: Detecting story connections

We read a JSON RDD from Elasticsearch and applied a range query using the batch ID. In the following example, we want to access all the vectors built over the past hour (four last batches) together with their original cluster ID and re-predict them against our updated model (accessed through the `latestModel` function):

```
import org.json4s.DefaultFormats
import org.json4s.native.JsonMethods._

val defaultVector = Array.fill[Double](256)(0.0d).mkString(",")
val minBatchQuery = batchId - 4
val query = "{"query":{"range":{"batch":{"gte": " + minBatchQuery +
",\"lte\": " + batchId + "}}}}"
val nodesDrift = sc.esJsonRDD(esArticles, query)
  .values
  .map { strJson =>
    implicit val format = DefaultFormats
    val json = parse(strJson)
    val vectorStr = (json \ "vector").extractOrElse[String](defaultVector)
    val vector = Vectors.dense(vectorStr.split(",").map(_.toDouble))
    val previousCluster = (json \ "topic").extractOrElse[Int](-1)
    val newCluster = model.latestModel().predict(vector)
    ((previousCluster, newCluster), 1)
  }
  .reduceByKey(_ + _)
```

Finally, a simple `reduceByKey` function will count the number of different edges over the past hour. In most of the cases, articles in story *s* will stay in story *s*, but in case of the Paris attacks, we may observe some stories to drift over time towards different *epics*. Most importantly, the more connections two branches have in common, the more similar they are (as many of their articles are interconnected) and therefore the closest they seem to be in a force directed layout. Similarly, branches that are not sharing many connections will seem to be far from another in the same graph visualization. A force atlas representation of our story connections is done using Gephi software and reported in the following *Figure 18*. Each node is a story at a batch *b*, and each edge is the number of connections we found between two stories. The 15 lines are our 15 *topics* that all share a common ancestor (the initial cluster spawn when first starting the streaming context).

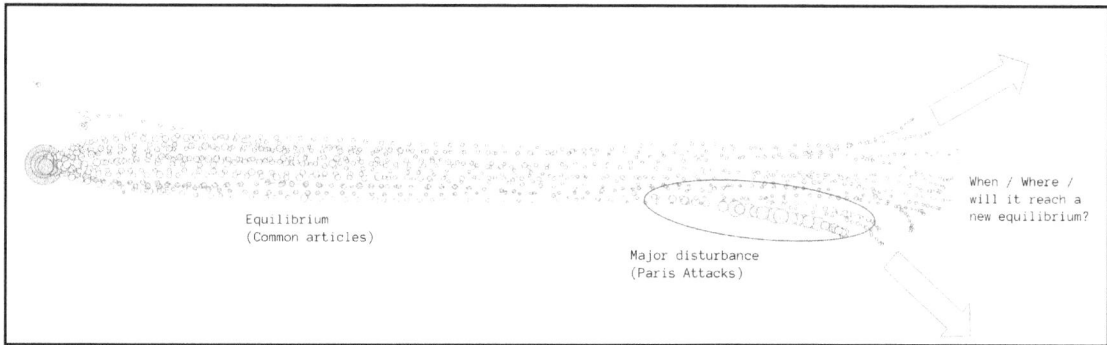

Figure 18: Force-directed layout of story mutation

The first observation we can make is this line shape. This observation surprisingly confirms our theory of an Equilibrium state where the world nicely fitted in 15 distinct *topics* until the Paris attacks happened. Before the event, most of the *topics* were isolated and intraconnected (hence this line shape). After the event, we see our main *Paris Attack epic* to be dense, interconnected, and drifting over time. It also seems to drag few branches down with it due to the growing number on interconnections. These two similar branches are the two other clusters mentioned earlier (social network and tributes). This *epic* is being more and more specific over time, it naturally becomes more different from others, hence pushing all these different stories upwards and resulting in this scatter shape.

We also want to know what these different branches were about, and whether or not we could explain why a story may have split into two. For that purpose, we find the main article of each story as being the closest point to its centroid.

```
val latest = model.latestModel()
val topTitles = rdd.values
  .map { case ((content, v, cId), gkg) =>
    val dist = euclidean(
                  latest.clusterCenters(cId).toArray,
                  v.toArray
                  )
    (cId, (content.title, dist))
  }
  .groupByKey()
  .mapValues { it =>
    Try(it.toList.sortBy(_._2).map(_._1).head).toOption
  }
  .collectAsMap()
```

In *Figure 19*, we report the same graph enriched with the story titles. Although it is difficult to find a clear pattern, we found an interesting case. A *topic* was covering (among others) an event related to *Prince Harry* joking around about his hair style, that slightly migrated to *Obama* offering a statement on the attack in Paris, and finally turned into the Paris attack and the tributes paid by politicians. This branch did not come out of nowhere but seemed to follow a logical flow:

1. [ROYAL, PRINCE HARRY, JOKES]
2. [ROYAL, PRINCE HARRY]
3. [PRINCE HARRY, OBAMA]
4. [PRINCE HARRY, OBAMA, POLITICS]
5. [OBAMA, POLITICS]
6. [OBAMA, POLITICS, PARIS]
7. [POLITICS, PARIS]

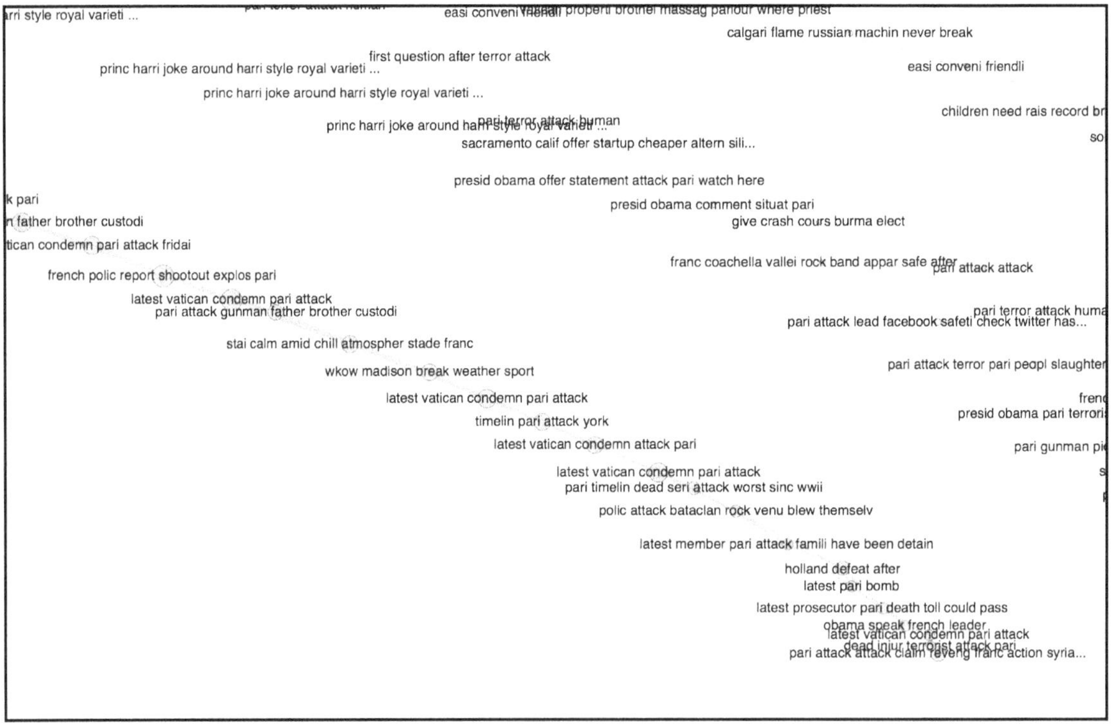

Figure 19: Force-directed layout of story mutation – title

To summarize, it seems that a breaking news event acts as a sudden perturbation of an Equilibrium state. Now we may wonder how long would that disturbance last, whether or not a new Equilibrium will be reached in the future and what would be the shape of the world resulting from that *wound*. Most importantly, what effect a different decay factor would have on that world shape.

With enough time and motivation, we would potentially be interested in applying some concepts of physics around *perturbation theory* (`http://www.tcm.phy.cam.ac.uk/~bds10/a qp/handout_dep.pdf`). I personally would be interested in finding harmonics around this Equilibrium. The reason of the Paris attacks events being so memorable is because of its violent nature for sure, but also because it happened only a few months after the *Charlie Hebdo* attacks in Paris.

Summary

This chapter was really complex and the story mutation problem could not be easily solved in the time frame allowed for delivering this chapter. However, what we discovered is truly amazing as it opens up a lot of questions. We did not want to draw any conclusion though, so we stopped our process right after the observation of the Paris attack disturbance and left that discussion open for our readers. Feel free to download our code base and study any breaking news and their potential impacts in what we define as an Equilibrium state. We are very much looking forward to hearing back from you and learning about your findings and different interpretations.

Surprisingly, we did not know anything about the *Galaxy Note 7 fiasco* before writing this chapter, and without the API created in the first section, the related articles would surely have been indistinguishable from the mass. De-duplicating content using *Simhash* really helped us get a better overview of the world news events.

In the next chapter, we will try to detect abnormal tweets related to the US elections and the new president elect (*Donald Trump*). We will cover both *Word2Vec* algorithm and Stanford NLP for sentiment analysis.

11
Anomaly Detection on Sentiment Analysis

When we look back at the year 2016, we will surely remember it as a time of many significant geo-political events ranging from Brexit, Great Britain's vote to leave the European Union, to the untimely passing of many beloved celebrities, including the sudden death of the singer David Bowie (covered in `Chapter 6`, *Scraping Link-Based External Data* and `Chapter 7`, *Building Communities*). However, perhaps the most notable occurrence of the year was the tense US presidential election and its eventual outcome, the election of President Donald Trump. A campaign that will long be remembered, not least for its unprecedented use of social media, and the stirring up of passion among its users, most of whom made their feelings known through the use of hashtags: either positive ones, such as *#MakeAmericaGreatAgain* or *#StrongerTogether*, or conversely negative ones, such as *#DumpTrump* or *#LockHerUp*. Since this chapter is about sentiment analysis, the election presents the ideal use case. However, instead of trying to predict the outcome itself, we will aim to detect abnormal tweets during the US election using a real-time Twitter feed. We will cover the following topics:

- Acquiring Twitter data in real-time and batch
- Extracting sentiment using Stanford NLP
- Storing sentiment time series in *Timely*
- Deriving features from only 140 characters using *Word2Vec*
- Introducing the concepts of graph *ergodicity* and *shortest paths*
- Training a KMeans model to detect potential anomalies
- Visualizing models with *Embedding Projector* from *TensorFlow*

Following the US elections on Twitter

On November 8, 2016, American citizens went in millions to polling stations to cast their votes for the next President of the United States. Counting began almost immediately and, although not officially confirmed until sometime later, the forecasted result was well known by the next morning. Let's start our investigation a couple of days before the major event itself, on November 6, 2016, so that we can preserve some context in the run-up. Although we do not exactly know what we will find in advance, we know that *Twitter* will play an oversized role in the political commentary given its influence in the build-up, and it makes sense to start collecting data as soon as possible. In fact, data scientists may sometimes experience this as a *gut feeling* - a strange and often exciting notion that compels us to commence working on something without a clear plan or absolute justification, just a sense that it will pay off. And actually, this approach can be vital since, given the normal time required to formulate and realize such a plan and the transient nature of events, a major news event may occur (refer to `Chapter 10`, *Story De-duplication and Mutation*), a new product may have been released, or the stock market may be trending differently (see `Chapter 12`, *TrendCalculus*); by this time, the original dataset may no longer be available

Acquiring data in stream

The first action is to start acquiring Twitter data. As we plan to download more than 48 hours worth of tweets, the code should be robust enough to not fail somewhere in the middle of the process; there is nothing more frustrating than a fatal `NullPointerException` occurring after many hours of intense processing. We know we will be working on sentiment analysis at some point down the line, but for now we do not wish to over-complicate our code with large dependencies as this can decrease stability and lead to more unchecked exceptions. Instead, we will start by collecting and storing the data and subsequent processing will be done offline on the collected data, rather than applying this logic to the live stream.

We create a new Streaming context reading from Twitter 1% firehose using the utility methods created in `Chapter 9`, *News Dictionary and Real-Time Tagging System*. We also use the excellent GSON library to serialize Java class `Status` (Java class embedding Twitter4J records) to JSON objects.

```
<dependency>
  <groupId>com.google.code.gson</groupId>
  <artifactId>gson</artifactId>
  <version>2.3.1</version>
</dependency>
```

We read Twitter data every 5 minutes and have a choice to optionally supply Twitter filters as command line arguments. Filters can be keywords such as *Trump*, *Clinton* or *#MAGA*, *#StrongerTogether*. However, we must bear in mind that by doing this we may not capture all relevant tweets as we can never be fully up to date with the latest hashtag trends (such as *#DumpTrump*, *#DrainTheSwamp*, *#LockHerUp*, or *#LoveTrumpsHate*) and many tweets will be overlooked with an inadequate filter, so we will use an empty filter list to ensure that we catch everything.

```
val sparkConf  = new SparkConf().setAppName("Twitter Extractor")
val sc = new SparkContext(sparkConf)
val ssc = new StreamingContext(sc, Minutes(5))

val filter = args

val twitterStream = createTwitterStream(ssc, filter)
  .mapPartitions { it =>
    val gson = new GsonBuilder().create()
    it.map { s: Status =>
      Try(gson.toJson(s)).toOption
    }
  }
```

We serialize our `Status` class using the GSON library and persist our JSON objects in HDFS. Note that the serialization occurs within a `Try` clause to ensure that unwanted exceptions are not thrown. Instead, we return JSON as an optional `String`:

```
twitterStream
  .filter(_.isSuccess)
  .map(_.get)
  .saveAsTextFiles("/path/to/twitter")
```

Finally, we run our Spark Streaming context and keep it alive until a new president has been elected, no matter what happens!

```
ssc.start()
ssc.awaitTermination()
```

Acquiring data in batch

Only 1% of tweets are retrieved through the Spark Streaming API, meaning that 99% of records will be discarded. Although able to download around 10 million tweets, we can potentially download more data, but this time only for a selected hashtag and within a small period of time. For example, we can download all tweets related to the *#LockHerUp* or *#BuildTheWall* hashtags.

The search API

For that purpose, we consume Twitter historical data through the `twitter4j` Java API. This library comes as a transitive dependency of `spark-streaming-twitter_2.11`. To use it outside of a Spark project, the following maven dependency should be used:

```
<dependency>
  <groupId>org.twitter4j</groupId>
  <artifactId>twitter4j-core</artifactId>
  <version>4.0.4</version>
</dependency>
```

We create a Twitter4J client as follows:

```
ConfigurationBuilder builder = new ConfigurationBuilder();
builder.setOAuthConsumerKey(apiKey);
builder.setOAuthConsumerSecret(apiSecret);
Configuration configuration = builder.build();

AccessToken token = new AccessToken(
  accessToken,
  accessTokenSecret
);

Twitter twitter =
  new TwitterFactory(configuration)
      .getInstance(token);
```

Then, we consume the `/search/tweets` service through the `Query` object:

```
Query q = new Query(filter);
q.setSince(fromDate);
q.setUntil(toDate);
q.setCount(400);

QueryResult r = twitter.search(q);
List<Status> tweets = r.getTweets();
```

Finally, we get a list of `Status` objects that can easily be serialized using the GSON library introduced earlier.

Rate limit

Twitter is a fantastic resource for data science, but it is far from a non-profit organization, and as such, they know how to value and price data. Without any special agreement, the search API is limited to a few days retrospective, a maximum of 180 queries per 15 minute window and 450 records per query. This limit can be confirmed on both the Twitter DEV website (`https://dev.twitter.com/rest/public/rate-limits`) and from the API itself using the `RateLimitStatus` class:

```
Map<String, RateLimitStatus> rls = twitter.getRateLimitStatus("search");
System.out.println(rls.get("/search/tweets"));

/*
RateLimitStatusJSONImpl{remaining=179, limit=180,
resetTimeInSeconds=1482102697, secondsUntilReset=873}
*/
```

Unsurprisingly, any queries on popular terms, such as *#MAGA* on November 9, 2016, hit this threshold. To avoid a rate limit exception, we have to page and throttle our download requests by keeping track of the maximum number of tweet IDs processed and monitor our status limit after each search request.

```
RateLimitStatus strl = rls.get("/search/tweets");
int totalTweets = 0;
long maxID = -1;
for (int i = 0; i < 400; i++) {

  // throttling
  if (strl.getRemaining() == 0)
    Thread.sleep(strl.getSecondsUntilReset() * 1000L);

  Query q = new Query(filter);
```

```
    q.setSince(fromDate);
    q.setUntil(toDate);
    q.setCount(100);

    // paging
    if (maxID != -1) q.setMaxId(maxID - 1);

    QueryResult r = twitter.search(q);
    for (Status s: r.getTweets()) {
      totalTweets++;
      if (maxID == -1 || s.getId() < maxID)
       maxID = s.getId();
       writer.println(gson.toJson(s));
    }
    strl = r.getRateLimitStatus();
  }
```

With around half a billion tweets a day, it will be optimistic, if not Naive, to gather all US-related data. Instead, the simple ingest process detailed earlier should be used to intercept tweets matching specific queries only. Packaged as main class in an assembly jar, it can be executed as follows:

```
java -Dtwitter.properties=twitter.properties /
  -jar trump-1.0.jar #maga 2016-11-08 2016-11-09 /
  /path/to/twitter-maga.json
```

Here, the `twitter.properties` file contains your Twitter API keys:

```
twitter.token = XXXXXXXXXXXXXX
twitter.token.secret = XXXXXXXXXXXXXX
twitter.api.key = XXXXXXXXXXXXXX
twitter.api.secret = XXXXXXXXXXXXXX
```

Analysing sentiment

After 4 days of intense processing, we extracted around 10 million tweets; representing approximately 30 GB worth of JSON data.

Massaging Twitter data

One of the key reasons Twitter became so popular is that any message has to fit into a maximum of 140 characters. The drawback is also that every message has to fit into a maximum of 140 characters! Hence, the result is massive increase in the use of abbreviations, acronyms, slang words, emoticons, and hashtags. In this case, the main emotion may no longer come from the text itself, but rather from the emoticons used (`http://dl.acm.org/citation.cfm?id=1628969`), though some studies showed that the emoticons may sometimes lead to inadequate predictions in sentiment (`https://arxiv.org/pdf/1511.02556.pdf`). Emojis are even broader than emoticons as they include pictures of animals, transportation, business icons, and so on. Also, while emoticons can easily be retrieved through simple regular expressions, emojis are usually encoded in Unicode and are more difficult to extract without a dedicated library.

```
<dependency>
   <groupId>com.kcthota</groupId>
   <artifactId>emoji4j</artifactId>
   <version>5.0</version>
</dependency>
```

The `Emoji4J` library is easy to use (although computationally expensive) and given some text with emojis/emoticons, we can either `codify` – replace Unicode values with actual code names – or `clean` – simply remove any emojis.

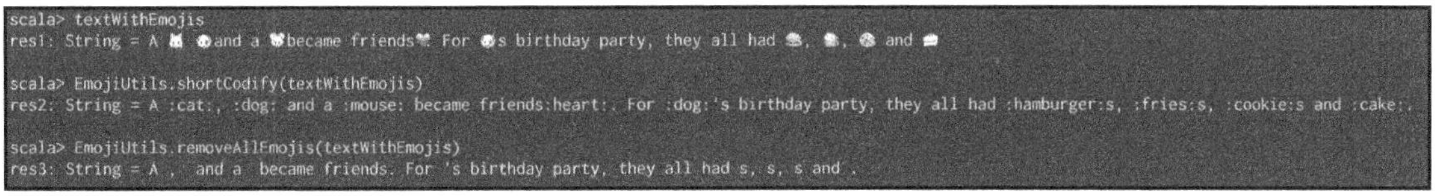

Figure 1: Emoji parsing

So firstly, let's clean our text from any junk (special characters, emojis, accents, URLs, and so on) to access plain English content:

```
import emoji4j.EmojiUtils

def clean = {
  var text = tweet.toLowerCase()
  text = text.replaceAll("https?:\\/\\/\\S+", "")
  text = StringUtils.stripAccents(text)
  EmojiUtils.removeAllEmojis(text)
    .trim
    .toLowerCase()
    .replaceAll("rt\\s+", "")
```

```
    .replaceAll("@[\\w\\d-_]+", "")
    .replaceAll("[^\\w#\\[\\]:'\\.!\\?,]+", " ")
    .replaceAll("\\s+([:'\\.!\\?,])\\1", "$1")
    .replaceAll("[\\s\\t]+", " ")
    .replaceAll("[\\r\\n]+", ". ")
    .replaceAll("(\\w)\\1{2,}", "$1$1") // avoid looooool
    .replaceAll("#\\W", "")
    .replaceAll("[#':,;\\.]$", "")
    .trim
}
```

Let's also codify and extract all emojis and emoticons and keep them aside as a list:

```
val eR = "(:\\w+:)".r

def emojis = {
  var text = tweet.toLowerCase()
  text = text.replaceAll("https?:\\/\\/\\S+", "")
  eR.findAllMatchIn(EmojiUtils.shortCodify(text))
    .map(_.group(1))
    .filter { emoji =>
      EmojiUtils.isEmoji(emoji)
    }.map(_.replaceAll("\\W", ""))
    .toArray
}
```

Writing these methods inside an *implicit class* means that they can be applied directly a String through a simple import statement.

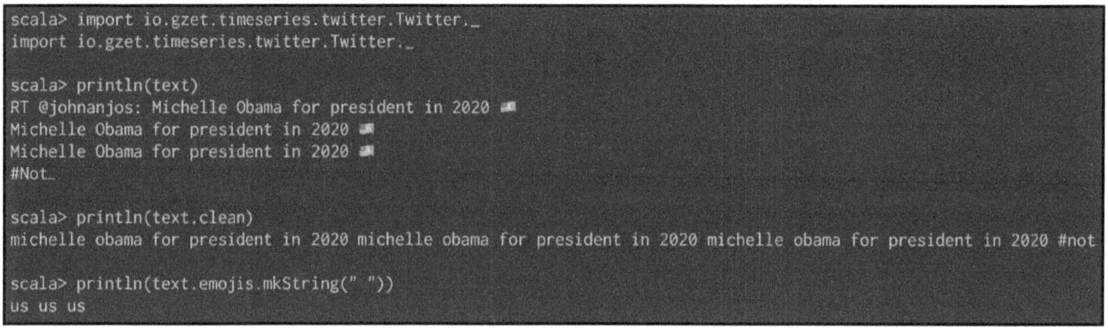

```
scala> import io.gzet.timeseries.twitter.Twitter._
import io.gzet.timeseries.twitter.Twitter._

scala> println(text)
RT @johnanjos: Michelle Obama for president in 2020 
Michelle Obama for president in 2020 
Michelle Obama for president in 2020 
#Not...

scala> println(text.clean)
michelle obama for president in 2020 michelle obama for president in 2020 michelle obama for president in 2020 #not

scala> println(text.emojis.mkString(" "))
us us us
```

Figure 2: Twitter parsing

Using the Stanford NLP

Our next step is to pass our cleaned text through a *Sentiment Annotator*. We use the Stanford NLP library for that purpose:

```xml
<dependency>
  <groupId>edu.stanford.nlp</groupId>
  <artifactId>stanford-corenlp</artifactId>
  <version>3.5.0</version>
  <classifier>models</classifier>
</dependency>

<dependency>
  <groupId>edu.stanford.nlp</groupId>
  <artifactId>stanford-corenlp</artifactId>
  <version>3.5.0</version>
</dependency>
```

We create a Stanford `annotator` that tokenizes content into sentences (`tokenize`), splits sentences (`ssplit`), tags elements (`pos`), and lemmatizes each word (`lemma`) before analyzing the overall sentiment:

```scala
def getAnnotator: StanfordCoreNLP = {
  val p = new Properties()
  p.setProperty(
    "annotators",
    "tokenize, ssplit, pos, lemma, parse, sentiment"
  )
  new StanfordCoreNLP(pipelineProps)
}

def lemmatize(text: String,
              annotator: StanfordCoreNLP = getAnnotator) = {

  val annotation = annotator.process(text.clean)
  val sentences = annotation.get(classOf[SentencesAnnotation])
    sentences.flatMap { sentence =>
    sentence.get(classOf[TokensAnnotation])
  .map { token =>
    token.get(classOf[LemmaAnnotation])
  }
  .mkString(" ")
}

val text = "If you're bashing Trump and his voters and calling them a
variety of hateful names, aren't you doing exactly what you accuse them?"
```

```
println(lemmatize(text))

/*
if you be bash trump and he voter and call they a variety of hateful name,
be not you do exactly what you accuse they
*/
```

Any word is replaced by its most basic form, that is, *you're* is replaced with *you be* and *aren't you doing* replaced with *be not you do*.

```
def sentiment(coreMap: CoreMap) = {

  coreMap.get(classOf[SentimentCoreAnnotations.ClassName].match {
      case "Very negative" => 0
      case "Negative" => 1
      case "Neutral" => 2
      case "Positive" => 3
      case "Very positive" => 4
      case _ =>
        throw new IllegalArgumentException(
          s"Could not get sentiment for [${coreMap.toString}]"
        )
    }
}

def extractSentiment(text: String,
                     annotator: StanfordCoreNLP = getSentimentAnnotator) =
{

  val annotation = annotator.process(text)
  val sentences = annotation.get(classOf[SentencesAnnotation])
  val totalScore = sentences map sentiment

  if (sentences.nonEmpty) {
    totalScore.sum / sentences.size()
  } else {
    2.0f
  }

}

extractSentiment("God bless America. Thank you Donald Trump!")
 // 2.5

extractSentiment("This is the most horrible day ever")
 // 1.0
```

A sentiment spans from *Very Negative* (0.0) to *Very Positive* (4.0) and is averaged per sentence. As we do not get more than 1 or 2 sentences per tweet, we expect a very small variance; most of the tweets should be *Neutral* (around 2.0), with only extremes to be scored (below ~1.5 or above ~2.5).

Building the Pipeline

For each of our Twitter records (stored as JSON objects), we do the following things:

- Parse the JSON object using `json4s` library
- Extract the date
- Extract the text
- Extract the location and map it to a US state
- Clean the text
- Extract emojis
- Lemmatize text
- Analyze sentiment

We then wrap all these values into the following `Tweet` case class:

```
case class Tweet(
          date: Long,
          body: String,
          sentiment: Float,
          state: Option[String],
          geoHash: Option[String],
          emojis: Array[String]
      )
```

As mentioned in previous chapters, creating a new NLP instance wouldn't scale for each record out of our dataset of 10 million records. Instead, we create only one `annotator` per `Iterator` (which means one per partition):

```
val analyzeJson = (it: Iterator[String]) => {

  implicit val format = DefaultFormats
  val annotator = getAnnotator
  val sdf = new SimpleDateFormat("MMM d, yyyy hh:mm:ss a")

  it.map { tweet =>

    val json = parse(tweet)
    val dateStr = (json \ "createdAt").extract[String]
```

```scala
    val date = Try(
      sdf.parse(dateStr).getTime
    )
     .getOrElse(0L)

    val text = (json \ "text").extract[String]
    val location = Try(
      (json \ "user" \ "location").extract[String]
    )
     .getOrElse("")
     .toLowerCase()

    val state = Try {
      location.split("\\s")
        .map(_.toUpperCase())
        .filter { s =>
          states.contains(s)
        }
        .head
    }
    .toOption

    val cleaned = text.clean

    Tweet(
     date,
     cleaned.lemmatize(annotator),
     cleaned.sentiment(annotator),
     state,
     text.emojis
    )
  }
}

val tweetJsonRDD = sc.textFile("/path/to/twitter")
val tweetRDD = twitterJsonRDD mapPartitions analyzeJson
tweetRDD.toDF().show(5)

/*
+-------------+---------------+---------+--------+----------+
|         date|           body|sentiment|   state|    emojis|
+-------------+---------------+---------+--------+----------+
|1478557859000|happy halloween|      2.0|    None [ghost]   |
|1478557860000|slave to the gr|      2.5|    None|[]        |
|1478557862000|why be he so pe|      3.0|Some(MD)|[]        |
|1478557862000|marcador sentim|      2.0|    None|[]        |
|1478557868000|you mindset tow|      2.0|    None|[sparkles]|
+-------------+---------------+---------+--------+----------+
```

```
*/
```

Using Timely as a time series database

Now that we are able to transform raw information into a clean series of Twitter sentiment with parameters such as hashtags, emojis, or US states, such a time series should be stored reliably and made available for fast query lookups.

In the Hadoop ecosystem, *OpenTSDB* (http://opentsdb.net/) is the default database for storing millions of chronological data points. However, instead of using the obvious candidate, we will introduce one you may not have come across before, called *Timely* (http s://nationalsecurityagency.github.io/timely/). Timely is a recently open sourced project started by the **National Security Agency** (**NSA**), as a clone of OpenTSDB, which uses Accumulo instead of HBase for its underlying storage. As you may recall, Accumulo supports cell-level security, and we will see this later on.

Storing data

Each record is composed of a metric name (for example, hashtag), timestamp, metric value (for example, sentiment), an associated set of tags (for example, state), and a cell visibility:

```
case class Metric(name: String,
                  time: Long,
                  value: Double,
                  tags: Map[String, String],
                  viz: Option[String] = None
                  )
```

For this exercise, we will filter out data for tweets only mentioning Trump or Clinton:

```
def expandedTweets = rdd.flatMap { tweet =>
  List("trump", "clinton") filter { f =>
    tweet.body.contains(f)
  } map { tag =>
    (tag, tweet)
  }
}
```

Next, we build a `Metric` object with names `io.gzet.state.clinton` and `io.gzet.state.trump` and an associated visibility. For the purpose of this exercise, we will assume that a junior analyst without the `SECRET` permission will not be granted access to highly negative tweets. This allows us to demonstrate Accumulo's excellent cell-level security:

```
def buildViz(tone: Float) = {
  if (tone <= 1.5f) Some("SECRET") else None: Option[String]
}
```

In addition, we will also need to handle *duplicate records*. In the event where multiple tweets are received at the exact same time (with potentially different sentiments), they will override an existing cell on Accumulo:

```
def sentimentByState = {
  expandedTweets.map { case (tag, tweet) =>
    ((tag, tweet.date, tweet.state), tweet.sentiment)
  }
  .groupByKey()
  .mapValues { f =>
    f.sum / f.size
  }
  .map { case ((tag, date, state), sentiment) =>
    val viz = buildViz(sentiment)
    val meta = Map("state" -> state)
    Metric("io.gzet.state.$tag", date, sentiment, meta, viz)
  }
}
```

We insert data either from a `POST` request or simply by piping data through an opened socket back to the Timely server:

```
def toPut = {

  val vizMap = if(viz.isDefined) {
    List("viz" -> viz.get)
  } else {
    List[(String, String)]()
  }

  val strTags = vizMap
    .union(tags.toList)
    .map { case (k, v) => s"$k=$v" }
    .mkString(" ")

  s"put $name $time $value $strTags"
}
```

```
implicit class Metrics(rdd: RDD[Metric]) {

  def publish = {

    rdd.foreachPartition { it: Iterator[Metric] =>

      val sock = new Socket(timelyHost, timelyPort)
      val writer = new PrintStream(
        sock.getOutputStream,
        true,
        StandardCharsets.UTF_8.name
      )

      it.foreach { metric =>
        writer.println(metric.toPut)
      }
      writer.flush()
    }

  }
}

tweetRDD.sentimentByState.publish
```

Our data is now securely stored in Accumulo and available to anyone with the correct access permissions.

We have created a series of input formats to retrieve Timely data back into a Spark job. This will not be covered here but can be found in our GitHub repository:

```
// Read  metrics from Timely
val conf = AccumuloConfig(
           "GZET",
           "alice",
           "alice",
           "localhost:2181"
           )

val metricsRDD = sc.timely(conf, Some("io.gzet.state.*"))
```

> **TIP**
> At the time of writing, Timely is still under active development and, as such, does not yet have a clean input/output format that can be used from Spark/MapReduce. The only ways to send data are via HTTP or Telnet.

Using Grafana to visualize sentiment

Timely does not come with a visualization tool as such. However, it does integrate well, and securely, with *Grafana* (https://grafana.net/) using the timely-grafana plugin. More information can be found on the Timely website.

Number of processed tweets

As a first simple visualization, we display the number of tweets for both the candidates on November 8 and 9, 2016 (UTC):

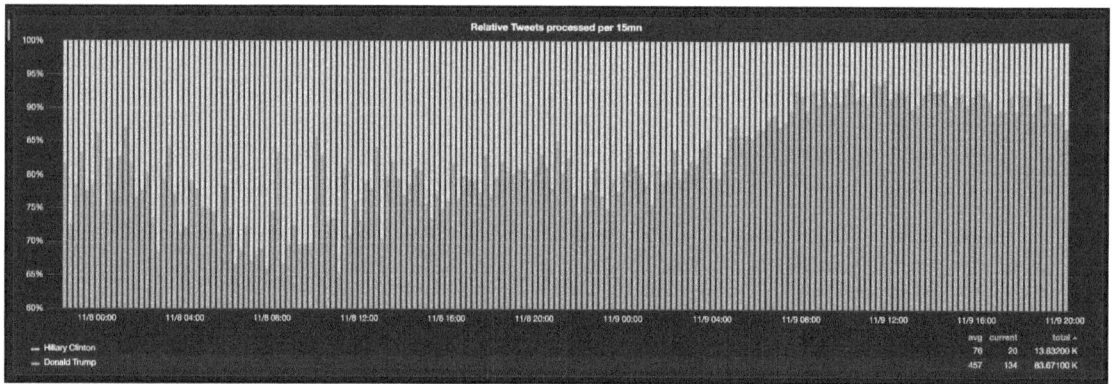

Figure 3: Timely-processed tweets

We observe more and more tweets related to Trump as the results of the election are published. On average, we observe around 6 times more Trump-related tweets than Clinton-related tweets.

Give me my Twitter account back

A quick study of the sentiment shows that it's relatively negative (1.3 on an average) and there's no significant difference between the tweets of both the candidates that would have helped predict the outcome of the US election.

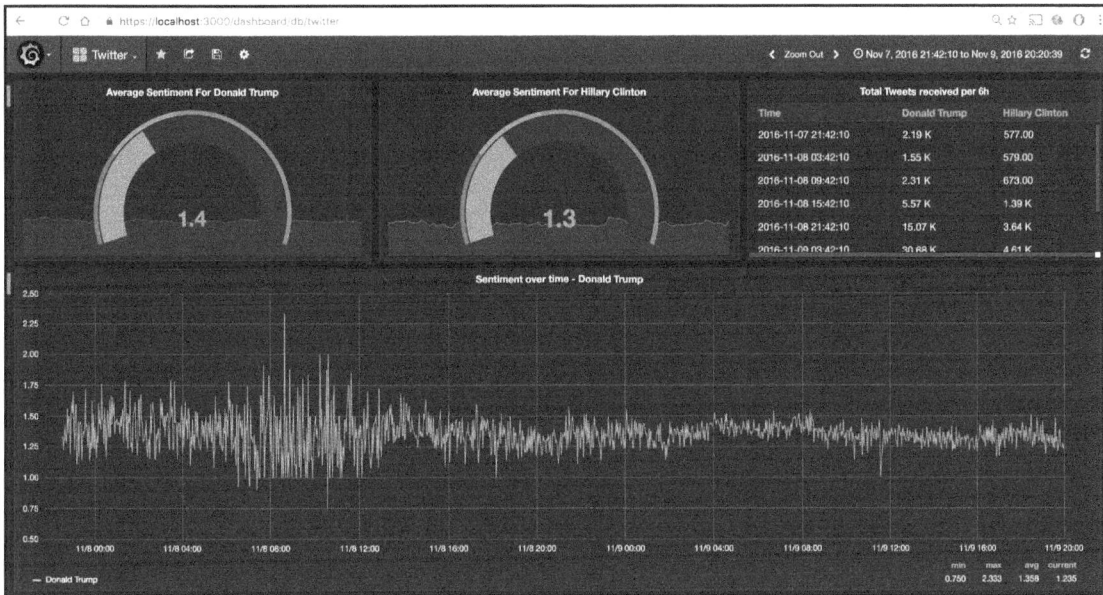

Figure 4: Timely-timeseries

However, on closer inspection, we find a truly interesting phenomenon. On November 8, 2016, around 1pm GMT (8am EST, that is, when the first polling stations opened in New York), we observe a massive drop-off in the *sentiment variance*. An oddity, seen in the preceding figure, which can't be completely explained. We can speculate that either the first vote cast officially marked the end of the turbulent presidential campaign and was the starting point of a retrospective period after the election – perhaps, a more *fact-based* dialog than before – or maybe Trump's advisors taking away his Twitter account really was their greatest idea.

Now we give an example of the versatility of Accumulo security by logging into Grafana as another user, this time with no SECRET authorization granted. As expected, in the proceeding image , the sentiment looks much more positive (as extremely negative sentiment is hidden), hence confirming the visibility settings on Timely; the elegance of Accumulo speaks for itself:

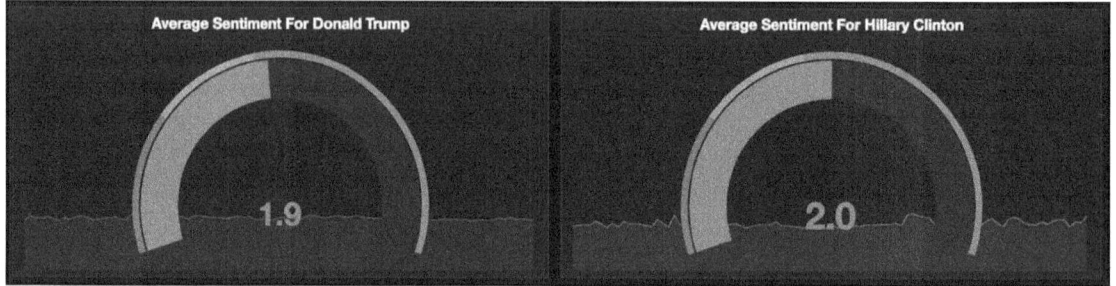

Figure 5: Timely-timeseries for non-SECRET

An example of how to create an Accumulo user can be found in Chapter 7, *Building Communities*.

Identifying the swing states

The last interesting feature we will leverage from Timely and Grafana is tree map aggregations. As all the US states' names are stored as part of the metric attributes, we will create a simple tree map for both the candidates. The size of each box corresponds to the number of observations, while the color is relative to the observed sentiment:

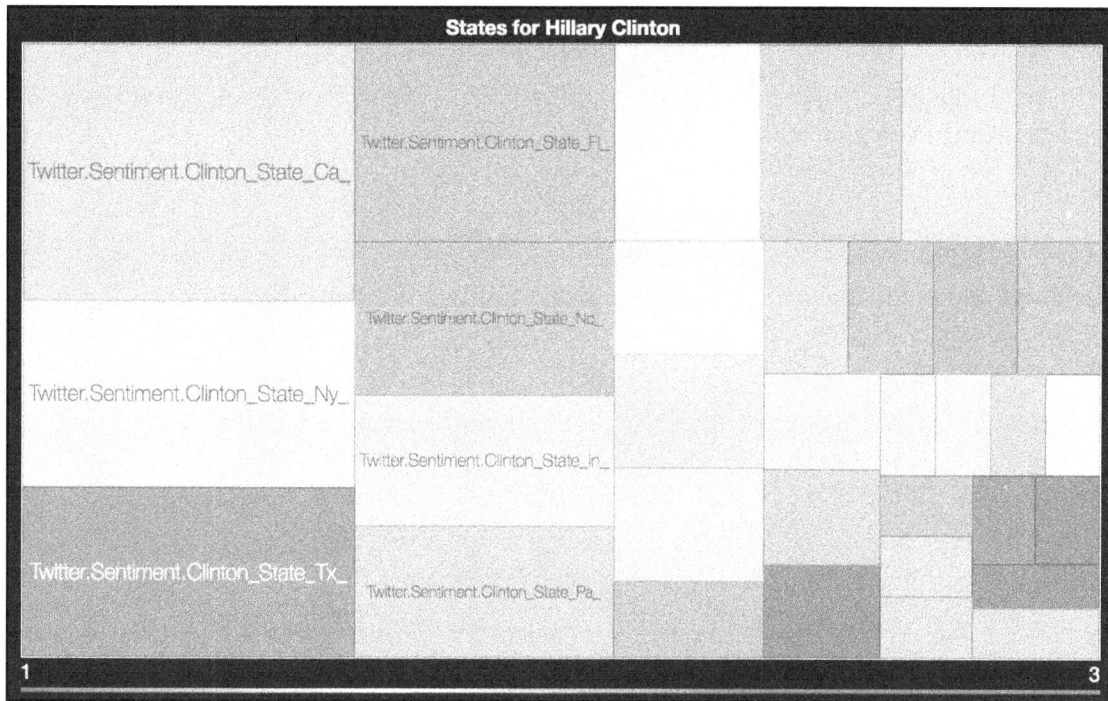

Figure 6: Timely – Tree map of the US states for Hillary Clinton

When we used the 2-day sentiment average previously, we couldn't differentiate between the republican and democrat states as the sentiment was statistically flat and relatively bad (1.3 on average). However, if we consider only the day prior to the election, then it seems much more interesting because we observed much more variance in our sentiment data. In the preceding image, we see Florida, North Carolina, and Pennsylvania – 3 of the 12 swing states-showing unexpectedly bad sentiment for Hillary Clinton. Could this pattern be an early indicator of the election outcome?

Twitter and the Godwin point

With our text content properly cleaned up, we can feed a *Word2Vec* algorithm and attempt to understand the words in their actual *context*.

Learning context

As it says on the tin, the *Word2Vec* algorithm transforms a word into a vector. The idea is that similar words will be embedded into similar vector spaces and, as such, will look close to one another contextually.

> More information about `Word2Vec` algorithm can be found at
> `https://papers.nips.cc/paper/5021-distributed-representations-of`
> `-words-and-phrases-and-their-compositionality.pdf`.

Well integrated into Spark, a `Word2Vec` model can be trained as follows:

```
import org.apache.spark.mllib.feature.Word2Vec

val corpusRDD = tweetRDD
    .map(_.body.split("\\s").toSeq)
    .filter(_.distinct.length >= 4)

val model = new Word2Vec().fit(corpusRDD)
```

Here we extract each tweet as a sequence of words, only keeping records with at least 4 distinct words. Note that the list of all words needs to fit in memory as it is collected back to the driver as a map of word and vector (as an array of float). The vector size and learning rate can be tuned through the `setVectorSize` and `setLearningRate` methods respectively.

Next, we use a Zeppelin notebook to interact with our model, sending different words and asking the model to obtain the closest synonyms. The results are quite impressive:

```
model.findSynonyms("#lockherup", 10).foreach(println)

/*
(#hillaryforprison,2.3266071900089313)
(#neverhillary,2.2890002973310066)
(#draintheswamp,2.2440446323298175)
(#trumppencelandslide,2.2392471034643604)
(#womenfortrump,2.2331140131326874)
(#trumpwinsbecause,2.2182999853485454)
```

```
(#imwithhim,2.1950198833564563)
(#deplorable,2.1570936207197016)
(#trumpsarmy,2.155859656266577)
(#rednationrising,2.146132149205829)
*/
```

While hashtags generally pass through standard NLP unnoticed, they do have a major contribution to make to tone and emotion. A tweet marked as neutral can be, in fact, much worse than it sounds using hashtags like *#HillaryForPrison* or *#LockHerUp*. So, let's attempt to take this into account using an interesting feature called *word-vector association*. A common example of this association given by the original *Word2Vec* algorithm is shown here:

```
[KING] is at [MAN] what [QUEEN] is at [?????]
```

This can be translated as the following vector:

```
VKING - VQUEEN = VMAN - V????
V???? = VMAN - VKING + VQUEEN
```

The nearest point should therefore be [WOMEN]. Technically speaking, this can be translated as follows:

```
import org.apache.spark.mllib.linalg.Vectors

def association(word1: String, word2: String, word3: String) = {

  val isTo = model
    .getVectors
    .get(word2)
    .get
    .zip(model.getVectors.get(word1).get)
    .map(t => t._1 - t._2)

  val what = model
    .getVectors
    .get(word3)
    .get

  val vec = isTo
    .zip(what)
    .map(t => t._1 + t._2)
    .map(_.toDouble)

  Vectors.dense(vec)

}
```

```
val assoc = association("trump", "republican", "clinton")

model.findSynonyms(assoc, 1)
    .foreach(println)

// (democrat,1.6838367309269164)
```

Saving/retrieving this model can be done as follows:

```
model.save(sc, "/path/to/word2vec")

val retrieved = Word2VecModel.load(sc, "/path/to/word2vec")
```

Visualizing our model

As our vectors are 100 dimensions wide, they are difficult to represent in a graph using traditional methods. However, you may have come across the *Tensor Flow* project and its recently open sourced *Embedding Projector* (http://projector.tensorflow.org/). This project offers a nice way to visualize our models due to its ability to quickly render high-dimensional data. It's easy to use as well – we simply export our vectors as tab-separated data points, load them into a web browser, and voila!

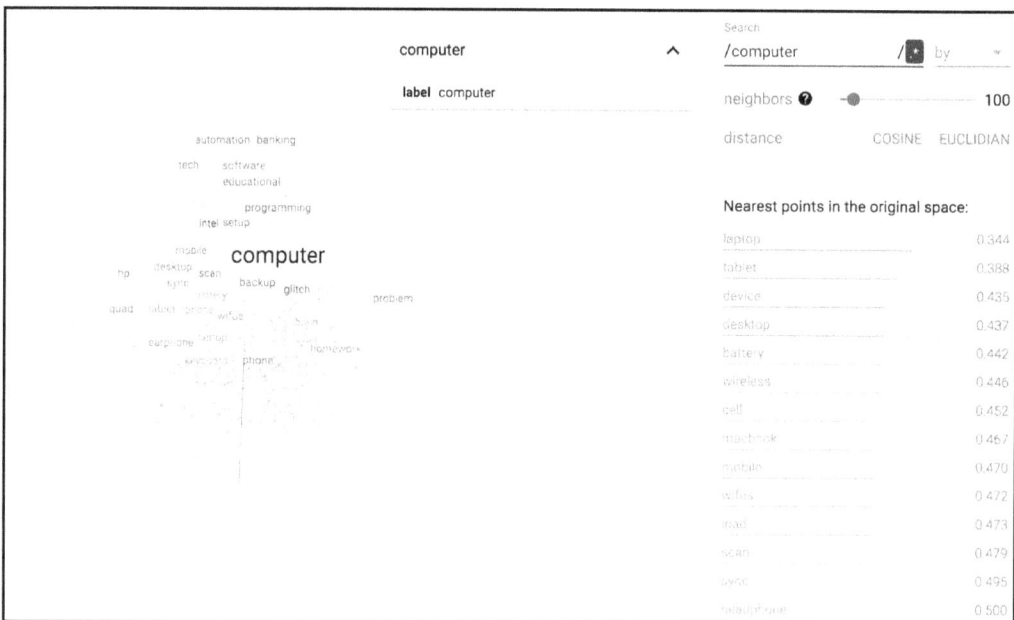

Figure 7: Embedding project. neighbours of Computer

Embedding Projector projects high-dimensional vector onto 3D space, where each dimension represents one of the first three **principal components** (**PCA**). We can also build our own projection where we basically stretch our vectors toward four specific directions. In the following representation, we stretch our vectors left, right, up, and down to [Trump], [Clinton], [Love], and [Hate]:

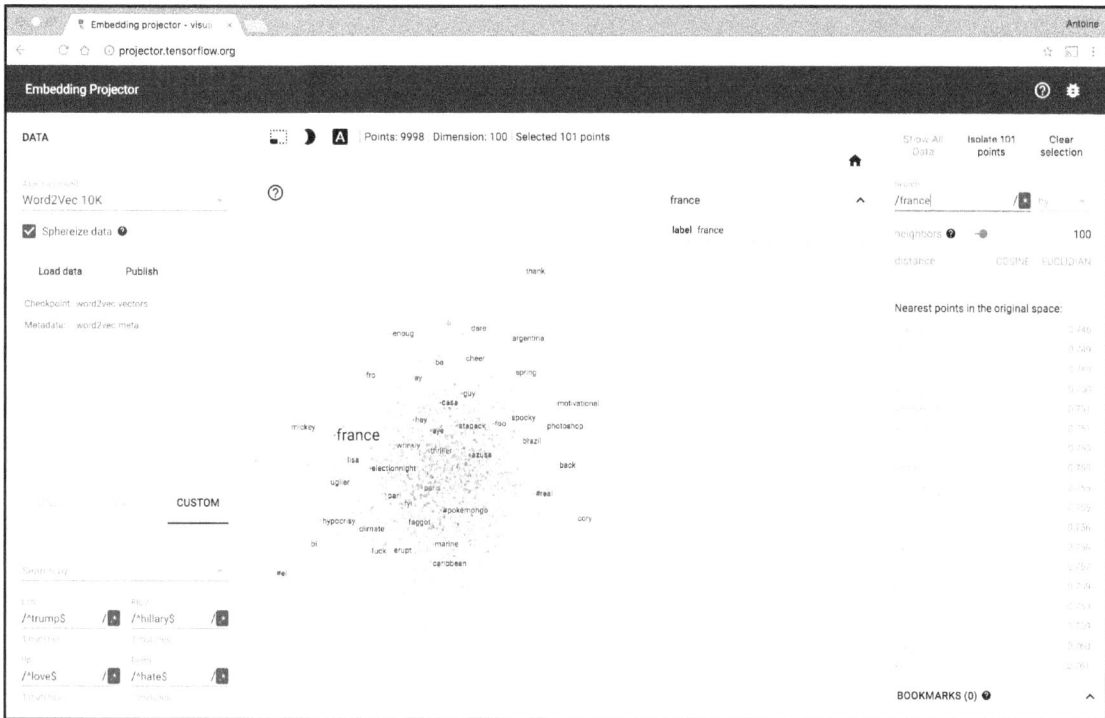

Figure 8: Embedding project. custom projection

Now that we have a greatly simplified vector space, we can more easily understand each word and how it relates to its neighbors (democrat versus republican and love versus hate). For example, with the French election coming up next year, we see that France is closer to Trump than it is to Clinton. Could this be seen as an early indicator of the upcoming election?

Word2Graph and Godwin point

You don't have to play around with the Twitter *Word2Vec* model for very long before you come across sensitive terms and references to World War II. In fact, this is an occurrence that was originally asserted by Mike Godwin in 1990 as Godwin's Law (`https://www.wired.com/1994/10/godwin-if-2/`), which states as follows:

> *As an online discussion grows longer, the probability of a comparison involving Nazis or Hitler approaches 1*

As of 2012, it is even part of the Oxford English Dictionary.

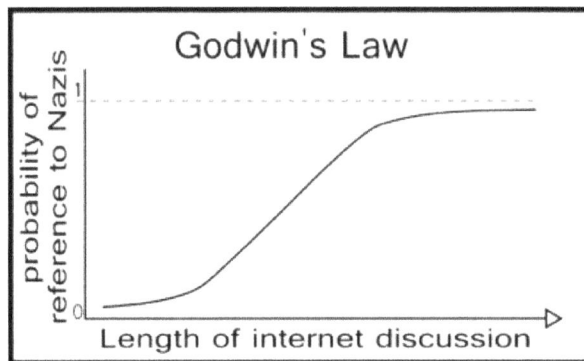

Figure 9: The Godwin law

Building a Word2Graph

Although more of a rhetorical device than an actual mathematical law, Godwin's Law remains a fascinating anomaly and seems to be relevant to the US election. Naturally, we will decide to explore the idea further using the graph theory. The first step is to broadcast our model back to the executors and parallelize our list of words. For each word, we output the top five synonyms and build an `Edge` object with word similarity as edge weight. Let's take a look:

```
val bModel = sc.broadcast(model)
val bDictionary = sc.broadcast(
  model.getVectors
    .keys
    .toList
    .zipWithIndex
    .map(l => (l._1, l._2.toLong + 1L))
    .toMap
```

```
)

import org.apache.spark.graphx._

val wordRDD = sc.parallelize(
  model.getVectors
    .keys
    .toSeq
    .filter(s => s.length > 3)
)

val word2EdgeRDD = wordRDD.mapPartitions { it =>
  val model = bModel.value
  val dictionary = bDictionary.value

  it.flatMap { from =>
    val synonyms = model.findSynonyms(from, 5)
    val tot = synonyms.map(_._2).sum
    synonyms.map { case (to, sim) =>
      val norm = sim / tot
      Edge(
          dictionary.get(from).get,
          dictionary.get(to).get,
          norm
        )
      }
    }
}

val word2Graph = Graph.fromEdges(word2EdgeRDD, 0L)

word2Graph.cache()
word2Graph.vertices.count()
```

To prove Godwin's law, we will have to prove that no matter the input node, we can always find a path from that node to the *Godwin point*. In mathematical terms, this assumes the graph to be *ergodic*. With more than one connected component, our graph cannot be ergodic as some nodes will never lead to the Godwin point. Therefore:

```
val cc = word2Graph
  .connectedComponents()
  .vertices
  .values
  .distinct
  .count

println(s"Do we still have faith in humanity? ${cc > 1L}")
// false
```

As we only have one connected component, the next step is to compute the shortest path for each node to that Godwin point:

```
import org.apache.spark.graphx.lib.ShortestPaths

val shortestPaths = ShortestPaths.run(graph, Seq(godwin))
```

The shortest path algorithm is quite simple and can be easily implemented with *Pregel* using the same techniques described in Chapter 7, *Building Communities*. The basic approach is to start Pregel on the target node (our Godwin point) and send a message back to its incoming edges, incrementing a counter at each hop. Each node will always keep the smallest possible counter and propagate this value downstream to its incoming edges. The algorithm stops when no further edge is found.

We normalize this distance using a Godwin depth of 16, calculated as the maximum of each of the shortest paths:

```
val depth = sc.broadcast(
  shortestPaths.vertices
    .values
    .filter(_.nonEmpty)
    .map(_.values.min)
    .max()
)

logInfo(s"Godwin depth is [${depth.value}]")
// 16

shortestPaths.vertices.map { case (vid, hops) =>
  if(hops.nonEmpty) {
    val godwin = Option(
      math.min(hops.values.min / depth.value.toDouble, 1.0)
    )
    (vid, godwin)
  } else {
    (vid, None: Option[Double])
  }
}
.filter(_._2.isDefined)
.map { case (vid, distance) =>
  (vid, distance.get)
}
.collectAsMap()
```

The following figure shows a depth of 4 – we normalize the scores of 0, 1, 2, 3, and 4 to **0.0**, **0.25**, **0.5**, **0.75**, and **1.0** respectively:

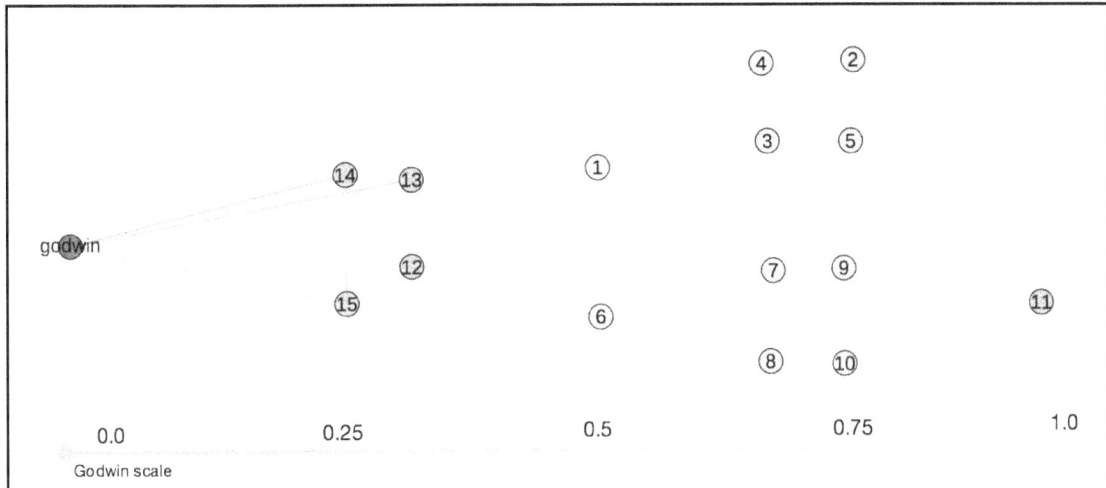

Figure 10: The normalized Godwin distance

Finally, we collect each vertex with its associated distance as a map. We can easily sort this collection from the most to the least-sensitive word, but we will not report our findings here (for obvious reasons!).

On November 7 and 8, 2016, this map contained all the words from our Twitter dictionary, implying a full ergodicity. According to Godwin's Law, any word, given enough time, can lead to the Godwin point. We will use this map later in the chapter when we build features from Twitter text content.

Random walks

One way to simulate random walks through the *Word2Vec* algorithm is to treat the graph as a series of **Markov chains**. Assuming N random walks and a transition matrix T, we compute the transition matrix T^N. Given a state, S_1 (meaning a word w_1), we extract the probability distribution to jump from S_1 to an S_N state in N given transitions. In practice, given a dictionary of ~100k words, a dense representation of such a transition matrix will require around 50 GB to fit in memory. We can easily build a sparse representation of T using the `IndexedRowMatrix` class from MLlib:

```
val size = sc.broadcast(
  word2Graph
```

```
        .vertices
        .count()
        .toInt
    )

    val indexedRowRDD = word2Graph.edges
      .map { case edge =>
        (edge.srcId,(edge.dstId.toInt, edge.attr))
      }
      .groupByKey()
      .map { case (id, it) =>
        new IndexedRow(id, Vectors.sparse(size.value, it.toSeq))
      }

    val m1 = new IndexedRowMatrix(indexedRowRDD)
    val m3 = m1.multiply(m2)
```

Unfortunately, there is no built-in method in Spark to perform matrix multiplication with sparse support. Therefore, the m2 matrix needs to be dense and must fit in memory. A solution can be to decompose this matrix (using SVD) and play with the symmetric property of the word2vec matrix (if word w_1 is a synonym to w_2, then w_2 is a synonym to w_1) in order to simplify this process. Using simple matrix algebra, one can prove that given a matrix M:

$$M = USV^T$$

and M symmetric, then

$$M^{2k} = US^{2k}U^T$$

$$M^{2k+1} = US^{2k+1}V^T$$

for even and odd value of *n* respectively. In theory, we only need to compute the multiplication of *S* that is a diagonal matrix. In practice, this requires lot of effort and is computationally expensive for no real value (all we want is to generate random word association). Instead, we generate random walks using our Word2Vec graph, the Pregel API, and a Monte Carlo simulation. This will generate word associations starting from a seed `love`. The algorithm stops after 100 iterations or when a path reaches our Godwin point. The detail of this algorithm can be found in our code repository.

```
Godwin.randomWalks(graph, "love", 100)
```

It is also worth mentioning that a Matrix, *M*, is said to be ergodic (hence also proving the Godwin Law) if there exists an integer, *n*, such that $M^n > 0$.

A Small Step into sarcasm detection

Detecting sarcasm is an active area of research (`http://homes.cs.washington.edu/~nasmith/papers/bamman+smith.icwsm15.pdf`). In fact, detecting sarcasm is often not easy for humans, so how can it be easy for computers? If I say *"We will make America great again"*; without knowing me, observing me, or hearing the tone I'm using, how could you know if I really meant what I said? Now, if you were to read a tweet from me that says *"We will make America great again :(:(:("*, does it help in a sense?

Building features

We believe that sarcasm cannot be detected using plain English text only, especially not when the plain text fits into less than 140 characters. However, we showed in this chapter that emojis can play a major role in the definition of emotion. A naive assumption is that a tweet with both positive sentiment and negative emojis can potentially lead to sarcasm. In addition to the tone, we also found that some words were closer to some ideas/ideologies that can be classified as fairly negative.

#LoveTrumpsHates

We have demonstrated that any word can be represented in a highly dimensional space between words such as [clinton], [trump], [love], and [hate]. Therefore, for our first extractor, we build features using the average cosine similarity between these words:

```
case class Word2Score(
                      trump: Double,
                      clinton: Double,
                      love: Double,
                      hate: Double
                      )

def cosineSimilarity(x: Array[Float],
                     y: Array[Float]): Double = {

  val dot = x.zip(y).map(a => a._1 * a._2).sum
  val magX = math.sqrt(x.map(i => i*i).sum)
  val magY = math.sqrt(y.map(i => i*i).sum)

  dot / (magX * magY)
}

val trump = model.getVectors.get("trump").get
val clinton = model.getVectors.get("clinton").get
val love = model.getVectors.get("love").get
val hate = model.getVectors.get("hate").get

val word2Score = sc.broadcast(
   model.getVectors.map { case (word, vector) =>
     val scores = Word2Score(
                     cosineSimilarity(vector, trump),
                     cosineSimilarity(vector, clinton),
                     cosineSimilarity(vector, love),
                     cosineSimilarity(vector, hate)
                     )
       (word, scores)
   }
)
```

We expose this method as a user-defined function so that each tweet can be scored against each of these four dimensions:

```
import org.apache.spark.sql.functions._
import collection.mutable.WrappedArray

val featureTrump = udf((words:WrappedArray[String]) => {
  words.map(word2Score.value.get)
```

```
      .map(_.get.trump)
      .sum / words.length
})

val featureClinton = udf((words:WrappedArray[String]) => {
  words.map(word2Score.value.get)
      .map(_.get.clinton)
      .sum / words.length
})

val featureLove = udf((words:WrappedArray[String]) => {
  words.map(word2Score.value.get)
      .map(_.get.love)
      .sum / words.length
})

val featureHate = udf((words:WrappedArray[String]) => {
  words.map(word2Score.value.get)
      .map(_.get.hate)
      .sum / words.length
})
```

Scoring Emojis

We can extract all emojis and run a basic word count to retrieve only the most used emojis. We can then categorize them into five different groups: love, joy, joke, sad, and cry:

```
val lov = sc.broadcast(
  Set("heart", "heart_eyes", "kissing_heart", "hearts", "kiss")
)

val joy = sc.broadcast(
  Set("joy", "grin", "laughing", "grinning", "smiley", "clap", "sparkles")
)

val jok = sc.broadcast(
  Set("wink", "stuck_out_tongue_winking_eye", "stuck_out_tongue")
)

val sad = sc.broadcast(
  Set("weary", "tired_face", "unamused", "frowning", "grimacing",
"disappointed")
)

val cry = sc.broadcast(
  Set("sob", "rage", "cry", "scream", "fearful", "broken_heart")
)
```

```
val allEmojis = sc.broadcast(
  lov.value ++ joy.value ++ jok.value ++ sad.value ++ cry.value
)
```

Again, we expose this method as a UDF that can be applied to a DataFrame. An emoji score of 1.0 will be extremely positive, and 0.0 will be highly negative.

Training a KMeans model

With the UDFs set, we get our initial Twitter DataFrame and build the feature vectors:

```
val buildVector = udf((sentiment: Double, tone: Double, trump: Double,
clinton: Double, love: Double, hate: Double, godwin: Double) => {
  Vectors.dense(
    Array(
      sentiment,
      tone,
      trump,
      clinton,
      love,
      hate,
      godwin
    )
  )
})

val featureTweetDF = tweetRDD.toDF
  .withColumn("words", extractWords($"body"))
  .withColumn("tone", featureEmojis($"emojis"))
  .withColumn("trump", featureTrump($"body"))
  .withColumn("clinton", featureClinton($"body"))
  .withColumn("godwin", featureGodwin($"body"))
  .withColumn("love", featureLove($"words"))
  .withColumn("hate", featureHate($"words"))
  .withColumn("features",
    buildVector(
      $"sentiment",
      $"tone",
      $"trump",
      $"clinton",
      $"love",
      $"hate",
      $"godwin")
    )

import org.apache.spark.ml.feature.Normalizer
```

```
val normalizer = new Normalizer()
  .setInputCol("features")
  .setOutputCol("vector")
  .setP(1.0)
```

We normalize our vectors using the `Normalizer` class and feed a KMeans algorithm with only five clusters. Compared to `Chapter 10`, *Story De-duplication and Mutation*, the KMeans optimization (in terms of *k*) does not really matter here as we are not interested in grouping tweets into categories, but rather detecting outliers (tweets that are far away from any cluster center):

```
import org.apache.spark.ml.clustering.KMeans

val kmeansModel = new KMeans()
  .setFeaturesCol("vector")
  .setPredictionCol("cluster")
  .setK(5)
  .setMaxIter(Int.MaxValue)
  .setInitMode("k-means||")
  .setInitSteps(10)
  .setTol(0.01)
  .fit(vectorTweetDF)
```

We recommend the use of the ML package instead of MLlib. There have been huge improvements to this package over the past few versions of Spark in terms of dataset adoption and catalyst optimization. Unfortunately, there is a major limitation: all ML classes are defined as private and cannot be extended. As we want to extract the distance alongside the predicted cluster, we will have to build our own Euclidean measure as a UDF function:

```
import org.apache.spark.ml.clustering.KMeansModel

val centers = sc.broadcast(kmeansModel.clusterCenters)
import org.apache.spark.mllib.linalg.Vector

val euclidean = udf((v: Vector, cluster: Int) => {
  math.sqrt(centers.value(cluster).toArray.zip(v.toArray).map {
    case (x1, x2) => math.pow(x1 - x2, 2)
  }
  .sum)
})
```

Finally, we predict our clusters and Euclidean distances from our *featured tweets* DataFrame and register this DataFrame as a persistent Hive table:

```
val predictionDF = kmeansModel
    .transform(vectorTweetDF)
    .withColumn("distance", euclidean($"vector", $"cluster"))

predictionDF.write.saveAsTable("twitter")
```

Detecting anomalies

We consider a tweet as abnormal if its feature vector is too far from any known cluster center (in terms of Euclidean distance). Since we stored our predictions as a Hive table, we can sort all points through a simple SQL statement and only take the first few records.

An example is reported, as follows, when querying Hive from our Zeppelin notebook:

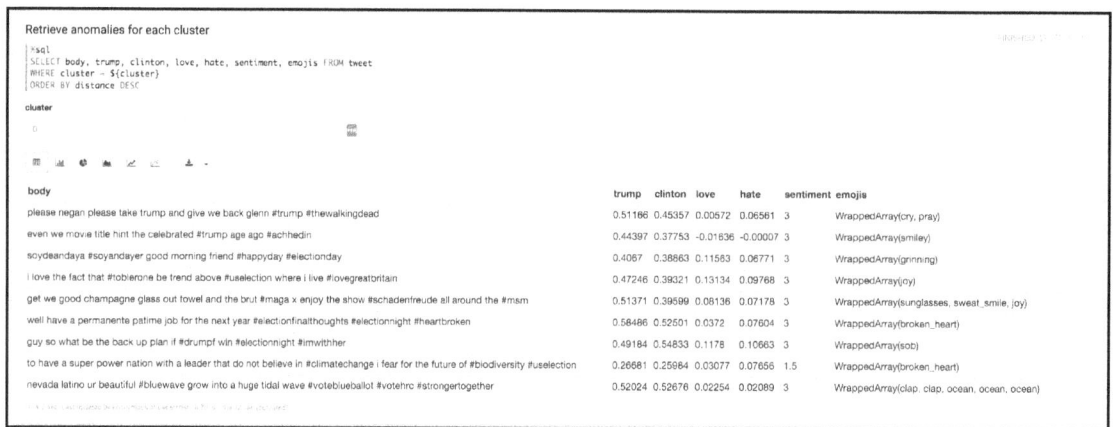

Figure 11: Zeppelin notebook for detecting anomalies

Without getting into too much detail (abnormal tweets can be sensitive), a few examples extracted from Hive queries are listed here:

- good luck today america #vote #imwithher [grimacing]
- this is so great we be america great again [cry, scream]
- we love you sir thank you for you constant love [cry]
- i can not describe how incredibly happy i am right now #maga [cry, rage]

Note, however, that the outliers we found were not all sarcastic tweets. We have only just begun our study of sarcasm, and lots of refining (including manual work) and probably more advanced models (such as *neural networks*) will be needed in order to write a comprehensive detector.

Summary

The purpose of this chapter was to cover different topics around time series, word embedding, sentiment analysis, graph theory, and anomaly detection. It's worth noting that the tweets used to illustrate the examples in no way reflect the authors' own opinions: "Whether or not America will be great again is out of scope here":(:(– sarcasm or not?

In the next chapter, we will cover an innovative approach to detect trends out of Time Series data using the *TrendCalculus* method. This will be used against market data, but can easily be applied in different use cases, including the *Sentiment Time Series* we built here.

12
TrendCalculus

Long before the concept of what's trending became a popular topic of study by data scientists, there was an older one that is still not well served by data science: it is that of Trends. Presently, the analysis of trends, if it can be called that, is primarily carried out by people "eyeballing" time series charts and offering interpretations. But what is it that people's eyes are doing?

This chapter describes an implementation in Apache Spark of a new algorithm for studying trends numerically, called TrendCalculus, invented by Andrew Morgan. The original reference implementation is written in the Lua language and was open-sourced in 2015, the code can be viewed at `https://bitbucket.org/bytesumo/trendcalculus-public`.

This chapter explains the core method, which delivers the fast extraction of trend change points on a time series; these are the moments when trends change direction. We will describe our TrendCalculus algorithm in detail while implementing it in Apache Spark. The result is a set of scalable functions to quickly compare trends across time series, to make inferences about trends and examine correlation across timeframes. Using these disruptive new methods, we demonstrate how to construct a causal ranking technique to extract potential causal models from across the thousands of time series inputs.

In this chapter we will learn:

- How to construct time windowed summary data efficiently
- How to effectively summarize time series data to reduce noise, for further trend studies
- How to extract trend reversal *change points* from the summary data using the new TrendCalculus algorithm
- How to create **User Defined Aggregate Functions** (**UDAFs**) that operate on partitions created by complex *window* functionality as well as more common *group by* methods

- How to return multiple values from UDAFs
- How to use lag functions to compare current and previous records

When presented with a problem, amongst the first hypotheses that data scientists consider are those related to trends; trends are an excellent way to provide a visualization of data and lend themselves particularly well to large datasets, where the general direction of change of the data can often be seen. In Chapter 5, *Spark for Geographic Analysis*, we produced a simple algorithm to attempt to predict the price of crude oil. In that study, we concentrated on the direction of change in the price, that is, by definition the trend of the price. We see that trends are a natural way to think, explain, and forecast.

To explain and demonstrate our new trend methods, this chapter is organized into two sections. The first is technical, to deliver the code we need to execute our new algorithm. The second section is about the application of that method on real data. We hope it demonstrates that the apparent simplicity of trends as a concept can often be more complicated to calculate than we may have first thought, particularly in the presence of noise. Noise results in many local highs and lows (referred to as jitter in this chapter), which can make finding trend turning points and discovering the general direction of change over time difficult to determine. Ignoring noise in time series, and extracting interpretable trend signals, provides the central challenges we demonstrate how to overcome.

Studying trends

The dictionary definition of trend is a general direction in which something is developing or changing, but there are other more focused definitions that might be more helpful for guiding data science. Two such definitions are from Salomé Areias, who studies social trends, and Eurostat, the official statistical agency in the European Union:

"A trend is the slow variation over a longer period of time, usually several years, generally associated with the structural causes affecting the phenomenon being measured." – EUROSTAT, official statistical agency in the European Union (`http://ec.europa.eu/eurostat/statistics-explained/index.php/Glossary:Trend`)

"A Trend is defined by a shift in behavior or mentality that influences a significant amount of people." – Salomé Areias, social trend commentator (`https://salomeareias.wordpress.com/what-is-a-trend/`)

We generally think of trends as nothing more than a long rise or fall in stock market prices. However, trends can also refer to many other use cases that relate to economics, politics, popular culture, and society: for example, the study of sentiments revealed by media outlets when they report on the news. In this chapter, we will use the price of oil as a simple demonstration; however, the technique could be applied to any data where trends occur in the following manner:

- **Rising trends**: When successive peaks and troughs are higher (higher highs and higher lows), referred to as an upward or rising trend. For example, the first arrow in the following diagram is the result of a series of peaks and troughs where the overall effect is an increase.

- **Falling trends**: When successive peaks and troughs are lower (lower highs and lower lows), referred to as a downward or falling trend. For example, the second arrow in the following diagram is the result of a series of peaks and troughs where the overall effect is a decrease.

- **Horizontal trends**: This is not strictly a trend on its own, but a lack of a well-defined trend in either direction. We are not specifically concerned with this at this stage, but it is discussed later in the chapter.

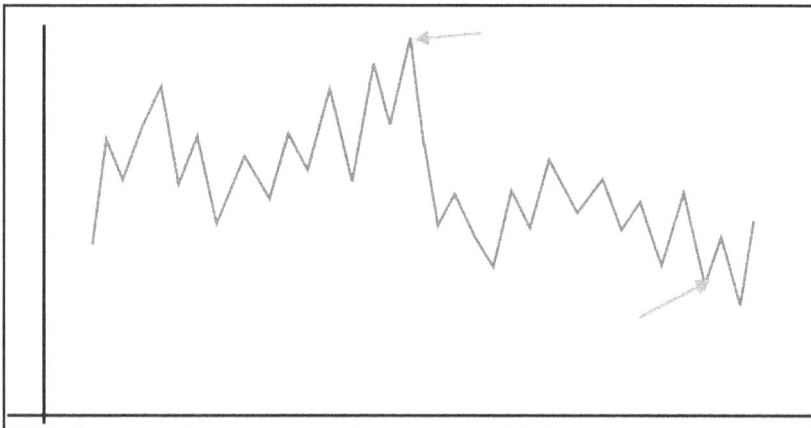

If you search for "higher highs" "higher lows" "trend" "lower highs" "lower lows" you will see over 16,000 hits including many high profile financial sites. This is a standard practice, rule of thumb definition of a trend in the finance industry.

The TrendCalculus algorithm

In this section we will explain the detail of the TrendCalculus implementation, using the Brent oil price data set seen in Chapter 5, *Spark for Geographic Analysis*, as an example use case.

Trend windows

In order to measure any type of change, we must first quantify it in some way. For trends, we are going to define this in the following manner:

- Overall positive change (usually expressed as a value increase)

    Higher highs and higher lows => +1

- Overall negative change (usually expressed as a value decrease)

    Lower highs and lower lows => -1

We must therefore translate our data into a time series of trend direction, being either +1 or -1. By splitting our data into a series of windows, size n, we can calculate the dated highs and lows for each of them:

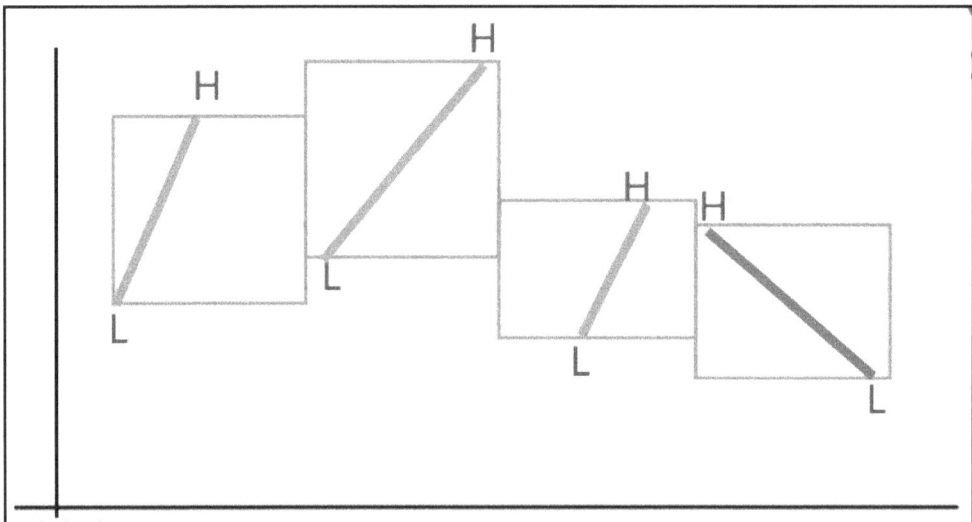

Since this type of windowing is a common practice in data science, it is reasonable to think there must be an implementation in Spark; if you have read Chapter 5, *Spark for Geographic Analysis* you will have seen them, in the form of Spark SQL windows functions. Let's read in some Brent oil data, which in this case is simply a date and the closing price of oil on that date (example data is located in our code repository):

```
// Read in the data
val oilPriceDF = spark
    .read
    .option("header","true")
    .option("inferSchema", "true")
    .csv("brent_oil_prices.csv")
```

Next, we should ensure the date field schema is correct so that we can use it in the `window` function. Our example dataset has a `String` date in the format `dd/MM/yyyy` so we shall convert it to `yyyy-MM-dd` using `java.text.SimpleDateFormat`:

```
// A date conversion UDF
def convertDate(date:String) : String = {
    val dt = new SimpleDateFormat("dd/MM/yyyy").parse(date)
    val newDate = new SimpleDateFormat("yyyy-MM-dd").format(dt)
    newDate
}
```

This will allow us to create a **User Defined Function (UDF)** that we can use to replace the date column we already have in the `oilPriceDF` DataFrame:

```
val convertDateUDF = udf {(Date: String) => convertDate(Date)}
val oilPriceDatedDF = oilPriceDF
    .withColumn("DATE", convertDate(oilPriceDF("DATE")))
```

As a quick aside, if we want to concentrate on a particular range of the data, we can filter it:

```
val oilPriceDated2015DF = oilPriceDatedDF.filter("year(DATE)==2015")
```

And now we can implement the window using the window function introduced in Spark 2.0:

```
val windowDF = oilPriceDatedDF.groupBy(
    window(oilPriceDatedDF.col("DATE"),"1 week", "1 week", "4 days"))
```

The arguments in the preceding statement allow us to provide a size of window, window offset and data offset, so this schema actually produces a tumbling window with an offset at the beginning of the data. This allows us to ensure that each window is constructed so that it always contains data for Monday to Friday (the trading days for oil), and each subsequent window contains data for the following week.

View the DataFrame at this stage to ensure all is in order; we cannot use `show` method in the usual way as `windowDF` is a `RelationalGroupedDataset`. So we can run a simple inbuilt function to create a readable output. Counting each window content, showing the first twenty lines and not truncating the output:

```
windowDF.count.show(20, false)
```

Which will appear similar to this:

```
+-------------------------------------------+-----+
|window                                     |count|
+-------------------------------------------+-----+
|[2011-11-07 00:00:00.0,2011-11-14 00:00:00.0]|5    |
|[2011-11-14 00:00:00.0,2011-11-21 00:00:00.0]|5    |
|[2011-11-21 00:00:00.0,2011-11-28 00:00:00.0]|5    |
+-------------------------------------------+-----+
```

Here, count is the number of entries in the window, that is, the number of prices in our case. Depending upon the data used, we may find that some windows contain less than five entries, due to missing data. We will keep these in the dataset, otherwise there will be gaps in our output.

> Data quality should never be overlooked, and due diligence should always be performed before working with a new dataset, see Chapter 4, *Exploratory Data Analysis*.

Changing the size of the window n (in this case, 1 week) will adjust our scale of investigation. For example, an n sized 1 week will provide a weekly change, and an n sized 1 year will provide a yearly change (each window will be sized: [no. of weeks' oil traded * 5] using our data). Of course, this is entirely related to how the dataset is structured, that is, depending on whether it be hourly or daily prices, and so on. Later in the chapter we will see how we can easily examine trends on an iterative basis, taking the change points from one pass over the data as the inputs to a second iteration.

Simple trend

Now that we have windowed data, we can calculate the +1 or -1 values for each window (the simple trend), so we need to develop a trend calculation equation. We can do this visually using an example from the previous graph diagram:

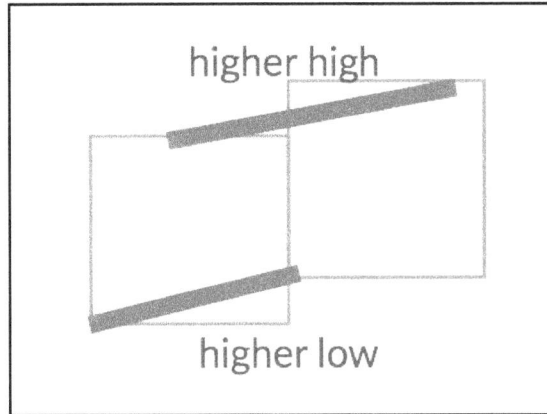

For the set of calculated windows, we can compare the current window to the previous window thereby showing the higher highs, higher lows and lower highs, lower lows.

We do this by selecting the following from each window:

- The earliest high price
- The latest low price

Using this information, we can derive our TrendCalculus equation:

$$ sign(sign(H_{p_i} - H_{p_{i-1}}) + sign(L_{p_i} - L_{p_{i-1}})) $$

where:

- **sign**: is the function (x > 0) ? 1 : ((x < 0) ? -1 : 0)
- **H**: high
- **L**: low
- **Pi**: current window
- **Pi -1**: previous window

For example, given the following scenario:

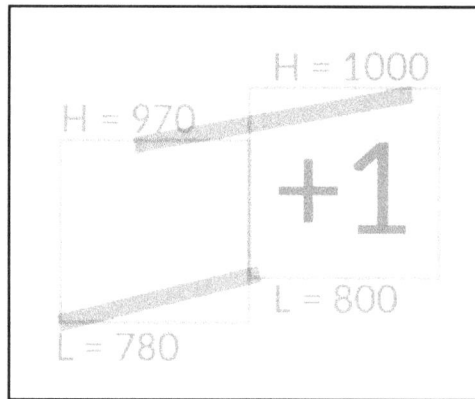

- Simple trend = sign(sign(HighDiff) + sign(LowDiff))
- Simple trend = sign(sign(1000-970) + sign(800-780))
- Simple trend = sign(sign(30) + sign(20))
- Simple trend = sign(1 + 1)
- Simple trend = sign(2)
- Simple trend = +1

It is also possible to obtain an answer of 0. This is explained in detail later in the chapter., see *Edge Cases*.

User Defined Aggregate Functions

There are a number of ways to perform the above task programmatically, we are going to look at UDFs for aggregated data (Spark `UserDefinedAggregateFunction`) so that we can use the windowed data collected earlier.

We would like to be able to use a function on our windows in a similar way to our previous UDF example. However, a standard UDF would not be possible, since our windows are represented as `RelationalGroupedDataset`. At runtime, the data for such a set may be held on more than one Spark node, so that functions are performed in parallel, as opposed to the data for a UDF, which must be co-located. The UDAF is therefore great news for us, as it means that we can implement our program logic safe in the knowledge that the concerns of parallelization efficiencies are abstracted away and the code will automatically scale to massive datasets!

In summary, we are looking to output the earliest high price along with its date and the latest low price with date (for each window) so that we can use this data to calculate the simple trend as described previously. We will write a Scala class that extends the `UserDefinedAggregateFunction`, which contains the following functions:

- `inputSchema`: The structure of the input data supplied to the function
- `bufferSchema`: The structure of the internal information (aggregation buffer) held for this instance
- `dataType`: The type of the output data structure
- `deterministic`: Whether the function is `deterministic` (that is, the same input always returns the same output)
- `initialize`: The initial state of the aggregation buffer; merging two initial buffers together must always return the same initial state
- `update`: Update the aggregation buffer with the input data
- `merge`: Merge two aggregation buffers
- `evaluate`: Calculate the final result based on the aggregation buffer

The full code for our class is shown below, refer back to the preceding definitions as you're raeding through to understand the purpose of each. The code has deliberately been left quite verbose so that the functionality can be more easily understood. In practice, we could certainly refactor the `update` and `merge` functions.

```
import java.text.SimpleDateFormat
import java.util.Date
import org.apache.spark.sql.Row
import org.apache.spark.sql.expressions.{MutableAggregationBuffer,
UserDefinedAggregateFunction}
import org.apache.spark.sql.types._

class HighLowCalc extends UserDefinedAggregateFunction {

// we will input (date, price) tuples
def inputSchema: org.apache.spark.sql.types.StructType = StructType(
  StructField("date", StringType) ::
  StructField("price", DoubleType) :: Nil)

// these are the values we will keep a track of internally
def bufferSchema: StructType = StructType(
  StructField("HighestHighDate", StringType) ::
  StructField("HighestHighPrice", DoubleType) ::
  StructField("LowestLowDate", StringType) ::
  StructField("LowestLowPrice", DoubleType) :: Nil
)
```

```scala
  // the schema of our final output data
  def dataType: DataType = DataTypes.createStructType(
    Array(
      StructField("HighestHighDate", StringType),
      StructField("HighestHighPrice", DoubleType),
      StructField("LowestLowDate", StringType),
      StructField("LowestLowPrice", DoubleType)
    )
  )

  // this function is deterministic
  def deterministic: Boolean = true

  // define our initial state using the bufferSchema
  def initialize(buffer: MutableAggregationBuffer): Unit = {
    // the date of the highest price so far
    buffer(0) = ""
    // the highest price seen so far
    buffer(1) = 0d
    // the date of the lowest price so far
    buffer(2) = ""
    // the lowest price seen so far
    buffer(3) = 1000000d
  }

  // how to behave given new input (date, price)
  def update(buffer: MutableAggregationBuffer,input: Row): Unit = {

    // find out how the input price compares
    // to the current internal value - looking for highest price only
    (input.getDouble(1) compare buffer.getAs[Double](1)).signum match {
      // if the input price is lower then do nothing
      case -1 => {}
      // if the input price is higher then update the internal status
      case  1 => {
        buffer(1) = input.getDouble(1)
        buffer(0) = input.getString(0)
      }
      // if the input price is the same then ensure we have the earliest date
      case  0 => {
        // if new date earlier than current date, replace
        (parseDate(input.getString(0)),parseDate(buffer.getAs[String](0)))
        match {
          case (Some(a), Some(b)) => {
            if(a.before(b)){
              buffer(0) = input.getString(0)
            }
          }
        }
```

```
          // anything else do nothing
          case _ => {}
        }
      }
    }
    // now repeat to find the lowest price
    (input.getDouble(1) compare buffer.getAs[Double](3)).signum match {
      // if the input price is lower then update the internal state
      case -1 => {
        buffer(3) = input.getDouble(1)
        buffer(2) = input.getString(0)
      }
      // if the input price is higher then do nothing
      case  1 => {}
      // if the input price is the same then ensure we have the latest date
      case  0 => {
        // if new date later than current date, replace
        (parseDate(input.getString(0)),parseDate(buffer.getAs[String](2)))
        match {
          case (Some(a), Some(b)) => {
            if(a.after(b)){
              buffer(2) = input.getString(0)
            }
          }
          // anything else do nothing
          case _ => {}
        }
      }
    }
  }
}

// define the behaviour to merge two aggregation buffers together
def merge(buffer1: MutableAggregationBuffer, buffer2: Row): Unit = {
  // first deal with the high prices
  (buffer2.getDouble(1) compare buffer1.getAs[Double](1)).signum match {
    case -1 => {}
    case  1 => {
      buffer1(1) = buffer2.getDouble(1)
      buffer1(0) = buffer2.getString(0)
    }
    case  0 => {
      // work out which date is earlier
      (parseDate(buffer2.getString(0)),parseDate(buffer1.getAs[String](0)))
      match {
        case (Some(a), Some(b)) => {
          if(a.before(b)){
            buffer1(0) = buffer2.getString(0)
          }
```

```
        }
        case _ => {}
      }
    }
  }
  // now deal with the low prices
  (buffer2.getDouble(3) compare buffer1.getAs[Double](3)).signum match {
    case -1 => {
      buffer1(3) = buffer2.getDouble(3)
      buffer1(2) = buffer2.getString(2)
    }
    case  1 => {}
    case  0 => {
      // work out which date is later
      (parseDate(buffer2.getString(2)),parseDate(buffer1.getAs[String](2)))
      match {
        case (Some(a), Some(b)) => {
          if(a.after(b)){
            buffer1(2) = buffer2.getString(2)
          }
        }
        case _ => {}
      }
    }
  }
}


// when all is complete, output:
// (highestDate, highestPrice, lowestDate, lowestPrice)
def evaluate(buffer: Row): Any = {
  (buffer(0), buffer(1), buffer(2), buffer(3))
}

// convert a String to a Date for easy comparison
def parseDate(value: String): Option[Date] = {
  try {
    Some(new SimpleDateFormat("yyyy-MM-dd").parse(value))
  } catch {
    case e: Exception => None
  }
}

}
```

You will notice that there is common use of the `signum` function. This is very useful for comparison, as it produces the following outcomes:

- If the first value is less than the second, output -1
- If the first value is greater than the second, output +1
- If the two values are equal, output 0

This function will really show its worth later in the chapter when we write the code to calculate the actual simple trend value. We have also used the `option` class (in `parseDate`), which enables us to return an instance of `Some` or `None`. This has a number of advantages: primarily it promotes a separation of concerns by removing the need to check for null immediately, but also enables the use of pattern matching, allowing us to chain together many Scala functions without the need for verbose type-checking. For example, if we write a function that returns either `Some(Int)` or `None`, then we can `flatMap` those values with no additional checking:

```
List("1", "2", "a", "b", "3", "c").flatMap(a =>
   try {
      Some(Integer.parseInt(a.trim))
   } catch {
      case e: NumberFormatException => None
   }
}).sum
```

The preceding code returns `Int = 6`.

Simple trend calculation

Now that we have our aggregation function, we can register it and use this to output the values to our DataFrame:

```
val hlc = new HighLowCalc
spark.udf.register("hlc", hlc)

val highLowDF = windowDF.agg(expr("hlc(DATE,PRICE) as highLow"))
highLowDF.show(20, false)
```

Producing an output similar to this:

```
+------------------------------+----------------------+
|window                        |highLow               |
|                              |                      |
+------------------------------+----------------------+
|[2011-11-07 00:00:00.0,... ]  |[2011-11-08,115.61,... ]|
|[2011-11-14 00:00:00.0,... ]  |[2011-11-14,112.57,... ]|
|[2011-11-21 00:00:00.0,... ]  |[2011-11-22,107.77,... ]|
```

We have already mentioned that we will need to compare the current window to the previous one. We can create a new DataFrame with the inclusion of the previous window details by implementing the Spark `lag` function:

```
// ensure our data is in correct date order by sorting
// on each first date in the window column window
// Struct contains the values start and end
val sortedWindow = Window.orderBy("window.start")

// define the lag of just one row
val lagCol = lag(col("highLow"), 1).over(sortedWindow)

// create a new DataFrame with the additional column "highLowPrev"
// where the previous row does not exist, null will be entered
val highLowPrevDF = highLowDF.withColumn("highLowPrev", lagCol)
```

We now have a DataFrame where each row contains all of the information required to calculate the simple trend value. We can again implement a UDF, this time to represent the simple trend equation using the `signum` function mentioned previously:

```
val simpleTrendFunc = udf {
  (currentHigh : Double, currentLow : Double,
   prevHigh : Double, prevLow : Double) => {
     (((currentHigh - prevHigh) compare 0).signum +
     ((currentLow - prevLow) compare 0).signum compare 0).signum }
}
```

And finally, apply the UDF to our DataFrame:

```
val simpleTrendDF = highLowPrevDF.withColumn("sign",
    simpleTrendFunc(highLowPrevDF("highLow.HighestHighPrice"),
     highLowPrevDF("highLow.LowestLowPrice"),
     highLowPrevDF("highLowPrev.HighestHighPrice"),
     highLowPrevDF("highLowPrev.LowestLowPrice")
    )
)

// view the DataFrame
simpleTrendDF.show(20, false)

+---------------------+---------------------+-----+
|highLow              |highLowPrev          |sign |
+---------------------+---------------------+-----+
|[2011-11-08,115.61,...|null                 |null |
|[2011-11-14,112.57,...|[2011-11-08,115.61,... |-1   |
|[2011-11-22,107.77,...|[2011-11-14,112.57,...|1    |
```

Reversal rule

Having run the code across all of the identified windows we now have our data represented as a series of +1 and -1s, and we can analyze this further to progress our understanding of the trends. You will notice that the data appears random, but there is a pattern that we can identify: the trend values often flip, either from +1 to -1 or -1 to +1. On closer inspection of the graph at these points, we can see that these flips actually represent a reversal of the trend:

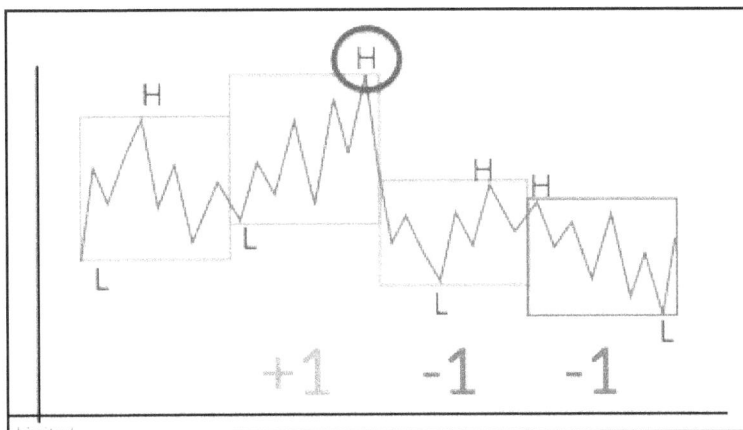

This can be summarized thus:

- If the trend moves from +1 to -1, then a previous high is a reversal
- If the trend moves from -1 to +1, then a previous low is a reversal

Using this simple rule, we can output a new time series that contains just the reversal points found on our scale. In this time series, we will create tuples of (date, price) that are equivalent to the higher high for a +1 reversal and the lower low for a -1 reversal as discussed earlier. We can code this by using the same method as before, that is, capture the previous sign using the `lag` function and implement a UDF to work out the reversals, like so:

```scala
// define the lag of just one row
val lagSignCol = lag(col("sign"), 1).over(sortedWindow)

// create a new DataFrame with the additional column signPrev
val lagSignColDF = simpleTrendDF.withColumn("signPrev", lagSignCol)

// define a UDF that calculates the reversals
val reversalFunc = udf {
  (currentSign : Int, prevSign : Int,
    prevHighPrice : Double, prevHighDate : String,
    prevLowPrice : Double, prevLowDate : String) => {
      (currentSign compare prevSign).signum match {
        case 0 => null
        // if the current SimpleTrend is less than the
        // previous, the previous high is a reversal
        case -1 => (prevHighDate, prevHighPrice)
        // if the current SimpleTrend is more than the
        // previous, the previous low is a reversal
        case 1 => (prevLowDate, prevLowPrice)
      }
    }
}

// use the UDF to create a new DataFrame with the
// additional column reversals
val reversalsDF = lagSignColDF.withColumn("reversals",
  reversalFunc(lagSignColDF("sign"),
    lagSignColDF("signPrev"),
    lagSignColDF("highLowPrev.HighestHighPrice"),
    lagSignColDF("highLowPrev.HighestHighDate"),
    lagSignColDF("highLowPrev.LowestLowPrice"),
    lagSignColDF("highLowPrev.LowestLowDate")
  )
)
```

```
reversalsDF.show(20, false)

+---------------------+------+--------+-------------------+
|highLowPrev          |sign  |signPrev|reversals          |
+---------------------+------+--------+-------------------+
|null                 |null  |null    |null               |
|[2011-11-08,115.61,...]|-1  |null    |null               |
|[2011-11-14,112.57,...]|-1  |-1      |null               |
|[2011-11-22,107.77,...]|1   |-1      |[2011-11-24,105.3] |
|[2011-11-29,111.25,...]|-1  |1       |[2011-11-29,111.25]|
```

In summary, we have successfully removed the jitter (non significant rise and fall) from our price data, and we could benefit from displaying this data straight away. It will certainly show a simplified representation of the original dataset and, assuming we are primarily interested in the points at which the price significantly changes, retains the key information, which is related to the important peaks and troughs. However, there is more that we can do to represent the data in a presentable and easily readable manner.

Introducing the FHLS bar structure

In the financial sector, **Open, High, Low, Close** (**OHLC**) charts are very common as they display the key data that every analyst requires; the price the item opened and closed at and the high and low price points for that period (usually one day). We can use this same idea for our own purposes. The **First, High, Low, Second** (**FHLS**) chart will enable us to visualize our data and build upon it to produce new insights.

The FHLS data format is described as follows:

- The open date
- **First** of High/Low value – whichever high or low occurs first
- **High** value
- **Low** value
- **Second** of High/Low value – the other value to first of High/Low
- High date
- Low date
- Close date

We have almost all of the data we need in the `reversalsDF` described perviously, the only items that we have not identified are the First and Second values, that is, whether the highest or the lowest price was first seen in any given window. We could calculate this using a UDF or select statement, however updating the `UserDefinedAggregateFunction` from earlier will enable us to make a small change whilst ensuring an efficient method. Only the evaluate function requires change:

```
def evaluate(buffer: Row): Any = {
  // compare the highest and lowest dates
  (parseDate(buffer.getString(0)), parseDate(buffer.getString(2))) match {
    case (Some(a), Some(b)) => {
      // if the highest date is the earlier
      if(a.before(b)){
        // highest date, highest price, lowest date,
        // lowest price, first(highest price), second
        (buffer(0), buffer(1), buffer(2), buffer(3), buffer(1), buffer(3))
      }
      else {
        // the lowest date is earlier or they are
        // both the same (shouldn't be possible)
        // highest date, highest price, lowest date,
        // lowest price, first(lowest price), second
        (buffer(0), buffer(1), buffer(2), buffer(3), buffer(3), buffer(1))
      }
    }
    // we couldn't parse one or both of the dates -shouldn't reach here
    case _ =>
      (buffer(0), buffer(1), buffer(2), buffer(3), buffer(1), buffer(3))
  }
}
```

Finally, we can write a statement to select the required fields and write our data to file:

```
val fhlsSelectDF = reversalsDF.select(
  "window.start",
  "highLow.firstPrice",
  "highLow.HighestHighPrice",
  "highLow.LowestLowPrice",
  "highLow.secondPrice",
  "highLow.HighestHighDate",
  "highLow.LowestLowDate",
  "window.end",
  "reversals._1",
  "reversals._2")
```

You will notice that the reversals column does not implement a `Struct` like the others, but a tuple. If you check `reversalsUDF`, you will see how this has been done. For demonstration purposes, we will show how to rename the component fields once they have been selected:

```
val lookup = Map("_1" -> "reversalDate", "_2" -> "reversalPrice")
val fhlsDF = fhlsSelectDF.select { fhlsSelectDF.columns.map(c =>
    col(c).as(lookup.getOrElse(c, c))):_*
}
fhlsDF.orderBy(asc("start")).show(20, false)
```

Writing the data to file:

```
fhlsDF.write
  .format("com.databricks.spark.csv")
  .option("header", "true")
  .save("fhls");
```

You could encrypt the data with the addition of the line:

```
.option("codec", "org.apache.hadoop.io.compress.CryptoCodec")
```

This important codec, and other security related techniques, are described in `Chapter 13`, *Secure Data*.

Visualize the data

Now that we have the data in a file, we can take the opportunity to display it; there are many packages available for creating charts, as a data scientist perhaps one of the key ones is D3.js. As we have mentioned D3 in other areas of the book, it is not our intention to explore here any more detail than is necessary to produce our end results. That said, it's worth outlining that D3 is a JavaScript library for manipulating documents based on data, and that there are many contributors to the ecosystem such that the number of data visualizations available is huge. Understanding the basics will allow us to provide truly impressive results with relatively little effort.

Using the FHLS format, we can convince chart software to accept our data as if it were OHLC formatted. So we should search the Internet for a D3 OHLC library that we can use. In this example, we have chosen `techanjs.org` as it provides not just OHLC, but also some other visualizations that may be useful later.

Implementing D3 code is usually as simple as cutting and pasting into a text file, having amended any paths to data directories in the source code. If you have never worked in this area before, there are some useful tips below to help you get started:

- If you are working with web technologies with the Chrome browser, there is a set of very useful tools located under **Options** | **More Tools** | **Developer Tools**. If nothing else, this will provide an output of errors from the code that you are trying to run, which otherwise will be lost, making a blank page result much easier to debug.

- If you are using a single file for your code, as in the example below, always use `index.html` for the filename.

- If your code references local files, which is usually the case when implementing D3, you will need to run a web server so that they can be served. By default, a web browser cannot access local files due to the inherent security risks (malicious code accessing local files). A simple way to run a web server is to execute: `nohup python -m SimpleHTTPServer &` in the source directory for your code. You must never give your browser access to local files, as it will be left wide open to attack. For example, do not run: `chrome --allow-file-access-from-files`

- When using D3 in your source, where possible always use `<script src="https://d3js.org/d3.v4.min.js"></script>` to ensure you import the latest version of the library.

We can use the code as is, the only change we should make is the way in which the columns are referenced:

```
data = data.slice(0, 200).map(function(d) {
  return {
    date: parseDate(d.start),
    open: +d.firstPrice,
    high: +d.HighestHighPrice,
    low: +d.LowestLowPrice,
    close: +d.SecondPrice
  };
});
```

This will produce a chart similar to this:

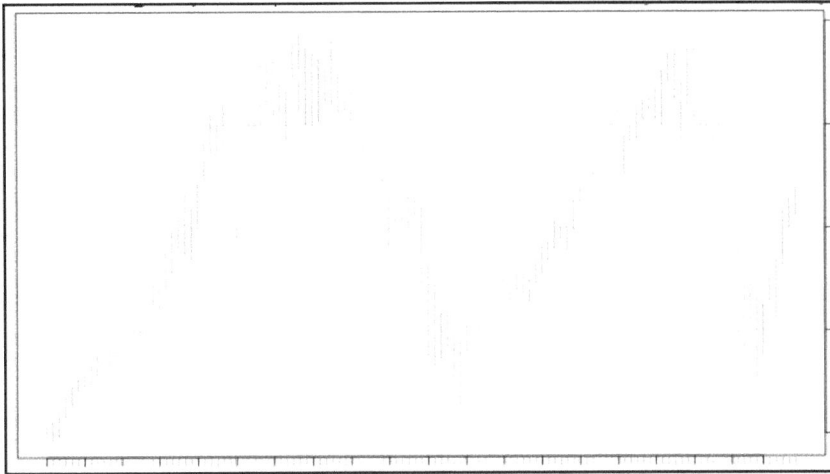

On this chart, green bars indicate an increase from the **First**, a low price, to the **Second**, a high price, and red bars indicate a decrease from a **first high** to **second low**. This subtle change from typical OHLC charts is critical. At a glance we can now easily see the flow of the time series as it rises and falls across the summarizing bars. This helps us to understand the flow of rises and falls in price on our fixed scale of enquiry, or window size, without having the disadvantage of having to interpret the effect of time scale as we would on a line chart of raw price values. The resulting chart offers a way to reduce noise on smaller timeframes, delivering a neat and repeatable way of summarizing our time series visually. There is still more that we can do, however.

FHLS with reversals

We have previously calculated the trend reversals, using our TrendCalculus equation, and plotting these together with the FHLS summary data above will really enhance our visualization, showing the high/low bars and the trend reversal points together. We can do this by modifying our D3 code to also implement D3 Scatterplot code. The code required can be found on the Internet in many places, as before; we have some code below which can be integrated by adding the relevant parts to <script>:

Add the reversalPrice field:

```
data = data.slice(0, 200).map(function(d) {
  return {
    date: parseDate(d.start),
    open: +d.firstPrice,
```

```
    high: +d.HighestHighPrice,
    low: +d.LowestLowPrice,
    close: +d.secondPrice,
    price: +d.reversalPrice
  };
}).sort(function(a, b) {
  return d3.ascending(accessor.d(a), accessor.d(b));
});
```

And draw the dots:

```
svg.selectAll(".dot")
  .data(data)
  .enter().append("circle")
  .attr("class", "dot")
  .attr("r", 1)
  .attr("cx", function(d) { return x(d.date); })
  .attr("cy", function(d) { return y(d.price); })
  .style("fill","black");
```

Once this is successfully integrated, we will see a chart similar to this:

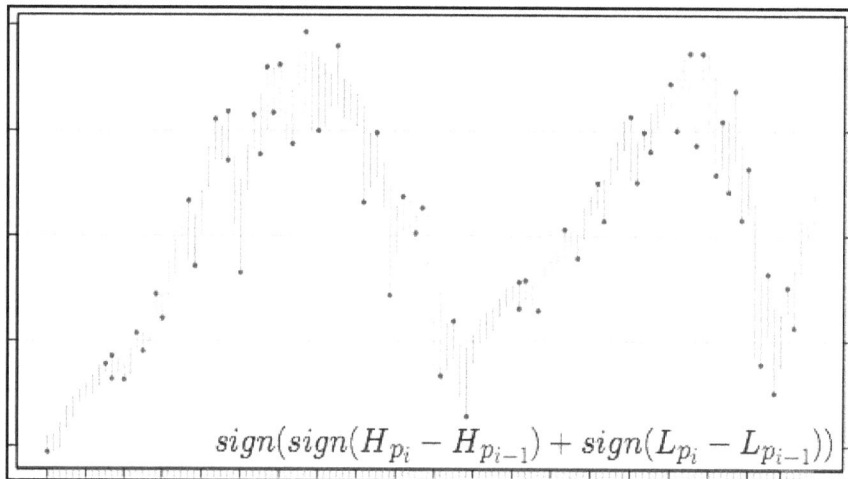

$$sign(sign(H_{p_i} - H_{p_{i-1}}) + sign(L_{p_i} - L_{p_{i-1}}))$$

Alternatively, the reversals can be very effective using just a simple line chart. The following is an example of such a chart to demonstrate the visual impact of trend reversal plotting:

Edge cases

During our previous calculations, we briefly mentioned that the value 0 could be produced when executing the simple trend algorithm. Given our algorithm, this can occur in the following scenarios:

- sign (-1 + (+1))
- sign (+1 + (-1))
- sign (0 + (0))

With an example graph we can identify the values using our algorithm thus:

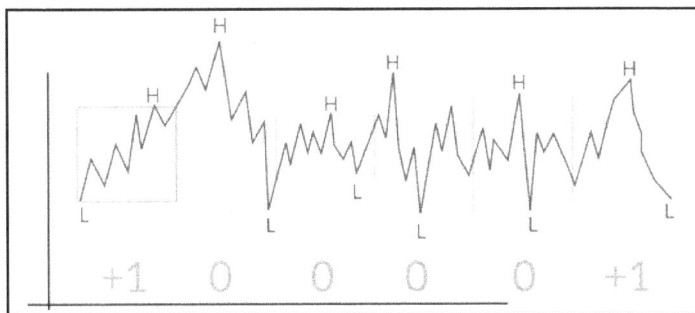

In the money markets we can identify each of the windows as being an inner bar or outer bar. Inner is a bar that defines uncertainty in the market; there is no higher high or lower low. Outer is where a higher high or lower low has been reached; of course these terms can only be assigned once the data is available.

From what we have seen so far, these zeroes appear to break our algorithm. However, this is not the case and indeed there is an efficient solution that enables us to take account of them.

Zero values

When reviewing the previous graph, we can imagine the path taken across the FHLS bars by the price, a process made easy considering that green bars mean rising prices in time, and red ones mean falling prices in time. How does understanding the path through time help solve the zero trend problem? There is a simple answer, but it is not necessarily intuitive.

We have previously kept a record of the dates of all highs and lows throughout our data processing; although we have not used all of them. Our **First** and **Second** values calculated using those dates actually indicate the flow or direction of that local trend, as in the following diagram, and once you study the summary charts for a while, your eye will naturally move with this flow to interpret the time series:

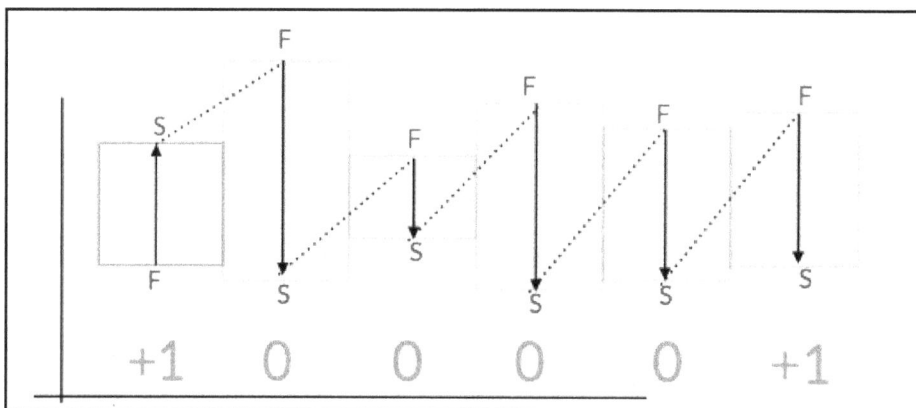

If we look at the next diagram, we can see that the dotted line showing how our eyes interpret the flow of time is not just implied. Between our dated highs and lows, there are data values that are not summarized in the chart by our specially constructed bars, meaning there are time gaps in coverage between the bars. We can leverage this property to solve the problem. Consider the following diagram, with the price line added back in:

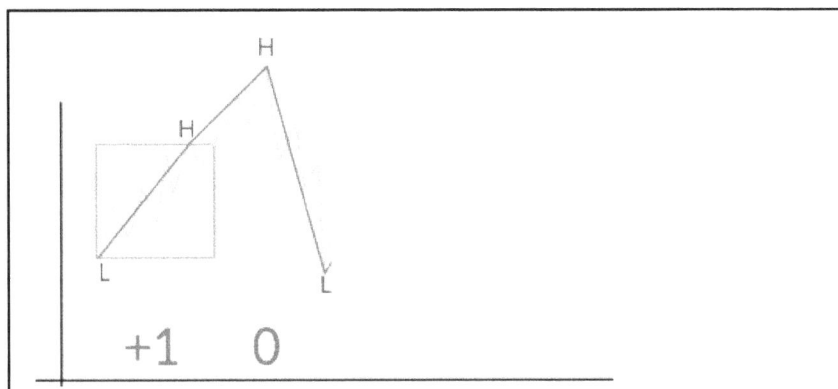

Completing the gaps

Using a continuation of the same example, we will take one of the identified gaps and demonstrate a method that we can use to fill them:

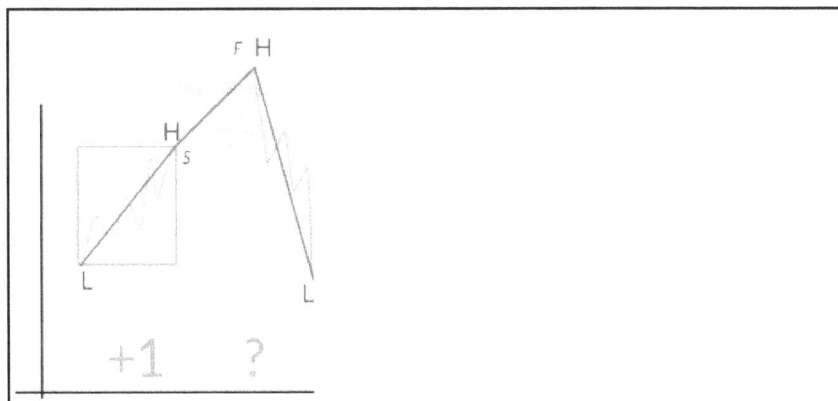

The steps are as follows:

- Find a 0 trend (inner/outer bar)
- Insert a new FHLS summary for the gap implied by borrowing the second value from the previous window, and the first value from the current window (see previous diagram)
- Emit these special bars during normal FHLS construction, format them as per regular windows of highs/lows and use them to find the trends in the normal way

Now that we have created a new bar, we can use it in the already defined manner; one of the signs of our equation (the high diff or low diff) will have a value of 0, the other will now be +1 or -1. The reversals are then calculated as before. In the previous example, the question mark becomes a -1 under our new system as we find a lower low; therefore the last high was a reversal.

We can modify the code in the following way, starting with the `simpleTrendDF` from our previous efforts:

1. Filter all of the rows with a sign of 0.

```
val zeroSignRowsDF = simpleTrendDF.filter("sign == 0").
```

2. Drop the sign column as we are going to use the schema of this new DataFrame.

```
val zeroRowsDF = zeroSignRowsDF.drop("sign").
```

3. Iterate each row and output an updated row that has been amended in the following way:

   The `window.start` date is the date of the **Second** value from the `highLowPrev` column

   The `window.end` date can remain the same, as it is not used in the FHLS calculation

The `highLow` entry is constructed thus:

1. `HighestHighDate`: The earlier of the **First** `highLow` date and **Second** `highLowPrev` date

2. `HighestHighPrice`: The price related to above

3. `LowestLowDate`: The later of the **First** `highLow` date and **Second** `highLowPrev` date

4. `LowestLowPrice`: The price related to above

5. `firstPrice`: The price related to the earliest new `highLow` date

6. `secondPrice`: The price related to the latest new `highLow` date

- The `highLowPrev` column can remain, as it will be deleted in the next step

```
val tempHighLowDF =
spark.createDataFrame(highLowDF.rdd.map(x => {
            RowFactory.create(x.getAs("window")., x.getAs("highLow"),
                        x.getAs("highLowPrev"))

        }), highLowDF.schema)
```

1. Drop the `highLowPrev` column

```
val newHighLowDF = tempHighLowDF.drop("highLowPrev")
```

2. Union the new DataFrame with `highLowDF`, which has the effect of inserting new rows

```
val updatedHighLowDF = newHighLowDF.union(highLowDF)
```

3. Proceed with the simple trend process as before, using `updatedHighLowDF` instead of `highLowDF` and starting with:

```
val sortedWindow = Window.orderBy("window.start")
```

Continuing with the preceding example, we see that there are (probably) no longer any zeroes, and the reversals are still clear and quick to compute. If the selected time window is very small, for example, seconds or minutes, then there may still be zeroes in the output, indicating that the price has not changed for that period. The gap process can be repeated, or the size of the window can be changed to something that extends the period of static price:

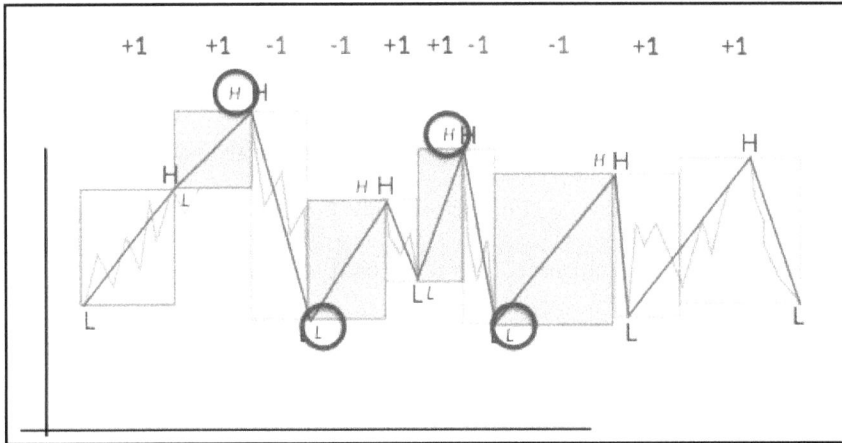

We have already seen the time series using D3, but can now use charting software to show where the new bars covering the implied gaps have been added, which are the white bars shown in the following diagram. The overall results are so intuitive, we can easily see the trends and their reversals just with our eyes:

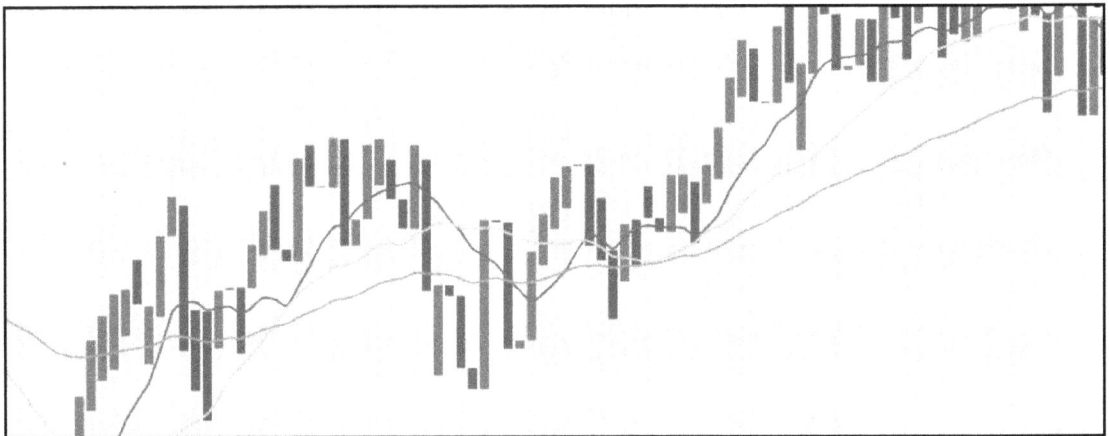

Stackable processing

Now we have this capability, we can treat the list of trend reversals as an input to a second pass of the algorithm. To do this we can adjust our windowing functions so that the inputs are windows of N-ordered observations, rather than fixed blocks of time. If we do this, we can *stack* and create multi-scale *trees of trends* TrendCalculus, meaning we can feed the output of the algorithm back into it on a subsequent pass. This creates a multi-scale reversal finder. Processing data in several passes, in this *stacked* way, is a highly efficient process due to the inherent data reduction on later passes. With multiple runs partitions build, bottom up, into a hierarchical structure. Working in this way, we can use this method to *zoom* in and out of the longer and shorter ranges of trends depending upon the level of detail we require; trend patterns become easier to see with the naked eye as we *zoom* out.

Selecting the relevant data from our `reversalsDF` DataFrame would enable us to simply run the process again; the `highLow` column contains:

- The date and price of the `HighestHigh`
- The date and price of the `LowestLow`

Which can be selected and output as a file containing (date, price); exactly the format we used to ingest our original file:

```
val newColumnNames = Seq("DATE", "PRICE")

val highLowHighestDF = simpleTrendDF.select("highLow.HighestHighDate",
"highLow.HighestHighPrice").toDF(newColumnNames:_*)

val highLowLowestDF = simpleTrendDF.select("highLow.LowestLowDate",
"highLow.LowestLowPrice").toDF(newColumnNames:_*)

val stackedDF = highLowHighestDF.union(highLowLowestDF)

stackedDF.write
    .option("header", "true")
    .csv("stackData.csv")
```

Let's review what we have built:

- We have constructed code to process a time series and to summarize it effectively into windows of dated highs and lows over fixed windows of time
- We have assigned a positive or negative trend to each time window
- We have a method to cope with edge cases, eliminating the zero valued trend problem
- We have a calculation to find the actual moments in time, and values of the prices when trend reversals occurred.

The effect of this is that we have constructed a very fast proxy method for delivering something akin to a piecewise linear regression of our time series. Seen in another way, the list of trend reversals represents a simplification of our time series into a compressed form that ignores noise on small timeframes.

Practical applications

Now that we have our algorithm coded, let's look at practical applications for this method on real data. We will start by understanding how the algorithm performs, so that we can determine where we might use it.

Algorithm characteristics

So, what are the characteristics of this algorithm? Below is a list of strengths and weaknesses.

Advantages

The advantages are as follows:

- The algorithm is general, lending itself well to both stream based and Spark implementations
- The theory is simple, yet effective
- The implementation is fast and efficient
- The result is visual and interpretable
- The method is stackable and allows for multi scale studies; this is very simple when using Spark windows

Disadvantages

The disadvantages are as follows:

- A lagging indicator the algorithm finds trend reversals that occurred in the past, and cannot be used directly to predict a trend change as it happens
- The lag accumulates for higher scales, meaning much more data (and thus time lag) is required to find long-range trend changes versus finding trend reversals on shorter timeframes

It's important to understand the limitations of this algorithm. We have created a very useful analysis tool that can be used for researching trends. However, it is not in itself a prediction tool, rather a tool to more easily identify trends for follow-on processing.

Possible use cases

With our newly found ability to convert a time series into a list of change points, many use cases that were once difficult become easy. Let's take a look at some potential applications.

Chart annotation

We can retrieve News Headlines from the GDELT feed at moments when trend changes occur, at major highs or lows, thus annotating our charts with context.

Co-trending

We can use the reduction in noise to compare trends across different time series, and devise calculations to measure which are co-trending.

Data reduction

We can use the algorithm to simplify time series and reduce data volumes, while retaining critical moments, stacking the algorithm allows for greater reductions.

Indexing

We can view the change points as a novel form of index to the time series, allowing, for example, the retrieval of portions of the data where things were on a short time frame running counter to a trend on a longer time frame.

Fractal dimension

We can find change points on different time scales, and use the information to investigate the fractal dimensions of the time series.

Streaming proxy for piecewise linear regression

The method can be used as a very fast way to compute proxy for piecewise linear regression, where such methods are needed.

Summary

In this chapter, we have introduced a method for analyzing trends with TrendCalculus. We have outlined the fact that despite analysis of trends being a very common use case, there are few tools to aid the data scientist in this cause apart from very general-purpose visualization software. We have guided the reader through the TrendCalculus algorithm, demonstrating how we implement an efficient and scalable realization of the theory in Spark. We have described the process of identifying the key output of the algorithm: trend reversals on a named scale. Having calculated reversals, we used D3.js to visualize time series data that has been summarized for one-week windows, and plotted trend reversals. The chapter continued with an explanation of how to overcome the main edge case: the zero values found during simple trend calculation. We have concluded with a brief outline of the algorithm characteristics and potential use cases, demonstrating how the method is elegant and can be easily described and realized in Spark.

In the next chapter, we will be demystifying the topic of data security. We'll describe the most important areas of security from a data science perspective, concentrating on the theory and implementation of sanctioned access for the handling of highly confidential data.

13
Secure Data

Throughout this book, we have visited many areas of data science, often straying into those that are not traditionally associated with a data scientist's core working knowledge. In particular, we dedicated an entire chapter, `Chapter 2`, *Data Acquisition*, to data ingestion, which explains how to solve an issue that is always present, but rarely acknowledged or addressed adequately. In this chapter, we will visit another of those often overlooked fields, secure data. More specifically, how to protect your data and analytic results at all stages of the data life cycle. This ranges from ingestion, right through to presentation, at all times considering the important architectural and scalability requirements that naturally form the Spark paradigm.

In this chapter, we will cover the following topics:

- How to implement coarse-grained data access controls using HDFS ACLs
- A guide to fine-grained security, with explanations using the Hadoop ecosystem
- How to ensure data is always encrypted, with an example using Java KeyStore
- Techniques for obfuscating, masking, and tokenizing data
- How Spark implements Kerberos
- Data security – the ethical and technical issues

Data security

The final piece to our data architecture is security, and in this chapter we will discover that data security is always important, and the reasons for this. Given the huge increase in the volume and variety of data in recent times, caused by many factors, but in no small part due to the popularity of the Internet and related technologies, there is a growing need to provide fully scalable and secure solutions. We are going to explore those solutions along with the confidentiality, privacy, and legal concerns associated with the storing, processing, and handling of data; we will relate these to the tools and techniques introduced in previous chapters.

We will continue on by explaining the technical issues involved in securing data at scale and introduce ideas and techniques that tackle these concerns using a variety of access, classification, and obfuscation strategies. As in previous chapters, ideas are demonstrated with examples using the Hadoop ecosystem, and public cloud infrastructure strategies will also be present.

The problem

We have explored many and varied topics in previous chapters, usually concentrating on the specifics of a particular issue and the approaches that can be taken to solve them. In all of these cases, there has been the implicit idea that the data that is being used, and the content of the insights gathered, does not need protecting in any way; or at least the protection provided at the operating system level, such as login credentials, is sufficient.

In any environment, whether it is a home or a commercial one, data security is a huge issue that must always be considered. Perhaps, in a few instances, it is enough to write the data to a local hard drive and take no further steps; this is rarely an acceptable course of action and certainly should be a conscious decision rather than default behavior. In a commercial environment, computing resources are often provided with built-in security. In this case, it is still important for the user to understand those implications and decide whether further steps should be taken; data security is not just about protection from malicious entities or accidental deletion, but also everything in-between.

As an example, if you work in a secure, regulated, commercial, air-gapped environment (no access to the Internet) and within a team of like-minded data scientists, individual security responsibilities are still just as important as in an environment where no security exists at all; you may have access to data that must not be viewed by any of your peers and you may need to produce analytical results that are available to different and diversified user groups, all of whom are not to see each other's data. The emphasis may be explicitly or implicitly on you to ensure that the data is not compromised; therefore, a strong understanding of the security layers in your software stack is imperative.

The basics

Security considerations are everywhere, even in places that you probably hadn't even thought of. For example, when Spark is running a parallel job on a cluster, do you know the points at which data may touch physical disk during that life cycle? If you are thinking that everything is done in RAM, then you have a potential security issue right there, as data can be spilled to disk. More on the implications of this further on in this chapter. The point here is that you cannot always delegate security responsibility to the frameworks you are using. Indeed, the more varied the software you use, the more security concerns increase, both user and data related.

Security can be broadly split into three areas:

- **Authentication**: determining the legitimacy of the identity of a user
- **Authorization**: the privileges that a user holds to perform specific actions
- **Access**: the security mechanisms used to protect data, both in transit and at rest

There are important differences between these points. A user may have full permissions to access and edit a file, but if the file has been encrypted outside of the user security realm, then the file may still not be readable; user authorization intervenes. Equally, a user may send data across a secure link to be processed on a remote server before a result is returned, but this does not guarantee that the data has not left a footprint on that remote server; the security mechanisms are unknown.

Authentication and authorization

Authentication is related to the mechanisms used to ensure that the user is who they say they are and operates at two key levels, namely, local and remote.

Authentication can take various forms, the most common is user login, but other examples include fingerprint reading, iris scanning, and PIN number entry. User logins can be managed on a local basis, as you would on your personal computer, for example, or on a remote basis using a tool such as **Lightweight Directory Access Protocol** (**LDAP**). Managing users remotely provides roaming user profiles that are independent of any particular hardware and can be managed independently of the user. All of these methods execute at the operating system level. There are other mechanisms that sit at the application layer and provide authentication for services, such as Google OAuth.

Alternative authentication methods have their own pros and cons, a particular implementation should be understood thoroughly before declaring a secure system; for example, a fingerprint system may seem very secure, but this is not always the case. For more information, refer to `http://www.cse.msu.edu/rgroups/biometrics/Publications /Fingerprint/CaoJain_HackingMobilePhonesUsing2DPrintedFingerprint_MSU-CSE-16-2.pdf`. We are not going to explore authentication any further here, as we have made the assumption that most systems will only be implementing user logins; a feature, by the way, that is often not a secure solution in its own right and indeed, in many cases, provides no security at all. For more information, refer to `http://www.cs.arizona.edu/~collberg/Tea ching/466-566/2012/Resources/presentations/2012/topic7-final/report.pdf`.

Authorization is an area that is of great interest to us as it forms a critical part of basic security, is an area that we most often have greatest control over, and is something that we can use natively in any modern operating system. There are various different ways of implementing resource authorization, the two main ones being:

- **Access control lists** (**ACL**)
- **Role-based access control** (**RBAC**)

We'll discuss each of these in turn.

Access control lists (ACL)

In Unix, ACLs are used throughout the filesystem. If we list directory contents at the command line:

```
drwxr-xr-x 6 mrh mygroup 204 16 Jun 2015 resources
```

We can see there is a directory called resources that has an assigned owner (mrh) and group (mygroup), has 6 links, a size of 204 bytes, and was last modified on the 16 June 2015. The ACLs drwxr-xr-x indicate:

- d this is a directory (- if it is not)
- rwx the owner(mrh) has read, write, and executable rights
- r-x anyone in the group (mygroup) has read and execute rights
- r-x everyone else has read and execute rights

Using ACLs is an excellent first step towards securing our data. It should always be the first thing considered, and should always be correct; if we do not ensure these settings are correct at all times, then we are potentially making it easy for other users to access this data, and we don't necessarily know who the other users on the system are. Always avoid providing full access in the *all* part of the ACL:

```
-rwx---rwx 6 mrh mygroup 204 16 Jun 2015 secretFile.txt
```

It doesn't matter how secure our system is, any user with access to the filesystem can read, write, and delete this file! A far more appropriate setting would be:

```
-rwxr----- 6 mrh mygroup 204 16 Jun 2015 secretFile.txt
```

Which provides full owner access and read-only access for the group.

HDFS implements ACLs natively; these can be administered using the command line:

```
hdfs dfs -chmod 777 /path/to/my/file.txt
```

This gives full permissions to the file in HDFS for everyone, assuming the file already had sufficient permissions for us to make the change.

> When Apache released Hadoop in 2008, it was often not understood that a cluster set at all of its defaults did not do any authentication of users. The superuser in Hadoop, hdfs, could be accessed by any user if the cluster had not been correctly configured, by simply creating an hdfs user on a client machine (sudo useradd hdfs).

Role-based access control (RBAC)

RBAC takes a different approach, by assigning users one or more roles. These roles are related to common tasks or job functions, such that they can be easily added or removed dependent upon the user's responsibilities. For example, in a company, there may be many roles, including accounts, stock, and deliveries. An accountant may be given all three roles, so that they can compile the end of year finances, whereas an administrator booking deliveries would just have the deliveries role. This makes it much easier to add new users and manage users when they change departments or leave the organization.

Three key rules are defined for RBAC:

- **Role assignment**: a user can exercise a permission only if the user has selected or been assigned a role
- **Role authorization**: a user's active role must be authorized for the user
- **Permission authorization**: a user can exercise a permission only if the permission is authorized for the user's active role

The relationships between users and roles can be summarized as follows:

- **Role-Permissions**: a particular role grants specific permissions to the user.
- **User-Role**: the relationships between types of users and specific roles.
- **Role-Role**: the relationships between roles. These can be hierarchical, so *role1 =>* *role2* could mean that, if a user has *role1*, then they automatically have *role2*, but if they have *role2*, this does not necessarily mean they have *role1*.

RBAC is realized in Hadoop through Apache Sentry. Organizations can define the privileges for datasets that will be enforced from multiple access paths, including HDFS, Apache Hive, Impala, as well as Apache Pig and Apache MapReduce/Yarn via HCatalog. As an example, each Spark application runs as the requesting user and requires access to the underlying files. Spark cannot enforce access control directly, since it is running as the requesting user and is untrusted. Therefore, it is restricted to filesystem permissions (ACLs). Apache Sentry provides role-based control to resources in this case.

Access

We have thus far concentrated only on the specific ideas of ensuring that a user is who they say they are and that only the correct users can view and use data. However, once we have taken the appropriate steps and confirmed these details, we still need to ensure that this data is secure when the user is actually using it; there are a number of areas to consider:

- Is the user allowed to see all of the information in the data? Perhaps they are to be limited to certain rows, or even certain parts of certain rows.
- Is the data secure when the user runs analytics across it? We need to ensure that the data isn't transmitted as plain text and therefore open to man-in-the-middle attacks.
- Is the data secure once the user has completed their task? There's no point in ensuring that the data is super secure at all stages, only to write plain text results to an insecure area.
- Can conclusions be made from the aggregation of data? Even if the user only has access to certain rows of a dataset, let's say to protect an individual's anonymity in this case, it is sometimes possible to make links between apparently unrelated information, for example. If the user knows that $A=>B$ and $B=>C$, they can guess that, probably, $A=>C$, even if they are not allowed to see this in the data. In practice, this kind of issue can be very difficult to avoid, as data aggregation problems can be very subtle, occurring in unforeseen situations and often involving information gleaned over an extended period of time.

There are a number of mechanisms that we can use to help us protect against the preceding scenarios.

Encryption

Arguably the most obvious and well known method of protecting data is encryption. We would use this whether our data is in transit or at rest, so, virtually all of the time, apart from when the data is actually being processed inside memory. The mechanics of encryption are different depending upon the state of the data.

Data at rest

Our data will always need to be stored somewhere, whether it be HDFS, S3, or local disk. If we have taken all of the precautions of ensuring that users are authorized and authenticated, there is still the issue of plain text actually existing on the disk. With direct access to the disk, either physically or by accessing it through a lower level in the OSI stack, it is fairly trivial to stream the entire contents and glean the plain text data.

If we encrypt data, then we are protected from this type of attack. The encryption can also exist at different levels, either by encrypting the data at the application layer using software, or by encrypting it at the hardware level, that is, the disk itself.

Encrypting the data at the application layer is the most common route, as it enables the user to make informed choices about the trade-off decisions that need to be made, thereby making the right choice of product for their situation. Because encryption adds an extra level of processing overhead (the data needs to be encrypted at write and decrypted at read), there is a key decision to make regarding the processor time versus security strength trade-off. The principal decisions for consideration are:

- **Encryption algorithm type**: the algorithm to use to perform encryption, that is, AES, RSA, and so on
- **Encryption key bit length**: the size of the encryption key roughly equates to how difficult it is to crack, but also influences the size of the result (possible storage consideration), that is, 64 bit, 128 bit, and so on
- **Processor time allowed**: longer encryption keys generally mean greater processing time; this can have a serious impact on processing, given data of sufficient volume

Once we have decided upon the correct combination of factors for our use case, bearing in mind that some algorithm key length combinations are no longer considered safe, we need the software to actually do the encryption. This could be a bespoke Hadoop plugin or a commercial application. As mentioned, Hadoop now has a native HDFS encryption plugin, so you will not need to write your own! This plugin uses a Java KeyStore to safely store the encryption keys, which can be accessed through Apache Ranger. Encryption takes place entirely within HDFS, and is essentially linked to the ACLs on files. Therefore, when accessing HDFS files in Spark, the process is seamless (apart from some extra time to encrypt/decrypt files).

If you wish to implement encryption in Spark to write data to somewhere that is not covered in the aforementioned scenarios, then the Java javax.crypto package can be used. The weakest link here is now the fact that the key itself must be recorded somewhere; therefore, we have potentially simply moved our security issue elsewhere. Using a suitable KeyStore, such as Java KeyStore would address this issue.

At the time of writing, there is no obvious way of encrypting data when writing from Spark to local disk. In the next section, we'll write our own!

The idea is to replace the `rdd.saveAsTextFile(filePath)` function with something as close as possible to the original, with the further capability of encrypting the data. However, that's not the whole story, as we'll need to be able to read the data back too. To do this, we'll take advantage of an alternative to `rdd.saveAsTextFile(filePath)` function, which also accepts a compression codec argument:

```
saveAsTextFile(filePath, Class<? extends
    org.apache.hadoop.io.compress.CompressionCodec> codec)
```

On the face of it, the way Spark uses the compression codec appears to be similar to what we'd want for data encryption. So, let's adapt one of the existing Hadoop compression implementations for our purposes. Looking at a few different existing implementations (`GzipCodec`, `BZip2Codec`), we find that we must extend the `CompressionCodec` interface to derive our encryption codec, named `CryptoCodec` from here on. Let's look at an implementation in Java:

```java
import org.apache.hadoop.io.compress.crypto.CryptoCompressor;
import org.apache.hadoop.io.compress.crypto.CryptoDecompressor;

public class CryptoCodec implements CompressionCodec, Configurable {

    public static final String CRYPTO_DEFAULT_EXT = ".crypto";
    private Configuration config;

    @Override
    public Compressor createCompressor() {
        return new CryptoCompressor();
    }
    @Override
    public Decompressor createDecompressor() {
        return new CryptoDecompressor();
    }
    @Override
    public CompressionInputStream createInputStream(InputStream in)
            throws IOException {
        return createInputStream(in, createDecompressor());
    }
```

```
    @Override
    public CompressionInputStream createInputStream(InputStream in,
        Decompressor decomp) throws IOException {
      return new DecompressorStream(in, decomp);
    }
    @Override
    public CompressionOutputStream createOutputStream(OutputStream out)
        throws IOException {
      return createOutputStream(out, createCompressor());
    }
    @Override
    public CompressionOutputStream createOutputStream(OutputStream out,
        Compressor comp) throws IOException {
      return new CompressorStream(out, comp);
    }
    @Override
    public Class<? extends Compressor> getCompressorType() {
      return CryptoCompressor.class;
    }
    @Override
    public Class<? extends Decompressor> getDecompressorType() {
      return CryptoDecompressor.class;
    }
    @Override
    public String getDefaultExtension() {
      return CRYPTO_DEFAULT_EXT;
    }
    @Override
    public Configuration getConf() {
      return this.config;
    }
    @Override
    public void setConf(Configuration config) {
      this.config = config;
    }
  }
```

It's worth noting here that this codec class just serves as a wrapper for integrating our encryption and decryption routines with the Hadoop API; this class provides the entry points for the Hadoop framework to use when the crypto codec is called. The two main methods of interest are createCompressor and createDeompressor, which both perform the same initialization:

```
public CryptoCompressor() {
    crypto = new EncryptionUtils(); }
```

We have used plain text passwords to make things simpler. When using this code, the encryption key should be pulled from a secure store; this is discussed in detail further on in this chapter:

```
public EncryptionUtils() {
    this.setupCrypto(getPassword());
}

private String getPassword() {
    // Use a Java KeyStore as per the below code, a Database or any other
secure mechanism to obtain a password
    // TODO We will return a hard coded String for simplicity
    return "keystorepassword";
}

private void setupCrypto(String password) {
    IvParameterSpec paramSpec = new IvParameterSpec(generateIV());
    skeySpec = new SecretKeySpec(password.getBytes("UTF-8"), "AES");
    ecipher = Cipher.getInstance(encoding);
    ecipher.init(Cipher.ENCRYPT_MODE, skeySpec, paramSpec);
    dcipher = Cipher.getInstance(encoding);
}

private byte[] generateIV() {
    SecureRandom random = new SecureRandom();
    byte bytes[] = new byte[16];
    random.nextBytes(bytes);
    return bytes;
}
```

Next, we define the encryption methods themselves:

```
public byte[] encrypt(byte[] plainBytes, boolean addIV)
        throws InvalidAlgorithmParameterException,
                InvalidKeyException {

    byte[] iv = "".getBytes("UTF-8");
    if (!addIV) {
        iv = ecipher.getParameters()
                    .getParameterSpec(IvParameterSpec.class)
                    .getIV();
    }
    byte[] ciphertext = ecipher.update(
            plainBytes, 0, plainBytes.length);
    byte[] result = new byte[iv.length + ciphertext.length];
    System.arraycopy(iv, 0, result, 0, iv.length);
    System.arraycopy(ciphertext, 0,
                    result, iv.length, ciphertext.length);
```

```
        return result;
    }

    public byte[] decrypt(byte[] ciphertext, boolean useIV)
            throws InvalidAlgorithmParameterException,
                InvalidKeyException {

        byte[] deciphered;
        if (useIV) {
            byte[] iv = Arrays.copyOfRange(ciphertext, 0, 16);
            IvParameterSpec paramSpec = new IvParameterSpec(iv);
            dcipher.init(Cipher.DECRYPT_MODE, skeySpec, paramSpec);
            deciphered = dcipher.update(
                ciphertext, 16, ciphertext.length - 16);
        } else {
            deciphered = dcipher.update(
                ciphertext, 0, ciphertext.length);
        }
        return deciphered;

    }

    public byte[] doFinal() {
        try {
            byte[] ciphertext = ecipher.doFinal();
            return ciphertext;
        } catch (Exception e) {
            log.error(e.getStackTrace());
            return null;
        }
    }
}
```

Each time a file is encrypted, the *Initialization Vector* (IV) should be random. Randomization is crucial for encryption schemes to achieve semantic security, a property whereby repeated usage of the scheme under the same key does not allow an attacker to infer relationships between segments of the encrypted message.

The main issue when implementing encryption paradigms is the mishandling of byte arrays. A correctly encrypted file size will usually be a multiple of the key size when using padding, 16 (bytes) in this case. The encryption/decryption process will fail with padding exceptions if the file size is incorrect. In the Java libraries used previously, data is fed to the internal encryption routine in stages, size `ciphertext.length`, which are encrypted in chunks of 16 bytes. If there is a remainder, this is prepended to the data given in the next update. If a `doFinal` call is made, the remainder is again prepended and the data is padded to the end of the 16 byte block before encryption, whereby the routine completes.

We can now proceed to complete the rest of our `CryptoCodec`, that is, the compress and decompress implementations that will implement the preceding code. These methods are located in the `CryptoCompressor` and `CryptoDecompressor` classes and are called by the Hadoop framework:

```
@Override
public synchronized int compress(byte[] buf, int off, int len) throws
IOException {
    finished = false;
    if (remain != null && remain.remaining() > 0) {
        int size = Math.min(len, remain.remaining());
        remain.get(buf, off, size);
        wrote += size;
        if (!remain.hasRemaining()) {
            remain = null;
            setFinished();
        }
        return size;
    }
    if (in == null || in.remaining() <= 0) {
        setFinished();
        return 0;
    }
    byte[] w = new byte[in.remaining()];
    in.get(w);
    byte[] b = crypto.encrypt(w, addedIV);
    if (!addedIV)
        addedIV = true;
    int size = Math.min(len, b.length);
    remain = ByteBuffer.wrap(b);
    remain.get(buf, off, size);
    wrote += size;
    if (remain.remaining() <= 0)
        setFinished();
    return size;
}
```

You can see the full implementation for the `CryptoCodec` class in our code repository.

Now that we have our working `CryptoCodec` class, the Spark driver code is then straightforward:

```
val conf = new SparkConf()
val sc = new SparkContext(conf.setAppName("crypto encrypt"))
val writeRDD = sc.parallelize(List(1, 2, 3, 4), 2)
writeRDD.saveAsTextFile("file:///encrypted/data/path",classOf[CryptoCodec])
```

And we have local disk encryption! To read an encrypted file, we simply define the codec class within the configuration:

```
val conf = new SparkConf()
conf.set("spark.hadoop.io.compression.codecs",
         "org.apache.hadoop.io.compress.CryptoCodec")
val sc = new SparkContext(conf.setAppName("crypto decrypt"))
val readRDD = sc.textFile("file:///encrypted/data/path")
readRDD.collect().foreach(println)
```

Spark will automatically use the CryptoCodec class when it recognizes an appropriate file and our implementation ensures a unique IV is used for each file; the IV is read from the beginning of the encrypted file.

Java KeyStore

Depending upon your environment, the preceding code may be enough to keep your data secure. However, there is a flaw, in that the key used to encrypt/decrypt the data has to be provided in plain text. We can solve this issue by creating a Java KeyStore. This can be done via the command line or programmatically. We can implement a function to create a JCEKS KeyStore and add a key:

```
public static void createJceksStoreAddKey() {

        KeyStore keyStore = KeyStore.getInstance("JCEKS");
        keyStore.load(null, null);

        KeyGenerator kg = KeyGenerator.getInstance("AES");
        kg.init(128); // 16 bytes = 128 bit
        SecretKey sk = kg.generateKey();
        System.out.println(sk.getEncoded().toString());

        keyStore.setKeyEntry("secretKeyAlias", sk,
            "keystorepassword".toCharArray(), null);

        keyStore.store(new FileOutputStream("keystore.jceks"),
                "keystorepassword".toCharArray());
}
```

We can achieve the same via the command line:

```
keytool -genseckey-alias secretKeyAlias /
        -keyalg AES /
        -keystore keystore.jceks /
        -keysize 128 /
        -storeType JCEKS
```

And check it exists:

```
keytool -v -list -storetype JCEKS -keystore keystore.jceks
```

To retrieve the key from this KeyStore:

```
public static SecretKey retrieveKey()
        throws KeyStoreException,
               IOException,
               CertificateException,
               NoSuchAlgorithmException,
               UnrecoverableKeyException {

    KeyStore keyStore = KeyStore.getInstance("JCEKS");
    keyStore.load(new FileInputStream("keystore.jceks"),
        "keystorepassword".toCharArray());

    SecretKey key = (SecretKey) keyStore.getKey("secretKeyAlias",
        "keystorepassword".toCharArray());

    System.out.println(key.getEncoded().toString());
    return key;
}
```

> We have hardcoded the specifics for ease of reading, this should not be done in practice, as Java byte code is relatively simple to reverse engineer and, therefore, a malicious third party could easily obtain this secret information.

Our secret key is now protected in a KeyStore and is only accessible using the KeyStore password and secret key alias. These still need to be protected, but would usually be stored in a database, where they are accessible only to authorized users.

We can now modify our `EncryptionUtils.getPassword` method to retrieve the JCEKS key rather than the plain text version, like so:

```
private String getPassword(){
    return retrieveKey();
}
```

Now that we have a `CryptoCodec` class, we can use it throughout Spark to secure data anytime we need data encryption. For example, if we set the Spark configuration `spark.shuffle.spill.compress` to true, and set `spark.io.compression.codec` to `org.apache.hadoop.io.compress.CryptoCodec`, then any spill to disk will be encrypted.

S3 encryption

HDFS encryption is great for providing what is essentially a managed service. If we now look at S3, this can do the same, but it also offers the ability to provide server-side encryption with:

- AWS KMS-Managed keys (SSE-KMS)
- Customer-Provided keys (SSE-C)

Server-side encryption can provide more flexibility should you be in an environment where the encryption keys need to be explicitly managed.

Hardware encryption is handled within the physical disk architecture. Generally, this has the advantage of being quicker (due to the bespoke hardware designated for encryption) and being easier to secure, as physical access to the machine is required in order to circumvent. The downside being that all data written to disk is encrypted, which can result in reduced I/O performance for heavily utilized disks.

Data in transit

If end-to-end security is your goal, an area that is often of concern is that of data in transit. This could be the reading/writing from disk or transportation of data around a network during analytics processing. In all cases, it is important to be aware of the weaknesses of your environment. It is not enough to assume that the framework or network administrator have covered these potential issues for you, even if your environment does not allow changes to be made directly.

A common mistake is to assume that data is secure when it is not human-readable. Although binary data itself isn't human-readable, it is often readily translated to the readable content and it can be captured over the network using tools such as Wireshark (www.wireshark.org). So, never assume data security on the wire, regardless of whether it's human-readable.

As we have seen previously, even when encrypting data on disk, we cannot assume it is necessarily secure. For example, if the data is encrypted at hardware level, then it is unencrypted as soon as it leaves the disk itself. In other words, the plain text is readable as it traverses the network to any machine and, therefore, completely open to being read by unknown entities at any point on that journey. Data encrypted at software level is generally not decrypted until it is used by the analytic, therefore, generally making it the safer option if the network topology is not known.

When considering the security of processing systems themselves, such as Spark, there are issues here too. Data is constantly moved between nodes with no direct control from the user. So, it is vital that we understand where the data may be available in plain text at any given time. Consider the following diagram that shows the interactions between entities during a Spark YARN job:

We can see that every connection transmits and receives data. Spark input data is transferred via broadcast variables and all channels support encryption apart from UI and local shuffle/cache files (see JIRA SPARK-5682 for more information).

Furthermore, there is a weakness here, in that cached files are stored as plain text. The fix is either to implement the preceding solution, or to set up YARN local directories to point to local encrypted disks. To do this, we need to ensure that `yarn.nodemanager.local-dirs` in yarn-default.xml are encrypted directories on all DataNodes, either using a commercial product or hosting these directories on encrypted disks.

Now that we have considered the data as a whole, we should address the individual parts of the data itself. It is very possible that data may contain sensitive information, for example, names, addresses, and credit card numbers. There are a number of ways to handle this type of information.

Obfuscation/Anonymizing

With obfuscation, the sensitive parts of the data are transformed into something that can never be linked back to the original content – providing security through obscurity. For example, a CSV file containing fields: `Forename, Surname, Address line 1, Address line 2, Postcode, Phone Number, Credit Card Number` might be obfuscated like so:

- Original

      John, Smith, 3 New Road, London, E1 2AA, 0207 123456, 4659 4234 5678
      9999

- Obfuscated

      John, XXXXXX, X New Road, London, XX 2AA, XXXX 123456, 4659
      XXXXXXXXXXXXX

Obfuscating data is great for analytics, as it protects sensitive data while still allowing useful calculations, such as counting completed fields. We can also be intelligent about the way we obfuscate the data in order to preserve certain details while protecting others. For example, a credit card number: `4659 42XX XXXX XXXX` can give us a surprising amount of information, as the first six digits of payments cards, called the **Bank Identification Number** (**BIN**), tell us the following:

- BIN 465942
- Card brand: VISA
- Issuing bank: HSBC
- Card type: debit
- Card level: classic
- ISO country number 826 (Great Britain)

Data obfuscation should not necessarily be random, but should be carefully tailored to ensure that sensitive data is definitely removed. The definition of sensitive will entirely depend upon the requirements. In the preceding example, it may be very useful to be able to summarize the distribution of customer payments cards by type, or it could be deemed as sensitive information that should be removed.

Another phenomenon to be aware of here, as you may recall from previous chapters, is data aggregation. For example, if we know that the name of the individual is John Smith AND that his credit card starts with 465942, then we know that John Smith has an account with HSBC in the UK, a great piece of information for a malicious entity to start building on. Therefore, care must be taken to ensure that the right amount of obfuscation is applied, bearing in mind that we can never recover the original data, unless we have another copy stored elsewhere. Non-recovery of data can be a costly event, so data obfuscation should be implemented wisely. Indeed, if storage allows, it is not unreasonable to want to store several versions of data, each with a different level of obfuscation and different levels of access.

When thinking about implementing this in Spark, it is most likely that we will have a scenario where there are many input records that require transformation. Thus, our starting point is to write something that works on a single record, and then wrap this in an RDD so that the functions can be run across many records in parallel.

Taking our preceding example, let's express its schema in Scala as an enumeration. Along with the definition, we'll include in our Enumeration class information about how any particular field should be obfuscated:

- *x*, *y* mask the char positions from *x* to *y*
- 0, len mask the entire field from 0 to the length of the field text
- prefix mask everything before the last space character
- suffix mask everything after the first space character
- "" do nothing

This information is encoded in the enumeration as follows:

```
object RecordField extends Enumeration {
type Obfuscation = Value
val FIRSTNAME       = Value(0,  "")
val SURNAME         = Value(1,  "0,len")
val ADDRESS1        = Value(2,  "0,1")
val ADDRESS2        = Value(3,  "")
val POSTCODE       = Value(4,  "prefix")
val TELNUMBER      = Value(5,  "prefix")
val CCNUMBER        = Value(6,  "suffix")
}
```

Next, we can split the input string and write a function that applies the correct obfuscation argument to the correct field:

```
def getObfuscationResult(text: String): String = {
  text
    .split(",")
    .zipWithIndex
    .map { case (field, idx) =>
      field match {
        case s: String if idx >= 0 && idx <= 6 =>
          stringObfuscator(s,RecordField(idx).toString, 'X')
        case _ => "Unknown field"
      }
    }
    .mkString(",")
}
```

To keep things simple, we have hardcoded some of the items that you may want to change later, for example the split argument (,), and also made the obfuscation symbol constant in all cases (X).

And finally, the actual obfuscation code:

```
def stringObfuscator(text: String,
                     maskArgs: String,
                     maskChar: Char):String = {
  var start = 0
  var end = 0

  if (maskArgs.equals("")) {
    text
  }

  if (maskArgs.contains(",")) {
    start = maskArgs.split(',')(0).toInt
    if (maskArgs.split(',')(1) == "len")
      end = text.length
    else
      end = maskArgs.split(',')(1).toInt
  }

  if (maskArgs.contains("prefix")){
    end = text.indexOf(" ")
  }

  if (maskArgs.contains("suffix")){
    start = text.indexOf(" ") + 1
    end = text.length
```

```
    }

    if (start > end)
      maskChar

    val maskLength: Int = end - start

    if (maskLength == 0)
      text

    var sbMasked: StringBuilder  = new StringBuilder(
          text.substring(0, start))

    for(i <- 1 to maskLength) {
      sbMasked.append(maskChar)
    }
    sbMasked.append(text.substring(start + maskLength)).toString
  }
```

Again, we have kept things simple and do not go to great lengths to check for exceptions or edge cases. Here is a practical example:

```
getObfuscationResult(
    "John,Smith,3 New Road,London,E1 2AA,0207 123456,4659 4234 5678 9999")
```

It provides the desired result:

```
John,XXXXXX,X New Road,London,XX 2AA,XXXX 123456,4659 XXXXXXXXXXXXXX
```

This handy bit of code provides a great basis for obfuscating at scale. We can easily extend it to more complicated scenarios, such as the obfuscation of different parts of the same field. For example, by changing `StringObfuscator`, we could mask the house number and road name differently in the `Address Line 1` field:

```
val ADDRESS1 = Value(2, "0,1;2,len")
```

Of course, if you were wishing to scale this out for many different use cases, you could also apply the strategy pattern over `StringObfuscator` to allow an obfuscation function to be provided at runtime.

A key software engineering technique, the strategy pattern is described here: `https://sour cemaking.com/design_patterns/strategy`.

At this point, it's worth thinking about obfuscating data using an algorithm, such as one-way hashing function or digest, rather than simply replacing with characters (XXX). This is a versatile technique and is applicable in a wide range of use cases. It relies on the computational complexity of performing an inverse calculation for some calculations, such as finding factors and modular squaring, meaning that once applied they are impractical to reverse. However, care should be taken when using hashes because, despite digest calculations being NP-complete, there are some scenarios where hashing is still susceptible to compromise using implicit knowledge. For example, the predictability of credit card numbers means that they have been proved to be cracked quickly by a brute-force approach, even using MD5 or SHA-1 hashes.

For more information, refer to `https://www.integrigy.com/security-resources/hashing-credit-card-numbers-unsafe-application-practices`.

Masking

Data masking is about creating a functional substitute of data while ensuring that important content is hidden. This is another anonymization method whereby the original contents are lost once the masking process has taken place. Therefore, it is important to ensure that the changes are carefully planned, as they are effectively final. Of course, an original version of the data could be stored for emergencies, but this would add additional burden to the security considerations.

Masking is a simple process and it relies on generating random data to replace any sensitive data. For example, applying a mask to our previous example gives:

```
Simon,Jones,2 The Mall,London,NW1 2JT,0171 123890,1545 3146 6273 6262
```

We now have a row, which is functionally equivalent to the original data. We have a full name, address, phone number, and credit card number, but they are *different*, such that they cannot be linked to the original.

Partial masking is very useful for processing purposes, as we can keep some data while masking the rest. In this way, we can perform a number of data auditing tasks that are not necessarily possible using obfuscation. For example, we could mask data actually present, allowing us to guarantee that populated fields will always be valid whilst also being able to detect empty fields.

It is also possible to use complete masking in order to generate mock data without having seen the original data at all. In this case, data could be completely generated, say, for testing or profiling purposes.

Whatever the use case, care should be taken when using masking, as it is possible to unwittingly insert real information into a record. For example, `Simon Jones` might actually be a real person. This being the case, it is certainly a good idea to store the data provenance, that is, the source and historical record for all data held. Therefore, should the real "`Simon, Jones`" submit a **request for information** (**RFI**) under the data protection act you have the necessary information in order to provide the relevant justifications.

Let's extend our previously built code to implement a basic masking approach using a completely random selection. We have seen that the masking method requires that we replace fields with some meaningful alternative. To have something working quickly we could simply provide arrays of alternatives:

```
val forenames = Array("John","Fred","Jack","Simon")
val surnames = Array("Smith","Jones","Hall","West")
val streets = Array("17 Bound Mews","76 Byron Place",
    "2 The Mall","51 St James")
```

Later, we can extend these to read from a file containing many more alternatives. We can even replace multiple fields in one go using a composite mask:

```
val composite = Array("London,NW1 2JT,0171 123890",
                      "Newcastle, N23 2FD,0191 567000",
                      "Bristol,BS1 2AA,0117 934098",
                      "Manchester,M56 9JH,0121 111672")
```

The processing code is then straightforward:

```
def getMaskedResult(): String = {

  Array(
    forenames(scala.util.Random.nextInt(forenames.length)),
    surnames(scala.util.Random.nextInt(surnames.length)),
    streets(scala.util.Random.nextInt(streets.length)),
    composite(scala.util.Random.nextInt(composite.length)).split(","),
    RandomCCNumber)
  .flatMap {
    case s:String => Seq(s)
    case a:Array[String] => a
  }
  .mkString(",")
}
```

We can define a `RandomCCNumber` function to generate a random credit card number. Here's a simple function that provides four sets of randomly generated integers using recursion:

```
def RandomCCNumber(): String = {

    def appendDigits(ccn:Array[String]): Array[String] = {
      if (ccn.length < 4) {
        appendDigits(ccn :+ (for (i <- 1 to 4)
          yield scala.util.Random.nextInt(9)).mkString)
      }
      else {
        ccn
      }
    }
    appendDigits(Array()).mkString(" ")
}
```

Putting this code together and running against our original example, gives the following:

```
getMaskedResult(
  "John,Smith,3 New Road,London,E1 2AA,0207 123456,4659 4234 5678 9999")
```

The output of the preceding code is as follows:

```
Jack,Hall,76 Byron Place,Newcastle, N23 2FD,0191 567000,7533 8606 6465 6040
```

Alternatively:

```
John,West,2 The Mall,Manchester,M56 9JH,0121 111672,3884 0242 3212 4704
```

Again, there are many ways we could develop this code. For example, we could generate a credit card number that is valid under the BIN scheme, or we could ensure that name selection doesn't randomly choose the same name that it's trying to replace. However, the outlined framework is presented here as a demonstration of the technique and can be easily extended and generalized to account for any additional requirements you might have.

Tokenization

Tokenization is the process of substituting sensitive information with a token that can be later used to retrieve the actual data, if required, subject to the relevant authentication and authorization. Using our previous example, tokenized text might look like:

```
John,Smith,[25AJZ99P],[78OPL45K],[72GRT55N],[54CPW59D],[32DOI01F]
```

Where the bracketed values are tokens that can be exchanged for the actual values when the requesting user fulfills the correct security criteria. This method is the most secure of those discussed and allows us to recover the exact original underlying data. However, it comes with a significant processing overhead to tokenize and detokenize data and, of course, the tokenizer system will require administration and careful maintenance.

This also means that there is a single point of failure in the tokenization system itself and, therefore, it must be subject to the important security processes we have discussed: audit, authentication, and authorization.

Due to the complexities and security issues with tokenization, the most popular implementations are commercial products covered by extensive patents. The bulk of the effort with this type of system, particularly with big data, is in ensuring that the tokenizer system can provide a full, completely secure, robust and scalable service at very high levels of throughput. We can, however, build a simple tokenizer using Accumulo. In Chapter 7, *Building Communities*, there is a section on setting up Apache Accumulo such that we can use cell-level security. Apache Accumulo, is an implementation of the Google BigTable paper, but it adds the additional security functionality. This means that a user can have all of the advantages of loading and retrieving data in parallel and at scale, but also be able to control the visibility of that data to a very fine degree. The chapter describes all of the information required to set up an instance, configure it for multiple users, and load and retrieve data with the required security labels (achieved through Accumulo Mutations).

For our purposes, we want to take a field and create a token; this could be a GUID, hash, or some other object. We can then write an entry to Accumulo using the token as the RowID and the field data itself as the contents:

```
val uuid: String = java.util.UUID.randomUUID.toString
val rowID: Text = new Text("[" + uuid + "]")
val colFam: Text = new Text("myColFam")
val colQual: Text = new Text("myColQual")
val colVis: ColumnVisibility = new ColumnVisibility("private")
val timestamp: long = System.currentTimeMillis()
val value: Value = new Value(field..getBytes())
val mutation: Mutation = new Mutation(rowID)

mutation.put(colFam, colQual, colVis, timestamp, value)
```

We then write the `uuid` to the related field in the output data. When tokenized data is read back in, anything starting with `[` is assumed to be a token and the Accumulo read procedure is used to obtain the original field data, assuming that the user invoking the Accumulo read has the correct permissions:

```
val conn: Connector = inst.getConnector("user", "passwd")
val auths: Authorizations = new Authorizations("private")
val scan: Scanner = conn.createScanner("table", auths)

scan.setRange(new Range("harry","john"))
scan.fetchFamily("attributes")

for(Entry<Key,Value> entry : scan) {
    val row: String = e.getKey().getRow()
    val value: Value = e.getValue()
}
```

Using a Hybrid approach

Obfuscation and masking can be used very effectively together to maximize the advantages of both methods. Using this hybrid approach, our example might become:

```
Andrew Jones, 17 New Road London XXXXXX, 0207XXXXXX, 4659XXXXXXXXXXXX
```

Using a combination of masking and tokenization is the emerging banking standard for securing credit card transactions. The **Primary Account Number** (**PAN**) is replaced with a token made up of a unique, randomly generated sequence of numbers, alphanumeric characters, or a combination of a truncated PAN and a random alphanumeric sequence. This enables the information to be processed as if it were the actual data, for example, audit checks or data quality reports, but it does not allow the true information to exist in plain text. Should the original information be required, the token can be used to request it and the user is only successful if they meet the authorization and authentication requirements.

We can refactor our code to perform this task; we will define a new function that mixes obfuscation and masking together:

```
def getHybridResult(text: String): String = {

  Array(
    forenames(scala.util.Random.nextInt(forenames.length)),
    RecordField.SURNAME,
    streets(scala.util.Random.nextInt(streets.length)),
    RecordField.ADDRESS2,
    RecordField.POSTCODE,
    RecordField.TELNUMBER,
```

```
    RandomCCNumber,
    "Unknown field")
  .zip(text.split(","))
  .map { case (m, field) =>
    m match {
      case m:String => m
      case rf:RecordField.Obfuscation =>
        stringObfuscator(field,rf.toString,'X')
    }
  }
  .mkString(",")
}
```

Once again, our example becomes:

```
Simon,XXXXXX,51 St James,London,XX 2AA,XXXX 123456,0264 1755 2288 6600
```

As with all tokenization, you will need to be careful to avoid side effects with the generated data, for example, `0264` is not a real BIN code. Again, requirements will dictate as to whether this is an issue, that is, it's not an issue if we are only trying to ensure that the field is populated in the correct format.

In order to run any of these processes at scale, we simply need to wrap them in an RDD:

```
val data = dataset.map { case record =>
    getMixedResult(record)
}
data.saveAsTextFile("/output/data/path", classOf[CryptoCodec])
```

Data disposal

Secure data should have an agreed life cycle. This will be set by a data authority when working in a commercial context, and it will dictate what state the data should be in at any given point during that life cycle. For example, a particular dataset may be labeled as *sensitive – requires encryption* for the first year of its life, followed by *private – no encryption*, and finally, *disposal*. The lengths of time and the rules applied will entirely depend upon the organization and the data itself – some data expires after just a few days, some after fifty years. The life cycle ensures that everyone knows exactly how the data should be treated, and it also ensures that older data is not needlessly taking up valuable disk space or breaching any data protection laws.

The correct disposal of data from secure systems is perhaps one of the most mis-understood areas of data security. Interestingly, it doesn't always involve a complete and/or destructive removal process. Examples where no action is required include:

- If data is simply out of date, it may no longer hold any intrinsic value – a good example is government records that are released to the public after their expiry date; what was top secret during World War Two is generally of no sensitivity now due to the elapsed time.
- If data is encrypted, and no longer required, simply throw the keys away!

As opposed to the examples where some effort is required, leading to the potential for mistakes to be made:

- **Physical destruction**: we often hear of disks being destroyed with a hammer or similar, even this is unsafe if not completed thoroughly.
- **Multiple writes**: relies upon writing over data blocks multiple times to ensure that the original data is physically overwritten. Utilities such as shred and scrub on Linux achieve this; however, they still have limited effectiveness depending upon the underlying filesystem. For example, RAID and cache type systems will not necessarily be overwritten beyond all retrieval with these tools. Overwriting tools should be treated with caution and used only with a complete understanding of their limitations.

When you secure your data, start thinking about your disposal strategy. Even if you are not made aware of any organizational rules in existence (in a commercial environment), you should still be thinking about how you are going to make sure the data is unrecoverable when access is no longer required.

Kerberos authentication

Many installations of Apache Spark use Kerberos to provide security and authentication to services such as HDFS and Kafka. It's also especially common when integrating with third-party databases and legacy systems. As a commercial data scientist, at some point, you'll probably find yourself in a situation where you'll have to work with data in a Kerberized environment, so, in this part of the chapter, we'll cover the basics of Kerberos – what it is, how it works, and how to use it.

Kerberos is a third-party authentication technique that's particularly useful where the primary form of communication is over a network, which makes it ideal for Apache Spark. It's used in preference to alternative methods of authentication, for example, username and password, because it provides the following benefits:

- No passwords are stored in plain text in application configuration files
- Facilitates centralized management of services, identities, and permissions
- Establishes a mutual trust, so both entities are identified
- Prevents spoofing – trust is only established temporarily, just for a timed session, meaning replay attacks are not possible, but sessions are renewable for convenience

Let's look at how it works with Apache Spark.

Use case 1: Apache Spark accessing data in secure HDFS

In the most basic use case, once you're logged on to an edge node (or similar) of your secure Hadoop cluster and before running your Spark program, Kerberos must be initialized. This is done by using the `kinit` command that comes with Hadoop and entering your user's password when prompted:

```
> kinit
Password for user:
> spark-shell
Spark session available as 'spark'.
Welcome to
      ____              __
     / __/__  ___ _____/ /__
    _\ \/ _ \/ _ `/ __/  '_/
   /___/ .__/\_,_/_/ /_/\_\   version 2.0.1
      /_/
Using Scala version 2.11.8 (Java HotSpot(TM) 64-Bit Server VM, Java
1.8.0_101)
Type in expressions to have them evaluated.
Type :help for more information.

scala> val file = sc.textFile("hdfs://...")
scala> file.count
```

At this point, you will be fully authenticated and able to access any data within HDFS, subject to the standard permissions model.

So, the process seems simple enough, let's take a deeper look at what happened here:

1. When the `kinit` command runs, it immediately sends a request to the Kerberos **key distribution centre** (**KDC**), to acquire a **ticket granting ticket** (**TGT**). The request is sent in plain text, and it essentially contains what is known as the **principal**, which is basically the "username@kerberosdomain" in this case (you can find out this string using the `klist` command). The **Authentication Server** (**AS**) responds to this request, with a TGT that has been signed using client's private key, a key that was shared ahead of time and is already known to the AS. This ensures secure transfer of the TGT.

2. The TGT is cached locally on the client, along with a **Keytab** file – which is a container for Kerberos keys and it is accessible to any Spark processes running as the same user.

3. Next, when the spark-shell is started, Spark uses the cached TGT to request that the **Ticket Granting Server** (**TGS**), provide a **session ticket** for accessing the HDFS service. This Ticket is signed using the HDFS NameNode's private key. In this way, the secure transfer of the Ticket is guaranteed, ensuring that only the NameNode can read it.

4. Armed with a ticket, Spark attempts to retrieve a **delegation token** from the NameNode. The purpose of this token is to prevent a flood of requests into the TGT when the executors start reading data (as the TGT was not designed with big data in mind!), but it also helps overcome problems Spark has with delayed execution times and ticket session expiry.

5. Spark ensures that all executors have access to the delegation token by placing it on the distributed cache so that it's available as a YARN local file.

6. When each executor makes a request to the NameNode for access to a block stored in HDFS, it passes across the delegation token it was given previously. The NameNode replies with the location of the block, along with a **block token** that is signed by the NameNode with a private secret. This key is shared by all of the DataNodes in the cluster and is only known by them. The purpose of this added block token is to ensure that the access is fully secured and, as such, it is only issued to authenticated users and it can only be read by verified DataNodes.

7. The last step is for the executors to supply the block token to the relevant
   DataNode and receive the requested block of data.

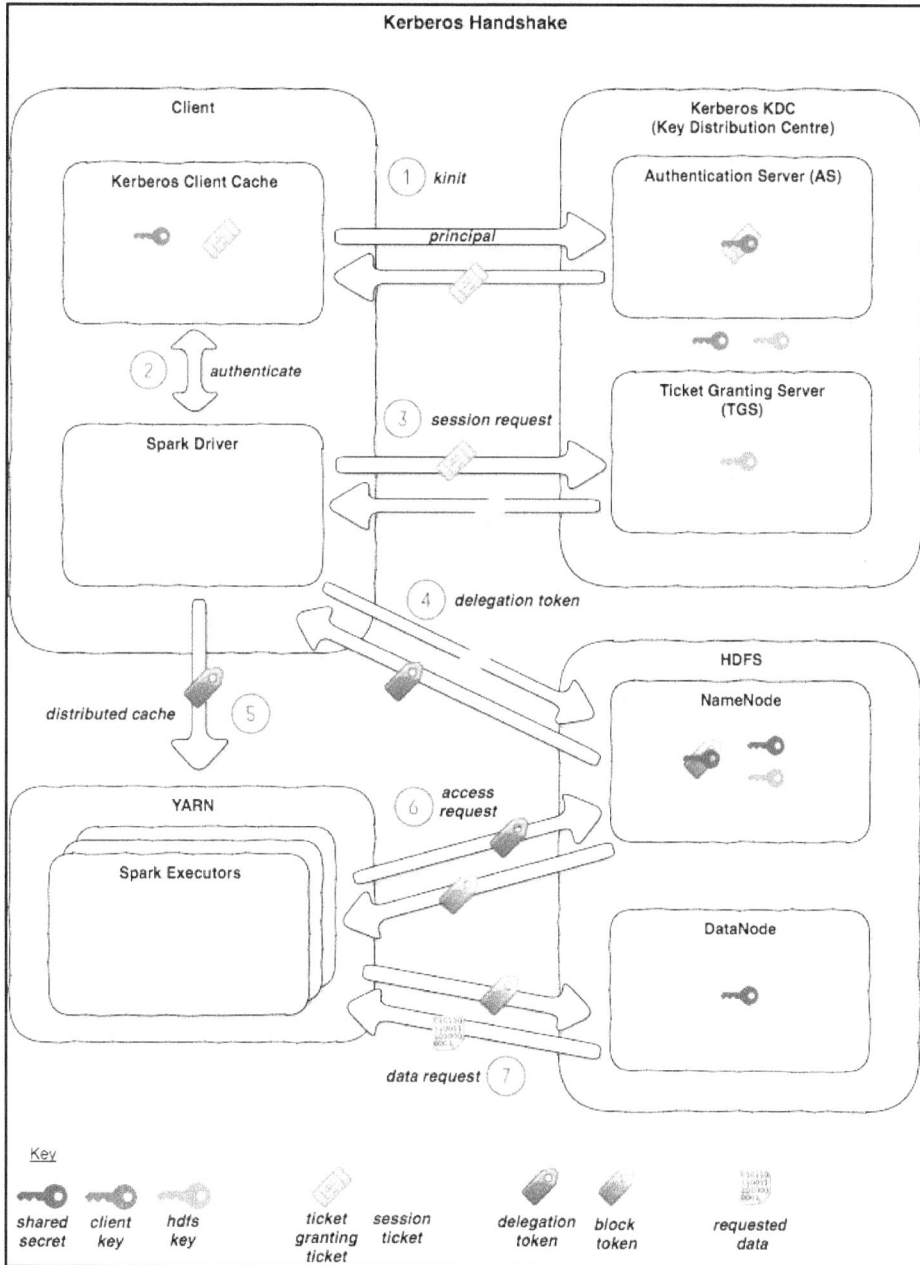

Use case 2: extending to automated authentication

By default, Kerberos tickets last for 10 hours and then expire, making them useless after this time, but they can be renewed. Therefore, when executing long-running Spark jobs or Spark Streaming Jobs (or jobs where a user is not directly involved and `kinit` cannot be run manually), it is possible to pass enough information upon starting a Spark process in order to automate the renewal of tickets issued during the previously discussed handshake.

This is done by passing in the location of the keytab file and associated principal using the command line options provided, like so:

```
spark-submit
    --master yarn-client
    --class SparkDriver
    --files keytab.file
    --keytab keytab.file
    --principal username@domain
ApplicationName
```

When attempting to execute a long running job as your local user, the principal name can be found using `klist` otherwise, dedicated **service principals** can be configured within Kerberos using `ktutils` and `ktadmin`.

Use case 3: connecting to secure databases from Spark

When working in a corporate setting, it may be necessary to connect to a third-party database that has been secured with Kerberos, such as PostgreSQL or Microsoft SQLServer.

In this situation, it is possible to use JDBC RDD to connect directly to the database and have Spark issue an SQL query to ingest data in parallel. Care should be taken when using this approach, as traditional databases are not built for high levels of parallelism, but if used sensibly, it is sometimes a very useful technique, particularly well-suited to rapid data exploration.

Firstly, you will need the native JDBC drivers for your particular database – here we've used Microsoft SQLServer as an example, but drivers should be available for all modern databases that support Kerberos (see RFC 1964).

You'll need to configure spark-shell to use the JDBC drivers on startup, like so:

```
> JDBC_DRIVER_JAR=sqljdbc.jar
> spark-shell
  --master yarn-client
  --driver-class-path $JDBC_DRIVER_JAR
  --files keytab.file    --conf spark.driver.extraClassPath=$JDBC_DRIVER_JAR
  --conf spark.executor.extraClassPath=$JDBC_DRIVER_JAR
  --jars $JDBC_DRIVER_JAR
```

Then, in the shell, type or paste the following (replacing the environment specific variables, which are highlighted):

```
import org.apache.spark.rdd.JdbcRDD

new JdbcRDD(sc, ()=>{
        import org.apache.hadoop.security.UserGroupInformation
        import UserGroupInformation.AuthenticationMethod
        import org.apache.hadoop.conf.Configuration
        import org.apache.spark.SparkFiles
        import java.sql.DriverManager
        import java.security.PrivilegedAction
        import java.sql.Connection

        val driverClassName =
"com.microsoft.sqlserver.jdbc.SQLServerDriver"
        val url = "jdbc:sqlserver://" +
                "host:port;instanceName=DB;" +
                "databaseName=mydb;" +
                "integratedSecurity=true;" +
                "authenticationScheme=JavaKerberos"

        Class.forName(driverClassName)
        val conf = new Configuration
        conf.addResource("/etc/hadoop/conf/core-site.xml")
        conf.addResource("/etc/hadoop/conf/mapred-site.xml")
        conf.addResource("/etc/hadoop/conf/hdfs-site.xml")
        UserGroupInformation.setConfiguration(conf)

        UserGroupInformation
           .getCurrentUser
           .setAuthenticationMethod(AuthenticationMethod.KERBEROS)
        UserGroupInformation
           .loginUserFromKeytabAndReturnUGI(principal, keytab.file)
           .doAs(new PrivilegedAction[Connection] {
             override def run(): Connection =
                   DriverManager.getConnection(url)
           })
```

```
},
"SELECT * FROM books WHERE id <= ? and id >= ?",
1,           // lowerBound    - the minimum value of the first placeholder
20,          // upperBound    - the maximum value of the second placeholder
4)           // numPartitions - the number of partitions
```

Spark runs the SQL passed into the constructor of JdbcRDD, but instead of running it as a single query, it is able to chunk it using the last three parameters as a guide.

So, in this example, in fact, four queries would be run in parallel:

```
SELECT * FROM books WHERE id <= 1 and id >= 5
SELECT * FROM books WHERE id <= 6 and id >= 10
SELECT * FROM books WHERE id <= 11 and id >= 15
SELECT * FROM books WHERE id <= 16 and id >= 20
```

As you can see, Kerberos is a huge and complicated subject. The level of knowledge required for a data scientist can vary depending upon the role. Some organizations will have a DevOps team to ensure that everything is implemented correctly. However, in the current climate, where there is a big skills shortage in the market, it could well be the case that data scientists will have to solve these issues themselves.

Security ecosystem

We will conclude with a brief rundown of some of the popular security tools we may encounter while developing with Apache Spark – and some advice about when to use them.

Apache sentry

As the Hadoop ecosystem grows ever larger, products such as Hive, HBase, HDFS, Sqoop, and Spark all have different security implementations. This means that duplicate policies are often required across the product stack in order to provide the user with a seamless experience, as well as enforce the overarching security manifest. This can quickly become complicated and time consuming to manage, which often leads to mistakes and even security breaches (whether intentional or otherwise). Apache Sentry pulls many of the mainstream Hadoop products together, particularly with Hive/HS2, to provide fine-grained (up to column level) controls.

Using ACLs is simple, but high maintenance. The setting of permissions for a large number of new files and amending umasks is very cumbersome and time consuming. As abstractions are created, authorization becomes more complicated. For example, the fusing of files and directories can become tables, columns, and partitions. Therefore, we need a trusted entity to enforce access control. Hive has a trusted service – **HiveServer2** (**HS2**), which parses queries and ensures that users have access to the data they are requesting. HS2 runs as a trusted user with access to the whole data warehouse. Users don't run code directly in HS2, so there is no risk of code bypassing access checks.

To bridge Hive and HDFS data, we can use the Sentry HDFS plugin, which synchronizes HDFS file permissions with higher level abstractions. For example, permissions to read a table = permission to read table's files and, similarly, permissions to create a table = permission to write to a database's directory. We still use HDFS ACL's for fine-grained user permissions, however we are restricted to the Filesystem view of the world and therefore cannot provide column-level and row-level access, it's "all or nothing". As mentioned previously, Accumulo provides a good alternative when this scenario is important. There is a product, however, that also addresses this issue – see the RecordService section.

The quickest and easiest way to implement Apache Sentry is to use Apache Hue. Apache Hue has been developed over the last few years, starting life as a simple GUI to pull together a few of the basic Hadoop services, such as HDFS, and has grown into a hub for many of the key building blocks in the Hadoop stack; HDFS. Hive, Pig, HBase, Sqoop, Zookeeper, and Oozie all feature together with integrated Sentry to handle the security. A demonstration of Hue can be found at `http://demo.gethue.com/`, providing a great introduction to the feature set. We can also see many of the ideas discussed in this chapter in practice, including HDFS ACLs, RBACs, and Hive HS2 access.

RecordService

One of the key aspects of the Hadoop ecosystem is decoupling storage managers (for example, HDFS and Apache HBase) and compute frameworks (for example, MapReduce, Impala, and Apache Spark). Although this decoupling allows for far greater flexibility, thus allowing the user to choose their framework components, it leads to excessive complexity due to the compromises required to ensure that everything works together seamlessly. As Hadoop becomes an increasingly critical infrastructure component for users, the expectations for compatibility, performance, and security also increase.

RecordService is a new core security layer for Hadoop that sits between the storage managers and compute frameworks to provide a unified data access path, fine-grained data permissions, and enforcement across the stack.

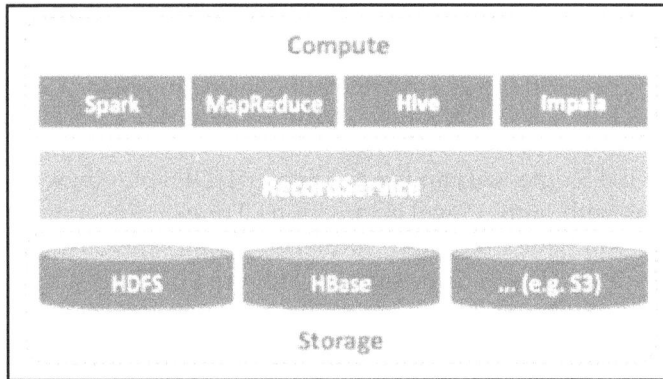

RecordService is only compatible with Cloudera 5.4 or later and, thus, cannot be used in a standalone capacity, or with Hortonworks, although HDP uses Ranger to achieve the same goals. More information can be found at www.recordservice.io.

Apache ranger

The aims of Apache ranger are broadly the same as RecordService, the primary goals being:

- Centralized security administration to manage all security related tasks in a central UI, or using REST APIs
- Fine-grained authorization to perform a specific action and/or operation with a Hadoop component/tool and manage through a central administration tool
- Standardize authorization methods across all Hadoop components
- Enhanced support for different authorization methods including role-based access control and attribute based access control
- Centralized auditing of user access and administrative actions (security related) within all components of Hadoop

At the time of writing, Ranger is an Apache Incubator project and, therefore, is not at a major point release. Although, it is fully integrated with Hortonworks HDP supporting HDFS, Hive, HBase, Storm, Knox, Solr, Kafka, NiFi, YARN, and, crucially, a scalable cryptographic key management service for HDFS encryption. Full details can be found at http://ranger.incubator.apache.org/ and http://hortonworks.com/apache/ranger/.

Apache Knox

We have discussed many of the security areas of the Spark/Hadoop stack, but they are all related to securing individual systems or data. An area that has not been mentioned in any detail is that of securing a cluster itself from unauthorized external access. Apache Knox fulfills this role by "ring fencing" a cluster and providing a REST API Gateway through which all external transactions must pass.

Coupled with a Kerberos secured Hadoop cluster, Knox provides authentication and authorization, protecting the specifics of the cluster deployment. Many of the common services are catered for, including HDFS (via WEBHDFS), YARN Resource Manager, and Hive.

Knox is another project that is heavily contributed to by Hortonworks and, therefore, is fully integrated into the Hortonworks HDP platform. Whilst Knox can be deployed into virtually any Hadoop cluster, it can be done with a fully integrated approach in HDP. More information can be found at `knox.apache.org`.

Your Secure Responsibility

Now that we've covered the common security use cases and discussed some of the tools that a data scientist needs to be aware of in their everyday activities, there's one last important item to note. *While in their custody, the responsibility for data, including its security and integrity, lies with the data scientist.* This is usually true whether or not you are explicitly told. Therefore, it is crucial that you take this responsibility seriously and take all the necessary precautions when handling and processing data. If needed, also be ready to communicate to others their responsibility. We all need to ensure that we are not held responsible for a breach off-site; this can be achieved by highlighting the issue or, indeed, even having a written contract with the off-site service provider outlining their security arrangements. To see a real-world example of what can go wrong when you don't pay proper attention to due diligence, have a look at some security notes regarding the Ashley-Madison hack here:
`http://blog.erratasec.com/2015/08/notes-on-ashley-madison-dump.html#.V-AGgT4rIU v.`

Another area of interest is that of removable media, most commonly DVDs and memory sticks. These should be treated in the same way as hard drives, but with the assumption that the data is always unsafe and at risk. The same options exist for these types of media, meaning data can be secured at the application level or at the hardware level (excepting optical disks, for example, DVD/CD). With USB key storage, there exists examples that implement hardware encryption. The data is always secure when written to them, therefore removing the bulk of the responsibility from the user. These types of drive should always be certified to **Federal Information Processing Standards** (**FIPS**); generally, FIPS 140 (Cryptographic modules) or FIPS 197 (AES Cipher).

If an FIPS standard is not required, or the media is optical in nature, then data can be encrypted at the application layer, that is, encrypted by software. There are a number of ways to do this, including encrypted partitions, encrypted files, or raw data encryption. All of these methods involve using third-party software to perform the encrypt/decrypt functions at read/write time. Therefore, passwords are needed, introducing the issues around password strength, safety, and so on. The authors have experienced situations where an encrypted disk was handed from one company to another, and the handwritten password handed over at the same time! Apart from a risk to data security, there are also possible consequences in respect of disciplinary action against the individuals involved. If data is put at risk, it's always worth checking best practice and highlighting issues; it is very easy to become lax in this area, and sooner or later, data will be compromised and someone will have to take responsibility – it may not necessarily be the individual who lost the media itself.

Summary

In this chapter, we have explored the topic of data security and explained some of the surrounding issues. We have discovered that not only is there technical knowledge to master, but also that a data security mindset is just as important. Data security is often overlooked and, therefore, taking a systematic approach, and educating others, is a key responsibility for mastering data science.

We have explained the data security life cycle and outlined the most important areas of responsibility, including authorization, authentication and access, along with related examples and use cases. We have also explored the Hadoop security ecosystem and described the important open source solutions currently available.

A significant part of this chapter was dedicated to building a Hadoop `InputFormat` *compressor* that operates as a data encryption utility that can be used with Spark. Appropriate configuration allows the codec to be used in a variety of key areas, crucially when spilling shuffled records to local disk where *currently no solution exists*.

In the next chapter, we will explore Scalable Algorithms, demonstrating the key techniques that we can master to enable performance at a truly "big data" scale.

14
Scalable Algorithms

In this chapter, we discuss the challenges associated with writing efficient and scalable analytics running on Spark. We will start by introducing the reader to the general concepts of distributed parallelization and scalability and how they relate to Spark. We will recap over Spark's distributed architecture giving the reader an understanding of its underlying principles and how this supports the parallel processing paradigm. We will learn about the characteristics of scalable analytics and the elements of Spark that underpin these (for example, `RDD`, `combineByKey`, and `GraphX`).

Next, we will learn about why sometimes even basic algorithms, despite working at small scale, will often fail in big data. We'll see how to avoid issues when writing Spark jobs that run over massive datasets, including an example using mean/variance. The reader will learn about the structure of algorithms and how to write custom data science analytics that scale over petabytes of data.

Later, we will move on to discuss some of the limitations of Spark's in-memory model (such as excessive memory usage, the pitfalls of traditional data models including the object-oriented approach [OOP] and 3rd normal form [3NF], the benefits of a denormalized data representation, and the dangers of fixed precision number representations) and how these relate to writing efficient Spark jobs.

This chapter completes by describing the main performance-related features and patterns that facilitate efficient runtime processing in Spark, and shows when to take advantage of them. We will introduce features such as parallelization strategies, caching, shuffle strategies, garbage collection optimization, and probabilistic models; and explain how these help you to get the most out of Spark.

This chapter also emphasizes the importance of having a good overall approach to the development process when analytic authoring. It reveals the tips and tricks of the professionals that will ensure that your algorithm writing experience is a success.

General principles

Throughout this book we have demonstrated many data science techniques that, by using the power of Spark, will scale across petabytes of data. Hopefully, you have found these techniques sufficiently useful that you want to start using them in your own analytics and, indeed, have been inspired to create data science pipelines of your own.

Writing your own analytics is definitely a challenge! It can be huge fun at times and it's great when they work well. But there are times when getting them to run at scale and efficiently (or even at all) can seem like a daunting task.

Sometimes, with scarce feedback, you can get stuck in a seemingly endless loop waiting for task after task to complete not even knowing whether your job will fail at the very last hurdle. And let's face it, seeing a dreaded `OutOfMemoryError` at the end of a 20-hour job is no fun for anyone! Surely there must be a better way to develop analytics that run well on Spark and don't lead to wasted time and poorly performing code?

One of the main characteristics of a well written Spark job is the concept of *scalability*. Scalability is a distinct concept from performance. While performance is a measure of the speed of the response of a computation, scalability is a measure of how well a computation performs when you increase demand (or in the case of Spark, increase the amount of data).

The holy grail of scalability is known as *linear scalability*. This refers to the ideal condition where there are no performance constraints imposed on scalability when additional resources are added to the cluster. In this case, doubling the number of machines in a cluster will lead to double the performance, or similarly doubling the volume of data would yield the same performance on a cluster twice the size.

This chapter will serve as an introduction to writing analytics that seek to take advantage of this linear scalability. It will demonstrate best practice for maximizing scalability and explain the barriers to achieving it. And while it will not provide an exhaustive description of optimization techniques, it will get you started by giving you a feel for how to write efficient Spark jobs.

Before we dive into the details, let's establish some basic principles that will assist and guide throughout:

1. **Preserve data locality where possible**: Moving data around is expensive. It's usually much quicker to process data in place by moving the processing to the data. In Spark, this is known as *data locality*. And indeed, Spark is designed to take full advantage of it. Therefore, you might assume that you don't need to worry much about it as the framework will handle it for you. While this is partly true, it's prudent to test this assumption at every stage to ensure that it's behaving as expected. And if not, use the levers that Spark provides in order to prevent moving data around when it's not necessary. In fact, the principle of data locality is so important that we even need to consider it throughout the entire development process. At each stage, considering whether it's really necessary to move data at all. In some cases, it's possible to decompose the problem in a different way in order to minimize or avoid movement altogether. If so, it's always worth considering the approach where less data is transferred.

2. **Ensure even distribution of data**: When running a Spark job, the ideal situation is to have all of your executors equally utilized. Having executors sit idle while a select few do all of the work is indicative of a poorly performing job. By arranging even distribution of data across executors, one can ensure the maximum utilization of cluster resources.

3. **Favor faster stores**: Not all methods of randomly accessing data are the same. The following snippet shows the approximate time taken to reference data in various states:

L1 cache	0.5 ns
L2 cache	7 ns
Main memory	100 ns
Disk (random seek)	2,000,000 ns

Fortunately, Spark provides in-memory processing capabilities, including many optimizations that take advantage of the fast caches available (L1/L2/L3 caches). Therefore, it can avoid unnecessarily reading from main memory or spilling to disk it's important that your analytics take full advantage of these efficiencies. This was introduced as part of Project Tungsten, `https://databrick s.com/blog/2015/04/28/project-tungsten-bringing-spark-closer-to-bare- metal.html`.

4. **Only optimize after observation**: There's a famous saying by Donald Knuth, the legendary computer scientist and author, that *premature optimization is the root of all evil*. While this sounds extreme, what he means is that all performance-related tweaks or optimizations should be based on empirical evidence rather than preemptive intuition. As such predictions very often fail to correctly identify performance problems, and instead give rise to poor design choices that are later regretted. But contrary to what you might think, the suggestion here is not that you just forget about performance until the end, in fact quite the reverse. In an environment where the size of the data and hence the length of time any operation takes dictates everything, it's fundamental to begin optimization early in the analytic design process. But isn't this a contradiction of Knuth's law? Well, no. In terms of performance, simplicity is often the key. The approach should be evidence-based so start simple, carefully observe the performance of your analytic at runtime (through the use of analytic tuning and code profiling, see the next section), perform targeted optimizations that correct the problems identified, and repeat. Over-engineering is usually as much to blame in poorly performing analytics as choosing slow algorithms, but it can be much harder to fix down the line.

5. **Start small and scale-up**: Start with small data samples. While an analytic may *eventually* be required to run over a petabyte of data, starting with a small dataset is definitely advisable. Sometimes only a handful of rows are required to determine whether an analytic is working as expected. And more rows can be added to prove out the various test and edge cases. It's more about breadth of coverage here rather than volume. The analytic design process is extremely iterative and judicious use of data sampling will pay dividends during this phase; while even a small dataset will allow you to measure the impact on performance as you incrementally increase the size of the data.

The bottom line is that writing analytics, particularly over data you are unfamiliar with, can take time and there are no shortcuts.

Now that we have some guidelines, let's focus on how they apply to Spark.

Spark architecture

Apache Spark is designed to simplify the laborious, and sometimes error prone task of highly-parallelized, distributed computing. To understand how it does this, let's explore its history and identify what Spark brings to the table.

History of Spark

Apache Spark implements a type of *data parallelism* that seeks to improve upon the MapReduce paradigm popularized by Apache Hadoop. It extended MapReduce in four key areas:

- **Improved programming model**: Spark provides a higher level of abstraction through its APIs than Hadoop; creating a programming model that significantly reduces the amount of code that must be written. By introducing a fluent, side-effect-free, function-oriented API, Spark makes it possible to reason about an analytic in terms of its transformations and actions, rather than just sequences of mappers and reducers. This makes it easier to understand and debug.

- **Introduces workflow**: Rather than chaining jobs together (by persisting results to disk and using a third-party workflow scheduler, as with traditional MapReduce), Spark allows analytics to be decomposed into tasks and expressed as **Directed Acyclic Graphs** (**DAGs**). This has the immediate effect of removing the need to materialize data, but also means it has much more control over how analytics are run, including enabling efficiencies such as cost-based query optimization (seen in the catalyst query planner).

- **Better Memory Utilization**: Spark exploits the memory on each node for in-memory caching of datasets. It permits access to caches between operations to improve performance over basic MapReduce. This is particularly effective for iterative workloads, such as **stochastic gradient descent** (**SGD**), where a significant improvement in performance can usually be observed.

- **Integrated Approach**: With support for streaming, SQL execution, graph processing, machine learning, database integration, and much more, it offers one tool to rule them all! Before Spark, specialist tools were needed, for example, Storm, Pig, Giraph, Mahout, and so on. Although there are situations where the specialist tools can provide better results, Spark's on-going commitment to integration is impressive.

In addition to these general improvements, Spark offers many other features. Let's take a look inside the box.

Moving parts

At a conceptual level, there are a number of key components inside Apache Spark, many of which you may know already, but let's review them within the context of the scalability principles we've outlined:

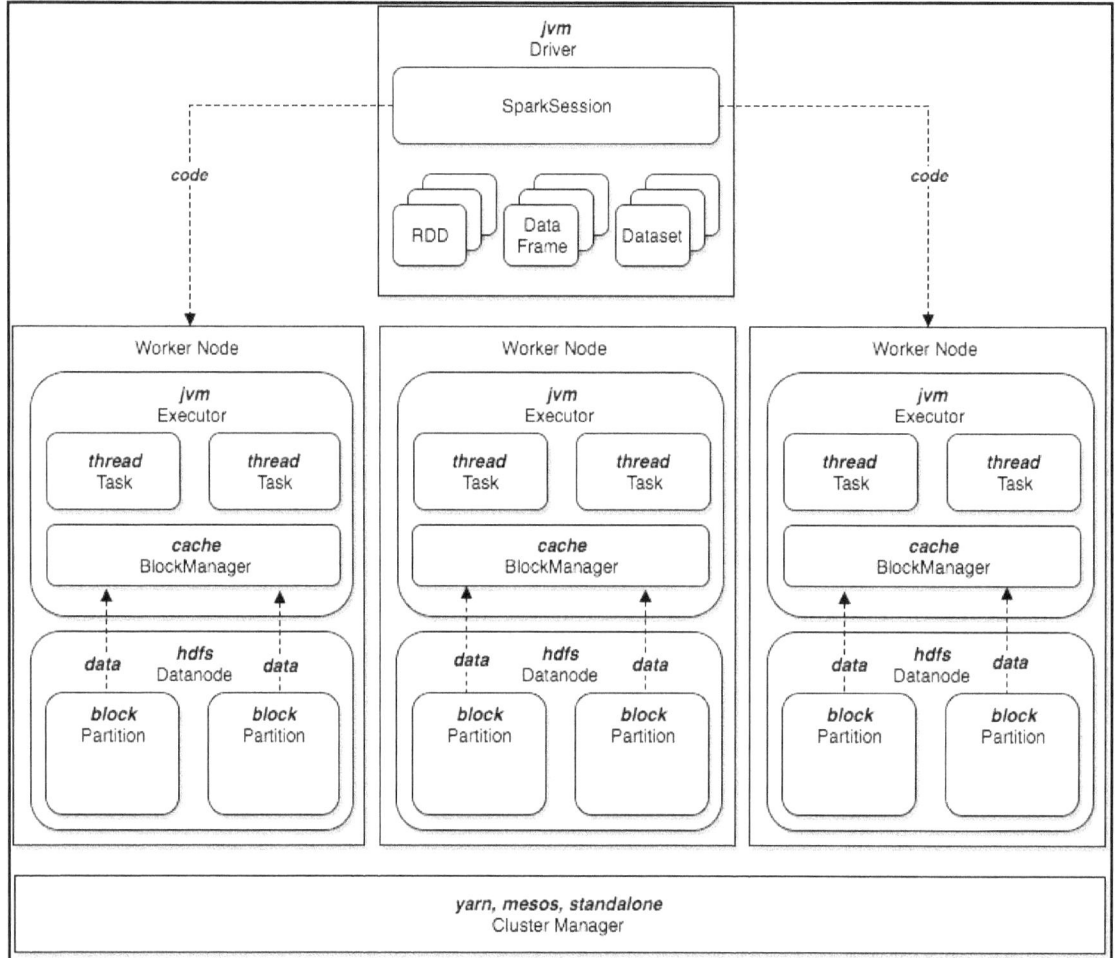

Driver

The **Driver** is the main entry point for Spark. It's the program that you start, it runs in a single JVM, and it initiates and controls all of the operations in your job.

In terms of performance, it's likely that you'll want to avoid bringing large datasets back to the driver, as running such operations (such as `rdd.collect`) can often cause an `OutOfMemoryError`. This happens when the size of data being returned exceeds the JVM heap size of the driver, as specified by `--driver-memory`.

SparkSession

As the driver is starting, the `SparkSession` class is initialized. The `SparkSession` class provides access to all of Spark's services, via the relevant context, such as `SQLContext`, `SparkContext`, and `StreamingContext` classes.

It's also the place to tune Spark's runtime performance-related properties.

Resilient distributed datasets (RDDs)

An **Resilient Distributed Dataset** (**RDD**) is the underlying abstraction representing a distributed set of homogenous records.

Although data may be physically stored over many machines in the cluster, analytics are intentionally unaware of their actual location: they deal only with RDDs. Under the covers, RDDs consist of partitions, or contiguous blocks of data, like slices of cake. Each partition has one or more replicas, or copies, and Spark is able to determine the physical location of these replicas in order to decide where to run transformation tasks to ensure data locality.

> For an example of how the physical location of replicas is determined, see `getPreferredLocations` in: `https://github.com/apache/spark/blob/master/core/src/main/scala/org/apache/spark/rdd/NewHadoopRDD.scala`.

RDDs are also responsible for ensuring that data is cached appropriately from the underlying block storage, for example, HDFS.

Executor

Executors are processes that run on the worker nodes of your cluster. When launched, each executor connects back to the driver and waits for instructions to run operations over data.

You decide on how many executors your analytic needs and this becomes your maximum level of parallelism.

> Unless using dynamic allocation. In which case, the maximum level of parallelism is infinity until configured using `spark.dynamicAllocation.maxExecutors`. See Spark configuration for details.

Shuffle operation

The **shuffle** is the name given to the transfer of data between executors that occurs as part of an operation whenever data must be physically moved, in order to compute a calculation. It typically occurs when data is grouped so that all records with the same key are together on a single machine, but it can also be used strategically to repartition data for greater levels of parallelism.

However, as it involves both (i) the movement of data over the network and (ii) its persistence to disk, it is generally considered a slow operation. And hence, the shuffle is an area of great significance to scalability more on this later.

Cluster Manager

The **Cluster Manager** sits outside of Spark, acting as a resource negotiator for the cluster. It controls the initial allocation of physical resources, so that Spark is able to start its executors on machines with the requisite number of cores and memory.

Although each cluster manager works in a different way, your choice is unlikely to have any measurable impact on algorithmic performance.

Task

A **Task** represents an instruction to run a set of operations over a single partition of data. Each task is serialized over to an executor by the driver and, is in effect, what is referred to by the expression moving the processing to the data.

DAG

A **DAG** represents the logical execution plan of all transformations involved in the execution of an action. Its optimization is fundamental to the performance of the analytic. In the case of SparkSQL and Datasets optimization is performed on your behalf by the catalyst optimizer.

DAG scheduler

The **DAG scheduler** creates a physical plan, by dividing the DAG into stages and, for each stage, creating a corresponding set of tasks (one for each partition).

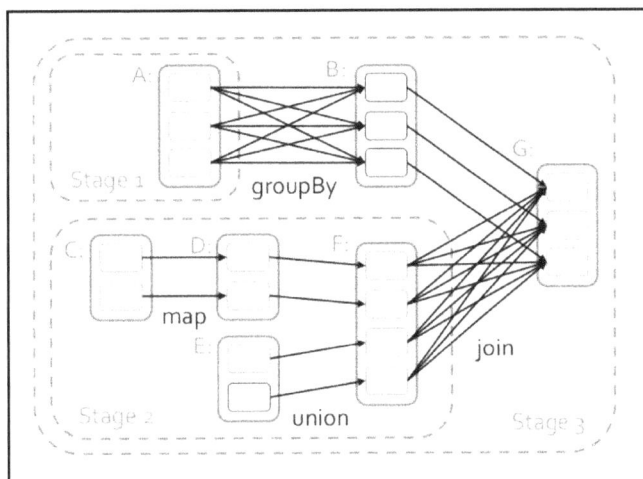

Transformations

Transformations are a type of operation. They typically apply a user-defined function to each record in an RDD. There are two kinds of transformation, *narrow* and *wide*.

Narrow transformations are operations that are applied locally to partitions and as such do not require data to be moved in order to compute correctly. They include: `filter`, `map`, `mapValues`, `flatMap`, `flatMapValues`, `glom`, `pipe`, `zipWithIndex`, `cartesian`, `union`, `mapPartitionsWithInputSplit`, `mapPartitions`, `mapPartitionsWithIndex`, `mapPartitionsWithContext`, `sample`, `randomSplit`.

In contrast, wide transformations are operations that require data to be moved in order to compute correctly. In other words, they require a shuffle. They include: `sortByKey`, `reduceByKey`, `groupByKey`, `join`, `cartesian`, `combineByKey`, `partitionBy`, `repartition`, `repartitionAndSortWithinPartitions`, `coalesce`, `subtractByKey`, `cogroup`.

> The `coalesce`, `subtractByKey` and `cogroup` transformations could be narrow depending on where data is physically situated.

In order to write scalable analytics, it's important to be aware of which type of transformation you are using.

Stages

A **stage** represents a group of operations that can be physically mapped to a task (one per partition). There are a couple of things to note about stages:

- Any sequence of narrow transformations appearing consecutively in a DAG are pipelined together into a single stage. In other words, they execute in order, on the same executor and hence against the same partition and do not need a shuffle.

- Whenever a wide transformation is encountered in a DAG, a stage boundary is introduced. Two stages (or more in the case of join, and so on) now exist and the second cannot begin until the first has finished (see `ShuffledRDD` class for more details).

Actions

Actions are another type of operation within Spark. They're typically used to perform a parallel write or transfer of data back to the driver. While other transformations are lazily evaluated, it is the action that triggers the execution of a DAG.

Upon invoking an action, its parent RDD gets submitted to the `SparkSession` or `SparkContext` classes within the driver and the DAG scheduler generates a DAG for execution.

Task scheduler

The **task scheduler** receives a set of tasks determined by the DAG scheduler (one task per partition) and schedules each to run on an appropriate executor in conjunction with data locality.

Challenges

Now that we have gained an understanding of the Spark architecture, let's prepare for writing scalable analytics by introducing some of the challenges, or *gotchas* that you might face if you're not careful. Without knowledge of these up-front, you could lose time trying to figure them out on your own!

Algorithmic complexity

As well as the obvious effect of the size of your data, the performance of an analytic is highly dependent on the nature of the problem you're trying to solve. Even some seemingly simple problems, such as a depth first search of a graph, do not have well-defined algorithms that perform efficiently in distributed environments. This being the case, great care should be taken when designing analytics to ensure that they exploit patterns of processing that are readily parallelized. Taking the time to understand the nature of your problem in terms of complexity before you start, can pay off in the long term. In the next section, we'll show you how to do this.

> Generally speaking, *NC-complete* problems are parallelizable, whereas P-complete problems are not: `https://en.wikipedia.org/wiki/NC_(compl exity)`.

Another thing to note is that distributed algorithms will often be much slower than single-threaded applications when run on small data. It's worth bearing in mind that in the scenarios where all of your data fits onto a single machine, the overhead of Spark: spawning processes, transferring data, and the latency introduced by interprocess communications, will rarely payoff. Investment in this approach only really starts to assist in the case where your datasets are large enough that they don't fit comfortably into memory, then you will notice gains in throughput, the amount of data you can process in unit time, as a result of using Spark.

Numerical anomalies

When processing large amounts of data, you might notice some strange effects with numbers. These oddities relate to the universal number representations of modern machines and specifically to the concept of *precision*.

To demonstrate the effect, consider the following:

```scala
scala> val i = Integer.MAX_VALUE
i: Int = 2147483647

scala> i + 1
res1: Int = -2147483648
```

Notice how a positive number is turned into a negative number simply by adding one. This phenomenon is known as a **number overflow** and it occurs when a calculation results in a number that is too large for its type. In this case, an `Int` has a fixed-width of 32-bits, so when we attempt to store a 33-bit number, we get an overflow, resulting in a negative. This type of behavior can be demonstrated for any numeric type, and as a result of any arithmetic operation.

> This is due to the signed, fixed-width, two's complement number representations adopted by most modern processor manufacturers (and hence Java and Scala).

Although overflows occur in the course of normal programming, it's much more apparent when dealing with large datasets. It can occur even when performing relatively simple calculations, such as summations or means. Let's consider the most basic example:

```scala
scala> val distanceBetweenStars = Seq(2147483647, 2147483647)
distanceBetweenStars: Seq[Int] = List(2147483647, 2147483647)

scala> val rdd = spark.sparkContext.parallelize(distanceBetweenStars)
rdd: org.apache.spark.rdd.RDD[Int] =  ...

scala> rdd.reduce(_+_)
res1: Int = -2
```

Datasets are not immune:

```
scala> distanceBetweenStars.toDS.reduce(_+_)
res2: Int = -2
```

Of course, there are strategies for handling this; for example by using alternative algorithms, different data types, or changing the unit of measurement. However, a plan for tackling these types of issues should always be taken into account in your design.

Another similar effect is the loss of significance caused by rounding errors in calculations limited by their precision. For illustrative purposes, consider this really basic (and not very sophisticated!) example:

```
scala> val bigNumber = Float.MaxValue
bigNumber: Float = 3.4028235E38

scala> val verySmall = Int.MaxValue / bigNumber
verySmall: Float = 6.310888E-30

scala> val almostAsBig = bigNumber - verySmall
almostAsBig: Float = 3.4028235E38

scala> bigNumber - almostAsBig
res2: Float = 0.0
```

Here, we were expecting the answer $6.3108875526456191453949933304824655E-30$, but instead we get zero. This is a clear loss of precision and significance, demonstrating another type of behavior that you need to be aware of when designing analytics.

To cope with these issues, Welford and Chan devised an online algorithm for calculating the mean and variance. It seeks to avoid problems with precision. Under the covers, Spark implements this algorithm, and an example can be seen in the PySpark StatCounter:

```
def merge(self, value):
    delta = value - self.mu
    self.n += 1
    self.mu += delta / self.n
    self.m2 += delta * (value - self.mu)
    self.maxValue = maximum(self.maxValue, value)
    self.minValue = minimum(self.minValue, value)
```

Let's take a deeper look into how it's calculating the mean and variance:

- `delta`: The `delta` is the difference between mu (the current running average) and the new value under consideration. It measures the change in value between data points and because of this it's always small. It's basically a magic number that ensures that the calculation never involves summing all the values as this would potentially lead to an overflow.

- `mu`: The mu represents the current running average. At any given time, it's the total of the values seen so far, over the count of those values. The `mu` is calculated incrementally by continually applying the delta.

- `m2`: The `m2` is the sum of the mean squared difference. It assists the algorithm in avoiding loss of significance by adjusting the precision during the calculation. This reduces the amount of information lost through rounding errors.

As it happens, this particular online algorithm is specifically for computing statistics, but the online approach may be adopted by the design of any analytic.

Shuffle

As we identified earlier in our section on principles, moving data around is expensive and this means that one of the main challenges when writing any scalable analytic is that of minimizing the transfer of data. The overhead of management and handling of data transfer is still, at this moment in time, a very costly operation. We'll discuss more on how to tackle this later in the chapter, but for now we'll build awareness of the challenges around data locality; knowing which operations are OK to use and which should be avoided, whilst also understanding the alternatives. Some of the key offenders are:

- `cartesian()`
- `reduce()`
- `PairRDDFunctions.groupByKey()`

But be aware, with a little forethought, using these can be avoided altogether.

Data schemes

Choosing a schema for your data will be critical to your analytic design. Obviously, often you have no choice about the format of your data; either a schema will be imposed on you or your data may not have a schema. Either way, with techniques such as "temporary tables" and schema-on-read (see `Chapter 3`, *Input Formats and Schema* for details), you still have control over how data is presented to your analytic – and you should take advantage of this. There are an enormous number of options here and selecting the right one is part of the challenge. Let's discuss some common approaches and start with some that are not so good:

- **OOP: Object-oriented programming** (**OOP**) is the general concept of programming by decomposing problems into classes that model real world concepts. Typically, definitions will group both data and behavior, making them a popular way to ensure that code is compact and understandable. In the context of Spark, however, creating complex object structures, particularly ones that includes rich behavior, is unlikely to benefit your analytic in terms of readability or maintenance. Instead, it is likely to vastly increase the number of objects requiring garbage collection and limit the scope for code reuse. Spark is designed using a *functional approach*, and while you should be careful about abandoning objects altogether, you should strive to keep them simple and reuse object references where it is safe to do so.

- **3NF**: For decades, databases have been optimized for certain types of schema – relational, star, snowflake, and so on. And techniques such as **3rd Normal Form** (**3NF**) work well to ensure the correctness of traditional data models. However, within the context of Spark, forcing dynamic table joins, or/and joining facts with dimensions, results in shuffles, potentially many shuffles, which is ultimately bad for performance.

- **Denormalization**: Denormalization is a practical way to ensure that your analytic has all the data it needs without having to resort to a shuffle. Data can be arranged so that records processed together are also stored together. This has the added cost of having to store duplicates of much of the data, but it's often a trade-off that pays off. Particularly as there are techniques and technologies that help overcome the cost of duplication, such as columnar-oriented storage, column-pruning, and so on. More on this later.

Now that we understand some of the difficulties that you might encounter when designing analytics, let's get into the detail of how to apply patterns that address these and ensure that your analytics run well.

Plotting your course

It's easy to overlook planning and preparation when you're preoccupied with experimenting on the latest technologies and data! Nevertheless, the *process* of how you write scalable algorithms is just as important as the algorithms themselves. Therefore, it's crucial to understand the role of planning in your project and to choose an operating framework that allows you to respond to the demands of your goals. The first recommendation is to adopt an *agile development methodology*.

The distinctive ebb and flow of analytic authoring may mean that there is just no natural end to the project. By being disciplined and systematic with your approach, you can avoid many pitfalls that lead to an under performing project and poorly performing code. Conversely, no amount of innovative, open source software or copious corpus will rescue a project with no structure.

As every data science project is slightly different, there's no right or wrong answers when it comes to overall management. Here we offer a set of guidelines, or best practice, based on experience, that should help navigate the data minefield.

When dealing with large quantities of data, even small mistakes in calculations may result in many lost hours – waiting for jobs to process without any certainty of when, or whether, they will finish. Therefore, generally speaking, one should approach analytic authoring with a similar level of rigor as one would the design of an experiment. The emphasis here should be on practicality and every care should be taken to anticipate the effect of changes on processing time.

Here are some tips for staying out of trouble during the development process.

Be iterative

Take an iterative approach to your everyday work and build your analytics incrementally. Add functionality as you go, and use unit testing to ensure that you have a solid base before adding more features. For each code change you make, consider adopting an iterative cycle, such as the one shown in the following diagram:

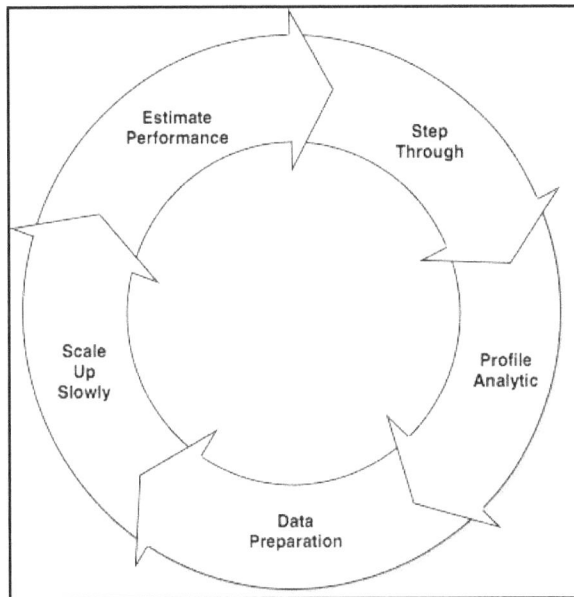

Let's discuss each of these steps in turn.

Data preparation

As always, the first step is to gain an understanding of the data you'll be processing. As discussed previously, it's likely that you'll have to attend to all the edge cases present in your corpus. You should consider starting with a basic data profile in order to understand whether the data meets your expectations, in terms of veracity and quality, where the potential risks are and how you might segment it into classes so that it can be processed. An approach to this is described in detail in Chapter 4, *Explorative Data Analysis*.

In addition to **Exploratory data analysis** (**EDA**), understanding the shape of your data will allow you to reason about the design of your analytic and anticipate additional demands that you may have to cater for.

For example, here is a quick data profile to show the completeness of some GDELT news article downloads for a given day:

```
content
  .as[Content]
  .map{
    _.body match {
      case b if b.isEmpty  => ("NOT FOUND",1)
      case _ => ("FOUND",1)
    }
  }
  .groupByKey(_._1)
  .reduceGroups {
    (v1,v2) => (v1._1, v1._2 + v2._2)
  }
  .toDF("NEWS ARTICLE","COUNT")
  .show
```

The results are in the following table:

```
+------------+------+
|NEWS ARTICLE| COUNT|
+------------+------+
|       FOUND|154572|
|   NOT FOUND|190285|
+------------+------+
```

For this particular day, you'll see here that in fact the majority of GKG records surveyed have no associated news article content. Although this could be for a variety of reasons, the point to note is that these missing articles form a new class of records that will require different processing. We'll have to write an alternate flow for these records, and that flow might have different performance characteristics.

Scale up slowly

In terms of data, it is important to *start small and scale up*. Don't be afraid to start with a subset of your corpus. Consider choosing a subset identified as significant during the data profile stage, or in many cases it's beneficial to use a handful of records in each subset. What's important here is that the subset you choose is representative enough to prove the particular use case, function or feature, yet small enough to allow for *timely iterations*.

In the preceding GDELT example, we could temporarily ignore records with no content and deal only with the subset containing news articles. In this way, we'll filter out any troublesome cases and handle them in later iterations.

Having said that, eventually you'll definitely want to reintroduce all the subsets and edge cases present in your corpus. While it's fine to do this in a piecemeal way, by including more important classes first and leaving edge cases until later, it is necessary to ultimately understand the behavior of every record in your dataset, even outliers, because the chances are they won't be one offs. You will also need to understand the effect that any data has on your analytic when it is seen in production, regardless of how infrequently, in order to avoid an entire run failing due to a single rogue record.

Estimate performance

As you write each transformation, be aware of the time-cost in terms of complexity. For example, it's good to ask yourself, "how would the running time be affected if i doubled the input?". When considering this, it's helpful to think in terms of the **Big O Notation**. Big O will not give you an exact performance figure; it does not take into account practical factors, such as number of cores, available memory, or network speed. However, it can be useful as a guide in order to get an indicative measure of the processing complexity.

As a reminder, here are some common notations, in order of time-complexity (preferred-first):

Notation	Description	Example Operations
O(1)	Constant (Quick) Not dependent on size	`broadcast.value` `printSchema`
O(log n)	Logarithmic *Grows with the height of a balanced tree of n nodes*	`pregel` `connectedComponents`

O(n)	Linear
	 Grows proportionally with n (rows)
		`map`
		 `filter`
		 `count`
		 `reduceByKey`
		 `reduceGroups`

O(n + m)	Linear
	 Grows proportionally with n and m (other dataset)
		`join`
		 `joinWith`
		 `groupWith`
		 `cogroup`
		 `fullOuterJoin`

O(n^2)	Quadratic *Grows as the square of n*	`cartesian`
O(n^2c)	Polynomial (Slow) *Grows with n and c (columns)*	`LogisticRegression.fit`

Using this kind of notation can assist you when choosing the most efficient operation during the design phase of your analytic. For an example of how to replace a `cartesian` join [O(n2)] with `connectedComponents` [O(log n)], see `Chapter 10`, *Story De-duplication and Mutation*.

It also allows you to estimate your analytics performance characteristics prior to executing your job. You can use this information in conjunction with the parallelism and configuration of your cluster to ensure that when it's time to do a full-run of your job, maximum resources are employed.

Step through carefully

Spark's fantastic, fluent, function-oriented API is designed to allow the *chaining together* of transformations. Indeed, this is one of its main benefits, and as we've seen it is especially convenient for building data science pipelines. However, it's because of this convenience that it is rather tempting to write a string of commands and then execute them all in one run. As you might have already found with this approach, if a failure occurs or you're not getting the results you expect, all processing up to that point is lost and must be replayed. As the development process is characteristically iterative, this results in an overly elongated cycle that can too often result in lost time.

To avoid this problem, it's important to be able to **fail fast** during each iteration. Therefore, consider getting into the habit of running one step at a time on a small sample of data before proceeding. By issuing an action, say a count or small take, after each and every transformation, you can check for correctness and ensure that each step is successful before moving onto the next step. By investing in a little up-front care and attention, you'll make better use of your time and your development cycles will tend to be quicker.

In addition to this, and whenever possible during the development life cycle, consider persisting intermediate datasets to disk to avoid having to repeatedly recalculate, particularly if they are computationally heavy, or potentially reusable. This is a form of on-disk caching and it is a similar approach to *checkpointing* (as used in spark streaming when storing state). In fact, it's a common trade-off when writing CPU-intensive analytics, and it is especially useful when developing analytics that run over large datasets. However, it is a trade-off, so to decide whether or not it's worthwhile, evaluate the amount time taken to compute the dataset from scratch, versus the time taken to read it from disk.

If you decide to persist, be sure to use `ds.write.save` and format as `parquet` (default) to avoid a proliferation of bespoke classes and serialization version issues. This way you'll preserve the benefits of schema on read.

Furthermore, as you're iterating through the analytic development lifecycle, writing your own highly-performant functions, it's a good idea to maintain a **regression test pack**. This has a couple of benefits:

1. It allows you to ensure that as you introduce new classes of data, you haven't broken existing functionality.
2. It gives you a level of confidence that your code is correct up to the step you're working on.

You can easily create a regression test pack using unit tests. There are many unit testing frameworks out there to aid with this. One popular approach is to test each function by comparing the actual results with what you expected. In this way, you can build up a pack over time, by specifying tests, along with the commensurate data for each of your functions. Let's explain how to do this with a simple example. Suppose we have the following model, taken from the GDELT GKG dataset:

```
case class PersonTone(article: String, name: String, tone: Double)

object Brexit {
  def averageNewsSentiment(df: DataFrame): Dataset[(String,Double)] = ???
}
```

We'd like to test that given a DataFrame of `PersonTone`'s, that the
`averageNewsSentiment` function correctly computes the average tone for various people
taken from all articles. For the purposes of writing this unit test, we're not too interested in
how the function works, just that it works as *expected*. Therefore, we'll follow these steps:

1. Import the required unit test frameworks. In this case, let's use `ScalaTest` and a
   handy DataFrame-style, parsing framework called `product-collections`:

```
<dependency>
  <groupId>com.github.marklister</groupId>
  <artifactId>product-
  collections_${scala.binary.version}</artifactId>
  <version>1.4.5</version>
  <scope>test</scope>
</dependency>

<dependency>
 <groupId>org.scalatest</groupId>
 <artifactId>scalatest_${scala.binary.version}  </artifactId>
 <scope>test</scope>
</dependency>
```

2. We'll also use a custom extension of the `ScalaTest FunSuite`, called
   `SparkFunSuite`, which we introduced in `Chapter 3`, *Input Formats and Schema*,
   which you can find in the code repository.
3. Next, mock-up some input data and define the *expected* results.
4. Then, run the function on the input data using and collect the *actual* result. Note:
   this runs locally and does not require a cluster.
5. Lastly, *verify* that the actual results match the expected results and if they don't,
   fail the test.

The complete unit test looks like this:

```
import java.io.StringReader
import io.gzet.test.SparkFunSuite
import org.scalatest.Matchers
import com.github.marklister.collections.io._

class RegressionTest extends SparkFunSuite with Matchers {

  localTest("should compute average sentiment") { spark =>

    // given
    val input = CsvParser(PersonTone)
```

```
                   .parse(new StringReader(
"""http://www.ibtimes.co.uk/...,Nigel Farage,-2.4725485679183
http://www.computerweekly.co.uk/...,Iain Duncan-Smith,1.95886385896181
http://www.guardian.com/...,Nigel Farage,3.79346680716544
http://nbc-2.com/...,David Cameron,0.195886385896181
http://dailyamerican.com/...,David Cameron,-5.82329317269076""")))

    val expectedOutput = Array(
      ("Nigel Farage", 1.32091823925),
      ("Iain Duncan-Smith",1.95886385896181),
      ("David Cameron",-5.62740678679))

    // when
    val actualOutput =
            Brexit.averageNewsSentiment(input.toDS).collect()

    // test
    actualOutput should have length expectedOutput.length
    actualOutput.toSet should be (expectedOutput.toSet)
  }
}
```

Tune your analytic

The purpose of analytic tuning is to ensure smooth running and maximum efficiency of your analytic within the practical limitations of your cluster. Most of the time, this means trying to confirm that memory is being used effectively on all machines, that your cluster is fully-utilized, and by ensuring that your analytic is not unduly IO-bound, CPU-bound, or network-bound. This can be difficult to achieve on a cluster due to the distributed nature of the processing and the sheer number of machines involved.

Thankfully, the Spark UI is designed to assist you in this task. It centralizes and provides a one-stop shop for useful information about the runtime performance and state of your analytic. It can help give pointers to resource bottlenecks and even tell you where your code is spending most of its time.

Let's take a closer look:

- **Input Size or Shuffle Read Size/Records**: Used both for narrow and wide transformations, in either case this is the total amount of data read by the task, regardless of its source (remote or local). If you're seeing large input sizes or numbers of records, consider repartitioning or increasing the number of executors.

Summary Metrics for 168 Completed Tasks

Metric	Min	25th percentile	Median	75th percentile	Max
Duration	71 ms	7 s	12 s	13 s	17 s
Scheduler Delay	1 ms	2 ms	3 ms	3 ms	5 ms
Task Deserialization Time	0 ms	1 ms	1 ms	2 ms	24 ms
GC Time	3 ms	0.2 s	0.4 s	0.4 s	0.6 s
Result Serialization Time	0 ms	0 ms	0 ms	0 ms	1 ms
Getting Result Time	0 ms	0 ms	0 ms	0 ms	0 ms
Peak Execution Memory	0.0 B	0.0 B	0.0 B	0.0 B	0.0 B
Input Size / Records	119.3 KB / 11	16.5 MB / 1397	32.1 MB / 2578	32.1 MB / 2728	35.2 MB / 2869
Shuffle Write Size / Records	1591.0 B / 32	61.9 KB / 6445	98.4 KB / 11595	104.9 KB / 12861	120.2 KB / 17005

Aggregated Metrics by Executor

Executor ID ▲	Address	Task Time	Total Tasks	Failed Tasks	Succeeded Tasks	Input Size / Records	Shuffle Write Size / Records
0	CANNOT FIND ADDRESS	14 min	88	0	88	2035.1 MB / 170712	6.7 MB / 809037
1	CANNOT FIND ADDRESS	14 min	80	0	80	2.0 GB / 174489	6.9 MB / 832305

Tasks (168)

Page 1 2 >   2 Pages. Jump to 1   Show 100   items in a page.   Go

Index ▲	ID	Attempt	Status	Locality Level	Executor ID / Host	Launch Time	Duration	Scheduler Delay	Task Deserialization Time	GC Time	Result Serialization Time	Getting Result Time	Peak Execution Memory	Input Size / Records	Write Time	Shuffle Write Size / Records	Errors
0	336	0	SUCCESS	PROCESS_LOCAL	1 / 192.168.1.67	2016/12/22 06:07:19	12 s	4 ms	24 ms	0.4 s	0 ms	0 ms	0.0 B	32.1 MB / 2644	48 ms	104.9 KB / 15620	
1	337	0	SUCCESS	PROCESS_LOCAL	0 / 192.168.1.67	2016/12/22 06:07:19	7 s	4 ms	24 ms	0.3 s	0 ms	0 ms	0.0 B	15.7 MB / 1286	44 ms	56.4 KB / 6727	
2	338	0	SUCCESS	PROCESS_LOCAL	1 / 192.168.1.67	2016/12/22 06:07:19	12 s	4 ms	23 ms	0.4 s	0 ms	0 ms	0.0 B	32.1 MB / 2627	45 ms	101.6 KB / 13084	
3	339	0	SUCCESS	PROCESS_LOCAL	0 / 192.168.1.67	2016/12/22 06:07:19	7 s	3 ms	24 ms	0.3 s	0 ms	0 ms	0.0 B	17.0 MB / 1397	37 ms	62.1 KB / 7047	
4	340	0	SUCCESS	PROCESS_LOCAL	0 / 192.168.1.67	2016/12/22 06:07:26	12 s	3 ms	2 ms	0.4 s	0 ms	0 ms	0.0 B	32.1 MB / 2720	35 ms	105.4 KB / 13534	
5	341	0	SUCCESS	PROCESS_LOCAL	0 / 192.168.1.67	2016/12/22 06:07:27	6 s	3 ms	1 ms	0.2 s	0 ms	0 ms	0.0 B	15.5 MB / 1306	39 ms	57.5 KB / 6523	
6	342	0	SUCCESS	PROCESS_LOCAL	1 / 192.168.1.67	2016/12/22 06:07:32	13 s	3 ms	1 ms	0.4 s	0 ms	0 ms	0.0 B	32.1 MB / 2717	35 ms	110.0 KB / 13248	

- **Duration**: The amount of time the task has been running. Although entirely dependent on the type of computational task underway, if you're seeing small input sizes and long durations, you may be CPU-bound, consider using thread-dump to determine what the time is being spent.

Pay particular attention to any variance in the duration. The Spark UI provides figures for the min, 25%, median, 75%, and max displayed on the **Stages** page. And from this it is possible to determine the profile of your cluster utilization. In other words, whether there is an even distribution of data across your tasks, meaning a fair distribution of computing responsibility, or whether you have a heavily skewed data distribution, meaning distorted processing with a long tail of tasks. If the latter is the case, review the section on handling data distribution.

- **Shuffle Write Size/Records**: The amount of data to be transferred as part of the shuffle. It may vary between tasks, but generally you'll want to ensure that the total value is as low as possible.

- **Locality Level**: A measure of data locality appears on the **Stages** page. Optimally, this should be PROCESS_LOCAL. However, you will see that it changes to any after a shuffle or wide transformation. This usually can't be helped. However, if you're seeing a lot of NODE_LOCAL or RACK_LOCAL for narrow transformations: consider increasing the number of executors, or in extreme cases confirm your storage system block size and replication factor or rebalance your data.

- **GC time**: The amount of time each task spends garbage collecting, that is, cleaning-up no longer used objects in memory. It should be no more than around 10% of the overall time (shown by **Duration**). If it's excessively high, it's probably an indication of an underlying problem. However, it's worth reviewing the other areas of your analytic relating to data distribution (that is, number of executors, JVM heap size, number of partitions, parallelism, skew, and so on) before attempting to tune the garbage collector.

- **Thread dump (per executor)**: Shown on the **Executors** page, the thread dump option allows you to take a peek at the inner workings of any of your executors, at any time. This can be invaluable when trying to gain an understanding of your analytic's behavior. Helpfully, the thread dump is sorted and lists most interesting threads at the top of the list look for threads labeled **Executor task launch worker** as these are the threads that run your code.

By repeatedly refreshing this view, and reviewing the stack trace for a single thread, it's possible to get a rough idea of where it's spending time and hence identify areas of concern.

> Alternatively, you can use a flame graph, for details see `https://www.paypal-engineering.com/2016/09/08/spark-in-flames-profiling-spark-applications-using-flame-graphs/`.

* **Skipped Stages**: The stages that were not required to run. Typically, when a stage is shown in this section on the Stages page, it means that a complete set of data for this section of the RDD lineage was found in the *cache*, which the DAG scheduler did not need to re-compute and instead skipped to the next stage. Generally, it is the sign of a good caching strategy.

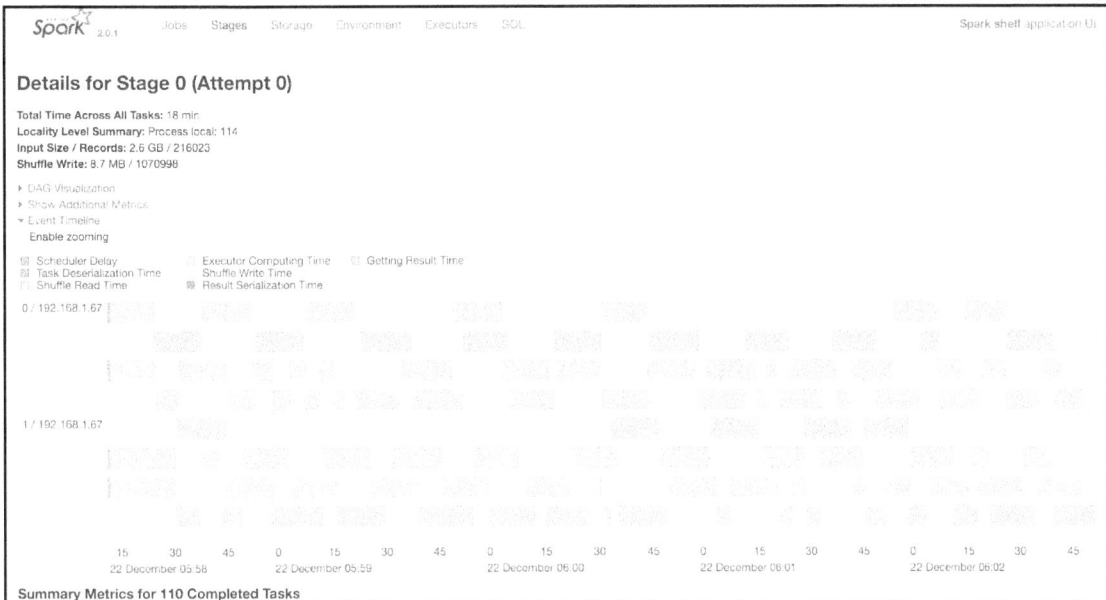

- **Event Timeline**: Again, shown on the **Stages** page the event timeline provides a visual representation of your running tasks. It's useful to see the level of parallelism, and how many tasks are executing on each executor at any given time.

If after initial investigations, should you need more in-depth information than the Spark UI provides, you can use any of the monitoring tools provided by your operating system in order to investigate the underlying conditions of your infrastructure. The following is a table of a selection of common Linux tools for this purpose:

Area Under Consideration	Tool	Description	Example Usage
General / CPU	htop	Process activity monitor that refreshes to show near real-time CPU, memory and swap (among other things) utilization per process	htop -p <pid>
	dstat	Highly-configurable reporting on system resource utilization	dstat -t -l -c -y -i -p -m -g -d -r -n 3
	ganglia	Aggregating system resource monitor designed for use on distributed systems	Web-based

Java Virtual Machine	jvmtop	Statistics about a JVM including resource utilization and a real-time view of its threads	jvmtop <pid>
	jps	Lists all JVM processes	jps -l
	jmap	JVM internal memory map including breakdown of all objects allocated on the heap	jmap -histo <pid> | head -20
	jstack	JVM Snapshot including full thread dump	jstack <pid>
Memory	free	Essential guide to memory utilization	free -m
	vmstat	Detailed system resource statistics based on sampling including breakdown of memory allocation	vmstat -s
Disk I/O	iostat	Provides disk I/O statistics, including I/O wait	iostat -x 2 5
	iotop	Disk I/O monitor, in a similar style to top. Show's I/O at a process level	iotop
Network	nettop	Network connection activity monitor including real-time I/O	nettop -Pd
	wireshark	Interactive network traffic analyzer	wireshark -i <iface> -k tshark -i <iface>

Design patterns and techniques

In this section, we'll outline some design patterns and general techniques for use when writing your own analytics. These are a collection of hints and tips that represent the accumulation of experiences working with Spark. They are offered up as guidelines for effective Spark analytic authoring. They also serve as a reference for when you encounter the inevitable scalability problems and don't know what to do.

Spark APIs

Problem

With so many different sets of API's and functions to choose from, it's difficult to know which ones are the most performant.

Solution

Apache Spark currently has over one thousand contributors, many of whom are highly experienced world-class software professionals. It is a mature framework having been developed for over six years. Over that time, they have focused on refining and optimizing just about every part of the framework from the DataFrame-friendly APIs, through the Netty-based shuffle machinery, to the catalyst query plan optimizer. The great news is that it all comes for "free" – providing you use the newest APIs available in Spark 2.0.

Recent optimizations (introduced by *project tungsten*), such as off-heap explicit memory management, cache-miss improvements, and dynamic stage generation, are only available with the newer `DataFrame` and `Dataset` APIs, and are not currently supported by the RDD API. In addition, the newly-introduced Encoders are significantly faster and more space-efficient than Kryo serialization or Java serialization.

For the most part, this means that Datasets usually outperform RDDs.

Example

Let's illustrate using an informal example of a basic count of people mentioned in articles:

```
personDS                          personRDD
  .groupBy($"name")                 .map(p => (p.person,1))
  .count                            .reduceByKey(_+_)
  .sort($"count".desc)              .sortBy(_._2,false)
  .show

36 seconds (Dataset API)          99 seconds (RDD API)
```

The preceding snippet shows the relative performance difference between the two API's. For this test, in each case 20 iterations were performed over 200 MB uncompressed text, running on 20 x 1 GB, 1-core executors with commodity hardware. Therefore, in terms of performance, it's a good idea to learn and use the dataset API, only turning to RDDs (using `ds.rdd`) when you need the flexibility to compute something not available on the higher level API.

Summary pattern

Problem

My timeseries analytic must run operationally within strict **service level agreements** (**SLAs**) and there is not enough time to compute the required result over the entire dataset.

Solution

For real-time analytics, or ones with strict SLAs, running lengthy computations over large datasets can be impractical. Sometimes it's necessary to design analytics using a two-pass algorithm in order to compute results in a timely fashion. To do this, we'll need to introduce the concept of the *Summary* pattern.

The Summary pattern is a two-pass algorithm where the end result is reconstructed from the aggregation of summaries only. Although only using summaries, and having never processed the entire dataset directly, the result of the aggregation is the same as if it were run over the entire raw dataset.

The basic steps are:

1. Calculate a summary over the appropriate interval (per minute, per day, per week, and so on).
2. Persist the summary data for later use.
3. Calculate an aggregate over the larger interval (per month, per year, and so on).

This is a particularly useful approach when designing incremental or online algorithms for streaming analytics.

Example

The GDELT GKG dataset is a great example of a summary dataset.

Certainly, it would be impractical to perform sentiment analysis or named entity recognition over say, a month's worth of global media news articles every 15 minutes. Fortunately, GDELT produces those 15 minute summaries that we are able to aggregate making this entirely possible.

Expand and Conquer Pattern

Problem

My analytic has a relatively small number of tasks, each with high *Input/Shuffle Size (Bytes)*. These tasks take a long time to complete, while sometimes there are idle executors.

Solution

The *Expand and Conquer* pattern tokenizes records for more efficient parallel execution by allowing you to increase parallelism. By decomposing or unpacking each record you enable them to be composed in different ways, spread over the cluster, and processed by different executors.

In this pattern, `flatMap` is used, usually in conjunction with shuffle or `repartition`, to *increase* the number of tasks and decrease the amount of data being processed by each task. This gives rise to an optimal situation whereby enough tasks are queued so that no executors are ever left idle. It can also help in the scenario where you're struggling to process large amounts of data in the memory of one machine, and hence receiving *out of memory errors*.

This useful and versatile technique comes in handy in almost every situation where you have large datasets. It promotes the use of simple data structures and allows you to take full advantage of the distributed nature of Spark.

A word of caution, however, as `flatMap` can also cause performance problems because it has the potential to *increase* the time complexity of your analytic. By using `flatMap`, you are generating many records for each and every row, hence potentially adding another dimension of data that requires processing. Therefore, you should always consider the impact of this pattern on algorithmic complexity, using the Big O Notation.

Lightweight Shuffle

Problem

The *Shuffle Read Blocked Time* of my analytic is a significant proportion of the overall processing time (>5%). What can I do to avoid having to wait for the shuffle to finish?

Solution

Although Spark's shuffle is carefully engineered to minimize both network and disk I/O by using techniques such as data compression and merge file consolidation, it has the following two fundamental problems that mean it will often become a performance bottleneck:

- **It's I/O Intensive**: The shuffle relies on (i) moving data over a network and (ii) writing that data to disk on the target machine. Therefore, it's much slower than local transformations. To illustrate how much slower, here are the relative timings for reading 1 MB sequentially from various devices: It's I/O intensive: The shuffle relies on (i) moving data over a network and (ii) writing that data to disk on the target machine. Therefore, it's much slower than local transformations. To illustrate how much slower, here are the relative timings for reading 1 MB sequentially from various devices:

Memory	*0.25ms*
10 GbE	*10ms*
Disk	*20ms*

  In this example, as a shuffle operation uses both network and disk, it would be around 120 times slower than one performed on a cached, local partition. Obviously, timings will vary depending on physical types and speeds of the devices used, figures here are provided as relative guidelines.

- **It's a synchronization point for concurrency**: Every task in a stage must complete before the next stage can begin. Given that stage boundaries involve a shuffle (see `ShuffleMapStage`), it marks a point in the execution where tasks that otherwise would be ready to start, must wait until all tasks in that stage have finished. This gives rise to a synchronization barrier that can have a significant impact on performance.

For these reasons, try to avoid the shuffle where possible, or at least minimize its impact.

Sometimes it's possible to avoid a shuffle altogether, in fact there are patterns, such as *Broadcast Variables* or *Wide Table patterns*, that offer suggestions on how to do this, but often it's inevitable and all that can be done is to lessen the amount of data that is transferred, and hence the impact of the shuffle.

In this case, try to construct a *Lightweight Shuffle* specifically minimizing data transfer – only necessary bytes should be transferred.

Once again, if you use the `Dataset` and `DataFrame` API, when the catalyst generates a logical query plan it will perform over 50 optimizations, including *pruning* any unused columns or partitions automatically (see `https://github.com/apache/spark/blob/master/sql/catalyst/src/main/scala/org/apache/spark/sql/catalyst/optimizer/Optimizer.scala`). But if you're using RDDs, you'll have to do this yourself. There's following few techniques that you can try:

- **Use map to reduce data**: Call `map` on your data immediately prior to a shuffle in order to get rid of any data that is not used in follow on processing.

- **Use keys only**: When you have key-value pairs, consider using `rdd.keys` instead of `rdd`. For operations such as counts or membership tests, this should be sufficient. Similarly, consider using `values` whenever appropriate.

- **Adjust order of stages**: Should you join and then `groupBy` or `groupBy` and then join? In Spark, this is mainly about the size of the datasets. It should be fairly trivial to do cost-based assessments using the number of records before and after each transformation. Experiment to find which one is more efficient for your datasets.

- **Filter first**: Generally speaking, filtering rows prior to a shuffle is an advantage as it reduces the number of rows transferred. Consider filtering as early as possible, provided your revised analytic is functionally equivalent.

  In some situations, you can also filter out entire partitions, like so:

  ```
  val sortedPairs = rdd.sortByKey()
  sortedPairs.filterByRange(lower, upper)
  ```

- **Use CoGroup**: If you have two or more RDDs all grouped by the same key, then `CoGroup` might be able to join them without instigating a shuffle. This ingenious little trick works because any `RDD[(K,V)]` using the same type `K` as a key, and grouped using a `HashPartitioner`, will always settle on the same node. Therefore, when joining by key `K`, no data needs to be moved.

- **Try a different codec**: Another tip for decreasing the amount of bytes transferred is to change the compression algorithm.

  Spark provides three options: `lz4`, `lzf`, and `snappy`. Consider reviewing each one to determine which works best for your particular type of data:

  ```
  SparkSession
    .builder()
    .config("spark.io.compression.codec", "lzf")
  ```

Wide Table pattern

Problem

The one-to-many or many-to-many relationships in my datasets are producing many shuffles that ruin all my analytics' performance.

Solution

In order to optimize your data structures, we advocate denormalizing your data into a form that's useful for your particular type of processing. The approach, described here as the *Wide Table pattern*, involves combining data structures that are frequently used together, so that they are composed into a single record. This preserves data locality and removes the need to perform expensive joins. The more often a relationship is used, the more you benefit from this data locality.

The process involves constructing a data representation, view, or table that contains everything you need to do for follow-on processing. You may construct this programmatically, or by standard *joins* SparkSQL statements. It is then materialized ahead of time and used directly inside your analytics whenever required.

Where necessary, data is duplicated across each row to ensure self-sufficiency. You should resist the urge to factor out additional tables, like those found in third-normal form or in snowflake designs, and instead rely on columnar data formats, such as Parquet and ORC, to provide efficient storage mechanisms without sacrificing fast sequential access. They can do this by arranging data by column and compressing data within each column, which helps alleviate concerns when duplicating data.

Similarly, nested types, classes, or arrays can often be used to good effect inside a record to represent children or composite data classes. Again, avoid necessary dynamic joins at analytic runtime.

Example

For an example of how to use denormalized data structures, including nested types, see `Chapter 3`, *Input Formats and Schema*.

Broadcast variables pattern

Problem

My analytic requires many compact reference datasets and dimension tables that, despite their smaller size, cause costly shuffles of all data.

Solution

While some datasets – such as transaction logs or tweets – are theoretically infinitely large, others have natural limits and will never grow beyond a certain size. These are known as *bounded datasets*. Although they may change occasionally over time, they are reasonably stable and can be said to be held within a finite space. For example, the list of all the postcodes in the UK could be considered a bounded dataset.

When joining to a bounded dataset or any small collection, there is an opportunity to take advantage of an efficiency pattern that Spark provides. Rather than using join as you would normally, which would instigate a shuffle that could potentially transfer all data, consider using a broadcast variable instead. Once assigned, the broadcast variable will be distributed and made available locally to all the executors in your cluster. You can use a broadcast variable like so:

Creating a broadcast variable

```
val toBeBroadcast = smallDataset.collect
val bv = spark.sparkContext.broadcast(toBeBroadcast)
```

Make sure you collect any data to be broadcast.

Accessing a broadcast variable

```
ds.mapPartitions { partition =>

    val smallDataset = bv.value
    partition map { r => f(r, bv.value) }
}
```

Removing a broadcast variable

```
bv.destroy()
```

Broadcast variables can be used by the RDD API or the Dataset API. Also, you can still exploit broadcast variables in SparkSQL – it will handle it automatically. Just ensure that the threshold is set above the size of the table to join, like so:

```
SparkSession
  .builder()
  .config("spark.sql.autoBroadcastJoinThreshold", "50MB")
```

Example

For examples of how to use broadcast variables to implement efficient joins and filters, see Chapter 9, *News dictionary and Real-time Tagging System*.

Combiner pattern

Problem

My analytic is performing an aggregation based on a set of keys, and hence, is having to shuffle *all data for all keys*. Consequently, it's very slow.

Solution

At the core of Apache Spark's shuffling abilities is a powerful and flexible pattern, referred to here as the *Combiner* pattern, which offers a mechanism for greatly reducing the amount of data in the shuffle. The Combiner pattern is so important that examples of it can be found in multiple locations in the Spark code – to see it in action here are some of those examples:

- `ExternalAppendOnlyMap`
- `CoGroupedRDD`
- `DeclarativeAggregate`
- `ReduceAggregator`

In fact, all high-level API's that use the shuffle operation, such as `groupBy`, `reduceByKey`, `combineByKey`, and so on, use this pattern as the core of their processing. However, there's some variation in the implementations mentioned previously, although the fundamental concept is the same. Let's take a closer look.

The Combiner pattern provides an efficient approach to compute a function across sets of records in parallel and then combines their output in order to achieve an overall result.

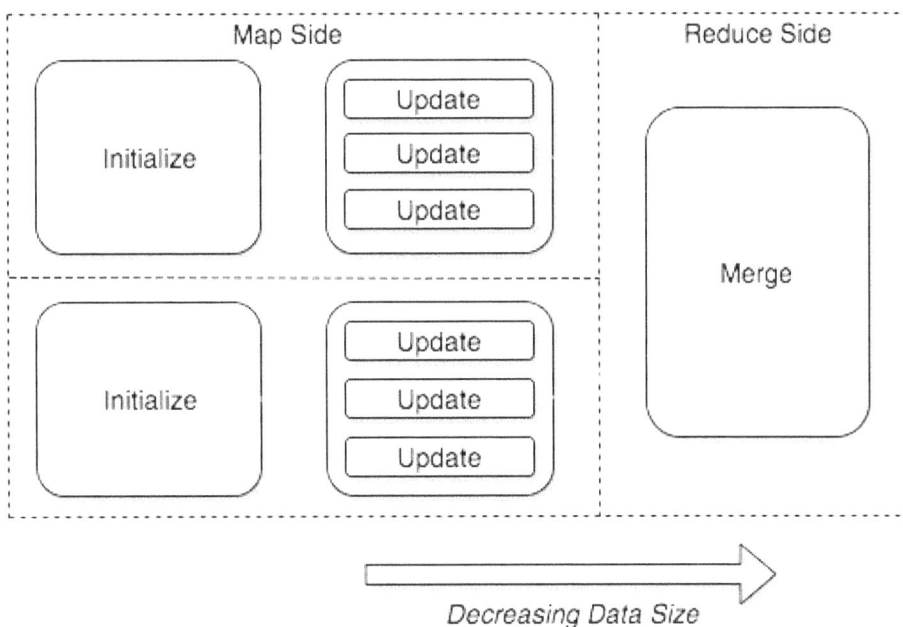

Generally, it consists of three functions that must be provided by the caller:

- **Initialize** *(e) -> C₀:* Creates the initial *container*, otherwise known as `createCombiner`, `type` constructor, or `zero`.

  In this function, you should create and initialize an instance that will serve as the container for all other combined values. Sometimes the first value from each key is also provided to pre-populate the container that will eventually hold all the combined values for that key. In this case, the function is known as *unit*.

  It's worth noting that this function is executed exactly once per key on every partition in your dataset. Therefore, it is potentially called multiple times for each key and consequently must not introduce any side-effects that would produce inconsistent results were the dataset to be distributed differently.

- **Update***(C₀, e) -> Cᵢ:* Adds an element to the container. Otherwise known as `mergeValue`, `bind` *function*, or `reduce`.

  In this function, you should add a record from the originating RDD into the container. This usually involves transforming or aggregating the value in some way and only the output of this calculation is taken forwards inside the container.

  As updates are executed in parallel and in any order, this function must be commutative and associative.

- **Merge***(Cᵢ, Cⱼ) -> Cₖ:* Combines together two containers. Otherwise known as `mergeCombiners` or `merge`.

  In this function, you should combine the values represented by each container to form a new value, which is then taken forwards.

  Again, because there are no guarantees on the order of merges, this function should be commutative and associative.

You may have noticed a similarity between this pattern and the concept of *monads*. If you haven't encountered monads yet, they represent an abstract mathematical concept, used in functional programming as a way of expressing functions so that they are composable in a general way. They support many features, such as composition, side-effect free execution, repeatability, consistency, lazy evaluation, immutability, and provide many other benefits. We will not give a full explanation of monads here, there are plenty of great introductions already out there – for example
`http://www.simononsoftware.com/a-short-introduction-to-monads/`, which takes a practical rather than a theoretical viewpoint. Instead, we will explain where the Combiner pattern is different and how it helps to understand Spark.

Spark executes the `update` function on every record in your dataset. Due to its distributed nature, this can happen in parallel. It also runs the *merge* function to combine results from the output of each partition. Again, because this function is applied in parallel and therefore could be combined in any order, Spark requires these functions to be *commutative*, meaning that the sequence in which they are applied should have no impact on the overall answer. It's this commutative, merge step that really provides the basis of the definition.

An understanding of this pattern is useful for reasoning about the behavior of any distributed aggregations. If you're interested in understanding this pattern further, a nice implementation can be found in
`https://github.com/apache/spark/blob/master/sql/core/src/main/scala/org/apache/spark/sql/expressions/Aggregator.scala`.

In addition to this, it's useful when trying to determine which high-level API to use. With so many available, it's sometimes difficult to know which one to choose. By applying an understanding of *types* to the preceding descriptions, we can decide on the most fitting and performant API. For example, where the types of e and C_n are the same, you should consider using `reduceByKey`. However, where the type of e is different to C_n, then an operation such as `combineByKey` should be considered.

To illustrate, let's consider some different approaches using four of the most common operations available on the RDD API.

Example

To provide some context, let's say we have an RDD of key-value pairs representing people mentioned in news articles, where the key is the name of the person referred to in the article, and the value is a pre-filtered, tokenized, bag-of-words, textual-version of the article:

```
// (person:String, article:Array[String])
val rdd:RDD[(String,Array[String])] = ...
```

Now suppose we want to find some statistics about articles in which a person is mentioned, for example, min and max length, most frequently used words (excluding stop-words), and so on. In this case, our result would be of the form, `(person:String,stats:ArticleStats)`, where `ArticleStats` is a case class designed to hold the required statistics:

```
case class ArticleStats(minLength:Long,maxLength:Long,mfuWord:(String,Int))
```

Let's start with the definition of the three combiner functions, as described previously:

```
val init = (a:Array[String]) => {
  ArticleStats(a)
}

val update = (stats:ArticleStats, a:Array[String]) => {
  stats |+| ArticleStats(a)
}

val merge = (s1:ArticleStats,s2:ArticleStats) => {
  s1 |+| s2
}
```

As you might notice, these functions are really just the syntactic sugar of our pattern; the real logic is hidden away in the companion class and the semigroup:

```
object ArticleStats {
  def apply(a:Array[String]) =
    new ArticleStats(calcMin(a),calcMax(a),findMFUWord(a))
  ...
}

implicit object statsSemiGroup extends SemiGroup[ArticleStats] {
  def append(a: ArticleStats, b: ArticleStats) : ArticleStats = ???
}
```

For our purposes, we won't cover these in detail, let's just assume that any computation necessary to calculate the statistics are carried out by the supporting code – including the logic for finding the extremities of two previously calculated metrics – and instead focus on the explanation of our different approaches.

GroupByKey approach:

Our first approach is by far and away the slowest option because `groupByKey` doesn't use the `update` function. Despite this obvious disadvantage, we can still achieve our result – by sandwiching the `groupByKey` between maps where the first map is used to convert into the desired type and the last to perform the reduce-side aggregation:

```
rdd.mapValues { case value => init(value) }
    .groupByKey()
    .mapValues { case list => list.fold(merge) } // note: update not used
```

However, you will notice that it does not perform any map-side combining for efficiency, instead preferring to combine all values on the reduce-side, meaning that all values are copied across the network as part of the shuffle.

For this reason, you should always consider the following alternatives before resorting to this approach.

ReduceByKey approach:

To improve on this, we can use `reduceByKey`. Unlike `groupByKey`, `reduceByKey` provides map-side combining for efficiency by making use of the `update` function. In terms of performance, it offers an optimum approach. However, it still requires each value to be manually converted to the correct type prior to invocation:

```
rdd.map(init(_._2)).reduceByKey(merge)
```

The result is achieved in two steps by mapping records from the originating RDD into the desired type.

AggregateByKey approach:

Again, `aggregateByKey` provides the same performance characteristics as `reduceByKey` – by implementing map-side combine – but this time as one operation:

```
rdd.aggregateByKey(ArticleStats())(update,merge)
```

In the preceding snippet we see `update` and `merge` being called, however `init` is not used directly. Instead, an empty container, in the form of a blank `ArticleStats` object, is provided explicitly for the purposes of initialization. This syntax is closer to that of `fold`, so it's useful if you're more familiar with that style.

CombineByKey Approach:

Generally, `combineByKey` is thought of as the most flexible key-based operation, giving you complete control over all three functions in the Combiner pattern:

```
rdd.combineByKey(init,update,merge)
```

While providing `init` as a *function* rather than just a single value might give you more flexibility in select scenarios, in practice for most problems the relationship between `init`, `update`, and `merge` is such that you don't really gain anything in terms of functionality or performance between either approach. And regardless, all three are backed by `combineByKeyWithClassTag`, so in this instance feel free to choose whichever one that is a better syntactic fit for your problem, or just pick the one you prefer.

Optimized cluster

Problem

I want to know how to configure my Spark job's executors in order to make full use of the resources of my cluster, but with so many options I'm confused.

Solution

As Spark is designed to scale horizontally, generally speaking, you should prefer having *more* executors over *larger* executors. But with each executor comes the overhead of a JVM, so it's advisable to make full use of them by running *multiple* tasks inside each executor. As this seems like a bit of a contradiction, let's look at how to configure Spark to achieve this.

Spark provides the following options (specified on the command line or in configuration):

```
--num-executors (YARN-only setting [as of Spark 2.0])
--executor-cores
--executor-memory
--total-executor-cores
```

Number of executors can be estimated using the following formula:

number of executors = (total cores – cluster overhead) / cores per executor

For example, when using a YARN-based cluster accessing HDFS and running in YARN-client mode, the equation would be as follows:

$$((T - (2*N + 6)) / 5)$$

where:

T: Total number of cores in the cluster.

N: Total of nodes in the cluster.

2: Removes the *per node* overhead of HDFS and YARN.

Assumes two HDFS processes on each node – `DataNode` and `NodeManager`.

6: Removes the *master process* overhead of HDFS and YARN.

Assumes the average of six processes – `NameNode`, `ResourceManager`, `SecondaryNameNode`, `ProxyServer`, `HistoryServer`, and so on. Obviously, this is an example and in reality it depends on what other services are running the cluster, along with other factors such as Zookeeper quorum size, HA strategy, and so on.

5: Anecdotally, the optimum number of cores for each executor to ensure optimal task concurrency without prohibitive disk I/O contention.

Memory allocation can be estimated using the following formula:

*mem per executor = (mem per node / number of executors per node) * safety fraction*

For example, when using a YARN-based cluster running in YARN-client mode with 64 GB per node, the equation would be as follows:

$$(64 / E)* 0.9 => 57.6 / E$$

where:

E:Number of executors per node (as calculated in the previous example).

0.9: Fraction of actual memory allocated to the heap after subtracting off-heap.

overhead (`spark.yarn.executor.memoryOverhead`, default 10%).

It's worth noting that while it is generally beneficial to allocate more memory to an executor (allowing more space for sorting, caching, and so on) increasing the memory also increases *garbage collection pressure*. The GC must sweep the entire heap for unreachable object references, therefore the larger the memory region it has to analyze, the more resources it must consume and at some point this leads to diminishing returns. Whilst there's no absolute figure as to at what point this happens, as a general rule of thumb, keep the memory per executor under 64 GB to avoid problems.

The preceding equations should provide a good starting-point estimation for sizing your cluster. For further tuning, you may wish to experiment by tweaking these settings and measuring the effect on performance using the Spark UI.

Redistribution pattern

Problem

My analytic always runs on the same few executors. How do I increase the level of parallelism?

Solution

When `Datasets` and `RDDs` are relatively small to begin with, even if you then expand them using `flatMap`, any child in the lineage will take the parents number of partitions.

So, if some of your executors are idle, calling the `repartition` function could improve your level of parallelism. You will incur the immediate cost of moving data around, but this could pay-off overall.

Use the following command to determine the number of partitions for your data and hence the parallelism:

```
ds.rdd.getNumPartitions()
```

If the number of partitions is less than the maximum number of tasks allowable on your cluster, then you're not making full use of your executors.

Conversely, if you have a large number of tasks (10,000+) and they aren't running for very long then you should probably call `coalesce` to make better use of your resources – starting and stopping tasks is relatively expensive!

Example

Here, we increase the parallelism of a `Dataset` to `400`. The physical plan will show this as `RoundRobinPartitioning(400)`, like so:

```
ds.repartition(400)
  .groupByKey($"key")
  .reduceGroups(f)
  .explain

. . .

+- Exchange RoundRobinPartitioning(400)
              +- *BatchedScan parquet
```

And here's the equivalent re-partitioning for an `RDD` performed by simply specifying the number of partitions to use in the `reduceByKey` function:

```
rdd.reduceByKey(f, 400)
    .toDebugString

res1: String =
(400) ShuffledRDD[11] at reduceByKey at <console>:26 []
  +-(7) MapPartitionsRDD[10] at map at <console>:26 []
     |    MapPartitionsRDD[6] at rdd at <console>:26 []
     |    MapPartitionsRDD[5] at rdd at <console>:26 []
     |    MapPartitionsRDD[4] at rdd at <console>:26 []
     |    FileScanRDD[3] at rdd at <console>:26 []
```

Salting key pattern

Problem

Most of my tasks finish in a reasonable time, but there's always one or two that take much longer (>10x) and repartitioning does not seem to have any beneficial effect.

Solution

If you're experiencing having to wait for a handful of slow tasks, then you could be suffering from a skew in your data distribution. Symptoms of this are that you're seeing some tasks taking far longer than others or that some tasks have far more input or output.

If this is the case, the first thing to do is check that the number of keys is greater than the number of executors, as coarse-grained grouping can limit parallelism. A quick way to find the number of keys in your RDD is to use `rdd.keys.count`. If this value is lower than the number of executors, then reconsider your key strategy. Patterns such as *Expand and Conquer* may be able to help out.

If the preceding things are in order, the next thing to review is key distribution. Where you find a small number of keys with large numbers of associated values, consider the *Salting Key* pattern. In this pattern, popular keys are subdivided by appending a random element. For example:

```
rdd filter {
    case (k,v) => isPopular(k)
}
.map {
    case (k,v) => (k + r.nextInt(n), v)
}
```

This results in a more balanced key distribution because during the shuffle, the `HashPartitioner` sends the new keys to different executors. You can choose the value of n to suit the parallelism you need – greater skew in the data necessitates a greater range of salts.

Of course, all this salting does mean that you'll need to re-aggregate back onto the old keys to ensure that you ultimately calculate the correct answer. But, depending on the amount of skew in your data, a two-phase aggregation may still be faster.

You can either apply this salting to all keys, or filter out as in the preceding example. The threshold at which you filter, decided by `isPopular` in the example, is also entirely your choice.

Secondary sort pattern

Problem

When grouping by keys, my analytic has to explicitly sort the values *after* they are grouped. This sorting takes place in memory, therefore large value-sets take a long time, and they may involve spilling to disk and sometimes give an `OutOfMemoryError`. Here is an example of the problematic approach:

```
rdd.reduceByKey(_+_).sortBy(_._2,false) // inefficient for large groups
```

Instead, when grouping by key, values should be pre-ordered within each key for immediate and efficient follow-on processing.

Solution

Use the *Secondary Sort* pattern to order the list of items in a group efficiently by using the shuffle machinery. This approach will scale when handling even the largest of datasets.

In order to sort efficiently, this pattern utilizes three concepts:

1. **Composite key**: Contains both the elements you want to group by *and* the elements you want to sort by.
2. **Grouping partitioner**: Understands which parts of the composite key are related to *grouping*.
3. **Composite key ordering**: Understands which parts of the composite key are related to *ordering*.

Each of these is injected into Spark so that the final dataset is presented as grouped and ordered.

Please note, in order to perform a secondary sort you need to use `RDD`s, as the new `Dataset` API is not currently supported. Track the progress on the following JIRA `https://issues.apache.org/jira/browse/SPARK-3655`.

Example

Consider the following model:

```
case class Mention(name:String, article:String, published:Long)
```

Here we have an entity representing the occasions where people are mentioned in news articles containing the person's name, the article they were mentioned in, and its publication date.

Suppose we want to group together all the mentions of people with the same name, and order them by time. Let's look at the three mechanisms we need:

Composite key:

```
case class SortKey(name:String, published:Long)
```

Contains both name and published date.

Grouping partitioner:

```
class GroupingPartitioner(partitions: Int) extends Partitioner {

    override def numPartitions: Int = partitions

    override def getPartition(key: Any): Int = {

      val groupBy = key.asInstanceOf[SortKey]
      groupBy.name.hashCode() % numPartitions
    }
}
```

It's only grouping by name.

Composite key ordering:

```
implicit val sortBy: Ordering[SortKey] = Ordering.by(m => m.published)
```

It's only sorting by published date.

Once we have defined these, we can use them in the API, like so:

```
val pairs = mentions.rdd.keyBy(m => SortKey(m.name, m.published))
pairs.repartitionAndSortWithinPartitions(new GroupingPartitioner(n))
```

Here the `SortKey` is used to pair the data, the `GroupingPartitioner` is used when partitioning the data, and the `Ordering` is used during the merge and, of course, it's found via Scala's `implicit` mechanism, which matches based on type.

Filter overkill pattern

Problem

My analytic uses a *whitelist* in order to filter relevant data for processing. The filter happens early on in the pipeline so that my analytic only ever has to process the data I'm interested in, for maximum efficiency. However, the whitelist frequently changes meaning my analytic must be executed afresh, each time, against the new list.

Solution

Contrary to some of the other advice you'll read here, in some scenarios calculating results across all the data, by removing filters, can actually *increase* the overall efficiency of an analytic.

If you are frequently rerunning your analytic over different segments of the dataset, then consider using a popular approach, described here as the *Filter Overkill pattern*. This involves omitting all filters in Spark and processing over the entire corpus. The results of this one-off processing will be much larger that the filtered version, but it can be easily indexed in a tabular data store and filtered dynamically at query time. This avoids having to apply different filters over multiple runs, and having to re-compute historical data when filters change.

Probabilistic algorithms

Problem

It takes too long to compute statistics over my dataset because it is too large. By the time the response is received, it's out of date or no longer relevant. Therefore, it's more important to receive a timely response, or at least provide a maximum bound to time-complexity, than a complete or correct answer. In fact, a well-timed estimate even with *a small probability of error* would be taken in preference to a correct answer where the running time is not known.

Solution

Probabilistic algorithms use *randomization* to improve the time complexity of their algorithms and guarantee worst case performance. If you are time sensitive and just about right is good enough, you should consider using a probabilistic algorithm.

In addition, the same can be said for the problem of memory usage. There are a set of Probabilistic algorithms that provide estimates inside restricted space-complexity. Examples include:

- **Bloom Filter** is a membership test that is guaranteed to never miss an element in a set, but could give you a false positive, that is, determine an element to be a member of a set when it is not. It's useful for quickly reducing the amount of data in a problem-space prior to a more accurate calculation.

- **HyperLogLog** counts the number of distinct values in a column, providing a very reasonable estimate using a fixed memory footprint.

- **CountMinSketch** provides a frequency table used for counting occurrences of events in a stream of data. Particularly useful in Spark streaming where a fixed memory footprint eliminates the potential for memory overflows.

Spark provides implementations of these in `org.apache.spark.sql.DataFrameStatFunctions` and they can be used by accessing `df.stat`. Spark also includes some access via the `RDD` API:

```
rdd.countApprox()
rdd.countByValueApprox()
rdd.countApproxDistinct()
```

Example

For an example of how to use a **Bloom Filter** see `Chapter 11`, *Anomaly Detection on Sentiment Analysis*.

Selective caching

Problem

My analytic is caching datasets, but if anything, it's running slower than before.

Solution

Caching is key to getting the most performance out of Spark; however, when used incorrectly, it can have a detrimental effect. Caching is particularly useful whenever you intend to use an RDD more than once. This generally happens when you are: (i) using the data across stages, (ii) the data appears in the lineage of multiple child datasets, or (iii) during iterative processes, such as stochastic gradient descent.

The problem occurs when you cache indiscriminately without considering reuse. This is because the cache adds overhead when it's created, updated and flushed, and then must be garbage collected when not used. Therefore, improper caching can actually *slow down your job*. So, the easiest way to improve caching is to stop doing it (selectively of course).

Another consideration is whether there's enough memory allocated and available to efficiently cache your RDD. If your dataset won't fit into memory, Spark will either throw an `OutOfMemoryError` or swap data to disk (depending on the storage levels, this will be talked about shortly). In the latter case, this could have a performance impact due to both (i) the time taken to move extra data in and out of memory and (ii) having to wait for the availability of the disk (I/O wait).

In order to determine whether you have enough memory allocated to your executors, first cache the dataset as follows:

```
ds.cache
ds.count
```

Then, look at the *Storage* page in the Spark UI. For each RDD, this provides the fraction cached, its size, and the amount spilled to disk.

This should enable you to adjust the memory allocated to each executor in order to ensure that your data fits in memory. There are also the following caching options available:

- **NONE**: No caching (default)
- **MEMORY**: Used when `cache` is called
- **DISK**: Spill to disk
- **SER**: Same as MEMORY, but objects are stored in a byte array
- **2 (REPLICATED)**: Keep a cached copy on two different nodes

The preceding options can be used in any combination, for example:

- If you're experiencing `OutOfMemoryError` errors, try changing to `MEMORY_AND_DISK` to allow spilling of the cache to disk

- If you're experiencing high garbage collection times, consider trying one of the serialized byte buffer forms of cache, such as `MEMORY_AND_SER`, as this will circumvent the GC entirely (at the slight cost of increased serialization)

The goal here is to ensure that the *Fraction Cached* is at 100%, and where possible, minimize the *Size on Disk* to establish effective in-memory caching of your datasets.

Garbage collection

Problem

The *GC time* of my analytic is a significant proportion of the overall processing time (>15%).

Solution

Spark's garbage collector works pretty efficiently out of the box, so you should only attempt to adjust it if you're sure that it's the cause and not the *symptom* of the problem. Before altering the GC settings, you should ensure that you have reviewed all other aspects of your analytic. Sometimes you might see high GC times in the Spark UI for reasons other than a poor GC configuration. Most of the time, it's worth investigating these first.

If you're seeing frequent or lengthy GC times, the first thing to do is confirm that your code is behaving sensibly and make sure that it's not at the root of excess/irregular memory consumption. For example, review your caching strategy (see the preceding section) or use the `unpersist` function to explicitly remove RDDs or Datasets that are no longer required.

Another factor for consideration is the number of objects you allocate within your job. Try to minimize the amount of objects you instantiate by (i) simplifying your domain model, or (ii) by reusing instances, or (iii) by preferring primitives where you can.

Finally, if you're still seeing lengthy GC times, try tuning the GC. There's some great information provided by Oracle on how to do this (`https://docs.oracle.com/javase/8/docs/technotes/guides/vm/gctuning/g1_gc_tuning.html`), but specifically there is evidence to suggest that Spark can perform well using the G1 GC. It's possible to switch to this GC by adding `XX:UseG1GC` to the Spark command line.

When tuning the G1 GC, the two main options are:

- **InitiatingHeapOccupancyPercent:** A threshold percent of how full the heap should be before the GC triggers a cycle. The lower the percentage, the more frequently the GC runs, but the less work it has to do on each run. Therefore, if you set it to *less than* 45% (the default value), you might see fewer pauses. It can be configured on the command line using –
  `XX:InitiatingHeapOccupancyPercent`.

- **ConcGCThread**: The number of concurrent GC threads running in the background. The more threads, the quicker the garbage collection can complete. But it's a trade-off as more GC threads means more CPU resource allocation. Can be configured on the command line using `-XX:ConcGCThread`.

In summary, it's a matter of experimenting with these settings and tuning your analytic to find the optimum configuration.

Graph traversal

Problem

My analytic has an iterative step that only completes when a global condition is met, such as all keys report no more values to process, and consequently the running time can be slow and difficult to predict.

Solution

Generally speaking, the efficiency of graph-based algorithms is such that, if you can represent your problem as a standard graph traversal problem, you probably should. Examples of problems with graph-based solutions include: shortest-path, depth-first search, and page-rank.

Example

For an example of how to use the *Pregel* algorithm in `GraphX` and how to interpret a problem in terms of graph traversal, see `Chapter 7`, *Building Communities*.

Summary

In this chapter, we have concluded our journey by discussing aspects of distributed computing performance, and what to exploit when writing your own scalable analytics. Hopefully, you've come away with a sense of some of the challenges involved, and have a better understanding of how Spark works under the covers.

Apache Spark is a constantly evolving framework and new features and improvements are being added every day. No doubt it will become increasingly easier to use as continuous tweaks and refinements are intelligently applied into the framework, automating much of what must be done manually today.

In terms of what's next, who knows what's round the corner? But with Spark beating the competition yet again to win the 2016 CloudSort Benchmark (`http://sortbenchmark.org/`) and new versions set to be released every four months, one thing is for sure, it's going to be fast-paced. And hopefully, with the solid principles and methodical guidelines that you've learned in this chapter, you'll be developing scalable, performant algorithms for many years to come!

Index

3

3rd Normal Form (3NF) 483

A

access 435
Accumulo
  about 31, 211
  AccumuloGraphxInputFormat 218
  advantages 32
  cell security 213
  database, using 211
  disadvantages 32
  EdgeWritable 218
  Elasticsearch to 214
  graph data model in 214
  graph, building 219
  Hadoop input 215
  installation 32
  iterators 213
  output formats 215
  reading 217, 218
  setting up 211
  URL 32, 211
actions 478
additional costs 20
advantages, Apache HDFS
  additional costs 20
  data balance 20
  data encryption 20
  data locality 20
  flexible storage 20
  load balancing 20
  redundancy 20
Amazon S3
  about 21
  advantages 22

disadvantages 22
  installation 22
analysis 168
analytic tuning
  about 491
  duration 492
  event timeline 495
  GC time 493
  input size 492
  locality level 493
  shuffle read size/records 492
  shuffle write size/records 493
  skipped stages 494
  thread dump 493
anonymizing 446, 447, 448, 450
Apache Avro
  about 25
  advantages 25
  disadvantages 26
  installation 26
Apache Bahir
  URL 301
Apache Dremel
  reference link 24
Apache HDFS
  about 19
  advantages 20
  disadvantages 20
  installation 21
Apache Kafka
  about 23
  advantages 23
  disadvantages 24
  installation 24
  reference link 24
Apache Knox
  about 465

reference link 465
Apache Lucene
  about 28
  advantages 29
  disadvantages 29
  installation 29
  URL, for downloading 29
Apache NiFi
  about 26
  advantages 27
  disadvantages 27
  installation 27
  references 27
Apache Parquet
  about 24
  advantages 24
  disadvantages 25
  installation 25
Apache ranger
  about 464
  references 464
Apache sentry 462, 463
Apache Software Foundation (ASF) 12
Apache Spark 18
Apache Thrift
  URL 31
Apache YARN
  about 27
  advantages 28
  disadvantages 28
  installation 28
Application Program Interface (APIs) 12
audio signatures
  extracting 258, 259, 261
Authentication Server (AS) 458
authentication
  about 432
  references 432
authorization
  about 432
  Access control lists (ACL) 433
  Role-based access control (RBAC) 434
Avro
  about 73
  pedagogical method 76, 79

Spark-Avro method 74
transformation, performing 80

B

Bank Identification Number (BIN) 446
big data ecosystem
  about 10
  Apache Software Foundation (ASF) 12
  data management 10
  data management responsibilities 10
Big O Notation 487
Bigtable design
  URL 211
block token 458
Bloom filter 191
bloom filter 518
bootstrap
  reference link 263
Brent
  URL 140
broadcast variables pattern
  about 503
  accessing 503
  creating 503
  example 504
  issues 503
  removing 504
  solution 503
bytes
  processing 250, 252

C

CAMEO codes
  reference link 160
CAMEO dataset
  reference link 65
CAP theorem
  about 292, 293, 294
  reference link 293
Cassandra
  about 333
  using 262
cell security 213
classification model
  bootstrapping 282

Naive Bayes model, training 287, 288, 289
Stack Exchange, learning 283
  text features, building 284, 285
  virtues of programmer 289, 290
cluster manager 476
collaborative filtering
  about 248
  reference link 248
combiner pattern
  about 504
  AggregateByKey approach 509
  CombineByKey Approach 510
  example 508
  GroupByKey approach 509
  initialize 506
  issues 504
  merge 506
  ReduceByKey approach 509
  reference link 507
  solution 505
  update 506
Common Query Language (CQL) 155
community detection algorithm
  about 220
  Louvain algorithm 221, 222
  Weighted Community Clustering (WCC)
    algorithm 222
companion tools
  about 19
  Accumulo 31
  Amazon S3 21
  Apache Avro 25
  Apache HDFS 19
  Apache Kafka 23
  Apache Lucene 28
  Apache NiFi 26
  Apache Parquet 24
  Apache YARN 27
  Elasticsearch 30
  Kibana 29
components, Spark
  actions 478
  cluster manager 476
  DAG scheduler 477
  Directed Acyclic Graphs (DAGs) 477

driver 475
executor 476
Resilient Distributed Dataset (RDD) 475
shuffle operation 476
SparkSession 475
stage 478
task 476
task scheduler 479
transformations 477
conquer pattern
  about 499
  solution 499
content deduplication
  about 194
  context learning 194
  location scoring 194
content registry
  about 47
  Kibana dashboard 50
  metadata model 49
  metadata model, capturing 48
  metadata model, selection 47
  metadata model, storing 48
content-based filtering 249
context
  learning 380, 381
Cooley algorithm
  reference link 255
core global knowledge graph model 58
CoreNLP processor 181
cosine distance
  reference link 341
curse of dimensionality
  about 339
  reference link 339
custom approach 249

D

DAG scheduler 477
data access 16
data architecture
  about 13
  data access 16
  data ingestion 13
  data lake 15

data science 16
  scalable data processing capability 15
data balance 20
data disposal 455, 456
data encryption 20
data lake
  about 15
  reliable storage 15
data management 10
data management responsibilities 10
data masking 450
data pipelines
  about 36
  Global Database of Events, Language, and Tone
    (GDELT) 38
  universal ingestion framework 36
data preparation 159
data schemes
  3rd Normal Form (3NF) 483
  about 483
  denormalization 483
  Object-oriented programming (OOP) 483
data science plague 339
data science
  about 16
  selling 261, 262
data security
  about 430
  basics 431
  issues 430, 431
  reference link 465
  responsibility 465, 466
data streams
  consuming 298
  GDELT data stream, creating 299
  Twitter data stream, creating 301, 302
data technologies
  about 17
  Apache Spark 18
data transit 444, 445
data visualization
  about 415
  edge cases 419
  FHLS, with reversals 417
  stackable processing 425

data
  classifying 311
  extracting, from Elasticsearch 208, 210
  GDELT data, predicting 314
  GKG ELT 70
  Java KeyStore 442
  loading 66
  Naïve Bayes model, training 311
  S3, encryption 444
  schema agility 67
  storing 373, 375, 436, 437, 439
  thread safety 313, 314
delegation token 458
denormalization 483
denormalized models 60, 61
design pattern
  broadcast variables pattern 503
  combiner pattern 504
  conquer pattern 499
  expand pattern 499
  filter overkill pattern 517
  garbage collection 520
  lightweight shuffle 500
  optimized cluster 510
  probabilistic algorithms 517
  redistribution pattern 512
  salting key pattern 513
  secondary sort pattern 515
  selective caching 518
  summary pattern 498
  wide table pattern 502
design patterns
  about 496
  Spark APIs 497
design techniques
  about 496
  broadcast variables pattern 503
  combiner pattern 504
  conquer pattern 499
  expand pattern 499
  filter overkill pattern 517
  garbage collection 520
  lightweight shuffle 500
  optimized cluster 510
  probabilistic algorithms 517

redistribution pattern 512
salting key pattern 513
secondary sort pattern 515
selective caching 518
Spark APIs 497
summary pattern 498
wide table pattern 502
Directed Acyclic Graphs (DAGs) 473, 477
Discrete Fourier transform (DFT) 254
distributed-graph-analytics
reference link 222
DoubleMetaphone algorithm 199
driver 475

E

edge cases, data visualization
gaps, completing 421
zero values 420
EdgeWritable 218
Elasticsearch
about 30
advantages 30
disadvantages 31
installation 31
URL, for installation 31
used, as caching layer 308, 309, 311
encryption
about 435
anonymizing 446, 447, 448, 450
data transit 444, 445
data, storing 436, 437, 439
masking 450, 452
obfuscation 446, 447, 448, 450
principle 436
tokenization 452, 453, 454
Equilibrium state 344
executor 476
expand pattern
about 499
solution 499
Exploratory data analysis (EDA) 486
Extract, Transform, Load (ETL)
about 13
reference link 66

F

Fast Fourier transform (FFT)
about 254, 255, 256
reference link 254
Federal Information Processing Standards (FIPS)
466
FHLS bar structure 413, 415
filter overkill pattern
about 517
issues 517
solution 517
First, High, Low, Second (FHLS) 413
flame graph
reference link 493
flattened data
challenges 61, 62, 64
flexible storage 20
Four V's of Big Data
reference link 14

G

garbage collection
about 520
InitiatingHeapOccupancyPercent 521
issues 520
reference link 521
solution 520
GCAM specification
reference link 60
GDELT data stream
content, publishing to Kafta topic 299
creating 299
Kafka topic, consuming from Spark Streaming
300
Kafka topic, creating 299
GDELT data
predicting 314
GDELT dataset
about 240
Accumulo cell level security, used 244
Bowie effect 241
smaller communities 243
GDELT Ingest 145
GeoMesa query API

analysis 168
  data preparation 159
  machine learning 165
  naive bayes 166
  oil prices, gauging with 156
  results 167
  using 157
GeoMesa
  about 143
  GDELT Ingest 145
  Geohash 149, 152
  GeoServer 152
  Ingest 145
  installing 144
  MapReduce (MR), to Spark 146
  URL 144
GeoNames
  about 188
  dataset 188
  URL 188
GeoServer
  about 152
  Common Query Language (CQL) 155
  map layers 153, 154
GIS lookup
  about 187
  join operation, building 189
GKG ELT
  about 70
  position matters 72
Global Database of Events, Language, and Tone
  (GDELT)
  about 35, 38, 140
  core global knowledge graph model 58
  data, viewing 58
  database, indexing 332
  denormalized models 60, 61
  dimensional modeling 57
  discovering, in real-time 38
  events 141
  feed 43
  flattened data, challenges 61
  GKG schema 142
  hidden complexity 60
  improving, with publish 45
  improving, with subscribe 45
  model 57
  near duplicates, detecting in 327, 328, 330
  news articles, improvement 336
  RDD, persisting 332
  reference link 38
  REST API, building 333, 334
Global Knowledge Graph (GKG) 57
Godwin point 380, 384
Goose library
  reference link 174
Grafana
  processed tweets, displaying 376
  swing states, identifying 378
  Twitter account 377, 378
  URL 376
  used, to visualize sentiment 376
Graph of Frequency Co-occurrence
  building 267, 268
graph of person entities
  building 206
  contact chaining 206, 208
  data, extracting from Elasticsearch 208, 210
graph
  building 219

H

Hadoop Distributed File System (HDFS) 15, 19
Hadoop
  reference link 21
hamming weight 326
Hash partitioning 193
hashing function
  reference link 450
hashtags
  extracting 303
hexagonal architecture
  reference link 266
hidden complexity 60
HiveServer2 (HS2) 463
Hortonworks
  reference link 18
HTML content
  fetching 307
Hue

reference link 463
human intelligence task 282

I

indexing web content
  hamming weight 326
  Simash 323
initial communities, Weighted Community
    Clustering (WCC) algorithm
  community back propagation 228, 230, 231,
    233
  message passing 226, 228
Internet of Things (IoT) 36, 139
Inverse Document Frequency (IDF) 165
iterative approach 485
  analytic tuning 491
  data preparation 485
  issues, avoiding 488, 490
  performance, estimating 487
  scaling up 487
iterators 213

J

Java Advanced Imaging (JAI) 152
join operation
  Bloom filter 191
  building 189
  Hash partitioning 193
jq utility
  reference link 310

K

Kafka topic
  consuming, from Spark Streaming 300
  content, publishing to 299
  creating 299
Kappa architecture
  about 294
  data immutability 294
  human fault tolerance 295
  significance 297, 298
Kerberos authentication 456, 457, 458, 460, 461
key distribution centre (KDC) 458
Kibana dashboard 50
Kibana

about 29
  advantages 30
  disadvantages 30
  installation 30
  URL, for downloading 30
KMeans clustering
  optimizing 340, 343
  reference link 340

L

Lambda architecture
  about 294
  Batch layer 296
  data immutability 294
  human fault tolerance 295
  Real Time layer 296
  Serving layer 296
  significance 295, 296, 297
Lightweight Directory Access Protocol (LDAP) 432
lightweight shuffle
  about 500
  issues 500
  solution 500, 501
load balancing 20
location scoring 194
Louvain algorithm 221, 222

M

machine learning 165
map layers 153, 154
MapReduce (MR)
  about 146
  to Spark 146
MapReduce
  reference link 17
masking 450, 452
mechanical Turk
  about 282
  classification model, bootstrapping 282
  human intelligence task 282
  references 282
metadata model
  about 49
  capturing 48
  storing 48

model
  visualizing 382, 383
monads
  reference link 507

N

naive bayes 166
Naive Bayes model
  training 311
Named Entity Recognition (NER) 181
named entity recognition
  about 180
  NLP walkthrough 181
  scala libraries 181
  scalable code, building 185
names de-duplication
  about 195
  DoubleMetaphone algorithm 199
  functional programming, with Scalaz 195
  simple clean mechanism 198
National Security Agency (NSA) 26, 373
Natural Language Processing (NLP) 180
NC (complexity)
  reference link 479
near duplicates
  detecting 319
  detecting, in GDELT 327, 328, 330
  hashing 322
  indexing web content, techniques 323
news index dashboard 201
NLP walkthrough
  about 181
  abstracting methods 184
  entities, extracting 182
number overflow 480
numerical anomalies 480, 481
Nyquist theorem
  about 251
  reference link 251

O

obfuscation 446, 447, 448, 450
object-oriented programming (OOP) 483
online machine learning
  reference link 296

OPEC
  URL 140
Open Geospatial Consortium (OGC) 152
Open, High, Low, Close (OHLC) 413
OpenTSDB
  URL 373
optimized cluster
  about 510
  issues 510
  solution 510, 512

P

PageRank algorithm
  about 267
  executing 269, 270
  Graph of Frequency Co-occurrence, building
    267, 268
  reference link 267
Parquet 81
pedagogical method 76, 79
personalized playlists
  building 270
perturbation theory
  reference link 359
Pipeline
  building 371
plan of action
  formulating 142
Play framework
  URL 263
  using 263, 264, 265, 266
playlist Service
  building 271
popular hashtags
  keeping 304
practical applications
  about 426
  advantages 426
  algorithm characteristics 426
  disadvantages 427
  use cases 427
Primary Account Number (PAN) 454
principal 458
principal components (PCA) 383
probabilistic algorithms

about 517
bloom filter 518
countminsketch 518
example 518
hyperloglog 518
issues 517
solution 518
production-ready library
creating 177
exception handling 177
mapPartitions transformation, used 177
performance tuning 179

Q

quality assurance
about 51
example 52, 53

R

Random Indexing
about 339
reference link 339
rate limit
reference link 365
RDD
persisting 332
recommendation system
approaches 248
collaborative filtering 248
content-based filtering 249
custom approach 249
recommender
building 267
PageRank algorithm 267
personalized playlists, building 270
user interface, expanding 271
RecordService
about 463, 464
reference link 464
redistribution pattern
about 512
example 513
issues 512
solution 512
redundancy 20

regression test pack 489
reliable storage 15
remote procedure call (RPC) 31
repository, GeoMesa
reference link 144
request for information (RFI) 451
Resilient Distributed Dataset (RDD) 475
reference link 475
REST API
building 333, 334
reversal rule 411, 413
Role-based access control (RBAC)
about 432, 434
relationships 434
rules 434

S

salting key pattern
about 513
issues 513
solution 514
Sampling by time window 256, 257
sarcasm
anomalies, detecting 394
detecting 389
example 390, 391, 392
features, building 389
scala libraries 181
scalable code
building 185
creating 253, 254
performance tuning 187
scalability 186
scalable data processing capability 15
ScalaNLP
about 181
URL 181
Scalaz
about 195
de-duplication strategy 195
functional programming with 195
mappend operator, used 197
URL 195
schema agility
about 68

reality check 69
secondary sort pattern
  about 515
  composite key 515
  composite key ordering 515
  example 516
  grouping partitioner 515
  issues 515
  reference link 515
  solution 515
security ecosystem
  about 462
  Apache Knox 465
  Apache ranger 464
  Apache sentry 462, 463
  RecordService 463, 464
selective caching
  about 518
  solution 519, 520
Sense
  references 31
sentiment
  analysing 366
  Pipeline, building 371
  Stanford NLP, used 369, 371
  Twitter data, messaging 367, 368
Service Level Agreement (SLA) 21
service level agreements (SLAs) 498
service principals 460
session ticket 458
shortened URLs
  expanding 305
Simhash
  about 323
  reference link 323
simple clean mechanism 198
simple trend 403, 404
simple trend calculation 409
song analyzer
  building 261
  Cassandra, used 262
  data science, selling 261, 262
  Play framework, used 263, 264, 265, 266
Spark APIs
  about 497

  example 497
  issues 497
  solution 497
Spark job server
  leveraging 273, 274
  reference link 273
Spark Streaming application
  architecture 292
  CAP theorem 292, 293, 294
  designing 291
  Kappa architecture 294
  Kappa architecture, significance 297, 298
  Lambda architecture 294
  Lambda architecture, significance 295, 296, 297
Spark-Avro method 74
Spark
  algorithmic complexity 479
  architecture 472
  challenges 479
  components 474
  data schemes 483
  history 473
  improved programming model 473
  integrated approach 473
  integration 175
  iterative approach 485
  memory utilization 473
  numerical anomalies 480, 481
  plotting 484
  principles 470, 471, 472
  Scala compatibility 175
  serialization issues 176
  shuffle 482
  workflow 473
spot instances
  reference link 16
Stack Exchange
  reference link 282
stage 478
stochastic gradient descent (SGD) 473
stories
  building 337
  curse of dimensionality 339
  data science plague 339
  KMeans clustering, optimizing 340, 343

term frequency vectors, building 337, 338
story mutation
  about 344
  Equilibrium state 344
  story connections, building 355, 356, 357, 359
  streaming application, building 346, 347
  tracking 345
  visualization 351, 354
strategy pattern
  reference link 449
structured data
  benefits 56
sum of the squared distances (SSE) 342
summary pattern
  about 498
  example 499
  issues 498
  solution 498

T

tag cloud visualizations
  reference link 316
task 476
task scheduler 479
Tensor Flow
  URL 382
term frequency vectors
  building 337, 338
thread safety 313, 314
Ticket Granting Server (TGS) 458
ticket granting ticket (TGT) 458
time domain
  audio signatures, extracting 258, 259, 261
  Fast Fourier transform (FFT) 254, 256
  Sampling by time window 256, 257
  to frequency domain 254
Time to live (TTL) 308
time
  mapPartitions forces, used 185
Timely
  data, storing 373, 375
  Grafana, used to visualize sentiment 376
  reference link 373
  used, as time series database 373
tokenization 452, 453, 454

Hybrid approach, using 454
transformations 477
trend windows 400, 402
TrendCalculus
  algorithm 400
  data visualization 415
  FHLS bar structure 413, 415
  reference link 397
  reversal rule 411, 413
  simple trend 403, 404
  simple trend calculation 409
  trend windows 400, 402
  User Defined Aggregate Functions (UDAFs) 404, 409
trends
  about 398
  falling trends 399
  horizontal trends 399
  references 399
  rising trends 399
Tukey algorithm
  reference link 255
Tungsten
  reference link 471
twiddle factor
  reference link 257
Twitter data
  hashtags, extracting 303
  messaging 367, 368
  popular hashtags, keeping 304
  processing 302, 303
  shortened URLs, expanding 305
  URLs, extracting 303
Twitter mechanical Turk 316, 317
Twitter
  about 380
  context, learning 380, 381
  data stream, creating 301, 302
  data, acquiring in batch 364
  data, acquiring in stream 362
  model, visualizing 382, 383
  rate limit 365
  search API 364
  URL 301
  US elections on 362

Word2Graph 384

U

uninformed data
   about 250
   bytes, processing 250, 252
   scalable code, creating 253, 254
   time domain, to frequency domain 254
universal ingestion framework 36
URLs
   extracting 303
use cases
   about 427
   chart annotation 427
   co-trending 427
   data reduction 427
   fractal dimension 428
   indexing 427
   proxy, streaming for piecewise linear regression 428
User Defined Aggregate Functions (UDAFs) 397, 404, 409
User Defined Function (UDF) 401
user interface
   about 277
   expanding 271
   playlist Service, building 271
   Spark job server, leveraging 273, 274

V

virtues of programmer 289, 290
visualization 351

W

WCC iteration

about 233, 238, 239
   gathering community statistics 234
   WCC computation 235, 236, 237
web content
   accessing 172
   Goose library 174
Web Feature Service (WFS) 152
Web Map Service (WMS) 152
web scale news scanner
   building 172
   production-ready library, creating 177
   Spark, integration 175
   web content, accessing 172
Weighted Community Clustering (WCC) algorithm
   about 222
   description 223
   initial communities 226
   iteration 233
   preprocessing stage 224, 225
West Texas Intermediate (WTI)
   about 140
   URL 140
wide table pattern
   about 502
   example 503
   issues 502
   solution 502
Word2Graph
   about 384
   building 384, 386, 387
   random walks 387
Word2Vec algorithm
   reference link 380

Y

Yet Another Resource Negotiator (YARN) 15

www.ingramcontent.com/pod-product-compliance
Lightning Source LLC
Chambersburg PA
CBHW060949210326
41598CB00031B/4766